THE WORLD ALMANAC OF THE
VIETNAM WAR

THE WORLD ALMANAC OF THE
VIETNAM WAR

Introduction by Fox Butterfield

General Editor: John S. Bowman

World Almanac
An Imprint of Pharos Books
New York, New York

A Bison Book

Library of Congress Catalog Card Number 85-052315

Pharos Books
ISBN 0-88687-272-3
Ballantine Books ISBN 0-345-33726-3

Printed in the United States of America

World Almanac
An imprint of Pharos Books

A Scripps-Howard Company
200 Park Avenue
New York, NY 10166
10 9 8 7 6 5 4 3 2 1

CONTENTS

INTRODUCTION

BY FOX BUTTERFIELD

INTRODUCTION

The Vietnam War defies description. It was certainly America's longest war, lasting from 1945 to 1975, or counting only the time American combat troops were involved, from 1965 to 1973. It was the first war the United States lost, though because of superior US firepower and mobility it won virtually every battle. It was the first war brought into the family living room by television. For the soldiers who fought it, it was a war maddeningly without front lines, against an enemy who often wore civilian clothes, and had no clear objective other than the 'body count.' By those cold numbers, it cost the lives of 57,939 Americans, $150 billion in US military spending and produced four million killed or wounded Vietnamese on both sides, a tenth of the total population of North and South Vietnam. It was also the most divisive conflict for Americans since the Civil War and perhaps the most misunderstood war in American history.

The Vietnam War was so frustrating and baffling and stirred such embittered passion on all sides in the United States, that with the signing of the Paris Peace Accords and the withdrawal of the last US forces in 1973, Americans went into a trance of collective amnesia. Even before the final collapse of the Saigon government in 1975, Americans somehow resolved simply to forget Vietnam. Returning veterans were ignored. Unlike the fall of Nationalist China to Mao Tse Tung in 1949, there were no postwar recriminations, no blame for who lost Vietnam.

But now, a decade later, Vietnam has quietly made the transition from controversial public issue to history, and gradually a better understanding of the war is emerging, based on new scholarship. *The Almanac of the Vietnam War* is part of this effort to demythologize the Vietnam War. It is now possible to see that the war was more complex, more morally ambiguous, than either the doves or hawks maintained.

Indeed, Vietnam was a war nobody won. North Vietnam achieved a military triumph, of course. But in 'liberating' South Vietnam the Communists themselves have become at least as corrupt and repressive as the regime they overthrew; they have impoverished both halves of the country through economic mismanagement and they have driven hundreds of thousands of their compatriots to flee by boat, an exodus unprecedented in Vietnam's long tragic history of warfare.

With the benefit of hindsight and the new scholarship, some facts about the war now emerge more clearly. Although most Americans were unaware of it at the time, US involvement really began in 1945 at the end of World War II with President Truman's decision to back France's reconquest of its former colony, Vietnam.

Each succeeding president then made a further commitment, narrowing the choices for their successor. Eisenhower helped empower Ngo Dinh Diem as South Vietnam's first leader after the 1954 Geneva agreement ended France's rule. Kennedy stepped up the number of American advisers and, by sanctioning the coup which led to Diem's death in 1973, increased America's sense of involvement. Johnson made the fateful decisions in 1965 to begin bombing North Vietnam and dispatch US combat troops to the south.

Paradoxically, none of these presidents had a plan to win the war. They were trapped between their fear of being blamed for the fall of Vietnam and widening the war so much it might bring in China or the Soviet Union. So each did only the minimum necessary not to lose it during his tenure in the White House. They nibbled the bullet rather than bit it. The strategic initiative was left to Hanoi, which calculated that in a war of attrition, America would eventually lose patience.

Much of this might have been avoided if Americans had realized Vietnam had a 2000-year history of battling for its independence against China, France and Japan and that for many Vietnamese, Ho Chi Minh was the legitimate inheritor of this tradition. The Saigon Government never had this appeal to nationalism.

But it is also clearer now that, much as Washington claimed, Hanoi was instrumental in organizing the Vietcong in the south and began infiltrating regular North Vietnamese army units into the south in 1964, before Johnson sent US troops there.

The critical turning point in the war may have been the Communists' Tet Offensive in 1968. We now know that Hanoi expected it would cause the collapse of Saigon. In fact, the opposite happened. By finally exposing themselves in open battle, the Communists suffered over 50,000 killed, a disasterous military defeat, as General William C Westmoreland claimed. But the ferocity of the Communist attack stunned Americans, who had been led to believe they were winning, and it greatly undermined remaining popular support for the war at home. In the aftermath of Tet, President Johnson announced he would not run for re-election and halted further escalation of the war.

Ironically, in the period after Tet the United States finally began to make progress in the war. Militarily the local Vietcong were largely wiped out while the North Vietnamese who came south to replace them were battered. Politically, the regime of President Nguyen Van Thieu proved more stable than its predecessors. And economically, American spending helped create a new affluence for many South Vietnamese. By 1970, 90 percent of the countryside was officially 'pacified,' compared with only 33 percent in 1965, a crude though significant index.

But the American public had tired of the war, liberals believing it was immoral, conservatives that it was unwinnable. With increasing domestic pressure to end the war, President Nixon in 1973 agreed to what turned out to be little more than a face-saving formula for withdrawal – The Paris Peace Accords. The POWs came back, but North Vietnam did not have to remove its troops from the south.

With the settlement, American interest in Vietnam rapidly waned, Congress cut back steeply on US aid to Saigon and the problems of corruption and incompetence which had long plagued the South Vietnamese were accentuated. In 1975 Saigon collapsed in panic after a Communist attack that was intended only to be preliminary to a full scale offensive a year later.

A decade later, the trauma of Vietnam is still with us. It has created doubts about US power and how and when to use it. But the lessons of Vietnam are unclear. What should have been done? Perhaps the one clear message is that the United States cannot go to war without popular support, as retired General Frederick C Weyand, the last American commander in Vietnam, once wrote. 'There is no such thing as a splendid little war,' he said. 'War is death and destruction ... The Army must have the price of involvement clear before we get involved, so that America can weigh the probable cost of involvement against the dangers of non-involvement. For there are worse things than war.'

January 1985

Fox Butterfield
Wellesley, Massachusetts

CHRONOLOGY

CHRONOLOGY

PREHISTORY

The Vietnamese emerge as an ethnically iden-tifiable group during the first millenium BC when the Nam ('South') Viet ('People'), one of several clan tribes living in China south of the Yangtse River, come under assimilative pressure from the Chinese and exodus south-ward to what is now the Red River Delta in North Vietnam. Intermingling with Indone-sian and Thai-speaking peoples who preceded them over the mountains and along the rivers from the north and west, they establish a primitive agricultural society which emerges by the fourth century BC into the Bronze Age culture known as Dong Son. Clearly distin-guishable from the Chinese to the north and the Chams and Khmer to the south, this Viet-namese blend of Austronesian and Mongo-lian peoples never quite escapes the influence of its powerful northern neighbor.

111 BC

The burning of the capital of Nam Viet by Han dynasty Chinese marks the beginning of the recorded, verifiable history of Vietnam. The fall of Nam Viet also marks the beginning of 1000 years of direct Chinese rule, which by all accounts is not oppressive and is more beneficial in the long run to the Viets than to their masters. Known as Giao Chi, the Red River valley and a coastal strip as far south as Hué becomes the southernmost Chinese pro-vince. The Vietnamese adopt the whole body of Chinese Confucian civilization from cen-tralized government to improved irrigation. The administrative institutions and political structure introduced by the Chinese eventu-ally give the Vietnamese the strength and cohesion to expel the northerners; by the time the Chinese leave a millenium later, practic-ally the only Vietnamese cultural survivals are their language and a fierce, almost inbred determination not to be assimilated. *Doc Lap*, the Vietnamese spirit of independence and resentment of foreign control, becomes a permanent feature of Vietnamese life; the heroes and heroines of Vietnamese history are always those who rebelled against in-vading armies from the north. For 1000 years the Vietnamese engage in constant low-grade resistance and periodic short-lived rebellions as their evolution toward national separate-ness reaches its final stage.

AD 939

With the defeat of the Chinese armies, Viet-nam becomes an independent state. Limited by infertile mountains to the west, China to the north, and the sea to the east, the national boundaries of Vietnam take shape as the growing nation pushes south along the coast in search of land suitable for use in their wet-rice economy. This 900-year period of expan-sion or *nam-tien* ('March to the South') takes the Vietnamese through Champa and eventu-ally into the Mekong River delta, where they encounter Buddhist and Indian influences.

1069

Emperor Thanh-Tong of the Le dynasty re-names the country Dai Viet ('Greater Viet'), the name by which it is most commonly known until the nineteenth century.

1427

After 20 years of Chinese reoccupation the northerners are expelled. Conquest of the Kingdom of Champa is completed by the end of the century, greatly expanding Vietnamese dominion.

1527

A 200-year period of regional strife and north-south contention begins when General Mac Dang Dung usurps the throne in the north and the Nguyen family sets up a de-scendant of the deposed Le dynasty south of Hanoi. Despite significant truces and bloody fighting, reunification eludes Vietnam until the nineteenth century.

1535

Under the command of Captain Antonio da Faria the Portuguese enter Danang Bay. First of the European colonial wave to reach Viet-nam, they confront a sophisticated people and do not succeed in creating a stronghold similar to Goa or Malacca. The Dutch, English, and French fare no better, nor do they find a stable market for Western goods. Trade, primarily in armaments, subsides after the north-south Nguyen-Trinh truce of 1673, and practically ceases after 1700.

1627

French missionary Alexandre de Rhodes adapts the Vietnamese language to the Roman alphabet. By the end of the next century French influence dominates mission-ary work in Vietnam.

1802

French missionary Pierre Pigneau de Béhaine helps Nguyen Anh overcome his enemies and reunify Vietnam. Nguyen Anh becomes Emperor Gia Long and renames the country Vietnam. Unlike his successors he does not persecute Christians, although like most of his countrymen he regards Christianity as potentially subversive because of its conflict with Confucianism on the relation of individual to state.

SEPTEMBER 1857
Unable to obtain trading privileges through diplomacy, the French attack Danang and take the city in 1858. They fail to meet the uprising of oppressed Christians they had expected. Decimated by disease, they push south and take Saigon in 1861. Vietnam is divided by a strong popular rebellion in the north, and under the weak Emperor Tu Duc, regional risings against the French are never coordinated effectively. Hanoi falls in 1883.

25 AUGUST 1883
The signing of a Treaty of Protectorate formally ends Vietnam's independence. The name 'Vietnam' is officially eliminated, and the French divide Vietnam into northern (Tonkin) and central (Annam) protectorates, both tightly under French control, although Annam retains its imperial Vietnamese administration. Southern Vietnam (Cochin China) has been a French colony since 1867. A general uprising in 1885 fails. In the Red River Valley of the north the French begin a period of twelve years of slaughter known as the 'pacification' of Tonkin.

1887
The French form the Indochinese Union, administered by a governor general under the ministry of colonies in Paris. The Union consists of Tonkin, Annam, Cochin China (which already includes parts of Cambodia), Cambodia (a French protectorate since 1863) and Laos, added in 1893.

1905
Japan's victory of Russia gives impetus to developing Vietnamese nationalist movements by demonstrating that an Asian nation can prevail over a Western nation. Phan Boi Chau – a scholar-patriot leader of Vietnamese anti-colonialism for the first quarter of the twentieth century – travels to Japan, where he is influenced by Sun Yat-sen's circle. Phan Boi Chau's vague program of modernization and constitutional monarchy, which appeals to an educated elite, relies on help from outside Vietnam to expel the French; other scholar-gentry groups seeking relief from within vainly turn to the French. Japan expels Phan Boi Chau in 1908 to please the French, and he continues to agitate from Siam. Although he fails to offer concrete immediate and long-range political and economic goals and never gains a broad base of popular support, probably every plan and act of resistance through World War I received direct help or inspiration from this old-guard Confucian anti-colonialist.

1919
During the Versailles Peace Conference, a few Vietnamese residing in Paris draw up an eight-point program for their homeland's independence. They have their program printed and send it to the conference secretariat, and one of the initiators, Nguyen Ai Quoc ('Nguyen the Patriot'), tries to meet with President Woodrow Wilson, who has inspired them with his 14-point program calling for independence for all peoples. But Nguyen is turned away and the eight points are never even officially acknowledged.

1925
Twelve-year-old Emperor Bao Dai ascends the throne. In Canton, China, Nguyen Ai Quoc founds the Revolutionary Youth League of Vietnam, the first truly Marxist organization in Indochina. The Vietnam Nationalist Party (VNQDD) is founded at the same time in opposition to the Youth League, which is clearly the precursor of the Indochinese Communist Party. Significantly, the enduring independence movements of the twentieth century, informed by French-imported knowledge of the West, tend to look beyond the end of foreign rule to the creation of a new social and political order.

1930
In Kowloon a unified Communist Party of Vietnam (Viet Nam Cong Sang Dang) is founded under the leadership of Nguyen Ai Quoc; in Hong Kong the Indochinese Communist Party is born, also under his leadership. An uprising at Yen Bay, northwest of Hanoi, is put down by the French, and the Vietnam Nationalist Party (VNQDD) is all but destroyed.

1932
Emperor Bao Dai returns from his education in France to a people hopeful he will be able

Emperor Bao Dai ascended the throne of Annam at the age of 12 in 1925.

to persuade the French to install a more liberal regime. His efforts are ignored by the French. Bao Dai loses interest. Colonial administration continues as before, and nationalist groups of several political persuasions continue to organize and resist within and without the country.

22 SEPTEMBER 1940

The Vichy government concludes an agreement permitting Japan to station troops and use facilities in Tonkin. Allegedly ignorant of the new agreement, Japanese troops cross the border from China and attack and take French-held Langson and Dong Dang after heavy fighting. The French order an end to all resistance. Although the French administrative machinery is left intact to 'rule,' the Japanese by degrees consolidate their position until by the opening of the general Asian War in December 1941, Vietnam is a virtual colony of Japan, and remains so for the duration of the war.

10 MAY 1941

The Vietminh or Vietnam Independence League (Viet Nam Doc Lap Dong Minh) is formed as a united front organization after the Eighth Plenum of the Communist Party at Pac Bo, chaired by Nguyen Ai Quoc, adopts a policy of collaboration with all nationalists. By far the most effective nationalist organization of any kind working from within or without Vietnam, under the direction of Vo Nguyen Giap the Vietminh organizes guerrilla and intelligence networks to operate against the Japanese and the French.

1942-1943
Nguyen Ai Quoc goes to China in 1942 with the hope of getting aid from Chiang Kai-shek in the fight against the Japanese, but he is arrested by the Chinese, who have their own designs on Vietnam, and held prisoner for 13 months. During this time, his Chinese captors set up their own front organization, the Vietnam Revolutionary League, or Dong Minh Hoi (short for Viet Nam Cach Nang Dong Minh Hoi), intended to seize the initiative from the Communist-led Vietminh in the struggle against the Japanese. When this new group fails to produce results, Nguyen convinces his captors that he will work on their behalf, so he is released and returns to Vietnam in the spring of 1943. By now he has adopted the name he will hereafter be known by, Ho Chi Minh ('Ho the Enlightened One'). During the ensuing months, backed with Chinese and American (via the OSS) funds, Ho and his Vietnamese colleagues help to rescue downed American and other Allied fliers, sabotage Japanese efforts and generally keep the Japanese off-balance in Vietnam. Meanwhile, Ho is secretly working against the other nationalist groups and on behalf of his own Communist Vietminh, led in the field by Vo Nguyen Giap.

22 DECEMBER 1944
With Ho Chi Minh's support, Giap sets up an armed propaganda brigade of 34 Vietnamese and within two days will begin to attack French outposts in northern Vietnam. This is essentially the beginning of the Vietminh's armed struggle against the French.

9 MARCH 1945
Alarmed by growing insurgent activity, the Japanese grant independence to Vietnam under Japanese protection and reinstall Bao Dai as head of state. Bao Dai is never able to gain much support for what is clearly a puppet government.

AUGUST 1945 – FEBRUARY 1946
Because of his relations with the OSS during World War II and because he regards the United States as the friend of all struggling peoples, Ho Chi Minh writes at least eight letters during these months to President Harry S Truman and the US State Department, asking for US aid in gaining Vietnam's independence from France. (There is no record of US officals ever answering these appeals.) The US Government at this time is in a quandry – not wanting to support French colonialism but not wanting to turn Vietnam over to a Communist Administration.

16-29 AUGUST 1945
Following the surrender of the Japanese, Ho Chi Minh and his 'Peoples Congress' create a National Liberation Committee of Vietnam to form a provisional government. On the 18th, the Japanese transfer power in Indochina to the Vietminh. Bao Dai abdicates on the 23rd, but Ho's Vietminh and its Peoples Liberation Committee establish a provisional government on the 29th and include Bao Dai as its 'supreme advisor.'

2 SEPTEMBER 1945
In Hanoi, with American OSS officers at his side, Ho Chi Minh proclaims the Independent Democratic Republic of Vietnam (DRV). Ho even quotes from the American Declaration of Independence, and he has high hopes of gaining support from the United States in maintaining an independent state of Vietnam.

12 SEPTEMBER 1945
British troops arrive in Saigon to accept surrender of the Japanese according to terms of the Potsdam Conference. Most Vietnamese expect the Allies to support their independence. While the United States in principle favors a provisional international trusteeship for Vietnam, after Roosevelt's death the United States signs a credit agreement with France for supply of vehicles and relief equipment to French authorities in Indochina. This is seen as US endorsement of the French reconquest.

21-24 SEPTEMBER 1945
Vietnam – and Saigon in particular – is in danger of being torn apart by violence from all sides. The Vietminh under Ho are trying to enforce their control but they are opposed by various nationalist Vietnamese groups, French colonials trying to regain power, and representatives of the French government determined to reassert sovereignty, while thousands of Nationalist Chinese troops are moving into northern Vietnam. On 21 Sep-

tember, the British General, Douglas Gracey declares martial law, and to aid his British, Indian and Gurkha troops he even allows Japanese troops to help maintain order. Gracey also arms 1400 French troops who had been interned by the Japanese, most of them tough French Legionnaires, and on the 22nd they go on a rampage in Saigon and remove the Vietminh's Executive Committee from city hall. The Vietminh then calls for a general strike on the 24th which effectively shuts down Saigon. But the day is also marked by considerable violence as armed Vietnamese attack French institutions and neighborhoods (and many Vietnamese will regard this day as the real beginning of their war against the French). Meanwhile, General Jacques Philippe Leclerc, newly appointed as France's military commander in Vietnam, arrives on the 24th in Saigon, and declares: 'We have come to reclaim our inheritance.'

26 SEPTEMBER 1945
In Saigon, Lieutenant Colonel A Peter Dewey, head of the American OSS mission in Vietnam, is driving a jeep to the airport when he is shot by Vietminh troops (who evidently mistake him for a Frenchman). Dewey thus becomes the first of some 60,000 Americans who will eventually die in the Vietnam War.

NOVEMBER 1945
To pave the way for Chinese support of resistance against the French, the Vietminh ostensibly dissolves the Indochinese Communist Party. In January 1946 it elects a National Assembly which includes VNQDD and Dong Minh Hoi members, and forms a coalition government headed by Ho Chi Minh. But in February China concludes a treaty with France, forcing the Vietminh to reconsider its policy towards the French.

6 MARCH 1946
Ho Chi Minh signs an agreement with France which recognizes the Democratic Republic of Vietnam as a free state within the (as yet unformed) Indochinese Federation and the French Union. The new state is not precisely defined and the French leave details to be decided by future agreement. French forces are permitted to land in the North; Bao Dai, to eliminate the possibility of his serving as a rallying point for opposing nationalist groups, departs on a 'goodwill' mission to China. Criticized by some Vietnamese for compromising, Ho Chi Minh supposedly retorted, 'It

is better to sniff French dung for a while than eat China's all our lives.'

1 JUNE 1946
A conference in Fontainebleau attended by Ho Chi Minh and a delegation of Vietnamese, hoping to clarify the status of the 'new state,' breaks up when Vietnam High Commissioner Georges Thierry d'Argenlieu violates the March agreement by proclaiming a separate government for Cochin China. In September Ho Chi Minh signs a *modus vivendi* he describes as 'better than nothing' which covers a cessation of hostilities and facilitates French resumption of economic and cultural activities in return for a more liberal regime.

19 DECEMBER 1946
In Hanoi the Democratic Republic of Vietnam launches its first attack against the French. Following months of steadily deteriorating relations, the bloody November 'pacification' of Haiphong, and unacceptable French demands including the disarmament of the Vietminh militia, the attack has the support of most Vietnamese and begins what comes to be known as the Indochina War.

APRIL 1947
The Vietminh have lost almost all towns in Tonkin and northern Annam. Preparing for a long war, the Vietminh Army, largely intact, moves into the Viet Bac, the mountainous region north of Hanoi.

15 AUGUST 1947
High Commissioner Emile Bollaert, with approval from Paris, plans an offer of independence for Vietnam within the French Union, accompanied by a unilateral cease-fire and an offer to negotiate with all Vietnamese parties and groups. The plan is never implemented. Largely an attempt to pressure Bao Dai, the French strategy to weaken the Vietminh by uniting all anticommunist nationalist groups behind the wary emperor (the 'Bao Dai Solution') fails because the French do not go far enough in granting real independence to Vietnam.

OCTOBER 1947
General Etienne Valluy, leading the biggest French colonial operation to date, fails to wipe out the Vietminh in one stroke. Although the Vietnamese lack the strength to expel the French, after Valluy's humiliating defeat it is clear that the French are unable to

The Vietcong base camps were village huts which could be abandoned easily.

Members of the 1st Marine Division in the midst of a firefight with the NVA.

The Chieu Hoi Armed Propaganda Teams encouraged the Vietcong to defect.

The first US troops in South Vietnam served as instructors and advisors.

An M48-A3 tank is pulled from the mud.

The M-60 machine gun was used throughout the war.

Marines of the Second Battalion on patrol.

An air strike on the old imperial city of Hué, in 1968.

The M-101A1 105mm howitzer was a standard artillery weapon of the Vietnam era.

Tanks appeared on the streets of Saigon during many demonstrations and riots.

An AH-1G 'Cobra' helicopter hovers, waiting for enemy positions to be marked.

Members of the 101st Airborne Division check their weapons during Operation Pickett.

A fire on the USS Forrestal *in 1967 destroyed 21 planes and killed 134.*

25

*The Aircraft Carrier **USS** Oriskany comes alongside the supply ship **Aludra**.*

An A-7E Corsair Attack Aircraft flies above her carrier, USS America.

The battleship USS New Jersey *spent 120 days in action during the Vietnam War.*

An Air Support Squadron aircraft of the US Air Force.

An F-100D Supersabre of the 416th Tactical Fighter Squadron over South Vietnam.

The US forces sprayed defoliants to diminish the jungle cover.

A badly damaged Skyhawk lands with the aid of a nylon emergency barrier.

Vietcong prisoners taken ashore from a US Navy patrol air cushion vehicle.

US Navy Assault Support Patrol boats on a canal in the Mekong Delta.

Public opinion against the war led to riots and demonstrations.

The colors pass in review in a departures ceremony for the 3rd Marine Division.

After the fall of Saigon, many Vietnamese fled their country in small boats.

Emile Bollaert, High Commissioner for France was greeted by Montagnards *on arrival in Indochina.*

dislodge the Vietnamese resistance. The Vietminh conduct guerrilla warfare based on tying down as many French troops as possible, biding their time until they are able to meet the French in large-scale open warfare.

5 JUNE 1948
High Commissioner Bollaert and General Nguyen Van Xuan sign the Baie d'Along Agreement. The Agreement names Bao Dai chief of state and France recognizes the independence of Vietnam within the French Union; however, the protocol governing other details makes this independence devoid of practical significance. Vietnamese statesmen from Ho Chi Minh to Ngo Dinh Diem denounce the Xuan government as a French tool. Although French attempts to establish Bao Dai as a focal point for anti-Vietminh nationalists never cease, from this point on no government formed by Bao Dai ever wins popular support.

8 MARCH 1949
The Elysée Agreement outlining general principles affecting French-Vietnamese relations is signed by French President Vincent Auriol and Bao Dai. The French promise to help build a national anti-Communist army.

14 JANUARY 1950
Despairing of any reconciliation with France, Ho Chi Minh declares that the only true legal government is his Democratic Republic of Vietnam. The Soviet Union and China extend recognition, and China will start supplying modern weapons to the Vietminh.

7 FEBRUARY 1950
The United States and Great Britain extend *de jure* recognition to the Bao Dai regime. Vietnam is now effectively becoming split between a communist-influenced north and an anti-communist south.

8 MAY 1950
US Secretary of State Dean G Acheson announces that an agreement has been reached with France for US arms assistance to the French Associated States of Indochina.

27 JUNE 1950
President Truman announces he is accelerating the program of military aid for Vietnam he

33

began in April. This includes a military mission and military advisors. Aid is funneled through Paris. The United States has been indirectly supporting a buildup of an anti-Communist Vietnamese Army since 1946. Fifteen million dollars is granted in military aid to the French for the war in Indochina on 26 July; by November 1952 the United States carries between one-half and one-third of the financial burden for the Indochina War.

3 AUGUST 1950
A US Military Assistance Advisory Group (MAAG) of 35 men arrives in Vietnam to teach troops receiving US weapons how to use them.

19 OCTOBER 1950
The Vietminh open up more of the Chinese border. Northern Tonkin is lost to the French from the sea to the Red River.

23 DECEMBER 1950
The United States signs a Mutual Defense Assistance Agreement with France, Vietnam, Cambodia and Laos (the French Associated States). In 1951 military aid tops $500,000,000. Congressman John F Kennedy asserts America has allied itself with a desperate French attempt to hang on to the remnants of its empire. By 1954 Amrican military aid to Vietnam tops $2 billion.

7 SEPTEMBER 1951
The United States signs an agreement with Saigon for *direct* aid to South Vietnam. American presence in Saigon is increased as civilian government employees join the military already there. General Jean de Lattre de Tassigny finds many in Washington who agree that France is preventing a 'red tide' from engulfing South Vietnam, the 'barrier in Southeast Asia' against Communism.

JULY 1952
President Truman promotes the American Legation in Saigon to an embassy. One sovereign country is dealing with another.

4 NOVEMBER 1952
Dwight David Eisenhower is elected president. With this administration the Indochina

French Generals Navarre and Coigny inspecting the French and Vietnamese parachute troops in 1953.

war ceases to be regarded as a colonial war, and the fighting in Vietnam becomes a war between Communism and the 'free world.' The possibility of direct Chinese intervention becomes a matter of urgent preoccupation for many of Eisenhower's closest advisors, in particular Secretary of State John Foster Dulles and Vice-President Richard Nixon.

20 MAY 1953

Using a phrase that will haunt Americans in later years – 'Now we can see (success in Vietnam) clearly, like light at the end of a tunnel' – General Henri Navarre assumes command of French Union Forces in Vietnam. He addresses himself to the grave deterioration of the French military position, particularly in the North, by advancing a plan for a buildup of French forces preparatory to a massive attack against the Vietminh. He receives more support from Dulles in Washington than he does from Paris, but his operations during the summer only underscore the inadequacy of French military means and French inability to deal with Vietminh tactics.

27 JULY 1953

With the signing of the Korean armistice, Chinese aid to the Vietminh (in trucks, artillery and anti-aircraft guns) increases.

30 SEPTEMBER 1953

Eisenhower approves $385,000,000 over the $400,000,000 already budgeted for military aid for Vietnam. By April 1954 aid to Indochina reaches $1,133,000,000 out of a total foreign aid budget of $3,497,000,000.

20 NOVEMBER 1953

Forced out of the strategically unimportant town of Dienbienphu he took from the French the year before, General Vo Nguyen Giap takes the last French stronghold in northwest Tonkin, and soon the entire Chinese border is open. A majority of the French National Assembly expresses hope for a negotiated settlement in Indochina, but in case the French believe it is important to turn the defense of Laos into a major clash, Giap sets up a supply base at Taum Giao near Dienbienphu. In December his troops push deeper into Laos.

25 JANUARY – 18 FEBRUARY 1954

Foreign ministers of the Big Four – the United States, Britain, France and the Soviet Union – meet in Berlin. In February they agree to hold a conference on Korea and Indochina in Geneva in April.

13 MARCH 1954

The Vietminh attack the French garrison at Dienbienphu. A force of 40,000 Vietminh with heavy artillery ring the 15,000 French troops General Navarre has placed 200 miles behind enemy lines as part of an exceptional effort to defend Laos and speed the inevitable French victory. With Chinese artillery the Vietminh shell the airstrip, and after five days it is clear the French are doomed, for all their supplies must arrive by air. With the Geneva Conference only six weeks away, General Giap knows a decisive Vietminh victory will demonstrate that France must negotiate.

20 MARCH 1954

News of Dienbienphu's impending fall reaches Washington. Dulles, a firm believer in the Navarre Plan, is shocked. Chairman of the Joint Chiefs of Staff Arthur Radford proposes nuclear strikes against the Viet Minh but settles for one massive US air strike. He favors back-up strikes, paratrooper drops, and mining of Haiphong Harbor.

25 MARCH 1954

The National Security Council approves the Radford plan. The United States has made a provisional decision to fight in Indochina.

7 APRIL 1954

At a news conference discussing the importance of defending Dienbienphu, Eisenhower explains: 'You have a row of dominoes set up, and you knock over the first one and what will happen to the last one is the certainty that it will go over very quickly. So you have the beginning of a disintegration that will have the most profound influences.'

16 APRIL 1954

Vice-President Nixon tells a convention of newspaper editors that the United States may be 'putting our own boys in [Indochina] ... regardless of allied support.' In Washington the desire to see colonialism end has given way to the desire to 'contain' Communism and to the belief that the war was fostered from the outside. Nixon claims there would be no war were it not for Communist China.

24 APRIL 1954

Radford and Dulles meet Anthony Eden in Paris and inform him that Eisenhower is pre-

CHRONOLOGY

Helicopters were used to evacuate wounded during the siege at Dienbienphu.

pared to ask Congress for a joint resolution approving the American air strike. Eden is opposed but presents their request for British approval to his government.

25 APRIL 1954
Prime Minister Winston Churchill rejects the US proposal, 'What we are being asked to do is assist in misleading the Congress into approving a military operation which would be in itself ineffective, and might well bring the world to the verge of a major war.'

29 APRIL 1954
At a press conference, President Eisenhower denies there was an US plan for massive air strikes and apparently abandons any thought of intervening in Vietnam, concluding: 'You certainly cannot hope ... for a completely satisfactory answer with the Communists. The most you can work out is a practical way of getting along.'

26 APRIL 1954
The Far Eastern Conference opens in Geneva. The siege at Dienbienphu continues to humiliate the French and bolster the Democratic Republic of Vietnam. The Vietminh are certain they can win the war and are not in the mood for compromise. US officials make a great point of avoiding the most casual contact with the Chinese, although the conference marks the international acceptance of China as one of the five great powers.

7 MAY 1954
Dienbienphu falls to the Vietminh. France has lost more than 35,000 men killed, 48,000 wounded in a war that has been financially and militarily humiliating. There is enormous pressure in France, as there has been for some time, for a rapid conclusion of the war. With the Western powers in disarray due to the US standoffishness, momentum and initiative in Geneva fall to the Vietminh and the East.

8 MAY 1954
Members of the nine delegations assemble in Geneva and start negotiations for ending the war in Vietnam as part of a larger settlement of Indochina problems. The French are pub-

licly opposed to any solution that involves a partition of Vietnam but behind the scenes they are considering this as a compromise. For the French and the West, partition would at least salvage half of the country. The Chinese indicate a willingness to support partition, for they have no desire to continue a war that might spill over into China and they have their own motives for wanting to keep the Vietnamese from becoming too strong. Negotiations will drag on for six weeks as the French reject the demands made by the Vietminh's chief delegate, Pham Van Dong.

1 JUNE 1954

Colonel Edward G Lansdale, USAF, arrives in Saigon as chief of the Saigon Military Mission (SMM). Called the Assistant Air Attache' at the US Embassy, Lansdale is in fact a member of the CIA assigned to run paramilitary operations against the Communist Vietnamese – specifically, covert operations to cause political-psychological disruption among the Communists (such as spreading rumors about their leaders and sabotaging North Vietnamese transportation). This 'cold war combat team' will be assembled by 11 August. Under the terms of the Geneva Agreements, that is the day by which each country must put a freeze on foreign military personnel in Vietnam.

16 JUNE 1954

China's Chou En-lai now negotiating for the Communists against the West, and he suggests that Vietminh troops withdraw from Laos and Cambodia. It is now clear that China and the Soviet Union, represented by Vyacheslav Molotov, are bringing pressure to bear on the Vietminh not to wreck the conference. Members of the Vietminh delegation will later complain that their revolution was halted on the verge of success, but without Chinese aid they cannot be certain of expelling the French. The French Parliament is so impatient with the proceedings in Geneva that it replaces Prime Minister Joseph Laniel with Pierre Mendès-France.

17 JUNE 1954

Newly elected Prime Minister of France Pierre Mendès-France declares he will resign as head of the French Government if he does not obtain a cease-fire in Indochina by 20 July. His vow to send conscripts to Indochina if he fails creates a make-or-break situation designed to test whether the Communists are really willing to reach a compromise; he travels to Bern to meet secretly with Chou En-lai. Allied strategy is becoming reasonably coordinated.

18 JUNE 1954

At his chateau in Cannes, France, Bao Dai personally selects Ngo Dinh Diem as the new prime minister of Vietnam. Diem will fly into Saigon on 26 June, where only a few hundred of his Catholic supporters greet him, and on 7 July will formally assume office as Premier.

24-29 JUNE 1954

Churchill, Eden, Eisenhower and Dulles endorse partiton and agreeing on seven points that offer a surprisingly accurate outline of the formal agreement at the conference.

20-21 JULY 1954

A cease-fire 'Agreement on the Cessation of Hostilities in Viet Nam,' is signed by General Ta Quang Buu for the Vietminh and General Henri Delteil for France. (Hostilities are to cease in Laos and Cambodia as well.) A second document, the 'Final Declaration of the Geneva Conference,' receives the general support of Britain, France, Laos, China, the Soviet Union, Cambodia and the Democratic Republic of Vietnam but is never signed. It states: (1) Vietnam is provisionally partitioned at the 17th parallel into North and South Vietnam, pending reunification or other permanent settlement to be achieved through nationwide elections, (2) for a period of 300 days all persons may pass freely from one zone to the other, (3) limits are imposed on foreign military bases North and South, on personnel movements, and re-armaments, (4) nationwide elections are scheduled for 20 July 1956, (5) an International Control Commission made up of representatives of India, Canada and Poland is established to supervise the implementation of these agreements. The Vietminh accept elections because their popular support is such that they would win; so the State of (South) Vietnam pushes the elections as far into the future as possible, and Molotov pressures the Vietminh to agree. The United States does not agree with the Final Declaration and does not support it, and Bao Dai's Government denounces all agreements. On 21 July, American 'observer' Walter Bedell Smith issues a unilateral declaration stating that the United States (1) 'will refrain from the threat or the use of force to disturb' the Geneva agreements, (2)

CHRONOLOGY

'view[s] any renewal of the aggression in violation of the aforesaid agreements with grave concern and as seriously threatening international peace and security,' and (3) supports the concept of unity through free elections supervised by the United Nations. Dulles remarks, 'The important thing from now on is not to mourn the past but to seize the future opportunity to prevent the loss in northern Vietnam from leading to the extension of Communism through Southeast Asia and the Southwest Pacific.' On 11 August after nearly eight years of war the cease-fire is operating throughout all Indochina. By this time, the US Military Assistance Advisory Group (MAAG), commanded by Lieutenant General John W O'Daniel, US Army, based in Saigon, has 342 men in South Vietnam.

AUGUST 1954
Under the terms of the Geneva Agreement, a flow of almost one million refugees from North to South Vietnam begins. CIA Colonel Lansdale plays a role in encouraging Catholics and providing transportation. France and the United States – especially the US Navy – provide aircraft and ships. US Marine Colonel Victor J Croizat, first US Marine assigned to the US Military Assistance Advisory Group (MAAG) in Saigon, creates refugee centers. The majority of the refugees are Catholics, led by their priests; others include various factions opposed to the Vietminh. They furnish Prime Mininster Diem, himself a Catholic, with a fiercely anti-Communist constituency in the South.

8-12 AUGUST 1954
In Washington, the National Security Council concludes that the Geneva settlement was a 'disaster' that 'completed a major forward stride of Communism which may lead to the loss of Southeast Asia.'

20 AUGUST 1954
President Eisenhower approves a National Security Council paper titled 'Review of US Policy in the Far East.' The paper supports Dulles's view that the United States should support Diem, while encouraging him to broaden his government and establish more democratic institutions.

8 SEPTEMBER 1954
The Manila Treaty is concluded, forming a military alliance which becomes the Southeast Asia Treaty Organization (SEATO). A result of efforts actually begun by Secretary of State Dulles before the Geneva Conference, but postponed by Britain's Anthony Eden, the signatories are France, the United States, Great Britain, Australia, New Zealand, the Philippines, Pakistan and Thailand. A Separate Protocol to SEATO designates Laos, Cambodia and 'the free territory under the jurisdiction of the State of Vietnam [South Vietnam]' as also being areas subject to the provisions of the treaty. SEATO does not go so far as the absolute mutual defense commitments of the NATO agreement. but its language provides a basis for justification for US support of anti-Communist regimes in Southeast Asia.

11 SEPTEMBER 1954
In an attempt to gain control of his military, Prime Minister Diem suspends his Chief of Staff, General Nguyen Van Hinh, and orders him to leave for France. This action follows the arrest of two staff officers accused of conspiring against the government. General Hinh refuses to relinquish his command or obey Diem's travel order.

19 SEPTEMBER 1954
Diem accuses General Hinh of rebellion after Hinh releases a statement demanding that the country be give a 'strong and popular' new government. A few days later Hinh stations tanks around the presidential palace, which is guarded by police controlled by Diem's enemies the Binh Xuyen. Diem stalls for time until loyal militia units can be brought up from Annam. Hoa Hao and Cao Dai sect leaders who have formed a united front with the Binh Xuyen in opposing Diem send Binh Xuyen leader Le Van Dien to Paris to seek permission from Emperor Bao Dai, nominally still head of state, for a coup against Diem.

20 SEPTEMBER 1954
Nine of Diem's 15 cabinet members resign, apparently convinced Diem is doomed. Diem begins to limit cabinet members to his family and friends. Colonel Lansdale and negotiators armed with US funds try to strike a bargain with Hoa Hao and Cao Dai leaders.

24 SEPTEMBER 1954
Forty-eight hours before the projected joint action of the sects against him, Diem announces the formation of a coalition government including four Hoa Hao and two Cao

Dai leaders. Although the National Army still enjoys the support of Bao Dai and influential French circles in Vietnam, Diem has maneuvered safely through his first great test in consolidating his regime.

OCTOBER 1954

The Vietnamese Marine Corps is formally organized with US Marine Colonel Croizat as its senior US advisor. At two-battalion strength by the end of the year, the Vietnamese Marine Corps enjoys the reputation of a well-disciplined unit.

11 OCTOBER 1954

The Vietminh formally take over Hanoi and North Vietnam. Unlike Diem in the South, Ho Chi Minh and his regime face no rebellious factions or challenges to their authority; but the long war against the French has devastated the North, and the incoming order is plagued by severe economic problems. In addition, on Diem's instructions, departing anti-Communist Vietnamese heading south dismantle public facilities and loot factories, crippling some essential services in Hanoi; and the North, long dependant upon the South for its rice, is now deprived of this traditional source.

24 OCTOBER 1954

President Eisenhower sends a landmark letter to Diem. Although Eisenhower makes it clear to Diem that US aid to his government in Vietnam's present 'hour of trial' is contingent upon his assurances of the 'standards of performance [he] would be able to maintain in the event such aid were supplied,' President Johnson later cites this letter as the starting point of US commitment to South Vietnam. Diem agrees to the 'needed reforms' stipulated as a precondition for receiving aid.

3 NOVEMBER 1954

On the basis of Diem's agreement to begin reforms, President Eisenhower announces he is sending General J Lawton Collins (then US representative on the military committee of NATO) to Vietnam to 'coordinate the operation of all US agencies in that country.'

17 NOVEMBER 1954

General Collins arrives in Saigon. Affirming $100 million in US aid, he announces, 'I have

Following the Geneva Accords, refugees fled south to avoid the Communist takeover.

CHRONOLOGY

Communist Vietminh troops marched into the city of Hanoi as the French marched out.

come to Vietnam to bring every possible aid to the Government of Diem and to his Government only. ... It is the legal government in Vietnam, and the aid which the United States will lend it ought to permit the Government to save the country.' Warning that the Army will receive US military aid only if it supports Diem, Collins announces, 'This American mission will soon take charge of instructing the Vietnamese Army.'

20 NOVEMBER 1954
Premier of France Mendès-France visits Washington. On his return to Paris, he discloses the results of Franco-American meetings: (1) the end of French control of the economy, commerce and finances of Vietnam; (2) transfer of command of the National Army to the Vietnamese government; (3) transfer of responsibility for training the Vietnamese Army to the United States; (4) US aid to go directly to Saigon; (5) withdrawal of the French Expeditionary Corps.

DECEMBER 1954
Hanoi Hanoi concludes its first aid agreement with China, providing for the delivery of road,

railroad, postal, telegraph, and water-works repair equipment. Chinese technicians supervise repair of the Hanoi-Langson railroad. Russian and Chinese technicians have begun to replace French experts.
Saigon General Collins, who has been given the rank of ambassador, writes from Saigon that he does not feel Diem is equal to the task of heading the government and ought to be removed; and that if the United States is not willing to replace him, plans for assisting Southeast Asia ought to be reevaluated.

30 DECEMBER 1954
Diem concludes economic agreements safeguarding French business interests in South Vietnam. He thus makes it easier for France to relinquish her political hold on Vietnam, and paves the way for US assumption of the military protection of South Vietnam.

1 JANUARY 1955
Washington In pledging new military assistance to South Vietnam, the United States cites the aid agreement of 23 December 1950 signed by the United States, France and the French Associated States of Indochina.

Hanoi At a five and one-half hour parade attended by over 200,000, Ho Chi Minh makes his first public appearance – he directed the war against the French from jungle and mountain headquarters – in over eight years.
Saigon Chief of the US Military Assistance Advisory Group (MAAG) Indochina Lieutenant General John W O'Daniel is assigned to assist the South Vietnamese government in organizing and training the South Vietnamese Army. All US aid to Vietnam goes directly to Saigon.

1 FEBRUARY 1955
The Training Relations and Instruction Mission is formed to implement the training of South Vietnamese forces by the United States military mission in Saigon.

3 FEBRUARY 1955
After months of prodding by US advisors, Diem introduces the first of a series of agrarian reform measures with a decree governing levels of rent for farm land. Critics maintain his land reform program begins too late too slowly and never goes far enough. Provisions for payment by peasants granted land create unnecessary hardships. Although one million tenants receive some relief, more than one million receive no land at all, and the lack of impartial enforcement agencies cripples many potential benefits. Instead of redistributing land to the poor, Diem's land reform program ends up by taking back what the peasants have been given by the Vietminh and returning it to the landlords, forcing peasants to pay for the land they considered theirs on terms they cannot meet. In 1960, 75 percent of the land is owned by 15 percent of the people. The Communists capitalize on unresolved peasant unrest throughout Diem's regime.

7 MARCH 1955
The United States and South Vietnam sign agreements supplementing the economic cooperation agreements of September 1951.

28 MARCH 1955
By transferring command of the Saigon police to the Prefect of the City, Diem attacks the Binh Xuyen, a private armed force of 40,000 who control the Saigon-Cholon police and the national security police. Troops are sent to take over the city's police headquarters. The Binh Xuyen withdraw, but the next night fighting breaks out, and Hoa Hao sect forces under Generals Ba Cut and Tran Van Soai join the Binh Xuyen in a blockade of Saigon.

26 APRIL 1955
Diem again attacks Binh Xuyen control of the police by dismissing Lai Van Sang, director-general of the national security police, and by ordering the Binh Xuyen to cease its deployments in Saigon. The Binh Xuyen refuse to hand over the security headquarters building, and Saigon turns into a battlefield. An attempt by Bao Dai to neutralize Diem fails when Diem refuses to honor a summons from Bao Dai to come to Cannes.

27 APRIL 1955
After a meeting with General J Lawton Collins in Washington, Secretary Dulles reluctantly agrees to replace Diem, and cables the embassy in Saigon to find an alternative. CIA Colonel Lansdale, who has already helped foil General Hinh's coup against Diem by organizing an effective palace guard and inviting General Hinh's two key aides on a visit to the Philippines for a tour of secret projects, once more rallies to Diem's side. He presses the embassy to support Diem and takes 'all measures possible under the narrow limits permitted by US Policy.' Details of 'a number of successful actions' are (uncharacteristically) not revealed.

28 APRIL 1955
Colonel Lansdale encourages Diem to persevere, and Diem orders a counterattack against the Binh Xuyen. Diem's troops are successful, and the American Embassy is told to burn Dulles's order of the preceeding day. After a few days most of the Binh Xuyen are expelled from their urban strongholds. By the end of May Diem has prevailed in Saigon, but most of the more than 2000 Binh Xuyen, Cao Dai and Hoa Hao fighters who withdrew into the Mekong Delta later reemerge to continue their opposition to Diem as Vietcong.

7-13 MAY 1955
Three-Power talks on the South Vietnamese question are held in Paris between French Premier Edgar Faure, Foreign Minister Pinay, British Foreign Secretary Harold Macmillan, and US Secretary of State Dulles. French Premier Faure announces that a complete understanding has been reached at Paris: Neither France nor the United States intend to interfere in South Vietnam's internal affairs, and both countries support Diem's

CHRONOLOGY

President Diem broadcasting during a government crisis over military disunity.

government, although they wish to see it become more representative. The next day Diem declares that as a sovereign country South Vietnam cannot be bound by decisions taken at conferences in which she is not a participant.

16 MAY 1955
The United States signs an agreement with Cambodia to supply direct military aid.

20 MAY 1955
The French command agrees to withdraw its troops from the Saigon-Cholon area. This means that remaining Cao Dai and Hoa Hao sect forces and their allies are deprived of French support, and must either submit to Diem or fight to bring him down. Bao Dai's fate is likewise sealed when it becomes clear that the French no longer guide the destiny of Vietnam.

5 JUNE 1955
Diem's troops begin an offensive against the Hoa Hao. Five Hoa Hao battalions surrender immediately, and on 18 June General Nguyen Gia Ngo rallies to the government. Troops massed by Generalissimo Tran Van Soai and

Generals Hinh and Vy at the Cambodian border are overrun and the generals flee into Cambodia. Hoa Hao resistance is reduced to sporadic guerrilla operations.

6 JUNE 1955
Foreign minister of North Vietnam Pham Van Dong states that his government is prepared to open consultations with South Vietnam in preparation for holding nationwide elections in July 1956, as stipulated in the Final Declaration of the Geneva Conference. He declares North Vietnam desires free elections in which 'all political parties, organizations, and individuals can take part.'

6 JULY 1955
Diem declares in a broadcast that since the Geneva Agreements were not signed, South Vietnam is not bound by them. Although he does not reject the 'principle of elections,' any proposals from the Vietminh are out of the question 'if proof is not given us that they put the higher interest of the national community above those of Communism.'

7 JULY 1955
China and Hanoi announce that Peking will extend Hanoi economic aid of 800 million yuan (about $200 million). This announcement follows a trip to Peking by Ho Chi Minh and his ministers of finance, industry, agriculture, education and health.

18 JULY 1955
Following a visit from Ho Chi Minh and his ministers, the Soviet Union announce it will grant Hanoi 400 million rubles ($100 million) in economic aid. A three-cornered deal between the Soviet Union, Hanoi and Burma supplying rice from Burma to Hanoi in exchance for Russian industrial equipment at the beginning of the year has prevented widespread famine. The July grants from Peking and Moscow initiate an ambitious industrialization program which in less than 10 years finds the North producing items not yet produced in the South.

19 JULY 1955
North Vietnam's Foreign Minister Pham Van Dong asks Diem to nominate delegates to a pre-elections conference.

20 JULY 1955
Diem rejects North Vietnam's invitation to discuss all-Vietnam elections on the grounds that the people will not be able to express their will freely.

26 JULY 1955
Britain, France and the United States formally pass notes to Diem urging him to open discussions with North Vietnam and to respect the Geneva Agreements.

10 AUGUST 1955
Declaring that South Vietnam is 'the only legal state,' Diem rejects any talks with North Vietnam, reaffirming his policy laid down in his broadcast of 6 July.

16 AUGUST 1955
The last French high commissioner in Vietnam departs.

6 OCTOBER 1955
Diem's Ministry of the Interior announces that a referendum is scheduled for 23 October to decide whether Bao Dai should be deposed and Diem replace him as head of state.

18 OCTOBER 1955
A communiqué from Bao Dai's office in Paris announces that he has dismissed Diem from the premiership and annulled his powers. In a message to the Vietnamese people, which Diem's censors suppress, Bao Dai prophetically declares, 'police methods and personal dictatorship must be brought to an end, and I can no longer continue to lend my name and my authority to a man who will drag you into ruin, famine and war.'

23 OCTOBER 1955
Diem's referendum in South Vietnam results in a 98.2 percent majority against Bao Dai and for Diem, who becomes chief of state. More a test of loyalty to authority than an exercise in democracy, the election is by all accounts rigged, with the CIA's Colonel Lansdale once again playing an important role. In Saigon, Diem receives one-third more votes than there are registered voters.

26 OCTOBER 1955
Diem proclaims the Republic of South Vietnam with himself as its first president. He is also prime minister, defense minister and supreme commander of the armed forces. The new regime is recognized immediately by France, the United States, Great Britain, Australia, New Zealand, Italy, Japan, Thailand and South Korea.

CHRONOLOGY

DECEMBER 1955
All of about 150 French companies still operating in North Vietnam are nationalized; and all, with the exception of coal mines and Hanoi public transportation, without compensation.

12 DECEMBER 1955
The United States consulate in Hanoi is closed.

13 DECEMBER 1955
According to an official announcement, by this date more than 100,000 people have taken part in trials of 'landlords' in villages near Hanoi. Agrarian reform, begun by the Vietminh in 1953 and halted for fear it might interfere with the war against the French, has been resumed. Peoples Agricultural Reform Tribunals composed of poor and landless try 'rich' landlords, many of whom own only two to four acres. The land reform campaign is ill-conceived and poorly executed. An unsavoury mixture of hate, greed and personal vengeance combine with official desires to eradicate a social class – which in this case has to be partly invented – in a rural reign of terror.

19 DECEMBER 1955
After approval by the US Senate and President Eisenhower, the Southeast Asia Collective Defense Treaty (SEATO) and its Protocol governing Vietnam, Cambodia and Laos comes officially into effect.

11 JANUARY 1956
The Diem administration issues Ordinance No 6 allowing the internment of former Vietminh members and others 'considered as dangerous to national defense and common security.' With his adversaries in the sects under control, at least in Saigon, Diem launches a drive against Vietminh who remain in the South. Those accused, frequently innocent peasants denounced by jealous neighbors, are tried by 'security committees,' which often employ torture. Many are executed or sent to concentration camps. Although by the end of 1956 Diem has smashed 90 percent of the former Vietminh cells in the Mekong Delta, his ruthless drive against all dissidents does little to enhance his popularity, and he loses many potential allies.

18 FEBRUARY 1956
On a visit to Peking, Prince Sihanouk renounces SEATO protection for Cambodia. He seeks neutrality for Cambodia.

13 APRIL 1956
Fanatical Hoa Hao guerrilla commander Ba Cut is finally captured by General Duong Van Minh. He is publically beheaded by guillotine at Cantho on 13 July. Ba Cut's death signifies the end of organized Hoa Hao resistance. With the Cao Dai already overcome, Diem has successfully neutralized two groups who long defied his regime.

28 APRIL 1956
The last French soldier leaves Vietnam and the French High Command for Indochina is officially dissolved. The US Military Assistance Advisory Group (MAAG) will assume responsibility for training South Vietnamese military forces.

MAY 1956
In violation of the Geneva Accords, the United States sends 350 additional military men designated Temporary Equipment Recovery Team (TERM) to Saigon under the pretext of helping recover and redistribute equipment abandoned by the French. They will stay on as a permanent part of MAAG.

25 MAY 1956
The South Vietnamese Government reiterates its refusal to recognize the Geneva Agreements. Promising not to 'have recourse to solutions of violence,' and to respect the demarcation line and the demilitarized zone, Diem declares South Vietnam is in favor of free elections, but states that 'the absence of all liberties in North Vietnam makes impractical at this moment any approach to the problem of electoral and pre-electoral discussions.'

JUNE 1956
Senator John F Kennedy, speaking on what must be done to defeat Communism in South Vietnam, declares: 'what we must offer [the Vietnamese people] is a revolution – a political, economic and social revolution far superior to anything the Communists can offer – far more peaceful, far more democratic, and far more locally controlled.'

7 JULY 1956
A constitution written at Diem's direction and bearing American and French precedents is officially promulgated on the second anni-

versary of Diem's accession to power. The president, whose term of office is six years, has veto power over the unicameral Legislative Assembly, whose members are elected for four years, and may rule by decree when the Assembly is not in session. Both the president and the Assembly are chosen by direct suffrage. Freedom of speech, press and assembly are guaranteed, but may be suspended during the next four years if the president declares a state of emergency.

20 JULY 1956
The deadline set at Geneva in 1954 for nationwide elections passes. Diem's intransigence convinces many dissidents that the struggle to demand the implementation of the Geneva agreements is futile. Although Diem's harsh security measures have efficiently decimated the Vietminh, disorganized and uncoordinated insurgency begins in the South.

24 AUGUST 1956
The official Hanoi newspaper *Nhan Dan* reports that former Vietminh fighters and even party members are among those wrongly classified, convicted and executed in the land reform campaign. Truong Chinh, head of the campaign, is dismissed as party secretary and replaced by Ho Chi Minh; the minister of agriculture is also dismissed. A 'Campaign for the Rectification of Errors' is established, although Ho, conceding that the introduction of liberal measures is inadequate to repair the damage, remarks with grim realism, 'One cannot awaken the dead.'

8 NOVEMBER 1956
North Vietnam's Peoples Agricultural Reform Tribunals are officially abolished. Between 10,000 and 15,000 persons are estimated to have been killed erroneously, another 50,000-100,000 deported and imprisoned. Most are eventually released. Although the reforms result in 1.5 million poor and landless families receiving slightly more than one acre each, the need for land is still not satisfied, and high taxes and demands for bigger harvests, combined with depressed prices, create growing dissatisfaction.

10-20 NOVEMBER 1956
About 1000 peasants are killed or wounded and several thousand arrested and deported when Hanoi sends its 325th Division to suppress an open rebellion that has broken out over its land reform campaign in Ho Chi

Minh's native Nghe An Province, a region long known for its pro-Vietminh sentiments. Smaller outbreaks occur in other parts of the country. The ending of land reform probably prevents other rebellions, but it is not until February 1957 that the government feels strong enough to withdraw its units from affected areas and return the maintenance of order to local militias. The Vietminh blame the Chinese for pushing them into this disastrous land reform campaign.

3 JANUARY 1957
The International Control Commission reports that neither North Vietnam nor South Vietnam have been fulfilling their obligations under the 1954 Geneva armistice agreement from December 1955-August 1956.

24 JANUARY 1957
The Soviet Union suggests that North and South Vietnam be admitted to the United Nations as 'two separate states . . . which differ from one another in political and economic structure. Russia's suggestion favoring a permanent division of Vietnam underscores the futility of Hanoi's policy of 'political struggle' to enforce the Geneva agreements.

1 MAY 1957
French responsibility for training the South Vietnamese Navy and Air Force terminates. The French naval and air force training mission is withdrawn in June.

8 MAY 1957
During Diem's visit (5-19 May) to the United States, Eisenhower calls him the 'miracle man' of Asia and reaffirms support for his regime. The Vietminh see a powerful America replacing a weak France as the major outside force in Indochina. After Diem's visit, some 6000 hard-core guerrillas, exhausted after eight years of war with the French and underground since 1954, begin a program of harassment, sabotage, and assassination. This murdering of officials – over 400 minor South Vietnamese officials are assassinated by the end of the year – is designed to disrupt social, political, and economic progress in South Vietnam which the guerrillas perceive as making reunification on their terms more difficult.

11 MAY 1957
President Diem and President Eisenhower issue a joint communiqué which declares that

CHRONOLOGY

President Diem visited the United States in 1957 to strengthen ties between the two nations.

both countries will work toward a 'peaceful unification' of Vietnam and reaffirms the United States' continuing assistance to South Vietnam in its stand against Communism.

24 JUNE 1957
The US Army's 1st Special Forces Group is activated in Okinawa. In the course of the year from this unit trains 58 men of the Vietnamese Army at the Commando Training Center in Nha Trang. These trainees become the nucleus of the Vietnamese Special Forces.

18 JULY 1957
In a letter to President Diem, Pham Van Dong suggests that discussions take place on the organization of elections, and that postal services between the two zones be restored as a step toward reunification. South Vietnam refuses, citing essentially the same reasons given in Diem's 6 July 1955 broadcast.

OCTOBER 1957
Communist insurgent activity in South Vietnam begins in earnest when a decision is reached in Hanoi to organize 37 armed companies in the Mekong Delta.

22 OCTOBER 1957
US military personnel suffer their first casualties in the Vietnam War when 13 Americans are wounded in three terrorist bombings of MAAG and US Information Service installations in Saigon. While the rising tide of guerrilla activity in South Vietnam reaches an estimated 30 terrorist incidents and at least 75 local officials assassinated or kidnapped in the last quarter of 1957, US intelligence in Saigon reports, 'there is only sparse evidence that North Vietnam was directing, or was capable of directing, that violence.'

DECEMBER 1957
By the end of 1957 the Diem government is able to announce that at least 300,000 refugees from the North have been settled in 300 new villages in the South. Local leadership, notably organized by refugee Catholic priests, plays an important role, along with US assistance and the natural wealth of one million acres of abandoned rice land, in achieving the most universally acknowledged success of the Diem regime. Although Diem does enjoy some popular support between 1955 and 1957, thereafter his policies create only discontent, and most of his energies and

the military and economic aid flowing from the United States are directed at maintaining himself and his family in power.

7 MARCH 1958
In a letter to President Diem, Phan Van Dong proposes that representatives of North Vietnam and South Vietnam meet at an early date to discuss a reduction in the number of troops on both sides and the establishment of trade relations with a view toward reunification. The letter strongly criticizes 'American interference in the internal affairs of Southeast Asian countries,' particularly Vietnam.

26 APRIL 1958
The South Vietnamese Government issues a statement rejecting Pham Van Dong's offer of 7 March. While stating that the South Vietnamese government also desires normalization of relations aimed at the country's unification, it characterizes North Vietnam's offer as 'phoney' and 'a propaganda trick,' and attaches a list of conditions to the opening of North-South discussions that the North is almost certainly unwilling or unable to meet.

JUNE 1958
The Communists form a coordinated command structure in the eastern Mekong Delta. Most of the 37 companies formed in October 1957 are located in the western Mekong Delta.

25 JUNE 1958
Cambodia alleges that South Vietnamese troops have invaded and occupied several Cambodian border villages, and accuses South Vietnam of 19 cases of violation of Cambodian territory since 1957. The allegation is repudiated by South Vietnam's foreign minister.

DECEMBER 1958
The CIA comes into possession of a directive from Hanoi to its headquarters for the Central Highlands stating that the Lao Dong (Communist) Party Central Committee has decided to 'open a new stage of the struggle' and move into overt insurgency.

JANUARY 1959
The CIA receives a copy of an order from Hanoi directing the establishment of two guerrilla operations bases, one in the western Central Highlands and one in Tayninh Province, near the Cambodian border.

APRIL 1959
The 559 Transportation Group is established directly under the Lao Dong Central Committee as a headquarters in charge of infiltration of insurgents into the South. Almost all infiltraters until 1964 are native southerners who went to the North in 1954 following the Geneva Agreements and expected to return to their homes in a reunited Vietnam after the elections agreed upon at Geneva were held.

4 APRIL 1959
Speaking at Gettysburg College in Gettysburg, Pennsylvania, of 'the inescapable conclusion that our own national interests damand' our support of South Vietnam, President Eisenhower delivers a speech which clearly links America's own 'national interest' to the survival of a non-Communist regime in South Vietnam.

MAY 1959
Saigon US advisors are assigned to the regimental level of South Vietnamese armed forces.

Hanoi At the 15th plenum of the Central Committee, North Vietnam's leaders formally decide to take control of the growing insurgency in the South. The tempo of the war speeds up as more southern cadre members infiltrate back to the South along an improved Ho Chi Minh Trail. Although infiltration from the North began in 1955, not until 1959 does the CIA pick up evidence of large-scale infiltration. Hanoi's decisions this month along with troop movements in preparation for an October offensive are viewed by intelligence in Washington as the beginnings of North Vietnamese intervention.

JULY 1959
The Lao Dong organizes Group 759 to study ways to ship men and supplies to the South by sea. The activities of this group and of group 559 are kept highly secret, as they are in clear violation of the Geneva agreements.

8 JULY 1959
Major Dale R Buis and Master Sergeant Chester M Ovnand become the first Americans killed in the Vietnam war when guerrillas strike a MAAG compound in Bienhoa, 20 miles northeast of Saigon.

AUGUST 1959
Diem promulgates a law authorizing severe repression of Communists and other dissi-

dents. The Vietcong campaign of assassination of local officials picks up dramatically – between 1959 and 1961 the number killed rises from 1200 to 4000 per year – and Diem reacts by appointing more military men to administrative posts, indirectly aiding the strategy of the insurgents by neglecting the social and economic needs of local populations.

30 AUGUST 1959
General elections held in South Vietnam result in an overwhelming victory for the government. Only government supporters are permitted to take part in the election; the vigorous non-Communist opposition is excluded. The two opposition members returned, Dr Phan Quang Dan and Nguyen Tran, are elected as independents when their party, the Democratic Bloc, is refused registration. They are refused seats when the Assembly meets, and later found guilty and fined on trumped-up charges of electoral law infractions.

12 SEPTEMBER 1959
North Vietnam Premier Pham Van Dong tells the French Consul: 'You must remember we will be in Saigon tomorrow.' In November he tells the Canadian Commissioner, 'We will drive the Americans into the sea.' The US Embassy in Saigon eventually passes these remarks along to Washington as evidence of the deteriorating situation in South Vietnam.

26 SEPTEMBER 1959
Vietcong ambush two companies of Saigon's 23rd Division killing 12 soldiers and capturing most of their weapons. The attack brings home Hanoi's decision to switch from 'political struggle' to 'armed struggle.'

17 JANUARY 1960
A popular uprising begins in Ben Tre Province, about 100 miles from Saigon in the Mekong Delta. Villagers armed with mattocks, machetes, spears, swords and sharpened bamboo join slightly better armed dissidents to storm civil guard posts and overthrow village administrations. Largely a reaction to oppressive measures employed by the Diem regime in the construction and maintenance of 'agrovilles,' the peasants, for the first time under the direction of the NLF, organize defense and survive a counterattack. For the first time a popular armed insurrection achieves victory on a provincial scale.

5 FEBRUARY 1960
The South Vietnamese Government requests that the United States double MAAG strength from 342 to 685.

17 APRIL 1960
Saigon The International Control Commission (ICC) agrees to the increase of American MAAG personnel to 685.
Hanoi North Vietnam protests to the chairmen of the 1954 Geneva Conference (Britain and the Soviet Union) against a 'formidable' increase in US MAAG personnel in South Vietnam; and accuses the United States of turning South Vietnam into 'a US military base for the preparation of a new war.'

AUGUST 1960
An American special national intelligence estimate notes that unless the South Vietnamese government can protect the peasants and win their cooperation and support, areas of Vietcong control will expand; and dissatisfaction and discontent with the government will continue to rise.

5 SEPTEMBER 1960
At the third congress of the Lao Dong Party, Hanoi leadership acknowledges that all hopes of achieving their objectives through elections are finally exhausted, and addresses the need to overthrow the Diem regime and liberate the South.

16 SEPTEMBER 1960
In a cable to Secretary of State Christian A Herter, US Ambassador in Saigon Elbridge Durbrow analyzes two separate but related threats to the Diem regime – danger from demonstration or coup, predominantly 'non-Communist' in origin; and the danger of the gradual Vietcong extension of control over the countryside. Durbrow explains that a coup would be partly motivated by a 'sincere desire to prevent Communist take-over in Vietnam.' He suggests methods Diem might use to mitigate both threats – including sending his brother Nhu abroad and improving relations with the peasantry – and ends by declaring, 'If Diem's position in country continues deteriorate as result failure adopt proper political, psychological, economic and security measures, it may become necessary for US government to begin consideration

alternative courses of action and leaders in order achieve our objective.'

8 NOVEMBER 1960
John F Kennedy is elected president of the United States.

11-12 NOVEMBER 1960
Paratroop battalions and a marine unit under the direction of Colonel Nguyen Van Thi and Lieutenant Colonel Vuong Van Dong surround Diem in the presidential palace in an effort to force reforms. Colonel Thi declares that Diem has 'shown himself incapable of saving the country from Communism and protecting national unity.' Diem feigns announcing concessions, and stalls until loyal

troops arrive. From this time on many in the military, including Diem's former allies, plot against him.

4 DECEMBER 1960
Ambassador Durbrow, reflecting weakening US leverage on Diem, who steadfastly resists pressures for economic and political reform, writes Washington, 'We may well be forced, in the not too distant future, to undertake the difficult task of identifying and supporting alternative leadership.'

20 DECEMBER 1960
Hanoi announces the formation of the National Front for the Liberation of the South

President-elect John F Kennedy confers with President Eisenhower shortly after the election.

– more commonly known as the National Liberation Front or NLF – at a congress held 'somewhere in the South.' One hundred delegates representing more than a dozen political parties and religious groups, including remnants of the Cao Dai, Hoa Hao, and Binh Xuyen, are in attendance. A broad yet Communist-controlled coalition, the NLF is truly the Vietminh reborn. The Saigon regime dubs the NLF the 'Vietcong,' a pejorative contraction of *Viet Nam Cong San* (Vietnamese Communists). This label, created by Diem's publicists, is designed to brand the rebels as Communists, and comes to be applied generally to the supporters and participants of the insurgency.

31 DECEMBER 1960
An estimated 4500 former South Vietnamese living in the North have infiltrated back to South Vietnam during the year. US forces in Vietnam now number 900.

6 JANUARY 1961
Soviet Premier Nikita Khruschev declares that the Soviet Union will back all 'wars on national liberation' around the world. This will greatly influence the incoming Kennedy administration to support a strategy of 'counterinsurgency,' particularly in Vietnam.

19 JANUARY 1961
Outgoing President Eisenhower cautions incoming President Kennedy that Laos is 'the key to the entire area of Southeast Asia' and might even require the direct intervention of US combat troops. Fearing the fall of Laos to the Communist Pathet Lao forces, President Kennedy increases US presence in the region by sending a carrier task force to the Gulf of Siam.

23 MARCH 1961
One of the first American casualties in Indochina, an SC-47 intelligence gathering plane en route from Vientiane in Laos to Saigon, is shot down over the Plain of Jars while checking radio frequencies used by Russian planes delivering arms to the Pathet Lao. Subsequently, at President Kennedy's suggestion, RT-33s borrowed from the Philippines Air Force and painted with Laotian markings are used for reconnaissance.

28 MARCH 1961
Citing that more than one-half of the rural region surrounding Saigon is under Communist control, and recalling the barely failed coup against Diem the preceeding November, a national intelligence estimate prepared for President Kennedy declares that Diem and the Republic of Vietnam are facing an extremely critical period. Not only are the Vietcong, who encircle the city, moving closer, but also the discontent which gave rise to the coup against Diem has not been dealt with. The report questions Diem's ability to rally the people against Communism.

1 APRIL 1961
Four hundred guerrillas attacking a village in Kienhoa Province are beaten off by South Vietnamese troops. Two days later, 100 guerrillas are killed in an attack on Bencat, north of Saigon.

12 APRIL 1961
Walt W Rostow, senior White House specialist on Southeast Asia and a principle architect of the counterinsurgency doctrine, delivers a memorandum to President Kennedy proposing that the time has come for 'gearing up the whole Vietnam operation.' Rostow's proposals, almost all of which eventually become policy, include: a visit to Vietnam by the vice-president, increasing the number of American Special Forces, increasing funds for Diem, and 'persuading Diem to move more rapidly to broaden the base of his Government, as well as to decrease its centralization and improve its efficiency.'

26-29 APRIL 1961
President Kennedy meets with the National Security Council to decide whether to send troops into Laos. In the heat of the crisis, Deputy Secretary of Defense Roswell L Gilpatric recommends quick expansion of South Vietnam's forces by 40,000 to prevent an invasion of South Vietnam from Laos. Two 1600-man US training troops and 400 counterinsurgency Special Forces are also recommended. In addition to what would be the first major input of US troops, on 29 April the Joint Chiefs of Staff cable Admiral Harry Felt to be prepared to send one brigade with air elements to northeastern Thailand and another to Danang, as a threat to intervene in Laos. Kennedy finally orders 100 additional advisors to the US mission in Saigon. The United States has clearly signaled its willingness to go beyond the 685-man limit on its Saigon mission.

4 MAY 1961
At a press conference Secretary of State Dean Rusk reports that Vietcong forces have grown to 12,000 men and have killed or kidnapped more than 3000 persons in 1960. While declaring that the United States will supply South Vietnam with every possible help, he refuses to say whether the United States will intervene militarily. At a press conference the next day President Kennedy says consideration is being given to the use of US forces.

9 MAY 1961
At a National Security Council meeting Gilpatric's recommendations are thoroughly revised, hinging on a new 'bilateral security arrangement with Vietnam.' Vice-President Johnson departs for Saigon.

11 MAY 1961
President Kennedy approves sending 400 special Forces troops and 100 other US military advisors to South Vietnam, on the same day ordering the start of a clandestine warfare against North Vietnam to be conducted by South Vietnamese agents under the direction and training of the CIA and US Special Forces troops. Kennedy's orders also call for infiltration of South Vietnamese forces into Laos to locate and disrupt Communist bases and supply lines.

12 MAY 1961
Vice-President Johnson meets with Diem in Saigon during his tour of Asian countries. Calling Diem the 'Churchill of Asia,' he encourages Diem to view himself as indispensible to the United States. On his return home Johnson echoes domino theorists, foreshadowing his future fears that the loss of Vietnam would compel the United States to fight 'on the beaches of Waikiki' and eventually on 'our own shores.' He finds Diem uninterested in US combat troops except in the event of open invasion.

16 MAY 1961
A fourteen-nation conference on Laos convenes in Geneva.

23 MAY 1961
Vice-President Johnson reports to President Kennedy on his visit to Asia. Giving Thailand and Vietnam pivotal significance, he reports that the United States must either aid these countries or 'pull back our defenses to San Francisco and a "Fortress America" concept.' He feels Asian leaders would welcome US troops if openly attacked.

4 JUNE 1961
President Kennedy and Premier Khrushchev of Russia, meeting in Vienna about the situation in Berlin, strike a bargain to support a neutral and independent Laos. While satisfied with this solution for Laos, Kennedy rejects neutrality for Vietnam even though Hanoi appears prepared to agree, believing that South Vietnam is the place to make US power credible.

9 JUNE 1961
Diem requests US assistance in increasing the South Vietnamese Army by 100,000 men. In August Washington agrees to finance a 30,000-man increase, but continues to postpone the build-up of US advisors Diem also requested.

16 JUNE 1961
Following a meeting between President Kennedy and South Vietnam's Nguyen Dinh Thuan, an agreement is reached for direct training and combat supervision of Vietnamese troops by US instructors.

JULY 1961
General Lansdale submits a report on the 'First Observation Group,' the clandestine warfare unit ordered by President Kennedy in May. About to expand from 340 to 805 men, the group's activities are soon to shift from actions against Vietcong in the South and focus entirely on North Vietnam.

2 JULY 1961
Hanoi captures at least three members of Lansdale's US-trained First Observation Group when their US C-47 aircraft is shot down (or experiences engine trouble).

16 JULY 1961
In what is described as the bloodiest battle since the 1954 armistice with the French, 169 guerrillas are killed by South Vietnamese forces in the Plain of Jars marsh area 80 miles west of Saigon.

18 SEPTEMBER 1961
A Communist force of over 1500 besieges Phuoc Vinh, a provincial capital 60km north of Saigon. During August there were 41 engagements between government troops and insurgent units in South Vietnam.

CHRONOLOGY

President Kennedy with Brigadier General Yarborough of the newly established Special Forces.

21 SEPTEMBER 1961
The US Army's 5th Special Forces Group, 1st Special Forces, is activated at Fort Bragg, North Carolina, and eventually becomes in charge of all Special Forces operations in Vietnam. Based on his belief in the potential of the Special Forces in counterinsurgency, President Kennedy visits the Special Warfare Center to review the program, and authorizes the Special Forces to wear the headgear that becomes their symbol, the Green Beret.

1 OCTOBER 1961
SEATO experts meet in Bangkok to discuss

guerrilla warfare in South Vietnam; the United States considers sending troops.

2 OCTOBER 1961
Addressing the National Assembly, President Diem declares that the Vietcong guerrilla campaign has grown into a 'real war.' The enemy 'attacks us with regular units fully and completely equipped,' and 'seeks a strategic position in Southeast Asia in conformity with the orders of the Communist International.'

5 OCTOBER 1961
Intelligence estimates that 80-90 percent of the 17,000 Vietcong in South Vietnam have been locally recruited and do not depend on external supplies. The same report deals realistically with the political and psychological rewards the Vietcong could expect from operations against SEATO forces.

11 OCTOBER 1961
At a meeting of the National Security Council, President Kennedy is asked to accept 'as our real and ultimate objective the defeat of the Vietcong.' The Joint Chiefs of Staff estimate that 40,000 US troops could clean up 'the Vietcong threat,' and another 120,000 could cope with possible North Vietnamese or Chinese Communist intervention. Kennedy decides to send General Maxwell Taylor to Vietnam to study the situation.

13 OCTOBER 1961
The Diem government sends an urgent request through Ambassador Frederick Nolting for US combat units or units introduced as 'combat trainer units,' as well as for additional aircraft and a symbolic US presence in the Central Highlands.

18-24 OCTOBER 1961
General Taylor arrives in Saigon and is greeted by President Diem's formal declaration of a state of emergency, a result of increased Vietcong activity and severe floods. Diem does not renew his request for American combat troops, but asks for tactical aviation, helicopter companies, coastal patrol forces, and ground transport; and reiterates his desire for a bilateral defense treaty with the United States. General Taylor perceives the disastrous flooding in the Mekong Delta as a potential cover for the introduction of 6000-8000 US combat troops, which might be withdrawn or augmented after the work of flood rehabilitation is completed.

NOVEMBER 1961
US Special Forces medical specialists are deployed to provide assistance to the *montagnard* tribes around Pleiku; out of this will develop the Civilian Irregular Defense Group (CIDG), a program of organized paramilitary forces among the ethnic and religious minorities of South Vietnam and the chief work of the US Special Forces during the war.

1 NOVEMBER 1961
Writing President Kennedy from the Philippines, General Taylor urges commitment of a 'US military task force' to Vietnam and advocates a 'massive joint effort' with the South Vietnamese to cope with the flood and the Vietcong. He feels the presence of US ground troops is essential to 'reverse the present downward trend of events.' Cabling from Japan, Secretary of State Dean Rusk acknowledges the great importance of the security of Southeast Asia, but questions Diem's abilities as well as the ability of South Vietnam to succeed against the Communists even with US help.

3 NOVEMBER 1961
General Taylor's final report proposes a hard commitment of US ground forces and introduces the concept of US 'limited partnership' in Vietnam, suggesting that the US military mission in Saigon become something nearer to an operational headquarters in a theater of war. The report assumes that the Americans can supply the South Vietnamese with the fervor needed to win, and asserts that if all else fails the United States can count on the bombing of North Vietnam or even the threat of bombing to hold Hanoi and other Communist nations at bay, avoiding the risk of a major land war. Kennedy eventually rejects this approach, but soon after Taylor's visit USAF Globemasters begin shuttling in US instructors and advisors, and Kennedy authorizes sending SC-47s, B-26s, and T-28 fighter bomber trainers to Bien Hoa Air Base, just north of Saigon.

12 NOVEMBER 1961
It is reported that four US F-101 reconnaissance jets are engaged in photo-spotting guerrillas units in remote areas vulnerable to air attack.

11 DECEMBER 1961
The ferry-carrier USNS *Core* arrives in Saigon with the first US helicopter units, 33

CHRONOLOGY

Vertol H-21C Shawnees and 400 air and ground crewmen to operate and maintain them. Their assignment will be airlifting South Vietnamese Army troops into combat.

14 DECEMBER 1961
A public exchange of letters between Presidents Kennedy and Diem formally announces the decisions on troop build-up. Kennedy writes, 'we shall promptly increase our assistance to your defense effort.' At first Diem refuses to heed US demands that he liberalize his regime. Threatened with a reduction in aid, Diem finally consents to the reforms in return for a heavy increase in US aid.

16 DECEMBER 1961
Operation 'Farm Gate' aircraft are authorized to fly combat missions, provided a Vietnamese crew member is aboard. Because the 1954 Geneva Agreements prohibit introduction of bombers into Indochina, US B-26 and SC-47 bombers are redesignated 'reconnaissance bombers.'

20 DECEMBER 1961
According to *The New York Times*, about 2000 uniformed US troops and specialists are 'operating in battle areas with South Vietnamese forces,' and are authorized to fire back if fired upon.

31 DECEMBER 1961
According to MAAG, US military forces in South Vietnam have reached 3200. The number of US servicemen in November was 948; total insurgent forces are estimated at 26,700. Fourteen Americans have been killed or wounded in combat. Two Army helicopter units are flying combat missions; 'Jungle Jim' air commandoes are instructing the South Vietnamese Air Force; US Navy Mine Division 73 (a tender and five sweepers) is sailing from Danang along the coastline; US aircraft from Thailand and Seventh Fleet carriers are flying surveillance and reconnaissance missions over Vietnam; and six C-123 aircraft equipped for support of defoliant operations have received 'diplomatic clearance' to enter South Vietnam. $65 million of US military equipment and $136 million in economic aid have been delivered to South Vietnam in 1961.

JANUARY 1962
The United States installs a tactical air control system in South Vietnam and furnishes additional aircraft for combat and airlift support.

4 JANUARY 1962
The United States and South Vietnam announce in a joint communiqué that they will cooperate in starting 'a broad economic and social program aimed at providing every Vietnamese with the means for improving his standard of living ... Measures to strengthen South Vietnam's defense in the military field are being taken simultaneously.'

10 JANUARY 1962
The Soviet Union denounces the United States for 'gross interference' in South Vietnam's internal affairs and for 'open violations of the international agreements on Indochina, placing primary responsibility 'for the present worsening of the situation in South Vietnam' on the United States and accuses Diem of abolishing all democratic liberties and of creating 'a military dictatorship based on ruthless terror.'

12 JANUARY 1962
The USAF launches Operation Ranch Hand, a 'modern technological area-denial technique', designed to expose the roads and trails used by Vietcong forces. Flying C-123 Providers, US personnel will dump an estimated 19 million gallons of defoliating herbicides (Agent Orange – so named from the color of its metal containers – is the most frequently used) over 10-20 percent of Vietnam and parts of Laos between 1962-1971. The operation will succeed in killing vegetation but not in stopping the Vietcong. Furthermore, the herbicides have a small proportion of dioxin, a chemical that at least in larger doses is considered a carcinogen and/or otherwise dangerous to human beings. Long after the war ends, thousands of veterans of Vietnam will attribute many medical, genetic (in their offspring), and psycholgical problems to exposure to dioxin.

13 JANUARY 1962
In the first Farm Gate combat mission, T-28 fighter-bombers are flown in support of a South Vietnamese outpost under Vietcong attack. By the end of the month USAF planes have flown 229 Farm Gate sorties.

15 JANUARY 1962
Washington Asked at a news conference if US troops are fighting in Vietnam, President Kennedy answers, 'No.'

South Vietnam The Peoples Revolutionary Party is founded. Ostensibly independent of the Communist Party in the North, it consolidates Marxist control of the NLF.

27 JANUARY 1962
Secretary of Defense McNamara forwards a memorandum from the Joint Chiefs of Staff to President Kennedy which urges the deployment of US forces to Vietnam. Recapitulating the domino theory, the Joint Chiefs of Staff assert that failure to deploy now will only delay the time when it must be done, and will make the task more difficult.

FEBRUARY 1962
The 39th Signal Battalion, a communications unit, is the first unit of US regular ground forces to arrive in Vietnam.

4 FEBRUARY 1962
The first US helicopter is shot down in Vietnam, one of 15 ferrying troops in an attack against the village of Hong My.

8 FEBRUARY 1962
The Military Assistance Command, Vietnam (MACV) headed by former US Army Deputy Commander-in-Chief in the Pacific General Paul D Harkins, is installed in Saigon as the United States reorganizes its military command in South Vietnam. Henceforth the conduct of the war is directed by MACV, which supervises MAAG.

11 FEBRUARY 1962
The first Farm Gate mission casualties occur when nine US and South Vietnamese crew members are killed in an SC-47 crash about 70 miles north of Saigon.

14 FEBRUARY 1962
President Kennedy reiterates in a news conference that 'the training missions we have [in South Vietnam] have been instructed that if they are fired upon, they are of course to fire back, but we have not sent combat troops in [the] generally understood sense of the word.' The next day former Vice-President Nixon expresses hopes that President Kennedy will 'step-up the build-up and under no circumstances curtail it because of possible criticism.'

27 FEBRUARY 1962
In a dramatic display of opposition to Diem's regime, two Vietnamese pilots flying US AD-6 fighter-bombers bomb, napalm and strafe the presidential palace, primarily out of frustration at Diem's failure to prosecute the war effectively. Diem and family miraculously escape injury. The attack confirms Diem's conviction that his main adversaries are domestic, and as a result he retreats deeper into himself, delegating more authority to his brother Nhu.

22 MARCH 1962
Operation Sunrise, South Vietnam's first long-range counteroffensive against the Vietcong, is launched in Binh Duong province, 35 miles north of Saigon. Central to the operation is the forced relocation of peasants in 'strategic hamlets,' fortified stockades in what is essentially a resumption of Diem's 'agroville' program. The plan to corral peasants into armed stockades, depriving the Vietcong of their support, proves ill-conceived, expensive and ineffective; it is used by Diem and his brother Nhu more to extend their influence and control than to encourage peasants to resist Vietcong. Nhu's chief lieutenant for the program, Colonel Pham Ngoc Thao, a secret Communist, welcomes the chance to estrange South Vietnamese peasants and drive them into the arms of the Vietcong.

9 APRIL 1962
Two US soldiers are killed in a Vietcong ambush while on a combat operation with Vietnamese troops. Questioned about the deaths in a news conference two days later, President Kennedy remarks, 'We are attempting to help Vietnam maintain its independence and not fall under the domination of the Communists ... We cannot desist in Vietnam.'

15 APRIL 1962
The first Marine air units sent to Vietnam, 15 Sikorsky UH-34D combat helicopters of the US 362nd Marine Medium Helicopter Squadron (HMM-362), arrive from the aircraft carrier *Princeton*. Based near Soc Trang, 100 miles southwest of Saigon, the 450 Marines and their craft, a task unit dubbed 'Shoofly,' reinforce the three US Army helicopter companies already in Vietnam, and carry supplies and troops to isolated or threatened villages and troop concentrations.

22 APRIL 1962
Twenty-nine US helicopters airlift about 600 Vietnamese troops to the Mekong Delta in

CHRONOLOGY

Kein Phong Province (about 80 miles south of Saigon) to double the number of troops used in a mopping up operation there.

MAY 1962
Some 5000 US troops (including US Special Forces, or Green Berets) are serving in South Vietnam, and there are a total of 124 US aircraft including two USAF C-123 squadrons and four helicopter companies. The Communists are forming battalion-size units in central Vietnam.

11 MAY 1962
Secretary of Defense McNamara makes the first of many trips to Vietnam and meets with Diem. After 48 hours in the country he concludes, 'every quantitative measurement ... shows that we are winning the war.'

17 MAY 1962
Three thousand US Marines begin landing at Bangkok, Thailand, in response to troop movements near the Thai border by the Soviet-supported Laotian Pathet Lao army. The Marines are flown 350 miles north to Udorn, which is 35 miles from the Laotian capital of Vientiane. This US show of force, ordered by President Kennedy at the request of the Thai government, is out of Thailand by the beginning of August. In Saigon President Diem publishes several presidential decrees forbidding the holding of any meeting for any purpose without prior governmental approval.

25 MAY 1962
A report of the International Control Commission (ICC) for Vietnam charges North Vietnam with subversion and aggression in South Vietnam. It also charges that the United States is violating the Geneva Agreements with its military buildup in South Vietnam, and accuses South Vietnam of violating the 1954 Geneva Accords by accepting US military aid and establishing 'a factual military alliance' with the US. The report is adopted by the Indian and Canadian members of the ICC but is opposed by the Polish member.

18 JULY 1962
The largest helicopter lift in Vietnam thus far takes Vietnamese troops north of Saigon in 18 Marine helicopters, 12 US Army helicopters, and 11 helicopters belonging to the Vietnamese Air Force.

23 JULY 1962
The declaration and protocol on the neutrality of Laos is signed at the 14-nation conference in Geneva. At a Honolulu conference on Vietnam strategy, Secretary of Defense McNamara orders planning for US withdrawal from Vietnam and the reduction of aid to Saigon. His orders reflect what is perceived as 'tremendous progress' during early 1962, as well as reservations concerning domestic support for longterm US involvement.

1 AUGUST 1962
Marine helicopter unit Shoofly (HMM-362) is replaced by HMM-163 after flying 50 combat troop lifts involving 130 landings against the Vietcong. The Marines suffer no casualties this tour. HMM-163 relocates at Danang in September.

22 AUGUST 1962
Kennedy administration officials quoted in The New York Times estimate there are 20,000 guerrilla troops in South Vietnam. Despite hundreds of engagements during the preceding two months and encouraging victories for South Vietnamese forces, the Vietcong has grown in numbers, and US officials feel the war has reached a point of stalemate.

OCTOBER 1962
In a major showdown with the Soviet Union, President Kennedy forces the Soviets to withdraw missiles from Cuba.

15 OCTOBER 1962
Despite State Department denials, several sources report that US helicopter crewmen have begun to fire first on Vietcong formations encountered during missions with South Vietnamese troops.

19 OCTOBER 1962
Operation Morning Star, a major South Vietnamese effort to clear Tayninh Province, north of Saigon near the Cambodian border, ends in failure. Five thousand South Vietnamese troops ferried by US helicopters kill 40 Vietcong in eight days and capture two others. One HU-IA attack helicopter is lost. US officials call the operation a waste and disclaim any responsibility for it.

2 DECEMBER 1962
Following a trip to Vietnam at President Kennedy's request, Senate Majority Leader

Robert McNamara was Secretary of Defense during the Kennedy and Johnson administrations.

Mike Mansfield (D-MT) becomes the first major US official to refuse to make an optimistic public comment on the progress of the war. Originally a supporter of Diem, what he sees prompts him to reverse himself and report that the $2 billion the United States has poured into Vietnam during the past seven years has accomplished nothing. He places blame squarely on the Diem regime for its failure to share power, suggesting that the Americans are simply taking the unenviable place formerly occupied by the French. His reversal surprises and irritates President Kennedy.

3 DECEMBER 1962

In a memorandum to Dean Rusk, Roger Hilsman, director of the State Department Bureau of Intelligence and Research, points out that the Vietcong are obviously prepared for a long struggle. While government control of the countryside has improved slightly, the Vietcong has expanded considerably in size and influence, both through its own efforts and because of its attraction for 'increasingly

frustrated non-Communist anti-Diem elements.' Successful counterinsurgency will take several years of greater effort by both the United States and the South Vietnamese Government. Real success hinges upon Diem gaining the support of the peasants through social and military measures he has failed to implement. Hilsman feels that a non-Communist coup against Diem 'could occur at any time,' and would seriously disrupt or reverse counterinsurgency momentum.

29 DECEMBER 1962

Saigon announces that 4077 strategic hamlets have been completed out of a projected total of 11,182, and now house 39 percent of the South Vietnamese population. These figures are considered questionable. Approximately 11,000 US advisory and support personnel are now in Vietnam, including 29 Special Forces detachments. One hundred and nine Americans have been killed or wounded this year, almost eight times as many as in 1961. US Army aviation units have flown over 50,000 sorties, about one-half of which are combat

CHRONOLOGY

Troops of the Vietnamese 21st Division prepare to search a village for Vietcong.

support missions. China claims to have armed the Vietcong with more than 90,000 rifles and machine guns this year, and trained guerrilla forces in South Vietnam are estimated at 25,000, with active Vietcong sympathizers numbered at 150,000. The Vietcong are now killing or kidnapping 1000 local officials per month. South Vietnamese government regular troops number 200,000 and 65,000 Self Defense Corps members have been trained to defend their villages.

2 JANUARY 1963
At Ap Bac in the Mekong Delta 30-50 miles southeast of Saigon 2500 troops of South Vietnam's 7th Infanry Divison equipped with automatic weapons, armored amphibious personnel carriers, and supported by bombers and helicopters fail to defeat a group of 300 guerrillas who escape almost intact after inflicting heavy losses on the army. The engagement is a landmark in revealing that government troops can neither cope with the strategy nor match the fighting spirit of the Vietcong. South Vietnamese officials in Saigon are irate with US advisors' candid assessments of the action.

11 FEBRUARY 1963
Senior White House aide Michael V Forrestal advises President Kennedy to expect a long and costly war. 'No one really knows how many of the 20,000 "Vietcong" killed last year were only innocent, or at least persuadable, villagers, whether the strategic hamlet program is providing enough government services to counteract the sacrifices it

requires, or how the mute class of villagers react to the charges against Diem of dictatorship and nepotism.' He points out that Vietcong recruitment in South Vietnam is effective enough to continue the war without any infiltration from the North.

26 FEBRUARY 1963
US helicopters are ordered to shoot first at enemy soldiers while escorting government troops. Two days before, one US soldier was killed when Vietcong ground-fire downs two of three US Army H-21 helicopters airlifting government soldiers about 100 miles north of Saigon.

11 APRIL 1963
One hundred US troops of the Hawaiian-based 25th Infantry Division have reinforced military units in South Vietnam to serve as machine gunners aboard Army H-21 helicopters.

17 APRIL 1963
Diem broadcasts an 'Open Arms' (Chieu Hoi) appeal, promising clemency and material benefits to Vietcong guerrillas if they abandon the war against his government. As a result of this plea, 2787 defect from Communist ranks, 1789 of them peasants living in Vietcong strongholds.

5 MAY 1963
The Americans for Democratic Action (ADA) issues a resolution demanding that the United States Government withdraw its troops from Vietnam.

58

8 MAY 1963

Twenty thousand Buddhists in Hué celebrating the traditional celebrated as the birthday of Gautama Siddhartha Buddha are fired upon by order of Catholic deputy province chief Major Dang Xi, who chooses to enforce an old French decree forbidding them from flying their multicolored flag. Nine persons are killed, including seven children and one woman. and about 20 are wounded. Diem blames the incident on the Vietcong and refuses Buddhist demands that the officials responsible be punished, although Major Xi and two others are eventually dismissed. In Vietnam, Buddhists form at least 70 percent of the population and Catholics less than 10 percent, but the government is dominated by Catholics – Diem and his family are Catholics – and in the armed forces, the police, the civil service, the universities and the trade unions Buddhists have been removed from key positions and replaced by Catholics, because Diem regards them as more politically reliable. Buddhist protests begin to crystallize the growing resentment against Diem's regime. Thich Tri Quang, a politically sophisticated monk of North Vietnamese origin twice arrested by the French on suspicion of Vietminh connections, stirs up the people against Diem and informs US officials in Saigon, whom he holds responsible for Diem because of US support, that they must make Diem reform or get rid of him. Ambassador Nolting urges Diem to conciliate, but Diem refuses.

7 JUNE 1963

Diem's sister-in-law Madame Nhu, self-styled First Lady of Vietnam, alleges the Buddhists are being manipulated by the Americans, publicly contradicting Diem. Pressure from Deputy Ambassador William Trueheart forces Diem to create a cosmetic committee to investigate the Hué incident.

Wounded Vietnamese being evacuated from the fighting along the Kinh Xang canal.

CHRONOLOGY

10 JUNE 1963
MACV Commander General Paul Harkins is reported to warn US military personnel to avoid duty with Vietnamese military units involved in the suppression of Buddhists.

11 JUNE 1963
Buddhist monk Quang Duc publicly burns himself in a plea for Diem to show 'charity and compassion' to all religions. Diem remains stubborn, despite repeated US requests, and his special committee of inquiry confirms his contention that Vietcong are responsible for the Hué incident. More Buddhist monks immolate themselves during ensuing weeks. In an orgy of bad taste, Madame Nhu refers to the burnings as 'barbecues' and offers to supply matches.

27 JUNE 1963
Pesident Kennedy appoints Henry Cabot Lodge, his former Republican political opponent, to succeed Nolting as ambassador to Vietnam (beginning 1 August). In Washington, the Kennedy administration begins seriously speculating on a coup against Diem.

4 JULY 1963
General Tran Van Don informs Lucien Conein of the CIA, that certain officers are planning a coup against Diem.

30 JULY 1963
Ninety Vietcong are killed in a four-hour battle in the Camau Peninsula. Three government soldiers die.

20 AUGUST 1963
Diem accepts the proposal of Tran Van Don and other generals that he declare martial law in order to prosecute the war more effectively. The generals' real purpose is to consolidate control for a coup; Diem accepts in order to implicate the army in a scheme to crack down on the Buddhists conceived by his brother Nhu.

21 AUGUST 1963
Shortly after midnight, troops loyal to Diem and Nhu disguised as regular soldiers attack Buddhist temples and sanctuaries in Saigon, Hue' and other cities, destroying property and beating, jailing and murdering hundreds of monks, nuns, students, student activists and ordinary citizens. Diem closes universities in Saigon and Hué. Spontaneous demonstrations against the regime fill the streets in several cities. At first Diem's ruse works, and even the Voice of America announces that the army has attacked the Buddhist temples. Buddhist leader Tri Quang takes refuge in the US Embassy. President Kennedy, a Roman Catholic, denounces the armed attacks, joining all US officials who have for some time considered the repressive tactics a hindrance to the war against the Communists.

22 AUGUST 1963
Diem's Foreign Minister Vu Van Mau (a Buddhist) resigns, as does his Ambassador to the United States, Tran Van Chuong (Madame Nhu's father), who shaves his head like a Buddhist monk to join Vu Van Mau in protest over Diem's treatment of the Buddhists. Ambassador Henry Cabot Lodge lands in Saigon and reports back to Washington that Nhu is behind the attacks against the Buddhists. Lodge confirms as well that the generals seek US support for a coup against Diem and Nhu, but counsels prudence. Admiral Felt suggests that the US Government act tough with Nhu.

24 AUGUST 1963
A policy decision reaches Lodge from Washington that Diem must be given the chance to remove Nhu, but will himself have to go if he does not. Lodge is advised to pass on this decision to the generals, in effect assuring them of support for a coup against Diem if he does not remove Nhu and make the necessary reforms.

26 AUGUST 1963
Lodge meets with Diem for the first time. Diem refuses to drop Nhu, and refuses to discuss reforms. Lodge now presses the Kennedy administration, still badly divided over the issue of encouraging a coup, to support the dissident generals. Chief of Saigon CIA John Richardson agrees with Lodge, reporting to Washington that the situation has reached a point of no return.

27 AUGUST 1963
Cambodia severs diplomatic relations with South Vietnam in protest over border violations and persecution of the Buddhists.

29 AUGUST 1963
French President Charles de Gaulle proposes that North and South Vietnam be united into a neutral state and offers French aid and co-

operation in helping Vietnam throw off US and Communist foreign influence.

30 AUGUST 1963
Two US pilots are killed and three other Americans injured when gunfire brings down their helicopter in the Tayninh area, 55 miles north of Saigon.

31 AUGUST 1963
At a National Security Council meeting Paul Kattenburg, just returned from Saigon, suggests that the United States is backing the wrong man in Diem, and that this might be a good time to get out of Vietnam honorably. Dean Rusk replies that the United States will stay until victorious, McNamara asserts that the United States is winning, and Lyndon Johnson suggests that the war be prosecuted vigorously. Subsequently, Kennedy wonders aloud whether any government in Saigon can successfully resist the Communists.

2 SEPTEMBER 1963
Washington In a television interview President Kennedy rebuffs de Gaulle's proposal for a neutral, reunited Vietnam, rejecting any policy that would lead to the withdrawal of US troops from Vietnam before the Vietcong menace has been eliminated. While reasserting the US commitment to stay in Vietnam, Kennedy calls South Vietnam's repressive actions against the Buddhists 'very unwise.'
Saigon The *Times of Vietnam* charges that the CIA had planned a coup against Diem for 28 August. On the same day Mieczyslaw Maneli, chief of the Polish delegation of the ICC, meets with Nhu. At the urging of French Ambassador Roger Lalouette, who is in turn acting on instructions from de Gaulle, Maneli has consulted with Hanoi to see if the Communists would be receptive to economic and cultural exchanges with South Vetnam; Pham Van Dong reminds Maneli that he made such an overture years before. Maneli returns to Hanoi after meeting with Nhu, where the Communists authorize him to tell Nhu that he can rely on their help in the event of a clash with the Americans. Roger Hilsman hears of these schemes and advises Rusk that the generals be encouraged to move promptly with their coup, and suggests attacking North Vietnam if Hanoi interferes.

10 SEPTEMBER 1963
General Victor Krulak, USMC, and Joseph Mendenhall of the State Department report to President Kennedy on a fact-finding mission to Vietnam. Krulak concludes after speaking to US and South Vietnamese military officers that the war is going well; Mendenhall concludes from talks with bureaucrats and politicians that Diem is near collapse. Kennedy responds, 'You two did visit the same country, didn't you?'

11 SEPTEMBER 1963
At least 90 persons, soldiers and civilians, are killed in fighting for Damdoi during a government counterattack to retake the Camau Peninsula towns of Cainouc and Damdoi.

24 SEPTEMBER 1963
McNamara and General Taylor arrive in Vietnam at President Kennedy's request to determine whether the country's military situation has deteriorated as a result of the clash between the government and the Buddhists. They find 'great progress' in the war but suggest sanctions against Diem. Lodge and civilian officials feel the anti-Buddhist campaign has hurt the war effort; General Harkins insists the anti-Communist campaign is progressing on schedule. General Taylor receives no information about the coup from General Minh and erroneously concludes it has been cancelled.

2 OCTOBER 1963
Acting on Taylor's belief that the coup has been called off, Kennedy cables Lodge that no encouragement to a coup should be given, although contacts should be made with potential alternative leader.

5 OCTOBER 1963
Lodge reports to Kennedy that the coup is on, and General Minh, meeting with CIA operative Conein, asks for assurances that the United States will not thwart a coup, and that economic and military aid will continue. Kennedy approves, cautioning that the United States should avoid getting involved with operational details. Conein keeps in touch with rebel activity through meetings with General Tran Van Don. In the wake of another Buddhist monk's self-immolation, intensified political repression including the arrest of scores of children and the reaction to it, US officials from Kennedy on down attempt to control US newsmen in Saigon

CHRONOLOGY

without success. Lodge's dismissal of Saigon CIA chief John Richardson, who has doubts about the coup, encourages the dissident generals.

7 OCTOBER 1963
Madame Nhu arrives in the United States for a short visit despite the displeasure of the Kennedy administration, which refuses officially to acknowledge her presence or to extend diplomatic courtesies to her.

21 OCTOBER 1963
The United States announce it will (1) deny funds to the Vietnamese Special Forces (active in attacks against Buddhists) if they are used for purposes other than fighting the Vietcong, and (2) not renew the annual agreement supplying the government with surplus food which is sold to pay South Vietnamese troops.

22 OCTOBER 1963
General Harkins informs General Don at a British Embassy reception that he knows of the coup and considers it a mistake. The following day Don tells Conein that he has postponed the coup set for 26 October. Conein assures Don that Harkins speaks only for himself. General Taylor passes Harkins misgivings on to President Kennedy, who becomes uneasy about the possibility of the coup wrecking the war effort against the Vietcong.

29 OCTOBER 1963
Saigon A US military spokesman reports that government troops have killed 44 guerrillas in a battle at three strategic hamlets in Quang-ngai Province during the past two days.
Washington Kennedy's confidence in the coup is shaken at a National Security Council meeting when Diem's performance is supported by General Taylor citing messages from General Harkins. Kennedy's main concern is now whether the coup can succeed. He cables Lodge to ask the generals to postpone; Lodge never delivers the message. In the end, Kennedy leaves the final judgment of the matter to Lodge.

1 NOVEMBER 1963
Saigon Dissidents organized by the key generals of the South Vietnamese Army lay siege to the presidential palace, which is captured by the following morning. Diem and Nhu at first believe the attack to be the open-ing of a countercoup engineered by Nhu and General To That Dinh, who controls nearly all forces in and around Saigon, but Dinh has joined the insurgent generals. Diem is unable to summon any support, and he and Nhu escape.

2 NOVEMBER 1963
At about 0600 hours Diem begins negotiating with the generals, who have assured Lodge that Diem's life will be spared. Diem finally agrees to surrender, and an US-built M113 armored personnel carrier is sent to pick him and Nhu up from St Francis Xavier Church in Cholon. Major Duong Huu Nghia and General Minh's bodyguard, Captain Nhung, murder Diem and Nhu on their way to staff headquarters, at Minh's orders. President Kennedy is shocked. Saigon rejoices as prisoners are released. In the countryside peasants demolish the strategic hamlets. The Soviet newspaper *Izvestia* expresses satisfaction at Diem's end while asserting that ' ... new American puppets have come to power.' Ambassador Lodge calls the insurgent generals to his office to congratulate them, and cables Kennedy that the prospects are for a shorter war.

4 NOVEMBER 1963
The United States recognizes the new provisional government of South Vietnam. Former Vice-President Nguyen Ngoc Tho, a Buddhist, becomes premier but the real power is held by the Revolutionary Military Committee headed by General Duong Van Minh. The new government pledges not to become a dictatorship and announces, 'the best weapon to fight communism is democracy and liberty.' Two days later Information Minister Oai announces in Saigon, 'the mission of the provisional government will not end until real democracy is established.'

6 NOVEMBER 1963
Ambassador Lodge cables President Kennedy, 'we could neither manage nor stop [the coup] once it got started ... It is equally certain that the ground in which the coup seed grew into a robust plant was prepared by us, and that the coup would not have happened [as] it did without our preparation.'

9 NOVEMBER 1963
The United States announces resumption of its commodity-import aid to South Vietnam, suspended in August.

Local militiamen are trained in the use of modern weapons

15 NOVEMBER 1963
A US mlitary spokesman in Saigon reports that 1000 US servicemen will be withdrawn from South Vietnam beginning 3 December.

19 NOVEMBER 1963
Cambodia declares an end to all US military and economic aid. Sihanouk charges that the CIA is trying to oust him from power.

22 NOVEMBER 1963
Pesident Kennedy is assassinated in Dallas, Texas. He has failed to brief his successor, Lyndon B Johnson, about important details concerning the US role in the undeclared war against Communism in Vietnam.

24 NOVEMBER 1963
President Johnson confirms the US intention to continue military and economic support to South Vietnam. He instructs Lodge, in Washington for consultations following Diem's death, to communicate his intention to the generals. Johnson's first decision on Vietnam is a continuation of Kennedy's policy.

25 NOVEMBER 1963
South Vietnamese officals announce that 150 guerrillas have been killed in two days of fighting in the Mekong Delta.

DECEMBER 1963
Ho Chi Minh and senior staff assess accomplishments and plan for the future. While convinced that Vietnam must be reunited through their efforts, and happy with Vietcong progress during recent months, they know there will be no rapid victory. Krushchev and Mao Tse-tung (who is ready, in Pham Van Dong's words, 'to fight to the last Vietnamese') wish to avoid large-scale conflict with the United States; it is clear that Lyndon Johnson plans to continue the US involvement, perhaps deploying as many as 100,000 US combat troops in Vietnam. Vietminh veteran Colonel Bui Tin explores the Ho Chi Minh Trail for the Hanoi leadership and after five months of covert inspection in the South finds the Vietcong poorly organized, lacking in leadership and unprepared for a long campaign. Partly due to his report,

CHRONOLOGY

Hanoi decides to start sending regular army troops into the South.

2 DECEMBER 1963
The South Vietnamese junta orders a temporary halt to the strategic hamlet program. Peasants are not to be forced to move into or to contribute to the financial upkeep of the hamlets, and the conditions under which 'labor contributions' may be demanded are considerably restricted. Senior US representative in Long An Province Barl Young reports that three-quarters of the strategic hamlets in Long An have been destroyed, either by the Vietcong, the peasants, or a combination of both. Reporting that Minh and his government are ineffective at best, Young says, 'The only progress in Long An has been by the Vietcong.' His report typifies a rising flood of pessimistic news flowing from Saigon to Washington.

14 DECEMBER 1963
A US military spokesman in Saigon reports that guerrilla attacks on hamlets, outposts and patrols in November have resulted in 2800 government casualties and 2900 Vietcong losses. The Vietcong have captured enough weapons to arm five 300-man battalions.

19 DECEMBER 1963
Secretary of Defense Robert McNamara arrives in Saigon to evaluate the new government's war effort against the Vietcong. Publicly optimistic, in a complete about-face from the previous year, he privately tells Johnson that the situation is 'very disturbing.' McNamara feels that unless conditions change in the next two or three months, current trends 'will lead to neutralization at best or more likely to a Communist-controlled state.' He finds the US officials in Saigon grouped into warring factions headed by Ambassador Lodge and General Harkins. 'There is no organized government in South Vietnam ...'

21 DECEMBER 1963
In his formal report to President Johnson, McNamara calls Operation Hardnose, which provides intelligence and disrupts Vietcong movements along the Laos corridor 'remarkably effective,' and urges its expansion. Concluding that his appraisal of the Vietnamese situation may be overly pessimistic, he remarks, 'We should watch the situation very

carefully, running scared, hoping for the best, but preparing for more forceful moves if the situation des not show early signs of improvement.' Air Force Commander General Curtis LeMay has already suggested bombing North Vietnam, and others in the military promote no less drastic moves.

24 DECEMBER 1963
In response to growing pressure from the military to widen and 'Americanize' the war, President Johnson tells the Joint Chiefs of Staff, 'Just let me get elected, and then you can have your war.'

31 DECEMBER 1963
A total of 489 Americans have been killed or wounded in Vietnam this year, well over four times the previous year's total. There are at least 16,500 US servicemen in South Vietnam, which has received $500 million in US aid this year.

2 JANUARY 1964
Covert War President Johnson is sent a report prepared by Major General Victor H Krulak, USMC, Special Assistant for Counterinsurgency and Special Activities for the Joint Chiefs of Staff; as directed by Defense Secretary McNamara, Krulak and his staff have outlined an elaborate series of clandestine operations against North Vietnam 'to result in substantial destruction, economic loss and harassment.' Known as Oplan 34A, it will go into effect on 1 February, and calls for a three-pronged attack. The first involves a mixture of operations such as flights by U-2 spy planes over North Vietnam, kidnapping North Vietnamese for intelligence gathering, parachuting sabotage and psychological-warfare teams into North Vietnam, commando raids to blow up rail and highway bridges, and bombarding North Vietnamese coastal installations by PT boats; these operations are controlled in Saigon (although approved in Washington) by the chief of the US MACV, through its Studies and Observations Group, but most of the participants are to be South Vietnamese or Asian mercenaries. The second element of Oplan 34A's war involves bombing raids by T-28s in Laos against North Vietnamese and Pathet Lao forces there; although bearing Laotian Air Force markings, the 25-40 US-supplied planes are mostly manned by Thai and Air America pilots (Air America being the 'private' airline run by the CIA); photo-

graphic intelligence for the bombing raids will be gathered by regular USAF and USN jets, a reconnaissance operation code-named Yankee Team. The third prong consists of USN detroyer patrols in the Gulf of Tonkin, both as a show of force and to collect intelligence on North Vietnamese coastal defenses and warning radar (useful to raiding parties or planes involved in other Oplan 34A activities); these destroyer patrols are code-named DeSoto Mission, and have been conducted for years off the Soviet Union, China and North Korea.

4 JANUARY 1964

South Vietnam The 11 main Buddhist sects in South Vietnam, concluding a four-day convention in Saigon, announce that they are forming an Institute for Secular Affairs, to coordinate Buddhist political and social activities. This is clearly a move to present a united front against a government the Buddhists regard as insensitive to their goals.

USA: Military A US military spokesman in Saigon reports that there has been considerable increase in arms shipments from Communist nations to the Vietcong, so that the Vietcong are 'better equipped and better organized than 12 months ago.' US military sources also claim that the bulk of the arms come from Chinese and North Vietnamese ports via Cambodia and the Mekong River to South Vietnam.

Ground War An offensive that began on 31 December, when 10 ARVN battalions set out to crush a Vietcong force of two battalions in the Bensuc region some 40 miles west of Saigon, ends when the Communist force disappears. Only two Vietcong are killed while the ARVN lose 15, and US military advisers openly describe the operation as a failure.

5 JANUARY 1964

Ground War In Long An province, 25 miles southwest of Saigon, a 500-man Vietcong battalion escapes from an ARVN encircling movement; ground fire hits 15 US planes supporting the action, and five Americans are wounded; nine ARVN are killed, and Vietcong casualties are estimated at 60-70.

6 JANUARY 1964

South Vietnam Major General Duong Van Minh, chairman of the Military Revolutionary Council, issues decrees that centralize government and military power in himself and two other officers, Major General Tran Van Don and Major General Le Van Kim.

13 JANUARY 1964

Guerrilla War Vietcong take over two strategic hamlets in Pleiku province, burning 135 houses and kidnapping seven officials.

14 JANUARY 1964

South Vietnam A joint US-South Vietnamese survey of villages issues a report that concludes the government's war against the Vietcong in the Mekong Delta 'cannot ever be won' unless there are major reforms in the administration of the villages and strategic hamlets. The report calls for an end both to the forcible removal of peasants into strategic hamlets and to the corruption and mismanagement that prevails in such villages.

USA: Military Lieutenant General William Westmoreland is appointed to become deputy to General Paul Harkins, chief of the US MACV; it is generally accepted that Westmoreland will soon replace Harkins, whose insistently optimistic views on the progress of the war have increasingly come under criticism.

Guerrilla War Guerrillas down a US B-26 bomber, killing two Americans.

17 JANUARY 1964

South Vietnam Students in Saigon stage two anti-French demonstrations protesting De Gaulle's proposal to neutralize Vietnam.

Ground War Five US helicopter crewmen are killed and three are wounded while supporting a major ARVN attack on Communist bases in the Mekong Delta.

18 JANUARY 1964

South Vietnam The USNS *Providence*, flagship of the 7th Fleet, arrives at Saigon on what Washington describes as a 'goodwill mission'; in addition to underlining US support for South Vietnam, the action is also designed to show US commitment to all powers in the Far East.

22 JANUARY 1964

USA: Military The US Joint Chiefs of Staff inform Defense Secretary McNamara that 'we are wholly in favor of executing the covert actions against North Vietnam. ... We believe, however, that it would be idle to conclude that these efforts will have a decisive

CHRONOLOGY

Thousands of Vietnamese fleeing south were taken aboard US aircraft carriers.

effect on the Communist determination to support the insurgency; and it is our view that we must therefore be prepared fully to undertake a much higher level of activity. ...' Among their recommendations are 'aerial bombing of key North Vietnam targets' and 'commit[ment of] additional US forces, as necessary, in support of the combat action within South Vietnam.'

23 JANUARY 1964
Guerrilla War A Vietcong battalion-size force carries out the first sizable action in Camau Peninsula in two months when it makes a pre-dawn attack on Nam Can, an isolated district capital.

27 JANUARY 1964
USA: Government Defense Secretary McNamara appears before the House Armed Services Committee in a closed session (his testimony is made public on 18 February) and insists that the 'bulk of the US armed forces in Vietnam can be expected to leave by the end of 1965' but that 'the survival of an independent Government in South Vietnam is so important to the security of southeast Asia and to the free world that I can conceive of no alternative other than to take all necessary measures with our capability to prevent a Communist victory.'
Diplomatic France establishes diplomatic relations with Communist China.

29 JANUARY 1964
USA: Domestic Governor Nelson Rockefeller of New York, a candidate for the Republican nomination for president, at a news conference, attacks the 'double talk' of the Johnson administration and calls for a 'full accounting' of the situation in Vietnam.

30 JANUARY 1964
South Vietnam The junta government headed by Major General Duong Van Minh is overthrown in a bloodless coup led by Major General Nguyen Khanh, commander of the ARVN First Corps. General Minh is placed under house arrest, but five other junta leaders and the figurehead premier, Nguyen Ngoc Tho, are arrested. US Ambassador Lodge knew of Khan's plans but dismissed them as just another rumor.

31 JANUARY 1964
South Vietnam General Khanh assumes the chairmanship of the Military Revolutionary Council and moves quickly to gain US support for his regime.

1 FEBRUARY 1964
USA: Government At a press conference, President Johnson says he has General Khanh's pledge to spur the war effort and that he, in turn, has pledged full US support for the new regime. Johnson also says he is prepared to consider any plan that truly ensures the neutralization of both North and South Vietnam.
Covert War The official beginning of the Oplan 34A with its elaborate covert operations against North Vietnam.
Terrorism One US soldier is killed and five are injured by a bomb explosion in Saigon.

3 FEBRUARY 1964
Guerrilla War A Vietcong squad raids the US military compound at Kontum and one US officer is killed.

4 FEBRUARY 1964
Guerrilla War Vietcong troops smash an ARVN battalion headquarters at Hau My, killing 12 and wounding 20 ARVN troops; Vietcong forces also ambush an ARVN battalion in Thua Thien Province and kill eight.

5-6 FEBRUARY 1964
South Vietnam About 1000 students in Saigon demonstrate for the return to power of General Duong Van Minh, whom General Khanh has persuaded to stay on as a figurehead, and for a more effective war effort.

6 FEBRUARY 1964
Guerrilla War Some 500 Vietcong cross from a base in Cambodia and seize three strategic hamlets at Bencau; they are forced to withdraw after a 14-hour battle and reportedly lose 100 men, but ARVN losses are 114.

7 FEBRUARY 1964
Terrorism A bomb explodes in a Saigon bar, killing five Vietnamese and wounding six US servicemen and 20 civilians.

8 FEBRUARY 1964
South Vietnam General Khanh announces the formation of a new Vietnamese Government with himself as Premier; General Duong Van Minh is named chief of state, a titular position without authority.

CHRONOLOGY

9 FEBRUARY 1964
Terrorism A bomb explodes at the Saigon stadium, killing two Americans and injuring 20; US authorities in Saigon denounce such indiscriminate bombings but take steps to tighten security measures at all US installations in Saigon.

13 FEBRUARY 1964
South Vietnam General Khanh visits ARVN troops in the field as part of the Vietnamese New Year observances and announces a 20 percent pay increase for all servicemen up to and including the rank of corporal.
USA: Government Walt Rostow writes a memo to Secretary of State Rusk in which he argues that the United States should seriously consider bombing Hanoi; Rostow also suggests that President Johnson obtain a Congressional resolution to give him authority to wage war – evidently the first time this has been put into writing by an administration official.
Diplomatic British Prime Minister Alec Douglas-Home, visiting President Johnson, reaffirms his nation's support for the US defense of South Vietnam and attacks the statements by Britons who have been urging that the United States withdraw.

16 FEBRUARY 1964
North Vietnam An article in an official newspaper hails the Soviet Union's pledge of support for the struggle against 'US imperialists'; the North Vietnamese Communists are playing a delicate game of trying to balance support from both the Soviet Union and China.
Terrorism A bomb explodes in the US community's movie theater in Saigon, killing three Americans and wounding 50. US officials announce that the Vietcong are evidently conducting a terrorist campaign to force a face-losing evacuation of army and diplomatic dependants.

19 FEBRUARY 1964
USA: Government The CIA sends a memo to the secretaries of defense, state, and other top officials and concludes that, based on information from its Saigon office, South Vietnam is making little progress in its war against the Communists.
Air War The Vietcong shoot down two Vietnamese planes and one US pilot is killed.
Cambodia Prince Sihanouk proposes that the United States, Thailand, South Vietnam and Cambodia sign an agreement to 'recognize'

Cambodia's neutrality and territorial integrity.

20 FEBRUARY 1964
USA: Government After a strategy meeting, President Johnson orders that 'contingency planning for pressures against North Vietnam should be speeded up.'

21 FEBRUARY 1964
USA: Domestic In a speech in Los Angeles, President Johnson says that the war in Vietnam is primarily a domestic contest but warns that 'those engaged in external direction and supply' are playing a 'dangerous game.'

24 FEBRUARY 1964
Guerrilla War Vietcong guerrillas stage an unusual daylight ambush on an ARVN convoy in the Saigon area, killing six soldiers and wounding nine.

25 FEBRUARY 1964
USSR A statement issued by TASS demands the withdrawal of US military aid and a halt to 'interference' in South Vietnam's affairs; it also states that the Soviet Union will not stand by if the United States extends the war to North Vietnam.
Guerrilla War Vietcong forces blow up a train on the Saigon-Danang run, killing 11.
Ground War ARVN troops attack Vietcong positions near the border of Cambodia and South Vietnam.

26 FEBRUARY 1964
Ground War Although encircled by some 3000 ARVN troops, 600 men of the Vietcong's 514th Battalion fight their way out during an eight-hour battle near Long Dinh; the Vietcong lose 40 and only 16 ARVN troops are killed, but the ARVN forces had called in air and artillery strikes rather than engage the enemy directly. General Khanh is so angry that he dismisses three of his four corps commanders and five of his nine division commanders in an effort to make the ARVN more aggressive, but he only ends up demoralizing it.

27 FEBRUARY 1964
USA: Government At a press conference, Secretary of State Rusk says that recent US warnings to North Vietnam are reminders that aggression is 'serious business' but that Americans should not regard extending the war as a 'miracle' way to end the fighting;

Rusk rejects any political settlement that involves US withdrawal, leaving South Vietnam exposed to a Communist takeover.

MARCH 1964
Covert War After a temporary delay because of bad weather, the USNS destroyer *Craig* begins the DeSoto Mission called for by Oplan 34A to gather intelligence about North Vietnamese installations on the Gulf of Tonkin.

1 MARCH 1964
USA: Government William Bundy, Deputy Secretary of Defense for International Security Affairs, sends President Johnson a series of recommendations for extending the war against North Vietnam – including the blockading of Haiphong Harbor and the bombing of North Vietnamese railways. Beyond this, Bundy points out that such actions require some form of legislative endorsement short of a declaration of war, and he recommends that the President obtain a congressional resolution.

2 MARCH 1964
USA: Military The Joint Chiefs of Staff submit a memo (168-64) requesting 'Removal of Restrictions for Air and Ground Cross Border Operations,' effectively eliminating Laos as a sanctuary.
Terrorism Two Vietnamese are killed and 10 injured by a grenade tossed into a crowded market place in Duc Ton.

3 MARCH 1964
United Nations Secretary General U Thant says that he sees no effective role for the UN in the Vietnam conflict.

4 MARCH 1964
Diplomacy Although the US government is said to be advising South Vietnam not to sever ties with France – over Khanh's charge on 2 March that the French were plotting to assassinate him and impose a neutralist settlement – Americans in Vietnam report growing sentiment there for neutralism; to encourage the French, the Vietcong release four French citizens they have held prisoner.

5 MARCH 1964
USA: Military The Joint Chiefs of Staff order a USAF air commando training advisory team to Thailand to train Lao pilots in counterinsurgency tactics; this had been proposed in December 1963 and the plan was approved by Thailand's government in February 1964.

7 MARCH 1964
South Vietnam In a 15-page policy paper, General Khanh sets forth a comprehensive reform program to rebuild South Vietnam's political and administrative structures and raise the standard of living.
USA: Government In a press conference, President Johnson says that the United States will move armed forces to and from South Vietnam depending on the need; he also says no decision has been made on removing US dependents from Vietnam.
Ground War In scattered clashes, the ARVN reports killing 52 Vietcong and capturing 33.

8-12 MARCH 1964
South Vietnam Defense Secretary McNamara and General Taylor, Chairman JCS, visit Vietnam on a fact-finding mission; they are briefed by General Khanh and Ambassador Lodge and McNamara announces that 'We shall stay for as long as it takes to . . . win the battle.'

9 MARCH 1964
South Vietnam General Khanh takes McNamara and Taylor on a tour of the countryside to demonstrate US commitment to his regime. (One US helicopter accompanying the group crashes and two US airmen are killed.)
Diplomatic The South Vietnam government agrees to the four-power talks proposed by Cambodia to guarantee the latter's neutrality.
Guerrilla War Vietcong attack Cantho and destroy fuel tanks there.

14 MARCH 1964
Ground War ARVN troops claim to have trapped over 500 Vietcong suspects in a raid in Kieng Phong Province and to have captured about 300 Vietcong suspects in Cai Cai. In separate actions, a US helicopter and a spotter plane are downed and six Americans are killed.
Laos General Phoumi Nosavan, the Laotian rightist leader, and General Khanh of South Vietnam agree to allow South Vietnamese troops to enter Laos in 'hot pursuit' of Communist forces.

17 MARCH 1964
USA: Government President Johnson presides over a crucial session of the National

Security Council, at which McNamara and Taylor present a full review of the situation in Vietnam as they observed it. The statement issued to the public afterwards says that the United States will increase military and economic aid to support Khanh's new plan for fighting the Vietcong, including his intention to mobilize all able-bodied males, raise the pay and status of paramilitary forces, and provide more equipment for the armed forces. Various secret decisions are also taken, including the approval of covert intelligence-gathering operations in North Vietnam; a plan to launch retaliatory USAF strikes against North Vietnamese military installations and against guerrilla sanctuaries inside the Laotian and Cambodian borders; and a long-range 'program of graduated overt military pressure' – intensified bombing of North Vietnam. President Johnson directs that planning for the bombing raids 'proceed energetically,' and within two months this will result in Operation Plan 37-64 (the number of planes and tonnages needed for each phase of the bombing scenario) and Operation Plan 32-64 (US military requirements should other Communist powers enter the conflict).

18 MARCH 1964
USA: Domestic Senator Barry Goldwater (R-AZ), candidate for the Republican nomination for President, attacks Johnson's handling of the war and calls for 'victory.'

20 MARCH 1964
USA: Government President Johnson sends a cable to Ambassador Lodge in which he says he is intent on 'knocking down the idea of neutralization wherever it rears its ugly head.' US Senators are now beginning to divide in their public positions on the war in Vietnam.
Cambodia Recent efforts to end the tension between Cambodia and South Vietnam are stopped as South Vietnamese ground and air forces attack the Cambodian village of Chantrea; US military advisers participate, and a US observer plane is downed. The United Sates and South Vietnam governments will apologize to Cambodia for the raid, but Sihanouk demands reparations.

23 MARCH 1964
Cambodia The talks between Cambodia and South Vietnam over border violations collapse and the South Vietnamese delegation departs. Sihanouk calls for a Geneva conference on Cambodia.

24 MARCH 1964
Ground War The ARVN claims two major victories in Kien Phong and Hau Nghia Provinces, with high casualties for the Vietcong, but an US flyer is killed in the supporting action.

25-31 MARCH 1964
Cambodia Sihanouk continues to force his demands for reparations and apologies from the United States for the raid on Chantrea while demanding a full-scale conference in Geneva. France intervenes and persuades Sihanouk to soften his demands; he continues to deny that Cambodia provides sanctuaries for Vietcong.

28 MARCH 1964
Guerrilla War US Army and ARVN helicopters evacuate Vietnamese from Ap Giao Hiep, an outpost threatened by Vietcong.

29 MARCH 1964
USA: Government Defense Secretary McNamara announces that the United States will provide South Vietnam with $50,000,000 annually to finance the expansion of its armed forces (in addition to the current annual aid of $500,000,000).

30 MARCH 1964
South Vietnam General Khanh initiates a 'clear and hold' program of training ARVN officers to run local governments properly so that 'the Vietcong won't come right back.'

31 MARCH 1964
South Vietnam An unidentified US official in Saigon announces that the 'momentum' of the Vietcong has been checked.
USA: Domestic Governor Rockefeller demands that Ambassador Lodge resign and explain US policy in Vietnam.

APRIL 1964
Covert War It has been no secret that the North Vietnamese have been developing a network of infiltration trails from North Vietnam through Laos and into South Vietnam – which becomes known as the Ho Chi Minh Trail; some of the routes are capable of handling continuous truck traffic, while others can handle little more than bicycles and foot-traffic. Most of the several thousand Communist soldiers and civilian cadres who have been infiltrating into South Vietnam in the years up to now have been indigenous

The first US soldiers in the field served as advisors to the Vietnamese.

southerners returning to work for the Vietcong. In late 1963, the Hanoi leadership seems to have decided to commit units of the North Vietnamese Army (NVA), and by April a large group of North Vietnamese construction battalions has been deployed to further the development of the road network. Furthermore, during April, regular troops of the NVA are undergoing special military and political training for operations in the South, and large units are being formed preparatory to being sent South.

1-3 APRIL 1964
USA: Domestic Former Vice-President Richard Nixon visits Vietnam and issues a series of statements sharply criticizing US policies for 'compromises and improvisations,' calling for continued aid, and promising to make the situation an issue in the forthcoming US presidential campaign.

4 APRIL 1964
Ground War In a clash at the Phouc Tan outpost, six US troops are wounded, 12 ARVN and 15 Vietcong are killed.

5 APRIL 1964
South Vietnam A new draft law authorizes conscription into the Civil Guard and the Self-Defense Corps, the two paramilitary forces that bear the brunt of the fight against the Vietcong; both forces have suffered a lack of volunteers and a rise in desertions.

8 APRIL 1964
Guerrilla War South Vietnamese troops kill some 75 Vietcong in capturing a guerrilla base in Kontum Province, 300 miles north of Saigon; the base is considered an important distribution point for arms and personnel coming down the Ho Chi Minh Trail.

9-12 APRIL 1964
Ground War During four days of major fighting in the Mekong Delta, ARVN losses are over 50 while four Americans are killed; during one mortar barrage, a US helicopter base is forced to evacuate.

11-15 APRIL 1964
Ground War In a five-day battle, the longest and heaviest to date, at Kien Long, 135 miles south of Saigon, South Vietnamese forces regain their original position, but 70 South Vietnamese guardsmen are killed, 55 ARVN are dead, and 175 Vietcong are killed.

13-15 APRIL 1964
SEATO The Ministerial Council of the Southeast Asia Treaty Organization (SEATO) holds its 10th annual meeting in Manila. French Foreign Minister Maurice Couve de Murville argues on behalf of De

Gaulle's plan for 'neutralization' of Vietnam, but the other delegates reject this and agree on the final communique' that states 'that defeat of the Communist campaign is essential not only to the security of Vietnam but to that of Southeast Asia.'

14 APRIL 1964

USA: Military It is announced that the US Military Advisory Group (MAG) in Vietnam will be combined with the Military Assistance Command (MAC) to cut duplication of effort and make more efficient use of US service personnel.

15-18 APRIL 1964

USA: Domestic Former Vice-President Richard Nixon, returning from his 24-day trip through Asia, gives a number of speeches in New York City and Washington in which he calls for extending the war into North Vietnam and Laos.

17 APRIL 1964

USA: Military The Joint Chiefs of Staff approve Operation Plan 37-64, prepared in the Honolulu headquarters of CINCPAC; the plan details how many planes and what bomb tonnages would be required for each phase of air raids against North Vietnam and also lists the specific targets, for the US planes.
Terrorism Terrorists toss a bomb into an US military bus in the Saigon area and injure two US soldiers.

17-20 APRIL 1964

Covert War Secretary of State Dean Rusk, William Bundy and General Earle Wheeler, Army Chief of Staff, visit Saigon where they reviewed the latest US plans for covert actions against North Vietnam with Ambassador Lodge. In his public appearances, Rusk visits a fortified hamlet with General Khanh and tells the villagers that 'we are comrades in your struggle.' Back in Washington, Rusk concedes that the military situation is critical but says that Khanh is 'on the right track.'

17-23 APRIL 1964

Laos In a crisis that will have far-reaching consequences for the US role in Southeast Asia, Souvanna Phouma goes to the Plain of Jars in the north of Laos to confer with leaders of opposing factions in an effort to demilitarize and neutralize Laos. The talks fail, however, and Souvanna returns to Vientiane and announces his intention to resign. On the

19th several generals attempt a coup, but with the support of the US ambassador, Souvanna regains control of a coalition government. The United States supports Souvanna as the only hope for some kind of moderate and stable government, but the Communist Pathet Lao now reject this coalition and go on the offensive.

19 APRIL 1964

Guerrilla War Vietcong guerrillas strike in four provinces, in one place within 14 miles of Saigon, but the South Vietnam forces halt their advance.

20 APRIL 1964

Ground War After the Vietcong have seized the outpost at Huong Hoa Ha, the ARVN counterattacks and inflict heavy losses on the Vietcong. US officials publicly praise this as one of the most successful operations of the war, but in private many US military regard the apathy and inertia of the ARVN as major barriers to victory.

21 APRIL 1964

USA: Domestic The Republican leaders of the Senate, Everett Dirksen (IL) and the House, Charles Halleck (IN), hold a joint news conference in Washington and charge that the Johnson administration is concealing the extent of US involvement in the war. To support their charge, they read from the letters of an Air Force captain killed in Vietnam: 'They tell you people we're just in a training situation ... But we're at war, we are doing the flying and fighting ... the only reason [the Vietnamese "students"] are on board is, in case we crash, there is one American "adviser" and one Vietnamese "student".'

22 APRIL 1964

USA: Government President Johnson, trying to still the rising protests, summons Congressional leaders to the White House for briefings by Defense Secretary McNamara and CIA Director John McCone.

23 APRIL 1964

Guerrilla War In a clash with the Vietcong in Trung Lap, one American is killed and three are wounded.
France Premier Georges Pompidou reemphasizes his country's desire to see Vietnam neutralized and says that this will require that United States and Japan deal with Communist China.

24 APRIL 1964
USA: Domestic In a news conference, Defense Secretary McNamara says that he does not mind Senator Wayne Morse's term, 'McNamara's War.'

25 APRIL 1964
USA: Military President Johnson announces that General William Westmoreland will replace General Paul Harkins as head of the US MACV (as of 20 June).
Guerrilla War South Vietnamese forces rout a Vietcong battalion at Binh Chanh.

30 APRIL 1964
Diplomatic Secretary of State Rusk flies to Ottawa, Canada, to make secret arrangements with J Blair Seaborn, Canada's new representative on the International Control Commission; Seaborn will be visiting Hanoi in June and the United States wants him to convey to the North Vietnamese Government an offer of US economic aid if it calls off its forces and support for the Vietcong.
Guerrilla War Vietcong guerrillas penetrate Long An, a provincial capital, and capture 74 Vietcong defectors; other Vietcong raid Tan An and kill six women and five children.

2 MAY 1964
Terrorism An explosion of a charge assumed to have been placed by Vietcong terrorists sinks the USNS *Card* at its dock in Saigon; no one is injured (and the ship will be raised and repaired). The *Card*, an escort carrier being used as an aircraft and helicopter ferry, arrived in Saigon with its load on 30 April.

3 MAY 1964
Terrorism A terrorist throws a bomb into the crowd viewing the USNS *Card*, sunk at its dock, and 8 US servicemen are wounded.
Ground War One hundred ARVN Rangers are wiped out by a Vietcong attack, 25 miles northwest of Saigon.

4 MAY 1964
South Vietnam General Khan tells Ambassador Lodge that he feels it is necessary to declare fullscale war on North Vietnam, have the United States start bombing the North, and send 10,000 US Special Forces troops 'to cover the whole Cambodian-Laotian border.' Khanh is beginning to feel a lack of support for his efforts. Lodge does not inform him that the United States has already developed its own plan to bomb the North.

USA: Government In secret testimony before the House Armed Services Committee (released 19 June) William Bundy, now assistant secretary of state for East Asian and Pacific affairs, says that the United States must drive the Communists out of South Vietnam even if it means 'attacking countries to the north.'

5 MAY 1964
USA: Government The United States announces it is freezing all assets of North Vietnam and barring any further financial and commercial transactions between the two countries.
Air War Ten US servicemen are among 16 killed when an USAF transport plane crashes at Tan Hiep.

7 MAY 1964
South Vietnam The 10th anniversary of the fall of Dienbienphu is not recognized officially, but General Khanh says that his country would appreciate aid from other countries than the United States, and the United States is known to agree that such aid would be valued for psychological and political reasons.

8-14 MAY 1964
Cambodia A Cambodian armored vehicle destroys an ARVN armored troop carrier that strays into Cambodia in pursuit of Vietcong. Khanh immediately apologizes, but South Vietnam asserts that Cambodia does allow Vietcong to take refuge there. On the 9th, a clash between Cambodians and ARVN leaves seven Cambodians dead. Cambodian students demonstrate in demanding the ousting of all US military personnel in their country. It is then alleged (but later denied) that Cambodian jets strafed ARVN troops searching for Vietcong. The crisis cools when Cambodia asks that the UN send a mission to Cambodia to disprove charges it shelters Vietcong.

9 MAY 1964
Terrorism A terrorist is captured trying to place an explosive charge under a Saigon bridge over which Defense Secretary McNamara's car is to pass on 12 May.

12-13 MAY 1964
South Vietnam Defense Secretary McNamara and General Maxwell Taylor visit Vietnam (for their fifth fact-finding mission). While McNamara reiterates US support for South

CHRONOLOGY

Vietnam, he also tells Khanh privately that, although the United States does not 'rule out' bombing the North, 'we do not intend to provide military support nor undertake the military objective of "rolling back" Communist control in North Vietnam.'

12-14 MAY 1964
USA: Military Amid charges that US pilots in Vietnam are endangered (and even losing their lives) due to obsolescent planes, it is announced that 60 USN dive bombers are being sent to Vietnam (and that 40 revamped B-26s are being readied for Vietnam).

14 MAY 1964
USA: Government Defense Secretary McNamara, returned to Washington, presents a plan to President Johnson calling for increased aid to South Vietnam.
Ground War A Vietcong battalion wipes out an ARVN relief force, 20 miles north of Saigon; 54 ARVN are killed and 50 wounded. (The next day, a US military adviser, referring to this incident, says 'we make the same mistake all the time.')

15 MAY 1964
South Vietnam Premier Khanh signs a decree that abolishes restrictions imposed by the Diem regime on Buddhists and grants them the same rights as Catholics.
USA:Government Defense Secretary McNamara reports to the National Security Council on the situation in Vietnam; President Johnson informs Congressional leaders attending the session that he will probably seek more aid for South Vietnam.

16 MAY 1964
USA: Domestic Governor Rockefeller accepts President Johnson's offer to brief all Republican candidates for the presidency; afterwards, he will agree with a questioner that Americans are not getting the full story of the situation. Senator Goldwater openly charges that US pilots have died because of obsolescent planes.

16-17 MAY 1964
Laos On the 16th, the Communist Pathet Lao succeed in driving the neutralist forces led by Kong-Le from the Plain of Jars, marking the end of any efforts at a coalition government and leaving Souvanna Phouma and his rightists in control. When word of this loss reaches Washington, President Johnson

Two young members of the South Vietnamese Popular Forces.

orders a troop alert in Okinawa and orders the Seventh Fleet in the South China Sea to prepare for possible military action. Officials begin drawing up a resolution that Johnson might present to Congress to get it to declare that the independence and integrity of Laos are vital to US interests.

17-19 MAY 1964
USA: Government Secretary of State Rusk visits Saigon primarily to get Ambassador Lodge's support for the 'retaliatory' actions being effected or contemplated by the Johnson administration. Lodge counsels more reliance on the South Vietnamese forces and more attempts to apply the 'carrot' of inducements to North Vietnam before applying the 'stick' (of heavy bombing).

18 MAY 1964
USA: Government President Johnson, in a special message to Congress, asks for $125,000,000 more for economic and military aid to Vietnam.

19-21 MAY 1964
Laos The US initiates low-altitudes target reconnaissance flights over southern Laos (on the 19th) and northern Laos (on the 21st) by US Navy and Air Force jets; these flights are code-named Yankee Team. At the same time, the US releases bomb fuses and more T-28s to the Laotian Air Force. Souvanna

Phouma has been consulted about the flights and has given his approval.

20 MAY 1964
Laos France proposes reconvening a 14-nation conference on Laos in Geneva; it is rejected by the United States and Great Britain but accepted by the Soviet Union, Poland, Cambodia, India and Communist China.

21 MAY 1964
UN The UN Security Council meets to consider Cambodia's charge that the United States directs South Vietnam raids into Cambodia. US Ambassador Adlai Stevenson calls for a clear marking of the border and the stationing of some force to police the border.

22 MAY 1964
USA: Government In a major speech before the American Law Institute in Washington, Secretary of State Rusk explicitly accuses North Vietnam of initiating and directing the aggression in South Vietnam. US withdrawal, says Rusk, 'would mean not only grievous losses to the free world in Southeast and Southern Asia but a drastic loss of confidence in the will and capacity of the free world.' He concluded: 'There is a simple prescription for peace – leave your neighbors alone.'
Ground War ARVN forces wind up almost a month of campaigning in the Do Xa region by overrunning the headquarters of General Don, a top Vietcong leader; he escapes, but South Vietnam claims this will set back the Vietcong's efforts for many months.

22-31 MAY 1964
Thailand Thailand mobilizes its border provinces against incursions by the Pathet Lao and agrees to the use of bases by US Air Force for reconnaissance, search and rescue, and even attacks against the Pathet Lao. By the end of the year, some 75 US aircraft will be based in Thailand to assist in operations against the Pathet Lao.

23 MAY 1964
USA: Government Assistant Secretary of State William Bundy directs the drawing-up of a 3-day scenario that, while publicly pretending that the United States and South Vietnam are trying to avoid widening the war, actually assumes that the United States will begin fullscale bombing of North Vietnam.

24-28 MAY 1964
USA: Domestic Senator Barry Goldwater, regarded as a serious contender for the Republican nomination for the presidency, gives an interview in which he proposes the use of low-yield atomic bombs to defoliate forests and the bombing of bridges, roads and railroad lines bringing supplies from Communist China. During the storm of criticism that follows, Goldwater tries to back away from these drastic actions – claiming that he did not mean to advocate the use of atomic bombs, only that he was 'repeating a suggestion made by competent military people.' But Goldwater will never be able to shake the image of an extremist in his Vietnam policies and it will count heavily against him when he runs against Johnson.

25 MAY 1964
USA: Government Following his own suggestion of 1 March, William Bundy drafts a joint Congressional resolution that would give the President the authority to take whatever steps he deems necessary in Vietnam.
UN During a discussion of the Cambodian-South Vietnam issue in the UN Security Council, France splits from the United States and Great Britain's position and urges the Council to pass a resolution 'deploring' South Vietnam's violations of the border.

26 MAY 1964
Cambodia Sihanouk says he welcomes UN inquiry teams or UN troops to police the disputed border with South Vietnam.

27 MAY 1964
South Vietnam Premier Khanh announces that South Vietnam forces will 'liberate' North Vietnam after defeating the Communists in the south.

28 MAY 1964
Diplomatic Canada's Prime Minister Lester Pearson meets President Johnson in New York and they discuss the forthcoming trip to Hanoi by Canada's delegate to the International Control Commission, James Seaborn, who is to convey a message from the United States that is essentially a threat to bomb North Vietnam unless the North Vietnam leaders concur with certain US demands.
Guerrilla War Vietcong storm Nho Dung and kidnap the hamlet chief; and at Quang Ngai, snipers kill two ARVN soldiers.

CHRONOLOGY

1-2 JUNE 1964
USA: Government All the top US officials concerned with the war gather for two days of meetings in Honolulu – Rusk, McNamara, Lodge, Westmoreland, Taylor, William Bundy, McCone and others. Much of the discussion focuses on the projected air war against North Vietnam, including a list of 94 targets. There is also discussion of the plan for a joint Congressional resolution.

2 JUNE 1964
USA: Government In a news conference, President Johnson reasserts US commitment to defend Vietnam but says he knows of no plans to extend the war into North Vietnam.
UN The United States and Cambodia agree on a compromise proposal to form a three-nation commission to visit the Cambodia border within 45 days.

3 JUNE 1964
USA: Government Rusk, McNamara and the other officials return to Washington and report to President Johnson. William Bundy prepares the briefing paper for Secretary Rusk and advises more time to 'refine our plans and estimates,' as well as an 'urgent' public relations campaign to 'get at the basic doubts' about US interests in Vietnam.
Guerrilla War Vietcong guerrillas enter the strategic hamlet of Khanh Hoi-Dong Hung and, meeting no opposition, kidnap 47 men.

4 JUNE 1964
USA: Government As a result of the report to President Johnson, Defense Secretary McNamara orders the US Army to take 'immediate action ... to improve the effectiveness and readiness status of its matériel prestocked for possible use in Southeast Asia.' Specifically, he orders the Army to augment stocks at Korat, Thailand, near the Laotian border, to support potential combat operations by an US Army infantry brigade.
UN The Security Council approves the compromise plan for a commission to investigate the situation on the Cambodian-Vietnam border, and on the 6th names Brazil, the Ivory Coast and Morocco to form the commission.

6-9 JUNE 1964
Air War Two US Navy jets flying low-altitude target reconnaissance missions over Laos – part of the Yankee Team – are shot down by Pathet Lao ground fire. Washington immediately orders armed jets to escort the reconnaissance flights, and by 9 June escort jets are attacking Pathet Lao gun positions and a Pathet Lao headquarters. The downing of the two planes and the retaliatory strikes are made public, but the full extent of the US involvement is not.

7 JUNE 1964
South Vietnam Some 35,000 Roman Catholic Vietnamese demonstrate in Saigon against what they allege is government favoritism toward Buddhists.
Guerrilla War US officials report that the Vietcong are blockading a 600-square-mile area south of Camau to starve the residents and deprive South Vietnam of charcoal supplies.

8 JUNE 1964
Australia Australian training teams with ARVN forces exchange fire with guerrillas on the same day that the Australian Government sends six transport planes and more army instructors as combat advisers. The government also calls for all SEATO members to increase their support for South Vietnam.

9 JUNE 1964
USA: Government In reply to a formal question submitted by President Johnson – 'Would the rest of Southeast Asia necessarily fall if Laos and South Vietnam came under North Vietnamese control?' – the CIA submits a memo that effectively challenges the 'domino theory' that lies behind the Johnson administration's policies. The CIA concludes that Cambodia is probably the only nation in the area that would immediately fall: 'Furthermore, a continuation of the spread of Communism in the area would not be inexorable, and any spread which did occur would take time – time in which the total situation might change in any number of ways unfavorable to the Communist cause.' Although the CIA analysis did not deny that the loss of South Vietnam and Laos 'would be profoundly damaging to the US position in the Far East,' it concluded that the United States, with its Pacific bases and its allies such as the Philippines and Japan, would have enough power to deter China and North Vietnam from any further aggression or expansion. Having solicited this analysis, President Johnson appears to ignore it.

Members of the Australian Army, serving as advisors, came under attack by guerrillas.

10-11 JUNE 1964

Laos Embarrassed by the disclosure of US participation in air actions in Laos, Souvanna Phouma threatens to resign if the flights don't stop. The US Ambassador to Laos Leonard Unger persuades Souvanna to change his mind, and after a temporary suspension, the US State Department announces on the 11th that the reconnaissance flights will continue 'as necessary' but that 'operational aspects would not be discussed.' This translates into describing all US air operations in Laos during the coming years as 'reconnaissance flights.' On the 11th, Thai pilots in planes with Laotian Air Force markings bomb the Pathet Lao headquarters at Khang Khay, destroying the Chinese mission and killing one civilian.

12 JUNE 1964

Ground War ARVN troops attack a Communist convoy from Laos and kill 27 guerrillas.
France De Gaulle calls for an end to all foreign intervention in South Vietnam.
West Germany Chancellor Ludwig Erhard pledges more aid to South Vietnam.

13 JUNE 1964

Guerrilla War Seven ARVN and one US soldier are killed in an ambush.
Terrorism Vietcong mines derail three trains, blow up two trucks and kill six Vietnamese.

14 JUNE 1964

USA: Military General Westmoreland is in Malaysia to study the methods used by the British to defeat Communist guerrillas there.
Riverine War A South Vietnamese river patrol is ambushed by Vietcong but manages to kill 23 guerrillas.
Laos/Thailand The US Military allows its own pilots operating out of Thailand to hit 'targets of opportunity' in Laos.
Australia The opposition Labour Party attacks the government for failing to tell Australians more about the situation in Vietnam while supporting the South Vietnamese and US positions there.

15 JUNE 1964

USA: Government At a meeting of the National Security Council, McGeorge Bundy, the President's national security advisor, informs Rusk, McNamara and the others present that President Johnson has decided to postpone submitting a resolution to Congress asking for authority to wage war –

the resolution that William Bundy has been preparing. Johnson and his aides deny that this decision was based on politics.

Air War Vietnam Air Force bombers save a district capital, Lap Vo, from capture by Vietcong.

17 JUNE 1964

USA: Government Amid speculation that Ambassador Lodge will have to be replaced in Vietnam because of his possible role as a Republican presidential candidate, there is also rumour that Attorney General Robert Kennedy might be named to succeed Lodge.

USA: Military An unnamed top US military adviser leaving after three years in Vietnam reports on the improvement of the Vietcong in recent years and claims that over 90 percent of their weapons come from the US military aid program for South Vietnam.

Ground War ARVN forces beat back a Vietcong attack on Duchoa, killing 19 but taking 51 casualties of their own.

18 JUNE 1964

Diplomatic In a meeting with North Vietnam's Premier Pham Van Dong, J Blair Seaborn, the chief Canadian delegate to the ICC, is serving as a secret envoy for the US government for he has been authorized to appraise the situation in Hanoi – specifically, to see whether the North Vietnamese leaders are ready to pull back from the war. Although Seaborn is not authorized to make any literal threats, he leaves the Premier with little doubt that the United States was prepared to 'carry the war to the North ... if pushed too far.' However, Seaborn was not informed about, nor authorized to convey a package of proposals including the withdrawal of US forces and various forms of economic aid if Hanoi would halt all hostilities in South Vietnam. When Seaborn returns to Saigon and sends two long reports to the US State Department, no action is taken by the US authorities.

19 JUNE 1964

USA: Government Secretary of State Rusk, in a news conference, states that the US commitment to the security of Southeast Asia, is 'unlimited' and comparable to the commitment to West Berlin, and that the United States demands full compliance with the Geneva Accords both in South Vietnam and Laos.

Terrorism Guerrillas blow up four cars of a passenger train and kill 20 Vietnamese.

20 JUNE 1964

USA: Military General Paul Harkins is succeeded as head of the US MACV by his deputy, Lieutenant General William Westmoreland.

23 JUNE 1964

USA: Government At a news conference, President Johnson announces that Henry Cabot Lodge has resigned as ambassador to South Vietnam and that General Maxwell Taylor is to be his replacement. It is reliably reported that virtually every top official in the administration volunteered to serve as ambassador, and Johnson makes a point of insisting that this change will in no way affect the US commitment to Vietnam.

USA: Military It is announced that General Westmoreland is to become the 'executive agent' to supervise the civilian advisory and assistance programs in three provinces around Saigon, the first stage of a plan to coordinate the entire US military and civilian program in South Vietnam under the military command.

24 JUNE 1964

USA: Domestic A dispute among Republicans is already surfacing, with some supporting Lodge's claim that Vietnam should not become an issue in the campaign while others try to link his resignation to a disagreement with the Johnson administration's policies.

Guerrilla War Seventeen Vietcong are killed and 11 captured during a search for two missing US soldiers (who are reported dead).

25 JUNE 1964

North Vietnam Foreign Minister Xuan Thuy writes to Communist China and other signers of the Geneva Accords and urges them 'to demand that the US government give up its design of ... provocation and sabotage against North Vietnam.'

Guerrilla War Vietcong capture a civil guard platoon without firing a shot in Quang Tri Province.

26 JUNE 1964

Guerrilla War In Quengngai Province, South Vietnamese forces break into a Vietcong training center and kill 50 guerrilla recruits.

Terrorism A bomb explodes in an airport hangar near where General Westmoreland is

Despite bombing by the USAF, supplies continued to move down the Ho Chi Minh Trail.

addressing US servicemen returning to the United States; two Americans are injured, but Westmoreland is not.
Ground War Armored carriers of the ARVN engage with a Vietcong force in Baucot and kill some 100 guerrillas.

27 JUNE 1964
Ground War ARVN Rangers in Lonc Hoi trap a Vietcong battalion and inflict heavy casualties.
Air War Two Americans are killed when their fighter-bomber is shot down.

29 JUNE 1964
Ground War Two outposts are overwhelmed by Vietcong in the Saigon area.
Air War Four Americans are killed when their helicopter crashes during a mission in the Mekong Delta.
New Zealand Twenty-four New Zealand Army engineers arrive in Saigon as a token of that country's support for South Vietnam.

JULY 1964
Covert War Both sides are now engaged in a barely-secret war in violation of the Geneva Accords. The Ho Chi Minh Trail is being turned into a modern route to carry the tons of weapons, ammunition, food and other necessities for the Vietcong and the increas-
ing numbers of North Vietnamese regular troops infiltrating into South Vietnam. Engineer battalions using modern Soviet and Chinese machinery are building roads and bridges capable of handling heavy trucks and a whole network of support facilities are also being built – antiaircraft defenses, underground barracks, workshops, warehouses, fuel depots and hospitals. Meanwhile, the various clandestine activities called for by Oplan 34A are well underway. The Royal Laotian Air Force, strengthened by more T-28s, and US planes from Yankee Team are now conducting regular missions in Laos. The DeSoto Mission is operating off North Vietnam's coast, and Admiral Ulysses Grant Sharp, Jr, American commander in the Pacific, orders the Seventh Fleet to deploy the aircraft carrier *Ticonderoga* and its ancillary force, at the entrance of the Tonkin Gulf; the destroyer *Maddox* is ordered over from Japan to engage in DeSoto electronic 'eavesdropping.' And in Laos this month, US military advisers assist the Laotian army in a ground operation to clear the junction of the road from the Plain of Jars with the road between Vientiane and Luang Prabang; this Operation Triangle (or Three Arrows) involves US Army advisers with Laotian regiments also US ground controllers for strikes by US airplanes.

CHRONOLOGY

1 JULY 1964
Air War A US Army helicopter is downed and its pilot and gunner are killed; elsewhere, a Vietcong sniper kills a US helicopter pilot and injures three other Americans who have landed to pick up a wounded serivceman. At a news conference in Saigon, a US military spokesman reports that US helicopters are now flying 1300-1400 hours a week, and this explains the rising losses of US aircraft and personnel.

2 JULY 1964
USA: Domestic At a joint news conference, Senate Republican leader Everett Dirksen (IL) and House Republican leader Charles Halleck (IN) say that the war will be a campaign issue because 'Johnson's indecision has made it one.'
Guerrilla War The Vietcong ambush an ARVN 36-truck convoy in the Pleiku-Quinhon area, but its load of shells is saved when two US helicopters arrive; 29 ARVN troops are killed, 24 injured and five missing.
Terrorism Terrorists throw a bomb at a US officers billet in Saigon and two Americans are injured.

3 JULY 1964
Ground War Vietcong overrun an ARVN camp at Kontum and kill 44 ARVN soldiers, wounding 22, including three US advisers. In central Vietnam, Vietcong wipe out the defenders of three strategic hamlets.

4 JULY 1964
Ground War Vietcong raid a US Special Forces training camp at Polei Krong, seize the camp's arms and ammunition and leave 41 South Vietnamese dead and two Americans wounded.

6 JULY 1964
Ground War At Nam Dong in the northern highlands, an estimated 500-man Vietcong force attacks an American Special Forces training camp but are forced to withdraw after a bitter five-hour battle that kills 57 Vietnamese defenders, two Americans and one Australian military adviser and an estimated 40 Vietcong.

7 JULY 1964
South Vietnam General Maxwell Taylor, the new ambassador, arrives in Saigon. As a military man with considerable experience in Vietnam, he is looked upon by everyone – the South Vietnamese government, the US military establishment and the Johnson administration – as the ideal individual to coordinate and invigorate the war.
Terrorism Presumably in recognition of the arrival of General Taylor, a bomb is thrown at the US Embassy and two grenades explode elsewhere in Saigon; no one is injured and only slight damage is caused.

8 JULY 1964
UN Secretary General of the UN U Thant proposes that the Geneva conference that ended in 1954 be reconvened to negotiate peace in Vietnam.

9 JULY 1964
China Communist China pledges to help defend North Vietnam if that land is attacked by US forces.

11-12 JULY 1964
Ground War In what is regarded as the largest battle of the war to date, at least 1000 Vietcong troops twice attack the South Vietnamese outpost of Chuong Thien and then ambush the relief force. The Vietcong seize 100 weapons and 200 ARVN soldiers are killed or wounded.
Guerrilla War Two US servicemen are killed when two locomotives are made to collide by guerrillas.

13 JULY 1964
South Vietnam The Vietnamese Air Force commander, General Nguyen Cao Ky, claims he has 30 Vietnamese pilots trained to fly jet fighter-bombers against North Vietnam.
Guerrilla War Vietcong forces ambush an ARVN convoy, 40 miles south of Saigon, killing 16 ARVN soldiers and three US soldiers.

14 JULY 1964
Ground War US military intelligence publicly charges that North Vietnamese regular army officers command and fight in so-called Vietcong forces in the northern provinces, where Vietcong strength has doubled in the past six months. Only the day before, General Khanh had referred to the 'invasion' by North Vietnamese Army (NVA) forces.

15-16 JULY 1964
USA: Domestic Senator Barry Goldwater (AZ) is nominated by the Republican Party to run for president. Although he has gone to

great trouble to explain that he never meant to advocate using atomic weapons in tactical or strategic situations, he has definitely called for a more aggressive approach by the United States, and in the ensuing campaign he will be portrayed by the Democrats as a trigger-happy warmonger.

16 JULY 1964
Ground War ARVN claims that it has killed 100 Vietcong in a clash in Vinh Binh Province, with its own losses at 17 dead and 45 wounded. Within the past two days, there have been 15 other clashes between South Vietnamese and Communist forces throughout South Vietnam, indicative of the stepped-up activity by the Vietcong, evidently bolstered by NVA forces.

19 JULY 1964
South Vietnam On what the South Vietnamese call 'The Day of Shame' – the 10th anniversary of the signing of the Geneva Accords that partitioned Vietnam – Premier Khanh, at a rally in Saigon, calls for an expansion of the war to North Vietnam. Ambassador Taylor and other US officials present decline comment on Khan's position (but it is known that the United States regards this as breaking an agreement to consult with Washington before issuing such a call).

19-30 JULY 1964
Cambodia The UN team that has been inspecting the Cambodian-South Vietnamese border returns and on the 28th urges prompt action by the Security Council to avoid fur-

Members of the US 1st Special Forces served as advisors to Vietnamese Special Forces.

ther conflict. Meanwhile, Cambodia continues to accuse South Vietnam of new acts of aggression, and on the 29th, Cambodia charges that the United States and South Vietnam used chemical weapons in attacking an area, killing 76 Cambodians in six villages. The United States promptly denies any use of chemical weapons, and South Vietnam claims that it was Vietcong troops masquerading as ARVN forces that have been attacking Cambodian border villages.

20 JULY 1964
Ground War Vietcong forces overrun Caibe, the capital of Dinh Tuong Province, killing 11 South Vietnamese militiamen, 10 women, and 30 children. On 31 July, South Vietnam will charge that the troops involved in the attack were NVA regulars and that Chinese Communist advisers led the attack.

21 JULY 1964
Guerrilla War Vietcong ambush a convoy in Chuong Thien Province and kill 26 ARVN and wound about 100.

22 JULY 1964
South Vietnam Air Force General Nguyen Cao Ky, at a news conference, reveals that 'combat teams' have been sent on sabotage missions into North Vietnam and that South Vietnamese pilots are being trained for possible large-scale attacks. He further states that he personally flew a plane over North Vietnam on one such mission. US officials refuse to confirm all of Ky's statements but concede that some flights had been made in previous years.

23 JULY 1964
France At a news conference in Paris, De Gaulle proposes that the United States, France, the Soviet Union and Communist China negotiate an end to the hostilities in Vietnam and Laos by agreeing to leave the Indo-Chinese Peninsula, guaranteeing its neutrality and independence, and providing economic and technical aid.

23-24 JULY 1964
South Vietnam Ambassador Taylor meets with General Khanh to register US disapproval of the recent calls by Khanh and Ky to extend the war into North Vietnam. Both meetings are reported to have been 'heated' but it is also reported that Khanh stands firmly against Taylor's reprimands, arguing that the

war has changed because of the presence of North Vietnamese forces. Khanh offers to resign at the second meeting; Taylor not only dissuades him but ends up cabling Washington that the United States should undertake covert planning with the South Vietnamese for bombing the North. In a news conference in Washington on the 24th, President Johnson insists that US-South Vietnamese relations are good.

25 JULY 1964
USA: Government Following a meeting of the National Security Council to discuss the recent events in Saigon, the Joint Chiefs of Staff draw up a memo proposing air strikes – in unmarked planes flown by non-American crews – against targets in North Vietnam. It will be the 30th before the memo reaches Secretary Rusk.

26 JULY 1964
South Vietnam General Khan and the top South Vietnamese military leaders hold secret talks at Dalat, but it is reliably reported that some present call for expanding the war into North Vietnam and Laos; it is also known that some ARVN generals have visited Taiwan to discuss the possibility of Nationalist Chinese troops being sent to Vietnam.

27 JULY 1964
USA: Government It is announced that the United States will be sending an additional 5000 US troops to Vietnam; its present military force there is about 16,000. Military spokesmen and Washington officials insist that this does not represent any change in policy, that new troops will only intensify present US efforts.

29 JULY 1964
Ground War ARVN troops, aided by air strikes, inflict heavy casualties on Vietcong forces attacking Ben Cat.
Guerrilla War The US military raises its estimates of Communist forces in South Vietnam to 28-34,000 fulltime regular Vietcong troops, another 60-80,000 guerrillas, and claims that about 30 percent of units formed in past eight months have infiltrated from North Vietnam.

30-31 JULY 1964
Covert War About midnight, six 'Swifts,' the special PT boats used by the South Vietnamese for their covert raids, attack two islands in

the Tonkin Gulf, Hon Me and Hon Ngu; although unable to land any commandos, the boats fire on island installations. Radar and radio transmissions are monitored by the USNS *Maddox*, the DeSoto Mission ship about 120 miles away. The *Maddox* will report sighting patrol boats in the Gulf but will be told that these were the Swifts returning from their undercover raid.

31 JULY 1964

USA: Government Secretary of State Rusk, in a news conference, admits there are differences between the United States and South Vietnam on the issue of extending the war into North Vietnam, yet he insists there is agreement on the general conduct of the war and that US warnings to Communist China and North Vietnam indicate total US commitment.

South Korea The National Assembly approves aid to South Vietnam.

1 AUGUST 1964

North Vietnam The government accuses the United States and South Vietnam of having authorized the raids on the two islands in the Tonkin Gulf.

Terrorism A bomb explodes in a Saigon bar, wounding 5 US servicemen and 18 South Vietnamese.

1-2 AUGUST 1964

Covert War Thai pilots, flying US T-28s from their base in Laos, bomb and strafe North Vietnamese villages near the Laotian border. Souvanna Phouma will deny this on the 7th as part of the policy to deny any aspect of the covert operations.

2 AUGUST 1964

Sea War The USNS *Maddox* has been cruising around the Tonkin Gulf monitoring the radio and radar signals following the attack by the South Vietnamese. US crews interpret one North Vietnamese message as indicating they are preparing 'military operations,' which the *Maddox*'s Captain John Herrick assumes means some retaliatory attack; his superiors instruct him to remain in the area. Early in the afternoon, three North Vietnamese patrol boats begin to chase the *Maddox*. About 1500 hours, Captain Herrick orders his crew to commence firing as the craft come within 10,000 yards and he radios the US aircraft carrier *Ticonderoga* for air support. The North Vietnamese boats each fire

one torpedo at the *Maddox* but two miss and the third fails to explode. US gunfire hits one of the craft, and then three US Crusader jets proceed to strafe them. After about 20 minutes, Maddox gunners have sunk one of the boats, and two are crippled; only one bullet has hit the *Maddox* and there are no US casualties. The *Maddox* is ordered to withdraw and await further instructions.

USA: Government Because of the time difference, President Johnson is informed of the incident in the morning of the 2nd. With a presidential campaign underway, he must appear firm yet restrained. He rejects any reprisals against North Vietnam – and the Pentagon's first press release doesn't even refer to the North Vietnamese. In his first use of the 'hot line' to Russia, he tells Khrushchev that he has no need to extend the conflict; and in the first US diplomatic note ever sent to Hanoi, he warns that 'grave consequences would inevitably result from any further unprovoked offensive military action' against US ships 'on the high seas.'

USA: Military Despite President Johnson's measured response, the US military command takes several more critical actions. US combat troops are placed on alert and additional fighter-bombers are sent to South Vietnam and Thailand; the carrier *Constellation* is ordered to the South China Sea to join the *Ticonderoga*; finally, Admiral Sharp, CINCPAC, orders a second destroyer, the *C Turner Joy* to join the *Maddox* and to make daylight approaches to within eight miles of North Vietnam's coast and four miles of its islands to 'assert the right of freedom of the seas.'

3-4 AUGUST 1964

Covert War Two more clandestine attacks under Oplan 34A are carried out: PT boats manned by South Vietnamese attack the radar installations at Cape Vinhson and an installation at the Cua Ron estuary. The two US destroyer commanders are aware of this operation and try to avoid becoming associated with the South Vietnamese operation, but Admiral Sharp orders the US ships to stay close by 'to assert our legitimate rights' and even to serve as decoys for the South Vietnamese boats.

4 AUGUST 1964

Sea War About eight o'clock in the evening, the *Maddox* intercepts radio messages from the North Vietnamese that give Captain

Herrick 'the impression' that their patrol boats were planning an attack. Herrick calls for air support from the *Ticonderoga* again, and eight Crusader jets soon appear overhead. In the darkness, neither the pilots nor the ship crews can see any enemy craft, but about ten o'clock the sonar operators are reporting torpedoes approaching; the US destroyers maneuver to avoid the torpedoes and begin to fire. When the action ends about two hours later, US officers report sinking two, possibly three, North Vietnamese craft. In fact, no American will be sure of ever having seen any enemy boats nor any enemy gunfire. Captain Herrick will immediately communicate his doubts to his superiors and urges a 'thorough reconnaissance in daylight.' Shortly thereafter he will also inform Admiral Sharp that the radarscope blips were apparently 'freak weather effects' while the torpedoes were probably due to an 'over-eager' sonar operator.

USA: Government Because of the time difference, it is only 0920 hours in Washington when the Pentagon is alerted to a potential attack on the US destroyers (based on disputed interpretations of North Vietnamese radio messages about their military operations). When word of the 'engagement' arrives at 1100 hours, President Johnson is immediately informed and the JCS begin to select targets for reprisal air strikes (from a list drawn up by the end of May). At a meeting of the National Security Council about noon, McNamara, Rusk and McGeorge Bundy recommend such reprisal strikes to the president. Johnson is more cautious, but at a second session of the NSC that afternoon he orders that reprisal strikes be made, and discusses the deployment of US air strike and other military forces – as called for by Operation Plan 37-64 – should a major bombing campaign bring a response from Communist China or other powers supporting North Vietnam. Details of the reprisal strikes – code-named Pierce Arrow – are prepared by the JCS by late afternoon. Meanwhile Admiral Sharp in Honolulu is still trying to get absolute confirmation from the *Maddox* and *C Turner Joy* that an attack took place. By 1723 hours, Admiral Sharp calls to say he is satisfied that there was such an attack, and by 1845 hours President Johnson meets with 16 leaders from both parties in Congress to inform them of the second unprovoked attack, the imminent reprisal strikes and his

intention to ask for a Congressional resolution. By 2320 hours Defense Secretary McNamara is informed by Admiral Sharp that the US bombers are flying to their targets, so at 2336 hours President Johnson appears on national television and announces that the reprisal strikes are underway because of the unprovoked attack on US ships. The President assures the world that, 'We still seek no wider war.'

5 AUGUST 1964

Air War F-8 Crusaders, A-1 Skyraiders and A-4 Skyhawks, flying from the carriers USS *Ticonderoga* and *Constellation*, fly 64 sorties over a 100-mile area of North Vietnam along the Gulf of Tonkin. They destroy or damage an estimated 25 North Vietnamese PT boats (claimed by the United States to comprise about one-half of the North Vietnamese Navy) in attacking bases at Hongay, Loc Ghao, Phuc Loi and Quang Khe; practically destroy an oil storage depot at Phuc Loi (estimated to be about 10 percent of North Vietnam's oil storage facilities); and destroy seven anti-aircraft installations at the base at Vinh. Two US planes are damaged and two others shot down by anti-aircraft fire. (The pilot of one, Lieutenant (jg) Everett Alvarez, Jr, parachutes to safety – although he fractures his back when landing in shallow water – and is taken prisoner by the North Vietnamese; the first of some 600 US airmen who will be captured by the Communist forces during the war, Alvarez will not be released until the cease-fire agreement is signed in 1973.)

USA: Government President Johnson has his aides present the resolution drafted earlier by William Bundy, to the two Congressional leaders who are to sponsor its passage: Senator J William Fulbright (D-AR), chairman of the Senate Foreign Relations Committee, and Representative Thomas E Morgan (D-PA), chairman of the House Foreign Affairs Committee. The resolution would give the President authority to 'take all necessary measures to repel any armed attack against the forces of the United States and to prevent further aggression ... including the use of armed force, to assist any member or protocol state of the Southeast Asia Collective Defense Treaty.'

USA: Military At a news conference, Defense Secretary McNamara announces the results of the US air strikes, and that moves are underway to reinforce US forces in Vietnam: interceptor and fighter-bomber aircraft have

7 AUGUST 1964

been moved from the Philippines to South Vietnam and Thailand and transferred from the United States to advance bases in the Pacific; an attack carrier group has been transferred from the First Fleet off the US Pacific coast to the western Pacific; an anti-submarine task force group has been moved into the South China Sea; and 'selected Army and Marine forces have been alerted and readied for movement.' McNamara admits that these actions are being taken in case there is some form of military reaction from Communist nations, but he does not reveal that these actions are part of the Operation Plan 37-64 and other operations that the Johnson administration and the JCS have been planning for several months.

International There are reactions from governments and leaders throughout the world to the recent incidents in Vietnam, with the Communist nations inevitably supporting North Vietnam and attacking the United States, while America's allies, although generally supportive, tend to qualify their statements. British Prime Minister Douglas-Home defends the US action as 'in accordance with the inherent right of self-defense,' while France simply observed that the crisis shows the need to accept De Gaulle's proposal for an international conference on Southeast Asia. China warns that it will 'not sit idly by' while the US commits 'deliberate armed aggression' against North Vietnam.

UN The Security Council holds an emergency session to consider the US charges that the North Vietnamese attacked US destroyers in international waters in the Gulf of Tonkin. The Soviet delegate condemns the United States for 'acts of aggression' against North Vietnam, but US delegate Adlai Stevenson defends the air attacks as a 'defensive measure.' A resolution is passed asking both North and South Vietnam to participate in the Security Council debate.

6 AUGUST 1964
USA: Government Defense Secretary McNamara and Secretary of State Rusk appear before a joint Congressional committee on foreign affairs and present the Johnson administration's arguments for a resolution authorizing the president 'to take all necessary measures.' Senator Wayne Morse (D-OR) has received a tip from an officer in the Pentagon that the *Maddox* had been engaged in certain covert actions against North Viet-

nam, but when Morse asks if there was any link between the US ship and the South Vietnamese raids, McNamara replies flatly, 'Our Navy played absolutely no part in, was not associated with, was not aware of, any South Vietnamese actions, if there were any. ...' Morse is unable to win over any of his colleagues. When the Senate begins to debate on the resolution, only Senator Ernest Gruening (D-AK) joins Morse in opposing it. McNamara gives a news conference at which he denies US naval involvement in any South Vietnamese raids. He admits that China may now provide fighter planes to North Vietnam but he sees no sign of a general Chinese or Communist military response to the US raids.
USA: Military President Johnson rules out any further air raids against North Vietnam. But one US bomber is reported as crashing and three are damaged in the first day of the US military buildup in Thailand and South Vietnam.
USA: Domestic The New York stock market reacts to the news of the crisis in Vietnam with the sharpest decline since the death of President Kennedy. Various rallies and peace vigils are held to protest the US bombing raids. Republican presidential candiate Barry Goldwater says the he supports President Johnson's ordering the air raids on North Vietnam but that he intends to make the whole question of Vietnam a campaign issue.

6-13 AUGUST 1964
Diplomatic The US State Department instructs J Blair Seaborn, of the ICC who had made the contacts with the North Vietnamese on 18 June, to tell Hanoi that the United States does not understand the motives behind the North Vietnamese attacks on US ships but that the US response 'for the moment will be limited and fitting,' although additional air power is being deployed to South Vietnam and Thailand. When Seaborn gets to see Premier Pham Van Dong on the 13th, the latter is furious, indicates that North Vietnam is quite prepared to fight, but also states he wants to keep open channels of communication with the United States. Seaborn's report of this mission indicates he feels that Hanoi is convinced there 'was no need to compromise.'

7 AUGUST 1964
South Vietnam To exploit the mood of crisis surrounding the events in the Gulf of Tonkin, General Khanh declares a state of emergency

in South Vietnam, reimposes censorship, and announces other controls, the justification being that the nation is threatened by large-scale Communist.

North Vietnam The government charges that US airplanes 'again intrude repeatedly' into North Vietnam air space, but the Pentagon categorically denies this.

USA: Government The Senate, by a vote of 82-2, and the House of Representatives, 416-0, overwhelmingly approve Public Law 88-408 which becomes known as 'The Tonkin Gulf Resolution.' President Johnson will sign it on 10 August. It will become increasingly controversial as Johnson employs it to enlarge the US commitment to the war in Vietnam. Two Senators vote against it, but eventually many Senators and Representatives will have strong doubts about the resolution, which will be repealed in May 1970.

Release of the official summary of the US air strikes against North Vietnam prompts Defense Secretary McNamara to admit that President Johnson was announcing the raids about one hour before the first target was actually hit, but he defends this on grounds that this warned China that only North Vietnam was to be the target.

International The world continues to react. Foreign Minister Gromyko of the Soviet Union promises his nation's full support for North Vietnam. In Peking, thousands of demonstrators march to support North Vietnam; in London, Lord Russell condemns the US action, while in Calcutta, 1000 leftist students demonstrate against the United States. But Premier Souvanna Phouma of Laos supports the US action, as does the Inter-American Naval Conference, meeting in Rio de Janeiro, and Britain announces its Far East fleet is ready for any emergency action to support the United States.

8 AUGUST 1964

South Vietnam A US intelligence report states that the Communists are winning the struggle for the allegiance of the Vietnamese and that the Vietcong strength has increased despite heavy casualties.

USA: Government At a news conference, President Johnson says that the US air strike and the Congressional resolution show the United States' 'determination to resist and repel aggression' in Southeast Asia.

9 AUGUST 1964

North Vietnam The government rejects the bid from the UN to participate in a debate before the Security Council on the crisis, contending that only the Geneva Pact signatories have jurisdiction in this matter.

USA: Military The DeSoto Mission patrol by US ships off North Vietnam is suspended.

10 AUGUST 1964

USA: Government Ambassador Maxwell Taylor in Saigon cables President Johnson a report in which he claims that the Khanh regime has only 'a 50-50 chance of lasting out the year'; therefore Taylor advocates that the United States 'be prepared to implement contingency plans against North Vietnam with optimum readiness by January 1, 1965.'

11 AUGUST 1964

North Vietnam Hanoi reports that Lt Everett Alvarez, the US Navy pilot shot down in the raid on 5 August, is paraded through the streets of Hongay.

USA: Government William Bundy, Assistant Secretary of State for East Asia and Pacific Affairs, draws up a memorandum that calls for a 'short holding phase' of 'military silence' during August but a phase of 'limited pressures' from September through December to be followed by 'more serious pressures' against North Vietnam after 1 January 1965 – including systematic bombing raids and the mining of Haiphong Harbor. This memo will circulate among the high-level US civilian and military officials.

USA: Military The Defense Department announces that Communist China has moved MiGs into North Vietnam; it also insists that the USS *Maddox*, despite claims to the contrary, never went closer than 12 miles to North Vietnamese territory.

12 AUGUST 1964

USA: Domestic Presidential candidate Barry Goldwater charges that President Johnson's 'admonition' to US naval commanders during the crisis authorized them 'to use any weapon necessary,' which he claims includes nuclear weapons. Goldwater claims that this, plus Johnson's 'impulsive action' in Vietnam takes the sting out of charges that he is the impulsive individual who might resort to nuclear warfare. Rusk and McNamara immediately deny that Johnson authorized the use of nuclear weapons and label Goldwater's charge 'both unjustified and irresponsible.'

Guerrilla War In an attempt to neutralize resistance, the Vietcong distribute leaflets

Helicopters were used as troop transports throughout the war.

claiming they will fire only on South Vietnamese units accompanied by US advisers; this promise is soon broken.

Ground War Ninety US and 12 South Vietnamese helicopters airlift about 1000 ARVN troops close to a Vietcong base near Ap Bo Cang, while other ARVN ground troops converge on the area; but the 2000-man guerrilla force slips away, and only four Vietcong are killed, while one US helicopter is downed.

14 AUGUST 1964

North Vietnam Hanoi is reported as holding air-raid drills for fear of more US attacks, and the government is urging all civilians with non-essential posts to leave the city.

Ground War In various military actions, ARVN troops ambush a Vietcong platoon south of Saigon; Guerrillas sweep through three hamlets in Vinh Binh Province, and a US helicopter crashes 50 miles northwest of Saigon, killing three US airmen.

16 AUGUST 1964

South Vietnam Meeting in closed session, the Military Revolutionary Council elects Nguyen Khanh president of Vietnam and reduces Duong Van Minh to adviser to the council (although Khanh says he stepped down on his own) under a new constitution – claimed to be based on that of the United States – that consolidated power in the president. A 150-member advisory provisional National Assembly and a separate judicial branch are also to be established. Khanh rejects the suggestion he is becoming a military dictator but he clearly is now the chief power in the government.

16 AUGUST-1 SEPTEMBER 1964

Diplomatic Henry Cabot Lodge, former ambassador to South Vietnam, tours the capitals of Western Europe as a personal emissary of President Johnson, to explain US policy in Vietnam and to obtain more support from these allies. In Paris, he argues that the struggle in Vietnam is just as vital to the West as is the freedom of Berlin. Although Lodge will return with pledges from countries such as West Germany, Holland, Belgium, Great Britain and Spain to provide non-military technical aid to South Vietnam, no Western

CHRONOLOGY

European country will ever provide military support.

17-19 AUGUST 1964
Ground War In the Mekong Delta, ARVN troops upset a Vietcong ambush plan and in three days of fighting claim to have killed about 280 guerrillas; but US military advisers will report finding only 10 Vietcong dead and no sign of the other 270.

19 AUGUST 1964
Air War South Vietnamese fighter-bombers, some piloted by Americans, attack a major Vietcong headquarters south of Saigon.

20 AUGUST 1964
North Vietnam In a message to the Security Council, the government rejects the US charge that North Vietnam committed 'deliberate aggression' against US ships and says that the United States 'circulated an imaginary story' about the second attack.
Ground War Vietcong forces overrun the outpost of Phu Tuc, kill seven, injure 15 and capture the remaining defenders; when an ARVN infantry unit sets out to track down the Vietcong responsible, it is ambushed and four US military advisers are killed.

21-25 AUGUST 1964
South Vietnam As opposition to Khanh's new government mounts, Saigon is plunged into virtual anarchy. The Buddhists charge the government with 'anti-Buddhist' holdovers from the Diem era. Students mount widespread and violent demonstrations – marching on Khanh's office, storming the national radio station, stoning US Army billets. Khanh meets with the student leaders and promises that the new government will have a majority of civilian ministers, but the students are not satisfied, and the anti-government violence begins to spread to other cities. The Revolutionary Council issues a proclamation that withdraws the constitution devised on 16 August and promises to elect a new head of state who will convene a national assembly to reform the government 'consistent with the aspirations of the people.'

22 AUGUST 1964
Guerrilla War Over 1000 ARVN troops are reported as casualties in the Vietcong jungle stronghold of Tayninh.
Terrorism A bomb explosion in a Saigon theater kills one Vietnamese.

26 AUGUST 1964
USA: Domestic Lyndon B Johnson is nominated by the Democratic Party to run for the presidency, with Hubert Humphrey as his vice-president. Republican candidate Goldwater announces that he believes that talks with Communist China might be helpful in ending the war and that he sees the solution to the conflict as 'not military in the long run.'
USA: Military The JCS send a memo to Defense Secretary McNamara and concur with a cable from Ambassador Taylor (dated 18 August) calling for 'a carefully orchestrated bombing attack on North Vietnam' – 'essential,' the JCS state, 'to prevent a complete collapse of the US position in Southeast Asia.'

26-29 AUGUST 1964
South Vietnam Despite the apparent resignation of Khanh and the withdrawal of the constitution that gave him the presidency, demonstrations and violence continue. In Danang, at least nine people are killed in clashes between Buddhists and Roman Catholics; the Buddhists also attack a US-run hospital and kill four patients; and in an attack on a Roman Catholic hamlet of Thanh Bo, the Buddhists raze 450 out of the 500 houses as well as burn down the two Catholic churches. The Revolutionary Council meets but can only propose a compromise: a provisionary triumvirate – Nguyen Khanh, Duong Van Minh and General Tran Thien Khiem, Khanh to retain the title of prime minister – will rule for two months, by which time a national convention will elect a provisional leader. Even then the violence does not stop; Catholic activists converging on the military headquarters where the council is meeting are fired on by soldiers guarding the gates and six are killed and many others wounded. As exaggerated rumors of the incident sweep Saigon, gangs of youths riot; the police are powerless and paratroopers are required to restore order. Nguyen Khanh, after a news conference at which he denounces the politicians who thwarted him, leaves for Dalat. It is announced that he has suffered a physical and mental 'breakdown' and has gone there to recuperate. Meanwhile, Nguyen Xuen Oanh – a Harvard-educated economist – is named acting premier to lead the caretaker government for the next two months. Through all this turmoil, the United States – in the person of Ambassador Taylor – attempts to support Khanh without tainting either him or the

United States with the image of a 'puppet government,' but Taylor does postpone his planned visit to Washington.

28 AUGUST 1964
Laos Prince Souvanna Phouma has been in Paris through most of August trying to rebuild a coalition government with the various factions and to gain international support for his talks with the leftists. But with US advisors working behind the scenes, he is encouraged to make demands that only draw out the discussions. The United States is convinced that a negotiated ceasefire will not lead to a true end of the threat of a Communist takeover. Souvanna Phouma breaks off his conference with Prince Souphanouvong, the leader of the Pathet Lao, on the grounds that the latter's demands are too extreme, and by the end of September the negotiations in Paris break down completely.

29 AUGUST 1964
USA: Domestic President Johnson assures his fellow Americans that he has 'tried very carefully to restrain ourselves and not to enlarge the war,' but that 'it is better to lose 200 [US servicemen] than to lose 200,000. The United States will continue to aid the South Vietnamese but not fight a war for them. (The Defense Department issues the official casualty list revealing that 274 Americans have been killed in Vietnam between December 1961 and 17 August 1964.)

30 AUGUST 1964
South Vietnam In Saigon, 50,000 Catholics participate in the funeral procession for six riot victims. The procession deliberately passes through the Buddhist section of the city and there is no incident; acting premier Nguyen Xuan Oanh praises the Buddhist and Roman Catholic leaders' efforts to end the rioting. In Saigon, the government charges that Communists stirred up the recent troubles; 450 persons arrested in the riots are still detained; and the army says that demonstrators who go too far will now be shot.
China The Commnist China press agency charges that the Soviet Union is supporting the United States in a move to intervene in Vietnam through the agency the UN.

31 AUGUST 1964
South Vietnam Ambassador Taylor confers at Dalat with Nguyen Khanh and reports that Khanh appears 'rested and recovered' and

ready to return to Saigon as premier shortly. In Hué, the Buddhist professors announce formation of the People's Revolutionary Council. Although anti-Communist it will challenge US policies and offer its own program of economic reform.
USA: Military Admiral Thomas Moorer, chief of staff of US Navy, announces that US warships continue to remain on alert in the South China Sea off North Vietnam in case there is any counterattack by North Vietnamese forces.
Japan Admiral U S Grant Sharp, CINCPAC, at a meeting of the joint Security Consultative Committee in Tokyo, briefs the Japanese on the situation in Vietnam and acknowledges that the Japanese have just alloted $500,000 in aid to South Vietnam.

SEPTEMBER 1964
USA: Government The JCS organize Sigma II, a 'war game' that is to estimate the possible results of a US air offensive against North Vietnam. One team represents the United States, the other North Vietnam, and the conclusion is that the Communists are not going to stop fighting, no matter how much North Vietnam is bombed.
UN Secretary General U Thant secretly tries to set up direct talks in Rangoon, Burma, between the United States and the North Vietnamese; President Johnson agrees in principle, but when U Thant reports to his top aides that Hanoi is willing to meet, they do not inform Johnson. (Secretary of State Rusk will claim that to meet with North Vietnam would mean 'the acceptance or the confirmation of aggression.')
USSR Premier Khrushchev is also secretly trying to get the North Vietnamese to negotiate with the United States, and although the Vietnamese distrust the Russians, he offers the prospect of increased aid.

1 SEPTEMBER 1964
South Vietnam Reliable reports are coming from Saigon that top US officials are informing South Vietnamese leaders that if Khanh is not allowed back into the government, the United States may have to reconsider its role. The State Department will deny such claims.

2-3 SEPTEMBER 1964
South Vietnam Nguyen Khanh returns to Saigon on 2 September and holds talks with Generals Minh and Khiem, the two other members of the 'triumvirate'; unknown to

them, however, he has secretly met with two of the most influential Buddhist leaders and promised them $200,000 in return for pledges of mutual support. The following day Khanh resumes his position as premier, dissolves the triumvirate, reappoints Duong Van Minh as chief of state, and appeals to Buddhists and students to support the government.

Cambodia Cambodia charges that South Vietnamese planes spread poisonous chemicals on Cambodian territory in August, and South Vietnam charges that Vietcong forces are operating from five bases in Cambodia.

3 SEPTEMBER 1964
USA: Government Assistant Secretary of Defense John T McNaughton draws up a crucial memorandum to Secretary McNamara outlining a specific series of provocative actions that the United States might take, culminating in a sustained air war against North Vietnam.

4 SEPTEMBER 1964
Guerrilla War A US helicopter crewman is killed by Vietcong gunfire, five other US servicemen are injured in other operations and the ARVN claims it has killed 70 guerrillas in a major clash in Quang Ngai Province.

7 SEPTEMBER 1964
USA: Government Ambassador Taylor arrives in Washington to brief the administration on the current situation in South Vietnam. He joins President Johnson in a strategy session with top planners of the Vietnam war, including Rusk, McNamara, General Earle Wheeler, McGeorge Bundy and William Bundy. Most of those present reject the schedule of escalation outlined in the McNaughton memo of 3 September – among other reasons, Johnson is engaged in a presidential campaign and except for a few minor operations (e.g. resuming the DeSoto patrols) no major decisions are taken. But the consensus is that there will have to be air attacks on North Vietnam sooner or later.

Cambodia South Vietnam makes a new series of charges that Cambodians have been shelling South Vietnam territory to aid the Vietcong and that Cambodian planes are violating South Vietnam's air space.

8 SEPTEMBER 1964
South Vietnam General Duong Van Minh is named chairman of the military tribunal

(Khiem has been allowed to stay on, although in deference to the Buddhists he has resigned as defense minister); Minh will have the duties of chief of state, but the real power is still held by Khanh.

Guerrilla War Five US helicopters engage in a lengthy battle with a Vietcong machine-gun position but the South Vietnamese forces are unable and unwilling to provide support.

Cambodia USAF jets come to the aid of South Vietnamese planes that report being chased by Cambodian jets, but no fire is exchanged.

9 SEPTEMBER 1964
South Vietnam General Khanh lifts press censorship and appoints two civilians to government posts to replace military men, but he announces he will hold onto the post of defense minister.

USA: Government After reporting to Congress Ambassador Taylor holds a news conference, stating that Khanh is 'very definitely head of the interim government' and that the situation in Vietnam is 'essentially normal.'

Covert War A USN patrol plane crashes in the South China Sea with the loss of five US crewmen.

USSR The Soviet government warns Japan that it must expect some military retaliation if it allows US bases there to be used for military action against North Vietnam.

10 SEPTEMBER 1964
USA: Government Special Emissary Henry Cabot Lodge reports to President Johnson on his trip throughout Europe; a statement issued claims that all Western European governments except France's view the Vietnam struggle as a 'free world' issue, not just a regional problem. Ambassador Taylor returns to Vietnam. And President Johnson authorizes a series of measures 'to assist morale in SVN and show the Communists we still mean business.' Mostly these involve covert actions such as the resumption of the DeSoto patrols and the South Vietnamese coastal raids; but another crucial item calls for asking Premier Souvanna Phouma of Laos to allow the South Vietnamese to make air and ground operations into southeastern Laos along with air strikes by Laotian planes and US armed aerial reconnaissance.

Guerrilla War A Vietcong ambush of ARVN troops near the Cambodian border halts a planned attack by the ARVN. And 25 miles south of Saigon, another Vietcong ambush leaves one US officer and two ARVN soldiers dead.

11 SEPTEMBER 1964
Laos The US ambassadors to Thailand and Laos meet with Ambassador Taylor in Saigon and decide the South Vietnamese Air Force must not participate in the intensified air raids suggested in President Johnson's memo of 10 September. But T-28s based in Laos and USAF and USN planes – the Yankee Team – will continue their clandestine operations. And it is agreed that ARVN troops, possibly accompanied by US advisers, will be able to make incursions into Laos up to 20km (12 miles) but that Souvanna Phouma will not be informed (so that he can honestly deny such operations and not weaken his government).

12 SEPTEMBER 1964
South Vietnam In a letter to the ICC, the government says it is prepared to disarm and end all US support as soon as North Vietnam halts the activities of the Vietcong.
USA:Domestic In an interview, Senator Humphrey says that the United States must remain in Vietnam but make it clear that the primary responsibility for achieving peace rests with the Vietnamese. Presidential candidate Goldwater says that 'if there is a solution brewing' for Vietnam, this is the time to inform the American people.
Covert War The USN destroyers *Edwards* and *Morton* resume the DeSoto patrols in the Gulf of Tonkin (but are ordered to observe the 12-mile limit).

13-14 SEPTEMBER 1964
South Vietnam Dissident army officers attempt to overthrow Khanh's government. The coup is led by General Lam Van Phat, a Roman Catholic who was dismissed as interior minister on 3 September, and General Duong Van Duc, commander of 4th Corps. Calling their movement the People's Council for the Salvation of the Nation, they are motivated by the growing influence of the Buddhists and Khanh's reorganization of the top military commands. Ambassador Taylor is en route back to Saigon but his deputy, Alexis Johnson, meets with the cabinet and encourages them to remain loyal to Khanh. Meanwhile, government troops loyal to Khanh move against the coup's main base near Tan Sonnhut air base. But the final blow to the coup comes when Air Vice Marshal Nguyen Cao Ky orders air force planes over the insurgent generals' headquarters and threatens to bomb them if they do not surrender. By the 14th, Ky is holding a news conference with the dissident leaders and claiming 'there was no coup' and Khanh returns to Saigon from Dalat.

15 SEPTEMBER 1964
Guerrilla War The National Liberation Front, the formal organization behind the Vietcong, call for a general military offensive to take advantage of the 'disarray' among the South Vietnamese, particularly after the abortive coup.

16 SEPTEMBER 1964
South Vietnam The two chief leaders of the coup attempt, Generals Phat and Duc, are arrested, as are three other rebel generals.

18-19 SEPTEMBER 1964
Covert War The two US destroyers, *Edwards* and *Morton*, on DeSoto patrol are pursued at night by four unidentified vessels, presumed to be North Vietnamese torpedo boats; the US ships fire over 200 5-inch and 100 3-inch shells, but never see any ships and no torpedoes are detected. On the 19th, McNamara will publicly report the incident, stating that the destroyers were on 'routine patrol.' North Vietnam will also report the incident but does not refer to any of its ships being involved, simply accusing the United States of firing offshore. President Johnson does not authorize any retaliatory air raids this time and suspends the DeSoto patrols.

18 SEPTEMBER 1964
Ground War South Vietnam claims that two companies from the North Vietnamese Army invade South Vietnam, in Quangtri Province, but that they are defeated with heavy casualties. US military advisers will question whether these were North Vietnamese troops, but in fact they are now beginning to infiltrate the South.
River War Vietcong artillery sink two South Vietnamese landing craft attempting an operation on the Mekong River.

19 SEPTEMBER 1964
South Vietnam General Khanh's government makes several major changes in the military command, in part a response to demands from officers who have emerged as loyal in the recent coup.
Cambodia Khanh threatens to restrict the use

CHRONOLOGY

Montagnard *tribesmen were also trained by the Special Forces, or Green Berets.*

of the Mekong River as an international waterway to punish Cambodia if it continues its hostile actions.

21-28 SEPTEMBER 1964
South Vietnam Rhadé (or Edé) tribesmen in the central plateau, one of several so-called *montagnard* groups who have little sympathy for either the Saigon government or the Vietcong, revolt and demand autonomy for the tribes of the mountainous areas. The revolt begins on the 20th when about 500 tribesmen kill some 50 ARVN troops at a US Special Forces camp near Banmethout, the capital of Darlac Province. Eventually General Khanh will appear to negotiate an end, but US military plays a major role in keeping South Vietnamese from attacking the rebels. The tribesmen also seized a Special Forces camp at Bonsarpa, close to the Cambodian border; again, US military advisers negotiate. And on the 27th US helicopters are allowed to evacuate 60 South Vietnamese hostages in Bonsarpa. (Another *montagnard* group had surrendered on 26 September after US advisers mediated.) By the 28th, all the *montagnards* have capitulated. Khanh blames the uprising on 'Communists and foreigners' and it does appear that the National Libera-tion Front has begun to influence some of the *montagnards* by taking advantage of their age-old resentment of the South Vietnamese government. The US Special Forces work with the *montagnards* to train them to fight against the Vietcong but will never really be able to gain the full support of these independent people who essentially want to be left alone.

21 SEPTEMBER 1964
USA: Government At a news conference, President Johnson says that although urged by some of his advisers to bomb North Vietnam for the recent incident in the Gulf of Tonkin, he chose to hold back.

22-23 SEPTEMBER 1964
USA: Domestic Republican presidential candidate Goldwater charges that President Johnson lied to the American people and that he is committing the US to war 'recklessly.' Having previously called it 'McNamara's War,' Goldwater calls it 'Johnson's War.'

23 SEPTEMBER 1964
Guerrilla War Near Rach Gia, Vietcong ground fire downs two US-piloted planes; one pilot is safe but the other is missing.

25-27 SEPTEMBER 1964
South Vietnam Rumors of another coup bring government troops to take up key points around Saigon, but nothing materializes; however, younger officers demand that Khanh dismiss General Khiem, a member of the ruling triumvirate, and five other generals. (Khanh will announce the resignations of all six on 30 September.) Anti-government riots at Quinhon, one of the centers of Buddhist protests during August, are also put down by government forces.

26 SEPTEMBER 1964
South Vietnam The Khanh regime forms a 17-member civilian High National Council that is charged with setting up a provisional government to replace Khanh's regime and to hold a national convention to draft a permanent constitution. The council includes representatives of Buddhist and Roman Catholic groups, opposition civil organizations, and political activists.
Guerrilla War An ARVN battalion engages in a fierce battle in the Mekong Delta with Vietcong forces; one US-piloted plane is downed and one US soldier is killed.

28 SEPTEMBER 1964
Guerrilla War ARVN forces claim a victory over guerrillas in Gocong Province but are defeated in a clash in Kien Gian Province, where one US soldier is killed.

30 SEPTEMBER 1964
USA: Domestic The first major demonstration by students and faculty opposed to the US role in the war in Vietnam takes place at the University of California at Berkeley. But polls of Americans show a majority support the President's conduct.

OCTOBER 1964
USA: Government Under-Secretary of State George Ball dictates a private 67-page memo that he sees as 'a challenge to the assumptions of our current Vietnam policy,' in particular arguing that an intensified US air war against North Vietnam would lead to a still greater escalation on both sides, 'leading, at the end of the road, to the direct intervention of China and nuclear war.' As for the assumption behind the 'domino theory' – that a loss in Vietnam will inevitably lead to the loss of America's credibility and so to the loss of a series of nations – Ball concludes: 'What we might gain by establishing the steadfastness of our commitments, we could lose by an erosion of confidence in our judgments.' Ball sends copies of the memo to Rusk, McNamara and McGeorge Bundy, but no one bothers to send a copy to President Johnson until February 1965.
Covert War Both sides are now blatantly escalating their clandestine operations. Tactical units of the North Vietnamese Army are beginning a steady influx into the South over the Ho Chi Minh Trail, while the United States continues to support the various groups operating under Oplan 34A.

2 OCTOBER 1964
South Vietnam General Khanh announces that his government and US authorities are revising the program that has been arming the *montagnards*. In reference to the recent troubles with the tribesmen, he threatens to use force to put down any further disorder.

4 OCTOBER 1964
Covert War President Johnson issues the order to reactivate coastal raids by South Vietnamese boats as part of Oplan 34A.
Guerrilla War In an ambush some 15 miles north of Saigon, ARVN troops suffer heavy casualties from the Vietcong.

5 OCTOBER 1964
USA: Government Senator Gaylord Nelson (D-WI), disturbed by growing reports that Johnson administration is preparing to extend US operations in Vietnam, states that Congress did not intend the Gulf of Tonkin Resolution (7 August) to endorse escalation.
USA: Domestic Republican presidential candidate Barry Goldwater announces that if he is elected he will ask ex-President Eisenhower to visit Vietnam and report on the situation there; Eisenhower's aides, however, quickly announce that he has not committed himself.

7 OCTOBER 1964
South Vietnam General Tran Thien Khiem, a member of the government triumvirate leaves on a 'goodwill mission' to various Asian nations; in fact, he is being forced into exile.
USA: Domestic Former Vice-President Richard Nixon claims that Vietnam will be lost within a year and all of Southeast Asia within three years if the United States does not quickly change its policy.
Guerrilla War Vietcong ground fire brings down a US helicopter and five US servicemen are killed.

CHRONOLOGY

8 OCTOBER 1964
USA: Government Secretary of State Rusk, in a news conference, insists that the administration's decisions about the conflict in Vietnam have 'nothing to do' with the election and denies that information is being withheld.

9 OCTOBER 1964
South Vietnam General Khanh says that South Vietnam now has the capability of bombing North Vietnam or China without US aid, but he says no such action is imminent.
Guerrilla War The ARVN forces, with US support, announce they are to begin using the 'Hoptac' operation that, based on tactics used by the British in fighting the Communists in Malaya, will operate on several levels and proceed in a series of concentric circles around Saigon to eliminate the Vietcong.

10 OCTOBER 1964
South Vietnam The government claims that 16,101 Communist soldiers or agents have deserted during the last 20 months under the amnesty program known as 'Open Arms' (*Chieu Hoi*). (Some of these defectors will fight with the US and ARVN forces and will become known as the Kit Carson Scouts.)
International In Cairo, a conference of non-aligned nations urges that a conference be called in Geneva to negotiate an end to the conflict in Vietnam.

11 OCTOBER 1964
South Vietnam The Buddhists' policy-making group issues orders to monks to condemn political agitation in the name of Buddhism; this is viewed as an attempt to disassociate the Buddhists from pro-Communist actions and seems particularly aimed at Thich Tri Quang, the radical Buddhist leader.
Guerrilla War The Vietcong burn 200 structures in attacks on eight fortified hamlets in the area of Pleiku.
Terrorism Two US soldiers are killed by a landmine explosion.

13 OCTOBER 1964
USA: Military The United States announces it is setting up a third helicopter company in the Mekong Delta area controlled by the Vietcong; it is designed to cut down on the ambushes against ARVN troops.

14 OCTOBER 1964
Laos After considerable pressure from both sides, the United States authorizes its Yankee Team jets to fly cover missions with the Laotian Air Force T-28s that are bombing the trails and installations used by the Vietcong and North Vietnamese Army making their way through Laos. The US jets are to protect the Laotian planes from attacks from North Vietnamese MiGs.

14-15 OCTOBER 1964
USSR After ten years in power, Nikita Krushchev is ousted as both premier and chief of the Communist Party. The new Russian leaders will increase military aid to the North Vietnamese without trying to persuade them to attempt a negotiated end to hostilities.

19 OCTOBER 1964
Guerilla War Thirteen US servicemen and four US civilians believed to be held as prisoners by the Vietcong for over two years have not been allowed to contact their families and the Red Cross has been unable to make contact with them.
Cuba The National Liberation Front reveals that it has maintained an office in Havana, Cuba for over two years to propagandize its achievements.

20 OCTOBER 1964
South Vietnam The High National Council (established on 26 September) issues a new draft constitution providing for a chief of state, a premier, a cabinet and a legislative assembly; its preamble explicitly states that 'the armed forces have rightfully asserted that they would return to their purely military duties and gradually hand over the power to a civilian government.'
Guerrilla War The United States reports that a helicopter operation, 80 miles southwest of Saigon, killed 34 guerrillas.

20-28 OCTOBER 1964
Cambodia A series of incidents and charges bring relations between Cambodia, South Vietnam and the United States to their lowest point, but all three back away from a complete break. South Vietnamese planes strafe a Cambodian village on the 20th. When Cambodia protests, South Vietnam replies by charging Cambodia once again with providing refuge for Vietcong forces. On the 22nd, the United States charges that Cambodian troops crossed over into South Vietnam and seized a US officer advising ARVN forces; on the 25th, the officer's body is recovered just inside South Vietnam and Cambodia is accused

2 NOVEMBER 1964

of placing the body there to allow the rescue force to be fired on. Then on the 24th, a USAF C-123, loaded with ammunition for a Special Forces camp, is shot down by Cambodians; eight US servicemen are lost. By the 28th, the US admits that the plane did stray over Cambodian territory by mistake, but the United States argues that such incidents arise because of the poorly defined border and the activities of the Vietcong in the area. Despite the charges and threats from Sihanouk, and despite the US losses in personnel and planes, neither side pursues the matter.

22 OCTOBER 1964
North Vietnam It is reported that Hanoi's government radio is increasing its propaganda broadcasts into South Vietnam and is repeating with approval the criticisms of the Johnson administration's handling of the war being made by various US senators.

23 OCTOBER 1964
South Vietnam The 20 military officers and civilians on trial, charged with an attempted coup 13-14 September, are acquitted. This is clearly an attempt by Nguyen Khanh to placate dissidents in the armed forces. Khanh also appoints to high posts the five generals arrested when he seized power in January.

24-29 OCTOBER 1964
South Vietnam The High National Council chooses Phan Khac Suu, a 63-year-old engineer, as chief of state. Although a figurehead, he at least represents a break with the strong military influence on the government. Nguyen Khanh resigns as premier on the 26th, and on the 29th, Tran Van Huong, former mayor of Saigon, is named premier.

28 OCTOBER 1964
Cover War US T-28s, piloted by Thais, bomb and strafe North Vietnamese villages in the Mugia Pass area. The United States denies the public charge by North Vietnam, however, that any US naval units participated in recent attacks on North Vietnam.
Guerrilla War One US soldier is wounded when the Vietcong down a US Army helicopter, and one US soldier is killed and two wounded Vietcong ambush.

1 NOVEMBER 1964
South Vietnam One year after the overthrow and assassination of Ngo Dinh Diem, a survey of South Vietnam reveals it has deteriorated

in both the political and military spheres. Meanwhile, the High National Council confirms the appointment of Tran Van Huong as premier, and he promises to wage total war against the Communists while separating religion and politics.
Guerrilla War Vietcong raiders infiltrate the US air base at Bienhoa, 12 miles north of Saigon, and launch a heavy mortar attack in the darkness that catches the US and South Vietnamese offguard. Before the Vietcong flee without a known loss, they kill 5 US servicemen and two Vietnamese, wound about 76, destroy six B-57s, and damage some 20 other US and Vietnamese aircraft. A lengthy search of the area around Bienhoa fails to locate any of the Vietcong. Word of the attack reaches Washington early in the morning, and the JCS call for 'a prompt and strong response,' i.e., long series of military actions against North Vietnam and Laos. Ambassador Taylor calls for a more limited response, but also advocates retaliation bombing raids. President Johnson, well aware that the presidential election will be underway within 48 hours, essentially decides to do nothing except order the immediate replacement of the destroyed and damaged planes. Administration officials, when briefing the press about the Bienhoa raid, distinguish between it and the Tonkin Gulf attacks, where the destroyers were 'on United States business' – virtually implying that Americans must be prepared to accept such attacks when US armed forces are aiding other nations.
Cambodia The US Embassy in Pnompenh sends dependents out of Cambodia because of the increase in anti-US demonstrations following charges of US involvement in border incidents. Wreckage of the C-123 shot down on 24 October is now displayed in Pnompenh.

2 NOVEMBER 1964
USA: Domestic In the last day before the election, presidential candidate Barry Goldwater and ex-Vice-President Nixon attack the President's handling of events in Vietnam, charging that the Pentagon was warned two days before that Bienhoa was exposed to just such an attack and that security is inadequate; Goldwater challenges Johnson to admit to the American people that the United States is involved in an undeclared war in Vietnam.
Cambodia The Soviet Union delivers a major shipment of arms to Cambodia, to replace US

In Saigon, the Vietnam Independence Day was celebrated with parades and speeches.

equipment no longer available. Within two days, the Soviet Union will also be calling for a new international conference to guarantee Cambodia's neutrality.

3 NOVEMBER 1964
USA: Government An interagency 'working group,' headed by William Bundy, holds its first meeting. This group is charged with drawing up the various military and political options for the United States in Vietnam and then presenting these to the high-level officials such as Rusk, McNamara, Wheeler and Taylor, who will in turn refine and present them to the President. 'Bundy's group' will meet throughout the next three weeks.
USA: Domestic Lyndon Johnson is re-elected by a landslide over Goldwater – in part, at least, because so many Americans believe Johnson is less likely to escalate the US involvement in Vietnam.

5 NOVEMBER 1964
South Vietnam Buddhists charge that Premier Huong has deliberately denied them any role in the government, students are angry that they will lose their draft exemptions, some charge he has ignored political leaders, while others charge he has appointed ministers who

had served under Ngo Dinh Diem and Emperor Bao Dai. Huong warns he will not hesitate to use force to suppress violent demonstrations, but on the 6th he speaks in a more conciliatory way, admitting his government's weakness and appealing to all dissident groups to cooperate.
Guerrilla War Heavily armed Vietcong, attempting to kidnap a Vietnamese official, get within rifle-range of the US Embassy in Saigon.

6 NOVEMBER 1964
Ground War ARVN officers refuse to order their boats and troops along a canal they regard as militarily insecure, delaying a major operation planned to break the Vietcong's hold on the Mekong Delta town of Nam Can; the US military advisers openly express their disgust with such lack of aggression.

7 NOVEMBER 1964
South Vietnam The government bans the sale of the current issue of *Newsweek* because it carries a photograph showing a Vietcong prisoner being tortured by ARVN personnel.
Guerrilla War The latest US intelligence analysis claims that the Vietcong now number about 30,000 professional full-time soldiers,

On 3 November 1960, Lyndon B Johnson won the presidential election.

many of whom are North Vietnamese. It can no longer be claimed that the Vietcong is a movement of South Vietnamese simply opposed to the government.

7-10 NOVEMBER 1964
Guerrilla War On the 7th, the South Vietnamese Air Force raids a Communist stronghold near Bienhoa; then some 1200 ARVN troops push through the jungles in the area, all part of the attempt to find the guerrillas that attacked the US air base at Bienhoa.

10 NOVEMBER 1964
USA: Government Secretary of Defense McNamara, at a news conference, says the United States has no plans to send combat units into Vietnam; asked whether the United States intends to increase its activities in Vietnam, Rusk replies 'wait and see.'
Australia Prime Minister Robert Menzies announces that his country will strengthen its defenses to meet the growing Communist threat in Southeast Asia.

10-14 NOVEMBER 1964
South Vietnam Major floods in the region north of Saigon disrupt military operations, while Vietcong attack rescue operations and relief convoys.

11 NOVEMBER 1964
South Vietnam The Saigon police announce they have uncovered a ring involving officials from the Nguyen Khanh government that sold exemptions to Vietnamese youths called up for military service.
USA: Domestic Veterans Day. NBC-TV shows a film (provided by a Japanese agency) that gives the North Vietnamese version of events; among other film clips, it shows the first US POW, Lt Everett Alvarez.

12 NOVEMBER 1964
Guerrilla War In two attacks in Binh Tuy Province, Vietcong kill 34 ARVN soldiers and wound 40.

15-18 NOVEMBER 1964
Cambodia Prince Sihanouk says that if the United States wants to improve its relations with Cambodia, it must get the South Vietnamese to stop their attack on border areas and stop charging that the Vietcong are allowed to use Cambodia as a sanctuary and supply route. He claims that the South Vietnamese have killed 100 Cambodians and demands that the United States and South Vietnam pay one bulldozer or one million riels for each Cambodian killed.

17 NOVEMBER 1964
Guerrilla War In a skirmish in Bienhoa Province, one US military adviser and four ARVN soldiers are killed, one US adviser and six ARVN soldiers are wounded.

18 NOVEMBER 1964
Gound War In the largest airborne strike of the war till now, 116 US and South Vietnamese helicopters fly some 1100 ARVN troops into Bing Dyong and Tayninh Provinces to take what is claimed to be a major Vietcong stronghold; General Nguyen Khanh personally directs the operation, but it makes only light contact with the Vietcong.

19 NOVEMBER 1964
Guerrilla War ARVN troops kill 17 Vietcong and capture 21 in a helicopter operation in Quangnam province; and in a forested area near Thudaumot, over 7000 ARVN troops move in only to find that the Vietcong have slipped away.
Terrorism A Vietcong mine planted on the Saigon-Hué railroad derails a train, killing four railroad workers and injuring 17 South Vietnamese and one US military adviser.

20 NOVEMBER 1964
North Vietnam It is reported that delegations from 10 Communist countries are meeting in Hanoi to express 'solidarity with North Vietnam against US imperialism.'

22-28 NOVEMBER 1964
South Vietnam The moratorium on violent demonstrations that the Buddhists have voluntarily observed since 6 November ends with a march by thousands of Buddhists to the palace of chief of state Phan Khac Suu and a resultant clash with police. On the 23rd, Buddhist leaders decide to oppose the government of premier Huong and rioting continues in Saigon. On the 26th, the government declares martial law, banning demonstrations and giving the military control over the police; on the 28th, Buddhist leaders announce that they will resort to a non-violent campaign of non-cooperation.

24 NOVEMBER 1964
USA: Government A select committee of the National Security Council meets to discuss

5 DECEMBER 1964

the options prepared by the 'Bundy working group.' Except for Under Secretary of State George Ball, the leaders are prepared to escalate the bombing into North Vietnam; only the timing is in question.

25 NOVEMBER 1964
Laos William Sullivan arrives in Laos as the new US ambassador.

27 NOVEMBER 1964
USA:Government Ambassador Maxwell Taylor arrives in Washington for a meeting with the National Security Council and calls for an escalation of US bombing of North Vietnam.

28 NOVEMBER 1964
USA: Government Johnson's top advisers – Taylor, Rusk, McNamara and other members of the National Security Council – agree to recommend to the president that he adopt Taylor's plan for a two-stage escalation of bombing of North Vietnam.

DECEMBER 1964
The US Navy Task Group 77 (TF 77) – including the attack carriers *Hancock, Coral Sea* and *Ranger* – is assigned to rendezvous about 75 miles out in the Gulf of Tonkin. This is Yankee Station (as opposed to the US ships assigned to the waters off South Vietnam, which are on Dixie Station). US military command data released early this month shows November to have been one of the most successful months in the war to date, with some 1370 guerrillas reported killed, 370 captured, and with the ratio of guerrillas killed to South Vietnamese dead (the 'kill ratio') at its most favorable level since 1961.

1 & 3 DECEMBER 1964
USA: Government In two crucial meetings at the White House, President Johnson and his top-ranking advisers agree somewhat ambivalently to a two-phase bombing plan, Phase I to involve air strikes by the USAF and USN jets against infiltration routes and facilities in the Laotian panhandle, Phase II to extend the air strikes to widening selection of targets in North Vietnam. The more 'hawkish' advisers – particularly the JCS – would prefer a more immediate and intensive series of raids against many targets in North Vietnam, while 'doveish' advisers question whether bombing is going to have any effect in Hanoi's support of the war. President Johnson makes it clear

that the South Vietnamese leaders must cooperate and pull their government and people together. In a news conference on the 3rd, Taylor indicates he has been authorized to improve South Vietnam's war efforts and that this might involve changes 'in tactics and method,' but he says nothing about the bombing operations planned.

2 DECEMBER 1964
USA: Domestic Richard Nixon calls on the United States to bomb Vietcong supply routes, even if it requires extending the war.
Guerrilla War Vietcong overrun the district headquarters of Thiengao, supposedly an area controlled by the South Vietnamese government; the Vietcong kill the district chief and take many weapons.

3 DECEMBER 1964
USA: Military It is announced that the first US women to serve as military advisers will be assigned to a South Vietnamese Women's Army Corps training camp at Saigon.

4 DECEMBER 1964
South Vietnam Nguyen Khanh, still commander in chief of the military forces, meets with other high-ranking military leaders at Dalat, and they issue an appeal to all dissident groups, to support the government.
USA: Government William Bundy leaves for Australia and New Zealand to brief their governments' leaders on the two-phase bombing plan. Other governments supporting of the US efforts in Vietnam will also be briefed, although most governments will not be told of the plans for Phase II, the extension into North Vietnam.
Ground War The Vietcong move into Phuoc Ty Province, southeast of Saigon, and commence a series of movements and attacks that will culminate in a major defeat of the ARVN forces at Binh Gia, 40 miles from Saigon, from 28 December 1964-4 January 1965. About 1000 Vietcong have been making their way in small groups for several weeks from Tayninh Province, northwest of Saigon, and now having joined forces the Vietcong will conduct a series of surprise attacks.

5 DECEMBER 1964
USA: Military The first Congressional Medal of Honor awarded to a US serviceman for action in Vietnam is presented to Captain Roger Donlon for his heroic action on 6 July 1964: although wounded four times, Donlon

led his Special Forces team and the South Vietnamese in resisting a Vietcong attack on Camp Nam Dong.

Guerrilla War In the area of Tan Phu in the Mekong Delta, a major attack by the Vietcong leaves seven US advisers wounded, 23 ARVN soldiers dead and 50 wounded, and fifty Vietcong dead.

7-9 DECEMBER 1964

Guerrilla War The Vietcong attack and capture the district headquarters of Anlao and much of the surrounding valley, some 300 miles northeast of Saigon, driving off large ARVN and paramilitary forces. ARVN troops regain control only after reinforcements are airlifted in by US helicopters; one US Army officer and one US soldier are killed, there are some 300 South Vietnamese casualties and as many as 7000 villagers are temporarily forced to abandon their homes.

7-11 DECEMBER 1964

South Vietnam Ambassador Taylor, having returned from Washington, holds a series of conferences with Premier Huong, General Khanh and other South Vietnamese leaders. The communiqué issued on the 11th refers to the additional aid that the United States will supply to strengthen South Vietnam's military forces (which South Vietnam agrees to increase by 100,000 men) and to 'further economic assistance for a variety of reforms of industrial, urban, and rural development.' But nothing is said of the plans to start the new bombing raids; in fact, US officials deny that the United States has any intention of extending the war into North Vietnam.

10 DECEMBER 1964

Laos Ambassador Sullivan gets Souvanna Phouma to agree to the new operations that will allow US planes to raid the Communist supply routes in Laos.

11 DECEMBER 1964

South Vietnam As soon as the communiqué announcing increased US support for the government is released, the Buddhist leaders announce a campaign to oust Premier Huong, particularly because they claim he is being kept in power by the Americans. Thich Tri Quang and two other prominent Buddhist leaders go on a 48-hour hunger strike.

12 DECEMBER 1964

Terrorism A bomb planted in a Saigon bar explodes and injures two Americans and four Vietnamese.

Covert War A C-123 transport crashes during take-off at the Danang airport and two US servicemen are killed; because the Defense Department does not provide any explanation for the plane's mission, it leads to public speculation that the USAF is engaging in some kind of secret operations.

13-17 DECEMBER 1964

Cambodia US and Cambodian representatives meet in New Delhi, India, in an effort to work out such issues as the border raids and alleged support for the Vietcong, but the talks quickly break down.

14 DECEMBER 1964

USA: Domestic A survey of Americans reveals that one-quarter do not know there is any fighting going on in Vietnam.

Guerrilla War Four US Army officers are killed when the Vietcong attack an ARVN division headquarters in Thudaumot.

Laos Operation Barrel Roll, the name given to the first phase of the bombing plan approved by President Johnson on 1 December, begins with US planes attacking 'targets of opportunity' in northern Laos. (In Washington, it has been agreed that there will be no statements to the public about these raids unless a plane is lost, and then the government will insist the US plane was simply on escort duty as requested by the Laotians.)

15 DECEMBER 1964

Guerrilla War Reports reach Saigon of recent battles in Soctrang and Chuongthien Provinces and in the Anloa Valley that have left some 580 ARVN troops missing and 40 known dead – contributing to the highest casualties for a week among the South Vietnamese for the war till now.

NATO Secretary of State Rusk, addressing the ministers council of NATO, says that the entire non-Communist world has a stake in the war in Vietnam and he asks that NATO countries provide more tangible aid.

17 DECEMBER 1964

Guerrilla War ARVN forces blow up a network of Vietcong tunnels some 15 miles northeast of Saigon; tons of earth fall on the Vietcong hiding there, and only 16 are pulled out alive.

19 DECEMBER 1964
Guerrilla War Vietcong disguised in uniforms of ARVN paratroopers ambush an ARVN convoy returning to Saigon after escorting General Khanh to Cap St-Jacques; it is believed that the Vietcong expected to find Khanh with the convoy.

19-20 DECEMBER 1964
South Vietnam General Khanh and some younger generals led by Air Commodore Ky and General Theiu stage another bloodless coup by arresting about three dozen high officers and civilian officials. The generals announce on the 20th the High National Council, which has been serving as a temporary legislature, is dissolved but that an Armed Forces Council will support the civilian government of Suu and Huong while working to 'act as a mediator to achieve national unity' among the nation's feuding political groups. This move seems primarily aimed to stemming the Buddhists' growing demands. When Ambassador Taylor summons the leaders of the coup to the US Embassy, Ky and Thieu appear but Khanh does not; Taylor then proceeds to scold them: 'I told you all clearly ... we Americans were tired of coups. Apparently I wasted my words ... Now you have made a real mess. We cannot carry you forever if you do things like this.'

21-23 DECEMBER 1964
South Vietnam In a series of talks with General Khanh, Premier Huong and other Vietnamese leaders, Taylor tries to restore the constitutional civilian government. US officials announce the suspension of talks on increasing US military aid. But General Khanh deliberately gives an interview to the *New York Herald Tribune* and says that the High National Council 'will not be reactivated' just to satisfy, the United States. He also says that Taylor's attitude during the last 48 hours ... and his activity have been beyond imagination as far as an ambassador is concerned.' On the 22nd, Khanh also issues an order from the Armed Forces Council saying that the military will retain responsibility. Although Secretary Rusk and other US officials try to maintain a conciliatory stance, Khanh continues to call for defiance of US influence.

24 DECEMBER 1964
Terrorism Two Vietcong agents, disguised as ARVN soldiers, leave a car filled with explosives parked at the Brinks Hotel, used to house US officers. Two Americans are killed and 65 Americans and Vietnamese injured. Taylor, Westmoreland and some other senior US officials try to persuade President Johnson to respond with retaliatory raids against North Vietnam, but Johnson refuses. In his cable to Taylor explaining his decision Johnson for the first time indicates he is considering a commitment of US combat troops.

25 DECEMBER 1964
South Vietnam Premier Huong broadcasts a Christmas message to US personnel in Vietnam. (General Khanh will issue his own Christmas message with thanks to the US troops on the 27th).
USA: Military The Pentagon has just released figures showing that most of the approximately 23,000 US military personnel now serving in Vietnam did not volunteer but were assigned. The Red Cross announces that although it has tried to send packages to the 17 or more Americans believed held as POWs by the Vietcong or in North Vietnam, they have no assurance they were delivered.

26 DECEMBER 1964
South Vietnam The Armed Forces Council orders paratroops into Saigon and extends martial law primarily to signal Buddhists and any other potential resisters that the military will not allow opposition to its control.
USA: Military A report from Saigon says that the United States has suspended participation in advanced planning of non-routine operations until the status of US aid is clarified, which in turn has been linked to restoration of the constitutional civilian government.

27-28 DECEMBER 1964
Guerrilla War Although outnumbered, ARVN troops in a two-day battle capture a Vietcong headquarters, seize a record cache of enemy arms, and claim to kill 85 guerrillas; ARVN casualties include 19 dead and 49 wounded, and eight Americans are wounded.

28 DECEMBER 1964-4 JANUARY 1965
Ground War The culmination of the Vietcong's major campaign launched on 4 December sees the Vietcong moving into the village of Binh Gia, 40 miles southeast of Saigon, and holding it for about eight hours. ARVN forces recapture the village but only after three battalions are brought in on helicopters. ARVN forces suffer a terrific loss on

2 January when two companies of Rangers, accompanied by tanks, are ambushed by Vietcong in a rubber plantation near Binh Gia. Total losses for the operation around Binh Gia include some 200 South Vietnamese and five US dead, plus almost 300 more wounded or missing; Vietcong losses are reported at about 120 dead. 'But the big question,' says one US officer of this operation, 'is how [Vietcong] troops, a thousand or more of them, could wander around the countryside so close to Saigon without being discovered. That tells something about this war.'

31 DECEMBER 1964
State of the War Although none of the combatants have formally declared war, it is undeniable that a fullscale war is now being waged in Vietnam and the adjacent territories of Laos and Cambodia. The United States has about 23,000 military personnel in South Vietnam, all still designated as 'military advisers'; South Vietnam has some 265,000 in its regular armed forces but also supports paramilitary and militia forces of some 290,000; South Korea has already sent some 2000 military advisers, Australia and New Zealand have assigned small units and individuals as advisers and Thailand and the Philippines are readying some units. It is reliably estimated that there are some 34,000 Communist troops fighting fulltime in South Vietnam. Calling themselves members of the National Liberation Front and popularly known as the Vietcong, increasing numbers of them have been trained in North Vietnam and have made their way southward along the Ho Chi Minh Trail, which is being greatly expanded and developed as a major logistical supply network. By December 1964, a continuous stream of North Vietnamese-trained soldiers is moving into South Vietnam. Meanwhile, the Communists can count on another 80,000 part-time activists who, whether through acts of terrorism or political 'education,' are gaining power over perhaps as much as 50 percent of the Vietnamese people. The costs of all this in terms of money and matériel are already beginning to defy accounting. (The United States, for instance, admits to losing 38 fixed-wing aircraft and 24 helicopters in 1964 alone.) The human casualties are mounting. The US official figures show 140 dead in combat (versus 76 in 1963), 1138 wounded, and 11 missing in action. The South Vietnamese have not such sophisticated statistical methods but estimates show some 7000 military personnel killed, 16,700 wounded, and 500 missing or captured. US estimates of Communists killed are 17,000, with some 4200 captured.

2 JANUARY 1965
Ground War The six-day battle that has been fought in and around the village of Binh Gia ends with a clear defeat of South Vietnamese forces. Nearly 200 of their best troops are dead and some 300 wounded. Five Americans are killed, three are missing – the highest US casualties in a single battle to date. Most sobering, though, is the fact that the South Vietnamese, despite the advantage of tanks, artillery, and helicopters, could not withstand the more flexible tactics of the Vietcong. On 4 January, Vietcong remaining in the area will make another surprise attack and account for several more casualties among the South Vietnamese and Americans.

3 JANUARY 1965
South Vietnam The political crisis that has been undermining the South Vietnamese government and military for months is aggravated when thousands of antigovernment demonstrators in Saigon clash with government marines and police; there is also rioting in Hué, where students are organizing strikes. The main resistance comes from the Buddhists, who are strongly opposed to Tran Van Huong, who became premier on 4 November 1964.

4 JANUARY 1965
USA; Government In his State of the Union message, President Johnson reaffirms the US commitment to support South Vietnam in fighting Communist aggression. He gives two basic reasons: for ten years now US Presidents have pledged the help requested by the South Vietnamese; and secondly, says Johnson, 'Our own security is tied to the peace of Asia.'

6 JANUARY 1965
USA: Government An Associated Press survey of 83 US Senators shows considerable ambivalence and division on the situation in Vietnam. William Bundy submits a memo to Secretary of State Dean Rusk that expresses the bleak view held by some top administration officials: 'The sum total . . . seems to us to point - together with almost certainly stepped-up Vietcong actions in the current favorable weather – to a prognosis that the

situation in Vietnam is now likely to come apart more rapidly than we had anticipated.'

8 JANUARY 1965
Guerrilla War In a typical series of actions, an ARVN company is ambushed by Vietcong and one US officer is killed; a US soldier is wounded in an encounter at Tanbu; US and South Vietnamese planes drop bombs and napalm over Phuoc Tuy Province to destroy a Vietcong regiment; and the ARVN claims to have killed 53 guerrillas in a fight at Quangnam and to have routed attackers in the area of Hué.

9 JANUARY 1965
South Vietnam After several weeks of negotiations, Vietnamese civil and military leaders (under pressure from US officials) reach a compromise that agrees to restore the civilian government, with Tran Van Huong remaining as premier. The five High National Council members and some 50 others arrested on 20 December 1964 are to be released; the armed forces leaders pledge to confine their activities to the military sphere; and a national convention is to be convened to 'assume legislative powers' and to draw up a permanent constitution.

11-27 JANUARY 1965
South Vietnam The major cities – especially Saigon and Hué – and much of central Vietnam are disrupted by demonstrations and strikes led by the Buddhists. Refusing to accept any government headed by Tran Van Huong, because they see the United States as supporting that government, the Buddhists turn against US institutions. Thich Tri Quang, the Buddhist leader, and other monks go on a hunger strike and a Buddhist girl in Nhatrang burns herself to death on the 26th (the first such self-immolation since 1963). Although Tran Van Huong tries to appease the Buddhists by rearranging his government, they are not satisfied.

12 JANUARY 1965
Japan Prime Minister Sato, addressing the National Press Club in Washington, says that the problems in Vietnam cannot be solved by the 'rational approach' of the West but should be left to the Asians themselves.

13 JANUARY 1965
Laos The US press reports that the two USAF jet fighters have just been shot down in Laos

while escorting USAF bombers in attacks on the Communist supply trails passing from North Vietnam through Laos into South Vietnam. These planes are part of the secret air war in northern Laos, an extension of the Yankee Team that had begun in May 1964 with reconnaissance flights and then become Operation Barrel Roll – bombing raids that began in December 1964.

17 JANUARY 1965
South Vietnam The new government is empowered to draft Vietnamese youth into the armed forces for up to one year. At the same time, it is reported that about 30 percent of the draftees desert within the first six weeks in service.

20-24 JANUARY 1965
South Vietnam A revised cabinet assumes office, as Premier Tran Van Huong tries to placate the Buddhists, who continue their demonstrations and strikes. On 24 January the Armed Forces Council, headed by Nguyen Khanh, resolves to get rid of Tran Van Huong; the US Deputy Ambassador is informed secretly, but US officials can only stand by.

21 JANUARY 1965
Ground War Some 1500 ARVN troops are transported by helicopter to confront a large Vietcong unit in the Mekong Delta province of Kien Hoa; the ARVN reports killing 46 and capturing 61.

26 JANUARY 1965
USA: Domestic Former Vice-President Richard Nixon, in a speech in New York City, charges that the United States is 'losing the war in Vietnam' and calls for US bombing of Communist supply routes. He says that to negotiate with the Vietcong or 'neutralize' South Vietnam is 'surrendering on the installment plan.'

27-28 JANUARY 1965
South Vietnam The Armed Forces Council ousts Premier Huong and his civilian government in a bloodless coup; General Nguyen Khanh is empowered to establish a stable government, The Council says it will observe the constitution of October 1964 and that the promised elections for a national congress will proceed. The Buddhists immediately order their followers to stop the antigovernment demonstrations and hunger strikes, but their

leaders do not hide their dislike of Khanh and the US influence.

FEBRUARY 1965
Covert War Operation Open Arms (*Chieu Hoi*), the South Vietnamese government's plan to win over defectors from the Vietcong, is now underway and will report some success in ensuing months; at the same time, there are reliable reports of the 'shadow government' operated by the Vietcong – a stable, orderly political control over much of South Vietnam's territory.
Sea War The USS *Hancock* and the USS *Coral Sea* are ordered to leave their duty station off Vietnam and rejoin the 7th Fleet, as there is an apparent reduction in the number of aggressive actions.

1 FEBRUARY 1965
Cuba A Cuban publication admits that Cubans are helping to train Vietcong.

3 FEBRUARY 1965
USA: Domestic A poll of some 600 prominent Americans, conducted by the Foreign Relations Council, reveals that most approve of US aims in Vietnam but feel the policy is failing; many advocate immediate withdrawal, but some call for widening the war.

4-6 FEBRUARY 1965
South and North Vietnam McGeorge Bundy, Johnson's special assistant for national security, arrives in Saigon on 4 February; two days later Soviet Premier Aleksei Kosygin arrives in Hanoi. There is worldwide speculation that their visits are linked – that the United States and the Soviet Union have agreed to pressure their 'clients' into negotiations – but this is denied by all the principals. Bundy, in fact, seems to be there to confer with Ambassador Taylor on the best way to deal with the political situation. And although Kosygin will publicly proclaim continued Soviet Union support for North Vietnam and the Communist war, a Soviet participant in the talks will later describe the North Vietnamese as 'a bunch of stubborn bastards.'

7 FEBRUARY 1965
Guerrilla War Vietcong attack the US helicopter base at Camp Halloway and simultaneously blow up the barracks of the US military advisers near Pleiku, in the Central Highlands; the Vietcong also destroyed part of a fuel depot in Phuyan Province. Eight Americans are killed, 126 are wounded, and nine helicopters are destroyed along with one transport plane; another 15 planes are damaged. When word of the Pleiku attacks arrived; McGeorge Bundy joins Westmoreland and Taylor at the Saigon military headquarters, then telephones President Johnson to urge immediate retaliatory air raids against North Vietnam.
USA: Government President Johnson convenes his top advisers and says he is ordering retaliatory raids, and all present except Senator Mike Mansfield (D-MT) and Vice-President Hubert Humphrey concur. (Humphrey will be kept out of Johnson's Vietnam planning for about a year, until he satisfies Johnson that he will support presidential policies.)
Air War Forty-nine US Navy jets – A-4 Skyhawks and F-8 Crusaders – from the 7th Fleet carriers *Coral Sea* and *Hancock*, drop bombs and rockets on the barracks and staging areas at Donghoi, a guerrilla training camp 40 miles north of the 17th parallel – in North Vietnam. There will be speculation that the Vietcong deliberately timed their attacks at Pleiku to force just such a response by the United States, thus compelling Kosygin to give absolute support. This is never proven, but shipments of Soviet surface-to-air missiles will begin to arrive at Haiphong within two weeks.

8 FEBRUARY 1965
South Vietnam A prearranged plan for evacuating US dependents goes into effect as wives and children are airlifted out in case North Vietnam, or another Communist power, decides to retaliate for the US raid.
Air War A follow-up raid by South Vietnamese planes – led by Air Vice-Marshal Nguyen Cao Ky, and escorted by US jets – bombs a North Vietnamese military communications center at Vinhlinh. (It will later be revealed that Ky dropped his flight's bomb loads on an unassigned target; he claimed it was to avoid colliding with USAF planes.)
USA: Government Bundy, back from Vietnam, defends the air raids as 'right and necessary.' Senate Majority Leader Mansfield (D-MT) and GOP leader Everett Dirksen (IL) support the President's decision, but Senators Wayne Morse (D-OR) and Ernest Gruening (D-AK) attack the action.

9 FEBRUARY 1965
International There is considerable reaction

around the world to this new stage of US involvement in Vietnam. Predictably, both Communist China and the Soviet Union threaten to intervene if the United States continues to apply its military might on behalf of the South Vietnamese. In Moscow, some 2000 demonstrators, led by Vietnamese and Chinese students and clearly supported by the authorities, attack the US Embassy. Britain and Australia support the US action, but France calls for negotiations.

10 FEBRUARY 1965

Guerrilla War Vietcong guerrillas blow up the US barracks at Quinhon (75 miles east of Pleiku, on the central coast) by planting a 100-lb explosive charge under the building; 23 US personnel are killed (as are two of the Vietcong).

11 FEBRUARY 1965

Air War Some 160 US and South Vietnamese planes, both land- and carrier-based, carry out a third series of retaliatory raids; bombing the barracks and staging points at Chan Hoa and Chaple, 160 miles and 40 miles, respectively, north of the 17th parallel; 3 US Navy planes are downed; one pilot is rescued.

12-16 FEBRUARY 1965

International The world reacts to the US role in the war. The National Liberation Front threatens to launch an all-out attack; the Communist Chinese threaten to send 'volunteers' to aid the Vietcong; there are anti-US demonstrations in various cities – including a break-in at the US Embassy in Budapest, Hungary, by some 200 Asian and African students. U Thant, Secretary-General of the United Nations, calls for peace talks inside or outside the UN.

13 FEBRUARY 1965

USA: Government President Johnson decides to undertake the sustained bombing of North Vietnam that he and his advisers have discussed – and avoided – for a year. Called Operation Rolling Thunder, it will continue, with occasional suspensions, until President Johnson halts it on 31 October 1968.

16-17 FEBRUARY 1965

South Vietnam The Armed Forces Council, which seized power on 27 January, appoints Dr Phan Huy Quat as premier and reappoints Phan Khac Suu as chief of state. Quat, a physician with considerable experience in

government, appoints a cabinet that includes representatives from many of Vietnam's political, religious, and military factions. On 17 February, the Armed Forces Council also announces the formation of a 20-member National Legislative Council.

USA: Government Former President Harry Truman issues a statement that gives full support to Pesident Johnson's policies and attacks the 'irresponsible critics ... who have neither all the facts – nor the answers.' The following day, Johnson meets with former president Dwight D Eisenhower to demonstrate the caliber of his supporters.

18 FEBRUARY 1965

USA: Government The State Department sends secret cables to US ambassadors in nine nations advising of the forthcoming bombing operations over North Vietnam and instructing them to inform the government concerned 'in strictest confidence' and to report reactions.

Air War US-piloted jet planes attack guerrilla forces in Binhdinh Province to support ARVN troops; in the first raid in which no South Vietnamese airmen have participated, indicating an escalation in US involvement.

19-25 FEBRUARY 1965

South Vietnam Dissident officers move several battalions of troops into Saigon on the 19th with the intention of ousting General Khanh from leadership. (One of the leaders of the attempted coup is Colonel Pham Ngoc Thao, who will be revealed years afterward as a Communist agent.) General Khanh escapes to Dalat with the aid of Marshal Ky, who then threatens to bomb Saigon and the Tansonn-hut airport unless the rebel troops are withdrawn. Ky is dissuaded from this by General Westmoreland, and Khanh is able to get troops to take over from the insurgents without any resistance on 20 February. Meanwhile, Marshal Ky has met with the dissident officers and agreed to their demand for the dismissal of Khanh; on 21 February the Armed Forces Council dismisses Khanh as chairman and as commander of the armed forces. Next day Khanh announces he has accepted the council's decision, after which he is appointed a 'roving ambassador,' assigned first to go to the United Nations and present evidence that the war in South Vietnam is being directed by North Vietnamese.

Air War The first Rolling Thunder raid has been scheduled for 20 February but it is

American advisors learned to live off the land, like their Vietnamese troops.

postponed by the upheaval in the South Vietnamese government.

22-26 FEBRUARY 1965
USA: Military General Westmoreland cables Washington to ask for two battalions of US Marines to protect the US base at Danang. Ambassador Taylor, aware of Westmoreland's plan, disagrees and cables President Johnson to warn that such a step will encourage South Vietnam to 'shuck off greater responsibilities.' The JCS, however, support Westmoreland's request and on 26 February Washington cables Taylor and Westmoreland that the troops are to be sent, and that Taylor should 'Secure GVN [Government of South Vietnam] approval.' General Westmoreland will later insist that he did not regard his request as 'the first step in a growing American commitment,' but although Taylor foresees just such a possibility, he does not raise any objections in public.

23 FEBRUARY 1965
USA: Government Senator Thomas Dodd (D-CT), in a 2½-hour speech, charges that to advocate negotiating with the Vietnamese Communists 'is akin to asking Churchill to negotiate with the Germans at the time of Dunkirk.'

24 FEBRUARY 1965
Air War USAF B-57 bombers and F-100 fighter-bombers from the Bienhoa and Danang air bases attack concentrations of Vietcong forces in Binhdinh Province.

25-26 FEBRUARY 1965
Air War US jet bombers raid Vietcong concentrations in Phuoctuy Province.

26 FEBRUARY 1965
South Korea The first contingents of South Korean troops arrive in Saigon. Although assigned to non-combat duties, they will come under fire on 3 April.

27 FEBRUARY 1965
USA: Government The State Department releases a 14,000-word report entitled 'Aggression from the North – the Record of North Vietnam's Campaign to Conquer

South Vietnam.' Citing 'massive evidence,' including testimony of North Vietnamese who had defected or been captured in South Vietnam, this so-called White Paper claims that nearly 20,000 Vietcong military and technical personnel have entered South Vietnam through the 'infiltration pipeline' from the North and that they remain under military command from Hanoi.

MARCH 1965
Diplomatic Concern grows throughout the world about the direction of events in Vietnam. The French, for one, have sent a series of proposals to China calling for support for a neutralized Vietnam with wider powers for the ICC; the hope is that China will use its influence with Hanoi to gain support for this. In fact, when J Blair Seaborn, the Canadian member of the ICC, makes a third secret visit to Hanoi this month, he is informed that the North Vietnamese have lost any interest they might have had in negotiating.

1-4 MARCH 1965
South Vietnam Ambassador Taylor calls on Premier Phan Huy Quat to inform him that the United States is preparing to send 3500 US Marines to Vietnam. Three days later, a formal request is submitted by the US Embassy, asking the South Vietnamese government to 'invite' the United States to send the Marines. Premier Quat, a figurehead, has to obtain approval from the real, power, General Nguyen Van Thieu, chief of the Armed Forces Council. Thieu approves, but asks that the Marines be 'brought ashore in the most inconspicuous way feasible.' Rumors of the imminent arrival of American troops soon circulate in Saigon, but there is no official word from either government.

By coincidence, this is also the day that a South Vietnamese government first states conditions for ending the war 'the Communists have provoked': they must stop all infiltration, subversions, and sabotage, and offer 'concrete, efficient, and appropriate means' to guarantee South Vietnam's security.

2 MARCH 1965
Air War Over 100 USAF jet bombers strike an ammunition depot at Xombang, 10 miles inside North Vietnam, while 60 South Vietnam Air Force propeller planes bomb the Quangkhe naval base, 65 miles north of the 17th parallel. This is the first raid on North Vietnam that is not justified as retaliation for Communist assaults on US installations or personnel. (Six US planes are downed, but only one US pilot is missing.) This raid begins Operation Rolling Thunder (rescheduled from 20 February). President Johnson has not yet approved any extended series of bombing raids. For the next two weeks, Johnson will consider the conflicting proposals of various military and civilian leaders. The official position is that this raid does not represent a change in US policy, but it does imply the possibility of additional raids until North Vietnam ends its support of the Vietcong.

3 MARCH 1965
Laos Over 30 USAF jets strike targets along the Ho Chi Minh Trail. Now that such raids are being reported, the US State Department feels compelled to announce that they are authorized by the powers granted to President Johnson in the August 1964 Tonkin Gulf Resolution.

3-5 MARCH 1965
International The world responds again to the new role of the United States in the Vietnam War. Inevitably, Communists criticize this role strongly; Premier Fidel Castro promises that Cuba will aid North Vietnam. On 4 March 2000 students, led by Asians, attack the US Embassy in Moscow (because the Russian police disperse them, the Chinese allow an anti-Soviet demonstration at the Soviet Embassy in Peking on 6 March). However, the Soviet Union, although it issues the expected warnings, remains largely aloof. Meanwhile, Prime Minister Lester Pearson of Canada expresses concern about the risk of escalation, but says that Canada understands the US position; Canadian members of the ICC file a minority report on the raids of 5-6 February, blaming them on North Vietnam for its support of the Vietcong. In Britain, however, there is mounting pressure against the government's support for US policies. In New York City, Women Strike for Peace demonstrates outside the United Nations to urge an end to the war.

5 MARCH 1965
USA: Military Reports are surfacing of complaints by US servicemen in Vietnam about shortages of ammunition and equipment - while some of these items are being sold on the black market in Saigon. At the Danang Air Base, the United States is clearing a 500-yard peripheral zone and moving thousands

of South Vietnamese from the area; an eight-mile deep special military sector is being established around Danang. All this lends credance to rumors that US Marines are to be sent to Vietnam.

6 MARCH 1965
USA: Government The White House confirms that the United States is sending two battalions of US Marines (3500 men) at the request of South Vietnam to be deployed in security work at Danang base, freeing South Vietnamese troops for combat.

8 MARCH 1965
USA: Military The USS *Henrico, Union* and *Vancouver*, carrying the 9th Marine Expeditionary Brigade under Brigadier General Frederick J Karch, take up station some 4000 yards off Red Beach Two, north of Danang. First ashore is Battalion Landing Team 3/9, which arrives on the beach at 0918 hours. Wearing full battle gear and carrying M-16s, the Marines are met by sightseers, ARVN officers, Vietnamese girls with leis, and four American soldiers with a large sign: 'Welcome Gallant Marines.' (General Westmoreland is reportely 'appalled.') Within two hours, BLT 1/3 begins landing at Danang Air Base.

9 MARCH 1965
USA: Government President Johnson authorizes the use of napalm by US planes bombing targets in North Vietnam.
USA: Military The Marines continue to land. Among today's arrivals is the first US Armor – an M48A3 tank of the 3rd Marine Tank Battalion; it will be followed in a few days by more tanks,including those with flame-throwing capabiity. There is scattered firing from Vietcong hidden onshore, but no Marines are hit. The Marines are at once assigned to protect the base, both from the immediate perimeter and from the high ground along a ridge to the west.
UN The US State Department formally rejects U Thant's proposal of 24 February that the United States join with other major powers in negotiating a solution to the war, on the ground that the government cannot support any such plan until North Vietnam ceases its 'aggression.'

10 MARCH 1965
Ground War Marines at Danang report

making their first contact with Vietcong guerrillas.
USA: Domestic The Republican Coordinating Committee attacks Democratic Party members who raise 'disruptive voices of appeasement' and expresses support for the Johnson administration's policies in Vietnam.

12 MARCH 1965
Ground War The last of the 3500 US Marines arrive.

13 MARCH 1965
USA: Military General Westmoreland begins work on a report titled 'Commander's Estimate of the Situation in SVN' which he will complete on 26 March, with the advice that he needs 40,000 more US troops to forestall a Vietcong victory.

14-15 MARCH 1965
Air War Twenty-four South Vietnamese Air Force planes, led by Vice-Marshal Ky and supported by US jets, bomb the barracks and depots on Conco ('Tiger') Island, 20 miles off the coast of North Vietnam. Next day 100 USAF jets and carrier-based bombers strike the ammunition depot at Phuqui, 100 miles south of Hanoi. This is the second set of raids in Operation Rolling Thunder and the first in which US planes use napalm.

15 MARCH 1965
USA: Military General Harold Johnson, Army Chief of Staff, reports to President Johnson and Secretary McNamara on his recent visit to Vietnam. He admits that the recent air raids have not affected the course of the war and says he would like to assign an American division to hold coastal enclaves and defend the central highlands. General Johnson also advocates creating a four-division force of US and SEATO troops to patrol the DMZ along the border separating North and South Vietnam and Laos.

16 MARCH 1965
USA: Government Under-Secretary of State George Ball openly criticizes France for repudiating the 'common burden' of the anti-Communist world by failing to support US efforts in South Vietnam.

16-19 MARCH 1965
International The Soviet Foreign Minister confers with British government leaders in

London, but the British are unable to persuade the Russians to join in convening peace talks on the situation in Vietnam.

17 MARCH 1965
Air War The South Vietnamese Air Force bombs the village of Manguang in the area of Danang and kills some 45 civilians, including 37 children; the government explains that the Vietcong flag had been flying over the village.

18 MARCH 1965
USA: Government A controversy is emerging between the press corps in South Vietnam and the US military, with the former charging that curbs on coverage are so strict as to constitute censorship. The US government claims that South Vietnam has imposed some of the restrictions.

19 MARCH 1965
Air War In the fourth Rolling Thunder raid 110 US planes bomb military targets at Phuvan and Vinhson in North Vietnam.

21 MARCH 1965
Air War US and South Vietnamese planes attack the base at Vucan, 15 miles north of the DMZ.

22-24 MARCH 1965
USA: Military The State Department confirms a report out of Saigon that the United States has supplied the South Vietnamese armed forces with a 'non-lethal gas which disables temporarily' for use 'in tactical situations in which the Vietcong intermingle with or take refuge among non-combatants, rather than use artillery or aerial bombardment.' The gas has already been used three times – with little effect. This triggers off a storm of criticism around the world; the North Vietnamese and the Soviets loudly protest this introduction of 'poison gas' into the war. Secretary Dean Rusk insists at a news conference (24 March) that the United States is 'not embarking upon gas warfare,' but is merely employing 'a gas which has been commonly adopted by the police forces of the world as riot-control agents.' It will be revealed on 1 April that British personnel have used the same type of gas 124 times in the past five years.

23 MARCH 1965
Air War US and South Vietnamese planes bomb a radar station at Babinh, 10 miles north of the 17th parallel, and attack a North Vietnamese convoy on Route 1.
USSR Leonid Brezhnev hints that the Soviet Union may join North Vietnam in the war and claims that many Russians have already volunteered to serve. But US authorities and most Western diplomats continue to doubt that the Soviet Union will allow Russian personnel to become involved in the war.

24 MARCH 1965
USA: Government In testimony before a Senate committee, Secretary of Defense McNamara claims that if the Communists are allowed to win in Vietnam, the United States will have to renew the struggle elsewhere. On this same day, John McNaughton, Assistant Secretary of Defense for international security affairs and one of McNamara's most trusted associates, drafts a crucial memo titled 'Plan for Action for South Vietnam,' to be used in the National Security Council sessions on 1-2 April.
USA: Domestic The first so-called teach-in is conducted at the University of Michigan at Ann Arbor; some 200 faculty participate by holding special seminars. Regular classes are canceled, and rallies and speeches dominate a 12-hour period. On 26 March there will be a similar teach-in at Columbia University in New York City; this form of protest eventually spreads to many colleges and universities.
Air War US and South Vietnamese planes attack North Vietnam radar and military radio stations and sink four ships at Quangkhe harbor.
China The official Communist newspaper says that China is ready to aid the Vietcong with men and materiél if requested, but it is clear from the statement that the Chinese are releasing it to pre-empt the Soviet Union by appearing as a closer ally of the Vietnamese.

25 MARCH 1965
USA: Government President Johnson makes an indirect offer of 'economic and social co-operation' to North Vietnam if peace can be restored. His offer is made in the context of a general statement about aiding Southeast Asian nations, and nothing comes of it.

26 MARCH 1965
Air War Forty US planes bomb four radar sites in North Vietnam, as Operation Rolling Thunder continues.
USSR The Communist Party's Central Com-

mittee ratifies a defense accord with North Vietnam.

27 MARCH 1965
USA: Military Lightning strikes US camp defenses at Pleidolin and triggers off mine explosions that cost 88 casualties. It is revealed today that US and South Vietnamese planes are using herbicides to defoliate jungles and destroy crops.

29 MARCH 1965
Guerrilla War ARVN troops discover a Vietcong camp some 60 miles northwest of Saigon, in Tayninh Province, and confiscate supplies, rations, and ammunition.
Air War Forty-two US planes drop 45 tons of bombs on the Bachlong radar station in North Vietnam.

30 MARCH 1965
Terrorism A bomb explodes in a car parked in front of the US Embassy in Saigon, virtually destroying the building; 19 Vietnamese, 2 Americans, and a Filipino are killed and 183 others are injured. (Congress will quickly appropriate $1,000,000 to reconstruct the embassy.) Although some US military leaders will advocate special retaliatory raids on North Vietnam, President Johnson refuses permission.

31 MARCH 1965
USA: Government Responding to questions from reporters – following meetings with Ambassador Maxwell Taylor, who is in Washington – President Johnson says, 'I know of no far-reaching strategy that is being suggested or promulgated.' In fact, he is ready to authorize US troops to go from defensive to offensive tactics in Vietnam.
Air War Over 70 USAF planes make the largest incendiary attack to date on a Vietcong concentration in the Boiloi Forest, 25 miles northwest of Saigon. To establish that this is not a retaliatory raid for yesterday's bombing of the embassy, US spokesmen state that the raid was planned for months, and that preparations included spraying to defoliate trees and using leaflets and loudspeakers to warn the civilian population to leave the area.

APRIL 1965
Sea War In response to the supplies that continue to come down from the North, a blockade of the coast is established under control of the 7th Fleet in an operation code-named Market Time. Its main assignment is to monitor the movement of junks, of which some 1000 per day ply the coastline. Thus it is all but impossible to locate clandestine craft carrying supplies to the Vietcong. The US Navy assigns some six picket destroyer escorts (released from duty in the North Atlantic and Pacific) to this task.

1 APRIL 1965
International The heads of state of 17 non-aligned nations, in an appeal to the UN, the United States, Britain, the Soviet Union, North and South Vietnam, and several other bodies, call for a 'peaceful solution through negotiations.' President Johnson will formally respond on 8 April, saying that the United States agrees with the goals but cannot negotiate until North Vietnam ceases its aggression against South Vietnam.

1-2 APRIL 1965
USA: Government During two days of National Security Council meetings, President Johnson agrees to send more US ground forces to Vietnam and to allow them to take offensive action. In statements to the public at this time, no mention is made of this change to offensive assignments.
Ground War In one of the largest battles since early February, ARVN troops clash with Vietcong forces 25 miles south of Danang.

3-5 APRIL 1965
Air War US and South Vietnamese planes make a series of raids on bridges and roads in North Vietnam – in particular, against the Hamrong and Dongphuong Bridges, the major rail links to Hanoi. Four Russian-built MiG fighters attack the US planes, in the first reported combat by the North Vietnamese Air Force. These raids are also the farthest north in the Rolling Thunder operation, and the first explicitly aimed against non-military targets. The US will concede that six of its planes were shot down on these raids.

4 APRIL 1965
Australia Prime Minister Robert Menzies says that the US intervention in Vietnam is an act of moral courage, in that Americans have accepted the challenge to 'human freedom.'

5-7 APRIL 1965
Ground War A fierce three-day battle in the Mekong Delta leaves six Americans dead and a reported 276 Vietcong fatal casualties. In an

air and amphibious assault at Vinhloc, Camau Peninsula, 16 ARVN troops are killed.

6 APRIL 1965
USA: Government McGeorge Bundy drafts and signs National Security Action Memorandum 328 on behalf of President Johnson; this 'pivotal document' constitutes the 'marching orders' developed in NSC meetings on 1-2 April: it authorizes US personnel to take the offensive to secure 'enclaves' and to support ARVN operations.

7 APRIL 1965
USA: Government In a major policy speech broadcast from Johns Hopkins University (and seen or heard by an estimated 60,000,000 people), President Johnson says that the United States is ready to engage in 'unconditional discussions' to settle the war (although in fact he sets forth several conditions). He calls for a vast economic plan for Southeast Asia, for which he will ask Congress to approve $1 billion. Between 9-12 April, however, North Vietnam, China, and the Soviet Union will reject these proposals; Western nations and U Thant of the UN support Johnson's statement.

8 APRIL 1965
North Vietnam Premier Pham Van Dong, at a meeting of the National Assembly, sets forth the four points that the North Vietnamese see as conditions for negotiations and peace: independence for all Vietnamese, non-intervention by foreign powers, political settlement of all issues, and reunification of the country. These four points will remain fixed as the Communists' non-negotiable conditions.
Air War US jets fly 63 sorties against Vietcong concentrations in Kontum Province.

9 APRIL 1965
Air War In the course of US raids over North Vietnam, four US carrier-based F-4 Phantom jets clash with Chinese MiGs off Hainan Island, the Chinese island opposite Vietnam. On 12 April, the United States will admit that one Phantom and its two pilots were lost, but it will not confirm that they were shot down by one of their own missiles.

10-14 APRIL 1965
USA: Military The 5000 US Marines already stationed in the area of Danang are reinforced with the arrival of the 2nd Battalion, 3rd Marines; one of its reinforced companies is sent immediately to Phu Bai, eight miles south of Hué. On 14 April, the 3rd Battalion, 4th Marines, takes over at Phu Bai to secure an Army radio intelligence station and auxiliary airfield. Meanwhile, the first Marine fixed-wing tactical aircraft also arrive at Danang – the F-4B Phantom II jets of the VMFA-531.

11 APRIL 1965
Ground War Determined to gain control of Highway 1 through the central highlands, ARVN troops disperse a concentration of Vietcong north of Bongson.

12 APRIL 1965
South Vietnam Roman Catholic leaders, concerned about the previous day's purge of several high-ranking military officers charged with corruption, inform Premier Quat that they fear Catholic officers are being replaced because of Buddhist pressure to end the war. It is also reported that the Catholics are planning to lead a military stand against any threat of complete Communist domination.

13 APRIL 1965
Air War US and South Vietnamese planes wreck the Thanhyen Bridge and two radar stations previously hit in North Vietnam.

14 APRIL 1965
USA: Military The JCS order the deployment of the 173rd Airborne Brigade from Okinawa to Bienhoa-Vungtau. Ambassador Maxwell Taylor is still resisting the increase of US combat personnel and tries to persuade the Johnson administration to hold back, but he is overruled.
Guerrilla War It is reported that South Vietnamese forces have discovered some 4 million pounds of rice and 21 stolen trucks in a Vietcong stronghold 30 miles north of Saigon.
Air War Thirty USAF planes bombs on the radar installations on Honmatt Island.

15-16 APRIL 1965
Air War US planes conduct armed reconnaissance along Highways 7 and 8 in North Vietnam and drop nine tons of bombs on the boat landing at Muongsen; other US planes fly the first night operation in North Vietnam. It is being reported, meanwhile, that sites near Hanoi are being prepared for SAM II missiles to be provided by the Soviet Union. South Vietnamese bombers, led by Vice-

Marshal Ky, then sink four ships in another night raid. In the largest air strike of the war to date, US and South Vietnamese planes drop 1000 tons of bombs on a major Vietcong stronghold in Tayninh Province, preparatory to an airlift of ARVN troops the next day.

17 APRIL 1965

USA: Government President Johnson, in a statement from his ranch at Johnson City, Texas, says that the United States will continue its air strikes against North Vietnam but reaffirms his willingness to participate in 'unconditional discussion.'

USSR After secret talks in Moscow, Leonid Brezhnev and North Vietnamese foreign secretary Le Duan issue a communiqué repeating that the Soviet Union will send volunteers if North Vietnam requests them.

18 APRIL 1965

USA: Domestic Newspaper publishers claim there is widespread support for Johnson's policies. Two Queens College students report that they have collected 2000 signatures on a petition backing the President's policies.

Inernational In his annual Easter message, Pope Paul VI calls for 'constructive collaboration' to obtain peace but does not mention Vietnam by name.

Air War US planes hit several targets throughout Vietnam; some barracks at Dongthanh, a ferryboat in the Song Trac River, and highways in the southern section of North Vietnam.

19-20 APRIL 1965

USA: Government High-level US military and civilian leaders – including Secretary of Defense McNamara and JCS Chairman Earle Wheeler – meet at Honolulu with General Westmoreland and Ambassador Taylor. The conferees agree to double US military forces from the present approved level of 40,200 to 82,000 and to bring the forces of Australia and South Korea up to some 7250 men. Although Taylor opposes such a sudden increase in numbers and assignments for US military, he is outvoted and apparently won over.

21 & 24 APRIL 1965

South Vietnam To protest the conduct of the war by his government, a 16-year-old novice Buddhist monk immolates himself on 21 April; another Buddhist monk sets himself aflame three days later.

21 APRIL 1965

Covert War The CIA and the Defense Inelligence Agency report a 'most ominous' development: a regiment of the 325th PAVN (People's Army of Vietnam) division is now part of the enemy's forces in South Vietnam.

22 APRIL 1965

Guerrilla War Vietcong guerrillas infiltrate within three miles of Danang and fire on a South Vietnamese radio station.

Air War The virtual round-the-clock bombing raids by US and South Vietnamese Air Forces in recent weeks have destroyed so many bridges and highways that North Vietnamese supply routes and transportation are said to be seriously impaired.

23 APRIL 1965

USA: Domestic In a speech before the American Society of International Law, Secretary of State Rusk attacks the 'gullibility of educated men and the stubborn disregard of plain facts by men who are supposed to be helping our young to learn'; this in reference to the growing number of academics who are criticizing the bombing raids but not the violence perpetrated by the Communists.

24 APRIL 1965

USA: Military President Johnson issues an executive order designating Vietnam a 'combat area' for income-tax purposes, retroactive to 1 January 1964.

Air War Over 200 US and South Vietnamese planes raid bridges and ferries in North Vietnam in a concentrated effort to destroy supply routes to the South.

26 APRIL 1965

USA: Government Secretary McNamara reports that although the air raids against North Vietnam have 'slowed down the movement of men and matériel . . . infiltration of both arms and personnel into South Vietnam' has increased. McNamara, however, refuses to answer questions as to whether the United States plans to send more troops. The war, he says, is now costing the nation about $1,500,000,000 per year.

USA: Domestic A Lou Harris Poll shows that some 57 percent of Americans support Johnson's handling of the war.

Cambodia Some 20,000, mostly students, attack the US Embassy in Pnompenh and rip down the US flag in protest.

A squad of Infantry takes cover during a jungle operation.

27 APRIL 1965
USA: Government President Johnson renews his offer of 'unconditional discussions ... with any government concerned,' and defends the US bombing raids: 'Our restraint was viewed as weakness. We could no longer stand by while attacks mounted.'
USA: Domestic Former presidential candidate Barry Goldwater praises Johnson's policies as what he had advocated in 1964.

28 APRIL 1965
USA: Government CIA director John A McCone sends a personal memo to President Johnson stating his view that unless the United States is willing to intensify the bombing of North Vietnam, there is no use in committing more US ground troops.

30 APRIL 1965
USA: Military The JCS present a detailed program for deploying 48,000 US and 5250 third-country troops in Vietnam – an increase over the numbers agreed to in Honolulu.

MAY 1965
USA: Military The US Marines in Vietnam – now officially designated the III Marine Amphibious Force (MAF) instead of the Marine Expeditionary Brigade – are quickly settling into their three enclaves: Danang, Phu Bai, and most recently, Chu Lai. Inevitably, there will be disputes among American military commanders about chains of command and operational concepts. One of the most pervasive disputes revolves around the Marines' concept of enclave-defense and pacification as the best long-term strategy, as opposed to the offensive 'search-and-destroy' strategy that Westmoreland prefers. The Marines pursue their pacification strategy in the three provinces of I Corps within their area of responsibility; for the next two years, they will expend considerable energy in civic action and village welfare work. One such initiative will be the Combined Action Program (CAP) that is begun at the Phu Bai enclave and then taken up at Danang: a specially trained Marine rifle squad joins a

CHRONOLOGY

Popular Forces (militia) platoon to provide continuous security from the Vietcong in a rural area. A variation on this was a MEDCAP patrol, which provided immediate medical assistance to villagers. US Marines not only spent government funds to aid the villages, but some of their own money as well. In the end, this pacification strategy failed, partly because the ARVN and other representatives of the South Vietnamese government failed to provide consistent support.

2 MAY 1965
China A Peking radio broadcast charges that the Soviet Union has joined the 'US aggressors' in a 'peace negotiation swindle' – because the Soviets are reportedly backing some kind of peace conference before the total withdrawal of US forces.
Ground War The first patrols by US Marines in tanks are met only by scattered sniper fire.

2-6 MAY 1965
South Vietnam North Vietnam will claim (on 13 May) that during these days the Vietcong held their first 'congress' in a 'liberated area' of South Vietnam; it was attended by the National Liberation Front's president, Nguyen Huu Tho, and 150 'outstanding cadres and fighters' from the Vietcong.

3-12 MAY 1965
USA: Military About 3500 men of the 173rd Airborne Brigade, stationed in Okinawa, are brought into Vietnam – the first US Army combat unit assigned there. Some go to the Bienhoa air base, 20 miles northwest of Saigon, others to the base at Vungtau. The 173rd Airborne Brigade includes the 3rd Battalion, 319 Artillery; the first US artillery unit assigned to Vietnam.

4 MAY 1965
USA: Domestic A three-man 'truth team,' sent out by the State Department to explain the administration's policies in Vietnam, makes its first stop, at the University of Iowa. Here (and later) it meets considerable opposition, but its members claim that such opposition represents a minority view.
Air War US planes sink three boats said to be carrying Vietcong guerrillas near Danang.

4-7 MAY 1965
USA: Government President Johnson asks Congress to appropriate an additional $700 million 'to meet mounting military require-

ments in Vietnam.' The House passes the bill, 408-7, on 5 May; the Senate approves it, 88-3; Johnson signs it on 7 May.

6 MAY 1965
South Vietnam The Armed Forces Council dissolves; its leader, General Nguyen Van Thieu, says this shows that the civilian regime of Premier Quat can govern, and that the military leaders have no political ambitions.

7 MAY 1965
USA: Military A 6000-man brigade of the 4th Marines is brought to Chu Lai, a sandy pine barren along the coast some 55 miles south of Danang, to build a second jet air base including a new type of field, the Short Airfield for Tactical Support (SATS) - a 4000-ft airstrip of aluminium matting, with arrestor wires as on an aircraft carrier. (A catapult will be installed two years later; until then, the planes make rocket-assisted takeoffs.) By 1 June, Douglas A-4 Skyhawks and MAG-12s will be using the field.

9-10 MAY 1965
Ground War A two-day battle in the Haughhai-Binhduong area, 25 miles northwest of Saigon, begins when the Vietcong start shelling the capital town; afterward it will be revealed that ARVN troops fled from the engagement when they became frightened by their own planes flying overhead.

10-15 MAY 1965
Ground War Some 1000 Vietcong overrun Songbe, the capital of Phuoclong Province, and occupy it for seven hours before ARVN forces recover it under cover of a heavy air attack; 5 US military advisers and 48 South Vietnamese are killed, and the bodies of 85 Vietcong are reported. US and ARVN forces pursue the Vietcong during several days but fail to engage them. The Americans will charge that the Vietcong surprised them in their compound from the adjacent ARVN camp, which failed to offer any resistance.
Air War US and South Vietnamese planes strike at 12 bridges in North Vietnam and claim to have knocked out four.

11 MAY 1965
USA: Military General Westmoreland and Deputy Premier Nguyen Van Thieu make a parachute jump together. The 1st Marine Aircraft Wing flies in to establish its advance headquarters at Danang.

12 MAY 1965
USA: Government The US Ambassador in Moscow, Foy Kohler, tries without success to get the North Vietnamese Embassy there to consider his message from Washington: the United States will suspend bombing of North Vietnam for several days in hope of reciprocal 'constructive' gestures – clearly meant as a call for peace talks. This is known as Operation Mayflower (all subsequent diplomatic moves will be code-named for flowers).

13 MAY 1965
USA: Government President Johnson, in a nationally televised address, accuses Communist China of opposing a political solution that could be in the best interests even of North Vietnam, because China's goal is to dominate 'all of Asia.'
Guerrilla War Disguised as Vietnamese troops, Vietcong guerrillas attack a textile mill only five miles north of Saigon. Eight are killed and 11 injured.

13-18 MAY 1965
Air War The United States suspends air raids on North Vietnam, claiming at first that it is for 'operational' reasons, but it is soon clear that the United States hopes to give North Vietnam a chance to call for peace negotiations. North Vietnam and China will charge that the United States did not, in fact, stop the raids; in any case, North Vietnam makes no peace overtures. Instead, it charges (18 May) that the halt was only 'an effort to camouflage American intensification of the war and deceive world opinion.'

14 MAY 1965
USA: Domestic George Meany, president of the AFL-CIO, criticizes 'academic' opponents of President Johnson's conduct of the war. Organized labor largely supports the administration's Vietnam policies.

15 MAY 1965
Air War Despite a plea by South Vietnamese Buddhists for a pause in observance of the Buddha's birthday, US and South Vietnamese Air Forces fly 150 missions against Vietcong targets in South Vietnam.

15-16 MAY 1965
USA: Domestic A major 'teach-in' is held in a lecture hall in Washington, DC, and broadcast by radio-telephone network to over 100 colleges. It lasts 15½ hours and features prominent academic and governmental figures who defend or attack the administration's policies in Vietnam. McGeorge Bundy agreed to participate, but he has gone to the Dominican Republic to monitor the assignment of US forces there. President Johnson has sent troops to put down what he regards as an attempted Communist takeover.

16 MAY 1965
USA: Military What is described as 'an accidental explosion of a bomb on one aircraft which spread to others' at the Bienhoa air base leaves 27 US servicemen and 4 South Vietnamese dead and some 95 Americans injured; over 40 US and South Vietnamese planes, including 10 B-57s, are destroyed.
USA: Domestic A Gallup poll shows a slight decline in the number of Americans who support the administration's policies in Vietnam – from 55 to 52 percent.

18 MAY 1965
USA: Government President Johnson releases a memo from Secretary of Defense McNamara showing how the recently appropriated $700 million will be spent on the military; he promises US servicemen a 'blank check' for their needs.

19 MAY 1965
Inernational Henry Cabot Lodge, back from a trip through Asia, insists that the nations he visited did not want the United States to negotiate an end to the war but were concerned about US willingness to stay in Vietnam.
Air War The United States resumes bombing raids over North Vietnam, striking at oil storage tanks. There is disappointment that North Vietnam did not respond to the bombing pause.
Thailand The Soviet Union warns Thailand against allowing the United States to use bases there to raid over North Vietnam.

20-21 MAY 1965
South Vietnam The government alleges that there has been a plot to assassinate Premier Quat; most of those arrested are Roman Catholics and military personnel, whose main complaint seems to be that Quat is not taking a hard enough line against pro-Communist and neutralist elements.

22 MAY 1965
North Vietnam It is now officially confirmed by US intelligence that the Soviet Union is

building anti-aircraft missile sites in and around Hanoi – and more than expected.

USA: Domestic The mother of a Haverford College student who has been involved in showing Vietcong propaganda films on college campuses asks that his scholarship be revoked.

Air War US planes bomb a military complex at Quansouï, an ammunition depot at Phuqui, and five other targets in North Vietnam.

24 MAY 1965

International Cyrus Eaton, the industrialist who has dedicated himself to working for world peace, reports that at a recent meeting in Moscow, Premier Aleksei Kosygin warned him that the Soviet Union and China would combine their resources and turn against the United States unless it changed its policies in Vietnam. Eaton also reports that President Anastas Mikoyan suggests the world is threatened by nuclear war within four weeks. Secretary of State Rusk will respond to Eaton's caveats two days later, claiming that the United States does not give 'undue importance' to them, but warning the Soviet Union and China to avoid further military involvement.

Ground War Over 2200 ARVN troops undertake an offensive in Kontum, a strategic central area, in an attempt to disrupt a Vietcong buildup reportedly aimed at taking control there when the monsoon season begins.

25 MAY 1965

South Vietnam Another government crisis develops when President Phan Khac Suu refuses to sign a decree of Premier Quat's calling for some cabinet changes; the National Legislative Council will uphold all of Quat's demands on 4 June.

26 MAY 1965

Australia/New Zealand Eight hundred Australian troops depart for Vietnam, and New Zealand announces that it will send an artillery battalion.

27 MAY 1965

Sea War Augmenting the vital role now being played by US aircraft carriers, whose planes participate in many of the raids over South and North Vietnam, US warships begin today to fire on Vietcong targets in the central area of South Vietnam. At first this gunfire is limited to five-inch-gun destroyers, but cruisers will soon be called in.

28 MAY-1 JUNE 1965

Ground War In Quangngai Province, Vietcong forces ambush a battalion of ARVN troops near Bagia; reinforcements are called for, but a US Marine battalion fails to arrive in time, and the ARVN reinforcements are also ambushed. Only three US advisers and about 60 of the ARVN troops manage to get away. Although the Vietcong suffer a reported loss of several hundred, ARVN losses are 392 and 446 weapons. This battle instills a sense of urgency and dismay in US military leaders, as it reveals how vulnerable the South Vietnamese military remains facing a sizeable and flexible Communist force.

31 MAY 1965

Air War US planes bomb an ammunition depot at Hoijan, west of Hanoi, and try again to drop the Thanhoa highway bridge.

JUNE 1965

USA: Military US forces in Vietnam are still assigned to operate under the so-called enclave strategy. The Marines are now at Danang, Phubai, and Chulai, and the Army at Vungtau; US forces are expected to defend these coastal areas, leaving ARVN troops to take the offensive in the rest of the country.

1 JUNE 1965

China Communist China warns again that the increasing US role in the war justifies its own growing aid to North Vietnam.

1-14 JUNE 1965

Air War US planes continue their bombing raids on military installations throughout North Vietnam. Visitors to Hanoi report that the city is now encircled by anti-aircraft sites, citizens are building air raid shelters, some 15 percent of the people are now enrolled in the militia, and almost one-third of Hanoi's population has been evacuated.

2 JUNE 1965

USA: Domestic The prominent American poet Robert Lowell rejects an invitation to attend an arts festival at the White House because he opposes the administration's policies in Vietnam.

Ground War As US Marines and ARVN troops mount a joint operation against Vietcong forces in the area of the Chulai air base, they are supported by shells fired from the USN *Canberra* offshore.

Australia The first contingent of Australian

The Vietcong abandoned camps and moved into the jungle to avoid US patrols.

combat troops arrives by plane in Saigon; they will join the US 173rd Airborne Brigade at the Bienhoa air base; 400 more Australian combat troops will arrive by ship on 8 June. (There are already 80 Australian military advisers attached to the ARVN.)

3 JUNE 1965
Diplomatic Britain's Foreign Secretary Michael Stewart proposes calling a conference to end the fighting and remove all foreign troops from South Vietnam, with a cease-fire to begin either before or during the talks. Stewart also reveals that the Soviet Union has rejected Britain's plan for reconvening the Geneva conference.
Ground War In two ambushes in the area of Pleiku, at Binhchanh and Phubon, the Vietcong destroy another battalion of ARVN troops.

4 JUNE 1965
USA: Military Major General Lewis Walt takes command of the III Marine Amphibious Force and the 3rd Division from Major General William Collins. US officials confirm that at least six Russian Ilyushin-28 light jet bombers are now in North Vietnam.

5 JUNE 1965
USA: Military The State Department confirms that US troops assigned to guard US installations in Vietnam are in fact engaging in some combat against Communist forces.

7 JUNE 1965
USA: Military General Westmoreland requests a total of 35 battalions of combat troops, plus another 9 in reserve: this gives rise to the '44-battalion' debate within the Johnson administration, because it is clear that such a commitment will change the US role in Vietnam. When questioned as to how he will deploy so many troops, Westmoreland will reply (on 13 June) that he must be free to move US forces around Vietnam.

8-9 JUNE 1965
USA: Military An apparently innocuous statement by the State Department press

CHRONOLOGY

officer – that 'American forces would be available for combat support together with Vietnamese forces when and if necessary' – alerts the press to what appears to be a major change. Next day the White House tries to calm the protest by issuing a statement that claims 'There has been no change in the missions of United States ground combat units in Vietnam,' but it goes on to state that Westmoreland does have the authority to employ troops 'in support of Vietnamese forces faced with aggressive attack.'

10 JUNE 1965
USA: Government Amid rising criticism of the new combat role of US forces in Vietnam, Johnson's attorney general, Nicholas Katzenbach, writes to assure the president that he has the power to commit large-scale forces without going back to Congress.

10-13 JUNE 1965
Ground War Some 1500 Vietcong start a mortar attack on the district capital of Dongxoai, about 60 miles northeast of Saigon, and then quickly overrun the town's military headquarters and an adjoining militia compound. Other Vietcong also raid a US Special Forces camp about a mile away. US helicopters fly in ARVN reinforcements, and at first the Vietcong seem to be in retreat, but they renew their attack and soon isolate and cut down the ARVN troops. Heavy US air strikes eventually help to drive off the Vietcong, but not before the ARVN has lost some 800-900 troops and the US has lost 7 killed, 12 missing and presumed dead, and 15 wounded. The Vietcong are estimated to have lost 350 in the ground combat and perhaps several hundred more in air attacks. On the last day, it is revealed that a battalion of US paratroopers was flown into an airstrip near Dongxoai, but Westmoreland never sent them into battle.

11 JUNE 1965
USA: Government Ambassador Maxwell Taylor, in Washington, reports to President Johnson, Congress, and several public forums; he provides a pessimistic outlook.

12-19 JUNE 1965
South Vietnam Mounting Roman Catholic opposition to Premier Quat's government leads him to resign. Next day a military triumvirate – headed by General Thieu – takes over, and expands to a 10-man National Leadership Committee on 14 June. The Committee decrees the death penalty for Vietcong terrorists, corrupt officials, speculators, and black marketeers; the Catholics approve of Quat's resignation and warn the military against favoring the Buddhists, who ask for appointment of civilians to the new cabinet.

15 JUNE 1965
USA: Government Senator J William Fulbright, in a speech in the Senate, calls for a 'negotiated settlement involving major concessions by both sides,' yet he is opposed to 'unconditional withdrawal of American support from South Vietnam.'
Terrorism Communist terrorists explode a bomb in the Saigon airport that wounds at least 22 persons, including 20 US servicemen.

15-30 JUNE 1965
Air War US planes bomb targets in North Vietnam every day, but they still refrain from bombing Hanoi and the Soviet missile sites. On 17 June, two USN jets down two Communist MiGs, and another three days later. US planes also drop almost 3 million leaflets urging the North Vietnamese to get their leaders to end the war.

16 JUNE 1965
USA: Military Secretary of Defense McNamara announces that 21,000 more US troops are to be sent to Vietnam. He also claims that it is now known that North Vietnamese regular troops had infiltrated South Vietnam before the US bombing began.

17 JUNE 1965
USA: Domestic Former president Dwight D Eisenhower, while admitting the complexities of the situation, urges Americans to support President Johnson's policies.
International Representatives of four nations of the British Commonwealth – Ghana, Nigeria, Trinidad and Tobago – and Ceylon say they will visit the principal nations involved and try to find a way to end the war. North Vietnam, the Soviet Union and Communist China immediately reject their plan, so the mission never gets going.
Air War For the first time, 27 B-52s fly from Guam to bomb a Vietcong concentration in a heavily forested area of Binhduong Province. (Such flights, under the aegis of the Strategic Air Command, are known as Operation Arc Light. One B-52 is lost in a collision, and the raid is revealed to have cost $20 million. Some

military leaders question the worth of such raids.)

19 JUNE 1965
South Vietnam Air Vice-Marshal Nguyen Cao Ky assumes the premiership of the ninth government within the last 20 months. He promises to rule with an iron hand and will start by demanding full mobilization.

22 JUNE 1965
Air War US planes bomb targets only 80 miles from the Chinese border, the deepest raids into North Vietnam so far.

24 JUNE 1965
South Vietnam Premier Ky announces austerity measures. They include extending martial law and curfew, imposing price controls, and cutting salaries of top government officials. South Vietnam breaks off diplomatic relations with France.
POWs Hanoi Radio announces that the Vietcong have shot US Army Sergeant Harold G Bennett in retaliation for South Vietnam's execution of a convicted Vietcong terrorist on 22 June.

25 JUNE 1965
USA: Government President Johnson appeals to the United Nations to persuade North Vietnam to negotiate a peace.
Terrorism Thirty-one people, including 9 Americans, are killed in a bomb explosion in a riverboat restaurant in Saigon.

26 JUNE 1965
North Vietnam Hanoi Radio reports that the Vietcong now have 'death lists,' headed by the names of Ambassador Taylor, his deputy, Alexis Johnson, Premier Ky, and General Thieu.
USA: Military General Westmoreland is given formal authority to commit US forces to battle when he decides they are necessary 'to strengthen the relative position of the GVN [Government of Vietnam] forces.'
Ground War Using what is described as the 'human wave' tactic, about 1000 Vietcong attack near Duchoa, 20 miles northwest of Saigon; they are finally dispersed by aerial bombing.

28-30 JUNE 1965
Ground War In the first major offensive ordered for US forces, 3000 troops of the 173rd Airborne Brigade – in conjunction with

800 Australian soldiers and a Vietnamese airborne unit – assault a jungle area known as Vietcong Zone D, 20 miles northeast of Saigon. The operation is called off after three days when it fails to make any major contact with the enemy, but one American is killed, and nine Americans and four Australians are wounded. The State Department assures the American public that the operation was in accord with Johnson administration policy on the role of US troops.

30 JUNE 1965
South Vietnam Premier Ky suspends all Vietnamese-language newspapers.

JULY 1965
USA: Military There are now some 51,000 US servicemen in Vietnam, and General Westmoreland has requested another 125,000. Bombing sorties over North Vietnam have increased from 3600 in April to 4800 in June.

1 JULY 1965
USA: Government Under Secretary of State George Ball submits a memo to President Johnson titled 'A Compromise Solution for South Vietnam.' It begins bluntly: 'The South Vietnamese are losing the war to the Vietcong. No on can assure you that we can beat the Vietcong, or even force them to the conference table on our terms, no matter how many hundred thousand *white, foreign* (US) troops we deploy.' [sic] Ball advises that the US cease committing more troops, restrict the combat role of those in place, and seek to negotiate a way out of the war. By now, though, President Johnson feels there is no turning back from his chosen route.
Guerrilla War The US air base at Danang comes under attack by the Vietcong for the first time when an 85-man enemy demolition force infiltrates the airfield to destroy three planes and damage three others; one USAF man is killed and three US Marines are wounded.

2 JULY 1965
USA: Government The State Department reports that 20 percent fewer ships from non-Communist nations are calling at North Vietnamese ports – suggesting that whether by political or military pressure, the United States is beginning to isolate North Vietnam.
USA: Domestic The Reverend Martin Luther King Jr, leader of the civil-rights struggle by black Americans, says that he is so convinced

CHRONOLOGY

the end of the war must be negotiated that he may join the peace rallies and teach-ins.

4 JULY 1965
USA: Government Secretary of State Dean Rusk makes an Independence Day broadcast over the Voice of America, stating that the United States is still waiting to hear what North Vietnam will do in return for a cessation of US bombing.

4-7 JULY 1965
Ground War ARVN troops retake an outpost near Bagia from the Vietcong, who attack on several occasions during the next few days but are repulsed.

6 JULY 1965
USA: Military The headquarters unit of the 9th Marines begins to land at Danang.

6-9 JULY 1965
Ground War B-52s based on Guam bomb Vietcong Zone D again. Then a 2500-man task force of South Vietnamese, US, and Australian troops moves in to search the area. An Australian platoon is ambushed, and at the end of the operation, it is reported that 10 Americans and one Australian were killed. Some 150 Vietcong are reported dead (it is also reported that they removed many of their wounded through tunnels.

7 JULY 1965
USA: Government Representative Gerald Ford (R-MI) urges President Johnson to bomb anti-aircraft sites that are ready to receive Soviet missiles.

8 JULY 1965
USA: Military President Johnson decrees that a Vietnam Service Medal be awarded to Americans serving in the conflict, even though there has been no official declaration of war. At a court-martial in Okinawa, a US Captain pleads not guilty to charges of feigning mental illness while serving in Vietnam.
USA: Government Ambassador Maxwell Taylor resigns from his post in Vietnam; he will be replaced by former ambassador Henry Cabot Lodge. Although Taylor had initially opposed the employment of US combat troops, he has come to accept this strategy.

8-13 JULY 1965
Diplomatic Prime Minister Harold Wilson of Great Britain sends a Member of Parliament to Hanoi to persuade the North Vietnamese to consider peace negotiations, but he is rebuffed.

9 JULY 1965
USA: Government President Johnson, at a news conference, confirms that the government is considering limited mobilization - such as a call-up of reservists, larger draft quotas, increased defense expenditures – to cope with the situation in Vietnam.

9-13 JULY 1965
Ground War Vietcong attack Anhoa Island, and five Americans are killed in the first day's fighting; in the ensuing days, many civilians are killed in the crossfire. On 13 July, the Vietcong overrun the last outpost and kill all 26 ARVN defenders.

10 JULY 1965
Guerrilla War In an unexpected gesture, evidently to gain favor with the people, the Vietcong free 60 ARVN soldiers captured on 8 June at Dongxoai.
Air War US planes continued their heavy raids in South Vietnam and claim to have killed 580 guerrillas. In the air over North Vietnam, US Phantom jets, escorting fighter-bombers in a raid on the Yensen ammunition depot northwest of Hanoi, destroy two North Vietnamese MiG-17 jets with Sidewinder air-to-air missiles.
USSR The Russians sign an agreement with a North Vietnamese delegation to provide more aid for the war effort.

11 JULY 1965
North Vietnam The government announces that the first contingent of 'volunteers' has left to serve in South Vietnam.
USA: Government Secretary Rusk states that the 'idea of sanctuary is dead' – that is, that the United States will attack any part of North Vietnam it chooses to.
Air War US planes inflict heavy damage on a river shipping area northwest of Hué.

12 JULY 1965
USA: Government Vice-President Hubert Humphrey defends the administration's conduct of the war and warns its critics not to mistake appeasement for peace.
USA: Military USMC Lieutenant Frank Reasoner of Kellogg, Idaho, is leading his patrol of the 3rd Reconnaissance Battalion when it is ambushed by Vietcong. Wounded,

23 JULY 1965

Reasoner kills two Vietcong and organizes his men, then races through machine-gun fire to rescue his injured radio operator. Mortally wounded, Reasoner is the first Marine to earn the Congressional Medal of Honor in Vietnam.

14 JULY 1965
USA: Domestic It is revealed that just before his death in London, US Ambassador to the UN Adlai Stevenson taped an interview with the BBC in which he disagreed with the anti-war protester and supported Johnson's policies in Vietnam. This comes as disheartening news to those who had hoped Stevenson would withhold his unofficial support.
Air War US planes hit targets only 40 miles – the closest to date – from the border of China.

15 JULY 1965
South Vietnam In an English newspaper interview Premier Ky is quoted as saying that Adolf Hitler is one of his 'heroes.' Confronted with outraged protest, Ky will at first deny making this statement, then admit that he had meant only that he admired the way Hitler rallied the German people.
USA: Military With the arrival of 3000 US troops, the total US force in Vietnam is now 71,000. This same day the first unit of a 120-man New Zealand artillery battery arrives. The Department of Defense announces that it is imposing 'voluntary' curbs on the press in reporting such specifics as casualties, troop movements, and participating units.

16-21 JULY 1965
USA: Government Secretary McNamara conducts a fact-finding mission in South Vietnam, and Henry Cabot Lodge arrives in Saigon to resume his post as ambassador. McNamara is informed by secret cable that Johnson has decided to give General Westmoreland the troops he wants. On leaving Saigon, McNamara admits at a press conference that 'There has been deterioration since I was last here, 15 months ago.'

17 JULY 1965
Ground War A large ARVN force clears and reopens Route 19, the strategic route through the central highlands, for the first time in six weeks, and an armed convoy from Quinhon gets through to Pleiku without being attacked by the Vietcong. But it is reported that six of the ten main roads leading out of Saigon are completely controlled by the Vietcong.

18 JULY 1965
USA: Military Secretary of Defense McNamara, visiting the carrier USS *Independence*, assists in launching a bombing raid.
POWs In a raid over North Vietnam, Commander Jeremiah Denton is shot down and captured; he will remain one of the most prominent US POWs until the end of the war (and will later be elected to Congress).
Laos Souvanna Phouma holds elections, limited to an elite who must vote for carefully screened candidates. The Communist Pathet Lao inevitably boycotts these elections, but some of the new politicians elected will try to take more power.

20 JULY 1965
North Vietnam On the 20th anniversary of the signing of the Geneva accords, Ho Chi Minh says that his people will fight 20 years more or as long as it takes to achieve victory. Premier Ky, also speaking on this occasion, reaffirms his determination to fight for the 'liberation' of North Vietnam.
Laos Laotian government planes bomb trucks carrying supplies for the Vietcong on the Ho Chi Minh Trail.

21 JULY 1965
USA: Government With McNamara back from Vietnam, President Johnson begins a week-long series of conferences with his civilian and military advisers on Vietnam and also with private citizens he trusts. He appears to be considering all the options with an open mind, but it is clear that he has made up his mind to provide more combat troops.
Air War Thirty Guam-based B-52s bomb the Vietcong stronghold in Zone D again; fighter-bombers then move in for precision strikes.

22 JULY 1965
Air War US planes destroy a highway bridge only 42 miles from the border of China.

23 JULY 1965
South Vietnam Chief of State Thieu decrees that the death penalty may be imposed for those supporting 'neutralism.'
USA: Government President Johnson, in the course of conferences is told by some that he should give the American public all the facts, ask for an increase in taxes, mobilize the reserves, and declare a state of national emergency. But Johnson rejects this approach, and informs his staff that he wants any decisions implemented in a 'low-key

121

CHRONOLOGY

manner in order (a) to avoid an abrupt challenge to the Communists, and (b) to avoid undue concern and excitement in the Congress and in domestic public opinion.'

24 JULY 1965

USA: Military The Pentagon reports that since 1961 US wounded in Vietnam outnumber those killed by 5 to 1, the highest such ratio in any American conflict.

Air War Four US F-4C Phantom jets escorting a formation of US bombers on a raid over munitions manufacturing facilities at Kangchi, 55 miles northwest of Hanoi, are fired at for the first time by anti-aircraft missiles from an unknown launching site; one plane is destroyed and the other three damaged.

Sea War US destroyers bomb a fleet of suspected Vietcong junks and sink 23.

27 JULY 1965

USA: Government President Johnson informs some of the Democratic and Republican leaders of Congress of his decision but there is general awareness that he has already decided to commit more troops.

International The US government confirms that Secretary of State Rusk has talked with members of the International Red Cross about improving the treatment of POWs on both sides.

Air War Forty-six US F-105 fighter-bombers attack the missile installation that fired at US planes on 24 July and another missile installation 40 miles northwest of Hanoi; one missile launcher is destroyed, another damaged, but five US planes are lost.

28 JULY 1965

USA: Government President Johnson announces that he has ordered an increase in US military forces in Vietnam from the present 75,000 to 125,000 – and that he will order additional increases if the situation calls for it. To fill the increase in military manpower needs, the montly draft calls will be raised from 17,000 to 35,000. At the same time, Johnson reaffirms US readiness to seek a negotiated end to the war, and appeals to the UN and any of its member states to help further this goal. There is an immediate reaction throughout the world to this latest escalation, with Communist leaders inevitably attacking Johnson. Most members of Congress are reported to favor Johnson's decision, while most US state governors, now convened for their annual conference, also

support a resolution backing Johnson. This decision is regarded as a major turning point, as it effectively guarantees US military leaders a blank check to pursue the war.

Air War US and South Vietnamese bombers hit a Buddhist monastery by mistake, killing two monks and wounding 10.

29 JULY 1965

USA: Domestic One survey shows general support for Johnson's decision to send more troops, but another, more specialized, shows a shift from complete support to uncertainty.

USA: Military The first 4000 paratroopers of the 101st Airborne Division arrive in Vietnam, landing at Camranh Bay. They make a demonstration jump immediately after arriving, observed by General William Westmoreland and out-going Ambassador (formerly General) Maxwell Taylor. Both are former commanders of the division, which is known as 'the Screaming Eagles.'

30 JULY 1965

International It is reported that 29 nations now give some kind of aid – in personnel, matériel, or money – to South Vietnam.

UN The United States formally requests that the Security Council help settle the war in Vietnam.

1 AUGUST 1965

USA: Government President Johnson charges that a Republican Congressman has misrepresented events by claiming that prominent Democrats dissuaded Johnson from calling up the reserves. Gerald Ford (R-MI), who is immediately singled out, will deny that he ever said this. Underlying this passing feud lies one of the most controversial aspects of the war: President Johnson's refusal to call up the reserves.

International President Tito of Yugoslavia and Prime Minister Shastri of India call on all principals involved to enter into peace negotiations before the new US military buildup extends the war beyond control.

Guerrilla War The Vietcong strike against 20 South Vietnamese outposts.

Air War US planes bomb 11 bridges, destroying two, and hit three radar installations in North Vietnam.

Sea War Operation Market Time – monitoring the junks along the coast to cut off supplies to the Vietcong – is removed from US 7th Fleet command and assigned to a newly created Coastal Surveillance Force.

The Coastal Surveillance Force patrolled the sea in search of junks carrying contraband.

2 AUGUST 1965
Ground War US troops end a six-day operation in Phuoctuy Province, where they have been searching for reported Vietcong forces; they fail to make contact but kill three South Vietnamese soldiers accidentally.
Air War Thirty Guam-based B-52s bomb a suspected Vietcong base in the area of Doxa.

2-3 AUGUST 1965
USA: Military General Wheeler, Chairman of the JCS, General Westmoreland, and Admiral U S Grant Sharp, meet in Honolulu to begin planning for the stepped-up US commitment. New command changes are announced for US forces already in Vietnam, and a schedule for deploying troops into combat is worked out. A US Army spokesman in Washington confirms that the United States has begun transferring troops from West Germany on a 'volunteer' basis, although the German government has not

been formally notified of this change.

2-11 AUGUST 1965
Ground War The South Vietnamese Special Forces camp at Ducco, only seven miles east of the Cambodian border on strategic Highway 19, has been under siege by the Vietcong for some two months. On 2 August, a 3000-man Vietcong force makes a full-scale assault; next day two ARVN paratroop battalions are flown in by helicopter to relieve the Ducco garrison. The battle continues for several days, but it is not until troops of the US First Infantry Division and 173rd Airborne Brigade are flown in that the Vietcong withdraw.

3 AUGUST 1965
South Vietnam Peasants in Haunghia Province are reported to be demonstrating against both the Vietcong and the South Vietnamese government.

CHRONOLOGY

USA: Military The Department of Defense announces that it has increased the monthly draft quota from 17,000 in August to 27,400 in September and 36,000 in October; it also announces that the US Navy will require 4600 draftees, the first such action since 1956.

War Crimes The first charge that US troops have engaged in unacceptable actions against civilians is reported by CBS-TV, when it shows men of the 1st Battalion, 9th Marines, burning most of the village of Camne, six miles southwest of Danang.

5 AUGUST 1965
South Vietnam It is reported that about 500,000 refugees are now present in South Vietnam and that another 1,000,000 are expected within the next year.

Guerrilla War The Vietcong attack the Esso storage terminal on the Haivai Peninsula, across the bay from Danang, and destroy almost 2,000,000 gallons of fuel – 40 percent of the supply. US planes and the USN destroyer *Stoddard* move in quickly to strike at guerrillas, but they escape. The US military claims the loss does not affect its operations.

6 AUGUST 1965
South Vietnam A US B-57 crashes into a residential section of Nhatrang with a full load of bombs; the crew survives, but 12 Vietnamese are killed.

6 AUGUST 1965
USA: Government President Johnson rejects a request from Ghanian President Kwame Nkrumah·that the US stop bombing North Vietnam. He advises Nkrumah 'to tell Hanoi that our military resistance would end when aggression ends.' Meanwhile, a group of Republican Congressmen charges that Johnson is preparing for a 'coming surrender,' because he has indicated willingness to negotiate a peace with North Vietnam.

7 AUGUST 1965
Air War US planes bomb the explosive plant at Langchi, North Vietnam.

China The government warns again that it will send troops to fight for the Communists in Vietnam if necessary.

8 AUGUST 1965
Air War In over 250 missions, US planes bomb suspected Vietcong concentrations in South Vietnam and report numerous enemy troops and buildings destroyed.

12 AUGUST 1965
USA: Government At the swearing-in ceremony of Ambassador Lodge, President Johnson insists that they agree that the United States would not continue to fight in Vietnam 'if its help were not wanted and requested.'

USA: Domestic Reverend Martin Luther King Jr criticizes what he regards as President Johnson's failure to enter discussions with the Vietcong to end the war, and says he will appeal personally to the Communist leaders, even if this means violating Federal Law.

Air War A Navy A-4 Skyhawk becomes the second US plane downed by a missile over Vietnam, when it is hit by a rocket fired from an unknown site 50 miles southwest of Hanoi.

13 AUGUST 1965
Ground War ARVN forces score an important victory in the Mekong Delta, killing 250 Vietcong while taking only light casualties.

Air War Five USN planes are downed over North Vietnam by conventional anti-aircraft artillery fire.

14 AUGUST 1965
North Vietnam Hanoi Radio broadcasts an appeal to American troops, particularly blacks, to 'get out'; this is purportedly a message from an American defector from the Korean War now living in Peking.

USA: Military With the landing of advance units of the 7th Marines at Chulai, the Marines now have four regiments and four air groups in Vietnam. The air base is a priority, because it gives the Marines an independent air force to support their operations in southern I Corps and northern II Corps.

Air War US and South Vietnamese planes damage hundreds of buildings and sink many sampans in widespread air attacks in South Vietnam.

South Korea The National Assembly approves sending troops to fight in Vietnam, but in return for this 15,000-man force, the US has agreed to equip five South Korean divisions.

16 AUGUST 1965
South Vietnam Two bomb-laden cars are driven into the compound of South Vietnamese National Police headquarters in Saigon. The ensuing explosion kills eight policemen and wounds 17; two other policemen are gunned down outside the gate. Although the Vietcong take credit for the

attack, there is some speculation that it was the work of a dissident clique of South Vietnamese who had attempted a coup.

Ground War The Vietcong attack a US Marine tank unit near Danang, but six of them are killed.

17-23 AUGUST 1965

USA: Domestic A minor controversy surfaces when former President Eisenhower – having been shown an advance copy of a pamphlet to be issued by the White House – says that his letter to Premier Diem of 1 October 1954 had intended to offer economic, not military, aid to Vietnam; this letter is the centerpiece of the White House pamphlet 'Why Vietnam?,' issued on 23 August. By 19 August, trying to squelch the dispute, Eisenhower has stated, 'I support the president.'

18-21 AUGUST 1965

Ground War In the first major ground action fought only by US troops, Operation Starlite, about 5500 US Marines destroy a Vietcong stronghold near Vantuong on a peninsula 16 miles south of the air base at Chulai. Marine jet planes and US warships support the operation. The Vietcong had fought tenaciously against superior Marine firepower. The Marines lose 45 and claim to have killed 688 Vietcong – most members of the 1st Vietcong Regiment and 'an undetermined number of persons caught in these caves, as indicated by the odor pervading the area.'

21 AUGUST 1965

Air War It is revealed that US pilots are now ordered to destroy any Soviet-made missiles they see while raiding North Vietnam (a change from previous orders to bomb only assigned targets). It is admitted, too, that Soviet citizens have almost certanly been killed and/or wounded in such raids.

23 AUGUST 1965

USA: Government Secretary of State Rusk, UN Ambassador Arthur Goldberg, and McGeorge Bundy appear on a TV panel and seem to offer a more conciliatory version of the US demands for ending the war.

Guerrilla War The Vietcong shell the air base at Bienhoa and damage 49 planes.

26 AUGUST 1965

Ground War The Vietcong overrun the ARVN post at Tonnhut, less than 10 miles from Saigon.

Air War B-52s raid suspected Vietcong concentrations in Zone D, while bombers strike a radar site in North Vietnam.

27 AUGUST 1965

Ground War ARVN forces clear Route 21 between Ninhoa and Banmethuot to allow supply convoys to pass.

Air War US and South Vietnamese planes fly over 300 missions in South Vietnam.

28 AUGUST 1965

Ground War After an all-night battle in the area of Cantho, in the Mekong Delta, a Vietcong battalion is forced to withdraw, leaving behind a reported 50 dead.

31 AUGUST 1965

South Vietnam Premier Ky says that South Vietnam will not negotiate with the Communists without guarantees of the withdrawal of North Vietnamese troops; he adds that his government now plans major reforms to correct economic and social injustices.

USA: Government President Johnson signs into law a bill making it a crime to destroy or mutilate a draft card, with penalties of up to five years in prison and a $1000 fine.

USA: Military It is announced that US and other foreign personnel in South Vietnam will now be paid in a special scrip, in an effort to curb the black-market economy.

Air War US planes continue to bomb targets in North Vietnam, while B-52s are still striking Vietcong concentrations in Zone D and in Quangtin Province.

SEPTEMBER 1965

China China's defense minister publishes an article urging the North Vietnamese not to attempt a head-on confrontation with South Vietnamese and US forces: 'Guerrilla warfare is the only way to mobilize and apply the whole strength of the people against the enemy. Mao Tse-tung is planning to begin his 'Great Proletarian Cultural Revolution' and needs his army and resources for his own purposes. China is trying to compete with the Soviet Union as a promoter of the Communist revolutionary approach. It will continue to attack the United States, resist any efforts to negotiate peace in Vietnam, and generally support the North Vietnamese.

2 SEPTEMBER 1965

USA: Military The United States announces that over 100 US servicemen a day are volun-

CHRONOLOGY

teering for duty in Vietnam – a sharp increase since the Marines landed in March.

3 SEPTEMBER 1965
Air War US and South Vietnamese planes fly a record 532 missions on one day, including a joint launch from three US carriers offshore.

7-10 SEPTEMBER 1965
Ground War US Marines and ARVN troops conduct Operation Piranha on the Batangan Peninsula, some 23 miles south of their base at Chulai, where they storm a Vietcong stronghold and claim to kill 200.

9 SEPTEMBER 1965
Air War US planes continue their heavy daily raids over North Vietnam, damaging a bridge only 17 miles from the border of China.

10 SEPTEMBER 1965
USA: Military US planes drop 10,000 tons of toys and supplies over five towns in South Vietnam for the annual celebration for children.

11 SEPTEMBER 1965
USA: Military The 1st Cavalry Division (Airmobile) begins to land at Quinhon; this brings US troop strength in Vietnam up to about 125,000.

USA: Government Representative Gerald Ford (R-MI) charges that the Johnson administration is deceiving Americans about the actual cost of the war.

14-15 SEPTEMBER 1965
Ground War ARVN paratroopers and some US advisers jump into the Bencat area, 20 miles north of Saigon; this is the first major parachute assault by the South Vietnamese. Although they fail to make contact with the enemy, they achieve their goal of driving the Vietcong from Route 13 temporarily.

15 SEPTEMBER 1965
South Vietnam To affirm their loyalty to the government of South Vietnam, 500 *montagnards* turn over their weapons at a ceremony at Banmethuot, attended by Premier Ky.

USA: Government In Tokyo, US Deputy Ambassador to Vietnam, Alexis Johnson, warns Japan and other non-Communist nations that they cannot continue to remain apart from the struggle in Vietnam, because fundamental issues are at stake.

16 SEPTEMBER 1965
Air War In their first strike over the Mekong Delta, B-52s bomb a Vietcong site in Vinhbinh Province.

17 SEPTEMBER 1965
South Vietnam ARVN troops claim that the Vietcong used gas grenades in attacking an ARVN outpost at Quangngai and that 22 soldiers were felled by them, but a US medical team will find no evidence.

17-19 SEPTEMBER 1965
Air War In three incidents, US planes strike so close to the DMZ that at least 60 South Vietnamese civilians are reported killed or wounded. General Westmoreland orders that special precautions be taken to avoid using undue force against civilians, but simultaneously calls for redrawing the borders of the free strike zone.

18-21 SEPTEMBER 1965
Ground War In one of the largest engagements thus far, US troops, including those of the 1st Airborne Division, take on the Vietcong at Ankhe; the US claims to have killed 226 guerrillas.

20 SEPTEMBER 1965
Air War In raids over North and South Vietnam, the US suffers a total loss of seven planes. The Chinese claim to have shot down a US-F104 jet over Hainan Island and captured its pilot; a US spokesman claims the plane developed a mechanical problem over the Gulf of Tonkin.

23 SEPTEMBER 1965
Ground War US troops report finding a large Vietcong arms cache in a village near Bencat and kill 12 guerrillas in the operation.

23-29 SEPTEMBER 1965
War Crimes The South Vietnamese government executes three accused Communist agents at Danang by night to prevent foreign photographers from recording it. Three days later, a clandestine Vietcong radio station announces the execution of two US soldiers, held captive since 1963, as 'war criminals.' On 29 September, the North Vietnamese reveal that they have written a letter to the International Red Cross to warn that US pilots captured while bombing North Vietnam will be treated as 'war criminals liable to go before tribunals'; they claim that the 1949 Geneva

agreements on war prisoners do not apply now. The US State Department protests.

30 SEPTEMBER 1965

USA: Military It is revealed that US troops are using non-toxic smoke, spread with crop dusters, on suspected Vietcong hideouts.

Air War Two USAF jets are shot down – one by a surface-to-air missile – while bombing the Minhbinh bridge.

5 OCTOBER 1965

USA: Military After a long debate, the administration authorizes the use of tear gas by US troops in Vietnam.

China Peking claims that Chinese gunners downed a US plane intruding into Kwangsi Province; the US Department of Defense will not confirm the incident, but acknowledges that one plane did not return from a bombing mission 50 miles northeast of Hanoi.

6 OCTOBER 1965

Air War US B-52s hit suspected Vietcong bases in Tayninh Province near the Cambodian border.

10-14 OCTOBER 1965

Ground War In its first operation since arriving the previous month, the US 1st Air Cavalry Division joins with South Vietnamese marines to mount a major drive against an estimated 2000 enemy troops about 25 miles from Ankhe in the Central Highlands. Faulty US-South Vietnamese co-ordination prevents allied forces from entrapping the NVA 325th Infantry Division, but they do reopen the Pleiku-Ankhe highway and destroy a 50-bed enemy hospital equipped with US medical supplies.

12 OCTOBER 1965

USA: Domestic Senator John Stennis (D-MS) states that it may be necessary to keep US forces in Vietnam for another 15 years.

15 OCTOBER 1965

USA: Domestic At a pacifist rally, David Miller, a relief program volunteer, becomes the first US war protester to burn his draft card; Miller is arrested by FBI agents.

16 OCTOBER 1965

International Demonstrators protesting US policy in Vietnam march through the streets of London, Rome, Brussels, Copenhagen, and Stockholm; the protests coincide with similar demonstrations in about 40 US cities, organized by the National Coordinating Committee to End the War in Vietnam.

Japan Premier Sato announces that Japan will send no troops to Vietnam, even if requested to do so by the US.

19-27 OCTOBER 1965

Ground War Enemy forces launch a heavy assault against the US Special Forces camp at Pleime in the Central Highlands, 215 miles north of Saigon. During a week of savage fighting, defenders of the besieged outpost – which is manned by 400 *montagnards*, 12 Green Berets and a handful of South Vietnamese guerrilla specialists – repel repeated Vietcong attacks, with the aid of several hundred ARVN reinforcements and numerous allied air strikes. Units from the US 1st Air Cavalry Division conduct a mop-up operation west of the camp.

21 OCTOBER 1965

USA: Domestic The United Automobile Workers' executive board issues a statement declaring its support of administration policy in Vietnam.

22 OCTOBER 1965

USA: Military In a Honolulu interview, Pacific area commander Admiral U S Grant Sharp asserts that allied forces have 'stopped losing' the war. Sharp also states that he does not believe China will enter the conflict.

23 OCTOBER 1965

USA: Domestic The Americans for Democratic Action denounce a Justice Department probe of Communist influence in the war protest and anti-draft movements as an effort to 'stifle criticism' of administration policy.

23 OCTOBER-20 NOVEMBER 1965

Ground War In an extension of the clash at the Pleime Special Forces camp, ARVN and US 1st Air Cavalry Division units seek to destroy enemy forces operating in Pleiku Province. The operation concludes with a week of bitter fighting when fleeing NVA troops decide to protect an important staging area and supply base in the Iadrang Valley. It is the bloodiest battle of the war to date: in one engagement, 500 North Vietnamese ambush a battalion, wiping out almost an entire company. Reported enemy casualties for the operation total 1771.

CHRONOLOGY

27 OCTOBER 1965
Guerrilla War Vietcong commandos damage and destroy numerous allied aircraft in two separate attacks on USMC air facilities. In one raid, the guerrillas row up the Danang River, dig in near the heliport runway at the Marble Mountain air base, and launch a mortar assault, thus providing cover for 20 comrades who run onto the runway and toss satchel charges into open helicopter cockpits. In subsequent fighting, US Marines kill at least 17 members of the 30-man assault force. The second raid occurs at Chulai, where a Vietcong mortar attack destroys two jet fighter planes and damages five others.

30 OCTOBER 1965
USA: Domestic In a New York City demonstration, 25,000 persons, led by five recipients of the Congressional Medal of Honor, march in support of US policy in Vietnam.
Ground War US Marines repel a 'human wave' assault 10 miles from Danang, killing 56 Vietcong attackers. A search of the dead uncovers a sketch of Marine positions on the body of a 13-year-old boy who had sold drinks to Marines the previous day.
Air War Two US planes accidentally bomb a friendly Vietnamese village, killing 48 civilians and wounding 55 others. An American civic action team is immediately dispatched to the scene, and a later investigation discloses that a map-reading error by South Vietnamese officers is responsible.

31 OCTOBER 1965
Air War US planes destroy three anti-aircraft missile sites and a highway bridge during a raid 35 miles northeast of Hanoi.

1 NOVEMBER 1965
Suth Vietnam South Vietnam celebrates National Day in memory of the coup which overthrew Ngo Dinh Diem.

2 NOVEMBER 1965
USA: Domestic To express his opposition to US actions in Vietnam, Norman Morrison, a 32-year-old Quaker from Baltimore, immolates himself in front of the Pentagon.

4 NOVEMBER 1965
Casualties Two US helicopters crash in midair near Ankhe, killing all nine crew members and passengers aboard both craft.

5 NOVEMBER 1965
USA: Domestic At a Los Angeles news conference, Senator Robert Kennedy (D-NY) defends 'the right to criticize and the right to dissent' from US policy in Vietnam in a statement asserting that donating blood to North Vietnam is 'in the oldest tradition of this country.' Former Senator Barry Goldwater believes otherwise and states that Kennedy's remarks come 'close to treason.'

5-8 NOVEMBER 1965
Air War During a series of raids against North Vietnam, US fighter-bombers from the aircraft carrier *Oriskany* damage or destroy nine anti-aircraft sites, five missile launchers and several support buildings; two planes are lost.

9 NOVEMBER 1965
USA:Government In a memorandum prepared by Ambassador Alexis Johnson, the State Department urges the administration to reject Defense Secretary McNamara's recent proposal for a bombing pause. The State Department is not persuaded by McNamara's argument and asserts that there are equally compelling reasons why the US should not slacken the air war against North Vietnam: Hanoi has given no indication that it is ready to negotiate and, even more importantly, such a pause would demoralize the Saigon regime and 'could adversely affect the Government's solidity.' 'On balance,' the memorandum concludes, 'arguments against the bombing pause are convincing to the Secretary of State, who recommends that it not be undertaken at the present time.'
USA: Domestic In the second such anti-war incident within a week, Roger Allen LaPorte, a 22-year-old member of the Catholic Worker movement, immolates himself in front of UN headquarters in New York. Before dying the next day, LaPorte declares that 'I'm against wars, all wars. I did this as a religious act.'

12 NOVEMBER 1965
USA: Military Defense Secretary McNamara states that allied troops have recently turned back an enemy offensive designed to split South Vietnam in two; he also reports that, despite a 100 percent increase in casualties since a similar period in 1964, Vietcong forces have continued to increase in number.

16 NOVEMBER 1965
Ground War Enemy troops overrun Hiep Duc, a district headquarters 25 miles west of

30 NOVEMBER 1965

Tamky. Although two ARVN battalions later retake the town, General Thi, commander of South Vietnamese forces in I Corps, is forced to abandon the town because he has too few regulars to leave any men there.

17 NOVEMBER 1965
USA: Domestic The 48th general assembly of Reform Judaism's Union of Hebrew Congregations adopts a resolution urging Pesident Johnson to order an immediate cease-fire in Vietnam so that peace talks might be arranged.

19 NOVEMBER 1965
Ground War Vietcong guerrillas, using string bows, fire arrows dipped in rancid animal fat at US troops guarding the air base at Quinhon.

22 NOVEMBER 1965
USA: Government Chairman L Mendel Rivers (R-SC) of the House Armed Service Committee calls for the bombing of Hanoi and Haiphong, declaring that it is 'folly to let the port of Haiphong and military targets at Hanoi remain untouched while war supplies being used against our troops are pouring into the port.'

22-23 NOVEMBER 1965
Ground War In an assault on the town of Thach Tru, the 18th PAVN Regiment encounters stiff resistance from a South Vietnamese Ranger battalion supported by gunfire from two US destroyers and Marine aircraft. The US 7th Marines arrive by helicopter the next day, driving enemy forces from the area.

24 NOVEMBER 1965
Casualties US casualty statistics reflect the intensified fighting in the Iadrang Valley and other parts of the Central Highlands: a record 240 troops were killed and another 470 wounded during the previous week.

26 NOVEMBER 1965
Sea War Two US Navy nuclear-powered vessels – the aircraft carrier *Enterprise* and guided-missile frigate *Bainbridge* - join the 7th Fleet and take up positions off Saigon.

27 NOVEMBER 1965
USA: Military The Pentagon informs President Johnson that during the coming year, US troop strength must be increased from 120,000 to 400,000 men if General Westmoreland is to conduct the major sweep operations he deems necessary to destroy enemy forces.

USA: Domestic In a demonstration organized by the National Committee for a Sane Nuclear Policy, an estimated 15,000 to 35,000 war protesters circle the White House for two hours before moving on to the Washington Monument, where they are addressed by Dr Benjamin Spock, Mrs Martin Luther King, Norman Thomas and other speakers.

POWs The Vietcong release two US Special Forces soldiers captured two years earlier during a battle at Hiephoa, 40 miles southwest of Saigon. At a news conference in Pnompenh three days later, the two Americans, Sgt George Smith and Sp 5/c Claude McClure, declare that they oppose US actions in Vietnam and will campaign for the withdrawal of US troops. Although Smith later denies having made the statement, US authorities announce that the two men face trial for co-operating with the enemy.

27-28 NOVEMBER 1965
Ground War Vietcong guerrillas kill several American advisers and maul two ARVN battalions during an attack on a South Vietnamese regimental headquarters at the Michelin rubber plantation; further casualties result when US planes accidentally bomb an ARVN relief unit.

30 NOVEMBER 1965
USA: Government In a memorandum to President Johnson, following a recent visit to South Vietnam, Defense Secretary McNamara reports that the Ky government 'is surviving, but not acquiring wide support or generating actions.' Even more worrisome, Vietcong recruiting successes coupled with a continuing heavy infiltration of North Vietnamese forces indicate that 'the enemy can be expected to enlarge his present strength of 110 battalion equivalents to more than 150 battalion equivalents by the end of 1966.' McNamara thus believes that US policymakers face two options: to seek a compromise settlement and keep further military commitments to a minimum, or continue to press for a military solution, which will require substantial increases in US troop strength and intensified bombing of North Vietnam. In conclusion, McNamara warns that there is no guarantee of military success: 'US killed-in-action can be expected

CHRONOLOGY

In North Vietnam, both men and women served in the People's Militia.

to reach 1000 a month, and the odds are even that we will be faced in early 1967 with a "no-decision" at an even higher level.'

30 NOVEMBER-2 DECEMBER 1965
Diplomatic At a series of meetings in Moscow, British Foreign Secretary Michael Stewart is unable to persuade Soviet leaders to join Britain in reconvening the Geneva conference on Indochina. The Soviet position, according to Foreign Minister Andrei Gromyko, is that peace talks cannot begin until the United States ceases bombing North Vietnam and withdraws its troops.

3 DECEMBER 1965
USA: Government In a confidential memorandum to Defense Secretary McNamara, Assistant Secretary John McNaughton outlines the terms which should precede a permanent bombing halt: North Vietnam must not only cease infiltration efforts, but take steps to withdraw troops currently operating in South Vietnam, while the Vietcong must terminate terror and sabotage activites and allow the Saigon regime to exercise 'governmental functions over substantially all of South Vietnam.' McNaughton does not believe that these conditions will soon be obtained, however, as they amount to 'capitulation by a Communist force that is far from beaten.'
USA: Domestic The general board of the National Council of Churches issues a statement approving the administration's commitment to unconditional negotiations and urging new peace initiatives.

4 DECEMBER 1965
USA: Domestic Fifty Catholic college students from Fordham University, protesting the 'suppression' of three priests who actively opposed US policy in Vietnam, picket the New York City chancery of Francis Cardinal Spellman.
Terrorism Vietcong commandos explode a bomb at a Saigon hotel housing US servicemen, killing one US Marine, a New Zealand artilleryman and six South Vietnamese civilians; another 137 persons are injured.

7 DECEMBER 1965
USA: Government In a memorandum to President Johnson, Defense Secretary McNamara states that US troop strength must be substantially augmented 'if we are to avoid being defeated there.' He cautions again that such deployments will not ensure military success. The North Vietnamese and Vietcong 'continue to believe that the war will be a long one, that time is their ally and their own staying power is superior to ours.' McNamara also expresses concern about Chinese intervention.

8-9 DECEMBER 1965
Air War In some of the heaviest raids of the war, 150 US Air Force and Navy planes sever North Vietnamese transport routes at 117 points to reduce enemy infiltration.

8-19 DECEMBER 1965
Ground War A joint South Vietnamese-USMC operation intended to clear Vietcong forces from the Que Son Valley begins on an inauspicious note when enemy units destroy two ARVN battalions before they can be reinforced by US Marines. In subsequent fighting, however, allied troops, supported by B-52 strikes, overcome stiff resistance and accomplish their objective.

9 DECEMBER 1965
USA: Military An article in *The New York Times* reports that US air attacks have neither destabilized North Vietnam's economy, nor appreciably reduced the flow of NVA forces into South Vietnam. These observations are strikingly similar to a recent Defense Intelligence Agency analysis which concluded that 'the idea that destroying, or threatening to destroy, North Vietnam's industry would pressure Hanoi into calling it quits seems, in retrospect, a colossal misjudgment.'

10 DECEMBER 1965
USA: Domestic Senator Ernest Gruening (D-AK) states that the conflict in Vietnam is a civil war which poses no threat to US security interests. Gruening also declares that, despite the President's repeated assertion that he is continuing a commitment undertaken by previous administrations, the United States has made no 'solemn pledge' to support South Vietnam.

11 DECEMBER 1965
USA: Military To prepare for an expected expansion of its role in Vietnam, the United States begins emergency construction of additional military installations in Thailand.

12 DECEMBER 1965
USA: Government Seventeen Democratic members of the House of Representatives sign a statement supporting President Johnson's refusal to bomb Hanoi and Haiphong.
USSR An article in the Soviet newspaper *Pravda* accuses Chinese leaders of refusing to co-operate with efforts by other Communist nations to defeat the United States in Vietnam.

14 DECEMBER 1965
USA: Domestic The Opinion Research Corporation releases a poll showing that only 20 percent of Americans believe the United States should have withdrawn from Vietnam before its troops became involved in combat.

15 DECEMBER 1965
Air War In the first raid on a major North Vietnamese industrial target, USAF planes destroy a thermal power plant at Uongbi, 14 miles north of Haiphong; the plant reportedly supplies about 15 percent of North Vietnam's total electric-power production.

16 DECEMBER 1965
USA: Military Defense Secretary McNamara receives a new troop request from General Westmoreland, stating that he needs 443,000 men by the end of 1966.

18-19 DECEMBER 1965
South Vietnam *Montagnard* tribesmen, seeking autonomy from the South Vietnamese government, stage a series of uprisings in the Central Highlands.

19 DECEMBER 1965
Terrorism A recent increase in Vietcong bombings prompts US authorities to impose a daily curfew on US forces stationed in Saigon.

21 DECEMBER 1965
USA: Domestic US Representative Emmanuel Cellar (D—NY) charges Selective Service director Lieutenant General Lewis Hershey with 'demeaning the draft act' by reclassifying students who participate in anti-war protests. Hershey denies the accusation.

22 DECEMBER 1965
China Peking issues a statement asserting that 'So far, a great part of the Soviet equipment supplied to Vietnam consisted of obsolete equipment discarded by the Soviet armed forces or damaged weapons cleaned out from the warehouse.'

23 DECEMBER 1965
Casualties A US C-123 transport plane crashes into a mountain 240 miles north of Saigon, killing four US crew members and 81 South Vietnamese soldiers.

26 DECEMBER 1965
USA: Military Heavy Vietcong attacks forced allied military authorities to abandon efforts to extend the Christmas truce and resume offensive operations.

CHRONOLOGY

27 DECEMBER 1965
Diplomatic In conjunction with a bombing pause which began three days earlier, the United Sates initiates a massive peace drive, as international missions conducted by UN Ambassador Goldberg, Ambassador-at-Large Harriman, Vice-President Humphrey and Presidential Assistant McGeorge Bundy depart for various world capitals. Their purpose is to explore the possibilitites of attaining a negotiated settlement.

30 DECEMBER 1965
Diplomatic The administration's current diplomatic campaign begins to make headway when Poland, Yugoslavia, and Italy agree to aid US peace efforts.

31 DECEMBER 1965
State of the War This has been the pivotal year of the war. Not only has the United States introduced large numbers of troops and equipment into Vietnam: those troops have been authorized to take the offensive. The United States has also begun bombing North Vietnam, with Operation Rolling Thunder, which will continue with occasional pauses till October 1968. Some 180,000 US military personnel are now in Vietnam, but General Westmoreland has made it clear that he wants another 250,000 during the coming year – and President Johnson has effectively assured him that he will get all the troops he wants. US forces are now beginning to report significant casualties: some 1350 killed, 5300 wounded, and 150 missing or captured during 1965. South Vietnam reports 11,100 killed, 22,600 wounded, and 7400 missing among the military alone. Increasing numbers of South Vietnamese civilians are also being killed by air raids and other military actions. South Vietnam also claims to have killed 34,585 of the Communist forces and captured 5746. Operation Rolling Thunder has already flown 55,000 sorties and dropped a total bomb tonnage of 33,000; 171 US aircraft have been lost, and direct operational costs for 1965 come to $460 million. There is no sign that these raids are having any effect on the North Vietnamese, in terms of the government's determination to pursue the war or its willingness to negotiate. It is estimated that some 36,000 North Vietnamese have now infiltrated South Vietnam, most coming down the Ho Chi Minh Trail. Since that traverses Laos, the United States has mounted a major secret bombing operation in that country (Opera-

tion Steel Tiger). It is controlled largely by the US Ambassador in Laos, William Sullivan. In 1965 US planes flew a daily average of 55 sorties over the network of trails in southern Laos. South Vietnam's government seems as unstable as ever, and in the United States, protests and demonstrations against the war are escalating. Many of the world's leaders are seeking desperately to find some solution to the widening war.

1 JANUARY 1966
USA: Domestic Senator Strom Thurmond (R-SC) declares that the United States should use nuclear weapons in Vietnam if military victory can be achieved by no other means.

3 JANUARY 1966
Cambodia In a letter to UN Secretary General U Thant, the Cambodian government warns that if allied forces violate its territory or airspace, it will seek aid from other nations and conduct armed attacks into South Vietnam. He also requests that the ICC expand its border patrols to investigate reports of arms shipments from Cambodia into South Vietnam, as well as Cambodian charges that US and ARVN units are attacking Khmer villages.

4 JANUARY 1966
North Vietnam The North Vietnamese Foreign Ministry finally acknowledges the bombing pause in a statement calling recent US diplomatic efforts 'a large scale deceptive peace campaign coupled with the trick of "temporary suspensions of air attacks".' Hanoi also asserts that the United States is preparing to double its strength in South Vietnam, while intensifying air attacks over Laos and sending American troops into central Laos and Cambodia.
USA: Domestic Returning from a recent trip to South Vietnam, Senator George McGovern (D-SD) contends that US peace proposals have little chance of success, because the administration refuses to recognize that the conflict is primarily a civil war between the Saigon regime and the NLF. Any talks which exclude either of these parties, McGovern adds, are doomed to failure.

5 JANUARY 1966
Diplomatic US Ambassador to the UN Arthur Goldberg circulates a letter asking that UN members help 'advance the cause of a peaceful settlement' in Vietnam. He also

informs them that the current American peace mission is intended to 'make sure that the channels of communication are open' and states that the United States is 'prepared for discussions or negotiations without prior conditions whatsoever or on the basis of the Geneva accords.'

6 JANUARY 1966
USA: Domestic John Lewis, chairman of the Student Nonviolent Coordinating Committee, issues a policy statement attacking US actions in Vietnam and announcing SNCC's support of 'the men in this country who are unwilling to respond to a military draft.' A few days later Roy Wilkins, executive director of the NAACP, asserts that the SNCC declaration does not represent the views of his organization or 'what is loosely called the civil rights movement.'
Ground War Vietcong forces employ 120-mm mortars for the first time during an attack on the allied camp at Khesanh in Quangtri Province. Following a five-day siege, Vietcong troops overrun the South Vietnamese outpost at Conghoa.

8 JANUARY 1966
USA: Government In a report to the Senate Foreign Relations Committee following a recent fact-finding tour of Vietnam, Senate majority leader Mike Mansfield (D-MT) offers a gloomy assessment. Noting that the war has already expanded into Laos and is now spreading into Cambodia, Mansfield warns that the entire Southeast Asian peninsula, 'cannot be ruled out as a potential battlefield.' He also observes that the military situation is no better than it had been 'at the outset.' Nor does there appear to be any prospect of meaningful negotiations. Even if peace talks, accompanied by a truce, could be arranged, Mansfield states, they would only 'serve to stabilize a situation in which the majority of the population remains under nominal government control but in which dominance of the countryside rests largely in the hands of the Vietcong.'
USA: Government Senate minority leader Everett Dirksen expresses opposition to President Johnson's offer of 'negotiations without prior conditions' in a statement asserting that total military victory must precede any peace talks. Dirksen further urges that the war be extended by blockading North Vietnam.

8-14 JANUARY 1966
Ground War In a massive search-and-destroy operation, US forces, supported by troops from Australia and New Zealand, converge on the Vietcong's Iron Triangle stronghold northwest of Saigon. Although they fail to make contact with any large enemy units, the allies do uncover and destroy a huge Vietcong tunnel network before pulling out.

12 JANUARY 1966
USA: Government: In his annual State of the Union message, President Johnson discloses that during the previous year administration officials engaged in '300 private talks for peace in Vietnam with friends and adversaries throughout the world.'

14 JANUARY 1966
USSR Moscow issues a communiqué pledging increased military aid to North Vietnam. The statement also reaffirms Soviet support of Hanoi's four-point peace formula as 'the only correct basis for solving the Vietnamese problem.'

16 JANUARY 1966
USA: Domestic Sixteen Harvard University professors and 13 other scientists assail the use of crop-destroying agents in Vietnam.

17 JANUARY 1966
Terrorism After ambushing his car, Vietcong guerrillas kidnap Douglas Ramsey, a US aid-mission representative.

19 JANUARY-21 FEBRUARY 1966
Ground War The 1st Brigade, 101st Airborne Division, Republic of Korea 2nd Marine Brigade, and ARVN 47th Regiment conduct operation to secure the rice fields in Phu Yen Province which claims 679 enemy casualties.

20 JANUARY 1966
USA: Government In a speech at Independence, Missouri, President Johnson urges Hanoi to respond positively to the bombing pause and peace campaign by agreeing to begin peace talks.
US: Military In testimony before a joint session of the Senate Armed Services and Appropriations Committees, General Earle Wheeler warns that a permanent bombing halt would deprive the United States of an important bargaining chip in any negotiations that might be arranged.

CHRONOLOGY

24 JANUARY 1966
North Vietnam Ho Chi Minh attacks American peace overtures in a statement demanding that Washington recognize the NLF 'as the sole representative of the people of South Vietnam' and adopt Hanoi's four-point peace formula as a basis for ending the war.
USA: Government In a memorandum to President Johnson, Defense Secretary McNamara recommends raising the number of US troops in Vietnam to more than 400,000 by year's end, but warns that planned deployments and increased bombing will not ensure military success.

24 JANUARY-6 MARCH 1966
Ground War In the largest search-and-destroy operation to date – Operation Masher/White Wing/Thang Phong II – the US 1st Air Cavalry Division, ARVN, and Korean forces sweep through Binh Dinh Province. It becomes the first large unit operation conducted across corps boundaries in late January, when the cavalrymen link up with Double Eagle, a USMC operation intended to destroy the 325A NVA Division. Altogether, reported enemy casualties number 2389.

25 JANUARY 1966
USA: Government President Johnson strongly suggests that he has decided to resume the bombing at a joint White House meeting of the National Security Council and a bi-partisan group of Congressional leaders. The administration also releases intelligence reports showing that North Vietnam is using the bombing pause to increase shipments of war supplies along the Ho Chi Minh Trail, infiltrate additional troops into South Vietnam, and repair bridges and other transport facilities damaged by US bombings.

26 JANUARY 1966
USA: Government There are new indications that the administration will soon resume air attacks against North Vietnam. In testimony before the House Foreign Affairs Committee, Secretary of State Rusk declares that despite the bombing suspension, Vietcong terrorists are still conducting bombings and assassinations in South Vietnam. Speaking at a New York luncheon the same day, special presidential adviser Maxwell Taylor (formerly Ambassador to South Vietnam) states that the reasons for halting the raids have been 'exhausted': 'We have shown friends

and foes the sincerity of our peaceful purposes.' Meanwhile, an Associated Press poll of 50 Senators shows that 25 favor a resumption of the bombing.

28 JANUARY 1966
USA: Military Defense Secretary McNamara receives a message from General William Westmoreland stating that in addition to the 443,000 troops already requested, he needs another 16,000 men by year's end.

30 JANUARY 1966
South Vietnam In honor of Tet, the Vietnamese lunar year, the Saigon government releases 21 North Vietnamese Army POWs.

31 JANUARY 1966
USA: Government In a televised address to the nation, President Johnson announces that after a 37-day bombing pause, the United States will resume air raids against North Vietnam. The President also discloses that he has instructed Ambassador Arthur Goldberg to ask the UN Security Council to arrange an international conference to end the conflict.

1 FEBRUARY 1966
North Vietnam In an article in the January issue of the North Vietnamese Communist Party journal *Hoc Tap*, General Giap asserts that US military efforts have failed 'to stabilize the very critical position of the puppet army and administration' of the South Vietnamese government. Moreover, Giap adds, US commitments elsewhere limit the number of men that can be sent to Vietnam.
North Vietnam Hanoi issues a statement declaring that because 'consideration of the United States war acts in Vietnam falls within the competence of the 1954 Geneva conference,' any UN Security Council resolution 'intervening in the Vietnam question would be null and void.'

2 FEBRUARY 1966
USA: Government Defense Secretary McNamara reveals that retired Lieutenant General James Gavin's proposal that US troops limit their activities to coastal enclaves had been considered by senior Pentagon officers, but that all had rejected it. Such a withdrawal would allow enemy forces to consolidate their hold on large areas of South Vietnam and leave ARVN units open to decimation.

3 FEBRUARY 1966
North Vietnam An article by Le Duc Tho in the North Vietnamese Communist Party newspaper *Nhan Dan* indicates that not all party members agree with Hanoi's war policy. Tho charges that some comrades 'have made an incorrect assessment of the balance of power between the enemy and us and of the enemy ruses. Now they entertain subjectivism and pacifism, slacken their vigilance and fail to get ideologically ready for combat.'

6-9 FEBRUARY 1966
USA: Government Accompanied by his leading political and military advisers, President Johnson confers with South Vietnamese Premier Nguyen Cao Ky in Honolulu. The talks conclude with issuance of a joint declaration in which the United States promises to help South Vietnam 'prevent aggression,' develop its economy and establish 'the principles of self-determination of peoples and government by the consent of the governed.' In his final statement on the discussions, Johnson warns conference participants that he will be monitoring their efforts to build democracy, improve education and health care, resettle refugees, and reconstruct South Vietnam's economy.

7 FEBRUARY 1966
South Vietnam South Vietnamese Rural Pacification Minister Nguyen Duc Thang reveals that current pacification efforts reach only 1900 of the country's 15,000 hamlets; he observes that it may require five to six years to place a typical province under government control.
Air War US planes strike a North Vietnamese training center at Dienbienphu.

8 FEBRUARY 1966
USA: Government In testimony before the Senate Foreign Relations Committee, retired Lieutenant General James Gavin declares that US policy in Vietnam is 'alarmingly out of balance'. Gavin also cautions that any further large increases in US troop strength in Vietnam could prompt Chinese intervention and even reopen the Korean front.

10 FEBRUARY 1966
USA: Government Former Ambassador to Russia and presidential adviser George Kennan tells the Senate Foreign Relations Committee that 'preoccupation with Vietnam' has caused the United States to neglect more important problems elsewhere. Kennan is particularly concerned about the war's impact on US-Soviet relations.
China Peking issues a statement charging that Soviet leaders are allied with the United States against China and that the principal purpose of Soviet aid to North Vietnam is 'to sow dissension in Sino-Vietnamese relations and to help the United States to realize its peace talks plot.'

11 FEBRUARY 1966
USA: Government At a Washington news conference, President Johnson discloses that additional US forces will be sent to Vietnam, but indicates that the build-up will be gradual. There are currently 205,000 US troops stationed in Vietnam.

14 FEBRUARY 1966
Terrorism Fifty-six South Vietnamese peasants are killed by three separate mine blasts along a road near Tuyhoa, 225 miles northeast of Saigon.

15 FEBRUARY 1966
France In response to a letter from Ho Chi Minh, asking that he use his influence to 'prevent perfidious new maneuvers' by the United States in Southeast Asia, President De Gaulle states that France is willing to do all that it can to end the war and outlines the French position on Vietnam: that the Geneva agreements should be enforced, that Vietnam's independence should be 'guaranteed by the nonintervention of any outside powers,' and that the Vietnamese government should pursue a 'policy of strict neutrality.'

16 FEBRUARY 1966
International The Central Committee of the World Council of Churches adopts a resolution proposing an immediate cease-fire in Vietnam.

17 FEBRUARY 1966
USA: Government In testimony before the Senate Foreign Relations Committee, General Maxwell Taylor states that a major US objective in Vietnam is to demonstrate that 'wars of liberation' are 'costly, dangerous and doomed to failure.' Discussing the American air campaign against North Vietnam, Taylor declares that its primary purpose is 'to change the will of the enemy leadership.'

22 FEBRUARY 1966
Ground War A USMC patrol rescues 23 men and 7 women from a Vietcong prison camp 350 miles northeast of Saigon.

23 FEBRUARY 1966
USA: Military The allied mission in Saigon discloses that 90,000 South Vietnamese soldiers deserted in 1965, a figure doubling that for 1964 and equalling almost 14 percent of ARVN troop strength; by contrast, the best estimates show that fewer than 20,000 Vietcong defected during the previous year.

25 FEBRUARY 1966
Ground War Elements of the US 1st Infantry Division uncover and destroy three Vietcong camps and an arms factory during an operation in the Boiloi forest.

27 FEBRUARY 1966
Ground War The 2nd Battalion, 1st US Marines, assault well-entrenched Vietcong forces to rescue an ARVN regiment in a battle northeast of Phubai.

1 MARCH 1966
USA: Government The Senate passes an emergency war funds bill after tabling an amendment by Senator Wayne Morse (D-OR) to repeal the Gulf of Tonkin Resolution.

2 MARCH 1966
USA: Military Defense Secretary McNamara denies charges that Vietnam requirements have overextended US military resources and asserts that the nation has the capacity to support a major buildup in Vietnam and remain 'fully capable of meeting our commitments elsewhere in the world.'

3 MARCH 1966
Air War In response to intelligence that the North Vietnamese are concentrating supplies USAF jets pound various Red River Valley transport facilities, 40 miles from the Chinese border.

4-8 MARCH 1966
Ground War USMC and ARVN forces engage NVA and Vietcong main-force units in the vicinity of Quang Ngai City; reported enemy casualties in this operation, code-named Utah/Lien Ket 26, number 632.

7 MARCH 1966
Air War In the heaviest air raids since the bombing began in February 1965, USAF and Navy planes fly an estimated 200 sorties against North Vietnam, hitting an oil storage area 60 miles southeast of Dienbienphu and a staging area 60 miles northwest of Vinh.

9 MARCH 1966
USA: Government The State Department issues a 52-page document contending that US intervention in Vietnam is legally justified under international law, the UN Charter and the US Constitution.
South Vietnam The US State Department reveals that as part of an effort to deny food to Vietcong guerrillas, South Vietnamese pilots flying US planes have destroyed 20,000 acres of crops.

9-11 MARCH 1966
Ground War Enemy troops wipe out the US Special Forces camp at A Shau near the Cambodian border after two days of savage fighting. Total disaster is averted when USMC helicopter pilots manage to lift out 12 of the 17 Green Berets and 172 of the 400-man Vietnamese garrison.

10 MARCH-15 APRIL 1966
South Vietnam Nine members of South Vietnam's ruling National Leadership Committee unanimously vote to dismiss the body's tenth member, Lieutenant General Nguyen Chanh Thi, and relieve him of his I Corps area command. Many consider Thi a potential rival of Premier Ky, whom Thi has often criticized for not eliminating government corruption. Thi is also a leading Buddhist, and his dismissal is followed by a violent Buddhist campaign intended to oust the Ky regime. Although Thi and Thich Tam Chau, the moderate chairman of the Unified Buddhist Church's Institute of Secular Affairs, urge their followers to practice restraint and nonviolence, the agitation continues into April and begins to exhibit a bitter anti-Americanism. Tensions gradually abate after 14 April, when Premier Ky and Chief-of-State Thieu pledge to dissolve the current ruling junta and hold elections for a constituent assembly with legislative powers. The statement mollifies Unified Buddhist Church leaders, and its issuance signals the beginning of an uneasy truce between Saigon and anti-government Buddhists.

12 MARCH 1966
USA: Domestic After a White House orienta-

Troopers of the 1st Cavalry Division (Airmobile) on patrol.

tion on the war, 38 state governors endorse a resolution declaring that they are fully committed to administration policies in Vietnam and 'believe the vast majority of Americans are, too.'

16 MARCH 1966
USA: Domestic Reporting on his observations during a visit to Vietnam, US Representative Clement Zablocki (D-WI) claims that for every Vietcong guerrilla killed in recent search and destroy missions, six civilians have died.

19 MARCH 1966
Korea The South Korean Assembly votes to send 20,000 additional troops to Vietnam; there are currently 21,000 ROK forces serving in the war zone.

20-24 MARCH 1966
Ground War In a reaction force operation (Texas/Lien Ket 28), US Marine, ARVN, and Vietnamese Marine Corps units retake An Hoa outpost in Quang Ngai Province; reported enemy casualties total 623.

22 MARCH 1966
USA: Military In a memorandum to Defence Secretary McNamara, Assistant Secretary John McNaughton contends that although air raids against North Vietnam bolster South Vietnamese morale and provide a bargaining chip for future negotiations, 'There is no evidence that they meaningfully reduce either the capacity or the will for the DRV to support the VC.' He recommends that the bombings be restricted to a narrow 'interdiction and verification zone' in Laos and that steps be taken to construct a physical anti-infiltration barrier.

23 MARCH 1966
China Peking rejects a Soviet invitation to a Communist Party congress and reiterates its charges that Soviet leaders are collaborating in a US 'plot' to impose peace talks on North Vietnam.

25 MARCH 1966
USA: Domestic At a New York City rally sponsored by the Veterans and Reservists to End the War in Vietnam, 15 veterans from both World Wars and the Korean conflict burn their discharge and separation papers.

1 APRIL 1966
Guerrilla War Vietcong commandos set off 200 pounds of explosives at a Saigon hotel housing US troops, heavily damaging the nine-story building and killing three Americans and four South Vietnamese.

CHRONOLOGY

4 APRIL 1966
Air War US F-4C Phantom bombers pound the main supply link between North Vietnam and Nanning, China, striking the Phulang-thuong railroad bridge, 25 miles northeast of Hanoi, and a road bridge 33 miles northeast of Hanoi; in a related raid, US planes destroy the Phutho railroad bridge northwest of Hanoi.

6 APRIL 1966
Ground War US Marines destroy a Vietcong hospital and storage complex during a sweep in the Saigon area.

7 APRIL 1966
Ground War Vietcong forces overrun a South Vietnamese outpost 25 miles south of Saigon.

9 APRIL 1966
USA: Government Fears that Premier Ky might be replaced by a neutralist Buddhist government prompt the administration to conduct a reassessment of Vietnam policy. Under Secretary of State George Ball urges that the United States cut its losses and 'halt the deployment of additional troops, reduce the level of air attacks on the North, and maintain ground activity at the minimum level required to prevent the substantial improvement of the Vietcong position.' Another position – supported by CIA analyst George Carver, Assistant Secretary of State William Bundy, and Defense Secretary McNamara – calls for a continuation of current policies. By and large, there is a striking absence of optimism, even among those who endorse present administration efforts.

11 APRIL 1966
USA: Government The administration publicly concedes for the first time that political turmoil in South Vietnam has begun to disrupt military operations by restricting the activities of ARVN forces.
USA: Military The USAF announces a new policy limiting pilots and crews stationed in Vietnam to a 12-month tour or 100 combat missions over North Vietnam; the USMC and Navy state that they will retain their current policy of no limit on the number of missions pilots fly over North or South Vietnam.

12 APRIL 1966
Ground War Vietcong guerrillas launch a mortar attack against Tansonnhut air base.

The assault kills seven US soldiers and South Vietnamese civilians, injures 160 US and ARVN troops, damages 23 helicopters and three planes and destroys two South Vietnamese transports.
Air War US B-52s from the Strategic Air Command base in Guam bomb North Vietnam for the first time in a raid on the Mugia Pass, the main route used to send supplies and infiltrators into South Vietnam through Laos.
China Peking claims to have downed a US 'attack plane' over the Liuchow Peninsula, north of Hainan Island. Although the US Department of Defense will not confirm the incident, it acknowledges that a tanker plane, flying from the Philippines to rejoin the carrier *Kitty Hawk* off South Vietnam, is 'overdue.'

13 APRIL 1966
USA: Domestic The Southern Christian Leadership Council adopts a resolution urging that the United States 'desist from aiding the military junta against the Buddhists, Catholics and students of Vietnam, whose efforts to democratize their government are more in consonance with our traditions than the policy of the military oligarchy.'

17 APRIL 1966
South Vietnam Speakers at a Bienhoa protest march involving thousands of Vietnamese Catholics demand that the government discipline Buddhist rioters.
Air War In the closest raids to Hanoi and Haiphong since the bombing began, US planes destroy two missile sites and damage the main railroad bridge between the two cities.

18 APRIL 1966
USA: Government In a speech to the Senate, majority leader Mike Mansfield (D-MT) declares that the current political crisis in Vietnam makes it urgent that the United States engage in direct talks with North Vietnam, Communist China, 'and such elements in South Vietnam as may be essential to the making and keeping of a peaceful settlement' of the war. Peking rejects the proposal.

21 APRIL 1966
South Vietnam The South Vietnamese government expels a group of six American pacifists, for seeking to stage anti-war demonstrations in Saigon.

Members of the 173rd Airborne await a helicopter which will evacuate their fallen comrade.

USA: Domestic In a lecture at the Johns Hopkins University School of Advanced International Studies, Senator William Fulbright (D-AR) warns that the US is 'succumbing to the arrogance of power.'

23 APRIL 1966

USA: Domestic Appearing at the annual convention of the Americans for Democratic Action Vice-President Humphrey states that the administration is willing 'to talk to anyone' at a Vietnam peace conference and would co-operate with 'any government the people of South Vietnam freely choose.'
Air War In an air clash over North Vietnam, involving at least 16 MiGs and 14 American planes, USAF F-4C Phantom jets shoot down two MiG-17s.

26 APRIL 1966

Air War In an air battle 20 miles from the Chinese border, a US pilot, firing Sidewinder missiles, downs a MiG-21, the most advanced Soviet-made fighter plane.

28 APRIL 1966

USA: Military The USAF announces that it is sending a team to Vietnam to investigate the efficiency and tactical usefulness of US missiles, after receiving a report that American pilots fired 11 rockets without scoring a hit during a recent clash with two MiG-21s.

29 APRIL 1966

Ground War US 1st Infantry Division troops uncover and destroy a huge cache of enemy war matériel during an operation in Tayninh Province.

USSR An article in the Soviet newspaper *Pravda* asserts that the television program 'Batman' is brainwashing American children into becoming 'murderers' in Vietnam.

2 MAY 1966

USA: Military In a speech before the US Chamber of Commerce, Defense Secretary McNamara reports that North Vietnamese infiltration into the South is up to 4500 men a month – three times the 1965 level.

3 MAY 1966

South Vietnam The Reverend Hoang Quynh, leader of South Vietnam's Roman Catholics, warns against early elections, because the Ky government controls only an estimated 10 percent of the country's territory.

5 MAY 1966

South Vietnam A 32-member committee, with representatives from all of South Vietnam's major religions, begins drafting an election law.

6 MAY 1966

USA: Military In a memorandum to Secretaries Rusk and McNamara, presidential adviser Walt Rostow contends that on the basis of US experience in Germany during World War II, a systematic bombing of North Vietnamese oil-storage facilities could seriously cripple the enemy war effort.

8 MAY 1966

South Vietnam Thich Thien Manh, cochairman of the leadership committee of the Unified Buddhist Church's Institute of Religious Affairs, issues a statement warning that Vietnamese Buddhists will launch another protest movement if the government does not hold elections as promised.

Air War A US military spokesman in Saigon reports that recent US air strikes have cut four major railroad links serving Hanoi, including a vital route to Nanning, China; reconnaissance photos also show that the raids have severed two main highways that share bridges with two of the rail lines.

10 MAY-30 JULY 1966

Ground War ARVN and 3rd Brigade, US 25th Infantry Division units conduct a border-screening and area-control operation, code-named Paul Revere/Than Phong 14, in Pleiku Province that claims 546 enemy casualties.

11 MAY 1966

Air War US Navy A-4 Skyhawk fighter-bombers destroy a surface-to-air missile site 10 miles northeast of Haiphong, as US air raids move increasingly closer to major North Vietnamese population centers.

13 MAY 1966

China Peking charges that five US planes 'flagrantly intruded' over Yunnan Province and downed a 'Chinese plane in training flight.'

Patrols routinely searched South Vietnamese villages for suspected Vietcong.

15 MAY-22 JUNE 1966

South Vietnam Premier Ky's decision to dispatch 1500 troops to Danang – which has been in a virtual state of rebellion since General Thi's dismissal on 10 March – touches off another wave of violent protest by Buddhist dissidents. During the next week, the Unified Buddhist Church issues a communiqué predicting that Ky's action will 'surely lead to civil war.' Besides deploying troops to troubled locales, the government also enters into negotiations with Buddhist leaders, and on 6 June the ruling National Leadership Committee of 10 generals is expanded to include 10 civilians. Two weeks later Premier Ky signs a decree setting 10 September as the date for the election of a constituent assembly with powers to appoint a civilian government. Meanwhile, on 22 June, a force of 300 pro-government troops takes control of Quangtri, the last remaining anti-government Buddhist stronghold.

17 MAY 1966

USA: Domestic Speaking at a Democratic Party fund-raiser in Chicago, President Johnson lashes out at critics of administration policy in Vietnam.

18 MAY 1966

USA: Domestic US Representative Melvin Laird (R-MI) states that because the administration is not providing the American public with precise information on planned troop deployments to Vietnam, a 'credibility gap' is developing. Informed sources report that 254,000 US troops are serving in Vietnam, and that another 90,000 are performing tasks directly concerned with the war.

19 MAY 1966

Casualties The US mission in Saigon reports that for only the third time since January 1961, more American than South Vietnamese soldiers were killed during the past week; the spokesman also discloses that the week's 6.1-to-1 kill ratio was the most favorable rating in nine months.

22 MAY 1966

USA: Military In a television interview, US Air Force Secretary Harold Brown reveals that President Johnson opposes widening the air war against North Vietnam, because such a move would not completely cut off North-South movement and might prompt Chinese intervention.

24 MAY 1966

Diplomatic UN Secretary General U Thant states that the United Nations does not possess sufficient influence to compel the warring sides in Vietnam to begin negotiations. Thant also urges that the NLF be allowed to participate in any peace talks which might be arranged.

30 MAY 1966

China Peking charges that US planes killed three persons during an attack on Chinese fishing boats north of the Gulf of Tonkin in international waters.

30-31 MAY 1966

Air War In the largest raids since air attacks on North Vietnam began in February 1965, US planes destroy five bridges, 17 railroad cars and 20 buildings in the Vinh-Thanhhoa area; other planes hit Highway 12 in four places north of the Mugia Pass and inflict heavy damage on the Yenbay arsenal and munitions storage area, 75 miles northeast of Hanoi. A US spokesman attributes the unprecedented number of planes taking part in the raids to an improvement in weather conditions.

2-21 JUNE 1966

Ground War The 1st Brigade, 101st Airborne Division, and ARVN units conduct an operation in Kontum Province (Hawthorne/Dan Tang 61) which claims 531 enemy casualties.

2 JUNE-13 JULY 1966

Ground War The US 1st Infantry Division and ARVN 5th Infantry Division account for 855 reported enemy casualties during Operation El Paso II in Binh Long Province.

4 JUNE 1966

USA: Domestic The Ad Hoc Universities Committee for the Statement on Vietnam takes a three-page advertisement in *The New York Times*, to urge the administration to cease all offensive military operations and 'evaluate seriously whether self-determination for the Vietnamese as well as our own national interest would not be best served by termination of our military presence.'

9 JUNE 1966

Ground War During the third day of a battle in Kontum Province, Captain W S Carpenter of the 101st Airborne Division calls for air strikes on his own position to prevent NVA attackers from wiping out his company. Carpenter and a handful of his men subsequently fight their way through machine-gun fire to safety. He will be recommended for the Congressional Medal of Honor.

USA: Military In a speech at Nashville, Major General Sternberg, commander of the 101st Airborne Division, states that an additional 500,000 men are needed to seal off South Vietnamese borders to enemy infiltration.

11 JUNE 1966
USA: Military Defense Secretary McNamara discloses that another 18,000 troops will be sent to Vietnam, raising the US commitment to 285,000 men.

15 JUNE 1966
USA: Military Intelligence sources report that two fresh NVA regiments have moved into the Central Highlands from Laos to serve as the vanguard for a coming enemy offensive.

17 JUNE 1966
South Vietnam In an effort to stabilize the economy and boost official morale, the South Vietnamese government devaluates its currency, lifts some controls on business transactions, and raises the salaries of military and civil servants.

18 JUNE 1966
USA: Military The JCS receive a new request from General Westmoreland, who states that he needs 542,588 troops for 1967 – an additional 111,588 men.

21 JUNE 1966
North Vietnam Hanoi reiterates its demand that an unconditional bombing halt precede negotiations, rejecting a new American proposal for the opening of peace talks.

21-27 JUNE 1966
Air War US planes strike North Vietnamese petroleum-storage facilities in a series of devastating raids.

23 JUNE 1966
USA: Domestic The American Baptist Association unanimously endorses a resolution denouncing 'the rash of protests and demonstrations' against US policy in Vietnam.

24 JUNE 1966
South Vietnam On a trip to Saigon to help develop civic-action programs, presidential adviser Robert Komer declares that pacification efforts should be given top priority. Komer's mission reflects renewed concern among US policymakers about the stability of the South Vietnamese government.

29 JUNE 1966
Air War US bombers attack fuel-storage installations near Hanoi and Haiphong, destroying an estimated 50 percent of North Vietnam's fuel supply. These are the first raids in the immediate vicinity of the two cities and constitute a major escalation of the air war.

30 JUNE 1966
USA: Government Congressional reaction to the Hanoi-Haiphong air attacks ranges from applause to denunciation. In voicing his approval, Senator Richard Russell (R-GA) states that the raids will reduce American casualties. Sixteen Democratic Representatives issue a joint statement declaring that the expanded air strikes commit the United States to 'a profoundly dangerous policy of brinkmanship' which challenges China.
China Peking calls the Hanoi-Haiphong raids a serious escalation of the war, warning that it is prepared for any eventuality.

1 JULY 1966
North Vietnam North Vietnamese authorities decide to evacuate all persons from Hanoi 'except those who have tasks of production or fighting, to assure the defeat of the United States war escalation.'
International The World Council of Churches in Geneva sends a cable to President Johnson saying that the latest bombing of North Vietnam is causing a 'widespread reaction' of 'resentment and alarm' among many Christians. Indian mobs protest the air raids on the Hanoi-Haiphong area with violent anti-American demonstrations in several cities. The Greek Orthodox Church of North and South America expresses 'wholehearted' support for the United States stand against all aggressors, particularly in Vietnam.

1-5 JULY 1966
Air War US Air Force and Navy jets carry out a series of raids on fuel installations in the Hanoi-Haiphong area. The Dongnham fuel dump, 15 miles northeast of Hanoi with 9 percent of North Vietnam's storage capacity, is attacked on 1 July. The Doson petroleum installation, 12 miles southeast of Haiphong,

is attacked for the second time on 3 July. The raids continue for two more days, as petroleum facilities near Haiphong, Thanhhoa, and Vinh are struck, and fuel tanks in the Hanoi area are hit. China reacts by calling the bombings 'barbarous and wanton acts that have further freed us from any bounds of restrictions in helping North Vietnam.'

4 JULY 1966
USA: Domestic The national convention of the Congress of Racial Equality (CORE) votes to adopt two resolutions on the Vietnam war. One calls for the withdrawal of US troops; the other attacks the draft as placing 'a heavy discriminatory burden on minority groups and the poor.'

5 JULY 1966
USA: Government During a press conference President Johnson expresses his disappointment at the reaction of a 'few' US allies. In New York, Australian Prime Minister Harold Holt says he agrees with Johnson that the bombing of the Hanoi-Haiphong area has been a 'military necessity.'

5-7 JULY 1966
USA: Domestic State and territorial governors meet in Los Angeles and adopt a resolution expressing 'support of our global commitments, including our support of the military defense of South Vietnam against aggression.' The vote is 49-1, with Governor Mark Hatfield (R-OR) casting the dissenting vote.

6 JULY 1966
International The seven active members of the Communist bloc's Warsaw Treaty military alliance announce their readiness to send 'volunteers' to aid North Vietnam in its fight against American 'aggression,' but only at Hanoi's request.

6-7 JULY 1966
Air War Fuel dumps are the main target again as US jets fly 80 missions within 65 miles of Hanoi. Next day, Navy jets from the carrier *Hancock* strike at fuel-storage tanks two miles northwest of Haiphong. Pentagon officials report that 80-90 percent of North Vietnam's fuel facilities have come under air attack and 55 percent have been destroyed.

6-9 JULY 1966
POWs Hanoi Radio reports that several captured US pilots have been paraded

Marines of the 4th Regiment attack North Vietnamese regulars near the DMZ.

through Hanoi and that angered mobs have demanded punishment for the 'American air pirates.' On 7 July and 9 July, statements are broadcast in which captured pilots allegedly confess their 'crimes' against North Vietnam.

7 JULY 1966
Great Britain The House of Commons defeats a Conservative motion (331-230) that would have committed Britain to support US policy on Vietnam without reservations. A government motion upholding Prime Minister Harold Wilson's support of American policy, but dissociating Britain from the US raids on the Hanoi-Haiphong area, is adopted 299-230.

8 JULY 1966
South Vietnam Premier Ky and Chief of Staff Thieu call for sterner military measures

including a land invasion of North Vietnam. Ky urges an allied invasion of North Vietnam even at the risk of a military confrontation with Communist China.

9 JULY-5 AUGUST 1966

USSR The Soviet Union sends a note to the US embassy in Moscow charging that the air strikes on the port of Haiphong endangered four Soviet ships that were in the harbor. The United States rejects the Soviet protest on 23 July, claiming that 'Great care had been taken to assure the safety of shipping in Haiphong.' A second Soviet note charging that a Russian ship had been hit by bullets during the raid on 2 August is also rejected by the US embassy (5 August).

11 JULY 1966

USA: Domestic A Harris survey taken shortly after the Hanoi-Haiphong raids shows that 62 percent of those interviewed favor the raids, 11 percent are opposed, and 27 percent are undecided. Of those polled, 86 percent felt the raids would hasten the end of the war.

Air war Officials in Saigon report increased air attacks in Laos to interdict North Vietnamese infiltration. More than 100 strikes a day are being carried out (this contrasts with fewer than 50 a day six months ago).

12-23 JULY 1966

POWs The National Committee for a Sane Nuclear Policy (SANE) and US Socialist Norman Thomas appeal to North Vietnam's President Ho Chi Minh on behalf of captured American pilots. On 15 July, 18 US Senators generally opposed to President Johnson's Vietnam policy sign a statement calling on North Vietnam to 'Refrain from any act of vengeance against American airmen.' Next day the UN Secretary General urges North Vietnam to exercise restraint in its treatment of American prisoners. Statements by North Vietnamese ambassadors in Peking and Prague assert (19 July) that the Americans will go on trial, but Ho gives assurances of a humanitarian policy toward the prisoners in response, he says, to the appeal he received from SANE and Norman Thomas.

15 JULY 1966

Air War A record 121 missions are flown by US planes against North Vietnam targets, as missile-launching sites in the Hanoi area are attacked. Navy jets strike at a fuel dump two miles from Vinh.

15 JULY-3 AUGUST 1966

Ground War A force of more than 8500 US Marines and 2500 South Vietnamese troops launch a massive drive (Operation Hastings) in Quangtri Province, in the vicinity of Cam Lo on east-west Route 9, below the Demilitarized Zone. The target of the allied force is a Communist force of 8000-10,000 soldiers, North Vietnam's 324-B Division. The division's mission, according to captured enemy troops, is to take control of Quangtri Province by destroying the South Vietnamese First Infantry Division, which is assigned to protect the area. After losing 824 men, North Vietnamese troops pull out of the area, and the operation ends 3 August.

22 JULY 1966

South Vietnam The government lodges a formal protest with the International Control Commission (ICC) accusing North Vietnam of using the DMZ to infiltrate troops into Quangtri Province. Specific mention is made of the North Vietnamese 324-B Division, the force engaged in Operation Hastings.

USA: Government Secretary of State Rusk says that bombing the port of Haiphong could lead to a 'larger war very quickly.' The bombing of Hanoi and Haiphong is part of the strategy of restricting Hanoi's ability to infiltrate men and supplies into South Vietnam.

USA: Domestic Senator J William Fulbright (D-AR) charges that President Johnson is following a policy of 'the United States taking on the role of policeman and provider for all non-Communist Asia.'

30 JULY-5 AUGUST 1966

Air War For the first time, US planes intentionally bomb targets in the DMZ. The initial target is a Communist camp and supply area a mile north of the Benhai River, the physical border between North and South Vietnam. The 15 B-52 jets fly from Guam, and return for five days to attack again.

31 JULY-13 AUGUST 1966

Cambodia Cambodia accuses the United States of bombing border villages and killing several people. A US spokesman first denies that the villages are in Cambodia, then admits that they are. The second raid (2 August) takes place as representatives of the International Control Commission (ICC) are en route to the area to inspect damage inflicted

Tanks were used throughout the war despite Vietnam's reputation for not being 'Tank Country.'

on Thlok and another village. The damage is confirmed, but a US Embassy spokesman in Saigon says on 12 August that all 'maps available to us show the two targets are in South Vietnam.' The statement expresses 'regret' for the error. Prince Sihanouk, Cambodian chief of state, cancels a scheduled September meeting with Ambassador-at-Large W Averell Harriman to discuss US-Cambodian diplomatic relations.

2 AUGUST 1966
Air War US bombers attack Haiphong's fuel installations for the third time; North Vietnam protests the raid to the International Control Commission. Department of Defense officials assert there are no homes or factories in the vicinity of the targets and that precision bombing techniques had been used.

3 AUGUST 1966
Air War US planes bomb a military headquarters 25 miles northeast of Haiphong, as well as barges and trucks at other locations.

3-7 AUGUST 1966
International The Association of Southeast Asia hold a conference in Bangkok in which Thailand, Malaysia, and the Philippines propose that a 'peace for Asia' committee be formed, composed solely of interested nations of the area and all the principals in the war in Vietnam.

3 AUGUST-18 SEPTEMBER 1966
Ground War US Marines begin a sweep just south of the DMZ (Operation Prarie) against three battalions of North Vietnam's 324-B Division. An additional 1500 Marines land from 7th Fleet ships off Quangtri Province (15 September) to assist. Two companies of the 4th Marine Regiment encounter a large North Vietnamese force three miles south of Zone 2: outnumbered, the Americans are unable to break out until 18 September. A total of 1099 enemy troops are fatal casualties.

4-6 AUGUST 1966
India India proposes expanding the International Control Commission (ICC) observations in the DMZ to prevent the spread of fighting there. Under the Indian plan, several teams of observers would move through the zone to investigate alleged violations of neutrality. The United States and Canada accept the proposal, but South Vietnam says its acceptance is conditioned on Hanoi's agreement.

CHRONOLOGY

6 AUGUST 1966
South Vietnam Thich Thien Hoa, acting chairman of the Secular Affairs Institute of the Unified Buddhist Church, appeals for international aid to halt what he calls religious persecution of the South Vietnamese people by Ky's government.

USA: Domestic Anti-war protests are staged across the country on the 21st anniversary of the atomic bombing of Hiroshima.

USA: Military A report from Saigon says that some military men in Washington want to increase US forces in Vietnam to 750,000 from the current 286,000. The reports are based on two recent assessments of the military situation. One assessment, from the Marine Corps, reportedly predicts that North Vietnam can continue to absorb casualties indefinitely at the current rate.

8 AUGUST 1966
Ground War A platoon of E Company, 4th Marines, is flown into an area four miles below the DMZ, near Cam Lo, to attack a large enemy unit. The Marines are unable to locate the NVA troops and are being flown out when the enemy opens fire, damaging two helicopters and stranding 21 Marines. Marine Captain Howard Lee returns by helicopter with seven of his men, and the Marines fight through the night until they are rescued the next day.

Air War A plane piloted by Major James H Kasler, regarded as the leading flyer of the war, and two other F-105 Thunderchiefs are shot down by North Vietnamese ground fire. Kasler bails out and is captured.

9 AUGUST 1966
Air War Two USAF jets mistakenly attack the villages of Truongtrung and Truongtay, about 80 miles south of Saigon; 63 people are killed and nearly 100 wounded.

10 AUGUST 1966
Ground War The 1st Battalion, 5th Marines, fights a tough battle against well-entrenched North Vietnamese troops in Quang Tin Province, six miles west of Tamky.

Thailand US-Thai co-operation in the Vietnam war is publicly acknowledged for the first time when a US-built air base in Sattihib is opened.

11 AUGUST 1966
Air War US jets fly 118 missions against targets in the Haiphong area. The Uongbi power plant is attacked, as well as 14 oil depots and storage areas.

13-14 AUGUST 1966
USA: Government General Westmoreland meets with President Johnson at the LBJ Ranch and gives a personal assessment of allied progress in the war.

16-19 AUGUST 1966
USA: Government The House Un-American Activities Committee holds hearings to investigate Americans who have aided the Vietcong. The purpose of the inquiry is to provide data for legislation to outlaw such aid. Disruptions begin even before the hearings get under way and the chairman of the subcommittee, Representative J R Pool (D-TX), instructs the police to remove demonstrators. After several disruptions by hostile witnesses, Pool announces (19 August) that the investigative stage of the hearings is completed. He says that the hearings revealed that key leadership of internal groups supporting the Vietcong is comprised of revolutionary, hard-core Communists. During the hearings, at least 50 people are arrested for disorderly conduct, including attorney Arthur Kinoy, who is forcibly ejected for arguing a legal point after being overruled by Chairman Pool. Seven other attorneys walk out of the hearing to protest.

19 AUGUST 1966
USA: Military After studying captured documents Sam Adams, a CIA analyst, will conclude that the irregular enemy forces (that is, those besides the Vietcong main force and North Vietnam Army units) are at least double the US military estimates. This will trigger off a debate still ongoing that pits the CIA's analysis and conclusions against the US military's.

23-29 AUGUST 1966
Sea War The US freighter *Baton Rouge Victory* strikes a Vietcong mine in the Long-tao River, 22 miles south of Saigon; seven crewmen are killed and one injured. The vessel is partially submerged, blocking traffic in the vital channel that links Saigon to the sea.

24 AUGUST 1966
USA: Government Secretary of State Rusk sends a letter to French Foreign Minister

Maurice Couve de Murville outlining US proposals for ending the war. US officials hope that President de Gaulle will use the proposals in discussions with Cambodian and North Vietnamese officials during his upcoming trip to Asia, but the French dismiss the letter as 'containing nothing new.'

26 AUGUST 1966

South Vietnam The Vietcong broadcast warnings that guerrilla forces are determined to frustrate the South Vietnamese elections scheduled for 11 September. The launching of terrorist attacks coincides with the start of the election campaign.

Air War US pilots fly a record 156 missions in strikes against North Vietnam's southern coast and panhandle region.

28 AUGUST 1966

Diplomatic The Vietcong's NLF president, Nguyen Huu Tho, invites other political groups to join the NLF in a coalition government for South Vietnam. Tho declares the NLF's goal is a broad and democratic coalition, and Tho lists three points as the basis for a political solution for South Vietnam, one of which is the withdrawal of all US troops and weapons.

USSR Three Soviet newspapers report that North Vietnam fighter pilots are being trained at an undisclosed Soviet air base to fly supersonic interceptors against US aircraft.

29 AUGUST 1966

China Peking charges that US planes sank a Communist Chinese merchant ship and damaged another in the Gulf of Tonkin, killing nine Chinese seamen and wounding seven.

30 AUGUST 1966

North Vietnam Hanoi Radio announces that Deputy Premier Le Thanh Nghi has signed an agreement by which Communist China will provide non-refundable economic and technical aid to North Vietnam.

1 SEPTEMBER 1966

North Vietnam Soviet leaders assure Ho Chi Minh that Soviet aid is being geared to 'the new phase of the war.'

1-2 SEPTEMBER 1966

Cambodia French President Charles de Gaulle, addressing an audience of 100,000 in Pnompenh, condemns US policy in Southeast Asia and argues that a withdrawal would bring the United States greater world influence than it could achieve by continuing its military commitment. He proposes that negotiations toward a settlement of the war could begin if the United States commited itself to withdrawing its troops by a certain date. On 2 September, Prince Norodom Sihanouk and de Gaulle sign a declaration calling for non-interference in the Indochinese peninsula by foreign nations.

4 SEPTEMBER 1966

USA: Government Assistant Secretary of State William Bundy on NBC-TV's 'Meet the Press,' rejects de Gaulle's proposal that the United States take the first step toward peace negotiations by announcing a timetable for the departure of its troops. Bundy says that the United States intends to withdraw when 'the North Vietnamese get out.' Bundy also officially reveals for the first time that the United States now has 25,000 military people in Thailand, principally air force units.

6 SEPTEMBER 1966

South Vietnam Thien Hoa of the Unified Buddhist Church issues an appeal to his followers to start a three-day hunger strike on 8 September protesting the elections to be held in South Vietnam on 11 September.

USA: Government President Johnson meets with officials of the Jewish War Veterans and complains about the many American Jewish leaders who oppose his policies on Vietnam. He expresses disappointment with this alleged lack of support in view of the Jews' concern about extended Communist rule and their interest in American support for other small nations like Israel.

Air War B-52 bombers strike twice at an infiltration route and a Communist base camp in the southern section of the DMZ.

6-9 SEPTEMBER 1966

USA: Domestic Three army privates are court-martialed at Fort Dix, New Jersey, for disobeying orders by refusing to go to Vietnam. The court rejects the defense argument that the Vietnam war is illegal and immoral.

7 SEPTEMBER 1966

Cambodia Two helicopters machine-gun the Cambodian border village of Sramar, killing one person and wounding two, according to Cambodian reports.

CHRONOLOGY

9 SEPTEMBER 1966
South Vietnam Reports in Saigon say that the United States plans a threefold increase in its aerial crop-destruction campaign against Vietcong-held territory.

11 SEPTEMBER 1966
South Vietnam Voters elect a 117-member Constituent Assembly that is to draft a new constitution and pave the way for a restoration of civilian government in 1967. The Vietcong seek to disrupt the election by terrorist attacks against civilians and government installations. About 81 percent of those registered voted.

12 SEPTEMBER 1966
Air War About 500 USAF planes attack coastal cities, transportation lines, supply areas, and missile sites in the heaviest air raid of the war on North Vietnam.

14 SEPTEMBER 1966
Ground War The South Vietnam village of Lienhoa, reportedly hostile, is burned by US troops. In the initial report of the incident, a US spokesman claimed that the village had been destroyed by air strikes and artillery fire, but newsmen on the scene alleged that members of the US First Cavalry Division set fire to the thatched-roof houses with matches. Before the village was burned, inhabitants had been warned to leave, and there are no reports of civilian casualties.

16-19 SEPTEMBER 1966
China Communist China charges that US planes have attacked Chinese territory at least twice during three intrusions. The Defense Ministry says that the planes bombed a main crossing point on the North Vietnamese border near Munankwan Pass on 5 September, and on 9 September strafed Chinese villages and commune members in the autonomous Kwangsi-Chuang region. The statement claims that Chinese planes had intercepted the US aircraft. Secretary of State Rusk replies on 16 September that US planes had encountered MiG fighters on 9 September about 30 miles south of the Chinese border. A State Department report of 19 September concedes the possibility of some intrusion into Chinese territory.

19 SEPTEMBER 1966
USA: Government House Republicans issue an update on a 1965 GOP White Paper on Vietnam in which they warn that the United States is becoming a 'full-fledged combatant' in a war that is becoming 'bigger than the Korean War.' The paper says that the United States must end the war 'more speedily and at a smaller cost, while safeguarding the independence and freedom of South Vietnam.'

USA: Domestic Twenty-two US scientists, including seven Nobel laureates, urge President Johnson to halt the use of anti-personnel and anti-crop chemical weapons.

UN Secretary General U Thant announces his willingness to continue in office after the expiration of his current five-year term. Thant proposes again his three-point plan for peace in Vietnam, including: (1) cessation of US bombing of North Vietnam, (2) de-escalation of the ground war in South Vietnam, (3) inclusion of the NLF in peace talks.

Diplomatic Pope Paul VI, in the encyclical *Christi Matri*, appeals to world leaders to end the Vietnam war.

19-23 SEPTEMBER 1966
Air War US B-52 bombers carry out heavy raids against North Vietnamese targets in the DMZ and the area just north of it. Targets include infiltration trails, troop concentrations, supply areas, and base camps. The purpose of the bombing is to interdict supplies destined for North Vietnamese forces.

22 SEPTEMBER 1966
USA: Government UN Ambassador Arthur Goldberg declares in an address to the General Assembly that the United States is prepared to halt the bombing of North Vietnam and begin de-escalation. Goldberg's speech is believed to indicate an acceptance of the major provisions of Thant's three-point proposal. His presentation of the administration's position differs from previous US statements only in its willingness to accept 'assurances' rather than 'evidence' of a North Vietnamese cutback and its readiness to accept the Vietcong at the bargaining table.

23 SEPTEMBER 1966
USA: Military The US military command discloses that US planes are defoliating dense jungle areas just south of the DMZ to deny cover and concealment to North Vietnamese Army units.

27 SEPTEMBER 1966
Air War Two US Marine jets mistakenly bomb the village of Hombe, five miles from

Quangngai, killing at least 35 civilians. The United States halts air strikes against the southeastern corner of the DMZ to allow the International Control Commission to resume patrols in the area.

30 SEPTEMBER 1966
USA: Domestic Former President Dwight D Eisenhower tells newsmen in Chicago that he favors using 'as much force as we need to win the war in Vietnam.'

1 OCTOBER-26 DECEMBER 1966
Air War US planes attack the city of Phuly, about 35 miles south of Hanoi. About 40 civilians are killed or wounded. After the bombings, Phuly is visited by Harrison Salisbury, assistant managing editor of *The New York Times*, who had gone to North Vietnam with the authorization of both Hanoi and Washington. Salisbury reports (on 25 December) the damage he observed in Phuly and Namdinh, another city he visited. According to his report, all the homes and buildings in Phuly (population 20,000) were destroyed. Next day, the US State Department concedes that North Vietnamese civilians had been bombed accidently during missions against military targets, but insists that 'All possible care is taken to avoid civilian casualties.'

2-3 OCTOBER 1966
USSR The Soviet Defense Ministry newspaper, *Krasnaya Zuezda*, reports that Russian military experts have come under fire during United States raids against North Vietnam missile sites while they were training the North Vietnamese in the use of Soviet-made anti-aircraft missiles. This is the first public acknowledgment that Soviets have trained North Vietnamese missile crews and observed them in action.

2-25 OCTOBER 1966
Ground War United States helicopter observers spot an estimated 300 enemy troops marching west in the central coastal area, 28 miles northwest of Quinhon and 305 miles northwest of Saigon. Two First Cavalry Division companies are sent in pursuit and kill more than 170 enemy troops. The Communist forces then flee east toward the South China Sea coast, where they come under heavy fire from South Vietnamese and South Korean soldiers, as well as US troops. The allied forces surround the Communists as US and

South Vietnamese patrol boats stationed offshore prevent escape by sea.

3 OCTOBER 1966
USSR Soviet Deputy Premier Vladimir N Novikov announces that he has negotiated an agreement with North Vietnam by which the Soviets will provide an undisclosed amount of economic and military assistance.

4 OCTOBER 1966
Air War B-52 bombers pound supply and staging areas in the DMZ. Pilots report destroying 25 structures.
Diplomatic Pope Paul VI addresses 150,000 people in St Peter's Square in Rome and calls for an end to the war in Vietnam through negotiations.

6-11 OCTOBER 1966
Diplomatic British Foreign Secretary George Brown outlines a plan, largely a restatement of previous British proposals, to end the war in Vietnam at a Labor Party conference. Brown renews the suggestion that the Soviet Union, as cochairman of the 1954 Geneva Conference, join Britain in reconvening the conference to seek an end to the war.

10-14 OCTOBER 1966
USA: Government US Defense Secretary Robert S McNamara makes his eighth fact-finding mission to South Vietnam. During his visit, McNamara confers with General Westmoreland, Ambassador Lodge, various military leaders, and South Vietnam's Premier Ky and Chief of State Thieu. At a news conference in Saigon (13 October), McNamara says that he found military operations have 'progressed very satisfactorily since 1965,' but conceded that 'progress is very slow indeed' in the pacification program.

13 OCTOBER 1966
USA: Government President Johnson, speaking in Washington, rules out any cessation of the bombing in North Vietnam in connection with a conference planned in Manila.
Air War US planes fly a record 173 multi-plane missions over North Vietnam's panhandle region, bombing radar sites, storage areas, transportation facilities, and missile centers.

15 OCTOBER-26 NOVEMBER 1966
Ground War A heavy concentration of US troops moves into Tayninh Province near the

Two marines assist a team from the Vietnamese Cultural Civil Action to repair a village bridge.

Cambodian border, 40-60 miles north of Saigon, on 15 October and sweeps the area in search of Vietcong (Operation Attleboro). On 3 November, they fight one of the war's biggest battles, involving the US First and 25th Infantry Divisions, the 196th Light Infantry Brigade, the 173rd Airborne Brigade, and at least two South Vietnamese battalions. Engagements continue through 12 November. At the height of the fighting, 20,000 allied troops – a record number – are committed. Communist troops are identified as major elements of the 9th Vietcong Division, the guerrillas' best-trained and best-equipped unit, and the 101st North Vietnamese regiment; 1100 of them will die in the offensive. Communist resistance is strong, because the Tayninh Province sector has been the site of the principal Vietcong command center for guerrilla operations in South Vietnam and the central office of the National Liberation Front.

17 OCTOBER 1966

Air War The United States resumes air strikes in the southeastern DMZ on 27 September,

after a pause for the International Control Commission (ICC) patrol. A US official attributes the resumption of bombing to the fact that the Hanoi regime has 'consistently rebuffed' efforts by ICC observers to enter and patrol that sector of the zone.

17 OCTOBER-2 NOVEMBER 1966

Diplomatic President Johnson leaves Washington for a 17-day trip to seven Asian and Pacific nations and a conference scheduled in Manila. En route to Manila, Johnson visits New Zealand and then Australia. In Melbourne, he encounters anti-war demonstrators. In Manila, Johnson meets with other allied leaders (24-25 October), and they pledge to withdraw troops from Vietnam within six months if North Vietnam 'withdraws its forces to the North and ceases infiltration of South Vietnam.' A communiqué signed by the seven participants includes a four-point 'Declaration of Peace' that stresses the need for a 'peaceful settlement of the war in Vietnam and for future peace and progress' in the rest of Asia and the Pacific. The signators include the United

States, Australia, New Zealand, South Korea, South Vietnam, Thailand, and the Philippines. President Johnson flies to South Vietnam on 26 October for a surprise 2½-hour visit with United States troops at Camranh.

21 OCTOBER 1966
Guerrilla War A terrorist mine explodes in the marketplace in Traon, a town in the Mekong Delta 75 miles southeast of Saigon, killing 11 persons and wounding 54.

21-22 OCTOBER 1966
South Vietnam Thich Tam Chau, head of the Institute of Secular Affairs of the Unified Buddhist Church, calls a meeting of church officials to reassert his control over the institute. Tam Chau, a moderate, has been challenged by militants who accuse him of 'treason' in his handling of the Buddhists' anti-government campaign during the spring.

24 OCTOBER 1966
Guerrilla War A bus detonates a Vietcong mine on a road 18 miles north of Hué, killing 15 Vietnamese civilians and injuring 19.

25 OCTOBER-23 NOVEMBER 1966
Sea War The US Navy increases attacks against North Vietnamese coastal shipping and shore installations in the Donghoi area. The four-week series of attacks begins when two US destroyers shell the North Vietnamese coast north of Donghoi after coming under fire from Communist coastal guns. By 23 November, more than 230 Communist vessels are reported sunk.

25 OCTOBER-13 FEBRUARY 1966
Ground War Operation Thayer II begins on 25 October in Binhdinh Province and ends almost four months later with a reported 1744 fatal Communist casualties.

26 OCTOBER 1966
Sea War In the Gulf of Tonkin, fire breaks out on the hangar deck of the 42,000-ton US aircraft carrier *Oriskany*, when a locker filled with night-illumination magnesium flares bursts into flame. The fire spreads quickly through most of the ship; 43 men are killed and another 16 injured. Crewmen throw 300 bombs overboard as a safety measure. After three hours, the fire is brought under control. Four jet bombers and two helicopters are destroyed.

27 OCTOBER-9 NOVEMBER 1966
Diplomatic US Ambassador-at-Large Averell Harriman visits ten nations to explain results of the Manila conference and the current US evaluation of the situation in Southeast Asia. Harriman, acting as President Johnson's personal emissary, visits leaders in Ceylon, Indonesia, India, Pakistan, Iran, Italy, France, West Germany, Britain, and Morocco. He reports to the President on 11 November and says later, at a news conference, that 'Every country in the world wants to see peace with the exception of Red China and North Vietnam.' There were indications, though, 'that Hanoi is willing to talk provided we do certain things.'

27 OCTOBER 1966
China The Communist Chinese news agency, Hsinhua, assails the decisions reached at the Manila conference and calls the allies' troop-withdrawal proposal 'out-and-out blackmail and shameless humbug.'

30 OCTOBER 1966
South Vietnam A South Vietnamese government announcement says that the National Police have smashed a guerrilla plot to blow up US and Vietnamese buildings in Saigon during National Day celebrations on 1 November.

31 OCTOBER 1966
Sea War US Navy patrol boats and helicopters prevent a Vietcong flotilla from crossing the Mekong Delta near Mytho. They sink 35 junks and sampans.

1 NOVEMBER 1966
Guerrilla War Two separate terrorist attacks occur in the center of Saigon. In the first incident, a 75-mm recoilless rifle is fired at a crowd of civilians waiting for the start of a parade celebrating South Vietnam's National Day. In the second incident, a Vietcong grenade is thrown at a crowded bus terminal in the city's central market. At least eight persons are killed in the two attacks.
Sea War A US minesweeper strikes a mine in the Longato River. The crew suffer casualties, as guerrillas fire on the sinking boat.

3 NOVEMBER 1966
USA: Military The Department of Defense drafts plans for intensified bombing of North Vietnam aimed at forcing Hanoi to negotiate and hindering North Vietnamese efforts to

transport materials to units in South Vietnam. Pentagon leaders admit disappointment that attacks on North Vietnam's oil facilities have done little to slow movement of supplies.

USA: Domestic Former Vice-President Richard Nixon criticizes the Manila conference, particularly the pledge to withdraw military forces from Vietnam if North Vietnam withdraws its forces.

4 NOVEMBER 1966

USA: Government President Johnson, reacting to Richard Nixon's criticism, says that Nixon does not 'serve his country well' by criticism, and that he confuses rather than clarifies issues. Johnson also cautions the North Vietnamese against interpreting the results of the Congressional elections as a test of administration policy on Vietnam.

Sea War Fire breaks out aboard the carrier *Franklin D Roosevelt* five decks below the flight deck. Eight enlisted men are killed.

5 NOVEMBER 1966

USA: Government Secretary of Defense McNamara confers with President Johnson before a press conference in which he says that no 'sharp increases' are planned in the number of air attacks in Vietnam (current monthly average is 25,000 sorties). During the press conference, which is held three days before the Congressional elections, McNamara states that the troop buildup in Vietnam will continue in 1967. He adds that the number of men drafted in the four-month period ending March 1967 will be 'significantly smaller' (80,000-100,000) than in the four-month period ending in November 1966 (estimated at 161,000).

7 NOVEMBER 1966

USA: Domestic Defense Secretary McNamara visits Harvard University to address a small group of students. As he leaves a dormitory, about 100 anti-administration demonstrators shout at him and demand a debate. When McNamara tries to speak, supporters of the Students for a Democratic Society shout him down. McNamara then tries to leave, but 25 demonstrators throw themselves under his automobile. Police finally escort the Secretary of Defense from the campus.

11 NOVEMBER 1966

Diplomatic The British Council for Peace in Vietnam opens in London, and a letter sent to council member Lord Brockway on 19 October is made public. In it, Secretary General of the United Nations U Thant calls for a final and unconditional halt in US air attacks on the North and disagrees with the conditional proposal advanced by Ambassador Goldberg at the UN on 22 September.

12 NOVEMBER 1966

South Vietnam A *New York Times* report from Saigon says that because of theft, bribery, black marketing, currency manipulation, and waste, about 40 percent of US economic and military assistance sent to South Vietnam has failed to reach its proper destination.

13 NOVEMBER 1966

USA: Domestic Freedom House issues a document titled *A Crucial Turning Point in Vietnam*, signed by 138 prominent Americans, which chides critics of the administration's Vietnam war policy for failing to make 'the distinction between responsible dissent and unfounded attacks upon our society.' The document urges 'men of stature in the intellectual, religious, and public service communities' to withdraw their support of the fantasies of extreme critics of the Johnson administration's policies.

14 NOVEMBER 1966

USA: Military US Navy Captain Archie C Kuntze, is found guilty by a general court-martial in California on a charge of 'conduct unbecoming of an officer and gentleman' while stationed in Saigon. (*The New York Times* had reported on 12 November that at least 400 US servicemen and civilians faced charges of corruption and black-market activities.)

15 NOVEMBER 1966

USA: Domestic General Earle Wheeler, Chairman of the Joint Chiefs of Staff, addresses a gathering at Brown University; some 60 students walk out to protest his defense of US involvement in Vietnam. Some of those who remain shout and heckle Wheeler, and others storm the stage. Outside, over 100 students from Brown University continue the protest.

17 NOVEMBER 1966

USA: Government Secretary of Defense McNamara sends a report to President Johnson advising that based on Pentagon

US Army advisors coach a Vietnamese Ranger on the use of a submachine gun.

calculations, previous US reinforcements have not brought sufficient increases in enemy casualties to justify additional heavy reinforcements in Vietnam. McNamara's secret report to the President is a challenge to General Westmoreland's strategy of attrition. The administration does not share McNamara's pessimism, and his recommendations are rejected.

18 NOVEMBER 1966

USA: Domestic The National Conference of Catholic Bishops, meeting in Washington, declares that the US 'presence in Vietnam is justified' and expresses support for the Johnson administration.

Sea War Two US destroyers shell a North Vietnamese radar site and 12 cargo boats two miles north of the DMZ in the Donghoi area.

CHRONOLOGY

23 NOVEMBER 1966
Sea War Two US destroyers sink or damage 47 of 60 Communist supply barges off the southern panhandle of North Vietnam.

30 NOVEMBER-1 DECEMBER 1966
China Communist China reports that two US planes have dropped 20 bombs on a fleet of Chinese fishing boats, killing 14 crewmen, wounding 20 and sinking five boats in international waters in the Gulf of Tonkin. A second raid takes place the next day.

30 NOVEMBER-22 DECEMBER 1966
South Vietnam The South Vietnam Constituent Assembly draws up draft articles for a new constitution. On 15 December, the Assembly approves a proposal for the future civil regime to be headed by a popularly elected president, also a proposal empowering the president, rather than the legislature, to appoint a premier. On 21 December, the assembly approves the establishment of a bicameral legislature made up of a senate and a house of representatives.

1 DECEMBER 1966
South Vietnam An American force of several battalions and a battalion of South Vietnamese Rangers begins guarding Saigon for the first time, in the wake of Vietcong terrorist attacks on the outskirts of the city.

2 DECEMBER 1966
Air War A truck-park five miles south of Hanoi is hit by Navy jets in the closest raid to the city since 29 June. The Hagia fuel storage depot, 14½ miles north of Hanoi, is bombed by 50 to 60 US F-4C Phantom jets. Their Thunderchief escorts destroy four radar missile sites and an anti-aircraft emplacement. About 40 miles northeast of Hanoi other Navy pilots hit a second fuel dump. During the day, eight US planes were downed, a record for a single day. The number of planes lost over North Vietnam is now 435.

2-14 DECEMBER 1966
Diplomatic US Ambassador Henry Cabot Lodge asks Janusz Lewandowski, Polish representative on the International Control Commission, to inform Hanoi of the United States' willingness to meet with North Vietnamese officials. On or about 4 December, Polish Foreign Minister Adam Rapacki discloses that Hanoi has accepted the proposal to take part in talks at the ambassadorial level. Hanoi does not repeat its usual demand for a cessation of US raids on the North as a condition for entering the talks. However, North Vietnam refuses to attend after US planes carry out raids in the Hanoi area on 13-14 December.

4 DECEMBER 1966
Guerrilla War A Vietcong unit penetrates the 13-mile defense perimeter around Saigon's Tansonnhut Airport, then shells the field in a 4½-hour attack. US and South Vietnamese security guards finally drive off the attackers killing 18 of them but also suffer casualties, and a US RF-101 reconnaissance jet is badly damaged. The guerrillas return that same night and resume the attack, until security guards kill 11 more Vietcong and repel the others.

Air War US fighter-bombers strike the Yenvien railroad yard six miles northeast of Hanoi. The Hagia fuel storage depot, 14½ miles north of the city, is hit again.

5 DECEMBER 1966
Sea War The US destroyer *Ingersoll* exchanges fire with a North Vietnamese coastal battery 11 miles northeast of Donghoi and is slightly damaged.

7 DECEMBER 1966
Terrorism Tran Van Van, 58, a prominent member of the South Vietnamese Constituent Assembly, is shot to death by two Vietcong terrorists while driving to an Assembly meeting in Saigon. One suspect, arrested and identified as Vo Van Em, says he was recruited for the assassination by the National Liberation Front.

8 DECEMBER 1966
USA: Military US Air Force Secretary Harold Brown releases a detailed assessment of the American air war over North Vietnam stating that the strikes have caused 'serious manpower, supply and morale problems' for North Vietnam but are still not severe enough to persuade Hanoi to enter peace talks.

8-9 DECEMBER 1966
POWs The International Red Cross (IRC) announces in Geneva that North Vietnam has rejected a proposal by President Johnson for joint discussion of fair treatment and possible exchange of war captives held by both sides. President Johnson had first broached the plan

on 20 July at a news conference, and the IRC had submitted the proposal to Hanoi in July. The US State Department confirms next day that the IRC had acted as Washington's intermediary.

8-14 DECEMBER 1966

Diplomatic Pope Paul VI proposes that the two separate 48-hour cease-fires (at Christmas and Tet) be merged 'into a single continuous period of time' to bring about an armistice that would be followed by 'sincere negotiations which will lead to peace.' On 14 December, White House Press Secretary Bill Moyers says the United States is willing to discuss the proposal if the Communists show interest.

9 DECEMBER 1966

USA: Domestic The General Assembly of the National Council of Churches, meeting at Miami Beach, approves a statement urging the administration to consider a halt in air strikes on North Vietnam.

10 DECEMBER 1966

USA: Domestic Governor-elect Ronald Reagan (R-CA) declares that he favors 'an all-out total effort' in Vietnam.

13-14 DECEMBER 1966

Air War US planes bomb the Yenvien railroad yard, six miles northeast of Hanoi and attack a truck depot two miles south of the city. Reaction to the raids, especially from Communist countries, is immediate. USSR and East German news agencies report that for the first time US planes are bombing residential areas in the city of Hanoi and causing civilian casualties. TASS, the Soviet news agency, says that US planes had bombed workers' districts along the Red River embankment. The Hanoi correspondent of the French press agency reports that the village of Caudat, outside Hanoi, has been 'completely destroyed by bombs and fire.' A spokesman at the US embassy in Saigon says on 14 December that 'If by some remote chance Hanoi was struck by bombs, it was an accident.'

14-16 DECEMBER 1966

USA: Government Robert J McCloskey of the US State Department meets with newsmen and at first denies that US planes had bombed Hanoi; he then adds: 'I took the question to mean that these are civilian targets or popu-lation centers . . . which one generally associates when talking about a city.' When asked whether these targets were inside Hanoi's limits, McCloskey says 'I don't know . . . how one defines what the city limits are.' On 15 December, the State Department reaffirms its position that 'There is no fixed geographical definition which can be called the city limits of Hanoi.' On 16 December, General Westmoreland issues a statement from Saigon that says, 'A complete review of pilot reports of the 13-14 December air strikes on Vandien and Yenvien showed that all ordnance expended by US air-strike aircraft was in the military target areas. None fell in the city of Hanoi.'

16 DECEMBER 1966

USA: Government The White House announces the appointment of David E Lilienthal to head the American section of a joint United States-South Vietnam effort to map long-range plans for South Vietnam's economy.

18-20 DECEMBER 1966

Air War US B-52s from Guam bomb North Vietnamese supply bases and staging areas just south of the DMZ, where the reorganized North Vietnamese 324-B division is believed to be massing for a new drive.

20 DECEMBER 1966

China The Chinese Communist Party newspaper *Jenmin Jih Pao* calls on North Vietnam and the Vietcong to spurn negotiations with the United States and to continue the war. The newspaper charges that the Soviet Union, 'in collusion with the United States' is 'resorting to the dirty tricks of forcing peace talks by coercion, inducement or persuasion . . . with the aim of compelling the Vietnamese people to lay down their arms and give up the struggle!'

23 DECEMBER 1966

USA: Government US intelligence sources confirm reports that North Korean pilots are in North Vietnam, presumably to train North Vietnamese pilots. A previous report indicated the presence of 100 new MiGs in North Vietnam, increasing the MiG force there to about 200.

23-28 DECEMBER 1966

USA: Domestic The Roman Catholic Archbishop of New York and military vicar of the

Ho Chi Minh, touring the anti-aircraft batteries outside Hanoi, with General Van Tien Dung.

US armed forces for Roman Catholics, Francis Cardinal Spellman, visits US servicemen in South Vietnam. In an address at Mass in Saigon, Spellman says: The Vietnamese conflict is 'a war for civilization – certainly it is not a war of our seeking. It is a war thrust upon us – we cannot yield to tyranny.' Anything 'less than victory is inconceivable.' On 26 December, Spellman tells US soldiers that they are in Vietnam for the 'defense, protection and salvation not only of our country, but ... of civilization itself.' Next day, Vatican sources express displeasure with Spellman's statements in Vietnam. One source says 'The Cardinal did not speak for the Pope or the Church.'

24 DECEMBER 1966
Air War A US cargo plane en route from Japan crashes in the village of Hoavang, near the Danang air base, killing over 100 civilians and all four crewmen.

25-26 DECEMBER 1966
USA: Military Harrison Salisbury, assistant managing editor of *The New York Times*, files a 25 December report describing US bombing destruction in several North Vietnamese cities. Salisbury states that Namdinh, about 50 miles southeast of Hanoi, has been bombed repeatedly by US planes since 28 June 1965. Salisbury also reports on destruction in the city of Phuly. Salisbury's press reports cause a stir in Washington where, it is reported, Pentagon officials express irritation and contend that he is exaggerating the damage to civilian areas. On 26 December, the US Defense Department concedes that North Vietnamese civilians have been bombed accidently by American pilots during missions against military targets. The spokesman restates administration policy that air raids are confined to military targets but add that 'It is sometimes impossible to avoid all damage to civilian areas.'

27-31 DECEMBER 1966
Ground War US planes overfly the eastern fringe of the U Minh Forest in the Mekong Delta, 125 miles southwest of Saigon, dropping hundreds of tons of bombs and napalm. An estimated 1200 South Vietnamese paratroopers are then dropped from allied Air Force planes. Some 6000 combined South Vietnamese troops attack a Vietcong force in the forest, considered one of the best-fortified Vietcong strongholds in South Vietnam. On

29 December the US destroyer *Herbert J Thomas* shells suspected Vietcong positions in the area for seven hours. The operation ends on 31 December with 104 Vietcong reported killed and 18 captured.

29 DECEMBER 1966
USA Military: Assistant Defense Secretary Arthur Sylvester says that the North Vietnamese city of Namdinh has been hit by US planes 64 times since mid-1965, and that the air strikes were directed only against military targets: railroad yards, a warehouse, petroleum storage depots, and a thermal power plant. He denounces *New York Times* correspondent Harrison Salisbury's reports on the Namdinh air raids as 'misstatements of facts.'
USA Domestic: Student-body presidents from 100 United States colleges and universities sign an open letter to President Johnson expressing anxiety and doubt over US involvement in Vietnam; they warn that many loyal youths may prefer prison to participation in the war.

30 DECEMBER 1966
Air War Hanoi charges that US planes bomb North Vietnamese residential and industrial targets in Vinhlin, Hatianh, Nghean, Thanhhoa, and Namha, and that US warships shell residential areas in the Quangbinh Province town of Quangtrac.

31 DECEMBER 1966
South Vietnam A New Year's truce begins and will extend to 2 January 1967. Both North and South Vietnam will charge each other with many violations during the truce.
USA: Government President Johnson responds to the controversy over North Vietnamese civilian casualties during US bombing raids by saying that there has been no change in orders 'to bomb only military targets.'
UN Secretary General U Thant, in a New Year's message, renews his plea to the United States for an unconditional cessation of the bombing of North Vietnam; in reply to Ambassador Goldberg's request that Thant use his position to obtain a cease-fire, he urges extension of the New Year's truce.
State of the War As the Vietnam War came to dominate the world's thoughts and actions during the year, opposing allied and Communist military forces could only intensify their conflict and augment their manpower and matériel. There are now approximately 1,138,000 men in the allied forces. During

CHRONOLOGY

1966, the United States has increased its forces in Vietnam from 180,000 to 280,000; there are also approximately 60,000 American servicemen aboard ships operating off Vietnam and an estimated 35,000 US servicemen in Thailand. South Vietnamese forces now number about 750,000 men, divided equally between regular army units and police, irregular, and regional-defense and militia units. South Korean forces were increased by 25,000 men this year, bringing their total in South Vietnam to 46,000. Australia contributed another 550 men, Thailand 180, New Zealand 150, and the Philippines 1000. Estimates of Communist forces in South Vietnam and their composition vary widely, but on 23 January 1967 Secretary of Defense McNamara will testify before a Senate committee that there are some 275,000 Communist troops, including 45,000 North Vietnamese regulars. Infiltration of personnel and supplies from the North continues unabated, despite the massive bombing raids on the Ho Chi Minh Trail: it is estimated that the Vietcong need only about 15 tons of supplies per day from the north to sustain their side of the war. Since the Soviet Union and China provide North Vietnam with 6000 tons of aid per day, only a small percentage need be brought down the trail, where most Vietnamese casualties are due to disease, rather than to US bombing.

Operation Rolling Thunder is now in overdrive. The total number of individual flights in 1966 was 148,000; the total bomb tonnage was 128,000; the number of aircraft lost was 318; and direct operational costs were $1,200,000,000. The CIA will produce a study in January 1967 that estimates North Vietnamese casualties from the bombing raids at 24,000 – of which 80 percent are civilian. It has been estimated that the bombing is costing the United States nearly $10 for every dollar's worth of damage done to the North Vietnamese.

The US Department of Defense reports that 5008 US servicemen have been killed and 30,093 wounded in the 1966 fighting, for a total of 6664 Americans killed and 37,738 wounded since 1 January 1961. Black Americans are beginning to suffer proportionately higher combat fatalities than their white comrades: blacks comprise about 10 percent of American forces now in Vietnam, but they are suffering about 16 percent of the fatalities. South Vietnam's combat fatalities totaled 19,110 during 1966, which brings the total to 43,582 since 1961. The South Vietnamese claim to have killed 61,631 Vietcong in combat this year (and a total of 168,631 since 1961). The North Vietnamese, meanwhile, claim that 240,000 allied troops have been killed in 1966, including 100,000 Americans.

But the war's cost is being measured in ways other than combat body counts. Individual servicemen on both sides are rejecting the war, and desertions are rising among both South Vietnamese and Vietcong troops. Some 116,858 South Vietnamese troops are reported to have deserted in 1966 – about 20 percent; this figure will remain relatively constant. In January 1967, a US spokesman will report that 20,242 Vietcong defected in 1966, raising to over 48,000 the number of Vietcong who have allegedly rwsponded to Saigon's *Chieu Hoi* ('Open Arms') program, which began in 1963.

More and more civilians are fleeing the areas of destruction. Saigon's population has exploded from perhaps half a million a few years ago to about 3 million, many of whom are war refugees; 200,000 juveniles are said to roam the streets. South Vietnam's civilian population has become the main victim of the war. A survey by a US study team has reported that South Vietnamese hospitals admitted 2510 war-wounded civilians in the month of December 1966; if a standard ratio of 2:1 is used (one dead for every two wounded), civilian deaths would number some 1250 a month, or almost 15,000 a year. Another study reveals that during one seven-month period this year, 3015 Rural Development personnel were murdered or kidnapped by the Vietcong.

1 JANUARY 1967

North Vietnam The Vietcong propose that the Tet truce be extended to 15 February.

USA: Military American troop strength in South Vietnam is increased to 380,000 with the arrival in Vungtau of 5000 soldiers of the 9th Infantry Division.

France French President Charles de Gaulle, in a New Year's message, calls on the United States to end its 'detestable intervention in Vietnam' by withdrawing its troops.

2 JANUARY 1967

USA: Government The New Year's truce, which began at 0700 on 31 December 1966, ends at 0700 today: the United States announces resumption of normal operations.

An infantryman waits for the rest of his squad to catch up during Operation Eagle Flight.

Air War In what is described as the biggest air battle of the war, US Air Force F-4 Phantom jets down seven Communist MiG-21s. The Phantoms were flying cover for F-105 Thunderchiefs attacking surface-to-air missile sites in the Red River Delta.

3 JANUARY 1967
North Vietnam In an interview with the *New York Times*, North Vietnam's Premier Pham Van Dong says that the North Vietnamese four-point plan for ending the war 'constitutes the basis for a settlement but should not be considered conditions.' Dong's apparent shift from his previous position raises international speculation as to whether Hanoi is modifying its conditions for ending the war.

4 JANUARY 1967
North Vietnam In an interview with Harrison Salisbury, *New York Times* correspondent, Nguyen Van Tien, a member of the National Liberation Front's Central Committee, insists on the NLF's right to a place at peace talks,

calling it a military and political force independent of North Vietnam.

Diplomatic The North Vietnam ministry rejects the British proposal for an international peace conference to end the war, attacking the plan, proposed by Foreign Secretary George Brown on 30 December 1966, for its failure to include the NLF in proposed negotiations.

5-16 JANUARY 1967

Ground War The 1st Battalion, 9th Infantry, Marines lands in the Mekong Delta, 62 miles south of Saigon, for the first time. Working with two Vietnamese marine battalions, the troops encounter no resistance in the first 36 hours. The delta target area, called the Thanhphu Secret Zone by the guerrillas, is reported by US intelligence sources to contain ammunition dumps, ordnance and engineering workshops, hospitals, and indoctrination centers.

8 JANUARY 1967

Guerrilla War Ten children are killed, and 25 other civilians are wounded, when two Vietcong companies in Kienhoa Province try to shield their advance behind civilian hostages during an exchange of gunfire with an ARVN Ranger Company.

8-26 JANUARY 1967

Ground War About 16,000 US and 14,000 South Vietnamese troops mount an attack (Operation Cedar Falls) to disrupt insurgent operations near Saigon. This offensive, the largest of the war to date, has as its primary targets the Thanhdien Forest Preserve and the Iron Triangle, a 60-square-mile area of jungle believed to contain base camps and supply dumps. US infantrymen discover a massive tunnel complex in the Iron Triangle, apparently a headquarters for guerrilla raids and terrorist attacks on Saigon. Bensuc, a village regarded as hostile, is leveled after its 3800 inhabitants are resettled, with 2200 other civilians suspected of Vietcong sympathies, in a camp 20 miles to the south. The operation ends with 711 of the enemy reported killed and 488 captured. The NLF claims that over 2500 US soldiers were killed in the 18-day operation, during which 1229 bombing sorties were flown by US planes.

9 JANUARY 1967

USA: Government Countering reports of widespread corruption and thievery of commodities sent to South Vietnam by the United States, the Agency for International Development (AID), in a report to the President, asserts that 'No more than 5-6 percent of all economic assistance commodities delivered to Vietnam were stolen or otherwise diverted.'

10 JANUARY 1967

USA: Government President Johnson, in his annual State of the Union message to Congress, asks for enactment of a 6-percent surcharge on personal and corporate income taxes to help support the Vietnam War for two years or 'for as long as the unusual expenditures associated with our efforts continue.'

UN Secretary General U Thant, during a press conference, says he has three basic differences with US policy in Vietnam: (1) the NLF is an independent entity and not a 'stooge' of the North Vietnamese; (2) the so-called domino theory is not credible; (3) 'South Vietnam is not strategically vital to Western interests and Western security.' Thant urges an unconditional halt to US bombing of North Vietnam.

15 JANUARY 1967

Air War US planes resume air strikes against the Hanoi area for the first time since December 1966. The attack is part of a 37-plane mission to destroy railroads, highways, bridges, and surface-to-air missile sites 15 miles from Hanoi.

18-26 JANUARY 1967

Australia/New Zealand South Vietnamese Premier Ky, in a visit to Australia and New Zealand, thanks the leaders of both countries for their aid in the war. The tour is marked by violent antiwar demonstrations.

19 JANUARY 1967

China Communist China joins North Vietnam in issuing a second warning to Thailand against any military intervention in the Vietnam war. The two countries threaten stern measures against Thailand if it permits the United States to base B-52s on its territory.

20 JANUARY 1967

USA: Domestic Former editor of the *Arkansas Gazette* Harry Ashmore arrives in Los Angeles after a visit to North Vietnam and says that the damage inflicted by US bombing there is offset by the raids' unifying influence on the North Vietnamese people.

21 JANUARY 1967
USA: Military US intelligence sources in Washington report that aerial photos show that North Vietnamese civilian structures as well as military targets have been heavily damaged. Some of this destruction is attributed to North Vietnamese anti-aircraft fire and accidental bombings by US planes.

25 JANUARY 1967
USA: Military The Joint Chiefs of Staff issue an order barring American pilots from bombing within a five-mile radius of the center of Hanoi. Planes will be permitted to penetrate the zone only to chase attacking aircraft. This appears to be yet another reaction by the Johnson administration to the controversy over civilian bombing casualties.
Ground War A 1000-man battalion of the 9th Infantry Division is being permanently assigned to the Mekong Delta. According to current plans, this combat team – camped near Mythr, 40 miles southeast of Saigon – is the first of what is expected to become a minimum 30,000-man force, whose goal will be to wrest control of the delta from the Vietcong.

28-29 JANUARY 1967
Ground War During an operation against the Vietcong in the Mekong River Delta, US helicopters accidently kill 31 Vietnamese civilians and wound 38. The civilians, apparently mistaken for Vietcong, were attacked as they crossed the Bassac River in 200 sampans at 2345 hours in violation of a curfew.

30 JANUARY 1967
USA: Domestic The US Court of Appeals for the 2nd Circuit rules unanimously in New York City that local draft boards cannot punish registrants who publicly protest the Vietnamese war and the draft by reclassifying them to a 1-A status.

31 JANUARY 1967
USA: Domestic About 2000 members of the National Committee of Clergy and Laymen Concerned About Vietnam march before the White House, demanding that President Johnson order a halt to bombing of North Vietnam.

1 FEBRUARY 1967
USA: Government Speaking with five British journalists Secretary of State Dean Rusk questions the NLF's claim to independence. 'The leadership of the Vietcong in the south is made up of North Vietnamese generals ... so we're not very much impressed with this alleged difference between the Liberation Front and Hanoi.'
Ground War US Marine artillery and planes accidently hit a South Vietnamese hamlet 12 miles southwest of Danang, killing eight civilians and wounding 18.

2 FEBRUARY 1967
Ground War US troops undertake a major offensive, Operation Gadsden, in War Zone C near the Cambodian border to discourage enemy troop movement. The US force consists of 6000-8000 troops of the 4th and 25th Infantry Divisions.

3 FEBRUARY 1967
Ground War Nearly 10,000 troops drive against War Zone D, a Communist stronghold near the Cambodian border, in Operation Big Spring.

5 FEBRUARY 1967
South Vietnam South Vietnamese and allied forces begin defoliation of jungle growth in the southern part of the DMZ because of alleged 'flagrant violations' of the buffer area by North Vietnamese troops. A US Embassy spokesman in Saigon says 'We fully support South Vietnam in this matter.'
USA: Domestic Leaders of 15 politically diverse student organizations sign a resolution calling for the end of the draft and urging establishment of a voluntary national service.

6 FEBRUARY 1967
USA: Government Senator Robert F Kennedy (D-NY) returns to the United States after holding informal discussions in Vietnam with Western leaders since 28 January. Kennedy says American participation in the Vietnam War has resulted in undermining US prestige abroad. After reporting to President Johnson on his visit, Kennedy denies a *Newsweek* magazine story reporting that he had received North Vietnamese peace proposals for ending the war.

8-10 FEBRUARY 1967
USA: Domestic The National Committee of Clergy and Laymen Concerned About Viet-

CHRONOLOGY

nam sponsor a three-day 'fast for peace' by Christians and Jews across the United States.

8-12 FEBRUARY 1967
Diplomatic The United States halts the bombing of North Vietnam during Tet. In London, Prime Minister Harold Wilson, acting on behalf of President Johnson, meets with Soviet Premier Aleksei Kosygin in an effort to stop the bombing permanently and begin peace talks.

11 FEBRUARY 1967
Ground War The Tet cease-fire ends at 0700 and allied ground forces immediately resume operations in South Vietnam. The United States and South Vietnam launch 16 separate operations. One of these, Operation Lam Son 67, involves several battalions of the First Infantry Division. Its purpose is to clear guerrillas from villages in an area 13 miles south of Saigon. The 1st Marines begin Operation Stone south of Danang.

13-14 FEBRUARY 1967
USA: Government Ignoring appeals for extension of the Tet truce from Pope Paul VI, UN Secretary General U Thant and other world leaders, President Johnson orders resumption of the bombing of North Vietnam and defends his action on the basis of what he calls the unparalleled magnitude of the North Vietnam supply effort.

13 FEBRUARY 1967
Ground War A US artillery shell accidentally hits the position of the First Cavalry Division, killing seven soldiers and wounding four. Operation Thayer II, which began on 25 October 1966 in Binhdinh, ends in the deaths of 1744 Communist soldiers.

15 FEBRUARY 1967
USA: Government Secretary of Defense McNamara, during a press conference, says that air raids on military targets in the North are accomplishing their objectives. As a result of the raids, the Communist buildup in the South has 'leveled off' and North Vietnam has been forced to divert 300,000 persons to repair supply lines. The raids have also raised morale in South Vietnam, according to McNamara.

16 FEBRUARY 1967
Ground War Communist ground-fire downs 13 US helicopters, a record number for a single day. Nine of the aircraft are hit during an operation in the Mekong Delta. US authorities report that four Americans were killed and eight wounded in the loss of the 13 helicopters.

21 FEBRUARY 1967
Ground War Writer and historian Bernard B Fall is killed by a Vietcong mine about 14 miles northeast of Hué, while gathering material for his eighth book on Vietnam. A US Marine photographer was also killed.

22 FEBRUARY 1967
USA: Domestic Hundreds of students at the University of Wisconsin demonstrate against the presence of Dow Chemical Company representatives on campus. Dow manufactures napalm used in Vietnam. A Harris poll shows that 55 percent of those polled favor continued military pressure on North Vietnam, 67 percent back continued bombing. President Johnson remains at a 43-percent approval rating, with 57 percent disapproving of the way he is handling the Vietnam War.
Ground War The first land-based artillery attack of the war takes place when 175-mm guns based near US Camp Carrol fire 63 shells at North Vietnamese anti-aircraft positions. The US command says that American artillery opened fire after a US spotter plane had been shot at just north of the buffer zone. Operation Junction City, an effort to smash the Vietcong's War-Zone-C stronghold near the Cambodian border and ease pressure on Saigon, begins with a force of over 25,000 US and South Vietnamese troops – the war's largest offensive so far. The first day's operation is supported by 575 US plane sorties, a record number for a single day in South Vietnam. Two South Vietnamese and 34 US battalions are participating.

24 FEBRUARY 1967
USA: Government Secretary of Defense McNamara denies that he disagrees with Secretary of State Dean Rusk on the bombing of North Vietnam. 'I can't recall a single instance when the Secretary of State and Secretary of Defense have differed on bombing policy.'

26 FEBRUARY 1967
Sea War US cruisers and destroyers of the 7th Fleet shell North Vietnamese supply routes along a 250-mile stretch between the DMZ and Thanhhoa.

27 FEBRUARY 1967
Ground War The Vietcong shell the US airbase at Danang, killing 12 Americans. Due to fires that sweep the adjacent village of Apdo, more than 150 buildings are destroyed and 35 South Vietnamese civilians are killed.
Air War The US command discloses that US planes have dropped 'a limited number of . . . non-floating mines in rivers in southern North Vietnam.'

1-4 MARCH 1967
Ground War Operation Junction City. The First Infantry Division, fighting in Tayninh Province, suffers heavy casualties while killing 150 enemy troops. The 173rd Airborne Brigade is ambushed near the Cambodian border, with additional heavy casualties.

2 MARCH 1967
USA: Government Senator Robert Kennedy (D-NY) proposes a three-point plan to help end the war. It includes suspension of US bombing of North Vietnam, and the gradual withdrawal of US and North Vietnamese troops from South Vietnam with replacement by an international force. Secretary of State Dean Rusk rejects Kennedy's proposal.
Ground War The village of Languei, 15 miles south of the DMZ, is accidentally hit by bombs dropped by two US F-4C Phantom jets, killing at least 83 civilians and wounding 176.

8 MARCH 1967
USA: Government Both Houses of Congress pass the Mansfield Resolution backing President Johnson's efforts to prevent expansion of the war and his attempts to gain a negotiated peace.
Diplomatic The US Chiefs of Mission of the East Asian and Pacific area meet in Baguio, the Philippines, and issue a statement supportive of the administration's policies: 'Any slackening of the collective military effort or the policy and programs in non-military fields would slow down the drive to achieve a stable and honorable peace.'

9 MARCH 1967
Thailand For the first time, Thailand acknowledges the use of Thai bases by US planes for air raids on North Vietnam.

10-11 MARCH 1967
Air War US planes bomb the Thainguyen iron and steel complex, 38 miles north of

Hanoi. This is the first bombing raid on a major industrial installation in North Vietnam. US sources in Saigon concede that this constitutes an escalation of the war.

11 MARCH 1967
Ground War US First Infantry Division troops of Operation Junction City kill 210 North Vietnamese soldiers in one of the heaviest battles of the operation.

13 MARCH 1967
USA: Military The House Appropriations Committee releases secret testimony given on 20 February 1967 by General Earle G Wheeler, Chairman of the Joint Chiefs of Staff. Wheeler had said that the North Vietnamese 'don't expect to win any military victory in South Vietnam' but 'expect to win a victory in the war right here in Washington, DC.'

15 MARCH 1967
USA: Government President Johnson addresses the Tennessee General Assembly in Nashville and defends his policy of continuing the bombing of North Vietnam. He announces that Ellsworth Bunker will replace Henry Cabot Lodge as Ambassador to South Vietnam. He also announces that Robert W Komer will head the pacification and economic-assistance programs in Vietnam.
USA: Military The Defense Department announces an increase in purchases of herbicides and defoliants in fiscal 1967 to triple the destruction of crops and defoliation of jungles in Vietcong areas.

18 MARCH 1967
South Vietnam The South Vietnamese Constituent Assembly adopts the draft of a new constitution that provides for a democratically elected civilian government, including a president, a vice-president, and a bicameral legislature. Provisions of the constitution call for local village elections to begin on 2 April 1967 and continue during four subsequent Sundays. The presidential election will be held in September.

20-21 MARCH 1967
USA: Government President Johnson and major administration officials, including Secretaries Rusk and McNamara, meet with Premier Nguyen Cao Ky, Chief of State Nguyen Van Thieu, and other South Vietnamese leaders in Guam to discuss military

CHRONOLOGY

and political aspects of the war. Premier Ky introduces a plan calling for a 100-mile fortified defensive zone to halt infiltration from North to South Vietnam.

20 MARCH-1 APRIL 1967
Ground War The Special Landing Force, 1st Battalion, 4th Marines, goes ashore four miles south of the DMZ near Gio Linh to help in Operation Prairie III. Before the landing force re-embarks on 1 April 1967, 29 men have been killed and 230 wounded.

21 MARCH 1967
North Vietnam The North Vietnamese press agency reports that an exchange of notes took place in February between President Johnson and Ho Chi Minh. The agency says that Ho rejected a proposal made by Johnson for direct talks between the United States and North Vietnam on ending the war, on ground that the United States 'must stop definitely and unconditionally its bombing raids and all other acts of war against North Vietnam.' The US State Department confirms the exchange of letters and expresses regret that Hanoi had divulged this information, since the secret letters were intended as a serious diplomatic attempt to end the conflict.
Ground War Operation Junction City produces what General Westmoreland describes as 'one of the most successful single actions of the year' when US forces kill 606 Vietcong in War Zone C.

22 MARCH 1967
USA: Military Washington officials announce that Thailand as agreed to the stationing of US B-52s on its territory for bombing raids against targets in North and South Vietnam.

25 MARCH 1967
USA: Government The Senate Preparedness Investigating Subcommittee recommends that the United States escalate the air war against North Vietnam by lifting restrictions on bombing targets. The report, based on a subcommittee staff investigation in Vietnam in October 1966, contends that curbing the raids has resulted in heavy losses for proportionately limited gains.
USA: Domestic The Reverend Martin Luther King Jr leads a march of 5000 anti-war demonstrators in Chicago. In an address to the demonstrators, King declares that the Vietnam war is 'a blasphemy against all that America stands for.'

28 MARCH 1967
USA: Domestic The *Phoenix*, a private US yacht with eight American pacifists aboard, arrives in Haiphong, North Vietnam, with $10,000 worth of medical supplies for the North Vietnamese. The trip, financed by a Quaker group in Philadelphia, was made in defiance of a US ban on American travel to North Vietnam.

31 MARCH 1967
USA: Government The House Committee on Un-American Activities (HUAC) charges that two anti-war demonstrations scheduled for 15 April 1967 were proposed by Communists, and that many of the organizations involved were infiltrated or dominated by Communists. The Reverend James L Bevel, national director of Spring Mobilization Committee to End the War in Vietnam, charges that the HUAC and its chairman, Representative Edwin E Willis (D-LA) are 'liars' and 'spreaders of trash.'

31 MARCH-1 APRIL 1967
Ground War In one of the bloodiest battles of Operation Junction City, US troops kill 591 Vietcong, suffering 10 fatalities themselves and 64 wounded. The US ground forces were assisted by continual air and artillery strikes on the estimated 2500 Vietcong troops.

2 APRIL 1967
South Vietnam As provided for in the new constitution, effective yesterday, local village elections are held. Balloting for legislative People's Councils are being held in 984 villages with a total population of 5 million.
USA: Government US officials express fear that the North Vietnamese may be brainwashing US prisoners of war to get anti-American-policy propaganda statements from them.

4 APRIL 1967
USA: Domestic The Reverend Martin Luther King Jr, head of the Southern Christian Leadership Conference, indicates that a link is forming between the civil rights and peace movements. King proposes that the United States (a) stop all bombing of North and South Vietnam; (b) declare a unilateral truce in the hope that it would lead to peace talks; (c) set a date for withdrawal of all troops from Vietnam; (d) give the National Liberation Front an role in negotiations.

6 APRIL 1967

Ground War About 2500 Vietcong and North Vietnamese troops carry out four closely coordinated attacks on the city of Quangtri, 15 miles south of the DMZ. US sources say 125 South Vietnamese troops are killed and 180 wounded. Four US Marines are killed and 27 wounded. South Vietnam charges that the Communist raiders had infiltrated from the DMZ, and attribute the success of the Quangtri raid to aid given to the Communists by disloyal South Vietnamese soldiers. A North Vietnamese force carries out the war's first attack across the bridge spanning the Benhai River at the 17th parallel; the South Vietnamese protest to the ICC.

7 APRIL 1967

USA: Military Secretary of Defense McNamara announces plans to build a fortified barrier just south of the eastern end of the DMZ to curb the inflow of arms and troops from North Vietnam.

USA: Domestic Governor George Rommey (R-MI) announces his position on the Vietnam war, which coincides with President Johnson's. 'It is unthinkable that the United States withdraw from Vietnam.'

9 APRIL 1967

USA: Domestic Former Republican presidential candidate Barry Goldwater praises the administration's policy on Vietnam in a TV interview: 'I think the President is now determined to win this war and end it, and all of us are behind him.'

11 APRIL 1967

USA: Government US officials report that Communist China and the Soviet Union have reached agreement on speeding the shipment of Soviet military supplies to North Vietnam across Chinese territory.

13 APRIL 1967

Guerrilla War Communist forces blow up two bridges between Danang and Quangtri on North-South Highway 2. The bridges were part of a major supply route to US forces along the DMZ.

15 APRIL 1967

South Vietnam South Vietnamese Premier Nguyen Cao Ky announces the start of construction on a fortified barrier south of the DMZ to halt infiltration from North Vietnam.

Moving tanks through a river ford during Operation Junction City, Phase II.

CHRONOLOGY

A protester burns his draft card during an anti-war demonstration in Central Park.

USA: Domestic Massive parades to protest US policy in Vietnam are held in New York and San Francisco. In New York, police estimate that 100,000 to 125,000 people hear speeches by Martin Luther King Jr, Floyd McKissick, Stokely Carmichael and Dr Benjamin Spock. Prior to the march, nearly 200 draft cards are burned by youths in Central Park. The San Francisco march is led by black nationalists, but most of the marchers, estimated at 20,000 by the police, are white.

Air War Two US Air Force F-100 Supersabre jets drop bombs off target, hitting a South Vietnamese army battalion position 23 miles northeast of Quinhon; 41 South Vietnamese troops are killed and at least 50 wounded.

18 APRIL 1967
South Vietnam An agreement is signed in Saigon for an additional $150 million worth of US economic aid to South Vietnam. This raises the total amount of assistance in 1967 to a record $700 million.

USA: Military General Westmoreland, back briefly from Vietnam, notifies the Joint Chiefs of additional troop needs: For an 'optimum force,' Westmoreland needs four and two-thirds divisions – 201,250 more troops – to boost the total strength of US forces in Vietnam to 671,616 men.

19-21 APRIL 1967
USA: Military The United States proposes that the six-mile-wide DMZ be extended 10

miles on each side and that troops on both sides be withdrawn behind the wider buffer. North Vietnam rejects the proposal on the ground that it does not include Hanoi's principal condition for peace talks – an end to air attacks against North Vietnam.

20 APRIL 1967

Air War For the first time, US planes bomb Haiphong, attacking two power plants inside the city. The raids were carried out by 86 planes from the aircraft carriers *Kitty Hawk* and *Ticonderoga*.

22 APRIL 1967

USA: Domestic Senator Charles Percy (R-IL) denounces the Johnson administration as unrealistic in its Vietnam policy and calls for Vietcong participation in peace talks.

Ground War A 15,000-man US task force is assigned to Quangtri and Thautien Provinces. An undisclosed number of Marines land by ship and helicopter in an area 21 miles southeast of the DMZ.

24 APRIL 1967

USA: Government In response to a reported division within the administration created by General Westmoreland's request for additional troops, Under Secretary of State Nicholas Katzenbach, acting in Secretary Rusk's absence, orders an intra-agency review of two major options facing the administration. Course A is to provide General Westmoreland with 200,000 more troops with 'possible intensification of military actions outside of South Vietnam, including invasion of North Vietnam, Laos, and Cambodia.' Course B is to confine troop increases 'to those that could be generated without calling up the reserves,' plus 'a cessation of the bombing of North Vietnam areas north of 20 degrees.'

Air War US planes bomb two MiG bases north of Hanoi. This appears to be a further relaxing of restrictions on air raids around the Hanoi and Haiphong areas.

24-30 APRIL 1967

USA: Domestic General Westmoreland arouses controversy by saying that the enemy had 'gained support in the United States that gives him hope that he can win politically that which he cannot win militarily.' He adds that the GI in Vietnam was 'dismayed, and so am I, by recent unpatriotic acts at home.' Westmoreland calls the attitude of the American

people toward the war 'wholesome.' 'Based on what I heard and saw, 95 percent of the people are behind the United States effort in Vietnam.

24 APRIL-5 MAY 1967

Ground War In a fierce battle, US Marines defeat North Vietnamese troops on three hills near the airstrip at Khesanh in Quangtin Province – less than 10 miles from the Laotian border. During the 12-day battle, US forces lose 160 men, with an additional 746 wounded, representing half the combat strength of the two battalions of the 3rd Marine Regiment. The Marines capture the last hill on 5 May. In a diversionary action, a North Vietnamese force of about 300 had moved down from the hills three miles west of Khesanh and attacked a comparable South Vietnamese force and a US Special Forces camp.

25 APRIL 1967

USA: Domestic A major speech attacking administration policies in Vietnam is delivered in the Senate by Senator George McGovern (D-SD). Democratic Senators Robert Kennedy (NY), Frank Church (ID), and Ernest Gruening (AK) join in the attack.

Air War US Navy jets from the carriers *Kitty Hawk* and *Bonhomme Richard* attack a cement plant a mile from the center of Haiphong, an oil depot, and an ammunition dump. The British freighter *Dartford* is hit by bullets during the raid, according to North Vietnamese sources. Six British seamen are reported as wounded by Hanoi.

China Peking Radio reports that two US F-4 Phantom jets were shot down 24 April after intruding into Chinese air space.

26 APRIL 1967

Air War US planes from Thailand attack a five-span bridge four miles north of the center of Hanoi. The raid's purpose was to sever North Vietnam's rail links with Communist China. An electrical transformer station seven miles north of Hanoi was also attacked.

28 APRIL 1967

USA: Government General Westmoreland addresses a joint session of Congress and evokes a standing ovation by declaring that 'Backed at home by resolve, confidence, patience, determination, and continued support, we will prevail in Vietnam over the Communist aggressor.'

Air War Waves of US planes drop hundreds

of bombs near the Danphuong highway, 12 miles west of Hanoi, and on the Gialam railroad repair yards, in one of the heaviest attacks of the war. Hanoi's power station in the northern outskirts is another target.

MAY-SEPTEMBER 1967
USA: Military A debate behind closed doors pits the CIA against US military leaders on the issue of how to measure the strength of Communist forces in Vietnam. Brigadier General Joseph A McChristian, Westmoreland's chief of intelligence, shows his superior a report that estimates available Communist forces at 400,000. Westmoreland feels this gives a distorted impression by lumping regular troops with guerrillas and including even those engaged primarily in political work.

1 MAY 1967
USA: Government Secretary of State Dean Rusk charges that the North Vietnamese have rejected at least 28 peace proposals presented by the United States and other nations. Rusk asserts that US acceptance of the proposals and their rejection by Hanoi 'throw a light . . . upon the question of who is interested in peace and who is trying to absorb a neighbor by force.' Assistant Secretary Bundy, in a memorandum to Under Secretary of State Katzenbach, says he is 'totally against' ground operations against North Vietnam.

1-4 MAY 1967
USA: Domestic Leading Republicans show a wide division in their party, as they react to a White Paper on Vietnam released 1 May. Questioning the administration's policy in Vietnam, the paper asks Republicans to address such questions as: 'Does the Republican Party serve America best by saying that politics stops at the water's edge? Must we rally behind the President? Does bipartisanship mean Democratic mistakes are Republican responsibilities?' A number of Republican Senators refute the paper.

2 MAY 1967
Air War Communist MiG bases at Kep, 37 miles northeast of Hanoi, and Hoalac, 19 miles west of Hanoi, are bombed for the third time. Pilots report heavy damage.

2-10 MAY 1967
International An 'International Tribunal on War Crimes' – created by opponents of US

policy in Vietnam – opens sessions in Stockholm on 2 May. The tribunal hands down a decision accusing the United States of aggression and 'widespread, deliberate and systematic bombing of civilian objectives.'

3 MAY 1967
China Communist China charges that four United States jets bombed the southern Chinese town of Ninmong, 20 miles north of the North Vietnamese border, on 2 May. The US Defense Department denies the incident.

4 MAY 1967
USA: Domestic The newspaper *Newsday* quotes Senator William Fulbright (D-AR) as saying he 'no longer believes' statements on Vietnam by President Johnson, Secretary Rusk, or Secretary McNamara. He also charges that some leading Congressional supporters of the war are influenced by their interest in defense industries in their home states. Later, Fulbright apologizes for 'any embarrassment the *Newsday* article may have caused members of Congress'

5-6 MAY 1967
USA: Government Assistant Secretary McNaughton sends Secretary of Defense McNamara a recommendation for cutting back the air war to the 20th parallel. The proposed cutback, he says, is to reduce US pilot and aircraft losses over heavily defended Hanoi and Haiphong, not primarily to get North Vietnam to negotiate. This paper is significant as the first recommendation to the President of such a cutback to the 20th parallel. On 6 May McNaughton expresses concern to McNamara about this memorandum, because it had also recommended giving General Westmoreland 80,000 more men. Limiting the troop request to 80,000 men, adds McNaughton, 'does the very important business of postponing the issue of a reserve call-up . . . but postpone is all it does.'

5-10 MAY 1967
USA: Government The US State Department discloses that a report was sent to Britain denying that US planes were responsible for damage inflicted on the British freighter *Dartford*. The report says the damage was probably caused by anti-aircraft missile debris. This version was supported by a British seaman aboard a nearby ship, but *Dartford* crewmen insist that their vessel was strafed by US pilots.

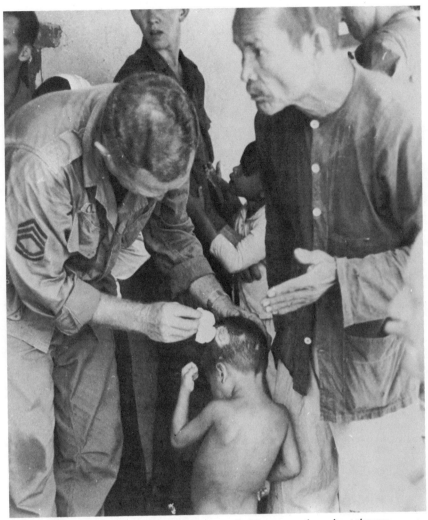

US forces gave first aid and other medical care to the Vietnamese throughout the war.

6 MAY 1967

North Vietnam Three US pilots shot down during a raid over Hanoi are paraded through the streets of Hanoi. North Vietnam says the three pilots had been based in Thailand.

South Vietnam Ambassador Ellsworth Bunker, in a report to President Johnson, describes an encouraging turnout in recent village council elections. He estimates that 77 percent of eligible voters in participating villages cast ballots.

8 MAY 1967

USA: Government Walt Rostow, generally described as a 'strong bombing advocate,' sends a memo to President Johnson recommending a bombing cutback. Rostow also rejects proposals for mining North Vietnam harbors and bombing port facilities. He recommends that the bombing be concentrated on the supply routes in southern North Vietnam.

USA: Domestic Senator Edward Kennedy (D-

CHRONOLOGY

Captured US pilots were interviewed by the press in Hanoi for propaganda purposes.

MA) says the civilian casualty rate in Vietnam is over 100,000 a year, based on a probe conducted by a Senate subcommittee.

Ground War The base camp at Conthien comes under a three-hour attack. The assault, backed by mortars, is repulsed after 179 North Vietnamese soldiers and 44 US Marines are killed. North Vietnam mortar teams also carry out attacks on nearby Marine camps at Dongha, Giolinh and Camp Carroll.

9 MAY 1967

Ground War A North Vietnamese force attacks a 3rd Marine Regiment unit nine miles northwest of Khesanh. In the five-hour clash, the Marines suffer 24 casualties.

10 MAY 1967

USA: Domestic US policy in Vietnam is assailed in a nationwide 'teach-in' staged at more than 80 colleges.

11 MAY 1967

South Vietnam Nguyen Cao Ky informs the cabinet that he will run for president on 3 September. Nguyen Van Thieu says it is 'entirely possible' that he will run against him.

USA: Military The civilian-operated pacification program in South Vietnam is turned over to the US military command. The project is aimed at re-establishing South Vietnamese government control over rural villages and hamlets.

UN UN Secretary General Thant expresses fear that the world is witnessing the initial phase of World War III, 'If the present trend continues, I am afraid direct confrontation, first of all between Washington and Peking, is inevitable.' In a statement issued later, US Ambassador Arthur Goldberg reaffirms US policy – that the United States would cease 'all bombing of North Vietnam the moment we are assured privately or otherwise that this step will be answered promptly by a corresponding and appropriate de-escalation on the other side.'

14-16 MAY 1967

China The *Chicago Daily News* reports that Premier Chou En-lai and four other Chinese officials, during an interview on 27-9 March, threatened to send troops into North Vietnam if US troops invaded there. The article quotes Chou as saying that China 'was ready tomorrow as need be to send a volunteer army into North Vietnam if Hanoi made such a request.' The Chinese Foreign Ministry denies that the interviews ever took place.

15 MAY 1967

Air War The US Defense Department reports that a US F-105 Thunderchief might have crashed in Communist China. The plane was hit during a raid on the Kep area in North Vietnam.

15-23 MAY 1967

Ground War US forces just south of the DMZ come under heavy fire, as Marine positions between Dongha and Conthien are pounded by North Vietnamese artillery. More than 100 Americans are killed or wounded during heavy fighting along the DMZ. On 17 and 18 May, the Conthien base is shelled heavily. Dongha, Giolinh, Camlo, and Camp Carroll are also bombarded. On 18 May a force of 5500 US and South Vietnamese troops invades the southeastern section of the DMZ to smash a Communist buildup in the area and to deny the zone's use as an infiltration route into South Vietnam. On 19 May the US State Department says the offensive in the DMZ is 'purely a defensive measure' against a 'considerable buildup of North Vietnam troops.' The North Vietnamese government (21 May) calls the invasion of the zone 'a brazen provocation' that 'abolishes the buffer character of the DMZ as provided by the Geneva agreements.'

USA: Domestic Sixteen Senate critics of administration policy on Vietnam issue a statement warning Hanoi that dissent on the war is a minority view in the United States, and that 'There are many more who either give their full endorsement to our government policy in Vietnam or who press for even greater action there.'

18-31 MAY 1967

Ground War The 26th Marines begin an offensive (Operation Prairie IV) east of Khesanh to clear the DMZ south of the Ben Hai River. Five battalions of the 1st ARVN Division work along the axis of Highway 1 between Giolinh and the Ben Hai River; three Marine battalions and the Special Landing Force operate along the river. At the end of May, seven Marine divisions finish up Prairie IV with hard action on Hill 174, southwest of Con Thien. During the operation, 164 Marines are killed and 999 wounded.

19 MAY 1967

USA: Government Secretary of Defense McNamara sends a memo to President Johnson that marshals the arguments against the strategy of widening the war and sharpens the case for curtailing the air war. He recommends a cutback of the bombing to the 20th parallel and the deployment of only 30,000 more troops for General Westmoreland. He also advocates a considerably more limited overall US objective in Vietnam.

21 MAY 1967

USA: Military General Earle G Wheeler, Chairman of the Joint Chiefs of Staff, says that the United States 'has no intention of invading North Vietnam.'

22 MAY 1967

USA: Government President Johnson issues a proclamation designating Memorial Day as a day of prayer for peace. He pledges to continue to resist aggression but to hold open the door to an honorable peace.

23 MAY-18 OCTOBER 1967

USA: Military A public controversy over the M-16, the basic combat rifle in Vietnam, begins after Representative James J Howard (D-NJ) reads to the House of Representatives a letter in which a Marine in Vietnam claims that almost all Americans killed in the battle for Hill 881 died as the result of jamming by their new M-16 rifles. The Defense Department acknowledges on 28 August that there had been a 'serious increase in frequency of malfunctions in the M-16.'

24 MAY 1967

USA: Military In response to Secretary of Defense McNamara's order for a new study of bombing alternatives on 20 May, the Joint Chiefs submit three memoranda renewing earlier recommendations for more than 200,000 new troops and for air attacks on Haiphong, mining of Haiphong harbors, and raids on eight major railways leading to China.

25 MAY 1967

Air War After a 24-hour truce in honor of the Buddha's birthday, air raids over North Vietnam are resumed with attacks on two rail-lines carrying supplies from Communist China to Hanoi.

25-27 MAY 1967

Ground War Fighting breaks out again in the southeastern section of the DMZ, when two US Marine battalions of about 1200 men assault a North Vietnamese position on Hill

CHRONOLOGY

The M-16 rifle was the basic combat weapon of the Vietnam War.

117, three miles west of the base at Conthien. Marines storm the hill and capture it on 27 May. They withdraw after blowing up enemy bunkers.

31 MAY 1967

USA: Military The Joint Chiefs issue a sharp rebuttal to the McNamara-McNaughton memorandum contending that 'the drastic changes' in our policy advocated by the Secretary 'would undermine and no longer provide a complete rationale for our presence in South Vietnam or much of our efforts over the past two years.'

1 JUNE 1967

Australia Prime Minister Holt gives President Johnson a pledge of Australia's support in the Vietnam conflict.

2 JUNE 1967

Ground War In Operation Union II, the 5th Marines in Quong Tin Province undertake a fierce battle with two North Vietnamese regiments that ends in bunker-to-bunker fighting.

2-3 JUNE 1967

USA: Military Captain Howard Levy, 30, a dermatologist from Brooklyn, is convicted by a general court-martial in Fort Jackson, South Carolina, of willfully disobeying orders and making disloyal statements about US policy in Vietnam. Levy had refused to provide elementary instruction in skin disease to Green Beret medics on ground that the Green Berets would use medicine as 'another tool of political persuasion.'

Ground War Fighting erupts near Tamky, 30 miles southwest of Danang, when a Marine battalion on patrol in the Hiepdus Valley comes under fire from a 2900-man North Vietnamese regiment. The US 5th Marine Regiment reports killing 540 North Vietnamese soldiers while suffering 73 losses themselves, with 139 wounded.

USSR The Soviet Union charges that US planes bombed the Soviet merchant ship

Turkestan in the port of Campha, 50 miles north of Haiphong, and files a protest claiming two crewmen were wounded. The Soviets warn that 'appropriate measures' will be taken to ensure the safety of other ships. On 3 June the United States attributes damage to anti-aircraft fire.

10 JUNE 1967
Ground War The Central Highland city of Pleiku is struck by two separate Communist mortar attacks. Most of the shells are directed against a pacification school for *montagnard* tribesmen, killing 27 people.

12 JUNE 1967
China The Chinese armed forces claim they shot down a pilotless US reconnaissance plane over the southern part of the Kwangsi Chuang Autonomous Region.

12-17 JUNE 1967
Ground War Troops of the US First Infantry Division launch a drive into War Zone D, 50 miles north of Saigon, in an effort to trap three Vietcong battalions. On 13 June the Americans kill 60 guerrillas in a four-hour battle. On 17 June in the same area US troops kill at least 196 soldiers. A Vietcong ambush costs the lives of 31 Americans, with 113 wounded.

14 JUNE 1967
Ground War In an all-day battle fought in the Mekong Delta 10 miles southwest of Cantho, a South Vietnamese force of about 1000, assisted by armed US helicopters, overwhelms a 450-man Vietcong battalion.

15 JUNE 1967
South Vietnam Premier Nguyen Cao Ky says informal contacts have been made with Laos to extend into Laos the proposed barrier against infiltration.

16 JUNE 1967
Guerrilla War The Vietcong's National Liberation Front Radio warns that captured Americans will be executed if 'the US Aggressors and their Saigon stooges' execute 'three Vietnamese patriots' sentenced to death by a special military tribunal in Saigon.

19-20 JUNE 1967
Ground War On the Rach-hui River, 19 miles south of Saigon, US Navy river assault boats and about 800 men of the US 9th Infantry

Division kill 169 Vietcong. US losses are 28 killed and 126 wounded.

20 JUNE 1967
USA: Government The United States apologizes to the Soviet Union for what it calls an inadvertent US air attack on the Soviet ship *Turkestan* on 2 June.

21 JUNE 1967
France In a policy statement to the cabinet, French President Charles de Gaulle links the Middle East conflict to US intervention in Vietnam. He sees no chance of a peaceful settlement in the present world situation, unless the Vietnam war is ended through 'termination of foreign intervention.'

22 JUNE 1967
Ground War A 130-man company of the 173rd US Airborne Brigade is virtually wiped out by a North Vietnamese ambush near Dakto, Kontum Province, 28 miles northeast of Saigon. Eighty Americans are killed and 34 wounded; 106 North Vietnamese soldiers are fatal casualties.

23-25 JUNE 1967
Diplomatic President Johnson and Soviet Premier Aleksei Kosygin meet in Glassboro, New Jersey, to discuss world problems.

26 JUNE 1967
China An unarmed US FY Phantom jet strays off course and is shot down by Chinese planes near Hainan Island. The two crewmen parachute from the plane and are rescued unhurt from the China Sea by a US Navy helicopter.

28 JUNE 1967
South Vietnam General Duong Van Minh, in exile in Bangkok, announces that he will be a candidate for the presidency in September. The Ky government forbids Minh to return.

30 JUNE 1967
South Vietnam The Armed Forces Council resolves rival claims to the presidency in favor of Nguyen Van Thieu, Chief of State. Ky, who had announced 11 May that he would run for president, is forced to accept second place on the presidential ticket.
Air War Several sources report attacks by US planes on foreign ships in Haiphong harbor. The Soviet government charges that a second Russian merchant vessel, *Mikhail Frunze*, was bombed by US planes in

CHRONOLOGY

Haiphong on 29 June. A protest is delivered to the US Embassy in Moscow 30 June. The North Vietnamese news agency reports that two other foreign ships were struck in Haiphong harbor.

2 JULY 1967

Ground War The US 9th Marine Regiment's 3rd platoon is ambushed by 500 troops of the North Vietnamese 90th Regiment about 1½ miles northeast of Conthien, just south of the DMZ: 35 Marines are killed. Reinforcements are rushed to the scene by both sides, and the fighting increases in intensity. US Marine casualties total 96 killed and 211 wounded.

2-14 JULY 1967

Ground War On 2 July B and C Companies of the 9th Marines are heavily attacked, with serious losses, near Con Thien. The 3rd battalion is helicoptered in, and the reinforced 1st battalion hits the enemy's flank. Two battalions of the 3rd Marines are flown into the battle area and the fighting continues until 14 July. The encounter costs the lives of 159 Americans, with 45 wounded. Communist losses are estimated at 1301 dead.

4-6 JULY 1967

Ground War North Vietnamese mortars, rockets, and artillery fire 300 rounds in eight separate attacks on US positions at Conthien and Dongha. The attack is resumed 6 July on Marine positions near Conthien. One of the artillery shells scores a direct hit on a Marine post, killing nine men and wounding 21.

6 JULY 1967

International A four-day conference on Vietnam, arranged by organizations of the international peace movement and the Swedish Society for Peace and Arbitration, begins in Stockholm.

7-12 JULY 1967

USA: Military Secretary of Defense McNamara goes to Saigon, reportedly with instructions from President Johnson to review with General Westmoreland his request for additional troops and 'reach an agreement on a figure well below the 200,000 he had requested.' On McNamara's final evening in Saigon, he and Westmoreland agree on a 55,000-man troop increase. Johnson approves the compromise.

10 JULY 1967

Ground War Outnumbered South Vietnamese troops repel an attack by two battalions of the 141st North Vietnamese Regiment on a military camp five miles east of Anloc and 60 miles north of Saigon. Communist forces capture a third of the base camp before they are thrown back with the assistance of US and South Vietnamese air and artillery strikes.

10-11 JULY 1967

Ground War US forces suffer heavy casualties in two separate battles in the Central Highlands. In the first action, about 400 men of the 173rd Airborne Brigade come under heavy fire from North Vietnamese machine guns and mortars during a sweep of the Dakto area near Kontum. Americans killed number 26, with 49 wounded. In the second Highlands clash, 35 soldiers of the US 4th Infantry Division are killed and 31 wounded five miles south of Ducco.

11 JULY 1967

USA: Government Secretary McNamara has reportedly said that resources now available in Vietnam are not being well used: despite the presence of 464,000 troops in South Vietnam, only 50,000 US troops are available for offensive ground operations.

USA: Domestic Senator Mike Mansfield (D-MT) warns against further escalation of the war and urges an alternative to expansion by (a) putting the entire question before the UN, and (b) containing the conflict by building a defensive barrier south of the DMZ separating North from South Vietnam. Senator George Aiken (R-VT) suggests that the administration pay more attention to its Senate leader than to 'certain military leaders who have far more knowledge of weapons than they have of people.' Republican leader Everett Dirksen of Illinois, asked if he favors an increase in US troops in Vietnam, replies, 'If General Westmoreland says we need them, yes, sir.'

12 JULY 1967

China Communist China claims that its planes chased four US jets after they had attacked a Chinese frontier post near Tunghing. The Peking report says the US planes fired two guided missiles.

13 JULY 1967

USA: Government During a press conference, President Johnson reveals that the United

The Vietcong were usually armed with Soviet or Chinese weapons, as well as captured ones.

CHRONOLOGY

Americans also served as advisors on the junks of the Vietnamese Coastal Patrol.

States has decided on a relatively modest increase in the buildup of US forces in Vietnam. This announcement comes amid renewed reports that administration officials disagree with Westmoreland and other US commanders in Vietnam who have requested a substantial increase in US forces.

15 JULY 1967
USA: Domestic The AFL-CIO conducts a survey of its membership and reports that 42 percent are uneasy about the war, but the majority believes that President Johnson is doing the best he can.
Air War The US air base at Danang is struck by 50 rounds of Communist rocket fire during a 45-minute attack in which 12 Americans are killed and 40 wounded.

16 JULY-31 OCTOBER 1967
Ground War Operation Kingfisher, a three-month action involving the 3rd Marine Division in northern South Vietnam ends with the loss of 340 Marines and 3086 wounded.

17 JULY 1967
POWs The White House calls on the NLF and North Vietnam to permit an impartial inspection of US POWs.

20 JULY 1967
USA: Government President Johnson is reported to have added 16 targets – including an airfield, a railroad yard, two bridges and 12 barracks and supply areas, all within the restricted circles around Hanoi and Haiphong to the approved list of bombing targets in North Vietnam. This represents a markedly different strategy from that of de-escalation recently urged by Defense Secretary McNamara.

22 JULY-3 AUGUST 1967
USA: Government General Maxwell Taylor, now a consultant to President Johnson, and Presidential Adviser Clark Clifford, tour South Vietnam, Thailand, Australia, New Zealand, and South Korea to sound out allied opinion on the possibility of another summit conference and, reportedly, to seek additional allied troops for the war. On their return, they report no major disagreement on any aspect of the war. During their visit to South Vietnam, Clifford and Maxwell deliver a personal message to the South Vietnamese leaders: 'If there was any one act on their part which would be calculated to alienate the American people, it would be to have a rigged election in South Vietnam.'

23 JULY 1967
Ground War In a five-hour battle, the US 4th Infantry Division virtually wipes out a North Vietnamese company four miles south of Ducco in the Central Highlands. The Communist force loses at least 148 of their 400-man force.

29 JULY 1967
USA: Government According to US intelligence, the number of non-Communist ships calling at North Vietnamese ports has increased from 20 during July-December 1966 to 39 during January-June 1967.
Ground War A battalion of US Marines is ambushed after penetrating the southern part of the DMZ.
Sea War Fire sweeps the aircraft carrier *Forrestal* off the coast of North Vietnam in the Gulf of Tonkin, in the worst US naval disaster in a combat zone since World War II. The accident takes the lives of 134 crewmen and injures 62. Of the carrier's 80 planes, 21 are destroyed and 42 damaged.

30 JULY 1967
USA: Domestic The Most Reverend Fulton J Sheen, Roman Catholic archbishop of Rochester, New York, appeals to President Johnson to 'Withdraw our forces immediately from South Vietnam for the sake of reconciliation.' A Gallup poll reports that 52 percent of the American people disapprove of President Johnson's handling of the Vietnam war; 41 percent think the United States made a mistake in sending troops to Vietnam in the first place. Over half, 56 percent, think the United States is losing the war or standing still.

1 AUGUST 1967
Diplomatic The US State Department reports that Cambodia rejected a 27 May suggestion for talks as a step toward preventing the use of Cambodian territory by North Vietnamese troops.

2 AUGUST 1967
Ground War Two US helicopters return fire against a group of Vietcong in a Mekong Delta village near Phuvinh, 60 miles south of Saigon, killing 40 South Vietnamese civilians and wounding 36.

3 AUGUST 1967
Air War US planes fly a record 197 missions, the highest total for a single day since 14

October 1966. They hit targets ranging from the Hanoi-Haiphong sector to the DMZ.

4 AUGUST 1967
USA: Domestic The US Court of Military Appeals in Washington upholds the 1965 court-martial of 2nd Lieutenant Henry H Howe, who had been sentenced to dismissal from service and a year of hard labor for participating in an anti-war demonstration.

6-8 AUGUST 1967
South Vietnam The election campaign opens amid opposition charges that the military slate headed by Thieu and Ky is deliberately impeding campaign efforts by the 10 civilian presidential candidates. The civilians charge harassment (6 August) at the start of their scheduled 22-day government-sponsored provincial tour. Thieu says the government had no intention of thwarting the Quangtri rally, and attributes the mix-up to 'an inadvertent technical error.'

7 AUGUST 1967
North Vietnam The North Vietnamese newspaper *Nhan Dan* reports that Communist China has signed an agreement to give Hanoi an undisclosed amount of aid in the form of an outright grant.
Ground War Vietcong gunfire downs five US helicopters along the Saigon River four miles from Saigon.

9-25 AUGUST 1967
USA: Government The Senate Preparedness Subcommittee holds closed hearings on the conduct of the air war. This subcommittee is known for its hard-line views and military sympathies. Testimony is given by high-ranking military officers, all of whom emphasize the need to continue and even expand the air war against North Vietnam. Secretary McNamara, on 25 August, offers a dissenting view, asserting that bombing of North Vietnam had not (1) reduced the movement of enemy supplies into South Vietnam; (2) seriously damaged the economy of North Vietnam; (3) broken the morale of the North Vietnamese people.

9 AUGUST 1967
Ground War US First Cavalry troops land near a North Vietnamese fortified position in the Songre Valley, 25 miles west of Ducpho; five US helicopters are lost to enemy gunfire.

CHRONOLOGY

11-14 AUGUST 1967
Air War US planes bomb North Vietnamese targets on the new list authorized 8 August by President Johnson. On 11 August, two Navy A-6 Intruder jets stray off course into China, after bombing the Ducnoi rail yard, seven miles north of Hanoi and 75 miles from the Chinese border. The Paul Doumer (Long-bien) bridge, which spans the Red River in the northeast part of Hanoi, is also attacked. On 12 August US planes carry out a series of attacks in the Hanoi area, including rail and highway bridges crossing the Canal des Rapides, ammunition dumps at the Kienan MiG airbase, five miles southwest of Hai-phong, and surface-to-air missile sites 11 miles southeast of Hanoi. The raids continue on 13 August, when US planes bomb the Langson rail and highway bridge spanning the Kikung River, ten miles from the Chinese border. It is the closest target to China ever hit by US planes. US pilots also bomb rail yards at Langgai and Langdang, 19 and 26 miles from the Chinese border.

13-19 AUGUST 1967
Air War US B-52s carry out raids against the southern part of North Vietnam on 13, 15, and 18 August. The bombings are directed against North Vietnamese troops and installations in the DMZ and in the sector just north of the buffer area. On 19 August a record 209 missions are directed against coastal shipping and infiltration traffic.

16-23 AUGUST 1967
USA: Government The US Senate Foreign Relations Committee holds hearings on the extent of foreign commitments; the Johnson administration's broad interpretation of the 1964 Gulf of Tonkin resolution comes under fire. At his press conference of 18 August, President Johnston says that 'Congress could rescind the resolution if it thought we have acted unwisely or improperly.'

19 AUGUST 1967
South Vietnam Presidential candidate Thieu seeks to dispel any idea that the military would oppose the accession of a civilian regime.
Ground War From his helicopter gunship, Captain Stephen Pless sees four Americans from a downed US Army helicopter being bayoneted and beaten by more than 30 Vietcong on a remote beach. Pless dives and fires his machine guns and rockets at the enemy soldiers as they race to the trees, then gets three wounded men from the downed helicopter aboard his aircraft. Under heavy fire from the Vietcong, he makes his escape in the overloaded craft.

21 AUGUST 1967
Air War Two US Navy A-6A Intruder Jet bombers from the carrier *Constellation* are pursued by North Vietnam MiG jets and stray over the Chinese border, where they are shot down. Peking claims its air force downed the planes.

25 AUGUST 1967
North Vietnam Hanoi's Administrative Committee orders all workers in light industry and all craftsmen and their families to leave the city; only persons vital to the city's defense and production are to remain.

25-27 AUGUST 1967
USA: Government Secretary of Defense McNamara refuses a request from military commanders to bomb all MiG bases in North Vietnam. McNamara estimates on 25 August that about 20 North Vietnamese MiGs are based there. Other Defense Department officials say this means that the remainder of North Vietnam's 75-MiG force is based in China. *The New York Times* reports on 27 August that Communist Chinese territory is being used by North Vietnamese MiGs 'to escape air clashes with US planes.'

26 AUGUST 1967
South Vietnam Presidential candidate Thieu denies opposition charges that he and Ky seek to rig the election. Thieu promises again to stop the bombing for a week as a 'good-will gesture' if he is elected.

27 AUGUST 1967
Guerrilla War Vietcong units kill an estimated 355 persons in a series of co-ordinated attacks ranging from the northern provinces to the Mekong Delta. Heaviest hit were the delta cities of Cantho and Hojan, 30 miles south of Hué.

28 AUGUST 1967
USA: Domestic Plans for a massive protest march on 21 October in Washington are announced by the Reverend Thomas Lee Hayes, speaking for the National Mobilization Committee.

Smoke grenades in a tree notify approaching aircraft of the position of allied infantry.

28 AUGUST-1 SEPTEMBER 1967
USA: Government Senator Mike Mansfield (D-MT) makes a proposal endorsed by 10 other senators to bring a peace plan before the United Nations.

29 AUGUST 1969
North Vietnam Hanoi declares that Communist activity has intensified in South Vietnam as a direct result of the increased US air war against North Vietnam. It vows to match every phase of US military escalation.

30 AUGUST 1969
Guerrilla War The US Marine helicopter base at Phubai, five miles south of Hué, is attacked by Vietcong. It is reported that two men are killed and 17 wounded, and 13 helicopters damaged. Later, US sources concede that 10 were killed and 30 wounded. The principal target of the raid is a secret radio station manned by Chinese Nationalists, who monitor North Vietnamese and Chinese Communist communications. The South Vietnamese military report that 18 helicop-

ters were damaged, 55 South Vietnamese troops killed, and 61 wounded in the Vietcong raid.

31 AUGUST 1967
USA: Government The Senate Preparedness Investigating Committee calls unanimously for intensification of bombing against North Vietnam and closing the port of Haiphong.

1 SEPTEMBER 1967
North Vietnam Premier Phan Van Dong reiterates his government's position that an unconditional halt in US raids on the North is Hanoi's prerequisite to peace negotiations.

1 SEPTEMBER-4 OCTOBER 1967
Ground War North Vietnamese artillery and mortars pound the US Marine base at Conthien, five miles below the DMZ throughout September. The adjacent bases of Dongha, Camp Carroll, and Camlo are also shelled. Since 13 August, B-52s have attacked 83 times along the DMZ; finally, with US artillery, they relieve pressure on Conthien.

CHRONOLOGY

2 SEPTEMBER 1967
South Vietnam Presidential candidate Thieu addresses election observers from 24 nations and says that he will abide by the result of the national election. Thieu asserts that 'during the campaign, everyone can see that there was complete freedom of speech and complete freedom for the press to report.' Later that day, the government announces the suppression of two Saigon newspapers.

3 SEPTEMBER 1967
South Vietnam The national election returns Chief of State Thieu to a four-year term as president of South Vietnam, with Premier Ky as vice-president. They received 35 percent of total votes cast, with the rest divided among the other 10 candidates.

4-5 SEPTEMBER 1967
South Vietnam Opposition candidates charge that the elections were rigged in favor of the Thieu-Ky military slate. A favorable impression of the election was reported by 22 prominent Americans who visited Vietnam as election observers.

4 SEPTEMBER 1967
USA: Domestic Governor George Romney (R-MI) seriously impairs his presidential prospects when he charges in a TV interview that he had undergone 'brainwashing' during his visit to Vietnam in 1965: 'I just had the greatest brainwashing that anyone can get when you go over to Vietnam, not only by the generals, but also by the diplomatic corps over there, and they do a thorough job.'

4-7 SEPTEMBER 1967
Ground War In a fierce four-day battle in the Queson Valley, 25 miles south of Danang, 114 men of the US 5th Marine Regiment are killed; there are 376 North Vietnamese casualties.

7-8 SEPTEMBER 1967
USA: Military Secretary of Defense McNamara announces plans to build a fortified barrier, including 'highly sophisticated equipment,' just south of the eastern end of the DMZ, to curb the flow of arms and troops from North Vietnam to the South. General Westmoreland and Marine commanders in Quangtri Province oppose the 'McNamara Line,' contending that surprise attacks inside the DMZ are more effective than a static defense would be.

9 SEPTEMBER 1967
USA: Domestic Governor George Romney attempts to correct the apparent damage to his presidential prospects arising from his 4 September reference to 'brainwashing. He charges that the administration has 'kept the American people from knowing the facts about the Vietnam war and its full impact on our domestic and foreign affairs.'

10 SEPTEMBER 1967
Air War US planes bomb the North Vietnamese port of Campha, in the first raid against the dock area of a major Communist port. Campha is 46 miles northeast of Haiphong.

11 SEPTEMBER 1967
Air War US jets carry out heavy raids on Haiphong and its suburbs in a major effort to isolate the port area from the rest of the country. All rail traffic from the port and most road movement from Haiphong is reportedly halted, with damage to several foreign ships in the harbor.

13-16 SEPTEMBER 1967
Ground War In Operation Coronado 5, the US 9th Infantry Division, flanked by South Vietnamese forces, battles the Vietcong in the Mekong Delta 47 miles southwest of Saigon. Allied troops are supported by 39 US Air Force strikes and by artillery fire.

14-15 SEPTEMBER 1967
Diplomatic Two separate news reports indicate that Hanoi has interest in peace talks. An *Agence France-Presse* dispatch from Hanoi quotes 'reliable sources' as saying that peace talks could begin 3-4 weeks after the cessation of US bombing attacks. The second report comes from Canadian External Affairs Minister Paul Martin, who says that officials in Hanoi had indicated that they were interested in opening discussions to end the war. US State Department officials express doubt that North Vietnam's position has changed.

14-16 SEPTEMBER 1967
North Vietnam General Vo Nguyen Giap, North Vietnam's defense minister, gives an analysis of the war that appears in the newspaper *Quang Doi Nhan Can*. Giap says the allied pacification program for winning control of the South Vietnamese countryside had failed because US troops needed to make it effective had to be shifted to the area below

the DMZ to reinforce US Marines under heavy attack there. Giap presents two options for the United States: to expand the ground war by invading North Vietnam, or to continue increasing military pressure with a limited number of troops.

15-16 SEPTEMBER 1967
Guerrilla War A flotilla of the US Navy's River Assault Task Force comes under heavy Vietcong attack in the Mekong Delta on the Rachba River. Fighting ends next day with 69 Vietcong killed. US casualties are 21 killed.

17 SEPTEMBER 1967
Air War US planes bomb the Thatkhe highway bridge, seven miles from the Chinese border – the closest that US bombing has come to Communist China's frontier.

19 SEPTEMBER 1967
South Vietnam The Chinese Nationalist embassy in Saigon is heavily damaged by a bomb explosion.

21 SEPTEMBER 1967
South Vietnam The first Thai combat troops arrive in Saigon and are greeted by General Westmoreland as they disembark. The arrival of the 1200-man force brings to six the number of allied countries that have sent troops to Vietnam.
Air War US Navy planes return to Haiphong and destroy the last intact bridge, on the Kienan highway leading from Haiphong.
UN Secretary Goldberg addresses the United Nations General Assembly and says that the UN has a 'right and duty to concern itself with the Vietnam problem.' Soviet Foreign Minister Andrei Gromyko tells the assembly the next day that 'the most serious threat to peace in the world is the United States.'

24 SEPTEMBER 1967
USA: Domestic The Americans for Democratic Action (ADA) adopts a resolution against the administration's position in Vietnam and charges that in Vietnam the United States is 'in league with a corrupt and illiberal government supported by a minority of the people.'
South Vietnam Demonstrations against the election of Thieu and Ky are held in Saigon, Sanang and Hué. The demonstrators, supported by the militant Buddhist faction, charge the elections had been rigged, and demand that the Constituent Assembly cancel the results.

26 SEPTEMBER 1967
USA: Domestic The Court of Military Appeals in Washington upholds the court-martial convictions of three army privates who had refused to go to Vietnam.
Air War Navy fighter-bombers attack two key bridges one mile and 1.7 miles from the center of Haiphong. Air force pilots pound the Thanhmoi railroad yard northeast of Hanoi.
Laos Laotian Premier Souvanna Phouma expresses opposition to any extension of the 'McNamara line' into Laos. To permit the barrier, he says, would 'enlarge the Vietnam conflict at a time when we are trying to limit and contain it.'

27 SEPTEMBER 1967
USA: Domestic Senator Thruston B Morton (R-KY) says that President Johnson had been 'brainwashed' by the 'military-industrial complex' into believing a military victory could be achieved in Vietnam. A group of 320 professors, writers, ministers and other professional people run an advertisement in the *New Republic* and the *New York Review of Books* requesting funds for a movement to help youths resist the draft.

28 SEPTEMBER 1967
Air War Navy pilots from the *Coral Sea* knock down part of the last intact bridge which carried the only major road and rail line out of Haiphong. Four bridges in Haiphong have been destroyed since 11 September, when a concerted drive was launched to cut off the port area.

29 SEPTEMBER 1967
USA: Government President Johnson, in a televised speech in San Antonio, Texas, restates US terms for a halt in the air and naval bombardment of North Vietnam.

30 SEPTEMBER-3 OCTOBER 1967
South Vietnam The South Vietnamese Constituent Assembly meets to debate whether to legalize the election results as 2000 students outside the assembly demonstrate against the elections. The Assembly concedes 2724 cases of irregularities affecting over 1 million of the 5,853,251 votes cast. But in discarding votes in precincts where these discrepancies had occurred, Thieu's margin over his nearest rival increased, the Assembly said. On 3 October, an Assembly vote of 58-43 validates the results of the national election.

CHRONOLOGY

Vietcong who defected to the South took part in indoctrination classes.

30 SEPTEMBER 1967
Air War Navy planes bomb the Loidong transshipment point on the Cua Cam estuary four miles northeast of Haiphong. Other planes pound the Kienan MiG base, the Kepha army barracks, and the Phucloi petroleum storage area near Vinh.

2 OCTOBER 1967
USA: Military The increased US aerial offensive that started against North Vietnam 11 August has slowed the flow of war supplies from Communist China to Hanoi, according to US State and Defense officials. The bombing of bridges has halted the movement of military material on the key rail line from Dongdang, near the Chinese border to Hanoi. US officials concede that Communist military equipment is reaching Hanoi by other means.
USA: Domestic Senator John Sherman Cooper (R-KY) urges the United States to take the 'first step' toward negotiations with an 'unconditional cessation' of the bombing of North Vietnam. Senator Gale McGee (D-WY) defends administration policy saying the

'stake is not only Vietnam but all the nations in Southeast Asia.'

3 OCTOBER 1967
USA: Domestic Senate Republican whip Thomas Kuchel (CA) warns that a unilateral halt in bombing would be of 'enormous value to the North Vietnamese' by permitting them to supply their forces in South Vietnam. Senator Stuart Symington (D-MO) proposes that the United States stop all military action and the South Vietnam government announce it will negotiate with the NLF.
Air War US raids center on key bridges at Locbinh and Caobang.

4 OCTOBER 1967
Ground War About 4000 troops of the US First Cavalry Division (Airmobile), 3rd Brigade are flown to two of South Vietnam's northernmost provinces – Quangtin and Quangngai – to relieve pressure on Marine units fighting in Quangtri, Thauthien and Quangngai. This move places these provinces under Army responsibility and may free Marines to move north along the DMZ.

17 OCTOBER 1967

Air War US planes again attack the Langson railroad bridge and the Chienchiang highway bridge close to the Chinese border.

5 OCTOBER 1967

USA: Government Senator Charles Percy (R-IL) with the support of 22 other Senators, introduces a resolution urging President Johnson to intensify efforts to have the free nations of Asia make a greater contribution of economic and military aid to the South Vietnamese cause.

Air War US planes strike the Kep, Kienan and Hoalac MiG bases and pound a petroleum storage area two miles northwest of the center of Haiphong. North Vietnam Minister of Education Nguyen Van Huyen charges that an US air raid on a North Vietnamese school on 20 September had killed 33 children and wounded 28.

6 OCTOBER 1967

Air War US Navy pilots fly 34 missions as they again strike the Chienchiang and the Langson bridges near the Chinese border, a bridge 39 miles northeast of Hanoi, a railroad yard near Motrang and two antiaircraft sites south of Donghoi. Also attacked are the Namdinh power plant, 45 miles southwest of Haiphong, a railway and highway bridge 24 miles southeast of Hanoi and eight buildings in the Yenbac military storage area.

7 OCTOBER 1967

USA: Government President Johnson, at a Democratic fund-raising event, says he will hold fast in Vietnam because that road 'leads to a more secure America and a free Asia.'

Air War US planes strike at Soviet-built helicopters on the ground, 30 miles west of Hanoi and destroy six of the aircraft. It is the first time in the war that Soviet helicopters have been bombed and destroyed.

11 OCTOBER 1967

USA: Domestic Speaker John W McCormack (D-MA) defends administration policy, by declaring, 'If I was one of those [whose dissent heartened the enemy], my conscience would disturb me the rest of my life.'

12 OCTOBER 1967

USA: Government During a news conference Secretary Dean Rusk says that Congressional proposals for peace initiatives – a bombing halt or limitation, UN Action or a new Geneva conference – were futile because of

Hanoi's opposition. Without the pressure of the bombing of North Vietnam, 'where would be the incentive for peace,' he asks.

12-14 OCTOBER 1967

Air War US Navy planes attack Haiphong shipyards and US officials report heavy damage, claiming direct hits on drydocks west of the city. Australian Communist correspondent Wilfred Burchett files a report 14 October saying that on personal observation these attacks were directed against a large hospital complex which was almost completely destroyed. Burchett says he visited the port area after the raid and found no evidence of air damage. He quotes the Haiphong mayor as saying that a third of the city's residential areas have been destroyed, principally since the heavy raids started 1 September.

13 OCTOBER 1967

Ground War Conthien, just below the DMZ, and the nearby Marine base at Giolinh come under heavy North Vietnamese shelling. The bases are pounded by 364 rounds of artillery and recoilless fire. The following day Communist troops, following a 130-round mortar barrage, attempt to penetrate the Marine positions near Conthien, but they are thrown back in fierce hand to hand combat.

14 OCTOBER 1967

USA: Domestic Senator William J Fulbright (D-AR) accuses Secretary Rusk of a 'McCarthy-type crusade' against war critics.

Air War US jets bomb several targets in the Hanoi-Haiphong area that hitherto had been spared. The planes pound a barge building and repair yard 1½ miles west of Haiphong and an early warning radar station at Kienan.

16-21 OCTOBER 1967

USA: Domestic Demonstrations against the draft are held throughout the United States by opponents of US policy in Vietnam. Major incidents occur in Oakland, California, where 125 protesters are arrested.

17 OCTOBER 1967

North Vietnam Hanoi radio reports that the NLF has formed a new organization designed to spur anti-war sentiment in the United States.

USA: Government In a televised press conference, President Johnson denies the charge that he is 'trying to label all criticism of his Vietnam policy as unpatriotic.' He says that

The three top men in the Vietnamese government, Ky, Thieu and Loc, watch planes of the Vietnamese Air Force fly past during a National Day parade.

he doesn't question the motives of dissenters. 'I do question their judgment.'

19 OCTOBER 1967

North Vietnam Hanoi rejects the Johnson terms for negotiations expressed in his San Antonio statement of 29 September.

USA: Domestic Senator Henry Jackson (D-WA) cautions against the 'negative' tone of anti-administration criticism saying he was speaking out because he fears 'that our frustrations are showing.'

21-23 OCTOBER 1967

USA: Domestic More than 50,000 people – liberals, radicals, black nationalists, hippies, professors, women's groups and war veterans – participate in massive demonstrations in Washington against US policy in Vietnam.' The demonstrators march in an orderly procession to the Pentagon where they hold another rally and a vigil that continues through the early hours of 23 October. A force of 10,000 troops surround the Defense Department. The Washington anti-war protest is paralleled by demonstrations in Western Europe and Japan.

22 OCTOBER 1967

USA: Domestic Representative Morris K Udall (D-AZ) says in a speech that the United States is on 'a mistaken and dangerous road' in Vietnam and should stop escalation and start 'bringing American boys home and start turning this war back to the Vietnamese.'

Air War For the first time, US Navy jets bomb the North Vietnamese naval base at Nuidong, seven miles northeast of Haiphong.

23-30 OCTOBER 1967

Air War US jets bomb many targets not previously touched as sustained attacks are carried out on the Hanoi-Haiphong area. US command acknowledges the loss of 13 US planes while Hanoi claims at least 35 US planes are shot down.

24-25 OCTOBER 1967

USA: Domestic Demonstrations are held on two university campuses against the Dow Chemical Company, a manufacturer of napalm used in Vietnam.

Air War The huge Phucyen airfield, 18 miles northwest of Hanoi is struck for the first time. It is believed to be the largest MiG base in North Vietnam. More than 65 US planes pound the field all day. The following day the planes return and bomb the airfield again.

25 OCTOBER 1967

USA: Government Senator Mike Mansfield (D-MT) and 54 co-sponsors introduce a resolution in the Senate urging the President to provide the initiative to have the UN Security Council take up a US proposal to discuss the Vietnam conflict.

25-30 OCTOBER 1967

Air War US planes carry on a sustained attack on targets in the Hanoi-Haiphong area. On 25 October, jets bomb the Longbien bridge, Hanoi's only rail and road link with Haiphong and the Chinese border. The following day Navy planes bomb a 32,000 kilowatt thermal power plant about a mile north of the center of Hanoi. Air Force planes from Thailand bomb targets three miles south of Hanoi on 27 October. The Longbien bridge and other targets are hit on 28 October. On successive days US planes pound the Kieana, Kep and Hoalac MiG bases and the Yenbai airfield.

29 OCTOBER-3 NOVEMBER 1967

Ground War The Vietcong's 273rd Regiment attacks a US Special Forces camp at Locninh and the defenders are quickly reinforced by two battalions of the US First Infantry Division, about 1400 men. The US forces fight the Vietcong through the streets from house to house and finally drive them from Locninh. More than 900 Vietcong are reported killed during the encounter.

31 OCTOBER 1967

North Vietnam Hanoi appeals to all governments to help stop the US bombing of Vietnam. The statement claims that 'the furious attacks on the area in recent days have killed or wounded 200 civilians and destroyed or set fire to more than 150 homes.'

2 NOVEMBER 1967

USA: Government President Johnson holds a secret meeting with some of the nation's most prestigious leaders, 'the Wise Men.' They include former Secretary of State Dean Acheson, General of the Army Omar Bradley, Ambassador-at-Large W Averell Harriman, and former ambassador to Vietnam, Henry Cabot Lodge. Johnson asks them for advice on 'How do we unite the country?' The conclusion they reach is that the administration must offer 'ways of guiding the press to show the light at the end of the tunnel.' In effect, they decide that the American people must be given more optimistic reports.

Confrontations were a standard part of anti-war demonstrations.

USA: Government Selective Service director Lewis B Hersey confirms that there is a policy to require early induction of draft-eligible persons interfering with draft procedures.

UN US Ambassador to the UN Arthur Goldberg says that the Johnson administration favors the participation of the NLF in UN Security Council discussions or in a reconvened Geneva conference on ending the war.

3-22 NOVEMBER 1967

Ground War One of the bloodiest and most sustained battles of the war is fought by US and North Vietnamese troops in the Central Highlands around Dakto. Dakto, about 280 miles north of Saigon near the Cambodian border, is the site of a large US military complex that includes an airfield, an ammunition dump and a South Vietnamese militia camp. The 1000 US troops in the Dakto area are reinforced before the battle starts with 3500-

4500 troops of the US 4th Division and the 173rd Airborne Brigade. They face four Communist regiments of about 6000 troops. The climax of the operation comes in a savage battle 19-22 November for Hill 875, 12 miles southwest of Dakto. The 173rd Brigade forces the North Vietnamese to abandon their last defense line on the ridge of Hill 875. The Brigade suffered a loss of 158 men, 30 of whom died as a result of an accidental US air strike on US positions 19 November. In the 19 days of action, North Vietnamese fatalities are estimated at 1455 while 285 US men are killed, 985 wounded and 18 missing.

6 NOVEMBER 1967

Air War The Giathuong storage complex, three miles from the center of Hanoi, a target hitherto on the restricted list, is bombed by USAF planes from Korat Air Base in Thailand.

CHRONOLOGY

7 NOVEMBER 1967

Air War US planes bomb rail facilities 21 miles from the Chinese border. Other planes attack the Anninhgoai shipyard and repair facilities 12 miles west of Haiphong, the first time these targets had been attacked.

9 NOVEMBER 1967

South Vietnam President Thieu announces the formation of a new 19 member cabinet. US officials in Saigon express disappointment that Thieu did not include at least some of the defeated civilian candidates so as to form a government of national unity. With the exception of two new officials, the cabinet is made up entirely of ministers who had served in the previous government.

11 NOVEMBER 1967

POWs Three US Army prisoners are released by the Vietcong in ceremonies held in Pnompenh, Cambodia. The three men are turned over to Thomas Hayden, a 'new Left' activist and member of the US committee formed to help the three Americans. US authorities in Saigon say they had been 'brainwashed' but this is denied by the State Department. The Vietcong say the men were released in response to opposition to the war in the United States and also to express support for the 'courageous struggle' of the Blacks in the United States.

11-12 NOVEMBER 1967

USA: Domestic Senator Eugene McCarthy (D-MN) addresses a convention of the College Young Democratic Club of America and asserts that Democrats who oppose administration policy on Vietnam 'have an obligation to speak out and party unity is not a sufficient excuse for their silence.' The next day the convention approves a resolution condemning the administration's Vietnam policy

14 NOVEMBER 1967

USA: Domestic Anti-war demonstrators clash with police in New York during a rally in protest against Secretary Rusk who is attending a dinner of the Foreign Policy Association.

19 NOVEMBER 1967

USA: Government The Senate Foreign relations Committee approves 14-0 a resolution to curb the commitment of US armed forces and a resolution urging the President to take the initiative to have the Vietnamese conflict brought before the UN Security Council.

19-24 NOVEMBER 1967

Cambodia AP Correspondents George McArthur and Horst Faas file stories from Pnomphenh reporting that they have visited a Vietcong base in Cambodia. The Cambodian government asserts 21 November that the reports of a new military complex constructed by the Vietcong in Cambodia are 'grotesque and a challenge to good sense.' In retaliation for the US press reports, Sihanouk says 24 November that 'from now on the door of Cambodia is hermetically sealed to all American journalists.'

20-21 NOVEMBER 1967

USA: Domestic Police attack San Jose (California) State College students demonstrating against Dow Chemical Company after they refuse to disperse. The next day the students defy Governor Ronald Reagan's warning against further demonstrations and again stage an anti-Dow demonstration.

22 NOVEMBER 1967

USA: Military General Westmoreland briefs officials at the Pentagon and says that the battle around Dakto was 'the beginning of a great defeat for the enemy.' He reveals that a document removed from the body of a dead North Vietnamese soldier on 6 November revealed that the Dakto battle was to be the beginning of a winter/spring offensive by the B-3 Front. Westmoreland was reportedly brought home from Vietnam by President Johnson to fulfill a public relations task and revive flagging morale throughout the country. His message on US military prospects in Vietnam is continually optimistic.

25 NOVEMBER 1967

USA: Domestic The Very Reverend Edward Swanstrom, auxiliary Roman Catholic Bishop of New York and head of Catholic Relief Services, writes in the weekly magazine *Ave Marie* (dated 2 December) that the overseas relief agency of the Roman Catholic Church in the United States has provided funds for sending medical supplies and hospital equipment to North Vietnam.

29 NOVEMBER 1967

USA: Government Robert S McNamara resigns as Secretary of Defense to be president of the World Bank.

30 NOVEMBER 1967

USA: Domestic Senator Eugene J McCarthy

A US Naval officer sets fire to a Vietcong bunker using a flaming arrow and a longbow.

(D-MN) announces at a Washington press conference that he would enter five or six Democratic Presidential primaries in 1968 to further the campaign for a negotiated settlement of the war in Vietnam.

1-7 DECEMBER 1967
South Vietnam South Vietnamese police arrest a Vietcong representative on his way to meet with US embassy officials. He is identified 2 December as Nguyen Van Huan and he was reportedly intercepted after the CIA had arranged a meeting between him and Ambassador Bunker. South Vietnamese Deputy Phan Xuan Huy charges the incident represents a 'flagrant act of American interference in the internal affairs of South Vietnam.' A Washington report concedes that the United States and South Vietnamese officials have been in touch with NLF representatives in previous months but the contacts had dealt with prisoners and similar matters and not peace negotiations. But the State Department does not concede until 6 December that a Vietcong representative had been blocked

in an effort to meet with US officials in Saigon. In a related matter, the *Washington Post* reports 1 December that the NLF had sought to send representatives to the UN in October to discuss the Vietnamese conflict with the UN General Assembly.

2 DECEMBER 1967
Thailand Thailand reports that it has received US ground to air missiles to protect it against possible retaliation for permitting its territory to be used for the launching of US air strikes against North Vietnam.

4 DECEMBER 1967
Ground War The United States 9th Infantry Division's riverine force and 400 South Vietnamese in armored troop carriers come under Vietcong fire in the Mekong Delta. In a coordinated action with the Vietnamese US troops surround and attack the Vietcong battalion. They are assisted by a helicopter drop of another 9th Division Battalion. They report killing 235 men of the 300-member Vietcong battalion.

CHRONOLOGY

4-8 DECEMBER 1967
USA: Domestic A coalition of about 40 anti-war organizations stage 'Stop the Draft Week' demonstrations.

6-8 DECEMBER 1967
Ground War US and South Vietnamese, troops encounter the North Vietnamese 3rd Division near Bongson, 140 miles south of Danang and engage in a fierce battle. US losses total 16 killed and 90 wounded while the North Vietnamese lose 252 soldiers.

8-10 DECEMBER 1967
Ground War A South Vietnamese force assisted by US air artillery traps two Vietcong battalions near Vithanh, 100 miles southwest of Saigon. The South Vietnam force claims to have killed 365 Communist troops but US officers question the claim.

10 DECEMBER 1967
Ground War A US artillery base camp 50 miles north of Saigon repells a North Vietnamese/Vietcong attack, killing 124.

14-19 DECEMBER 1967
Air War US planes bomb rail yards at Yenvien, six miles east of Hanoi. A North Vietnamese report claims that homes in the northeastern section of Hanoi are destroyed in the attack. On 19 December it is reported that US pilots have been granted permission to fly through two previously restricted target areas in North Vietnam – the 25 mile strip along the Chinese Communist border and the outer 20 miles circle around Hanoi. White House permission is still required to bomb targets in both sections.

15-16 DECEMBER 1967
Ground War Renewed fighting breaks out in the Bongson area resulting in the deaths of 219 Communist soldiers.

18 DECEMBER 1967
USA: Military General Earle G Wheeler, Chairman of the Joint Chiefs, suggests that the single most important factor prolonging the war is Hanoi's calculation that there is a reasonable possibility of a change in US policy before the collapse of the Vietcong.
USA: Domestic General David M Shoup, retired US Marine Commandant, says that it is 'pure unadulterated poppycock' to believe US presence is necessary in South Vietnam to prevent a Communist invasion of the USA.

Shoup derides the administration's efforts 'to keep the people worried about the Communists crawling up the banks of Pearl Harbor or crawling up the Palisades or crawling up the beaches of Los Angeles.'

18-19 DECEMBER 1967
USA: Domestic About 750 anti-war demonstrators try to block the armed forces induction center in Oakland and 268 are arrested.

20-24 DECEMBER 1967
USA: Government President Johnson attends a memorial service for the Australian Prime Minister Harold Holt and then visits Vietnam, Thailand and the Vatican. In a taped TV interview Johnson praises South Vietnam president Thieu for 'his statesmanlike position' in agreeing to hold informal talks with members of the NLF. But Thieu, before departing for Australia, says 20 December, 'we will never recognize the front as a government.' He says he is willing to talk to them on an individual basis but not as front representatives. Thieu and Johnson meet in Canberra on 21 December and later issue a joint communiqué affirming that Thieu is ready 'to discuss relevant matters with any individual now associated with the NLF' but the front would not be recognized as an independent organization by the Saigon government. Johnson visits the Korat air base in Thailand 23 December where he tells US pilots that the United States and its allies are 'defeating this aggression.' The President next visits US combat troops in Camranh Bay in South Vietnam and tells them that the enemy 'knows that he has met his master in the field.' Johnson then flies to Rome and meets with Pope Paul VI for over an hour with only interpreters present. A Vatican statement says the Pope had advanced proposals toward attaining peace in Vietnam.

21-22 DECEMBER 1967
Ground War To thwart plans for what Hanoi calls 'the winter-spring offensive,' US forces launch a drive in and around the DMZ. An estimated 35,000-45,000 Communist troops are in or just above the zone. About 1000 Marines land by boat and helicopter along the coast of Quangngai Province and exchange fire with entrenched Communists. USAF B-52s carry out raids on Communist positions inside the zone on 22 December. Guns of an US cruiser destroy a Communist bunker five miles east of Giolinh.

24-25 DECEMBER 1967
South Vietnam Ground action is largely halted and air operations suspended because of a Christmas truce. North Vietnam charges that the United States violates the truce by carrying out air strikes against eight targets.

26-27 DECEMBER 1967
Ground War South Vietnam troops, backed by US artillery and air strikes, encounter the Vietcong 416th Battalion during a search-and-destroy mission aimed at providing security for pacification teams in Quantri Province. South Vietnam claims 203 enemy killed.

Cambodia The US State Department on 26 December discloses that a note was sent to Cambodia assuring the Pnompenh regime that it has 'no hostile intentions toward Cambodia or Cambodia territory.' The note is made public after Cambodia broadcasts the text of its reply which says that Cambodia territory is not being used as a base for Communist forces involved in Vietnam. Cambodia further charges that the US and South Vietnamese forces commit 'flagrant violations of international law through daily incursions into Cambodian territory for purposes of sabotage and assassination.' The United States again disavows intentions of

Members of the Army of the Republic of Vietnam at a machine gun post armed with an M-60.

expanding the Vietnam war: 'The root cause of incidents affecting Cambodia territory is the Vietcong and North Vietnam presence in the frontier region and their use of Cambodian territory in violation of the neutrality of Cambodia.' Cambodian's Prince Sihanouk warns that if US troops invade Cambodia in search of North Vietnam and Vietcong forces, his government would ask China, Russia and 'other anti-imperialistic powers' for new military aid.

26-29 DECEMBER 1967
Laos Laotian Premier Souvanna Phooma reports that North Vietnamese troops have started a general offensive against government forces in southern Laos. Laotian sources report at least one battle is being waged near Phalane, but say Laotian troops appear to be in control of the situation. North Vietnam on 29 December denies that its forces had begun a drive in Laos.

27 DECEMBER 1967
Ground War US Marines battle North Vietnam troops in the coastal village of Thonthamkhe on the borders of Quangtri and Thathien Provinces and 48 Marines are killed and 81 wounded.

30 DECEMBER 1967
South Vietnam South Vietnam announces a 36 hour New Year's truce. A Vietcong ceasefire also goes into effect. Ho Chi Minh extends New Year's greetings to Americans opposed to US policies in Vietnam.

31 DECEMBER 1967
State of the War This past year was a time of continued build-up of forces on both sides to maintain the intensified hostilities. The US contingent increased from about 380,000 at the outset of 1967 to approximately 500,000 troops by its end. (The number is actually closer to 600,000 when Americans serving in Thailand as well as those of the 7th Fleet are included.) South Vietnamese regular forces now number some 200,000. Estimates of Vietcong/North Vietnamese forces have been debated throughout the year, but it is agreed that the regular forces now number about 250,000, with at least that many in the irregular and political units. Since February 1965, the US and South Vietnamese air forces have dropped more than 1,500,000 tons of bombs on North and South Vietnam, and it is estimated that these attacks have cut North

Vietnam's electrical-generating capacity by 85 percent. But during this year alone, the US has lost 328 airplanes over North Vietnam (bringing the total lost since February to 779). The United States has lost 225 other planes over South Vietnam since 1961; additionally, more than 500 helicopters have been lost in combat and 1000 other planes and helicopters have been lost in accidents. All this is becoming costly: for one fiscal year ending June 1967, the war had cost the US $21,000,000,000. Obtaining the Americans to fight in Vietnam is beginning to become something of a strain, too: the elite USMC had to take 19,000 draftees in 1967, and the Marines are finding it increasingly harder to find – and retain – qualified officers and noncommissioned officers and technical specialists. For one thing, US casualties are beginning to become significant: in 1976, the US lost 9353 – more than all the dead in all the previous years of the war in Vietnam (with a total of 15,997 since 1961). Another 99,742 US servicemen were wounded in 1967. The South Vietnamese armed forces report 11,135 dead while other allied troops fatalities totaled 189. The Vietcong reportedly killed 3820 South Vietnamese civilians and kidnapped 5318 during 1967. And the US and South Vietnamese claim to have killed about 90,400 enemy soldiers and some 25,000 enemy civilians in 1967, but it is becoming general knowledge that these 'body counts' are greatly inflated.

1 JANUARY 1968
USA: Military In his end of year progress report, Admiral Ulysses Grant Sharp, Commander in Chief, Pacific, declares that Operation Rolling Thunder has been successful not only in terms of matériel destroyed; it has also forced North Vietnam to divert considerable manpower from industrial and agricultural production to military tasks, thus compelling Hanoi to seek ever greater amounts of aid from its Communist allies.

2 JANUARY 1968
South Vietnam Saigon expels *Newsweek* reporter Everett Morton for writing articles critical of the South Vietnamese army.

4 JANUARY 1968
Cambodia The Cambodian government announces that it has accepted military aid from Communist China repeating claims that it feels threatened by the United States.

Two Marines on a village patrol investigate a grass hut.

USSR The Soviet Union charges that US planes damaged a Russian merchant ship during raids on Haiphong and demands that those responsible be punished. The United States expresses its regret, but adds that it is impossible to eliminate such risks.

8 JANUARY 1968
South Vietnam South Vietnamese police arrest 100 peasants in Danang for protesting against the US presence in Vietnam; government officials assert that the demonstration is part of a Vietcong campaign to destabilize the Saigon regime.

9 JANUARY 1968
Ground War Vietcong forces overrun a US airfield at Kontum, killing seven Americans and wounding 25.

12 JANUARY 1968
Cambodia Following talks between Ambassador-to-India Chester Bowles and Prince Sihanouk, the United States and Cambodia announce substantial agreement on measures designed to isolate Cambodia from the war.

13 JANUARY 1968
USA: Military The USAF announces that it will begin training 100 South Vietnamese pilots at a Louisiana base.

USA: Domestic In a statement denouncing administration fiscal policies, a group of 320 economists from 50 colleges and universities opposes any tax increases and asserts that the war is the major source of US economic problems.

Laos Royal Laotian troops suffer a major defeat when a combined North Vietnamese-Pathet Lao force captures the town of Nambac, a government supply center 60 miles north of the royal capital of Luang Prabang.

14 JANUARY 1968
South Vietnam A group of South Vietnamese intellectuals issues a call for elections with National Liberation Front participation.

17 JANUARY 1968
USA: Government In his State of the Union message, President Johnson declares: 'The bombing would stop immediately if talks would take place promptly and with reasonable hopes that they would be productive. And the other side must not take advantage of our restraint.'

18 JANUARY 1968
Cambodia The Cambodian government charges that allied forces entered 200 yards into her territory and killed three Cambodians. The United States acknowledges that

CHRONOLOGY

an allied patrol did make a limited incursion and expressed regret about any casualties.

20 JANUARY-14 APRIL 1968
Ground War One of the most publicized and controversial battles of the war occurs at Khesanh, 14 miles below the DMZ and six miles from the Laotian border. Seized and activated by the US Marines a year earlier, it is used as a staging area for forward patrols. The battle begins on 20 January with a brisk firefight involving the 3rd Battalion, 26th Marines and an NVA Battalion entrenched between two hills northwest of the base. The next day NVA forces overrun the village of Khesanh and North Vietnam long-range artillery opens fire on the base itself, hitting its main ammunition dump and detonating 1500 tons of explosives. An incessant barrage keeps Khesanh's Marine defenders pinned down in their trenches and bunkers. Because the base must be resupplied by air, Lieutenant General Robert Cushman is reluctant to put in any more troops and drafts a battle plan calling for massive artillery and air strikes; during the siege, US planes, dropping 5000 bombs daily, explode the equivalent of five Hiroshima-sized atomic bombs in the area. The relief of Khesanh, called Operation Pegasus, begins in early April as the 1st Air Cavalry Division and an ARVN Battalion approach the base from the east and south, while the 1st Marines push westward to re-open Route 9. The siege is finally lifted on 6 April when the cavalrymen link up with the 9th Marines south of the Khesanh airstrip. In a final clash on Easter Sunday a week later, the 3rd Battalion, 26th Marines drives enemy forces from Hill 881 North. General Westmoreland contends that Khesanh plays a vital blocking role at the western end of the DMZ, and asserts that, should the base fall, NVA forces could flank Marine defenses along the buffer zone. Various statements in *Nhan Dan*, the North Vietnamese Communist Party newspaper, suggest that Hanoi sees the battle as an opportunity to re-enact its famous victory at Dienbienphu. Some US military leaders take a similar view, and when the JCS indicate to President Johnson that Khesanh may indeed become another Dienbienphu, he demands formal assurances that it will not.

21 JANUARY 1968
Ground War Operation Lancaster II, a multibattalion search-and-clear operation involving elements of the 3rd Marine Division lasts until 23 November 1968; it claims 1081 enemy casualties.

22 JANUARY 1968
Guerrilla War The military command of the National Liberation Front issues orders calling for the 'annihilation' of all pacification teams and any forces supporting them.
Ground War The first operation conducted by the 1st Cavalry Division in northern I Corps, Operation Jeb Stuart terminates 31 March, with listed enemy casualties numbering 3268.
Cambodia In a joint communiqué, Prince Sihanouk and Yugoslav President Josip Tito express full support for North Vietnam and the NLF.

23 JANUARY 1968
USA: Military A USN intelligence vessel, the *Pueblo*, is seized along with its 83-man crew by North Korean patrol boats in the Sea of Japan; the US ship – allegedly in violation of the 12-mile territorial limit claimed by North Korea – has been on the same type DeSoto Operation patrol that the *Maddox* was on in the Gulf of Tonkin on 2 August.

25 JANUARY 1968
Laos NVA troops strengthen their position in the northwest corner of South Vietnam by capturing an outpost inside the Laotian border nine miles west of Khesanh.

26 JANUARY 1968
South Vietnam Major General Nguyen Duc Thang quits his position as head of South Vietnam's pacification program. Informed sources report that Thang is disillusioned with the failure of government efforts to curb corruption and frustrated by his inability to secure needed support from other generals. In honor of Tet, the Vietnamese lunar year, President Thieu grants amnesty to nearly 500 prisoners, including many political detainees; Saigon's nighttime curfew is also lifted.

29 JANUARY 1968
USA: Government In his annual budget message, President Johnson asks for $26.3 billion to continue the war and announces an increase in taxes.

30 JANUARY 1968
USA: Government The US Senate unanimously confirms Clark Clifford's appointment as Secretary of Defense.
Ground War At dawn on the first day of the

Tet truce, Vietcong forces, supported by large numbers of NVA troops, launch the largest and best coordinated offensive of the war, driving into the center of South Vietnam's seven largest cities and attacking 30 provincial capitals ranging from the Delta to the DMZ. Among the cities taken during the first days of the offensive are Hué, Dalat, Kontum, and Quangtri; in the north, all five provincial capitals are overrun. At the same time, enemy forces shell numerous allied airfields and bases, while in Saigon, a 19-man Vietcong suicide squad seizes the US Embassy and holds a section of it for six hours until they are routed by an assault force of US paratroopers landed by helicopter on the building's roof. Nearly 1000 Vietcong are believed to have infiltrated Saigon and it requires a week of intense fighting by an estimated 11,000 US and South Vietnamese troops to dislodge them. By 10 February the offensive is largely crushed. The former Imperial capital of Hué takes almost a month of savage house-to-house combat to regain. Efforts to assess the offensive's impact begin well before the fighting ends On 2 February President Johnson announces that the Vietcong have suffered complete military defeat, an appraisal which General Westmoreland echoes four days later in a statement declaring that allied forces have killed more enemy troops in the past seven days than the United States has lost in the entire war. Militarily, Tet is decidedly an US victory; but psycho-logically and politically, it is a disaster. In Saigon by the second week of February, the black-market rate for US dollars – a sure indicator of popular confidence in the government – is soaring out of sight.'

7 FEBRUARY 1968

Ground War After an 18-hour siege, North Vietnamese troops overrun the US Special Forces camp at Langvei, southwest of Khesanh. During the assault, NVA forces use nine PT-76 light tanks, the latest Soviet model, to shatter the camp's defenses. More than 300 allied troops, including eight Americans, are killed in the action.

11 FEBRUARY 1968

South Vietnam The South Vietnamese government announces that it is mobilizing 65,000 more troops as a result of the recent enemy offensive.

13 FEBRUARY 1968

USA: Military Secretary of Defense McNamara approves the deployment of 10,500 troops – a brigade of the 82nd Airborne Division and a Marine regimental landing team – to cope with threats of a second offensive. The JCS, who had argued against dispatching any reinforcements at this time because it would seriously deplete the strategic reserve, immediately send McNamara a memorandum asking that 46,300 reservists and former servicemen be activated.

The citadel at Hué was badly bombed during the Tet Offensive.

CHRONOLOGY

14 FEBRUARY 1968
Air War In the heaviest assault against North Vietnam in six weeks, US planes bomb targets near Hanoi, hitting a bridge, two airfields, and several missile sites.

15 FEBRUARY 1968
USA: Domestic Presidential candidate George Romney (R-MI) states that the Vietnam war will be his principal campaign issue in the New Hampshire primary.

16 FEBRUARY 1968
South Vietnam US officials report that – in addition to the 800,000 listed as refugees prior to 30 January – the Tet Offensive has created 350,000 new refugees.
Air War To bolster allied defenses around Khesanh, the US command deploys the AC-130, equipped with electronic detectors capable of locating the enemy despite fog, darkness, and jungle.
POWs North Vietnam turns over three US pilots shot down the previous fall to representatives of the American Mobilization Committee against the Vietnam War. They are the first prisoners freed by Hanoi and in late March the United States reciprocates by releasing three North Vietnamese sailors.

20 FEBRUARY 1968
USA: Government The Senate Foreign Relations Committee opens hearings to investigate American policy in Vietnam. Early sessions focus on the Gulf of Tonkin incident and lead to a 'credibility gap' dispute with the White House. At issue is whether the administration provided Congress with truthful data at the time it was seeking passage of the Tonkin Gulf resolution, in August 1964, which considerably broadened the President's war-making authority in Southeast Asia.

21 FEBRUARY 1968
USA: Domestic In a major policy statement, the National Council of Churches calls for an immediate bombing halt as a prelude to peace talks.
Sea War The aircraft carrier *Bonhomme Richard* arrives in Vietnam for its fourth combat deployment.

23 FEBRUARY 1968
USA: Military General Earle Wheeler, Chairman of the JCS, departs for South Vietnam to confer with General Westmore-land. During their talks, Wheeler tells Westmoreland that the administration might mobilize the reserves and allow allied forces to move into Laos and Cambodia. Westmoreland replies that the expanded effort will require additional troops – 206,000 more. There is now a basic disagreement that will influence future troop deployments developing between the American and South Vietnamese commands concerning enemy military objectives during the recent offensive: General Westmoreland and his staff believe that Saigon and Khesanh are major targets; ARVN General Cao Van Vien contends that the enemy's primary goal is to split South Vietnam.

24 FEBRUARY 1968
South Vietnam The US mission to Saigon admits for the first time that pacification efforts suffered a severe setback as a result of the Tet Offensive.
Diplomatic UN Secretary-General U Thant issues a statement asserting that if the United States unconditionally halts its bombing of North Vietnam, 'meaningful talks will take place much earlier than is generally supposed.' Thant bases his prediction on the results of recent talks with Soviet Premier Alexei Kosygin, British Prime Minister Harold Wilson, French President de Gaulle, and various North Vietnamese officials. Reacting to Thant's declaration, Senator Mike Mansfield (D-MT) calls for a trial suspension of the bombing.
Ground War South Vietnamese troops retake the Imperial Palace in Hué. Although the Battle of Hué is not officially declared over for another week, this is the last major engagement of the Tet Offensive.
Air War US planes bomb the Red River wharves and warehouses of Hanoi for the first time.

26 FEBRUARY-12 SEPTEMBER 1968
Ground War Operation Houston, a 1st Marine Division operation in the Thua Thien and Quang Nam border region claims 702 enemy casualties.

28 FEBRUARY 1968
USA: Military General Wheeler returns from his recent round of talks with General Westmoreland and immediately delivers a written report to the President, stating that despite the heavy casualties incurred during the Tet Offensive, North Vietnamese and

Marines investigate the ruins of the old imperial capital of Hué.

Vietcong forces now have the initiative: they are 'operating with relative freedom in the countryside,' have pushed South Vietnamese forces back into a 'defensive posture around towns and cities,' seriously undermined the pacification program in many areas, and forced General Westmoreland to place half of his maneuver battalions in the still imperiled northernmost provinces, thus 'stripping the rest of the country of adequate reserves' and depriving the US command of 'an offensive capability.' To meet the new enemy threat and regain the initiative Westmoreland will need more men: 'The add-on requested totals 206,756 spaces for a new proposed ceiling of 731,756.' It is a major turning point in the war. To deny the request will be to concede that the US can impose no military solution to the conflict, but to meet it will require a call-up of reserves and vastly increased expenditures. Rather than making an immediate decision, President Johnson asks Defense Secretary Clark Clifford to conduct a high-level 'A to Z' review of US policy in Vietnam.

29 FEBRUARY 1968
USA: Government Representative L. Mendel Rivers (D-SC) Chairman of the House Armed Services Committee, declares that the US should either use tactical nuclear weapons at Khesanh or withdraw from the base.

29 FEBRUARY-9 DECEMBER 1968
Ground War A US Marine Corps operation, known as Napoleon/Saline, along the Cua Viet River designed to keep that supply line open to port facilities in the Dong Ha area of Quang Tri province; it accounts for 3495 reported enemy casualties.

1 MARCH 1968
South Vietnam President Thieu dismisses seven provincial chiefs in an unprecedented move which many consider a major step towards carrying out his promise to combat corruption and inefficiency.
USSR Asked to assess how the Soviet Union would react to various measures being considered by US policymakers, Ambassador-to-Russia Llewellyn Thompson reports that 'any serious escalation except in South Vietnam would trigger [a] strong Soviet response.'

1 MARCH-30 JULY 1968
Ground War Operation Truong Cong Dinh conducted by ARVN units and elements of the US 9th Infantry Division in the IV Corps provinces of Dinh Tuong and Kien Tuong

Members of a Vietnamese Artillery Battalion prepare a meal of chicken and rice.

which, on 21 May, is combined with Operation People's Road.

2 MARCH 1968
South Vietnam Pacification teams begin returning to hamlets abandoned a month earlier during the Tet Offensive.
Ground War In what is described as one of the costliest ambushes of the war, 48 US troops are killed and 28 wounded four miles north of Tansonnhut Air Base.

4 MARCH 1968
USA: Government In a draft memorandum to the President, the recently formed Clifford Group – which among its principal members incudes outgoing Secretary of Defense Robert McNamara, Deputy Secretary of Defense Paul Nitze, CIA Director Richard Helms, General Maxwell Taylor, Assistant Secretary of State for Far Eastern Affairs William Bundy, and Paul Warnke, head of the Pentagon's politico-military policy office – advises that the administration send 22,000 more troops to Vietnam, but make deployment of the remaining 185,000 men requested by General Westmoreland contingent on future developments. President Johnson asks that the memorandum be sent to General Westmoreland, who, in a reply four days later, welcomes the additional 22,000 troops, but insists that he still needs the full 206,756 reinforcement by year's end.

7 MARCH 1968
USA: Government Senate debate on civil rights is interrupted when several prominent Senators issue a demand that the administration consult Congress before making any troop increases.
Air War The US Navy deploys a new plane, the A-7 Corsair II, to help repel enemy troops threatening Khesanh.

10 MARCH 1968
South Vietnam Vice-President Nguyen Cao Ky declares that the recent offensive has made a general mobilization necessary.
USA: Domestic Public concern with recent developments in Vietnam is intensified when *The New York Times* discloses that General Westmoreland has requested 206,000 addi-

tional troops. President Johnson is reportedly 'furious' at the leak, which gives his political adversaries a focus for their criticism.

11 MARCH-7 APRIL 1968
Ground War Operation Quyet Thang the largest to date, involves elements of the US 1st, 9th, and 25th Infantry Divisions, airborne battalions from the ARVN 5th and 25th Divisions, and selected Vietnamese marine corps units – altogether a total of 22 US and 11 Vietnamese battalions. Conducted in the area of Saigon and its five surrounding provinces, it is designed to eliminate a persisting enemy threat to the capital.

12 MARCH 1968
USA: Domestic In a surprisingly strong showing, Senator Eugene McCarthy (D-MN), an outspoken critic of administration policy in Vietnam, polls 40 percent of the vote in New Hampshire's Democratic presidential primary. A Harris poll later shows that anti-Johnson, rather than anti-war, sentiment provided the basis for McCarthy's performance. Nevertheless, the primary's results embolden Senator Robert Kennedy (D-NY) to announce his candidacy for the presidency four days later.

14 MARCH 1968
South Vietnam North Vietnamese troops are sighted for the first time in the Mekong Delta.

16 MARCH 1968
War Crimes In what will become the most publicized war atrocity committed by US troops in Vietnam, a platoon from Charlie Company, 1st Battalion, 20th Infantry of the newly formed Americal Division, slaughters between 200 and 500 unarmed villagers at the hamlet of Mylai-4. The hamlet is located in a heavily mined region where Vietcong guerrillas are well entrenched and numerous members of Charlie Company have been killed or maimed during the preceeding month. Although the platoon receives no opposing fire as it approaches Mylai its commanding officer, Lieutenant William Calley, orders his men to go in firing. The scene which follows can only be described as horrific: several old men are bayoneted, some women and children praying outside the local temple are shot in the back of the head, and at least one girl is raped before being killed.

17 MARCH-30 JULY 1968
Ground War Operation Duong Cua Dan (People's Road) involving elements of the 9th

Residents of Hué dig through the rubble to find possessions after the Tet Offensive.

CHRONOLOGY

Infantry Division designed to provide security for engineers working on Route 4, which, on 21 May, is combined with Operation Truong Cong Dinh; together, the two operations claim 1251 enemy casualties.

19 MARCH 1968
USA: Government The House of Representatives passes a resolution calling for an immediate Congressional review of US policy in Southeast Asia.
Air War Much to the embarrassment of US military officials, two NVA defectors report that North Vietnam's intelligence agencies provide as much as 24 hours notice of US B-52 raids.

20 MARCH 1968
USA: Military Retired USMC Commandant David Shoup estimates that up to 800,000 men are required just to defend South Vietnamese population centers. He further states that the United States can only achieve military victory by invading the North, but argues that such an operation would not be worth the cost.
USA: Military *The New York Times* publishes excerpts from General Westmoreland's classified end-of-year report which indicate that the US command did not believe the enemy capable of any action even approximating the Tet Offensive.'

22 MARCH 1968
USA: Military President Johnson announces the appointment of General Westmoreland as Army Chief of Staff; General Creighton Abrams will assume command of US forces in Vietnam.
Air War USAF F-111 fighterbombers go into action for the first time.

25 MARCH 1968
South Vietnam An outbreak of bubonic plague in Tayninh province has reached epidemic proportions and is beginning to spread toward Saigon.
USA: Domestic A Harris Poll reports that in the past six weeks 'basic' support for the war among Americans declined from 74 percent to 54 percent; it also reveals that 60 percent of those questioned regard the Tet Offensive as a defeat of US objectives in Vietnam.

25-26 MARCH 1968
USA: Government After being told by Defense Secretary Clifford that the Vietnam war is a 'real loser,' President Johnson is still uncertain about his future course of action and decides to convene a nine-man panel of retired presidential advisors. The group, which becomes known as the 'Wise Men,' includes the respected generals Omar Bradley and Matthew Ridgway, distinguished State Department figures like Dean Acheson and George Ball, and McGeorge Bundy, former National Security advisor in both the Kennedy and Johnson administrations. After two days of deliberation the group reaches a consensus: they advise against any further troop increases and recommend that the administration seek a negotiated peace. Johnson is furious at their conclusions.

30 MARCH 1968
South Vietnam President Thieu dismisses six more province chiefs as part of his campaign to eliminate corruption and inefficiency.

30 MARCH 1968-31 JANUARY 1969
Ground War A 173rd Airborne Brigade operation known as Cochise Green in Binh Dinh province accounts for 929 reported enemy casualties.

31 MARCH 1968
USA: Government In a televised speech to the nation, President Johnson announces that he has ordered – 'unilaterally' – a halt to air and naval bombardments of North Vietnam 'except in the area north of the DMZ where the continuing enemy build-up directly threatens allied forward positions.' He also states that he is sending 13,500 more troops to Vietnam and will request further defense expenditures – $2½ billion in fiscal 1968 and $2.6 billion in fiscal 1969 – to finance recent troop build-ups, reequip the South Vietnamese Army, and meet 'our responsibilities in Korea.' In closing, Johnson shocks the nation with an announcement which in effect concedes that his own presidency has become another casualty of the war: 'I shall not seek, and I will not accept, the nomination of my party for another term as your President.'

1 APRIL-17 MAY 1968
Ground War Operation Carentan II in the lowland areas of Quang Tri and Thua Thien provinces claims 2100 enemy casualties.

1-15 APRIL 1968
Ground War Operation Pegasus/Lan Son 207 is designed to relieve the siege at Khesanh,

conducted by the 1st Air Cavalry Division, 1st Marines, and four ARVN airborne battalions, which accounts for 1144 reported enemy casualties. The 77 day siege is officially lifted on 6 April, when elements of the 1st Air Cavalry Division link up with USMC forces south of the Khesanh airstrip.

2 APRIL 1968

USA: Government Following widespread criticism in reaction to continuing air strikes deep within North Vietnamese territory, the administration explains that the bombing limitation applies only to the region north of the 20th Parallel – an 'area of North Vietnam containing almost 90 percent of its population and three-quarters of its land.'

3 APRIL 1968

Diplomatic At the end of a government message broadcast by Hanoi radio denouncing the bombing limitation as a 'perfidious trick' intended 'to appease public opinion,' North Vietnam declares its 'readiness' to meet with US representatives to discuss 'the unconditional cessation of the US bombing raids and all other acts of war against the Democratic Republic of Vietnam so that talks may start.' In his response, President Johnson chooses to ignore the statement's abusive features and simply announces that 'we will establish contact with representatives of North Vietnam.'

8 APRIL-31 MAY 1968

Ground War The largest operation to date – involving 42 US and 37 Vietnamese battalions – Toan Thang (Complete Victory) is a combined II ARVN Corps and II Field Force, Vietnam, offensive designed to destroy Vietcong and NVA forces operating within the Capital Military District: reported enemy casualties number 7645.

8 APRIL-11 NOVEMBER 1968

Ground War Operation Burlington Trail, a combat sweep, conducted by the 198th Infantry Brigade of the American Division in Quang Tri province along the Quang Nam border claims 1931 enemy casualties.

10-12 APRIL 1968

Ground War In three days of intense fighting, US troops recapture the Special Forces camp at Langvei, are driven out by NVA forces, and then retake the camp.

11 APRIL 1968

USA: Government A recent intensification of fighting requires the United States to mobilize additional troops. At his first Pentagon press conference, Defense Secretary Clifford announces a call-up of 24,500 military reservists to serve as support forces in Vietnam and to replenish the Army's Strategic Reserve. He also states that the troop ceiling for US strength in Vietnam has been raised to 549,500.

Diplomatic The United States rejects a North Vietnamese proposal that preliminary talks be held in Warsaw, insisting that on 'serious matters of this kind, it is important to hold talks in a neutral atmosphere, fair to both sides.'

13 APRIL 1968

Laos US officials in Vientiane report that a recent North Vietnamese-Pathet Lao offensive – resulting thus far in the virtual encirclement of the two provincial capitals of Saravane and Attopeu in southern Laos – suggests that the enemy has adopted a new strategy of 'attacking towns and taking terrain.'

15 APRIL 1968-28 FEBRUARY 1969

Ground War A continuation of USMC operations known as Scotland II around Khesanh following termination of Pegasus which results in 3311 listed enemy casualties.

16-17 APRIL 1968

USA: Government At a series of meetings in Honolulu, President Johnson discusses recent allied and enemy troop deployments with US military leaders. He also confers with South Korean President Park Chung Hee to reaffirm US military commitments to Seoul and assure Park that his country's interests will not be compromised by a Vietnamese peace agreement.

18 APRIL 1968

South Vietnam The US command in Saigon discloses figures showing that the South Vietnamese government lost control over 1.1 million people as a result of the Tet Offensive.

19 APRIL-17 MAY 1968

Ground War An operation involving the 1st Air Cavalry Division, 101st Airborne Division, and elements of the US 196th Infantry Brigade, ARVN 1st Division, and ARVN Airborne Task Force Bravo is intended to

CHRONOLOGY

Near Khe Sanh, two troopers of the US 1st Air Cavalry prepare a defensive position.

preempt enemy preparations for another attack on Hué. Known as Operation Delaware/Lam Son 216 its focal point is the Ashau Valley, an area which the 1st Cavalry Division commander describes as one of the NVA's 'top logistical support bases, as important to him as Camranh Bay is to us'.

21 APRIL 1968
Ground War A high-ranking NVA defector exposes enemy plans to conduct a second wave of attacks on Saigon beginning 22 April.

22 APRIL 1968
USA: Government Defense Secretary Clifford declares that the South Vietnamese have 'acquired the capacity to begin to insure their own security [and] they are going to take over more and more of the fighting.' This is the first public announcement of a policy that, under the Nixon administration, will become known as 'Vietnamization.'

26 APRIL 1968
International Students throughout the world cut classes as part of an antiwar strike organized by the Student Mobilization Committee

to End the War in Vietnam.
Air War F-111 raids resume, after suspected technical malfunctions had caused the planes to be grounded for three weeks.

27 APRIL 1968
USA: Domestic Vice-President Hubert Humphrey announces his candidacy for the Democratic presidential nomination. In an interview, he supports the current US policy of sending troops 'where required by our own national security.'

28 APRIL 1968
South Vietnam North Vietnamese sources report the formation of a new political organization in South Vietnam, the Alliance of National, Democratic, and Peace Forces, which is prepared to conduct peace talks with the United States. Although the Alliance reportedly represents non-communist South Vietnamese nationalists, the US State Department refuses to recognize the group.

29 APRIL 1968
South Vietnam Opposition and independent members in the lower house of South Viet-

Sit-ins became popular with demonstrating students in the United States.

nam's National Assembly issue a statement calling for a change of government, because of corruption in high places.

30 APRIL 1968
South Vietnam The US embassy in Saigon reports that during the Tet Offensive in Hué, NVA and Vietcong forces executed more than 1000 civilians and buried them in mass graves, 19 of which have been recently uncovered.

3 MAY 1968
Negotiations After 34 days of discussions to select a talks site, the United States and North Vietnam agree to begin formal negotiations in Paris on 10 May or shortly thereafter. Hanoi discloses that ex-Foreign Minister Xuan Thuy will head the North Vietnamese delegation at the talks; and W Averell Harriman is named as his US counterpart. The next day each side restates its negotiating position: the North Vietnamese Communist Party newspaper

203

CHRONOLOGY

Nhan Dan declares that Hanoi's four-point program and the NLF's political program remain 'the correct basis for a political solution of the Vietnam problem'; and Secretary of State Rusk asserts that the United States regards an end to Communist infiltration of South Vietnam and neighboring countries as vital for 'an honorable peace in Southeast Asia.'

4 MAY-24 AUGUST 1968
Ground War A USMC operation known as Allen Brook which takes place west of Hoi An City in southern Quang Nam Province claims 1017 enemy casualties.

5-13 MAY 1968
Ground War The second large-scale Communist offensive of the year begins with the simultaneous shelling of 119 cities, towns, and military barracks. Heavy action continues for a week. The principal enemy target is Saigon, where, following a major ground assault, the fighting quickly spreads to Cholon, Tansonnhut airbase, and the Phutho racetrack. The battle climaxes on 12 May, when US jets, dropping napalm and high-explosive bombs, pound a final Vietcong stronghold in the slum district around the Y bridge, preparing the way for an assault by US Infantry troops. According to allied sources, 5270 North Vietnamese are killed in the offensive, compared with 154 Americans and 326 South Vietnamese.

9 MAY 1968
South Vietnam President Thieu declares that, even if the United States should negotiate an end to the war, his government will never recognize the National Liberation Front.
USA: Military The US Army announces that, in order to bolster its firepower and mobility, the 101st Airborne Division will be converted into an airmobile division; it also discloses that separate reconnaissance squadrons will be attached to each of the five remaining infantry divisions in Vietnam.

11 MAY 1968
Negotiations American and North Vietnamese negotiators complete procedural arrangements for the formal talks. They agree that, for the time being, participation will be restricted to representatives of the United States and North Vietnam, thereby excluding both Saigon and the NLF.

15-19 MAY 1968
Negotiations To break an impasse at the Paris talks, the United States asks that the meeting be moved into secret session, after intensifying its bombing of North Vietnam.

17 MAY-3 NOVEMBER 1968
Ground War A continuation of 1st Air Cavalry Division operations along the border of Quang Tri and Thua Thien provinces Operation Jeb Stuart III claims 2114 enemy casualties.

17 MAY 1968-28 FEBRUARY 1969
Ground War A continuation of 101st Airborne Division operations in central Thua Thien Province Operation Nevada Eagle accounts for 3299 reported enemy casualties.

18 MAY 1968
South Vietnam Newly appointed South Vietnamese Premier Tran Van Huong declares his opposition to negotiations with the National Liberation Front in a statement asserting that the peace talks should be between Saigon and Hanoi, rather than the United States and North Vietnam.

18 MAY-23 OCTOBER 1968
Ground War A 1st Marine Division operation Mameluke Thrust in central Quang Nam province claims 2728 enemy casualties.

21 MAY 1968
South Vietnam The allied command in Saigon announces the start of a new program, Operation Hearts Together, designed to resettle Saigon area families.

22 MAY 1968
Negotiations Xuan Thuy, chief NVN delegate to the peace talks, declares that negotiations will remain deadlocked until the United States unconditionally terminates all bombing raids on North Vietnam. If the talks should collapse, Thuy adds, 'the American side would bear the full and entire responsibility.' Ambassador Harriman replies that a bombing halt must be accompanied by mutual troop withdrawals along the DMZ; but Thuy rejects the proposal, charging that it is the United States, not North Vietnam, which has violated the buffer zone.

23 MAY 1968
South Vietnam At the conclusion of an experimental civic affairs program in Longan

The city of Cholon came under artillery fire several times during the Tet offensive.

province, John Paul Vann and other US advisors issue a report recommending widespread changes in the pacification effort. The report states that Saigon has little understanding of its people's needs and has consistently failed to provide adequate funds and services for grass-roots programs. As a result, the Vietcong continue to collect taxes and recruit troops from many hamlets that the government claims it has pacified.

25 MAY 1968

South Vietnam South Vietnamese Premier Tran Van Huong announces the formation of a new 19-member cabinet in which a faction supporting Vice-President Ky is given only one post; in the previous 17-member cabinet, the Ky faction had controlled seven ministries.

25 MAY-4 JUNE 1968

Ground War The Vietcong launch their third major assault of the year on Saigon. The heaviest fighting occurs during the first three days of June, and again centers in Cholon, where US and South Vietnamese forces use helicopters, fighterbombers, and tanks to dislodge deeply entrenched Vietcong infiltrators. A captured enemy directive, which the US command makes public on 28 May,

indicates that the Vietcong see the offensive as a means of influencing the Paris peace talks.

27 MAY 1968

Thailand Thai Premier Thanom Kittikachorn announces that, at President Johnson's request, his country will send 5000 more troops to Vietnam.

30 MAY 1968

South Vietnam South Vietnamese Information Minister Ton That Thien issues a directive lifting the press censorship which has been in effect since the Tet Offensive.

1 JUNE 1968

South Vietnam Recent government directives on pacification indicate that, since the Tet Offensive, the program's focus has shifted from school-building, health care, and providing other forms of aid to an emphasis on training self-defense teams and bolstering hamlet security.

3 JUNE 1968

Negotiations Le Duc Tho, a member of the North Vietnam Communist Party's Politburo, joins the North Vietnamese negotiating team as a special counselor.

CHRONOLOGY

5 JUNE 1968
USA: Domestic Senator Robert Kennedy (D-MA), a leading critic of administration policy in Vietnam, is shot after making a statement announcing his victory in California's Democratic presidential primary; he dies the next day.

10 JUNE 1968
South Vietnam South Vietnamese Information Minister Ton That Thien declares the US impact on Vietnamese culture, religion, and politics has been 'devastating' and 'disintegrating.'
USA: Military At a Saigon news conference on the day he is to turn over command of US forces in Vietnam to General Creighton Abrams, General Westmoreland offers his assessment of past and current trends in the war. In defense of his attrition policy, Westmoreland declares that it will ultimately make continued fighting 'intolerable to the enemy.' He also explains that, because it is impossible to 'cut a surface line of communication with other than ground operations,' Washington's ban on ground attacks to interdict Communist infiltration through Laos precludes the achievement of military victory. Westmoreland denies, however, that the military situation is stalemated.

13 JUNE 1968
South Vietnam South Vietnamese Open Arms Minister Phan Quang Dan is dismissed for suggesting that the government hold direct talks with the National Liberation Front.

14 JUNE 1968
USA: Domestic A Federal District Court jury in Boston convicts Dr Benjamin Spock and three others of conspiring to aid, abet, and counsel draft registrants to violate the Selective Service Law.

19 JUNE 1968
South Vietnam In a public ceremony at Hué, President Thieu signs a general mobilization bill. Under the new measure, men between the ages of 18 and 43 are subject to induction into the regular armed forces; men between the ages of 44 and 50 and 16 and 17-year-old youths are eligible to serve in the civilian part-time People's Self-Defense Organization; and an estimated 90,000 17-year-olds in the People's Self-Defense Organization can be transferred to the regular army. It is believed that, by the end of 1968, the law will provide for the induction of an additional 200,000 men.

26 JUNE 1968
South Vietnam Speaking on behalf of the South Vietnamese House of Representatives, Duong Van Ba demands that Saigon be given a role in the Paris peace talks, asserting that 'we should tell the United States government and the United States people that we suspect that there is now a plot to sell out South Vietnam to the Communists.'
Negotiations Cyrus Vance, deputy US delegate to the peace talks, seeks to break a continuing impasse in the negotiations by appealing to North Vietnam for some sign that it is taking steps to scale down the level of military violence. Although this is the first time that US negotiators have urged military reciprocity in such broad terms, Xuan Thuy rejects the initiative and repeats Hanoi's demand that all US bombing raids on North Vietnam be unconditionally terminated. Thuy also insists that the Saigon government be replaced by a coalition regime committed to a neutral foreign policy and eventual reunification.

27 JUNE 1968
Ground War The US command in Saigon confirms that US forces have begun to evacuate the military base at Khesanh. The command statement attributes the pullback to a change in the military situation. To cope with increased NVA infiltration and activity in the DMZ area, allied forces are adopting a more 'mobile posture,' thus making retention of the outpost at Khesanh unnecessary. The new western anchor of the US base system in I Corps will be located 10 miles east of Khesanh.

28 JUNE 1968
USA: Military Lieutenant Colonel Richard A McMahon denounces the body count as a 'dubious and possibly dangerous' method of determining the enemy's combat potential.
Laos Prince Souvanna Phouma declares that, until North Vietnam agrees to withdraw its forces from Laos, the United States should continue to reject Hanoi's demands for a bombing halt.

29 JUNE 1968
South Vietnam South Vietnamese Premier Tran Van Huong expresses concern that, because of its impatience to end the war, the

United States is making too many concessions at the peace talks – behavior which the North Vietnamese interpret as a sign of weakness.

Ground War For the second time in three days South Vietnamese forces patrolling the Saigon area uncover a huge arms cache containing rockets and other weapons. The allied command believes that capture of the matériel has caused the Vietcong to postpone plans for another assault on Saigon.

30 JUNE 1968

South Vietnam Militant anti-communist Phan Ba Cam announces the formation of a new South Vietnamese political party, Vietnam Force, committed to ending the war peacefully, unifying North and South Vietnam, and building a socialist economy.

1 JULY 1968

Air War US B-52 bombers resume raids north of the DMZ.

2 JULY 1968

USA: Government At President Johnson's request, Congress passes a $6 billion supplemental appropriations bill to sustain US operations in Vietnam.

3 JULY 1968

Casualties The US command in Saigon releases figures showing that more Americans were killed during the first six months of 1968 than in all of 1967.

Ground War US troops conducting a sweep near Saigon uncover an enemy arms cache containing 56 Soviet and Chinese rockets; three more caches are discovered two days later west and northwest of the capital.

4 JULY 1968

South Vietnam At a formal ceremony inaugurating the formation of a new multiparty pro-government political grouping, the People's Alliance for Social Revolution, President Thieu praises the organization as a 'major step toward grass roots political activity.' An Alliance manifesto asserts that it is 'determined to wipe out corruption, do away with social inequalities, and rout out the entrenched forces of militarists and reactionaries who have always blocked progress.'

Ground War In a two and a half hour battle, US infantrymen repulse a combined NVA-Vietcong attack on the 25th Infantry Division base at Dautieng, 40 miles northwest of Saigon.

8 JULY 1968

South Vietnam President Thieu announces that the possibility of another enemy offensive has caused him to postpone a planned visit to the United States.

Cambodia In a formal complaint to the UN, Cambodia charges that allied helicopters killed 14 Cambodians working in their rice fields more than 6000 yards from the border.

9 JULY 1968

South Vietnam Le Quang Chanh, a member of the NLF Central Committee, reaffirms the NLF's goal of overthrowing the present Saigon regime in a statement asserting that no elections can be held to form a post-war government in South Vietnam until all US and allied forces have withdrawn.

Negotiations Bui Diem, chief South Vietnamese observer at the Paris peace talks, reiterates Saigon's call for direct negotiations between North and South Vietnam. His statement reflects a growing fear on the part of the Saigon government that the United States and North Vietnam might conclude a settlement inimical to its interests.

13 JULY 1968

USA: Domestic Governor Nelson Rockefeller of New York, a Republican presidential candidate, reveals a four-stage peace plan, which, he argues, could end the war in six months if North Vietnam assents to it. The proposal calls for a mutual troop pullback and interposition of a neutral peacekeeping force, followed by the withdrawal of all North Vietnamese and most allied units from South Vietnam, free elections under international supervision, and direct negotiations between North and South Vietnam on reunification.

14-18 JULY 1968

USA: Military Defense Secretary Clifford visits South Vietnam to confer with US and South Vietnamese leaders. Upon his arrival in Saigon, Clifford states that the United States is doing all that it can to improve the fighting capacity of the South Vietnamese Army and intends to provide all ARVN units with M-16 automatic rifles.

16 JULY 1968

Ground War A senior US military source in Saigon reveals that enemy units have withdrawn toward the west, indicating that an attack on the capital has been postponed.

CHRONOLOGY

17 JULY 1968-4 MARCH 1969
Ground War Operation Quyet Chien conducted by the ARVN 7th, 9th, and 21st Infantry Divisions and the 44th Special Tactical Zone unit, claims 15,593 enemy casualties.

18-20 JULY 1968
USA: Government President Johnson meets President Thieu in Honolulu to discuss relations between Washington and Saigon. Johnson reaffirms his administration's commitment 'to defend South Vietnam.' Thieu states that he had 'no apprehensions at all' concerning the US commitment. In a joint communiqué, Thieu further asserts that his government is determined 'to continue to assume all the responsibility that the scale of the forces of South Vietnam and their equipment will permit,' thus tacitly accepting current US efforts to 'Vietnamize the war.' The two Presidents also agree that South Vietnam 'should be a full participant playing a leading role in discussions concerning the substance of a final settlement' to the conflict.

20 JULY 1968
South Vietnam South Vietnam observes National Shame Day, the anniversary of the 1954 Geneva Accords.
North Vietnam Ho Chi Minh marks the anniversary of the Geneva Accords by issuing an appeal to step up the war of resistance against US imperialism.

21 JULY 1968
South Vietnam The widows of six South Vietnamese military officers and government officials, killed during a tour of the Saigon battlefront on 2 June, by what US authorities say was a misdirected US helicopter rocket, charge that the United States deliberately murdered their husbands – all of whom were political allies of Vice President Ky, who was then seeking to assume control of the Saigon military district. Three days later, a joint US-South Vietnamese investigating board confirms that a malfunctioning rocket was responsible for the deaths.

22 JULY 1968
Negotiations Nguyen Thanh Le, North Vietnamese spokesman at the Paris talks, tells reporters that the Honolulu conference reveals that 'the position of the United States remains infinitely obstinate': the United States is still determined to support the 'puppet government' in Saigon.

26 JULY 1968
South Vietnam Truong Dinh Dzu, a peace candidate in the September 1967 presidential elections, is sentenced to five years of hard labor for urging the formation of a coalition government as a step toward ending the war. This is the first time that a major political figure has been tried and convicted under a 1965 decree ordering the prosecution of persons 'who interfere with the government's struggle against Communism.'

2 AUGUST 1968
POWs Three US pilots recently released by Hanoi arrive in Laos and report that they were well treated. Five days later, Ambassador Harriman informs North Vietnamese negotiators in Paris that the United States will reciprocate by turning over 14 seamen. Harriman also expresses the hope that more prisoner exchanges can be arranged in the future.

2 AUGUST 1968-24 APRIL 1969
Ground War Operation Lam Son 245 conducted by the ARVN 54th Regiment in Thua Thien province accounts for 636 reported enemy casualties.

4 AUGUST 1968
Ground War For the second time in 1968, US and South Vietnamese forces, supported by B-52 bomber strikes, move into the Ashau Valley to prevent the massing of NVA troops for a new offensive in the I Corps area. Although allied forces make only light contact with the enemy, substantial amounts of war matériel are uncovered during the sweep.

5-8 AUGUST 1968
USA: Domestic The Republican National Convention opens in Miami and adopts a Vietnam plank emphasizing the need for an honorable negotiated peace and 'progressive de-Americanization' of the war. In his speech accepting the presidential nomination, Richard Nixon pledges to 'bring an honorable end to the war in Vietnam' and inaugurate 'an era of negotiations' with leading Communist powers, while restoring 'the strength of America so that we shall always negotiate from strength and never from weakness.'

8 AUGUST 1968
Ground War During efforts to repel three

Members of the South Vietnamese Army (ARVN) board helicopters in the Ashau valley.

Vietcong ambushes, US troops of the 9th Infantry Division accidentally kill 72 civilians and wound 240 in the Mekong Delta town of Caireng.

10 AUGUST 1968
Ground War A USAF F-100 Super Sabre jet accidentally strafes a unit of the 101st Airborne Division in the Ashau Valley, killing eight and wounding five.

12-13 AUGUST 1968
Ground War Heavy fighting erupts again in the Delta when allied troops – part of a 75 battalion force guarding enemy infiltration routes into Saigon – kill 181 Vietcong.

15 AUGUST 1968
South Vietnam President Thieu denounces the Paris talks as a North Vietnamese 'trick' and declares that peace will become possible only when 'our armed forces can achieve an absolute victory in the future.'
Ground War Fighting intensifies in the northern I Corps area as ARVN forces pursue

a North Vietnamese battalion inside the DMZ and kill 165 enemy troops in a seven and a half hour battle; at the same time, US Marines attack three strategic positions just below the buffer zone, killing 56 NVA troops.

17 AUGUST 1968
Air War The US Defense Department reports that, since February 1965, US planes have flown 117,000 combat missions over North Vietnam, dropping 2,581,876 tons of bombs and rockets.

18 AUGUST 1968
Ground War In the heaviest fighting in three months, NVA and Vietcong forces conduct 19 separate attacks on allied positions throughout South Vietnam. Fifteen of the assaults occur in Tayninh and Binhlong provinces, northwest of Saigon near the Cambodian border. The struggle for Tayninh begins after 600 Vietcong, supported by elements of two NVA divisions, infiltrates the provincial capital during the night of 17 August and attacks government offices and

CHRONOLOGY

UH-1D Helicopters were used as troop transports throughout the war.

installations the following morning. To meet the threat, US reinforcements, led by an armored column of the 25th Infantry Division, are rushed to the scene and after a day of house-to-house fighting expel the attackers.

19 AUGUST 1968
USA: Government In a major address at the Veterans of Foreign Wars convention, Detroit, President Johnson declares that given recent US efforts to scale down the conflict – specifically, the 31 March bombing curtailment and subsequent offers to terminate all bombing of the North if Hanoi would take some reciprocal action – it is North Vietnam's turn to make the next move. To halt the bombing without serious assurances, Johnson contends, would allow North Vietnam to mass men and supplies at the DMZ, 'against our men and our allies, without obstruction.' Johnson addresses his closing remarks to critics of administration policy, commenting that 'there are some among us who appear to be searching for a formula which would get us out of Vietnam and Asia on any terms, leaving the people of South Vietnam and Laos and Thailand ... to an uncertain fate.'

USA: Domestic A Harris poll reports that 61 percent of those questioned oppose a bombing cessation, even after being reminded that North Vietnamese negotiators in Paris insist that the talks will not progress until the bombing is stopped.

22 AUGUST 1968
Ground War For the first time in two months, enemy forces launch a rocket attack on Saigon, killing 18 and wounding 59. US State Department officials afterwards denounce the shelling as a deliberate repudiation of President Johnson's call for de-escalation.

23 AUGUST 1968
Ground War Vietcong forces conduct heavy rocket and mortar attacks on numerous cities, provincial capitals, and military installations; the heaviest shellings focus on the US airfield at Danang, the cities of Hué and Quang Tri, and US Special Forces camp at Duclap, 130 miles northeast of Saigon near the Cambodian border. The attack at Duclap is followed by a ground assault involving between 1200 and 1500 NVA troops. The camp is retaken on 25 August, when an allied relief column,

led by US Special Forces men, forces the North Vietnamese to withdraw from the area. A reported 643 NVA troops are killed during the three days of fighting.

24 AUGUST-9 SEPTEMBER 1968
Ground War Operation Tien Bo conducted by the ARVN 23rd Infantry Division in Quang Duc province claims 1091 enemy casualties.

26-29 AUGUST 1968
USA: Domestic The Democratic National Convention opens in Chicago. Divisions arise when the platform committee is asked to consider two Vietnam planks calling for markedly different approaches to the conflict. An antiwar plank fashioned by supporters of Senators Eugene McCarthy (D-MN) and George McGovern (D-SD) advocates unconditionally halting the bombing of North Vietnam; negotiating a mutual withdrawal of US and North Vietnamese forces from South Vietnam; encouraging the Saigon regime to open talks with the National Liberation Front and accept a coalition government; and reducing US offensive operations in South Vietnam. A competing plank, selected as the majority choice of the platform committee, endorses administration policies, applauds President Johnson's effort to scale down the war and begin peace talks, and asks Hanoi to 'respond affirmatively to this act of statesmanship.' On 28 August, the convention adopts the administration plank by a vote of 1567 to 1041, but only after a heated three-hour debate punctuated by prolonged demonstrations. Events that afternoon and evening are even more raucous outside the convention hall, where a week of mounting tensions and intermittent violence is climaxed by a full-scale riot pitting police and National Guardsmen against youthful antiwar demonstrators. In his speech accepting the Democratic presidential nomination the next day, Hubert Humphrey acknowledges that differences exist within the party.

30 AUGUST 1968
Ground War Acting on information supplied by an NVA defector, US paratroopers seize and destroy a North Vietnamese regimental headquarters 12 miles south of Hué, killing 176 enemy troops and capturing seven anti-aircraft guns and 435 other weapons.
Ground War Enemy forces overrun a US Special Forces camp at Hathanh, 14 miles west of Quangngai, but allied troops retake the outpost three days later.

2 SEPTEMBER 1968
Air War The US command orders the heaviest bombing in weeks along infiltration routes leading into Saigon. The increased raids reflect an allied concern that North Vietnam will celebrate its annual National Day with another assault on the capital.

8 SEPTEMBER 1968
South Vietnam Brigadier General Truong Quang An, commander of the ARVN 23rd Infantry Division, is killed when NVA gunners down his helicopter near Duclap – the first South Vietnamese general to die in combat.

10 SEPTEMBER 1968
USA: Government In a speech before the American Legion convention President Johnson states that, according to General Abrams, if the bombing of the North Vietnamese panhandle were terminated without reciprocal deescalation on Hanoi's part, 'the military capacity of the enemy to hurt our forces would greatly increase.' At another point in the speech, the President reveals his concern over mounting war expenditures.

11-16 SEPTEMBER 1968
Ground War In the second assault on Tayninh in less than a month, two columns of about 1500 NVA-Vietcong troops enter the city following rocket and mortar attacks on allied military bases in the surrounding area. The next day about 2000 ARVN forces are sent in to reinforce the local garrison and after four days of heavy fighting drive enemy attackers from the city. The last engagement during the current outbreak of activity occurs 16 September, when a US 25th Infantry Division convoy is ambushed 9 miles southeast of Tayninh. Allied military sources believe fighting in the general area will remain heavy, due to increased enemy infiltration from Cambodia.

11 SEPTEMBER 1968-24 APRIL 1969
Ground War Operation Lam Son 261 conducted by the ARVN 1st Regiment in Thua Thien and Quang Tri provinces accounts for 724 reported enemy casualties.

13 SEPTEMBER-1 OCTOBER 1968
Ground War The largest sustained allied

drive inside the DMZ opens when US and ARVN infantry and armored troops, supported by planes, artillery, and US Navy ships, move two miles into the buffer zone. The operation has two objectives: to relieve enemy pressure on allied bases along the 40 mile stretch of South Vietnam's northern frontier and to prevent an anticipated offensive by two North Vietnamese divisions currently operating within the DMZ. On 17 September another 2000 Marines are airlifted into the area and US B-52s, striking for the first time in a month, hit targets on both sides of the Benhai River, part of the demarcation between North and South Vietnam. In a final phase of the drive ten days later, an additional 4000 Marines sweep into the buffer area in a coordinated pincer movement designed to trap remaining NVA forces. Altogether, 742 North Vietnamese are reported killed during the operation; US casualties number 65 dead and 77 wounded.

18 SEPTEMBER 1968

South Vietnam In an article in *Foreign Affairs*, Major General Duong Van Minh argues that only the introduction of participatory democracy at the village level can restore unity to South Vietnam and create a political system capable of defeating the communists.

20 SEPTEMBER 1968

South Vietnam At a news conference in Saigon, US officials claim that the use of defoliants in selected areas of South Vietnam has neither appreciably altered the country's ecology, nor produced any harmful effects on human or animal life. Another report released at the conference – a study prepared by Dr Fred Tschirley, a US Agriculture Department investigator – states that defoliants have caused 'undeniable ecological change' and that 'recovery may take a long time.'

26 SEPTEMBER 1968

UN In the introduction to his annual report to the UN General Assembly, U Thant characterizes the Vietnam War as a nationalist struggle and declares that major world powers should 'let the Vietnamese themselves deal with their own problems.' Thant also reiterates his appeal for a bombing halt and asserts that the parties to the Paris talks should seek to reunify North and South Vietnam and neutralize the entire Indochinese peninsula.

28 SEPTEMBER 1968

USA: Military The US command in Saigon discloses that the enemy has substantially increased its use of Cambodia as a staging area and sanctuary. Recent intelligence reports indicate that NVA-Vietcong military activity in the region nearest Saigon has 'increased three-fold' since November 1967.

28 SEPTEMBER-19 OCTOBER 1968

Ground War NVA forces attack the US Special Forces camp at Thuong Duc, midway between Danang and the Laotian border, briefly capturing two outposts before being driven out by air and artillery strikes. They then decide upon a more deliberate siege, which is lifted when a relief column, led by the 7th Marines, reaches the base and expels enemy forces from Hill 163 two miles from the camp. By 19 October the road to Thuong Duc is once again open.

30 SEPTEMBER 1968

USA: Domestic In a major campaign speech, Vice President Hubert Humphrey declares that, if elected President, he would end the bombing of North Vietnam if there was any 'evidence, direct or indirect, by deed or word, of Communist willingness to restore the DMZ zone between North and South Vietnam.'
Sea War The world's only active battleship, the USS *New Jersey*, arrives in Vietnamese waters and goes into action, shelling NVA positions in the DMZ.

3 OCTOBER 1968

Air War In the heaviest raid over North Vietnam since 2 July, US planes destroy 45 supply craft and 31 trucks and sever roads in more than 20 places.
Casualties A US Army Chinook helicopter collides with a two-engine US C-7 Caribou cargo plane near the airstrip at Camp Evans, 11 miles north of Hué; all 24 Americans aboard the two aircraft are killed.

4 OCTOBER 1968

Ground War US Marines reoccupy the abandoned base at Khesanh to secure a hill for two artillery batteries.

5 OCTOBER 1968

North Vietnam A statement issued by the North Vietnamese Water Conservation Ministry charges that the United States is intensifying its air strikes against dikes, dams, and other water-management projects.

9-14 OCTOBER 1968
Negotiations A North Vietnamese representative in Paris asks Ambassador Harriman
whether the United States would 'stop the
bombing if we give you an affirmative clear
answer to the question of Saigon participation' in the talks. Harriman immediately
relays the proposal to President Johnson, who
turns to General Abrams and Ambassador-
to-South Vietnam Ellsworth Bunker for their
assessment of the query. When they respond
that they 'interpret the exchange to mean that
Hanoi is ready for a shift in tactics from the
battlefield to the conference table,' Johnson
instructs Bunker to present the matter to
President Thieu. The South Vietnamese
leader assents to a bombing halt, but insists
that allied military pressure in South Vietnam
be continued.

11 OCTOBER 1968
USA: Domestic In the first antiwar demonstration organized and led by soldiers, more
than 7000 protestors – including 200 soldiers,
700 veterans, and 100 reservists – march
through downtown San Francisco.

12 OCTOBER 1968
USA: Domestic In an address to a symposium
at De Pauw University, former presidential
advis0r McGeorge Bundy advocates an unconditional bombing halt and a substantial
withdrawal of US forces from South Vietnam.

14 OCTOBER 1968
USA: Military US Defense Department
sources disclose that the Army and Marines
will be sending about 24,000 men back to
Vietnam for involuntary second tours in a
move made necessary by the length of the
war, high turnover of personnel resulting
from the one year tour of duty, and a tight
supply of experienced officers.

15 OCTOBER 1968
USA: Military The US military command in
Saigon reports that most, if not all, North
Vietnamese regulars appear to have withdrawn from positions near South Vietnamese
population centers and that infiltration into
the South has also declined. Although US
officials believe the enemy is using the current
battlefield lull to prepare for another offensive, they do not reject the possibility that it is
a political signal intended to break the present
impasse in the Paris negotiations.

16 OCTOBER 1968
Negotiations Aware that a breakthrough in
the talks may be imminent, Ambassador
Harriman attempts to sweeten the pot by
suggesting that Hanoi would be eligible for
various forms of economic aid.

16-22 OCTOBER 1968
South Vietnam In a series of meetings with
Ambassador Bunker, President Thieu insists
that North Vietnam assent to three conditions
prior to a bombing halt: that it respect the
neutrality of the demilitarized zone, stop
shelling South Vietnamese cities and towns,
and agree to South Vietnamese participation
in the Paris talks. He also demands that the
NLF be excluded from the negotiations.
Despite his reservations, Thieu's stance
appears to have softened as a result of the
discussions with Bunker, and on 22 October,
he announces that he does not oppose a
bombing halt.

16 OCTOBER 1968-24 APRIL 1969
Ground War Operation Lam Son 271 con-
ducted by the ARVN 2nd Regiment in Quang
Tri province claims 603 enemy casualties.

18 OCTOBER 1968
USA: Domestic Rumors that the administration will soon announce a bombing halt send
sales volume on the New York Stock
Exchange soaring; US bond prices also climb.

24 OCTOBER-6 DECEMBER 1968
Ground War A search and clear operation,
known as Henderson Hill, is conducted by the
5th Marines in north central Quang Nam
province. It accounts for 700 reported enemy
casualties.

26 OCTOBER 1968
Ground War In the first major ground assault
in a month, an enemy force of 500 to 600 men
storms a US 1st Infantry Division base in
Tayninh province, 59 miles north of Saigon
near the Cambodian border.

26-29 OCTOBER 1968
Air War US B-52s conduct 22 strikes over the
Tayninh area in an effort to disperse a re-
ported massing of North Vietnamese forces.

27 OCTOBER 1968
Britain An estimated 50,000 persons march
through the streets of London to protest the
Vietnam war.

CHRONOLOGY

Navy SEALS rappelling into the jungle to set up an ambush.

29 OCTOBER 1968

USA: Government General Abrams secretly returns to Washington and in talks with President Johnson states that, given current battlefield conditions, he can accept the military consequence of a complete cessation of the bombing over North Vietnam. This represents a significant change in Abrams' views.

31 OCTOBER 1968

USA: Government In a televised address to the nation, President Johnson announces that, on the basis of recent developments in the Paris negotiations, he has ordered a cessation of all bombing raids over North Vietnam. The President further discloses that Hanoi has agreed to allow the South Vietnamese government to participate in the peace talks, while the United States has consented to a role for the NLF, though the latter concession 'in no way involves recognition of the National Liberation Front in any form.' Domestically, the President's action draws widespread acclaim: both major presidential candidates express their full support. The reaction in Saigon, however, is much more subdued: President Thieu issues a communiqué declaring that the United States has acted unilaterally in its decision to halt the bombing.

1 NOVEMBER 1968

Guerrilla War The US mission in Saigon initiates two operations designed to bolster pacification efforts. One is the Le Loi program, an intensified civic action campaign intended to repair the damage done by the enemy's 1968 offensives and to return control of the rural population to pre-Tet levels. The other is the Phoenix program, a hamlet security initiative relying on centralized, computerized intelligence gathering aimed at destroying the Vietcong infrastructure – the upper echelon of NLF political cadres and party members. It becomes one of the most controversial operations undertaken by US personnel in Vietnam. Critics charge that it involved the routine use of extreme torture by participating South Vietnamese 'hit teams' who indiscriminately arrested and murdered many suspects on the flimsiest of pretexts. Whatever the program's intentions, US officials familiar with the effort estimate that it accounted for the deaths of more than 20,000 persons.

Air War US officials in Washington disclose that, to compensate for the bombing cessation over North Vietnam, there will be a three-fold increase in the number of air strikes along the Ho Chi Minh trail in Laos. It is believed that President Johnson approved the intensified attacks on enemy infiltration routes to obtain support from US military commanders for his decision to terminate air raids against the North.

2 NOVEMBER 1968

South Vietnam In a speech before the South Vietnamese National Assembly, President Thieu states that Saigon will boycott the Paris negotiations. Thieu's principal objection is to NLF participation in the talks as a separate delegation. Thieu's position is apparently shared by Vice President Ky, who afterwards tells a group of legislators that President Johnson's decision to terminate the bombing indicates that 'we can trust the Americans no longer – they are just a band of crooks.'

6 NOVEMBER 1968

USA: Domestic Richard Milhous Nixon is elected President of the United States.

8 NOVEMBER 1968

South Vietnam As a condition for South Vietnamese participation in the expanded Paris talks, President Thieu proposes a two-sided conference: 'Each side is to consist of a single delegation headed by the principal party. Our side – the victims of aggression – will be headed by South Vietnam. Our delegation will include the United States and, if necessary, our other allies. The other side is the side of the Communist aggressors, to be headed by North Vietnam. Their delegation can include members of Hanoi's auxiliary forces, labeled as the National Liberation Front.' Both Washington and Hanoi reject the formula.

8-9 NOVEMBER 1968

Air War US B-52s conduct heavy raids against a suspected enemy force of 35,000 men about five miles from the Cambodian border in Tayninh province; the US command also transfers the 1st Air Cavalry Division from northern I Corps to an area northwest of Saigon.

9 NOVEMBER 1968

South Vietnam The Saigon government files a protest with the International Control Commission charging that enemy forces have shelled population centers in 14 provinces since the bombing halt.

10 NOVEMBER 1968
Ground War North Vietnamese guns, firing from inside the DMZ, shell US Marine positions just south of the buffer zone for the first time since President Johnson announced the bombing halt; a Marine air and artillery counterattack destroys 10 enemy bunkers.

12 NOVEMBER 1968
USA: Government Speaking at a news conference in Washington, Defense Secretary Clifford warns that, if South Vietnam does not agree soon to participate in the talks, the US may conduct negotiations without them.

13 NOVEMBER 1968
USA: Government The administration charges that recent North Vietnamese artillery strikes from inside the DMZ violate the agreement upon which the bombing halt is based. A North Vietnamese official in Paris later denies the accusation in a statement asserting that the United States has violated the buffer zone with naval and ground fire. The spokesman also contends that US reconnaissance flights over the North constitute further violations.

14 NOVEMBER 1968
South Vietnam The South Vietnamese government closes down a Saigon newspaper for publishing a detailed account of Defense Secretary Clifford's criticisms of the Thieu regime. It is the tenth newspaper which the government has suspended or shut down in the past three weeks.

15 NOVEMBER 1968
Ground War US reconnaissance pilots report NVA troops and supply movements north of the DMZ have quadrupled since the bombing halt. Aerial observations also reveal that work crews have repaired all the bombed-out bridges between the 17th and 19th Parallels.

17 NOVEMBER 1968
Cambodia The Cambodian government charges that South Vietnamese patrol boats shelled the village of Prekkoeus in Kampot province, killing 12 civilians and wounding another 12.

20 NOVEMBER-19 DECEMBER 1968
Ground War Operating 10 miles south of Danang between the La Tho and Ky Lam Rivers, the US 9th Marines place a cordon of troops around an area believed to contain 1400 enemy troops and then move in to engage the trapped NVA and Vietcong forces. Reported enemy casualties total 1210.

23 NOVEMBER 1968
Ground War The US command in Saigon reports that 210 'indications of enemy activity and presence' inside the DMZ – ranging from sightings of enemy vehicles to artillery strikes – have been recorded since the bombing halt.

26 NOVEMBER 1968
South Vietnam South Vietnamese Foreign Minister Tran Chanh Thanh declares that, following several weeks of discussion with US officials, his government has decided to participate in the Paris talks.
Ground War Responding to intelligence reports that NVA troops 500 yards inside the DMZ pose a threat to the Marine base at Conthien, US and ARVN forces enter the buffer zone for the first time since the bombing halt and drive the enemy back from its advanced positions.

29 NOVEMBER 1968
Guerrilla War Hanoi Radio broadcasts an NLF directive calling for a new offensive to 'utterly destroy' allied forces. The broadcast adds that the operation is particularly concerned with eliminating the 'Phoenix Organization' units.

1 DECEMBER 1968
USA: Domestic The National Commission on Causes and Prevention of Violence issues a report, *Rights in Conflict*, characterizing the behavior of the Chicago police during the Democratic National Convention as gratuitous and mindless.

1 DECEMBER 1968-31 MAY 1969
Ground War Operation Speedy Express is conducted by the US 9th Infantry Division in the IV Corps region south of Saigon and claims 10,899 enemy casualties.

6 DECEMBER 1968-7 MARCH 1969
Ground War A 1st Marine Division operation, Taylor Common, in Quang Nam province accounts for 1299 reported enemy casualties.

8 DECEMBER 1968-10 FEBRUARY 1969

Ground War An ARVN 1st Ranger Group operation, Le Loi I, in Quang Nam province claims 695 enemy casualties.

11 DECEMBER 1968
South Vietnam The US mission in Saigon issues a statement declaring that 73.3 percent of the South Vietnamese live in relatively secure areas controlled by the Saigon government; the report also claims an increase of 3.5 percent since the inception of the Le Loi and Phoenix programs.

12 DECEMBER 1968
Negotiations Responding to North Vietnamese and NLF demands that the four delegations to the Paris negotiations be seated at separate tables, Nguyen Cao Ky refuses to consent to any seating plan that would place the NLF on an equal footing with Saigon. The issue is one of several procedural points deadlocking the talks.

12-13 DECEMBER 1968
Air War US B-52s pound numerous targets north of Saigon in an apparent effort to disrupt an expected enemy offensive.

15 DECEMBER 1968
USA: Government Defense Secretary Clifford states that the United States has no 'obligation' to keep 540,000 troops in Vietnam until a final political settlement is concluded and suggests that the administration and North Vietnamese arrange a de-escalation once the expanded talks begin.

16 DECEMBER 1968
USA: Domestic In a decision concerning an appeal by 57 military reservists, the Supreme Court refuses to review the federal government's constitutional right to send reservists to Vietnam in the absence of an official declaration of war.

17 DECEMBER 1968
USA: Domestic Senator George McGovern (D-SD) characterizes Nguyen Cao Ky as a 'little tinhorn dictator' in a statement complaining that Saigon is deliberately trying to delay the peace talks. A Gallup Poll shows that the majority of Americans are now ready to let South Vietnam take over the fighting and assume a leading role in the peace talks.

18 DECEMBER 1968
USA: Domestic Dr Henry Kissinger in an article published in *Foreign Affairs*, proposes that the peace talks proceed on two tracks: the United States and North Vietnam arranging a mutual withdrawal of forces in one set of negotiations, while South Vietnam and the NLF forge a political settlement in separate discussions. He further asserts that the United States can neither awcept military defeat nor an externally imposed change in the South Vietnamese government, but that once North Vietnam has withdrawn its forces from the South, the United States has no obligation to maintain the Saigon government by force.

23 DECEMBER 1968
Negotiations NLF representative in Paris Tran Buu Kiem rejects any direct negotiations between the NLF and Saigon, adding that 'if one wants to settle a conflict, one settles it between the direct adversaries,' which in this case are the United States and the Vietcong.

27 DECEMBER 1968
Ground War The allied mission in Saigon reports that there were 140 enemy-initiated violations of the Christmas truce.
Negotiations The Saigon government issues a statement dismissing 30 members of its 80-man peace delegation for a 'violation of national discipline.'

30 DECEMBER 1968
Ground War Allied forces will not observe a 72-hour New Year's cease-fire unilaterally declared by the Vietcong.

31 DECEMBER 1968
State of the War The end of the year 1968 seems to be yet another threshold for a war that has now become the most pervasive concern of most of the world. Some US officials continue to claim that the allied forces are making increasing progress against the Communist forces, but few others really believe that the war is going to be decided on the battlefield. As it happens, the Tet offensive of the early weeks of 1968 is in fact something of a military defeat for the Communists (and unbeknownst to the rest of the world, the North Vietnamese leaders have been engaged in debates – and recriminations – over the strategy and tactics that are proving to be so costly in manpower). But the Tet offensive has such an impact on Americans that it leads President Johnson to stop

CHRONOLOGY

Members on the 199th Light Infantry Brigade take up positions at the racetrack near Cholon.

complying with the requests of his military chiefs to have infinite amounts of men and matériel. It also leads Johnson effectively to not seeking another term, and in turn to the tumultuous summer of 1968 that climaxes at the Chicago Democratic Convention. The election is won by Richard Nixon, and there is a general sense that he had both a plan and a mandate to bring the war quickly to an end. Since January 1961, some 31,000 US servicemen have died in Vietnam – 14,314 in 1968 alone – and some 200,000 US personnel have been wounded. During 1968, 20,482 South Vietnamese military personnel were killed in combat as were 978 other allied military personnel. Allied estimates of Vietcong and North Vietnamese military deaths are 35,774 for the year 1968, while a total of some 439,000 Communists are claimed to have been killed since January 1961. Even if these figures represent inflated 'body counts,' there is no denying that hundreds of thousanks of Vietnamese, civilians as well as military, Southern as well as Northern, have been killed in the war. Little wonder that as President Johnson ends the year with only a few weeks left in office, he is reported to be 'haunted' by the war.

1 JANUARY-31 AUGUST 1969
Ground War Military operations code-named Operation Rice Farmer are conducted throughout the Mekong Delta by elements of the 9th Infantry Division and the 5th ARVN Regiment along with other supporting forces. Enemy casualties of 1860 are reported.

1 JANUARY-31 DECEMBER 1969
Ground War A multi-division operation, Quyet Thang, involving the ARVN 7th, 9th and 21st Infantry Divisions in IV Corps Tactical Zone. Enemy casualties are reported at 37,874.

2 JANUARY 1969
Negotiations US and North Vietnamese negotiators meet in Paris for more than four hours in an attempt to break the deadlocked peace talks. Most of the meeting continues to focus on the shape of the conference table.
Ground War The New Year 72-hour ceasefire proclaimed by the Vietcong ends.

4 JANUARY 1969
USA: Government President-elect Richard Nixon announces he will ask Ellsworth Bunker to remain at his post as Ambassador to South Vietnam.

5 JANUARY 1969
USA: Government President-elect Nixon names Henry Cabot Lodge to succeed W Averell Harriman as chief negotiator at the Paris talks. Lawrence Edward Walsh, a New York lawyer and deputy attorney general (1957-60), is named deputy chief negotiator

to replace Cyrus R Vance, who will remain temporarily after 20 January. Marshall Green, an Asian affairs expert and ambassador to Indonesia, is assigned to assist the negotiating team.

Riverine War The US Navy announces it has established the final link of interlocking water patrols along a 150 mile stretch of the Cambodian-South Vietnamese border involving more than 100 vessels.

6 JANUARY 1969

Terrorism Le Minh Tri, education minister in the government of South Vietnam, dies 10 hours after a bomb is thrown into his car. The police refuse to specifically blame the Vietcong as Tri had made many enemies fighting corruption in the educational system and had received many death threats.

10 JANUARY 1969

Diplomatic Sweden announces it will establish full diplomatic relations with North Vietnam.
Guerrilla War The Vietcong ambush and wipe out a nine-man US patrol near Dongtam. The Vietcong also open mortar attacks on several towns and military bases. At least 17 are reported killed and 155 wounded.
Air War North Vietnam reports downing an unmanned US reconnaissance plane over Thaibinh province.

11 JANUARY 1969

Cambodia A US helicopter is shot down by Cambodian anti-aircraft gunners. One crew member is killed and three are rescued. Prince Norodom Sihanouk charges that the helicopter intruded into Cambodian territory.

13 JANUARY 1969

South Vietnam In a move to prepare for a possible guerrilla assault, all special leaves for South Vietnam troops are cancelled.
Ground War US and South Vietnamese troops take into custody 470 Vietcong suspects as they begin a drive to clear guerrilla forces from Cape Batangan in Quangngai province.

14 JANUARY 1969

South Vietnam A government spokesman proposes that US forces start 'a gradual, phased withdrawal' from South Vietnam.
USA: Government President Johnson, in a combined State of the Union message and final address to the nation, urges the country

to press its 'quest for peace' in Vietnam.
Ground War US forces kill 122 enemy troops while beating back an attack on a supply convoy northwest of Saigon. Seven Americans are killed and 10 wounded.

15 JANUARY 1969

USA: Military President Johnson sends his final budget to Congress calling for Vietnam war-related expenditures of $25,733,000,000 for the fiscal year 1970. This includes a $3,500,000,000 reduction in spending for the war in Vietnam, the first since the United States entered the war.

16 JANUARY 1969

Negotiations An agreement is reached in Paris for the opening of expanded talks. Representatives of the United States, South Vietnam, North Vietnam and the National Liberation Front will sit at a circular table without nameplates, flags or markings. The ambiguous compromise allows the United States and South Vietnam to speak of only two sides, while allowing North Vietnam and the NLF to speak of four sides.

17 JANUARY 1969

Negotiations At a Paris news conference, Tran Hoai Nam, chief spokesman for the National Liberation Front, says the NLF will participate in the talks as a 'fully independent and equal party.'

18 JANUARY 1969

South Vietnam President Nguyen Van Thieu confirms he has requested the withdrawal of some US troops from South Vietnam in 1969.
Negotiations The expanded Paris peace talks open. Negotiators agree to hold the first plenary session on substantive issues early next week.

20 JANUARY 1969

USA: Government Richard Milhous Nixon is inaugurated as President of the United States and says that 'after a period of confrontation, we are entering an era of negotiation.'

22 JANUARY 1969

Ground War US troops find 56 Vietcong and 100 women and children in a tunnel complex on Cape Batangan.

22 JANUARY-18 MARCH 1969

Ground War The US 9th Marine Regiment (Reinforced) conducts military operations,

CHRONOLOGY

known as Dewey Canyon, north of the Ashau Valley in Quangtri province. Enemy casualties are reported at 1335.

24 JANUARY 1969
South Vietnam The government bans firecrackers during the Lunar New Year because the Vietcong used firecracker noise during Tet in 1968 to conceal its attack.

25 JANUARY 1969
Negotiations The first plenary meeting of the Paris peace talks is held. Ambassador Henry Cabot Lodge, chief negotiator for the United States, urges an immediate restoration of a genuine DMZ as the first 'practical move toward peace.' Lodge also suggests a mutual withdrawal of 'external' military forces and an early release of prisoners of war. On one side, Ambassador Pham Dang Lam, chief delegate from South Vietnam, and on the other, Tran Buu Kiem and Xuan Thuy, heads of the National Liberation Front and North Vietnamese delegations respectively, trade charges of 'aggression.'
Ground War A force of 800 Americans, after a six-day battle, finally succeed in entirely seizing a village seven miles northwest of Quangngai which had been occupied by about 200 Communist troops.

28 JANUARY 1969
Negotiations At the Paris talks, the NLF delegation rejects the US proposal for a prisoner-of-war exchange and other proposals as a basis on which progress could be made in the talks. Their statement reaffirms that the United States must accept the program of the NLF and North Vietnam which calls for a political settlement, the withdrawal of US and allied troops, and the settlement of South Vietnamese internal affairs without foreign interference.

29 JANUARY 1969
Ground War The Vietcong proclaim a week's ceasefire, 15-22 February, for Tet, the Vietnamese Lunar New Year.

30 JANUARY 1969
Negotiations At the second plenary session, North Vietnam and the NLF reject the proposals by the United States and South Vietnam for a DMZ, a mutual withdrawal of troops and an exchange of prisoners. North Vietnam and the NLF state that a reduction in the fighting must be tied to a political settlement.

31 JANUARY-1 FEBRUARY 1969
UN The UN Secretariat receives documents and charges issued by the Cambodian government that US and South Vietnamese forces had killed and wounded civilians on Cambodian territory on 14 December 1968 and in three raids in November 1968.

1 FEBRUARY 1969
South Vietnam A three-month pacification program ends as officials report more than one million South Vietnamese have been added to those under the 'relatively secure' control of the Saigon government. US officials claim, that as of mid-January, 76.3 percent of the population is 'relatively secure.' A drihe is set for the remainder of 1969 with the goal of bringing 90 percent of the South Vietnamese population under government control.
South Vietnam The US Navy turns over 25 heavily-armed river boats to the South Vietnamese Navy.

6 FEBRUARY 1969
USA: Government President Nixon, at a news conference, says that while a troop reduction is high on his list of priorities, there will have to be progress in the peace talks before he can announce any reduction.
Negotiations In Paris, there is a restatement of earlier proposals and positions. The United States and South Vietnam urge North Vietnam and the NLF to reconsider their proposal to take military steps to reduce the fighting; North Vietnam and NLF negotiators restate their earlier rejection and accuse the United States of trying to separate the military questions from the political problems.

7 FEBRUARY 1969
Ground War The US Navy announces that the military operation on Cape Batangan in Quangngai province is a success and reports 200 enemy killed and 251 captured since the operation began 13 January.

10 FEBRUARY 1969
Negotiations South Vietnamese Vice-President Nguyen Cao Ky, political adviser to the delegation from South Vietnam, says his government will negotiate a political settlement with the Vietcong after North Vietnam withdraws its forces from South Vietnam. Ky states that he would like to see the United States and North Vietnam agree on a mutual withdrawal of forces while leaving the settle-

ment of political problems to the South Vietnamese government and the NLF. Meanwhile, on leaving Paris for Hanoi, Le Duc Tho, political adviser to the North Vietnamese delegation, says the Nixon administgation is 'pursuing the same policy as the administration of President Johnson.'

15 FEBRUARY 1969
South Vietnam The seven-day Tet ceasefire proclaimed by the Vietcong begins. Allied forces announce they will observe a 24-hour Tet truce.
USA: Military There are now 539,000 American soldiers in South Vietnam as allied troops strength reaches an all-time high of 1,610,500.

22 FEBRUARY 1969
Guerrilla War The Tet ceasefire ends. Communist forces fire rocket and mortar rounds into Saigon and approximately 70 other cities and allied military positions. In raids throughout South Vietnam, 28 Americans and eight civilians are reported killed and 128 Americans and 81 civilians wounded. It is the first shelling of Saigon since the last days of October.
Sweden Sweden grants asylum to more than 200 draft evaders and military deserters from the US armed services.

23 FEBRUARY 1969
Ground War Communists forces, striking at Saigon and at least 115 other targets begin what the allied command considers to be the long-predicted general offensive (which becomes known as 'post-Tet'). Approximately 100 US soldiers are reported killed in the first 15 hours of fighting; enemy losses are estimated at 1000.
USA: Government President Nixon, responding to the series of enemy attacks, orders a full investigation to determine whether the attacks violate the accord that was responsible for the US bombing halt of North Vietnam on 1 Novemser 1968.

24 FEBRUARY 1969
Ground War Communist forces continue shelling towns and military bases but the attacks diminish as only about 60 targets are struck. It is reported that nearly 200 Americans have been killed in the offensive.

Nixon confers with Kissinger and Admiral John McCain, Commander of the Pacific Fleet.

CHRONOLOGY

24 FEBRUARY-10 MARCH 1969
Ground War The ARVN 2nd Division conducts military operations code-named Quyet Thang 22 in Quangngai province. Enemy casualties are reported at 777.

25 FEBRUARY 1969
North Vietnam The North Vietnamese Foreign Ministry, in a Hanoi radio broadcast, asserts that the 'South Vietnamese people' have a right to attack US forces 'at any place on Vietnamese territory.' North Vietnam also denies it agreed to any conditions in return for a bombing halt.
Ground War Communist troops assault two major installations near Saigon and shell more than 50 towns and bases in the fourth consecutive day of attacks. Near Bienhoa airbase 150 enemy soldiers are reported killed. Meanwhile, two US positions, just south of the DMZ come under heavy attack. Following one attack by a North Vietnamese suicide squad, 36 United States Marines are killed. The US losses are described as the highest in a single battle in nearly six months.

27 FEBRUARY 1969
Negotiations At the sixth plenary session in Paris the United States argues that the attacks, particularly the shelling of population centers in the South, violate the US-North Vietnamese understanding that led to a halt of the bombing of North Vietnam.
Ground War Communist forces shell 30 military installations and nine towns. The United States estimates that 5300 of the enemy have been killed during the offensive, while US losses are put at 250-300 men. South Vietnamese officials report 200 civilians killed and 12,700 made homeless.

27 FEBRUARY-20 JUNE 1969
Ground War The ARVN 1st Ranger Group conducts Operation Quang Nam in Quangnam province. Enemy casualties are reported at 688.

28 FEBRUARY 1969
Ground War The Communist offensive continues as gunners shell about 30 targets. US troops fight a day-long battle near Saigon.

1 MARCH 1969
South Vietnam President Thieu states that the Communist offensive has been a 'complete failure.' The enemy 'no longer have the ability to sustain offensives.'

1 MARCH-14 APRIL 1969
Ground War Military operations, known as Wayne Grey, by the 4th Infantry Division are carried out in Kontum province. There are 608 enemy casualties reported.

1 MARCH-29 MAY 1969
Ground War Operation Oklahoma Hills by the US 7th and 26th Marine regiments is conducted southwest of Danang in Quangnam province. There are 596 enemy casualties reported.

2 MARCH 1969
Diplomatic President Nixon meets in Paris with Ambassador Lodge and South Vietnamese Vice-President Nguyen Cao Ky.

4 MARCH 1969
USA: Government President Nixon declares that the United States 'will not tolerate' additional attacks and warns that an appropriate response will be made.

5 MARCH 1969
Guerrilla War Communist forces fire at least seven rockets into Saigon as at least 22 civilians are reported killed and scores wounded.

6 MARCH 1969
USA: Government Secretary of Defense Melvin Laird and Chairman of the Joint Chiefs of Staff General Earle Wheeler arrive in South Vietnam for a five-day visit.
Negotiations The seventh plenary session is broken off when South Vietnam's chief negotiator, Pham Dang Lam, requests to adjourn because an 'atmosphere favorable to useful discussions does not exist.' Ambassador Lodge reminds North Vietnam and the NLF that the understanding which led to the bombing halt is still in effect.
Ground War The US military command reports that 453 Americans were killed during the first week of the post-Tet offensive and 2593 were wounded. There are 521 South Vietnamese ank 6752 enemy soldiers reported killed in the fighting.
Cambodia Prince Norodom Sihanouk says he will release four US fliers, captured after their observation plane was downed 12 February. Cambodia protests the violation of its airspace.

8 MARCH 1969
Ground War Communist gunners increase attacks on military targets. About 50 targets

are struck as ground fighting also increases.
Laos US military sources report an incursion of about 100 US Marines into Laos. About a dozen hilltops were seized recently just south of Dongha, as part of Operation Dewey Canyon, begun in late January.

9 MARCH 1969

Ground War Attacks continue as Communist gunners strike at 35 military positions and six civilian communities.

12 MARCH 1969

South Vietnam President Thieu establishes five new cabinet positions and fills several other government positions in a further consolidation of his political power.
Diplomatic Four US fliers, captured by Cambodia, arrive in Thailand after a letter by President Nixon to Prince Sihanouk brings them freedom.

13 MARCH 1969

Ground War The US command reports 336 US soldiers were killed during the second week of the offensive and 1694 were wounded. There are 259 South Vietnamese soldiers, 4063 enemy soldiers and 72 civilians also reported killed.

14 MARCH 1969

USA: Government At a news conference, President Nixon says there is no prospect for a US troop reduction in the foreseeable future because of the enemy offensive. Nixon states that the prospects for withdrawal will hinge on the level of enemy activity, progress in the Paris talks and the ability of the South Vietnamese to defend themselves.

15 MARCH 1969

Ground War US Marines move about one mile into the southern section of the DMZ, the first US military force in the area since November 1968. Fighting breaks out three miles northeast of Giolinh after a US patrol observes Communist rocket emplacements firing into South Vietnam.

16 MARCH 1969

North Vietnam Ho Chi Minh urges the Vietnamese people and armed forces to press the fight until the United States is defeated.

17 MARCH 1969

USA: Government Senator George McGovern (D-SD) accuses President Nixon

of continuing the 'tragic course' of the Johnson administration. The Nixon administration, says McGovern, rather than seeking a military disengagement and settlement, seems intent on pursuing a 'policy of military attrition and moral disaster.' Other Senate leaders, notably Senate Majority Leader Mike Mansfield (D-MT), say that Nixon should be given 'a further chance.'
Diplomatic Cuba establishes formal diplomatic relations with the NLF.

18 MARCH 1969

Covert War US B-52 bombers are ordered diverted from their targets in South Vietnam to attack suspected Communist base camps and supply areas in Cambodia for the first time in the war. The mission, formally designated Operation Breakfast, was approved by President Nixon at a meeting of the National Security Council on 15 March. The B-52 strikes inside Cambodia became known as the 'Menu' bombings. A total of 3630 flights over Cambodia will drop 110,000 tons of bombs over a 14 month period through April 1970. This bombing of Cambodia and all subsequent 'Menu' operations are kept secret from the American public and the US Congress.

19 MARCH 1969

USA: Government Secretary of Defense Melvin Laird, appearing before the Senate Armed Services Committee, asks for $156,000,000 for a program to increase the capability of South Vietnamese troops so they can replace US forces even before all outside forces have been withdrawn by mutual agreement.

20 MARCH 1969

USA: Domestic A federal grand jury, under anti-riot provisions of the 1968 Civil Rights Act, indicts eight persons on charges of conspiracy to incite riot during the 1968 Democratic convention in Chicago. Eight Chicago policemen are also indicted, seven of them on charges of assaulting demonstrators.
Ground War The US command reports 351 Americans were killed from 9-15 March, the third week of the enemy offensive. Also reported killed were 325 South Vietnamese and 4137 enemy soldiers.

20-31 MARCH 1969

Ground War Military action by the ARVN 4th Regiment operating in Quangngai province continues as Operation Quyet Thang

US Marines patrol a jungle road in search of North Vietnamese tracked vehicles.

25. Enemy casualties are reported at 592.

22 MARCH 1969
USA: Domestic A Gallup Poll conducted recently among 1535 Americans records 32 percent favor greatly escalating the war or 'going all-out,' 26 percent favor pulling out, 19 percent favor a continuation of the current policy and 21 percent have no opinion.

USA: Domestic Nine anti-war demonstrators, including five Roman Catholic clergymen, are arrested after ransacking the Dow Chemical offices in Washington, DC.

24 MARCH 1969
USA: Military President Nixon names Lieutenant General William B Rosson as deputy commander of US forces in Vietnam and nominates him for four-star rank.

28 MARCH 1969
Terrorism US officials find a mass grave near Hué containing at least 57 bodies of civilians killed in last year's Tet offensive.

1 APRIL 1969
USA: Government Secretary of Defense Laird announces that B-52 bomber raids in South Vietnam will be decreased by more than 10 percent as a result of further cuts in next year's defense budget.

Ground War The Vietcong's Liberation News Agency, the news organ of the National Liberation Front, claims that the offensive has 'shattered' the strategic plan conceived by General Abrams following the 1968 Tet offensive.

2 APRIL 1969
Terrorism A South Vietnamese government spokesman announces the Vietcong had assassinated 201 civilians in the last week of March, bringing the total for the first three months of 1969 to 1955.

3 APRIL 1969
USA: Government Secretary Laird contends that the United States is moving to 'Vietnamize' the war as rapidly as possible, but warns it does not serve the United States' purpose to discuss troop withdrawals while the enemy is conducting an offensive.

Ground War US combat deaths for the week of 23-29 March raised the toll to 33,641 Americans killed in eight years of US involvement in Vietnam, or 12 more than fell during the Korean War.

5-6 APRIL 1969
USA: Domestic Thousands of anti-war demonstrators march in New York City to Central Park demanding the United States withdraw from Vietnam. The weekend of anti-war protests ends with demonstrations and parades in San Francisco, Los Angeles, Washington, DC and other cities.

7 APRIL 1969
South Vietnam President Thieu, in a State of the Union address to the opening session of the National Assembly in Saigon, offers the enemy a policy of 'national reconciliation' in which former Vietcong members would enjoy full political rights in exchange for the withdrawal of North Vietnamese troops from South Vietnam, Laos and Cambodia. Thieu stresses that Vietcong members would be able to participate in South Vietnamese politics only as individuals, and not as members of the NLF or any official Communist party.

8 APRIL 1969
Diplomatic A Vietcong spokesman in Paris rejects Nguyen Van Thieu's proposals.
Air War The US military command reports five waves of B-52s raid suspected enemy camps near the Cambodian border.

9 APRIL 1969
USA: Domestic The Chicago Eight indicted 20 March on federal charges of conspiracy to incite riot at the 1968 Democratic convention in Chicago plead not guilty. A Gallup Poll reports that three out of every five persons who express an opinion back President Nixon on the Vietnam War. In a poll conducted 28-31 March, 44 percent approve of the way Nixon is handling the situation in Vietnam, 30 percent reserved judgement or gave no opinion, while 26 percent disapproved.
Terrorism Workers uncover another 65 bodies of victims of Vietcong execution squads in Hué during the 1968 Tet offensive.

10-11 APRIL 1969
Ground War The Communist offensive flares sharply with 45 mortar and rocket attacks during the night. Increased ground fighting is reported in the Mekong Delta and in the area northwest of Saigon. The town of Vinhlong, 60 miles southwest of Saigon, suffers the heaviest mortar attack on a provincial capital since the offensive began as it is struck by 100 mortar rounds; 15 persons are reported killed and 103 wounded.

14 APRIL 1969
Ground War US troops kill 198 communist soldiers in a massive enemy attack against an infantry camp 33 miles northwest of Saigon. Thirteen Americans are reported killed and three wounded.

15 APRIL 1969-1 JANUARY 1971
Ground War The 173rd Airborne Brigade conducts a pacification operation, Washington Green, in the An Lao Valley in Binhdinh province. There are 1957 enemy casualties reported.

16 APRIL 1969
Diplomatic President Nixon, in a message to Prince Sihanouk of Cambodia, declares: 'In conformity with the UN Charter, the United States recognizes and respects the sovereignty, independence, neutrality and territorial integrity of the kingdom of Cambodia within its present frontiers.' Sihanouk reports he is ready to resume diplomatic relations with the United States.

17 APRIL 1969
Negotiations At the 13th plenary session, the Paris talks continue to show no progress as Communist negotiators reject allied proposals for mutual troop withdrawals and repeat their earlier demand that US forces must leave unconditionally and at once.

18 APRIL 1969
USA: Government President Nixon, at a news conference, says he feels the prospects for peace have 'significantly improved' since he took office, largely because of what he terms the greater political stability of the Saigon government and the improvement in the South Vietnamese armed forces.

18 APRIL-31 DECEMBER 1969
Ground War The ARVN 22nd Division conducts military operations, Dan Thang 69, in Binhdinh province. Enemy casualties are reported at 507.

19 APRIL 1969
South Vietnam The United States turns over the first 20 of 60 jet fighter-bombers to the South Vietnamese Air Force.

20 APRIL 1969
South Vietnam A new political party is formed in Saigon opposed to both Communism and critical of President Thieu. The

party is officially called the Progressive Nationalist Movement and is headed by Dr. Nguyen Ngoc Huy, a member of South Vietnam's delegation to the Paris talks.

24-25 APRIL 1969
Air War In two days of the heaviest bombing raids of the war, almost 100 B-52 bombers, based in Thailand and Guam, are reported to drop close to 3000 tons of bombs on a border area 70 miles northwest of Saigon.

26 APRIL 1969
Ground War US forces report killing 213 enemy troops near the Cambodian border, 45 miles northwest of Saigon, in one of the bloodiest battles fought in almost a year, but only one American is reported killed and one wounded. US planes and artillery attack North Vietnamese gun positions in Cambodia near the border following a Communist assault on a US artillery base on the frontier.

27 APRIL 1969
Ground War Heavy fighting erupts near the Cambodian border for the second consecutive day as US forces turn back an attack by 300 enemy troops; 100 Communist soldiers and 10 Americans are reported killed.

30 APRIL 1969
Diplomatic Prince Sihanouk withdraws his assent to the resumption of diplomatic relations with the United States because the United States fails to mention its stand regarding the status of a group of offshore islands, including Dao Phu Duoc, claimed by both Cambodia and South Vietnam.

1 MAY 1969
USA: Government In a speech on the floor of the Senate, George Aiken (R-VT), senior member of the Senate Foreign Relations Committee, urges the Nixon administration to begin an immediate 'orderly withdrawal' of US forces from South Vietnam. Aiken says that 'it may take some time to complete this operation, but it should be started without delay.' The speech is widely regarded as the end of the self-imposed moratorium on criticism Senators have been following since the Nixon administration took office.

1 MAY-16 JULY 1969
Ground War The US 9th Marine Regiment conducts military operations Virginia Ridge in northern Quangtri province along the

DMZ. Enemy casualties are reported at 560.

5 MAY 1969
Ground War Communist soldiers attack a US military camp 65 miles northwest of Saigon; 125 enemy soldiers are reported killed and four are captured. Nine Americans are killed and 59 wounded.

6 MAY 1969
Ground War A US helicopter crashes and burns 75 miles north of Saigon, killing 34 and injuring 35 in what is believed to be the worst helicopter disaster of the war. To date 2595 helicopters are reported to have been lost.

8 MAY 1969
Negotiations At the 16th plenary session of the Paris talks, the NLF presents a 10-point program for an 'overall solution' to the war. The program includes an unconditional withdrawal of United States and allied troops from Vietnam, the establishment of a coalition government and the holding of free elections, the demand that the South Vietnamese settle their own affairs 'without foreign interference', and the eventual reunification of North and South Vietnam.

9 MAY 1969
South Vietnam The South Vietnamese Foreign Ministry says Saigon is prepared to discuss, in private or at a plenary session, three of the NLF's 10 points: the exchange of captives, the restoration of the neutrality of the DMZ and the application of the 1962 agreement on Laos.

USA: Government William Beecher, military correspondent for *The New York Times*, publishes a page-one dispatch from Washington, 'Raids in Cambodia by US Unprotested,' which accurately describes the first of the secret B-52 bombing raids in Cambodia. Within hours, Henry Kissinger, presidential assistant for national security affairs, contacts J Edgar Hoover, the director of the FBI, asking him to find the governmental sources of Beecher's article. During the next two years, Alexander Haig, a key Kissinger assistant, will transmit the names of National Security Council stafz members and reporters who are to have their telephones wiretapped by the FBI.

Ground War US Marines, supported by aircraft, report killing 129 enemy soldiers 18 miles southwest of Danang. Six Americans are killed and 12 are wounded.

10 MAY-7 JUNE 1969
Ground War Military operations (Apache Snow) by the US 9th Marine Regiment and elements of the 101st Airborne Division are conducted in western Thauthien province. Enemy casualties stand at 977.

10-20 MAY 1969
Ground War US and South Vietnamese forces battle North Vietnamese troops for Apbia mountain (Hill 937), one mile east of the Laotian border. The battle is part of a 2800-man allied sweep of the Ashua valley (Operation Apache Snow). The purpose is to cut off the North Vietnamese there and stop any infiltration from Laos menacing Hué to the northeast and Danang to the southeast. US paratroopers, pushing northeast, find the Communist forces entrenched on Apbia mountain. In fierce fighting, directed by Major General Melvin Zais, the mountain comes under heavy allied air strikes, artillery barrages and 10 infantry assaults. The Communist stronghold is captured in the 11th attack when 1000 troops of the US 101st Airborne Division and 400 South Vietnamese fight their way to the summit. There are 597 North Vietnamese reported killed. US casualties are listed as 56 killed and 420 wounded. Due to the intense fighting and the high loss of life, Apbia mountain is dubbed 'Hamburger Hill.'

11-12 MAY 1969
Ground War Communist forces shell 159 cities, towns and military bases throughout South Vietnam, including Saigon and Hué, in the largest number of attacks since the 1968 Tet offensive; 14 persons are reported killed and about 100 wounded in a series of terrorist attacks near Saigon. Initial reports claim at least 500 Communist soldiers killed.

13 MAY 1969
Ground War In a Communist attack on a US camp near the Laotian border 20 Americans are killed and 65 wounded; 20 North Vietnamese are reported killed.

14 MAY 1969
Diplomatic Singapore Prime Minister Lee Kuan Yew meets with President Nixon at the White House and cautions against hasty US withdrawal from Vietnam.
USA: Government In his first full-length report to the American people on the Vietnam War, President Nixon responds to the

10-point plan offered by the NLF. Nixon proposes a phased, mutual withdrawal of major portions of US, allied and North Vietnamese forces from South Vietnam over a 12-month period with the remaining non-South Vietnamese forces withdrawing to enclaves and abiding by a ceasefire until withdrawals are completed. Nixon also insists that North Vietnamese forces withdraw from Cambodia and Laos at the same time and offers internationally supervised elections for South Vietnam. Nixon's offer of a 'simultaneous start on withdrawal' represents a revision of the last formal proposal offered in October 1966 – known as the 'Manila formula' – in which the United States stated the withdrawal of US forces would be completed within six months after the North Vietnamese left South Vietnam.
Negotiations Tran Buu Kiem, speaking at a luncheon in Paris, says the 10-point program put forth by the NLF 'forms a whole' and says that he is opposed to only partial acceptance of the NLF program.
Ground War Communist forces shell Danang as 22 South Vietnamese are reported killed and 21 are wounded.

15 MAY 1969
USA: Government Eight Democratic members of the House of Representatives introduce legislation asking President Nixon to withdraw 100,000 troops unconditionally and to call for a ceasefire.

15 MAY-7 JUNE 1969
Ground War Military operations Dan Quyen 38-A (Peoples Rights) are conducted by the 42nd ARVN Regiment and 22nd Ranger Group in the Benhet-Dakto area, with 945 enemy casualties reported.

16 MAY-13 AUGUST 1969
Ground War Operation Lamar Plain is conducted southwest of Tamky in Quangtin province by elements of the 23rd Infantry and 101st Airborne Divisions. Enemy casualties stand at 524.

18 MAY 1969
Ground War More than 1500 Communist troops attack US and South Vietnamese camps near Xuanloc, 38 miles east of Saigon and are driven off after five hours of intense fighting. At the US camp, 14 Americans are killed and 39 wounded and 24 enemy soldiers are killed. At the South Vietnamese camp,

four South Vietnamese are killed, 14 wounded with 54 Communist soldiers reported killed and nine captured. In another battle near the Laotian border, 12 Americans are killed and 79 wounded with 125 enemy soldiers reported killed.

20 MAY 1969

USA: Government As part of a growing outcry over US military policy in Vietnam, Edward Kennedy (D-MA), in a Senate speech, scorns the military tactics of the Nixon administration, in particular the battle for Apbia mountain, as 'senseless and irresponsible.'

21 MAY 1969

USA: Military A US military command spokesman in Saigon defends the battle for Apbia mountain as necessary to stop enemy infiltration and protect Hué.

22 MAY 1969

USA: Military In Phubai, South Vietnam, Major General Melvin Zais, commander of the 101st Airborne Division which took Apbia mountain, says his orders were 'to destroy enemy forces' in the Ashua valley and says that he did not have any orders to reduce casualties by avoiding battles. The US military command in Saigon states that the recent battle for Apbia mountain is an integral part of the policy of 'maximum pressure' that it has been pursuing for the last six months and confirms that no orders have been received from President Nixon to modify the basic strategy.

Negotiations Ambassador Lodge, at the 18th plenary session of the Paris talks, says he finds common ground for discussion in the proposals of President Nixon and the NLF. In reply, Nguyen Thanh Le, spokesman for the North Vietnamese says the programs are 'as different as day and night.'

24 MAY 1969

Negotiations Xuan Thuy, head of the North Vietnamese delegation, says that while there are 'points of agreement' between the proposals of President Nixon and the NLF, it is necessary for the United States to abandon the South Vietnamese government for the conference to progress.

25 MAY 1969

South Vietnam President Thieu assumes personal leadership of the National Social Democratic Front at its inaugural meeting in Saigon. Thieu says the group is 'the first concrete step in unifying the political factions in South Vietnam for the coming political struggle with the Communists,' and emphasizes the new party will not be 'totalitarian or despotic.' The six major parties comprising the NSDF are: the Greater Union Force, composed largely of militant Roman Catholic refugees from North Vietnam; the Social Humanist Party, successor to the Can Lao party, which had held power under the Diem regime; the Revolutionary Dai Viet, formerly the Dai Viet, created to fight the French; the Social Democratic Party, a faction of the Hoa Hao religious sect; the United Vietnam Kuomintang, formed as an anti-French party; the People's Alliance for Social Revolution, a pro-government bloc formed in 1968.

28 MAY 1969

USA: Military US troops abandon Apbia mountain. A spokesman for the 101st Airborne Division says that the US troops 'have completed their search of the mountain, and are now continuing their reconnaissance-in-force mission throughout the Ashua valley.'

30 MAY 1969

South Korea South Vietnamese President Thieu, concluding a four-day visit to South Korea, says at a news conference that he will 'never' agree to a coalition government with the NLF. Regarding the role of the NLF in possible elections, Thieu says that 'if the Communists are willing to lay down their weapons, abandon the Communist ideology and abandon atrocities, they could participate in elections.'

3 JUNE 1969

Taiwan South Vietnamese President Thieu, on a four-day state visit to Taiwan, issues a joint communiqué with Chiang Kai-shek declaring that the 'absurd demand' for 'a coalition government must be resolutely rejected.'

7 JUNE 1969

Ground War In Tayninh and Binhlong provinces allied officers report finding the bodies of 399 Communist soldiers strewn over 11 battlefields after two nights of fighting along the Cambodian border. Four Americans are killed-in-action and 21 are wounded. In another battle, 10 US Marines are killed and 24 wounded near Khesanh. During the night

65 Communist shellings are reported. Danang is struck by 45 rockets in three separate attacks. Four US airmen are killed and 37 wounded.

8 JUNE 1969
USA: Government President Nixon and South Vietnamese President Thieu meet at Midway Island in the Pacific. Nixon announces 25,000 US troops will be withdrawn before the end of August. Nixon and Thieu underscore the point that US forces will be replaced by South Vietnamese forces.

9 JUNE 1969
South Vietnam President Thieu, in a televised news conference in Saigon, attempts to counter the gloom following his meeting with President Nixon by saying 'this is a replacement, not a withdrawal. Withdrawal is a defeatist and misleading term.'
Negotiations A NLF spokesman says that the refusal of Nixon and Thieu to accept a coalition government for South Vietnam is 'an obstacle to progress' in the Paris negotiations.

10 JUNE 1969
USA: Government President Nixon says the Midway meeting has 'opened wide the door to peace' and invites North Vietnam to 'walk with us through that door.' Nixon challenges North Vietnam to begin withdrawing forces or to begin serious negotiations or both.
France The NLF announces the establishment of a Provisional Revolutionary Government (PRG) to rule South Vietnam. The position of the new government is declared to be no different in substance from NLF policy. The formation of the PRG is seen as a challenge to the Thieu government for political control of South Vietnam.

11 JUNE 1969
Ground War Communist forces stage heavy ground attacks on two US bases south of Danang. Vietcong troops at a base at Tamky, 35 miles south of Danang, cut through the base defense perimeter and fight the defenders hand-to-hand; 16 Americans and 62 Communist soldiers are reported killed.
France A 12-point 'program of action' of the Provisional Revolutionary Government is presented at a news conference. The program is basically the same as that set forth by the NLF in its 10-point program and at the Paris talks. Under the new political arrangement,

the NLF remains the 'organizer and leader' of the resistance to the 'aggression' by the United States, while the PRG will be responsible for internal and foreign policy.

12-15 JUNE 1969
Diplomatic Bulgaria, Cambodia, China, Cuba, Czechoslovakia, East Germany, Hungary, Mongolia, North Korea, North Vietnam, Poland, Rumania, Syria, Soviet Union and Yugoslavia recognize the Provisional Revolutionary Government.

13 JUNE 1969
USA: Domestic The US government discloses it used wiretapping devices to eavesdrop on the 'Chicago Eight' anti-war activists who have been indicted for inciting riots during the 1968 Democratic convention. The government contends it has the right to eavesdrop without court approval on members of organizations it believes to be seeking to attack and subvert the government.
Laos Souvanna Phouma, premier of Laos, acknowledges publicly for the first time that US planes regularly carry out bombing raids in Laos and says the bombing will continue as long as North Vietnam uses Laotian bases and infiltration routes.
Air War B-52 bombing missions over the Ho Chi Minh trail in southern Laos rise to 5567 in 1969, up from 3377 in 1968, according to official Pentagon statistics. The B-52s, no longer permitted to bomb North Vietnam since the November 1968 bombing halt, are increasingly diverted to Laos and, in secret, to Cambodia. Nearly 160,000 tons of bombs are dropped on the Ho Chi Minh trail in 1969, a 60 percent increase from 1968. The total number of bombing sorties by US land and sea-based warplanes rises to 242,000 in 1969.

14 JUNE 1969
USA: Military The US command announces that three combat units are to be withdrawn, the First and Second Brigades of the 9th Infantry Division and Regimental Landing Team 9 of the 3rd Marine Divison, a total of about 13,000-14,000 men. The remainder of the 25,000 to be withdrawn are support troops.

14-15 JUNE 1969
Ground War North Vietnamese forces twice attack Third Brigade headquarters of the 101st Airborne Division atop a 2000-foot peak just east of Apbia mountain. Eighty-one North Vietnamese are reported killed. US losses are 18 killed and 47 wounded.

CHRONOLOGY

Patrolling a Delta village from a helicopter.

16 JUNE 1969
Ground War Troops of Thailand's Black Panther Division repel 500 Vietcong soldiers who assault their base 20 miles east of Saigon three times. The defenders, aided by the supporting fire of US jets, helicopters and artillery, report killing 212 enemy soldiers. Thai losses are six killed and seven wounded.

17 JUNE 1969
USA: Military US intelligence reports that an estimated 1000 North Vietnamese troops have reoccupied Apbia mountain.
Ground War US officials disclose the launching of a combined US-South Vietnamese search-and-destroy operation 8 June in the Ashua valley, 28 miles southwest of Hué. Twenty-one Americans have been killed and 130 wounded thus far. The drive started the day Operation Apache Snow, which included

the fight for Apbia mountain, ended with 113 Americans killed and 627 wounded.

17-21 JUNE 1969
Ground War The US military command reports increased fighting below the DMZ. An estimated 250 enemy troops are reported killed during the five-day period, while 30 Americans are killed and 71 wounded.

19 JUNE 1969
USA: Government Former Secretary of Defense Clark Clifford, writing in the journal *Foreign Affairs*, proposes a timetable for withdrawal from Vietnam which calls for the removal of 100,000 combat troops in 1969 and an additional 100,000-150,000 troops by the end of 1970. President Nixon, speaking at a news conference, expresses the 'hope that we could beat Mr. Clifford's timetable.'

Ground War Communist forces shell 12 targets near the city of Tayninh, 50 miles northwest of Saigon and 12 miles from the Cambodian border, followed by six attacks on the city itself and its surrounding villages. About 1000 civilians flee their homes as allied and Communist troops fight in the city streets. It is reported that 146 Communist soldiers were killed. Three Americans are killed and 14 wounded.

21 JUNE 1969
Ground War Approximately 600 Communist soldiers storm a US base near Tayninh. Seven Americans are killed and 18 wounded. Communist losses around Tayninh in the last two days are put at 194 killed.

23 JUNE 1969
Ground War Benhet, a US Special Forces camp located 288 miles northeast of Saigon and six miles from the junction of the Cambodian, Laotian and South Vietnamese borders, is beseiged and cut off by 2000 North Vietnamese troops using artillery and mortars. The base is defended by 250 US soldiers and 750 South Vietnamese *montagnards*.

25 JUNE 1969
South Vietnam The US Navy turns over to the South Vietnamese Navy 64 river patrol gunboats valued at $18.2 million in what is described as the largest single transfer of military equipment in the war thus far. The transfer raises the total number of boats in the South Vietnamese Navy to more than 600.

26 JUNE 1969
Ground War A force of 180 South Vietnamese troops are airlifted into Benhet. A US military spokesman reports that 100 US servicemen have been killed or wounded at Benhet since 1 June.

27 JUNE 1969
Ground War A total of 445 artillery shells strike Benhet, more than double the total for any previous day. The Vietcong radio claims the situation at Benhet is desperate.

28 JUNE 1969
Ground War US sources in Saigon report that North Vietnamese infiltration into South Vietnam in January-May is 40 percent lower than the corresponding 1968 period.
USA: Domestic A Gallup Poll shows 42 percent of the American people favor a faster withdrawal of US troops than that ordered by President Nixon, while 16 percent favor a slower rate: 29 percent favor a total withdrawal, 61 percent are opposed with 10 percent undecided.
Ground War A 1500-man South Vietnamese force begins new sweeps around Benhet. US units remain in an advisory role and supply only air and artillery support. The US command reportedly considers the Benhet campaign a test of the ability of the South Vietnamese forces to stand-up against the North Vietnamese and Vietcong.

2 JULY 1969
South Vietnam Ninety-two of 135 South Vietnamese House Deputies send a letter to President Thieu asking him to dismiss Premier Tran Van Huong.
USA: Government Senator George McGovern (D-SD) reveals that he met privately with the chief North Vietnamese and NLF negotiators in Paris on 22 May. McGovern says that he is convinced fruitful peace negotiations could not begin unless the United States agreed to 'unconditional withdrawal' from Vietnam and discontinued its 'unqualified embrace' of the Thieu-Ky government.
Ground War A convoy of South Vietnamese armored personnel carriers reaches Benhet over a road from Dakto that was closed for a week by North Vietnamese troops. Allied commanders say the siege of Benhet has been broken as combat activity in the last 24 hours declines to its lowest level in a month.

3 JULY 1969
Ground War The US military command in Saigon reports that three North Vietnamese regiments (about 7500 men) have withdrawn across the DMZ during the past three weeks.

7 JULY 1969
USA: Military A battalion of the US 9th Infantry Division leaves Saigon in the initial withdrawal of US troops.

9 JULY 1969
France David Dellinger, member of the Chicago Eight and chairman of the National Mobilization Committee to End the War in Vietnam, arrives in Paris at the invitation of the North Vietnamese delegation to arrange the release of three US prisoners-of-war with the encouragement of the State Department.

CHRONOLOGY

10 JULY 1969
Ground War The US command in Saigon announces the lowest casualty figures in six months for the week ending 5 July; 153 soldiers are reported killed and 722 wounded as a battlefield lull moves into its third week. Also reported are 247 South Vietnamese soldiers killed and 586 wounded.

France David Dellinger announces that a team of US pacifists will fly to Hanoi to bring home three US prisoners-of-war.

11 JULY 1969
South Vietnam President Thieu, in a televised speech, makes a 'comprehensive offer' for a political settlement which challenges the NLF to participate in free elections organized by a joint electoral commission and supervised by an international body. Following the speech, Foreign Minister Tran Chanh Thanh explaining the Thieu proposal, says Communists can never participate in elections in South Vietnam 'as communists' nor have any role in organizing elections and that only the South Vietnamese government can organize elections.

USA: Domestic The US First Circuit Court of Appeals in Boston reverses the 1968 conviction of Dr Benjamin Spock on charges of conspiracy to counsel evasion of the draft.

12 JULY 1969
Guerrilla War Communist gunners shell a US 9th Division center processing troops to be returned home. Two are killed and 21 are wounded.

13 JULY 1969
USA: Domestic George Wallace criticizes President Nixon for his handling of the war and says he favors an all-out military victory if the Paris talks fail to produce peace soon.

15 JULY 1969
South Vietnam Vice-President Nguyen Cao Ky, in a speech made during his first public appearance in five months, says President Thieu's offer (11 July) to the enemy constitutes a 'grave step backward' in the national policy of anti-communism.

USA: Government President Nixon sends a secret letter to North Vietnamese President Ho Chi Minh declaring he solemnly desires 'to work for a just peace.' Nixon defends his proposal of 14 May as 'fair to all parties' and says 'there is nothing to be gained by waiting.' At the same time Jean Sainteny, a retired French diplomat, after conferring with Nixon and his assistant for national security affairs, Henry Kissinger, relays a US proposal for secret negotiations to Xuan Thuy, the chief North Vietnamese representative to the Paris talks, for transmittal to Hanoi. Hanoi accepts.

USA: Government Secretary of Defense Laird, testifying before a Senate committee, says there has been no change in the battlefield orders to US commanders to maintain 'maximum pressure' on the enemy. Laird, however, admits that the present military strategy is under review.

USA: Domestic A US Federal Appeals judge overrules a lower court judge, allowing anti-war activist Rennie Davis, under federal indictment on charges of having conspired to incite disorders during the 1968 Democratic convention, to fly to Hanoi to aid in the release of three US prisoners-of-war.

17 JULY 1969
Negotiations At the 26th plenary session of the Paris talks, the Communist delegations formally reject President Thieu's offer of 11 July of free elections in South Vietnam with non-organized Communist participation.

17-20 JUNE 1969
USA: Military General Earle Wheeler, chairman of the Joint Chiefs of Staff, conducts four days of conferences and inspections with US commanders in South Vietnam in an effort to assess the battlefield lull, determine the progress of the South Vietnamese armed forces and to discuss future strategy.

19 JULY 1969
North Vietnam Ho Chi Minh, marking the anniversary of the 1954 Geneva accords, says no free elections can be held in South Vietnam while US troops remain there and the present South Vietnamese government stays in power.

20 JULY 1969
USA: Government A top-secret study, commissioned by presidential assistant Henry Kissinger, is completed by the office of the Chief of Naval Operations. Code-named Duck-Hook, the study proposes measures for military escalation against North Vietnam. The military options include: a massive bombing of Hanoi, Haiphong and other key areas of North Vietnam; a ground invasion of North Vietnam; the mining of harbors and

rivers; and, a bombing campaign designed to sever the main railroad links to China. Altogether 29 major targets in North Vietnam are pinpointed for destruction in a series of air attacks planned to last four days and to be renewed until Hanoi capitulates.

21 JULY-25 SEPTEMBER 1969
Ground War Operation Idaho Canyon is conducted by the US 3rd Marine Regiment in Quangtri province. Enemy casualties are reported at 565.

22 JULY 1969
USA: Government As President Nixon begins his Asian trip, he meets with Secretary of Defense Laird and General Wheeler, who has just returned from South Vietnam. Wheeler reports that the situation there is 'good' and that the program to improve the South Vietnamese armed forces is on schedule.

23 JULY 1969
USA: Military US troops of the First Brigade of the 9th Infantry Division, departing for the United States, turn over a fire support base at Cailay in the Mekong Delta to the ARVN 7th Division.

25 JULY 1969
USA: Government President Nixon, at a briefing in Guam for the news media accompanying him on his trip to Asia, discusses at length the future role the United States should play in Asia and the Pacific after the conclusion of the Vietnam war. The president's remarks are quickly earmarked as the 'Nixon Doctrine' and are interpreted to mean that while the United States will have primary responsibility for the defense of allies against nuclear attack, the non-communist Asian nations must bear the burden of defense against conventional attack and responsibility for internal security.

26 JULY 1969
South Vietnam President Thieu says his proposal of free elections with Vietcong participation is 'the final solution we can afford to offer.'
Ground War US combat deaths drop to 110 for the week of 20-26 July. This is the lowest weekly toll since 1 January and the fourth lowest in two years.

28 JULY 1969
Ground War In the biggest battle since the combat lull began, more than 1000 US troops, supported by tanks and armored personnel carriers, surround a suspected Vietcong stronghold known as 'the Citadel,' 25 miles north of Saigon. In day-long fighting the Americans fight their way through hedgerows and bunkers before overwhelming the Vietcong force identified as elements of two battalions of the 268th Vietcong Regiment. Vietcong losses at 53 are reported. Losses suffered by the Second Brigade of the US 25th Infantry Division total three dead and 14 wounded.

30 JULY 1969
USA: Government President Nixon makes an unscheduled five-and-a-half hour visit to South Vietnam. Nixon meets with President Thieu and privately discusses US troop withdrawals and possible changes in military tactics with US commanders. Nixon also visits US troops of the US 1st Infantry Division at Dian, 12 miles south of Saigon.

31 JULY 1969
USA: Government President Nixon visits India and discusses the Vietnam war with Prime Minister Indira Gandhi. Nixon says he visited South Vietnam to demonstrate his solidarity with President Thieu and praises Thieu as one of the four or five best leaders in the world.

1 AUGUST 1969
Air War The US command reports 27 US planes lost last week, for a total of 5690 planes lost since the fighting began.

3-9 AUGUST 1969
Ground War Ninety-six Americans are reported killed. This is the lowest weekly US death toll since 12 August 1967.

4 AUGUST 1969
North Vietnam Hanoi Radio announces the release of three US prisoners-of-war who will be returned in the custody of a pacifist group led by Rennie Davis. The men are identified as Captain Wesley Rumble, Lieutenant Robert Frishman and Seaman Douglas Hegdahl. They are the first US prisoners freed by North Vietnam since 2 August 1968.
Diplomatic Henry Kissinger and Xuan Thuy hold their first secret meeting in Paris at the apartment of Jean Sainteny. Kissinger presses the US 14 May proposal for a mutual withdrawal of North Vietnamese and US troops

CHRONOLOGY

President Nixon greeting troops during an unscheduled visit to South Vietnam.

and also warns that if by 1 November no progress toward ending the war has been made, the United States would consider measures of 'grave consequence.' Xuan Thuy replies that North Vietnam considers the NLF's 10-point plan to be the only 'logical and realistic basis for settling the war.' The only agreement is to keep open the new secret channel of communication.

6 AUGUST 1969

War Crimes The US Army announces that Colonel Robert Rheault and seven other Green Berets have been charged with premeditated murder and conspiracy to commit murder of a South Vietnamese national and are in confinement at Longbinh prison, 12 miles northeast of Saigon. US authorities refuse to disclose further details of the case, but US press reports indicate that the Vietnamese national had been a spy for the Green Berets and was slain after it was discovered that he was a double-agent, also in the employ of the North Vietnamese. The CIA is reported to have ordered the execution.

7 AUGUST 1969

Terrorism Vietcong commandos raid an US convalescent hospital at Camranh bay killing two Americans and wounding 99, including 53 patients. Before withdrawing without suffering casualties, the Communist commandos, reportedly numbering six men, destroy 10 wards and damage three others, and blow up the hospital's water tower and officer barracks. In another incident, explosions rip through the South Vietnamese Air Force school in Saigon killing eight and injuring 62, including four Americans.

8 AUGUST 1969

Ground War Fourteen Americans and 17 South Vietnamese are killed in military actions ranging from the DMZ to the Saigon area. A total of 174 Communist soldiers are reported killed with the heaviest combat reported near the DMZ where 102 enemy soldiers are reported killed. In the same action 164 Americans and 51 South Vietnamese are wounded.

9 AUGUST 1969

Ground War In military action near Danang, 600 US troops go to the aid of two US units. There are 148 Communist soldiers reported killed. US losses are 15 killed and more than 50 wounded.

Ground War About 50 US B-52 bombers raid North Vietnamese troops concentrations 65-75 miles north of Saigon, along the Cambodian border. After being forced from cover, a North Vietnamese force of about 100 men come under ground attack by US infantry. A total of 64 Communist soldiers is reported killed and six captured.

10 AUGUST 1969

Ground War North Vietnamese soldiers attack two US Marine bases 1500 yards apart near the DMZ. The attackers, using grenades and dynamite bombs, kill 17 Marines and wound 83. Seventeen enemy bodies are found inside the perimeter of one Marine camp.

12 AUGUST 1969

Ground War Communist forces attack more than 150 cities, towns and bases, including Danang and Hué. The heaviest attacks are centered on Anloc, a provincial capital 60 miles north of Saigon; Quanloi, northeast of Anloc; and Tayninh and Locninh where 2000 North Vietnamese attack. Communist commandos fight their way into the US First Marine Division headquarters in Danang, but are driven out with 11 enemy killed and four captured. Two US Marines are killed. US Marines fight off an attack 22 miles south of Danang, killing 40 North Vietnamese. US losses are five killed and 23 wounded.

13 AUGUST 1969

Ground War Allied military sources report 1450 enemy killed during the last 24 hours in the heaviest fighting in three months. Ninety Americans and 107 South Vietnamese are killed, and 500 Americans and 371 South Vietnamese wounded in the attacks on 150 bases and towns.

14 AUGUST 1969

USA: Military In response to congressional criticism, the Department of Defense concedes that the number of US troops in Vietnam has actually increased since President Nixon took office, but attributes the increase to troop arrivals scheduled during the Johnson administration.

14-15 AUGUST 1969

Ground War US troops kill 96 Communist soldiers as enemy troops unsuccessfully attempt to storm US camps in Haunghia, Tayninh and Binhlong provinces. The Vietcong radio announces a new offensive.

15 AUGUST 1969

USA: Military The Defense Department releases figures revealing that US troops strength in Vietnam had reached its lowest point in 1969 – 532,500 – only two days prior to President Nixon's inauguration, and rose to its highest point on 22 February. It is reported as of 14 August the US total stands at 534,200 men.

17-26 AUGUST 1969

Ground War US troops report killing at least 650 North Vietnamese in a fierce battle in the Queson valley, 30 miles south of Danang. More than 60 Americans are reported killed in the fighting. The clash breaks out when 1200 troops of the US Americal Division and South Vietnamese soldiers find 1000 North Vietnamese in a complex of tunnels and bunkers. The battle assumes its greatest intensity 20 August when the allied force steps up its drive to reach the wreckage of a US command helicopter shot down by ground-fire on 19 August. The fighting to get to the downed aircraft reaches its climax on 23 August when four companies of the Americal Division, about 250 men, occupy a knoll (known as Hill 102) about 1000 yards from the wreckage of the helicopter. The knoll had been a major obstacle to the allied advance due to North Vietnamese machine-gun emplacement there which had inflicted heavy losses to US troops and helicopters. The US units had tried repeatedly to outflank the hill but were forced to withdraw under heavy fire. On 24 August Company A of the 196th Light Infantry Brigade, refuses the order of its commander, Lieutenant Eugene Shurtz, Jr, to continue combat operations toward attempting to reach the downed helicopter. The unit had attempted to make the push during the previous five days but was thrown back with heavy losses. Shurtz phones Lieutenant Colonel Robert C Bacon, the battalion commander, informing him that his men refuse to carry out the mission because they had 'simply had enough' and that they were 'broken.' The company finally moves out after Bacon dispatches his executive officer and a sergeant to Company A, to 'give them a pep talk.' US infantrymen fight their way to the helicopter on 25 August and report all eight men aboard dead. Schurtz is relieved of his post and transferred to another assignment in the division. Neither he nor his men are disciplined.

CHRONOLOGY

21-22 AUGUST 1969
USA: Government President Nixon and South Korean President Park Chung Hee meet in San Francisco. In his welcoming address, Nixon notes that South Korea has 'more fighting men in South Vietnam than any other nation' except the United States and South Vietnam. The United States will spend $250 million in 1969 to maintain South Korea's 50,000-man Tiger Division in South Vietnam.

22 AUGUST 1969
USA: Military The United States and Thailand agree to begin talks on reducing the 49,000-man US force in Thailand, which is primarily involved in air operations against Communist troops in Laos and South Vietnam.

23 AUGUST 1969
South Vietnam President Thieu chooses Deputy Premier and Interior Minister Tran Thien Khiem, a close and powerful friend, to replace Tran Van Huong as Premier. A new cabinet is to be presented 1 September.

24 AUGUST 1969
Ground War US troops battle Communist soldiers for more than seven hours 28 miles north of Saigon. A total of 48 enemy troops is reported killed. Another 30 Communist soldiers are reported killed in three other clashes near the city. Two Americans are killed and five wounded. Communist forces again shell the US hospital at Camran Bay.

25 AUGUST-31 DECEMBER 1969
Ground War The ARVN 4th Regiment conducts military operations Lien Ket 414 in Quangnai province. Enemy casualties are reported at 710.

26 AUGUST 1969
USA: Military The US command announces

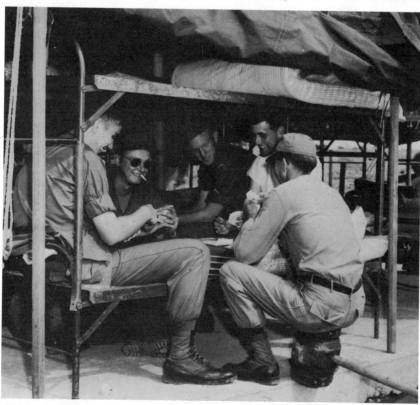

Soldiers relax with a hand of bridge at Long Binh Junction.

Ho Chi Minh (center) died in Hanoi on 3 September 1969.

the departure of troops in the next two days will complete the 25,000-man withdrawal announced by President Nixon on 8 June.

26 AUGUST-31 DECEMBER 1969
Ground War The ARVN 5th Regiment conducts military operations Lien Ket 531 in Quangtri province. A total of 542 enemy casualties is reported.

28 AUGUST 1969
Ground War Sharp fighting again erupts in the Danang area. Communist losses are reported at 18. US losses are 13 US Marines killed and 42 wounded. The Department of Defense reports that 93,653 Communist soldiers were killed during the first half of the year, 1 January-30 June. This figure compares with the 119,000 Communist troops reported killed during the same period in 1968.

30 AUGUST 1969
North Vietnam President Ho Chi Minh's reply to President Nixon's letter of 15 July is received in Paris. Ho accuses the United States of a 'war of aggression' against the Vietnamese people, 'violating our fundamental national rights' and warns that 'the longer the war goes on, the more it accumulates the mourning and burdens of the American people.' Ho says he favors the 10-point program of the NLF as 'a logical and reasonable basis for the settlement of the Vietnamese problem.' Ho declares that 'the United States must cease the war of aggression,' withdraw from Vietnam and allow self-determination for the Vietnamese people. The text of this letter dated 25 August is not revealed by President Nixon until 3 November.

1 SEPTEMBER 1969
South Vietnam President Thieu and Premier Tran Thien Khiem present a new 31-member cabinet strong in technicians and soldiers, but lacking political leaders. Tran Thien Khiem, in a ceremony at the presidential palace, says that there will be no radical changes in policy. The cabinet does not include any representatives of the non-communist opposition, leaders of religious groups or any leaders of the factions of the pro-government National Social Democratic Front.

3 SEPTEMBER 1969
North Vietnam President Ho Chi Minh dies in Hanoi at the age of 79.

CHRONOLOGY

4 SEPTEMBER 1969
Ground War The NLF announces it will halt military operations for three days, 8-11 September, in mourning for Ho Chi Minh.

4-5 SEPTEMBER 1969
North Vietnam Chinese Premier Chou En-lai and a delegation from China hold talks with First Secretary Le Duan and other members of the North Vietnamese Politburo. The Chinese leaders assure the North Vietnamese of their continued support in the war against the United States.

5 SEPTEMBER 1969
War Crimes Criminal charges are formally preferred against Lieutenant William Calley. The charges include six specifications of premeditated murder as Calley is accused of killing a total of 109 'Oriental human beings, occupants of the village of My Lai 4, whose names and sexes are unknown, by means of shooting them with a rifle.'
Ground War Vietcong gunners shell Danang and nearby military installations. At least 13 civilians are reported killed. In a Communist attack on a bridge south of Danang, three US Marines are killed and 30 wounded. A Vietcong rocket attack sets fire to tons of food at a US Navy storage area east of the city. Communist ground forces attack nine other allied bases. About 140 Communist soldiers are reported killed. Twenty Americans and 30 South Vietnamese are also killed.

6 SEPTEMBER 1969
North Vietnam The Communist Party newspaper *Nhan Dan* and Hanoi Radio announce the formation of a collective leadership to succeed Ho Chi Minh. The four-member leadership consists of: Le Duan, first secretary of the Communist Party; Truong Chin, member of the Politburo and chairman of the National Assembly; General Vo Nguyen Giap, defense minister; and, Premier Pham Van Dong.
Ground War Three battles rage in the jungles north of Saigon as Communist gunners shell 40 targets during the night. In the fighting 91 Communist soldiers, 35 Americans and 68 South Vietnamese are reported killed.

9 SEPTEMBER 1969
North Vietnam Funeral services, attended by 250,000 people, are held for Ho Chi Minh in Hanoi's Badinh Square. Among those in attendance are Soviet Premier Aleksei Kosygin, Chinese Vice-Premier Li Hsien-nien and Prince Norodom Sihanouk of Cambodia.
Ground War A South Vietnamese military spokesman says government troops have increased their offensive operations during the Vietcong-proclaimed ceasefire. US and Communist forces curtail their military activity. Nearly all US bombers in South Vietnam are grounded.

10 SEPTEMBER 1969
North Vietnam Norodom Sihanouk expresses Cambodian support for the 'just stand' of the North Vietnamese and calls on the United States to withdraw from South Vietnam.
Ground War As Communist forces shell more than 30 allied military installations, the United States announces US forces will resume military operations at the same level as before the ceasefire.

13 SEPTEMBER 1969
South Vietnam Vice-President Nguyen Cao Ky predicts that any attempt to form a coalition government in South Vietnam with the Communists will lead members of the armed forces to stage a coup 'inside of 10 days.'
USA: Military In response to increasing Communist attacks, the White House announces the resumption of B-52 raids following a 36-hour suspension.
Ground War Allied forces report killing 113 Communist soldiers repulsing a heavy attack on a village near Quangnai with 260 houses destroyed and eight civilians killed.

14 SEPTEMBER 1969
Ground War The US command reports that North Vietnamese regular army units have moved into the Mekong Delta for the first time in the war. This movement is reported to have taken place in the four weeks since US troops departed the region as part of President Nixon's withdrawal plan.

15 SEPTEMBER 1969
Ground War A regular North Vietnamese army unit, 2000 men of the 18th Regiment, attack a government training center six miles north of Triton in the Mekong Delta, but is thrown back with a reported loss of 83 killed.

16 SEPTEMBER 1969
USA: Government President Nixon announces a second round of US troop withdrawals of approximately 35,000 men.

Ground War US helicopter gunships mistakenly open fire on a group of civilians in the Mekong Delta, killing seven and wounding 17. Eight Americans are killed and 10 wounded in an explosion 33 miles northwest of Saigon. South of the DMZ 25 US Marines are killed and 63 are wounded in fighting with North Vietnamese soldiers.

17 SEPTEMBER 1969
Ground War North Vietnamese troops assault two US Marine outposts just below the DMZ killing 23 Americans and wounding 24. In one attack, several Communist soldiers manage to breach the camp perimeter of the Third Regiment of the 3rd Marine Division. The attacks are finally repelled by artillery and air strikes. A total of 23 North Vietnamese is reported killed in the two attacks.

18 SEPTEMBER 1969
USA: Military The US command announces two Marine Corps regiments stationed along the DMZ and an Army airborne brigade assigned to guard Saigon will make up the combat contingent of the additional troops to be withdrawn, a total of 19,500 men.
USA: Domestic A fall offensive is announced by Dr Benjamin Spock and 10 other representatives of the New Mobilization Committee to End the War in Vietnam. Planned activities include a 36-hour 'March Against Death' in Washington, 13-15 November, combined with a 15 November rally in San Francisco.

19 SEPTEMBER 1969
USA: Government President Nixon announces a 50,000-man reduction in planned draft calls for the remainder of 1969. Nixon says the scheduled draft calls of 32,000 men in November and 18,000 in December will be 'cancelled.'

21 SEPTEMBER 1969
Air War Thirty-five US B-52s drop more than 1000 tons of bombs on North Vietnamese troops concentrations, north of the 'Rockpile', a US Marine base near the DMZ, following attacks there 17 September.

23 SEPTEMBER 1969
USA: Domestic Eight anti-war activists – the 'Chicago Eight' – go on trial in Chicago as 1000 young people demonstrate.
Ground War A company of more than 130 South Vietnamese troops, led by Green Berets, suffer more than 50 percent casualties in heavy fighting six miles from the Cambodian border, about 65 miles northwest of Saigon. Seven South Vietnamese are killed and 62 are wounded. US fighter-bombers and artillery respond killing 35 Communist troops.

24 SEPTEMBER 1969
South Vietnam The US command reports all 62 South Vietnamese aboard and two on the ground are killed when a US jet collides with an Air Vietnam DC-4 at Danang Airport. The US jet lands safely.

25 SEPTEMBER 1969
USA: Government Senator Charles Goodell (R-NY) proposes legislation which would require the withdrawal of US troops by the end of 1970, and bar the use of congressionally appropriated funds after 1 December 1970 for maintaining US military personnel in Vietnam.
Terrorism Vietcong commandos throw a grenade into a meeting place near Danang killing four civilians and one policeman; twenty-six civilians are wounded. A bus strikes a mine 95 miles southeast of Danang killing 14 civilians.

26 SEPTEMBER 1969
USA: Government President Nixon, speaking at a news conference, cites 'some progress' in the effort to end the Vietnam war and says 'we're on the right course in Vietnam.' Nixon urges the American public to give him the support and time he needs to end the war honorably saying, 'If we have a united front, the enemy will begin to talk.' Nixon brands the attitude of Senator Goodell and others like him in Congress as 'defeatist.'
USA: Government A private caucus of 24 liberal Democratic congressmen is held. The group decides to endorse the nationwide protest scheduled for 15 October and press in Congress for resolutions calling for an end to the war and a withdrawal of US troops.
Ground War The US command discloses that an US helicopter mistakenly attacked a group of civilians near Tamky, killing 14.
China North Vietnam and China sign a new agreement of military and economic aid for an undisclosed sum for 1970 in Peking.

27 SEPTEMBER 1969
South Vietnam President Thieu says his government entertains no 'ambition or pre-

CHRONOLOGY

Members of the Popular Forces transported by a US Navy patrol boat.

tense' to take over all fighting by the end of 1970, but given proper support South Vietnamese troops could replace the 'bulk' of US troops in 1970. Thieu says his agreement on any further US troops withdrawals will hinge on whether his requests for equipment and funds for ARVN forces are granted.

29 SEPTEMBER 1969
War Crimes Secretary of the Army, Stanley Resor, announces that the US Army, conceding it is helpless to enlist the cooperation of the CIA, is dropping the murder charges (of 6 August) against eight Green Berets accused of killing a Vietnamese national.

29 SEPTEMBER-31 DECEMBER 1969
Ground War ARVN 32nd Regiment conducts military operation Quyet Thang 21/38 in Anxuyen province. There are 721 enemy casualties reported.

30 SEPTEMBER 1969
USA: Military The United States and Thailand announce that 6000 US troops and will be withdrawn from Thailand by 10 July 1970.

3 OCTOBER 1969
USA: Military US military planners in Saigon report shifting their major emphasis from battlefield support to military and technical training in a campaign to turn the war effort over to the South Vietnamese armed forces.

4 OCTOBER 1969
USA: Military General Wheeler, chairman of the Joint Chiefs of Staff, arrives in Saigon to review the progress being made in turning over the combat action to the South Vietnamese.

7 OCTOBER 1969
USA: Government President Nixon, in a meeting at the White House with Premier Souvanna Phouma of Laos, gives assurances that the United States will insist on a withdrawal of North Vietnamese forces from Laos and Cambodia as part of a settlement of the Vietnam war.
USA: Military At his departure following a four-day inspection of South Vietnam, General Wheeler reports 'progress in Vietnamization is being steadily and realistically

achieved,' but US forces will have to assist the South Vietnamese for 'some time to come.'

8 OCTOBER 1969

USA: Domestic Members of Students for a Democratic Society (SDS) clash with Chicago police during a demonstration as the trial of the 'Chicago Eight' continues. Forty demonstrators are arrested.

9 OCTOBER 1969

USA: Military Secretary of Defense Laird, reporting on General Wheeler's trip to South Vietnam at a news conference, says US commanders operate under formal new orders aimed at placing the 'highest priority' on shifting the burden of the fighting to the ARVN forces. Laird terms the new military tactics as 'protective reaction,' but says the new orders do not forbid US commanders seeking out and attacking enemy troops that pose threats.
USA: Domestic The National Guard is called out as demonstrations continue in Chicago protesting the trial of the Chicago Eight.

10 OCTOBER 1969

South Vietnam The US Navy transfers 80 river-patrol boats to the South Vietnamese Navy in the largest single turnover of naval equipment since the war began.
Ground War South Vietnamese armed forces assume complete responsibility for the defense of Saigon as the last US combat contingent in the city is moved to an area 20 miles away.

11 OCTOBER 1969

USA: Domestic A Gallup Poll reports 57 percent of Americans say they would like to see Congress pass legislation which calls for the withdrawal of all US troops by the end of 1970.

15 OCTOBER 1969

USA: Domestic Protests ranging from rallies to prayer vigils and involving a broad spectrum of the population are held across the United States to demonstrate opposition to the Vietnam war. The protest, as a nationally-coordinated anti-war demonstration, is considered unprecedented.

19 OCTOBER 1969

Ground War South Vietnamese forces report killing 116 North Vietnamese soldiers in two battles in the U Minh forest in the Mekong Delta. ARVN losses are six killed and 16 wounded. In another battle 85 miles northeast of Saigon, US troops report killing 14 enemy soldiers while suffering five dead.

21 OCTOBER 1969

Ground War Seven Americans are killed and 20 wounded in six sharp but short battles north and west of Saigon. Forty-six Communist soldiers are reported killed. Two more Americans are killed when their spotter plane is downed by enemy ground-fire.

22 OCTOBER 1969

USA: Military US field commanders contend there has been no basic changes in their orders on military strategy and tactics. The officers do admit, however, that there are refinements in certain areas, such as no ground assaults against fortified areas. The commanders deny that they have been ordered to keep casualties down and say that the battlefield situation does not even remotely resemble a ceasefire. The commanders add that they never even heard of Secretary of Defense Laird's phrase 'protective reaction.'

24 OCTOBER 1969

USA: Military The US Army Blackhorse base, 38 miles northeast of Saigon, headquarters of the US Army's 11th Armored Cavalry, is turned over to ARVN's 18th Division to be used as an infantry regiment base and training center.
Ground War A force of 200 soldiers of the 25th Infantry Division fight the biggest battle by US troops in more than a month 28 miles north of Saigon. Forty-seven Communist soldiers and 10 Americans are reported killed. Twelve Americans are wounded.

29 OCTOBER 1969

USA: Domestic Chicago Eight defendant Bobby Seale is gagged and chained to his chair at his trial for conspiracy to incite riot. The judge's order comes after Seale repeatedly shouts accusations and insults at the judge and prosecution. In November, Seale's conduct will force the judge to try him separately, and the remaining defendants will become known as the 'Chicago Seven.'

31 OCTOBER 1969

Air War In attacks designed to protect two US Special Forces camps at Duclap and Buprang, B-52s carry out heavy bombing

CHRONOLOGY

raids against suspected North Vietnamese troops concentrations along the Cambodian border in the Central Highlands.

1 NOVEMBER-28 DECEMBER 1969
Ground War The ARVN 23rd Division conducts military operation Dan Tien 33D in Quangduc province. A total of 746 enemy casualties is reported.

3 NOVEMBER 1969
USA: Government To gather support for his policies in Vietnam and in an attempt to blunt the renewed strength of the anti-war movement, President Nixon delivers his most expansive report to date on the Vietnam war before a nationwide television audience.

4 NOVEMBER 1969
USA: Domestic Congressional and public reaction to President Nixon's speech is overwhelmingly favorable. Fifty Democrats and 50 Republicans in the House of Representatives introduce legislation supporting the President. A Gallup Poll telephone survey reports 77 percent of those interviewed back President Nixon, while only six percent oppose him on the Vietnam war.
Ground War In the biggest battle in four months, South Vietnamese infantry, supported by US planes and artillery, clash with North Vietnamese troops for 10 hours near Duclop near the Cambodian border. Eighty North Vietnamese are reported killed. South Vietnamese losses are 24 killed and 38 wounded.

6 NOVEMBER 1969
Ground War US military officials, in a test of South Vietnamese units to take on tougher assignments, decide not to commit US ground forces to the fighting near Duclop.

7 NOVEMBER 1969
Ground War Saigon's outer defenses come under heavy attack for the first time since May 1968 as an estimated 100 Vietcong fire at two government police posts.

8 NOVEMBER 1969
Ground War Allied spokesmen report North Vietnamese troops assault a South Vietnamese navy-marine task force headquarters in the Mekong Delta for the second time in three days. South Vietnamese troops report killing 80 Communist soldiers in a day-long battle 15 miles from the base. Eight South Vietnamese are killed and 43 wounded.

9 NOVEMBER 1969
Ground War North Vietnamese forces maintain pressure on Duclop and three other allied outposts along the Cambodian border, setting off a day-long fight. The US military command still offers no infantry support to the South Vietnamese troops, giving only air and artillery support.

11 NOVEMBER 1969
Sweden Swedish Foreign Minister Torsten Nilsson announces Sweden will begin a three-year program of economic aid to North Vietnam 1 July 1970 valued at $45 million. This reverses a previous decision to provide only humanitarian assistance while the Vietnam war is in progress.

12 NOVEMBER 1969
USA: Domestic The federal government begins to assemble 9000 troops in the Washington area in anticipation of the massive protests and demonstrations planned for 14-15 November. The Defense Department announces that the men are being made available at the request of the Justice Department and will augment a 1200 National Guard and 3700-man police force. The New Mobilization Committee, sponsors of the planned demonstrations, promise to provide 2500 marshals to police the parade.
War Crimes Seymour Hersh, in a cable filed through Dispatch News Service and picked up by more than 30 newspapers the following day, reveals the extent of the US Army's charges against Lieutenant William Calley. Hersh writes that 'the Army says he deliberately murdered at least 109 Vietnamese civilians during a search-and-destroy mission in March 1968, in a Viet Cong stronghold known as 'Pinkville.'

12 NOVEMBER-28 DECEMBER 1969
Ground War The ARVN 23rd Division conducts Operation Dan Tian 40 in Quangduc province. A count of 1012 enemy casualties is reported.

13 NOVEMBER 1969
USA: Government President Nixon pays extraordinary separate visits to the House of Representatives and the Senate to convey his appreciation to those who support his Vietnam policy and to ask for understanding

US Navy SEALS return from a mission with captured Vietcong equipment.

and 'constructive criticism' from those congressional members who oppose him.

USA: Government In a speech, Vice-President Agnew criticizes news media coverage, particularly television, of the policies of the Nixon administration policies and demonstrations and protests aimed at them.

USA: Domestic The second moratorium opens as organizers concentrate on mass demonstrations in Washington, DC and San Francisco. The anti-war demonstrations begin with a symbolic 'March Against Death' which begins at Arlington National Cemetary and continues past the White House. The march is headed by relatives of servicemen killed in Vietnam and contains 46,000 marchers.

Ground War The US command reports 122 North Vietnamese killed in two days of fighting six miles southwest of an allied outpost at Conthien near the DMZ. US losses are 22 dead and 53 wounded. In a number of clashes near Danang 130 Communist soldiers are reported killed while US losses are 17 killed and 60 wounded.

14 NOVEMBER 1969

USA: Domestic Washington riot policemen use tear gas to rout 2000 demonstrators in an attempted march on the South Vietnamese embassy after a day of peaceful activities by protestors. At least 20 demonstrators are arrested and seven policemen are injured.

Ground War In fighting between Communist and South Vietnamese troops in the Central Highlands, South Vietnamese fighter-bombers strike both enemy and ARVN soldiers. Twenty South Vietnamese are killed and 53 are wounded. Communist losses are reported as 95 killed.

15 NOVEMBER 1969

USA: Domestic More than 250,000 protestors gather in Washington DC to participate in the largest anti-war demonstration in the nation's history. There is a march down Pennsylvania Avenue and a rally at the Washington Monument. Later, radicals split off from the main rally to march on the Justice Department in a demonstration led by members of the Youth International Party ('Yippies') and supporters of the 'Chicago Eight' defendants. The crowd, numbering about 6000, throw rocks and bottles and burn US flags but are repelled with tear gas. Almost 100 demonstrators are arrested.

War Crimes Survivors of Mylai 4, interviewed by reporters at a relocation hamlet in Songmy village, claim that 567 Vietnamese men, women and children were massacred by US troops on 16 March 1968.

Guerrilla War Nearly 20 helicopters are destroyed in a Vietcong commando attack on a US Army base, Camp Radcliffe, at Ankhe, 260 miles northeast of Saigon.

France Protests and demonstrations are held in Paris, where 2651 persons are arrested, and 42 other cities in France coinciding with the moratorium demonstrations in Washington and San Francisco. Major protests are also held in Frankfurt, Stuttgart, West Berlin and London.

16-17 NOVEMBER 1969

Ground War Allied bombers and artillery attack North Vietnamese positions inside Cambodia that have shelled allied camps at Buprand and Duclop. The US command calls the raids on Cambodian territory 'an inherent right of self-defense against enemy attacks.'

18 NOVEMBER 1969

Ground War South Vietnamese troops lose 60 men killed or wounded in a clash with North Vietnamese forces in the Mekong Delta. North Vietnamese losses are put at 14 killed. A South Vietnamese spokesman says the high ARVN casualties were 'due to bad fighting on our part.' The battle is the first major action in the northern delta since the US 9th Division was withdrawn.

20 NOVEMBER 1969

Negotiations Ambassador Henry Cabot Lodge and his deputy, Lawrence E Walsh, resign as the chief US delegates to the Paris peace talks effective 8 December. Philip C Habib, Lodge's chief adviser, will become the acting head of the delegation.

War Crimes The *Cleveland Plain Dealer* publishes graphic photographs by Ron Haeberle of the massacre at Mylai. Seymour Hersh files a second Mylai story based on interviews with Michael Terry and Michael Bernhardt, who served under Lieutenant William Calley. The American public is stunned.

24 NOVEMBER 1969

USA: Military The 35,000-man troop withdrawal announced 16 December 1968 is reached three weeks prior to the 15 December deadline.

War Crimes The US Army announces that

Lieutenant Calley has been ordered to stand trial at a general courtmartial for the premeditated murder of 109 Vietnamese civilians. In Washington, Army Secretary Stanley Resor and Army Chief of Staff William C Westmoreland announce the appointment of Lieutenant General William R Peers to 'explore the nature and scope' of an original Army investigation of the Mylai slayings in April 1968. The initial probe, conducted by members of the 11th Infantry Brigade, the unit involved in affair, concluded that no massacre had occurred and that no further action was warranted.

25 NOVEMBER 1969

Ground War Communist forces step up attacks against US troops shielding allied installations near the Cambodian border. Ten Americans are killed and 70 are wounded. US troops report killing 115 enemy soldiers. North Vietnamese troops destroy more than a dozen tanks and tons of ammunition at a US base near the Cambodian border.

28 NOVEMBER 1969

Ground War A 300-man ARVN unit is ambushed in the Mekong Delta losing 36 men dead. A counterattack in the same area, 72 miles southwest of Saigon, results in 45 Communist soldiers reported killed.

30 NOVEMBER 1969

Ground War North Vietnamese gunners shoot down four US Army helicopters about 10 miles from Songbe near the Cambodian border. Five crewmen are killed and four are wounded.

3 DECEMBER 1969

Ground War Communist troops attack the town of Tuyenbinh in the Mekong Delta and are repelled by defenders and US planes and are pursued into Cambodia. Fifteen civilians are killed and 30 are wounded. A total of 108 Communist soldiers is reported killed.

7-8 DECEMBER 1969

Ground War Communist forces launch 44 attacks throughout South Vietnam. Allied soldiers report killing 88 North Vietnamese troops in two clashes near Tayninh. One American is killed and four are wounded.

7 DECEMBER 1969-31 MARCH 1970

Ground War In an operation codenamed Randolph Glen, the 101st Airborne Division (Airmobile), in coordination with the ARVN 1st Infantry Division, is committed to provide a shield of security on the periphery of the populated lowlands of Thuathien province. A total of 670 enemy casualties is reported.

8 DECEMBER 1969

USA: Government President Nixon, at a news conference, says the Vietnam war is coming to a 'conclusion as a result of the plan that we have instituted' which calls for replacing US troops with South Vietnamese forces.

9 DECEMBER 1969

Ground War A Vietcong force attacks a national police field force training center in Dalat killing 13 police and wounding 25.

11 DECEMBER 1969

Negotiations North Vietnamese chief negotiator Xuan Thuy boycotts the Paris talks in protest against what the North Vietnamese delegation insists is the 'sabotage' and 'downgrading' of the talks by the US failure to name a replacement for Henry Cabot Lodge.

12-20 DECEMBER 1969

South Vietnam The Philippine army's 1350 noncombatant contingent withdraws from South Vietnam. The unit had been in the country since September 1966.

13 DECEMBER 1969

Ground War The second highway bridge in two days near Cantho is attacked by saboteurs. Eleven American soldiers are killed and 27 are wounded in scattered attacks which leave 130 Communist soldiers reported dead. Bienhoa airbase is hit by Communist rocket attacks. The US Americal Division reports killing 53 enemy soldiers in a battle two miles southeast of Mylai.

14 DECEMBER 1969

Ground War US troops of the Third Brigade, 3rd Cavalry Division, report killing 1177 enemy soldiers near the Cambodian border since 24 September.

15 DECEMBER 1969

USA: Government President Nixon announces a third US troop reduction of 50,000 men by 15 April 1970.

16 DECEMBER 1969

USA: Government Secretary of Defense Laird reports draft calls should be reduced by about 25,000 men next year as a direct result of plans to withdraw 50,000 troops from Vietnam.

Ground War South Vietnamese troops are airlifted into a Communist troop concentration in the Mekong Delta. Communist soldiers totalling 83 are reported killed. South Vietnamese losses are 17 killed and 61 wounded.

18 DECEMBER 1969
USA: Government Congress prohibits the use of current Defense Department appropriations to introduce ground combat troops into Laos or Thailand.

21 DECEMBER 1969
Thailand Thailand announces plans to withdraw its 12,000-man contingent from South Vietnam. South Korea will maintain its 50,000-man force.

24 DECEMBER 1969
South Vietnam A Vietcong-proclaimed three-day truce begins at 0100 hours.

25 DECEMBER 1969
South Vietnam Allied military forces suspend combat activity for 24 hours beginning at 1800 hours.

27 DECEMBER 1969
Ground War In their fiercest battle in six weeks, US forces report killing 72 of 250 North Vietnamese soldiers in a day-long battle nine miles northwest of Locninh, about 80 miles north of Saigon.

28 DECEMBER 1969
Guerrilla War Seven Americans of the 25th Infantry Division are killed and five are wounded when an explosive charge is thrown into a US field camp in darkness near Laikhe, 25 miles northwest of Saigon.

30 DECEMBER 1969
South Vietnam A Vietcong-proclaimed three-day truce begins at 0100 hours.

Negotiations Acting head of the US delegation to the Paris talks, Philip Habib, hands over to the Communist side a list of 1406 names of US servicemen missing in action as of 24 December. Habib says he hopes the other side will indicate which men are prisoners and which are known dead, as a 'matter of humanitarian concern for their families.'

31 DECEMBER 1969
South Vietnam Allied military fogces suspend combat activity for 24 hours starting at 1800 hours.

War Crimes The US Army announces it will courtmartial Staff Sergeant David Mitchell on charges of assault with intent to murder 30 South Vietnamese civilians at Mylai.

31 DECEMBER 1969
State of the War As the year comes to an end, it may definitely be said that the new administration has made changes. President Nixon is now withdrawing US forces, so that from a peak of some 543,000 in June they are now down to some 479,000, the lowest number in two years; US forces in Thailand are also being withdrawn, although there are still some 46,000 US personnel there. Although Australia and the Philippines are beginning to withdraw their forces from Vietnam, the South Koreans and Thais are not: there is still a 12,000-man Thai division fighting in Vietnam – fully paid for by US funds. The Communists also seem to be cutting back their forces somewhat, so that they are estimated to be some 240,000 (down from 290,000 in 1968) – approximately made up of 100,000 North Vietnamese troops, 100,000 guerrillas, and 40,000 'main force' Vietcong.

The second change is the obvious increase of South Vietnamese forces and the general increase of the South Vietnamese role that is now known as 'Vietnamization.' When Nixon assumed the presidency in January 1969, the South Vietnamese armed forces were numbered at about 850,000, now they are estimated at over a million; military schools are expanding and various militia and security organizations are being enlarged. Meanwhile, vast quantities of US weapons of all kinds are being turned over to the South Vietnamese: planes, ships, helicopters, vehicles of all kinds, and over a million M-16 rifles.

However the fighting is far from over. US combat deaths in 1969 come to 9414 (against 14,592 in 1968); some 40,000 US servicemen have now lost their lives in the fighting in Vietnam, while another 260,000 have been wounded and some 1400 are listed as missing or captured; at least 6000 South Vietnamese civilians were killed in 1969 by terrorist actions alone. The growing casualty list, coupled with the knowledge that US troops are being withdrawn, is beginning to lead to a

US Marines return fire from an M79 Grenade Launcher on the south bank of the Perfume River.

demoralized US fighting force: drug use is on the rise; 'fragging' incidents are increasing; and in 1969 there were 117 convictions in the US Army for 'mutiny and other acts involving willful refusal' to follow orders (against 82 such convictions in 1968). Opposition in Congress is also being more openly expressed and the anti-war forces are able to call out large numbers of Americans. Yet polls continue to show that a majority of Americans support President Nixon's policies in general, and with Ho Chi Minh now dead and President Thieu apparently consolidating his power in South Vietnam, Nixon is far from calling off the war.

2 JANUARY 1970
Ground War The US command reports 65 Americans were killed-in-action during the past week.

3 JANUARY 1970
Ground War North Vietnamese troops attack a US field camp near Ducpho, south of Quangnai, killing seven Americans and wounding 11.

6 JANUARY 1970
Ground War Three North Vietnamese sapper teams attack and penetrate a US Marine 7th

Regiment base in the Queson valley killing 13 Americans and wounding 40. Reported North Vietnamese losses are 38 killed.

8 JANUARY 1970
South Vietnam President Thieu states that it will be 'impossible and impractical' to withdraw all US combat troops in 1970. Thieu says that further US withdrawals will depend on the 'crucial question' of whether the United States supplies South Vietnam with the adequate equipment and funds to modernize its armed forces. Although Thieu says that he has been assured by the Nixon administration of the necessary assistance, he contends that US troop withdrawals will have to be phased over a number of years.

War Crimes Private Gerald Smith and Sergeant Charles Hutto, both due to leave the US Army next week, are charged with murder and sexual offenses in connection with the killing of civilians at Songmy; 11 more members of the Americal Division will be charged with complicity in the killings.

8-9 JANUARY 1970
Ground War US troops, supported by armor, artillery and air strikes report killing 109 Communist soldiers near Tayninh. US losses are two killed and 10 wounded.

CHRONOLOGY

15 JANUARY 1970
South Vietnam Senator Tran Van Don and 14 other senators announce the formation of a new political group, called the Peoples Bloc, which is dedicated to finding a political solution to the reunification of North and South Vietnam under a non-Communist government.

16 JANUARY 1970
Terrorism A Vietcong force moves into a refugee camp in the village of Chauthan on the Batangan peninsula hurling dynamite charges into houses, killing 16 civilians and wounding 21.

18 JANUARY 1970
Ground War Mines planted by the Vietcong explode at the Thuduc Officers Training School, 12 miles northeast of Saigon, killing 18 persons, including 16 South Vietnamese officer cadets and their instructor, and wounding 33.

22 JANUARY 1970
Ground War A combined force of North Vietnamese and Vietcong attack a South Vietnamese marine brigade command post in the Mekong Delta, killing 15 and wounding 41. The communist losses are reported at 72. At an artillery base, 55 miles north of Saigon, 13 US soldiers are killed and three are wounded in an ammunition explosion.

26 JANUARY 1970
Ground War The US command reports increased combat activity in all four military

Field telephone kept patrols in communication with their bases.

zones as Communist forces shell 29 targets. The Communists report 75 killed in various actions. Nine Americans are killed and five are wounded.

28 JANUARY 1970

Air War A US fighter-bomber attacks an anti-aircraft missile base 90 miles inside North Vietnam after missiles are fired at an unarmed US reconnaissance plane and its jet escorts. One F-105 jet is brought down by Communist ground fire. A rescue helicopter sent to search for the jet's two missing pilots is destroyed by a MiG-21 near the North Vietnamese-Laotian border. The downed helicopter's six-man crew is also listed as missing. These reconnaissance missions had been conducted daily since the November 1968 bombing halt.

30 JANUARY 1970

USA: Government President Nixon, at a news conference, states that 'the policy of Vietnamization is irreversible,' even without any progress at the Paris peace talks. Nixon warns that if North Vietnam steps up its military activity in South Vietnam during US withdrawals, he will deal with that situation 'more strongly than we have dealt with it in the past.' Nixon says that the planned US withdrawals will include only combat units and not necessarily US support troops.

USA: Military In announcing the combat action over North Vietnam involving the downing of a US jet and the attack on a North Vietnamese anti-aircraft missile base, the White House denies the incident signals any change in US policy. The US command acknowledges that there have been periodic air-to-ground engagements in North Vietnam since the bombing halt that were not made public because they were considered 'insignificant.'

Negotiatons At the Paris talks, the United States affirms it sends reconnaissance planes over North Vietnam with fighter escorts, but denies this violates the bombing halt understanding. The North Vietnamese delegation charges that the US planes bombed and strafed several populated areas.

31 JANUARY-1 FEBRUARY 1970

Ground War Communist forces carry out more than 100 rocket, mortar and ground attacks against allied bases and towns ranging from the DMZ to the Mekong Delta. Nineteen Americans are reported killed and 119 wounded. South Vietnamese losses are 11 killed and 86 wounded. More than 400 Communist soldiers are reported killed.

1 FEBRUARY 1970

North Vietnam Le Duan, first secretary of the Communist Party, speaking at a celebration in Hanoi marking the 40th anniversary of the Party, warns the North Vietnamese people that they 'must be prepared to fight for many more years' to force the withdrawal of US forces from Vietnam.

2 FEBRUARY 1970

USA: Domestic Members of the anti-war movement file suit against the Dow Chemical Company in a Washington DC court. The plaintiffs will try to force the company to disclose all government contracts to prove that the company still makes napalm.

Air War A US fighter-bomber attacks a North Vietnamese missile and gun position for the second time in a week after an unarmed reconnaissance jet comes under intense anti-aircraft fire. The action takes place in the area of the Bankarai Pass, an infiltration route leading into Laos through North Vietnamese mountains, 20 miles north of the DMZ.

3 FEBRUARY 1970

USA: Government The Senate Foreign Relations Committee reopens hearings on the Vietnam war. Senator Charles Goodell (R-NY) says Vietnamization has been a 'great public relations success'. Senators Harold Hughes (D-IA), Thomas Eagleton (D-MO) and Alan Cranston (D-CA) testify in support of Senate resolution calling for the termination of the American commitment to South Vietnam unless the Saigon government takes steps to broaden its cabinet, and press censorship and release political prisoners.

Ground War Vietcong gunners shell Bienhoa airbase. US helicopter gunships respond killing 23 enemy soldiers. Another 52 Communist soldiers are reported killed by US forces in two battles north of Saigon.

5 FEBRUARY 1970

Ground War In an accidental attack by a US helicopter gunship, 275 miles north east of Saigon, eight South Vietnamese soldiers are killed and 31 are wounded.

10 FEBRUARY 1970

USA: Government Arriving in South Vietnam, Secretary of Defense Melvin Laird states that the current pace of Vietnamization

CHRONOLOGY

is adequate, but that ways to improve it and push it forward are being examined.

11 FEBRUARY 1970
USA: Government Secretary of Defense Laird says that US warplanes will continue to take whatever steps are necessary to protect themselves during reconnaissance flights over North Vietnam. This policy of 'protective reaction' applies to action over North Vietnam as well as to ground action by US troops in Laos and Cambodia.

13 FEBRUARY 1970
Ground War In a Communist ambush in the Queson valley near Danang, 13 US Marines are killed and 12 are wounded. Six enemy soldiers are reported killed.

14 FEBRUARY 1970
USA: Domestic A Gallup Poll shows that a majority of those polled (55 percent) continue to oppose an immediate withdrawal of US troops from Vietnam, but that those that favor it has risen from 21 percent, in a November poll, to 35 percent.
USA: Domestic Following numerous violent courtroom outbreaks, Chicago Seven conspiracy trial judge, Julius Hoffman, sentences four defendants to lengthy prison terms for contempt of court.
Ground War In an ambush by North Vietnamese soldiers near the Cambodian border, eight US soldiers are killed and 30 are wounded. Thirty-one Communist soldiers are reported killed.

15 FEBRUARY 1970
USA: Domestic As the jury continues to deliberate in the trial of the Chicago Seven, defense attorneys William Kunstler and Leonard Weinglass, and three more defendants are sentenced to prison for contempt of court.
Ground War South Vietnamese soldiers and an armored brigade, with the aid of US firepower, kill 145 Communist soldiers belonging to a battalion apparently planning to attack Danang. South Vietnamese losses are four killed and 26 wounded.

17-18 FEBRUARY 1970
Air War B-52 raids in South Vietnam are halted for 36 hours while the bombers attack North Vietnamese and Pathet Lao forces threatening the Plain of Jars. The expansion of the B-52 bombing missions to northern

Laos is carried on the US military records as routine missions over South Vietnam or southern Laos, where bombing along the Ho Chi Minh trail had been conducted on a near-daily basis and fully reported. The raids over northern Laos are made public on 19 February provoking a new wave of congressional criticism regarding the policies of the Nixon administration in Indochina.

19 FEBRUARY 1970
USA: Domestic All seven defendants in the Chicago conspiracy trial are acquitted of plotting to incite riot during the 1968 Democratic National Convention.

20 FEBRUARY 1970
USA: Domestic In the maximum sentence possible under the law, five defendants convicted of inciting riot in Chicago are sentenced to five years in prison and fined $5000 each plus the costs of their prosecution.
Ground War An armored unit of the 196th Light Infantry Brigade, Americal Division, is ambushed by North Vietnamese forces south of Danang in the Queson valley. Fourteen Americans are killed and 29 are wounded.

21 FEBRUARY 1970
Negotiations Presidential assistant Henry Kissinger and Le Duc Tho, the fifth-ranking member of the Hanoi Politburo, hold the first of three clandestine meetings in Paris. Le Duc Tho states that the North Vietnamese position continues to be an unconditional US withdrawal on a fixed date and the abandonment of the Thieu government as a precondition for further progress in the stalled negotiations. The North Vietnamese reject Kissinger's proposals for a mutual withdrawal of military forces, the neutralization of Cambodia and a mixed electoral commission to supervise elections in South Vietnam. The other two meetings, in which there is a similar lack of progress, will be held on 16 March and 4 April.
Laos Following an offensive launched in northern Laos on 12 February, 3000 North Vietnamese troops capture the airfield at Xiengkhouong, 100 miles northeast of the capital of Vientiane. This is the last military stronghold of the Laotian government in the Plain of Jars.

26 FEBRUARY 1970
USA: Government Secretary of Defense, Laird, responding to strident congressional

An Essex class Aircraft Carrier moves alongside an ammunition ship for supplies.

criticism over US military activity in Laos, says that US airpower is being employed in Laos only to interdict North Vietnamese supply lines through Laos into South Vietnam.

28 FEBRUARY 1970
Terrorism After a bus strikes a mine near Danang. 10 South Vietnamese civilians are killed and 15 are wounded. Eleven other civilians are wounded by grenades thrown at a truck in the same area. Three civilians are killed and 19 are wounded following the shelling of a village by US Marine artillery.

2 MARCH 1970
South Vietnam US officials announce a new method for measuring progress in pacification programs in which district advisers answer 139 'more or less' objective questions. A computer then interprets the information and marks a scorecard. In the first month of operation using the new method, the number of hamlets reported to be relatively pacified is reduced from 92.7 percent to 89.9 percent.

9 MARCH 1970
USA: Military The US Marines turn over control of the I Corps area to the US Army.

The commanding officer of the 150,000 US troops in the five northernmost provinces in South Vietnam will be Lieutenant General Melvin Zais.

10 MARCH 1970
War Crimes The US Army accuses Captain Ernest Medina and four other soldiers of committing crimes at Songmy in March 1968. The charges range from premeditated murder to rape and the 'maiming' of a suspect under interrogation. Medina was the company commander of Lieutenant William Calley and other soldiers who are charged with murder and other crimes at Mylai 4 in Songmy village.

11 MARCH 1970
Cambodia An estimated 20,000 demonstrators, protesting the presence of Communist forces in Cambodia, assault the embassies of the Provisional Revolutionary Government of South Vietnam and North Vietnam causing heavy damage.

12 MARCH 1970
Cambodia The Cambodian government announces the cancellation of a trade agreement which allow North Vietnam and the Vietcong

CHRONOLOGY

to use the port of Sihanoukville as a source of supply for their military forces in Cambodia and South Vietnam. Premier Lon Nol formally apologizes for the attacks on the Vietnamese embassies, but also issues an ultimatum that their troops must leave Cambodia in 72 hours.

12-13 MARCH 1970
Cambodia Cambodian demonstrators continue to rampage in the streets of Phnompenh, attacking Vietnamese shops and homes.

16 MARCH 1970
Diplomatic North Vietnamese, NLF and Cambodian officials meet in Phnompenh to discuss the presence of Communist military forces in Cambodia.

17 MARCH 1970
War Crimes The US Army, following an investigation by a panel headed by Lieutenant General William Peers, accuses 14 officers of suppression of information relating to the incident at Songmy in March 1968. The charges include dereliction of duty, failure to obey lawful regulations and false swearing. The report says that US soldiers committed individual and group acts of murder, rape, sodomy, maiming and assault that took the lives of a large number of civilians and concludes that a 'tragedy of major proportions' occurred at Songmy. The Peers report says that each successive level of command received a more watered-down account of what actually occurred at Songmy; the higher the report went, the lower was its estimate of civilians allegedly killed by Americans. Americal Division headquarters, where accounts of the incident stopped, received information that 20-28 civilians were killed.

18 MARCH 1970
Cambodia While returning to Cambodia from Moscow and Peking Prince Norodom Sihanouk is ousted as Cambodian chief of state in a bloodless coup by Lieutenant General Lon Nol, premier and defense minister, and First Deputy Premier Prince Sisowath Sirik Matak.

19 MARCH 1970
Cambodia The National Assembly grants 'full power' to Premier Lon Nol, declares a state of emergency and suspends four articles of the constitution, permitting arbitrary arrest and banning public assembly.

20 MARCH 1970
Ground War In the first coordinated allied-Cambodian military operation of the war, a Cambodian army commander calls in a US spotter plane and South Vietnamese artillery to help repel a 150-man Vietcong attack on an outpost about 10 miles north of the South Vietnamese district capital of Anphu.

21 MARCH 1970
Diplomatic Pham Van Dong, prime minister of North Vietnam, flies secretly to Peking and meets with Chinese Premier Chou En-lai and deposed Cambodian head of state Norodom Sihanouk. Sihanouk agrees to accept the leadership of the Cambodian Communists.

22 March 1970
Terrorism At Hocman, seven miles northwest of Saigon, a Vietcong bomb explodes at a Buddist meeting, killing 14 women and children and wounding 20 others.

23 MARCH 1970
Diplomatic In Peking, Norodom Sihanouk issues a public call for arms against the Lon Nol government in Phnompenh and the establishment of a National United Front of Kampuchea (FUNK). North Vietnam, the NLF and the Pathet Lao immediately pledge their support to the new organization.

25 MARCH 1970
Diplomatic North Vietnam announces it is recalling its diplomats from Cambodia.

27-28 MARCH 1970
Ground War Following several days of consultations with the Cambodian government, South Vietnamese troops, supported by advance artillery and air strikes, launch their first major military operation into Cambodia. The South Vietnamese encounter a 300-man Vietcong force in Kandal province and report killing 53 communist soldiers. Two teams of US helicopter gunships take part in the action. Three South Vietnamese soldiers are killed and seven are wounded. US and South Vietnamese officials disavow any knowledge of the operation.

28 MARCH 1970
USA: Military The White House announces for the first time that US troops, depending on

Airboats were used by the Vietnamese Mobile Strike Force to patrol the shallow Delta.

the judgement of their field commanders, are permitted to cross the Cambodian border in response to enemy threats. US officials contend that this does not mean a widening of the war, but that it merely represents a restatement of the rules promulgated by the Pentagon and already in force.

29 MARCH 1970
Ground War North Vietnamese troops attack an American base near the Cambodian border killing 13 and wounding 30. The Communists report 75 killed.

1 APRIL 1970
War Crimes The United States formally charges Captain Ernest Medina of being 'responsible' for the murder of Vietnamese civilians killed by members of his infantry company at Songmy. Medina, speaking at a news conference, discloses that the Army accuses him of premeditated murder of not less than 175 civilians and repeats denials of having participated in or ordered or seen any mass killings at Songmy.
Ground War After six months of relative quiet the war flares up again as Communist forces launch 115 shellings and ground assaults throughout South Vietnam.
Air War In the first such action reported since

the November 1968 bombing halt, a US military spokesmen reports that a US Navy F-4 Phantom shot down a North Vietnamese MiG-21 while flying reconnaissance escort on the 28 March near Thanhhoa, about 85 miles south of Hanoi.

1 APRIL-5 SEPTEMBER 1970
Ground War Operation Texas Star is a follow-up to Operation Randolph Glen. One brigade of the 101st Airborne Division (Airmobile) retains responsibility for pacification and development support in Thauthien province, while the other two brigades conduct offensive operations in the western portions of Quangtri and Thauthien provinces. Enemy casualties are reported at 1782.

3 APRIL 1970
Ground War Communist forces shell 60 targets as heavy attacks continue for the third consecutive day. US troops pursuing a Communist battalion toward the Cambodian border meet heavy resistance. Ten Americans and 62 Communist soldiers are reported killed.

4 APRIL 1970
USA: Domestic About 15,000 people march up Pennsylvania Avenue to a rally at the

CHRONOLOGY

Washington Monument to support 'victory over the Communists in Vietnam.'

4-5 APRIL 1970
Ground War The allied command reports the heaviest fighting involving US troops along the DMZ in nearly five months and new clashes in Cambodia, where two South Vietnamese battalions move 10 miles into Cambodia. In fighting near the DMZ, centered four miles southwest of Conthien and one mile south of the 17th parallel, six Americans are killed and 40 are wounded.

6-7 APRIL 1970
Ground War Communist forces attack Cambodian troops at Chipou, near the eastern end of Svayrieng province. Cambodian losses are listed as 20 killed, 30 wounded and 30 missing.

8 APRIL 1970
Ground War Allied military officials announce 754 South Vietnamese soldiers were killed the week of 29 March-4 April. This is the second-highest South Vietnamese casualty toll for a week in the war. US losses for the same period are 138 dead, the highest since September 1969.

9 APRIL 1970
Cambodia Cambodia withdraws all of its military forces from Svayrieng province, also known as the 'Parrot's Beak', abandoning it to the Vietnamese Communists. One-half of the province's population, about 30,000 civilians, also withdraws westward. Most of those remaining are ethnic Vietnamese.

10 APRIL 1970
Cambodia Hundreds of ethnic Vietnamese are massacred by Cambodian troops in the village of Prasot in Svayrieng province. The Cambodian government reports the deaths of 89 villagers due to 'crossfire.'

11 APRIL 1970
USA: Domestic A Gallup Poll shows 48 percent of the public approve of President Nixon's policy in Vietnam, while 41 percent disapprove. This figure compares with a 65 percent approval rating in January.

14 APRIL 1970
Ground War Two thousand South Vietnamese troops, operating with a token Cambodian force, attack a North Vietnamese base camp one mile inside Cambodia. South Viet-

namese headquarters reports 179 Communist soldiers killed and claims that the entire operation took place entirely in South Vietnam. President Thieu denies South Vietnamese troops crossed the border.

15 APRIL 1970
USA: Military A force of 12,900 US Marines depart South Vietnam to complete the third phase of US troop withdrawals announced by President Nixon. Units departing include the 26th Marines, the 1st Antitank Battalion, most of the First Tank Battalion, the 3rd Amphibian Tractor Battalion and the 1st Shore Party Battalion. There are now 429,200 US troops in Vietnam.

Ground War The US command reports 25 Americans killed and 54 wounded yesterday in one of the year's highest one-day casualty tolls. The casualties include 14 Americans killed and 32 wounded in an explosion of a US artillery shell rigged as a Vietcong booby-trap near Ducpho, 105 miles south of Danang.

16 APRIL 1970
Cambodia At least 100 ethnic Vietnamese civilians are killed by rampaging Cambodian troops at Takeo, 50 miles south of Phnompenh.

19 APRIL 1970
USA: Domestic The Vietnam Moratorium Committee announces that it is disbanding. Committee leaders say that their sources of funding have run dry and acknowledge that President Nixon's withdrawal policy has undermined the non-radical opposition to the Vietnam war.

20 APRIL 1970
USA: Government President Nixon, in a televised speech, pledges to withdraw 150,000 more US troops over the next year 'based entirely on the progress' of Vietnamization.

Ground War South Vietnamese troops move into Cambodia in their third major cross-border offensive in the past week. South Vietnamese sources report killing 144 Communist soldiers. Twenty South Vietnamese soldiers are killed and 70 are wounded.

Cambodia Following reports by Cambodian military authorities that Communist forces have more than doubled their area of control, including Svayrieng province, Premier Lon Nol sends a personal appeal to President Nixon for military aid.

24-25 APRIL 1970

Diplomatic China sponsers a conference near Canton attended by Norodom Sihanouk; Prince Souphonouvong, leader of the Pathet Lao; Nguyen Huu Tho, president of the Provisional Revolutionary Government of South Vietnam; and, North Vietnamese Prime Minister Pham Van Dong. The leaders of the four Communist movements pledge joint action to expel the United States and other forces that oppose them in Indochina. Chinese Premier Chou En-lai attends the final session of the conference and gives it his endorsement.

28 APRIL 1970

USA: Government President Nixon gives his formal authorization to commit US combat troops, in cooperation with South Vietnamese units, against Communist troop sanctuaries in Cambodia. Secretary of State William Rogers and Secretary of Defense Melvin Laird, who have been excluded from the decision to use US troops, are informed for the first time. General Wheeler cables General Abrams, informing him of the decision that a 'higher authority has authorized certain military actions to protect US forces operating in South Vietnam.' Three National Security Council Staff members and key aides to presidential assistant Henry Kissinger resign in protest over the planned invasion of Cambodia.

Ground War Two US Marine Skyhawk jets accidentally bomb a South Vietnamese outpost during a battle in Quangnai province, killing 10 ARVN soldiers and wounding 20 others.

29 APRIL 1970

USA: Government As 6000 ARVN soldiers launch an attack into the Parrot's Beak area of Cambodia, supported by US warplanes and artillery, the United States announces that it will provide combat advisers, tactical air support, medical evacuation teams and some supplies to the South Vietnamese forces.

30 APRIL 1970

USA: Government President Nixon, in a nationally televised speech, announces he is sending US combat troops into Cambodia to destroy Communist sanctuaries and supply bases. Nixon says the objective of the US forces is the Fishhook area, 50 miles northwest of Saigon, which the President calls the 'key control center' for the enemy and its 'headquarters for the entire communist military operation in South Vietnam.' Nixon says the purpose of the military action is not to occupy Cambodian territory and insists 'this is not an invasion of Cambodia' since the border areas are 'completely occupied and controlled by North Vietnamese forces.' In defending his decision, Nixon argues that 'plaintive diplomatic protests' no longer are sufficient since they would only destroy American credibility in areas of the world 'where only the power of the United States deters aggression.' Nixon warns that 'if, when the chips are down, the world's most powerful nation, the United States of America, acts like a pitiful, helpless giant, the forces of totalitarianism and anarchy will threaten free nations and free institutions throughout the world.'

1 MAY 1970

Ground War The military operation into the Fishhook area is launched by a combined force of 8000 US and 2000 South Vietnamese soldiers.

1-2 MAY 1970

Air War Heavy bombing raids are carried out against supply depots and other targets in North Vietnam. One raid involves at least 128 US warplanes against targets in Quangbinh and Nghean provinces. A Hanoi radio broadcast charges that more than 100 planes struck targets in two provinces killing or wounding many civilians. On 2 May US spokesmen confirm the raids.

2 MAY 1970

USA: Government Alexander Haig, deputy to presidential assistant Henry Kissinger, requests FBI wiretaps on *New York Times* reporter William Beecher; Robert Pursley, Secretary of Defense Laird's military assistant; Richard Peterson, the State department counselor; and, William H Sullivan, an assistant secretary of state. Beecher will report the following day on the intensive bombing raids against North Vietnam. The wiretaps will remain in effect until 10 February 1971.

USA: Government Senators George McGovern (D-SD), Mark Hatfield (R-OR) and Charles Goodell (R-NY) announce they will offer an amendment to a pending military procurement authorization bill to cut off funds for all US military activity in Southeast Asia.

Ground War Fighting has raged for three days

Many draft evaders went to Canada via an 'underground railroad.'

in the northernmost zone of South Vietnam with the military action focused on the town of Hiepduc, 40 miles south of Danang, where North Vietnamese troops hold firm control of three hamlets. South Vietnamese troops report killing 219 enemy soldiers. Seven Americans and 12 ARVN soldiers have been killed.

USA: Domestic Ohio National Guardsmen and police subdue students on the campus at Kent State University after the ROTC building is attacked and burned to the ground. Student strikes spread to a number of campuses to protest the expansion of the war into Cambodia.

Ground War More than 2000 well-armed Cambodian mercenaries, serving in units in South Vietnam operated by the US Special Forces, are flown into Cambodia to reinforce the Cambodian army.

4 MAY 1970

USA: Domestic At Kent State 100 National Guardsmen fire their rifles into a group of students killing four and wounding 11. President Nixon issues a statement deploring the deaths and saying the incident should serve as a reminder that 'when dissent turns to violence it invites tragedy.' The National Student Association and former Vietnam Moratorium Committee leaders call for a national university strike of indefinite duration, beginning immediately, to protest the war. At least 100 colleges and universities pledge to strike. The presidents of 37 universities and colleges sign a letter urging President Nixon to clearly show his determination to end the war.

Ground War About 20 miles north of the Fishhook area, US troops reach the site of what is believed to be the largest Vietnamese base in the area, known as The City. Communist forces launch heavy attacks in the area around Phnompenh as North Vietnamese and Vietcong units cut the Phnompenh-Saigon highway at a point 29 miles from the Cambodian capital.

Soviet Union In a rare public news conference, Soviet Premier Alexsei Kosygin personally criticizes President Nixon for sending US troops into Cambodia.

5 MAY 1970

USA: Government President Nixon meets with congressional committees at the White House and gives the legislators a 'firm commitment' that US troops will be withdrawn

from Cambodia in 3-7 weeks. Nixon also pledges that he will not order US troops to penetrate deeper than 21 miles into Cambodia without first seeking congressional approval.

Ground War In Cambodia, a US force captures Snoul, 20 miles from the tip of the Fishhook area, after a squadron of nearly 100 tanks of the 11th Armored Cavalry Regiment and jet planes virtually level the village which had been held by the North Vietnamese.

6 MAY 1970

USA: Domestic More than 100 colleges and universities across the nation shut down as thousands of students join a nationwide campus protest. Governor Ronald Reagan closes down the entire California university and college system until 11 May involving more than 280,000 students on 28 campuses. Pennsylvania State University, with 18 campuses, is closed down for an indeterminate period. A National Student Association spokesman reports students from more than 300 campuses are boycotting classes.

Ground War Three new fronts are opened in Cambodia bringing to nearly 50,000 the number of allied troops in Cambodia. One US spearhead, by troops of the 25th Infantry Division, moves across the border from Tayninh province between the Fishhook and Parrot's Beak areas. In another US thrust, the First Cavalry Division (Airmobile), is airlifted into the jungles 23 miles west of Phocbinh, South Vietnam, northeast of the Fishhook area.

8 MAY 1970

South Vietnam President Thieu says he and Premier Lon Nol of Cambodia have worked out 'agreements in principle' for South Vietnamese troops to conduct continuing military operations in eastern Cambodia. Thieu makes clear that South Vietnamese troops will not be bound by the restrictions President Nixon has placed on the use of US forces and says there is no deadline or limits to the South Vietnamese operation in Cambodia.

USA: Government President Nixon, at a news conference, defends the US troop movement into Cambodia saying the operation will provide 6-8 months time for the training of South Vietnamese forces and thus will shorten the war for Americans. Nixon reaffirms his promise to withdraw 150,000 US soldiers by next spring.

USA: Government More than 250 State De-

CHRONOLOGY

partment and foreign aid employees sign a letter to Secretary of State Rogers criticizing US military involvement in Cambodia.

USA: Domestic College students across the nation intensify their anti-war protests with marches, rallies and scattered incidents of violence. About 400 schools are affected by strikes, with more than 200 colleges and universities closed completely.

USA: Domestic Helmeted construction workers break up a student anti-war demonstration on Wall Street in New York City, attacking demonstrators in a melee that leaves more than 70 persons injured.

9 MAY 1970

USA: Domestic Between 75,000 and 100,000 young people, mostly from college campuses, demonstrate peaceably in Washington DC at the rear of a barricaded White House, demanding the withdrawal of US military forces from Vietnam and other southeast Asian nations. Afterwards, a few hundred militants spread through surrounding streets, causing some damage. Police attack the most threatening crowds with tear gas.

Riverine War Thirty US gunboats join a flotilla of 110 South Vietnamese craft in a thrust up the Mekong River in a attempt to neutralize enemy sanctuaries along a 45-mile stretch of river between the South Vietnamese border and Phnompenh. The US vessels will move no farther north than Neak Luong, in compliance with the US policy of limiting US penetration of Cambodia to 21.7 miles.

12 MAY 1970

Naval War South Vietnamese Vice-President Ky announces that allied naval vessels have begun blockading a 100-mile stretch of the Cambodian coastline to prevent Communist forces from resupplying by sea. The blockade extends from Kompong Som (formerly Sihanoukville) to the South Vietnamese border.

14 MAY 1970

Ground War Allied military officials announce 863 South Vietnamese were killed the week of 3-9 May. This is the second-highest weekly death toll of the war for the South Vietnamese forces.

15 MAY 1970

USA: Domestic Congress is virtually buried under an avalanche of mail, telegrams and petitions heavily opposed to the use of US troops in Cambodia.

17 MAY 1970

Ground War A forced of 10,000 South Vietnamese troops, supported by 200 US advisers, aircraft and logistical elements move into Cambodia and reach Takeo in a 20-mile thrust. The Communist report 211 killed.

19 MAY 1970

Ground War Communist forces shell more than 60 allied positions to commemorate the 80th anniversary of Ho Chi Minh's birth.

20 MAY 1970

USA: Domestic More than 100,000 construction workers, dockmen and office workers lead a parade in New York City supporting the policies of President Nixon and attacking Mayor John Lindsay and other opponents of the Vietnam war.

Ground War About 2500 South Vietnamese soldiers, supported by US airpower and advisers, open a new front in Cambodia, 125 miles north of Saigon, bringing the number of South Vietnamese troops in Cambodia to 40,000. South Vietnamese troops link up with Cambodian forces 25 miles north of Takeo after a cross-country drive in which they report killing 400 Communist soldiers.

22 MAY 1970

USA: Government The White House announces the United States is prepared to continue air cover, if needed, for South Vietnamese forces that are considered almost certain to remain in Cambodia after US troops are withdrawn.

South Vietnam South Vietnam announces a halt in the repatriation of Vietnamese refugees in Cambodia. About 50,000-80,000 refugees have already been moved to South Vietnam since the start of evacuation efforts 10 May. 70,000 more refugees remain stranded in refugee camps. Pham Huy Ty, head of South Vietnam's permanent liaison mission in Phnompenh, says the halt is due to greater security measures for Vietnamese residents being instituted by the Cambodian government. The increasing presence of South Vietnamese troops in Cambodia has inflamed the traditional animosities existing between the two countries.

23-24 MAY 1970

Ground War About 10,000 South Vietnamese troops, led by Khmer Krom, ethnic

Cambodian mercenaries assigned to the Cambodian army, attack Cambodia's largest rubber plantation at Chup, about 50 miles northeast of Phnompenh. A regiment of North Vietnamese and Vietcong had been reported to have retreated into the 70-square mile plantation. South Vietnamese air assaults leave the plantation in a flaming ruin. The attacks kill 15 civilian workers and injure 80 others. Twelve Cambodian Communist soldiers, known as the Khmer Rouge, are reported killed and 15 captured. The plantation at Chup had accounted for 50 percent of Cambodia's rubber production.

26 MAY 1970

Diplomatic Norodom Sihanouk arrives in Hanoi and is greeted at the airport by Premier Pham Van Dong, Defense Minister Vo Nguyen Giap and Foreign Minister Nguyen Duy Trinh. Sihanouk urges the people of Indochina to unite in their fight against foreign intervention.

27 MAY 1970

Diplomatic Following three days of talks in Saigon, South Vietnam and Cambodia sign agreements re-establishing diplomatic relations (broken since 1963), providing for economic and military cooperation and dealing with the treatment of Vietnamese residents in Cambodia.

31 MAY 1970

Ground War About 75 Communist soldiers, who had seized key outposts in the resort city of Dalat, 145 miles northeast of Saigon, slip past 2500 South Vietnamese militiamen and soldiers who had surrounded their positions. In earlier fighting, 47 Communist soldiers are reported killed. South Vietnamese losses are 16 killed and 2 wounded.

1-3 JUNE 1970

Ground War In heavy fighting, 21 miles south of the DMZ, North Vietnamese sappers overrun part of a South Vietnamese fire base but are beaten back after inflicting heavy losses. On 3 June fresh South Vietnamese troops relieve the base. The Communist report 83 killed. South Vietnamese losses are 50 killed and 119 wounded.

3 JUNE 1970

USA: Government President Nixon, in a televised speech, claims the allied drive into Cambodia is the 'most successful operation of

this long and difficult war,' and that he is now able to resume the withdrawal of US troops from South Vietnam. Nixon reaffirms earlier pledges to bring the Cambodian operation to an end by 30 June with 'all of our major military objectives' achieved and reports that 17,000 of the 31,000 US troops in Cambodia have returned to South Vietnam. After 30 June, says Nixon, 'all American air support' for allied troops fighting in Cambodia will end, with the only remaining American activity being attacks on enemy troops movements and supplies threatening US forces in South Vietnam. Nixon promises that 50,000 of the 150,000 troops, whose withdrawal from Vietnam he had announced 20 April, 'will be out by 15 October.'

3-8 JUNE 1970

Ground War Communist forces attack Cambodian troops at Kompong Thom, 87 miles north of Phnompenh and at Siemreap, 80 miles to the northwest of the capital. Communist troops capture Kompong Thom and the nearby town of Am Leang 7 June, but are driven out 8 June. Cambodian officials report 128 Communist soldiers killed around both centers. Cambodian losses are officially listed as nine killed and 23 wounded.

6 JUNE 1970

Diplomatic South Vietnamese Vice-President Ky, in a speech to the Cambodian parliament, says South Vietnam has no territorial ambitions in Cambodia and will send military forces to help Cambodia wherever and whenever Phnompenh asks.

8 JUNE 1970

North Vietnam In a speech delivered in Hanoi, Norodom Sihanouk pledges Cambodians will fight with the Vietnamese Communists to defeat US 'imperialism.'

8-13 JUNE 1970

Ground War US troops battle Communist forces within an 11-mile radius of Memot in the Fishhook region. US losses are 13 killed and 60 wounded. Nine Communist soldiers are reported killed.

11 JUNE 1970

Terrorism 200 Vietcong guerrillas shoot their way through the hamlet of Thanhmy (also known as Baren), 17 miles southeast of Danang, firing mortars and rifles, and throwing satchel charges and grenades into civilian

Night defenses included the setting of flares on a trip wire around the perimeter of a camp.

homes. An estimated 114 civilians are killed and 316 homes are destroyed.

12-16 JUNE 1970
Ground War A force of 4000 South Vietnamese and 2000 Cambodian soldiers battle 1400 Communist troops for the provincial capital of Kompong Speu, 30 miles southwest of Phnompenh. It is the deepest penetration that South Vietnamese forces have made into Cambodia yet (50 miles). The town is captured by the Communists on 13 June, but retaken by allied forces 16 June. South Vietnamese officials report 183 enemy soldiers killed, while losing four killed and 22 wound-

ed. Civilian casualties in Kompong Speu are estimated at 40-50 killed.

15 JUNE 1970
Ground War South Vietnamese forces report killing 110 North Vietnamese in three battles around Prevyeng, 30 miles east of Phnompenh. Thirteen South Vietnamese are killed and 37 are wounded.

16-21 JUNE 1970
Ground War North Vietnamese and Vietcong attacks almost completely isolate Phnompenh. The principal fighting rages in and around Kompong Thom, about 90 miles

north of the capital. On 17 June Cambodia's last working railway line, which runs to the border with Thailand, is severed when Communist troops seize a freight train with 200 tons of rice and other food supplies at a station at Krang Lovea, about 40 miles northwest of Phnompenh. On 18 June, Communist forces sever Highway 1, linking Phnompenh with Saigon, 30 miles southeast of the capital and Highway 4, leading southwest to the port of Kompong Som.

24 JUNE 1970
USA: Government On an amendment offered by Senator Robert Dole (R-KS), to the Foreign Military Sales Act, the Senate votes, 81-10, to repeal the Tonkin Gulf Resolution. The Nixon administration takes a neutral stance on the vote, denying that it relies on the Tonkin resolution as the basis for its warmaking authority in Southeast Asia. The administration asserts that it primarily draws on the constitutional authority of the President as commander-in-chief to protect the lives of US military forces.
USA: Government The US embassy in Phnompemh discloses that the United States has stepped up the shipment of arms of Cambodia and that all of the $7.9 million in arms aid promised for the current fiscal year either had arrived or would arrive shortly.

26 JUNE 1970
USA: Government Secretary of State Laird affirms the US plans to continue bombing raids inside Cambodia after 30 June. Laird makes clear the 'primary emphasis' of the raids will be the denial of routes for enemy troops and supplies, but refuses to rule out air support for allied ground combat troops.

27 JUNE 1970
Cambodia All Cambodian troops are reported to have withdrawn from Ratanakiri province, virtually leaving the northeastern part of the country under Communist military control.

29-30 JUNE 1970
Ground War US ground combat troops end two months of operations in Cambodia and return to South Vietnam. Military officials report 354 Americans have been killed and 1689 wounded in the operation. The South Vietnamese report 866 killed and 3724 wounded. About 34,000 South Vietnamese troops remain in Cambodia.

30 JUNE 1970
USA: Government President Nixon, in a written report on the US operation in Cambodia, pronounces it a 'successful' operation. Nixon rules out the use of US troops there in the future, suggesting Cambodia's defense will be left largely to Cambodia and its allies. Regarding the use of US airpower in Cambodia, Nixon states the United States will not provide air or logistical support for South Vietnamese forces in Cambodia, but will continue bombing enemy personnel and supply concentrations 'with the approval of the Cambodian government.' Nixon notes that more than a year's supply of weapons and ammunition was captured and that 11,349 enemy soldiers were killed by allied forces.
USA: Government The Senate votes, 58-37, to adopt the Cooper-Church amendment to limit Presidential power in Cambodia. The amendment bars funds to retain US troops in Cambodia after 1 July or to supply military advisers, mercenaries or to conduct 'any combat activity in the air above Cambodia in direct support of Cambodian forces' without congressional approval. The amendment represents the first limitation ever voted on the President's powers as commander-in-chief during a war situation. The House of Representatives rejects the amendment 9 July and it is eventually dropped from the Foreign Military Sales Act.

1 JULY 1970
USA: Government President Nixon announces the appointment of David K E Bruce to head the US delegation to the Paris peace talks.

3 JULY 1970
Terrorism South Vietnamese civilians are killed when a passenger river boat strikes a Communist floating mine on the Cuaviet River near Dongha, about nine miles south of the DMZ.

8 JULY 1970
Ground War US troops kill 139 enemy soldiers near Khesanh when rocket-firing helicopters, along with units of the 101st Airborne Division, catch enemy soldiers of the North Vietnamese 304th Division in the open after crossing the border from Laos.

15 JULY 1970
South Vietnam President Thieu, in a speech honoring South Vietnamese troops who par-

CHRONOLOGY

ticipated in the Cambodian operation, vows to 'beat to death' those of his countrymen who call for an 'immediate peace' with the Communists.

23 JULY 1970
Ground War US troops abandon an artillery base north of the Ashua valley after heavy bombing strikes and artillery barrages fail to stop a North Vietnamese army buildup around the post. In three weeks of fighting at the base, US losses are 61 killed and 345 wounded.

26 JULY 1970
Ground War A force of 2500 South Vietnamese troops move into Cambodia from Danphuc, in South Vietnam's western Mekong Delta, raising the number of South Vietnamese soldiers in Cambodia to 20,000. In initial fighting, 35 Communist soldiers are reported killed.

31 JULY 1970
South Vietnam President Thieu declares South Vietnam's conditions for peace are unchanged and once again rules out any coalition government with the Communists, except one that might result from internationally supervised elections. Thieu puts the Communist side and those urging a more flexible negotiating position on notice that US negotiator David Bruce has no new proposals approved by the South Vietnamese government.

4 AUGUST 1970
Ground War In a battle in the Mekong Delta, South Vietnamese forces kill 44 Communist soldiers. Six South Vietnamese are killed and 29 are wounded.

6 AUGUST 1970
USA: Government In response to eyewitness reports that US planes are providing direct combat support to Cambodian ground troops, Secretary of Defense Laird says that recent US bombings were part of a general interdiction campaign aimed at protecting US forces in Vietnam. However, Laird makes it clear that the Nixon administration's definition of interdictory bombing encompasses virtually all of Cambodia.
Negotiations US chief negotiator David Bruce attends his first session of the Paris talks. The Communist negotiators declare the positions of both sides appear as frozen as ever. A

North Vietnamese spokesman says that the Nixon administration has corrected its 'error' in sending Bruce to the talks.

8 AUGUST 1970
USA: Military US military command issues a confidential set of instructions to all unit commanders on US air operations in Cambodia. These order the commanders to say that US air raids are for interdiction purposes to protect the remaining US troops in Vietnam and to aid the process of Vietnamization.

11 AUGUST 1970
Ground War South Vietnamese units take over from US forces the primary role of fending off enemy forces along the Cambodian and Laotian borders. US soldiers have been replaced by the South Vietnamese along almost all of the South Vietnamese frontiers.

15 AUGUST 1970
Ground War South Vietnamese militiamen, known as the 'Ruff Puffs', fall upon a Vietcong base area south of Danang and claim one of their biggest victories of the war. The South Vietnamese report killing 125 enemy soldiers and capturing 125 prisoners in a coordinated series of 80 raids. The South Vietnamese government reports their regional forces have killed 308 Communist soldiers in four days of fighting along a coastal strip south of the DMZ.

19 AUGUST 1970
Diplomatic In an agreement signed in Phnompenh between the United States and Cambodia, the United States agrees to provide Cambodia with $40 million worth of military equipment during the fiscal year ending 30 June 1971. The equipment includes small arms, ammunition, communications equipment, spare parts and training funds.

21 AUGUST 1970
Terrorism Vietcong mortars shell the Mekong Delta village of Buchuc in Chauduc province, killing 11 persons and wounding 42.

26 AUGUST 1970
Ground War A US helicopter is shot down while ferrying out troops during the closing down of the Khamduc combat base, 13 miles from the Laotian border, killing the 30 Americans aboard. Another helicopter is shot down the same day killing four more Americans. The loss of the two aircraft bring

Infantry on patrol at the Michelin Rubber Plantation with a tank to provide cover.

to 3998 the number of helicopters down since January 1961. Of this figure, 1777 have been reported lost to enemy ground fire.

27 AUGUST 1970
Diplomatic US Vice-President Spiro Agnew meets with South Vietnamese leaders Thieu and Ky. In a speech at Tansonnhut airfield in Saigon, Agnew lauds the South Vietnamese people for suffering 'so much in freedom's cause' and pledges that 'there will be no lessening' of US support.

Ground War The US command reports 52 Americans died in combat the week of 16-22 of August and 358 were wounded. This is the lowest casualty toll since the week of 3 December 1966.

28 AUGUST 1970
Thailand Thailand announces it intends to withdraw its 11,000-man contingent from South Vietnam. No date or timetable is set.

29 AUGUST 1970
Terrorism Communist forces attack a Buddhist orphanage and temple south of Danang,

killing 15 and wounding 45.

30 AUGUST 1970
South Vietnam As an estimated six million South Vietnamese cast ballots for 30 seats at stake in elections for the Senate, Communist forces attack at least 14 district towns, a provincial capital and a few polling places. Fifty-five civilians are reported killed and 140 wounded.

31 AUGUST 1970
South Vietnam Anti-government Buddhist candidates appear to win 10 of the 30 Senate seats contested in yesterday's election. However, the Senate as a whole remains in firm control of conservative, pro-government supporters. Catholics still hold 50 percent of the Senate seats, even though they constitute only 10 percent of the population of South Vietnam.

1 SEPTEMBER 1970
USA: Government The Senate rejects (55-39) the McGovern-Hatfield amendment, which set a deadline of 31 December 1971 for com-

CHRONOLOGY

plete withdrawal of American troops from South Vietnam. The Senate also turns down, 71-22, a proposal forbidding the Army from sending draftees to Vietnam.

USA: Government Vice-President Agnew, after briefing President Nixon on his Asian tour, reports that 'the Cambodian situation seems to be developing very well.'

USA: Government A bipartisan group of 14 Senators, including both the majority and minority leaders, sign a letter to President Nixon asking him to propose a comprehensive standstill ceasefire for South Vietnam at the Paris peace talks.

3 SEPTEMBER 1970

Negotiations Xuan Thuy, ending a nine-month boycott, returns to the Paris talks and declares that the positions of both the United States and North Vietnam remain unchanged. Thuy says the United States must agree to withdraw unconditionally and 'renounce' the Saigon government. Thuy describes as 'very flexible and generous' his side's proposal to support a coalition government.

4 SEPTEMBER 1970

Guerrilla War In a strike directed against South Vietnam's pacification program, Vietcong guerrillas attack a civil defense training center in Bindinh province. Fourteen South Vietnamese are killed and 26 are wounded.

5 SEPTEMBER 1970-8 OCTOBER 1971

Ground War Combat operations, including Jefferson Glen, are initiated by the 101st Airborne Division (Airmobile) in coordination with the ARVN 1st Infantry Division and government officials in Thuathien province. This is the last major military operation in which US ground forces will participate. The Communists report 2026 casualties.

7 SEPTEMBER 1970

Negotiations Presidential aide Henry Kissinger holds the first of two clandestine meetings with North Vietnamese representatives in Paris. Le Duc Tho does not attend either meeting and North Vietnam is represented by Xuan Thuy. A second meeting is held 27 September. There is no progress at either session.

8 SEPTEMBER 1970

Ground War More than 200 Communist troops attack the Trabong district headquarters and ranger camp south of Danang, killing 24 South Vietnamese and wounding 42. One US adviser is killed.

10 SEPTEMBER 1970

Ground War A 2000-man South Vietnamese force announces the completion of military operations in the Parrot's Beak area of Cambodia. Fifty eight enemy soldiers are reported killed.

12 SEPTEMBER 1970

Ground War The pattern of the war continues as it has in recent weeks with most military action taking place in the northern provinces and the Mekong Delta. Communist troops launch a third assault against South Vietnamese troops near Fire Base O'Reilly below the DMZ. South Vietnamese forces report killing 73 enemy soldiers in the Mekong Delta.

17 SEPTEMBER 1970

Negotiations Nguyen Thi Binh, foreign minister of the Provisional Revolutionary Government, returns to the Paris conference table for the first time in three months and issues an eight-point statement similar to the National Liberation Front 10-point plan of May 1969. The statement declares that in exchange for the withdrawal of all US and allied forces by 30 June 1971, Communist forces will refrain from attacking the departing troops and will also offer to begin immediate negotiations on the release of POWs once the withdrawal is agreed to. The PRG statement demands the purge of South Vietnam's top three leaders: President Thieu, Vice-President Ky and Premier Khiem.

Ground War The US command reports Communist forces have downed and destroyed nine US helicopters in the last six days and have damaged eight others, killing four Americans and wounding six. US troops report killing 54 enemy soldiers in four ground actions near Danang.

19 SEPTEMBER 1970

Riverine War A force of 200 South Vietnamese vessels and 1500 marines begin naval operations, 35 miles southeast of Phnompenh, aimed at destroying Communist base areas and infiltration corridors between the Bassac and Mekong Rivers.

20 SEPTEMBER 1970

Ground War North Vietnamese gunners down a US helicopter attempting to land a reconnaissance team and then shell an armored relief force attempting to reach the scene one mile south of the DMZ. Eleven Americans are killed and 11 are wounded.

21 SEPTEMBER 1970
South Vietnam The revised 'hamlet evaluation system' used by US officials to measure progress in pacification programs indicates that as of 31 August, 92.8 percent of South Vietnam's population was under government control and only 184,700 people were under Vietcong control. The report says 996,600 people live in areas where neither the Vietcong nor the government has control.

26 SEPTEMBER 1970
South Vietnam Vice-President Ky says he had decided not to attend a pro-war rally scheduled for 3 October in Washington DC. Ky, who had previously announced he would attend the rally, had been scheduled to meet with Henry Kissinger in Paris in an attempt by the Nixon administration to dissuade Ky from attending the rally.
USA: Domestic A Gallup Poll shows 55 percent of the American people favor the recently-defeated McGovern-Hatfield amendment to pull all US troops out of South Vietnam by 31 December 1971.

27 SEPTEMBER 1970
Ground War Twelve US soldiers are killed and five are wounded in accidents involving helicopter collisions and the accidental triggering of mines.

28 SEPTEMBER 1970
Riverine War South Vietnamese military headquarters announces the end of combat operations along the Bassac and Mekong Rivers in Cambodia. The enemy report 233 killed.

3 OCTOBER 1970
USA: Domestic More than 20,000 people gather at the Washington Monument for a Vietnam war victory rally. South Vietnamese embassy aide, Tran Khoa Hoc, reads a speech which was to have been delivered by South Vietnamese Vice-President Ky, pleading for continued assistance by Americans and other peoples of the world to South Vietnam.

4 OCTOBER 1970
USA: Government President Nixon confers privately in Dublin, Ireland with the US negotiators to the Paris talks, David Bruce and Philip Habib. Following the meeting, Nixon says that European leaders on his recent tour showed a more sophisticated understanding of US aims in Vietnam than they did when he toured Europe early in 1969.
Guerrilla War As Communist forces shell 19 targets, 15 South Vietnamese are killed and seven are wounded in two terrorist incidents north of Saigon. South Vietnamese troops report killing 19 enemy soldiers in the Mekong Delta.

5 OCTOBER 1970
Guerrilla War As the surge in Communist bombardments and attacks continues, 20 civilians are killed and 40 are wounded in an attack on a refugee camp 280 miles northeast of Saigon.

6 OCTOBER 1970
Guerrilla War Intensified Communist shellings continue for a third consecutive day, most of them in the coastal provinces of the central and northern parts of South Vietnam. Seven refugees are killed and 52 are wounded in an attack on a resettlement center near Phumy on the central coast.
Ground War South Vietnamese military headquarters announces the end of a three-month operation in southeastern Cambodia and the withdrawal of the task force involved. During the operation 453 enemy soldiers are reported killed. South Vietnamese losses are 93 killed and 642 wounded. South Vietnamese troop strength in Cambodia is 12,000 men.

7 OCTOBER 1970
USA: Government In a televised speech, President Nixon asks North Vietnam and the Vietcong to agree to a 'ceasefire in place' throughout Indochina and agree to attend an Indochina peace conference to negotiate an end to the fighting. Nixon proposes the eventual withdrawal of all US forces on a timetable to be worked out in negotiations, the immediate and unconditional release of all prisoners-of-war and his willingness to accept a political solution reflecting the will of the South Vietnamese people and the existing relation of political forces in the South Vietnamese countryside. Nixon says the communist proposals for the ouster of Nguyen Van Thieu, Nguyen Cao Ky and Tran Thiem Khiem are 'totally unacceptable' and rejects them.

CHRONOLOGY

8 OCTOBER 1970
USA: Government The United States publicly urges the Soviet Union to use its 'considerable influence' with the Communists to persuade them to accept President Nixon's new proposals.
USA: Government The Senate adopts a resolution expressing support for President Nixon's initiative, calling the proposals 'fair and equitable.'
Negotiations The Communist delegations to the Paris talks denounce President Nixon's proposals as 'a maneuver to deceive world opinion,' and continue their demand for an unconditional and total US withdrawal from Indochina and the overthrow of the 'puppet' leaders in Saigon.

11 OCTOBER 1970
Ground War A US helicopter gunship accidentally fires 12 rockets at South Vietnamese soldiers in the Mekong Delta, 132 miles southwest of Saigon, killing eight and wounding 23.

12 OCTOBER 1970
USA: Government President Nixon announces the United States will withdraw 40,000 more troops from South Vietnam before Christmas.

13 OCTOBER 1970
USA: Government Sir Robert Thompson, a renowned counterinsurgency and guerrilla warfare expert, meets with President Nixon. Following a five-week secret mission to South Vietnam in September and October at the request of the President, Thompson reports that US and allied intelligence and police efforts have failed to destroy the Communist subversive apparatus in South Vietnam. Thompson's report concludes that success in other areas of pacification cannot solve the basic political problems of South Vietnam after the withdrawal of the bulk of US forces so long as the Vietcong apparatus remains virtually intact.
Ground War In two days of fighting in Quangngai province, 10 Americans are killed and 24 are wounded. Communist losses are put at 13 killed.

14 OCTOBER 1970
Negotiations North Vietnam releases a statement officially rejecting President Nixon's peace proposal of 7 October and calls on the United States to reply to the 'concrete proposals' advanced by the Provisional Revolutionary Government on 17 September.
Guerrilla War Nine US soldiers and 15 South Vietnamese soldiers are killed and five

Infantrymen use an air mattress as a raft while crossing a canal in the Mekong Delta.

Americans are wounded by a Vietcong booby trap, 66 miles southeast of Danang.

15 OCTOBER 1970
Negotiations The Communist delegations to the Paris talks declare that their rejections of the recent peace proposals by President Nixon is 'firm, total and categorical.' The Communists reject the proposal on troop withdrawals because they say Nixon refuses to set a date for the withdrawal of US forces and continues to insist on mutual withdrawal.

21 OCTOBER 1970
Ground War In combat centered around the district town of Thuongduc and a nearby US Special Forces camp, 26 miles south of Danang, the allied command reports killing 163 Vietcong and capturing 20 in two days of fighting. Many of the Communist soldiers are killed by bombers, helicopter gunships and artillery.

23 OCTOBER 1970
USA: Military The US command reports Americal Division troops have violated a Pentagon order by continuing to use a chemical defoliant banned since April. An investigation reveals that troops used the chemical to strip away enemy cover and destroy crops 'on several occasions'.

25 OCTOBER 1970
Ground War Fourteen Americans are reported killed in mine and booby trap explosions in Quangtin and Quangnam provinces. In other action, as part of a South Vietnamese offensive in Quangtin province, allied forces report killing 37 Communist soldiers without suffering any casualties.

28 OCTOBER 1970
Ground War Forty one Vietcong are reported killed in various actions. Four persons are killed and nine are wounded in Vietcong shellings of two Mekong Delta towns.

30 OCTOBER-1 NOVEMBER 1970
South Vietnam Fighting in the five northernmost provinces comes to a virtual halt as the worst monsoon rains in six years strikes the region. The resultant floods kill 293 people and leave more than 200,000 homeless.

31 OCTOBER 1970
South Vietnam President Thieu delivers a speech on the state of the nation before a joint session of the National Assembly. Thieu declares the Communists have no intention of negotiating a settlement unless they are assured the domination of South Vietnam. Thieu says the Communists view negotiations merely as a way to gain time and to 'achieve victory gradually.' Thieu, repeats, once again, that he will never accept a coalition government with the Communists, citing 'countless past experiences' which show that it would not bring peace. Contending that the Saigon government now controls 99.1 percent of the people of South Vietnam, Thieu says that a military victory is close at hand and that 'we are seeing the light at the end of the tunnel.'

2 NOVEMBER 1970
Terrorism In their first attack on the capital since 20 July, Communist forces fire four rockets into Saigon, killing seven civilians and wounding 25.

4 NOVEMBER 1970
USA: Military The South Vietnamese Air Force takes over a Mekong Delta air base from the United States as part of the Vietnamization program. Secretary of the Air Force Robert Seamans and General Abrams, the commander of all US forces in Vietnam, attend the ceremony. The air base will be the home of two South Vietnamese helicopter squadrons with the United States providing 62 aircraft, 31 of which are turned over today.

5 NOVEMBER 1970
Ground War Fighting resumes in the northern provinces as US troops report killing seven North Vietnamese in a battle of 17 miles southwest of Hué, while suffering three killed and three wounded. In another engagement, 17 miles southeast of Danang, US Marines report killing 20 North Vietnamese while losing one soldier killed.
Ground War Releasing the lowest weekly death toll in five years, the US command reports 24 Americans died in combat in Indochina the week of 25-31 October. This is the lowest weekly death toll since the week ending 25 October 1965. It is also the fifth consecutive week that the US death toll has been below 50. The high number of 431 Americans wounded for the same period reflects the low-level of fighting, in which most US casualties result from booby traps, sniper fire and mortar attacks, which more often wound than kill.

CHRONOLOGY

6 NOVEMBER 1970
Ground War South Vietnamese troops advance across a 100-mile wide front in southeastern Cambodia in a new offensive aimed at cleaning out new enemy border sanctuaries and blocking the movement of North Vietnamese forces into South Vietnam.

9 NOVEMBER 1970
USA: Government The Supreme Court refuses to hear a challenge by the state of Massachusetts regarding the constitutionality of the Vietnam war. By a 6-3 vote, the justices reject the effort of the state to bring suit in federal court in defense of Massachusetts citizens who claim protection under a state law which allows them to refuse military service in an undeclared war.

10-11 NOVEMBER 1970
Ground War For the first time in five years, here are no US combat fatalities in Indochina.

11 NOVEMBER 1970
Ground War The 6000-man South Vietnamese task force pulls out of Cambodia after failing to find new Communist troop sanctuaries. Forty-one enemy soldiers are reported killed in the operation.

13 NOVEMBER 1970
Air War An unarmed US reconnaissance plane is shot down over North Vietnam, 42 miles south of Vinh, and its two crewmen apparently killed. It is the 13th US plane shot down over North Vietnam since the 1 November 1968 bombing halt.
USA: Government Speaking at a news conference, Secretary of Defense Laird says the shooting down of a US plane is a violation of 'certain understandings' between the United States and North Vietnam and that the United States is 'ready to take appropriate action in response' to such attacks.

14 NOVEMBER 1970
North Vietnam North Vietnam denies once again that it had accepted any conditions in exchange for the bombing halt of North Vietnam. Nguyen Thanh Le, spokesman for the Hanoi delegation at the Paris talks, insists 'there is absolutely no tacit accord' between the United States and North Vietnam and, instead, refers to 'acts of provocation' by the Nixon administration designed as a pretext for the expansion of the war.

Ground War North Vietnamese troops attack two US units in the northern jungles killing four Americans and wounding 25. Other action reported raises US casualties in the northern sector to eight killed and 49 wounded in the last 24 hours.

15 NOVEMBER 1970
Guerrilla War Booby traps and land mines kill nine Americans and wound 10.

16 NOVEMBER 1970
Diplomatic South Vietnamese Vice-President Ky, speaking at the US Military Academy at West Point, says Cambodia would be overrun by Communist forces 'without 24 hours' if South Vietnamese troops, currently operating there, are withdrawn, Ky describes the Cambodian operation of last May as the 'turning point' of the war and says that as a result the enemy has been forced to revert to low-level guerrilla warfare. Ky reports that his government is concerned that the Nixon administration may yield to the 'pressure of the anti-war groups' and pull out the remaining US troops too quickly.

17 NOVEMBER 1970
War Crimes The US Army opens its case against Lieutenant William Calley, charging that Calley ordered a large group of civilians to be pushed into a ditch and killed in an apparently mindless slaughter. Chief Army prosecutor, Captain Aubrey Daniel, says Calley ordered Sergeant David Mitchell to 'finish off the rest' after returning to the scene that he had left briefly. The prosecution stresses that all the killings were committed despite the fact that Calley's platoon met no resistance and that he and his men were at no time fired upon.
Guerrilla War Communist forces shell the Bienhoa airbase killing three Americans and two South Vietnamese. Fourteen civilians are wounded.
Ground War Premier Thonom Kittikachorn says Thailand will withdraw all of its 12,000 troops from South Vietnam by 1972.

18 NOVEMBER 1970
USA: Government President Nixon asks Congress for supplemental funds for the Cambodian government of Premier Lon Nol. Nixon asks for $155 million in new funds – $85 million for military assistance, mainly in the form of ammunition – as well as $100 million to restore funds taken from other foreign

appropriations during the year by 'presidential determination' and given to Cambodia.

Ground War A US Marine helicopter, returning from a rescue mission, crashes into the Queson mountains, 22 miles southwest of Danang. Fifteen Marines are killed, including members of the patrol that were rescued.

19 NOVEMBER 1970

Terrorism Nine civilians are killed and 43 are wounded when a Vietcong grenade is thrown into an open-air movie at Congthanh, 20 miles northeast of Saigon.

20 NOVEMBER 1970

USA: Government Secretary of Defense Laird says that congressional refusal to provide increased air to Cambodia could slow down the withdrawal of US forces from Vietnam and argues that the aid is a 'good investment.'

War Crimes Sergeant David Mitchell is acquitted in Fort Hood, Texas of intent to murder 30 South Vietnamese civilians at Mylai in March 1968.

21 NOVEMBER 1970

Covert War A combined Air Force and Army team of 50 Americans – led by Colonel 'Bull' Simon – in 10 large helicopters lands at the Sontay prison camp, 23 miles west of Hanoi, in an attempt to free 70-100 Americans suspected of being held there. US warplanes provide escort and attack North Vietnamese troop installations and anti-aircraft sites within two miles of the camp. The force finds no US prisoners, but reports killing 25 guards in 40 minutes at the camp. All Americans return safely.

Air War Approximately one hour after the Sontay raid, US warplanes carry out their heaviest and most sustained bombing of North Vietnam since 1 November 1968. About 200 fighter-bombers and 50 support planes take part in the raids against a wide variety of military targets.

The grenade booby-trap used by the Civilian Irregular Defense guard with devastating results.

CHRONOLOGY

North Vietnam Hanoi Radio reports 'wave after wave' of US bombers attack targets in North Vietnam and say the planes strike at targets ranging from Haiphong to Hoabinh province, southeast of Hanoi.

USA: Government Secretary of Defense Laird issues a statement confirming reports of US bombing raids against North Vietnam. Laird, however, contends that all of the air strikes took place below the 19th parallel in North Vietnam and says they are in response to continued attacks on US reconnaissance planes.

22 NOVEMBER 1970

Guerrilla War A Vietcong prison camp in the Mekong Delta is attacked by a joint raiding party composed of 15 US Navy men and 19 South Vietnamese. The operation results in the freeing of 19 South Vietnamese prisoners. No allied casualties are reported.

Ground War North Vietnamese forces attack the headquarters of a South Vietnamese task force operating just inside the Cambodian border near Krek. South Vietnamese losses are 10 killed and 20 wounded. The Communists report 48 killed.

23 NOVEMBER 1970

USA: Government Secretary of Defense Laird discloses the 21 November US raid on the North Vietnamese prison camp at Sontay and says that it was the only operation that took place north of the 19th parallel.

Negotiations The Communist delegations to the Paris talks say they will not attend the next session of the talks to protest the recent US bombing raids against North Vietnam. Xuan Thuy says that as an excuse for 'acts of war', the United States has 'invented the so-called understanding' permitting reconnaissance missons over North Vietnam.

24 NOVEMBER 1970

USA: Government Secretary of Defense Laird, in testimony before the Senate Foreign Relations Committee, says he will recommend to President Nixon the resumption of full-scale air attacks on North Vietnam if it engages in major violations of the tacit understanding with the United States regarding the bombing halt of North Vietnam. Laird notes these violations include the firing at unarmed US reconnaissance planes, the shelling of major South Vietnamese population centers and troop movements through the DMZ.

Ground War A helicopter carrying South Vietnamese soldiers collides with an US light plane in the Mekong Delta. Thirteen South Vietnamese and four Americans are killed.

26 NOVEMBER 1970

North Vietnam Nguyen Thanh Le, spokesman for the North Vietnamese delegation to the Paris talks, claims 49 civilians were killed and 40 were wounded in the recent US bombing raids. Of this total, 28 are reported to have died in the bombing of a restaurant in Hatinh, just below the 19th parallel.

27 NOVEMBER 1970

South Vietnam A US Air Force C-123 transport plane is reported missing with six Americans and 73 South Vietnamese aboard. On 7 December the wreckage of the plane is found in the Central Highlands. There are no survivors.

USA: Government Daniel Henkin, an assistant secretary of defense for public affairs, acknowledges US aircraft recently struck military targets near Hanoi during the attempted prisoner-of-war rescue mission at Sontay.

Ground War A South Vietnamese task force, operating in southeastern Cambodia, comes under North Vietnamese attack near the town of Krek. The South Vietnamese command reports repelling the assault and killing 48 enemy soldiers. The South Vietnamese command also reports killing 33 Vietcong in the Rungsat special zone, 23 miles southeast of Saigon.

29 NOVEMBER 1970

South Vietnam US Air Force C-123 transport plane en route to the United States, carrying 32 Americans and 12 South Vietnamese, crashes into a mountain near Camranh Bay. The US command reports 5 December that the only survivors are two US Air Force sergeants who are rescued by helicopter.

Air War The US command announces that a US fighter-bomber has attacked a North Vietnamese anti-aircraft position, five and one-half miles north of the DMZ, near the Laotian border. The raid is termed another 'protective reaction' attack.

30 NOVEMBER 1970

Ground War The Vietcong's Provisional Revolutionary Government announces that its forces in South Vietnam will observe three truces during Christmas, from midnight 24 December to midnight 27 December; for New

A UH-1D helicopter carrying supplies drops into a carefully cleared landing zone.

Year, from midnight 31 December to 3 January 1971; and, for Tet, from midnight 26 January 1971 to midnight 30 January 1971.
Ground War The allied commands announce an increase in battlefield activity throughout South Vietnam. Five Vietcong guerrillas are reported killed in a battle 100 miles southeast of Saigon and five more are reported killed 31 miles northeast of the capital. Near the city of Dalat, in the Central Highlands, the South Vietnamese report killing enemy soldiers in several clashes. Seven South Vietnamese are killed and 22 are wounded.

1 DECEMBER 1970
Ground War A 7000-man South Vietnamese force launches a major drive against a suspected Communist force of 3000 in the U Minh Forest in the southern part of the Mekong Delta.

2 DECEMBER 1970
Guerrilla War Communist forces shell 22 targets with rocket barrages against towns and military bases throughout South Viet-

nam. Nearly 100 attacks have been reported in the last four days.

4 DECEMBER 1970
Ground War South Vietnamese forces push deeper into the U Minh Forest and report killing 59 Vietcong in the first three days of the operation. South Vietnamese troops report killing 35 Vietcong in three small engagements.

5 DECEMBER 1970
North Vietnam A North Vietnamese army newspaper, replying to warnings by US Secretary of Defense Laird regarding the bombing of North Vietnam, says US reconnaissance planes will be downed, anti-aircraft installations will be set up anywhere and troops will be massed in any sector.

8 DECEMBER 1970
Ground War South Vietnamese troops continue their drive in the U Minh Forest and report killing 144 Vietcong in the first eight days of the operation. Eight South Vietnamese have been killed and 71 wounded.

CHRONOLOGY

9 DECEMBER 1970
South Vietnam The South Vietnamese government announces it will only observe one-day truces for Christmas and New Year's.

Ground War A force of 200 North Vietnamese, using mortars and rockets, attack a South Vietnamese force in the Fishhook area just inside Cambodia. Thirty South Vietnamese are killed and 41 are wounded. The Communist report 48 killed.

10 DECEMBER 1970
North Vietnam The North Vietnamese government and the Communist Party issue an extraordinary appeal to the North Vietnamese people and army for redoubled efforts to win the war. The North Vietnamese high command calls for the armed forces to heighten their preparedness and determination 'to fight victoriously.'

USA: Government President Nixon, holding his first news conference in four months, warns that if North Vietnam increases 'the level of fighting in South Vietnam...I will order the bombing of military sites in North Vietnam... That is the reaction that I shall take.' Nixon defends his request for an additional $250 million in foreign assistance, mostly military aid, for Cambodia as 'probably the best investment in foreign assistance that the United States has made in my lifetime.' Nixon notes that if the army of Premier Lon Nol was not fighting 40,000 North Vietnamese soldiers inside Cambodia, 'they'd be over killing Americans' in South Vietnam.

War Crimes The defense opens its case in the murder trial of Lieutenant William Calley. The defense contends that Calley had orders to 'kill every living thing' in Mylai. Defense Attorney George Latimer, cites 'superior orders' as one of several reasons why noncombants were killed. Other reasons include the poor training of the platoon, the rage of the men who had seen buddies killed and the expectation of fierce resistance. Latimer contends that Captain Ernest Medina, company commander, told the men that at long last they were going to fight the enemy and ordered 'every living thing' killed. Latimer also charges that the whole episode was observed by higher commanders, both on the ground and in the air, including Lieutenant Colonel Frank Barker, task force commander and General Samuel W Koster, commanding officer of the Americal Division.

14 DECEMBER 1970
Ground War Six of eight Americans in an infantry patrol are killed when they inadvertantly enter an old US mine field south of the DMZ.

17 DECEMBER 1970
War Crimes The trial of Lieutenant William Calley adjourns until 11 January 1971.

19 DECEMBER 1970
Ground War US troops report killing 10 enemy soldiers south of the DMZ. South Vietnamese forces report killing 26 Communist soldiers in the U Minh Forest and 39 Communist soldiers in two other engagements.

20 DECEMBER 1970
Ground War Communist forces, observing the 10th anniversary of the National Liberation Front, bombard four allied positions, down four US planes and ambush a US convoy. Five Americans are killed and six are wounded. The allied command reports killing 99 Communist soldiers in weekend actions ranging from the DMZ to the U Minh Forest.

22 DECEMBER 1970
North Vietnam Defense Minister Vo Nguyen Giap affirms that US unarmed reconnaissance flights over North Vietnam will be downed and says that the United States has no right to make such flights.

23 DECEMBER 1970
USA: Government Secretary of State Rogers acknowledges that President Nixon goes beyond the 1968 understanding in threatening to renew the bombing of North Vietnam if it steps up the level of fighting in South Vietnam. Rogers, however, contends that this is because the situation has been changed by US troops withdrawals.

24 DECEMBER 1970
Ground War Two hours before the start of the allied Christmas ceasefire, US artillery fires an 105-millimeter shell into a group of soldiers of the 1st Brigade, 101st Airborne Division killing nine American soldiers and wounding nine others. The accident takes place 11 miles south of Hué.

26-27 DECEMBER 1970
Ground War South Vietnamese troops report killing 38 more enemy soldiers in the U Minh Forest in the Mekong Delta.

Refugees find themselves in the middle of a firefight between US infantry and the Vietcong.

27 DECEMBER 1970

North Vietnam The Communist Party newspaper, *Nhan Dan*, commenting on US Secretary of State Rogers' news conference, says President Nixon will 'invite upon himself heavier setbacks' unless he learns from President Johnson's 'failure.' The newspaper says Nixon's proposal for a standstill ceasefire is not the 'key' to a settlement.

30 DECEMBER 1970

USA: Military In a ceremony in which the South Vietnamese Navy receives 125 US vessels, the US Navy ends its four-year role in inland waterway combat. This brings the total number of vessels turned over to South Vietnam to 650. About 17,000 Americans will remain with the South Vietnamese navy in shore positions and as advisers aboard South Vietnamese vessels.

31 DECEMBER 1970

State of the War The war in Vietnam is winding down, at least for US military forces there, as President Nixon withdraws troops; by year's end, they are down to about 280,000. As both sides avoid large-unit confrontations, US casualties are increasingly due to booby-traps, mortar attacks, and sniper fire; in this sense, the war is reverting to its earlier phase. The number of US military personnel killed in the fighting in 1970 is 4204; South Vietnamese military forces report 20,914 dead. At least 25,000 South Vietnamese civilians are killed, and another 6000 are reported by the Vietcong as having been executed for serving in the Saigon government. The invasion of Cambodia, and the turmoil it causes within the United States, serves to underline just how widespread and interrelated are the ongoing hostilities throughout Indochina. The total number of Americans killed in all combat in Indochina since 1961 is now some 44,200. In Paris, the peace talks are still stalemated, as all parties make demands that the others will not accept.

1 JANUARY 1971

USA: Government Congress forbids the use of US ground troops in Laos and Cambodia, but not the use of US air power in those countries.

2-25 JANUARY 1971

Cambodia In an attempt to lift the Communist blockade of the strategic Route 4 between Pnompenh and Kompong Som, the

CHRONOLOGY

nation's sole port facility, Cambodian and South Vietnamese forces continue a drive to clear the 115-mile road. In effect since 20 November 1970, the blockade has resulted in increasingly serious fuel shortages in Pnompenh, forcing the South Vietnamese to give armed escort to trucks and tanker ships carrying fuel to the Cambodian capital. On 5 and 6 January, Vietcong and North Vietnamese forces fire on several tankers and their armed escort as they travel along the Mekong River northwest toward Pnompenh. By mid-January some 6000 South Vietnamese and 8000 Cambodians are fighting three North Vietnamese battalions and a battalion of Khmer Rouge. On 22 January, the Saigon and Cambodian contingent report seizing control of Route 4 near the Pich Nil pass. The US aids the allied effort by placing two helicopter carrier warships off the Cambodian coast to provide support to the operation. On 25 January, Saigon reports the withdrawal of 5300 troops from Cambodia. Reportedly some 1800 Communist soldiers remain in the area, and the road itself is impassable because of numerous bomb craters and damaged bridges.

3 JANUARY 1971
Ground War At 0100 the Vietcong's 3-day New Year's truce ends. During the ceasefire, fighting continued intermittently, reaching a climax on 2 January as South Vietnamese troops entered the southern DMZ in pursuit of North Vietnamese forces who had attacked an ARVN patrol deployed just south of the DMZ. After a 10-hour battle, the South Vietnamese withdraw from the DMZ.

3 JANUARY 1971
Air War South Vietnam, Laos and Cambodia are the sites of intensive bombing raids by a large force of US B-52 bombers and some 300 fighter bombers against Communist supply and infiltration routes, and supporting Laotian and Cambodian troops along the Ho Chi Minh Trail. On 8 January US jets hit two North Vietnamese missile bases north of the DMZ in 'protective reaction' strikes. Other attacks on missile bases follow on 15-17 January by US jets escorting B-52s on bombing raids along the Laotian border. On 20 January a Hanoi communiqué accuses the United States of almost daily bombing raids, as well as defoliation missions, from 4-17 January inside North Vietnam. The US Defense Department at once denies the charges,

citing solely the use of 'protective reaction' strikes.

6 JANUARY 1971
USA: Military Following the orders of General Creighton Abrams, commander of US forces in Vietnam, the US Saigon command announces a program to combat widespread drug use by US soldiers. This action is taken after a Defense Department report cites narcotics use as a cause of breakdown in military discipline and leadership. The anti-drug program provides for amnesty and rehabilitation.

6 JANUARY-17 DECEMBER 1971
War Crimes The US Army Mylai massacre trials continue. On 6 January the Army drops charges of an alleged coverup against four officers, bringing to 11 the number cleared. Charges are pending only against three men, all officers – Lieutenant William Calley, Jr, Captain Ernest Medina and Captain Eugene Kotouc. On 29 March the Fort Benning court martial jury finds Calley guilty of the premeditated murder of at least 22 South Vietnamese civilians. Calley is seen by many as a scapegoat and the widespread public outcry against the sentence of life imprisonment moves President Nixon to intervene on 3 April. He has Calley removed from the Fort Benning stockade and vows to personally review the case. On 20 August, Calley's life term is reduced to 20 years. Captain Kotouc is cleared by a court martial on 29 April, and Medina is acquitted on 22 September. On 19 May, the Army disciplines two generals for failing to conduct an adequate investigation of Mylai, demoting Major General Samuel W Koster from two-star to one-star rank. At the same time, both Koster and Brigadier General George H Young, Jr, his assistant divisional commander at the time of the massacre, are stripped of their distinguished service medals, and letters of censure are placed in their files. The trials end with the 17 December acquittal of Colonel Oran K Henderson of coverup charges. He is the highest ranking officer to be tried. Of all those originally charged, only Calley is convicted.

7-11 JANUARY 1971
USA: Military Accompanied by chairman of the US Joint Chiefs of Staff Admiral Thomas H Moorer, Defense Secretary Melvin Laird visits Thailand and South Vietnam to assess the military situation. Laird announces the

end of US 'combat responsibility' by mid-summer, but later warns President Nixon and his cabinet of 'some tough days ahead.' Admiral Moorer, who makes a side trip to Pnompenh, sees the Cambodian situation as 'deteriorating.'

8 JANUARY 1971

USA: Military Opposing a scientific study made under Dr. Matthew Meselson, professor of biology at Harvard University, the Department of Defense denies that the US defoliation program has destroyed completely nearly 250,000 acres of mangrove forest in South Vietnam and defends the program by citing the advantages of cleared land for small Vietnamese farmers and for the lumber industry.

12 JANUARY 1971

USA: Domestic The Reverend Philip F Berrigan, serving a 6-year prison term on charges of destroying draft records, and five others are indicted by a grand jury on charges of conspiring to kidnap presidential adviser Henry Kissinger and of plotting to blow up the heating tunnels of federal buildings in Washington. The 'Harrisburg Six' deny the charges, denouncing them as a government effort to destroy the peace movement.

War Crimes In a Washington news conference, representatives of the antiwar Concerned Officers Movement, four Army officers and a Navy officer, formally request a military court of inquiry to investigate reported war crimes by US soldiers in Vietnam, citing 300 pages of testimony by Vietnam veterans given in December 1970 and holding as precedent the Nuremberg and Japanese war crimes trials.

17 JANUARY 1971

Cambodia Led by South Vietnamese Lieutenant General Do Cao Tri, and with US air support and advisers, some 300 paratroopers raid a communist POW camp near the town of Mimot on information that 20 US prisoners are held there. They find the camp empty, but take 30 enemy soldiers with no casualties.

18 JANUARY 1971

USA: Domestic In a television speech, Senator George S McGovern (D-SD) begins his antiwar campaign for the 1972 Democratic presidential nomination by vowing to bring home all US soldiers from Vietnam.

21 JANUARY 1971

USA: Government Amid reports of US air and ground presence in the Cambodian fighting, 64 Democratic congressmen present legislation to deny money to 'provide United States air or sea combat support for any military operations in Cambodia.' The Democrats also introduce a resolution to end at once 'all offensive actions by the United States in Southeast Asia' and to remove all US troops by June.

Negotiations For the third straight session the Paris peace talks stalemate continues. The session on 21 January marks the 100th meeting since the talks began on 25 January 1969.

22-24 JANUARY 1971

Cambodia Communist commandos shell central Pnompenh for the first time, at the same time penetrating the nation's major airport and destroying much of its military fleet. US air operations are greatly stepped up and later in the week, after fresh Communist terrorist attacks on the capital, Cambodian forces clash with the Communist forces in several battles near Pnompenh.

26-30 JANUARY 1971

Ground War The two sides declare separate truces in observance of Tet the Vietnamese lunar new year. Despite at least 53 reported violations during the truce (26-27 January), the allied commands term it the quietest in recent years. The Communists interrupt their own ceasefire (26-30 January) with a grenade explosion in a Binhdinh Province theater that kills 10 South Vietnamese, and a market-place bomb blast that kills nine others.

30 JANUARY-7 FEBRUARY 1971

Ground War The South Vietnamese ground offensive Operation Dewey Canyon II begins as the vanguard of the US 1st Brigade, 5th Infantry Division begins movement with an armored cavalry/engineer task force from Vandegrift toward Khesanh. Some 9000 GIs support the move of 20,000 South Vietnamese troops to reoccupy 1000 square miles of territory in northwest South Vietnam and to mass at the Laotian border in preparation for Operation Lam Son 719. US ground forces are not to enter Laos in accordance with a US congressional ban. Instead they give logistical support, with some 2600 helicopters on call to airlift Saigon troops and supplies, in addition to artillery fire into Laos from the border.

CHRONOLOGY

3-4 FEBRUARY 1971
Cambodia In what is proclaimed a new campaign to eradicate Communist border sanctuaries, a force of 2500 ARVN troops cross the frontier into Kompong Cham Province, already occupied by some 7500 ARVN troops. The drive is assisted by US air support and 7500 Cambodian troops. An engagement with the Communists on 4 February nets 69 enemy dead, with South Vietnamese losses reported at seven. The 9th North Vietnamese Division headquarters at Chup is the primary objective of a 1000-man Cambodian force. In related developments, the first gasoline convoy in over two months reaches Pnompenh from Kompong Som.

8 FEBRUARY-6 APRIL 1971
Ground War South Vietnamese troops, supported by heavy US airpower and artillery fire, cross into Laos for an extensive assault known as Operation Lam Son 719 on the Ho Chi Minh Trail. The drive on Hanoi's supply routes and depots is described as the 'bloodiest fighting' of the Indochina war by observers. Enemy resistance is light at first as a 12,000-man spearhead of the South Vietnamese army thrusts its way across the border into the Communists' deepest jungle stronghold, with the town of Tchepone, a major enemy supply center on Route 9, as their big target. But resistance stiffens in the second week. During the last week of February, the big push bogs down some 16 miles from the border, after bloody fighting in which the Communist troops overrun two ARVN battalions.

8 FEBRUARY 1971
Cambodia Premier Lon Nol suffers a paralyzing stroke, and turns his duties over to Deputy Premier Sisowath Sirik Matak. Still debilitated by the stroke, he resigns on 20 April. A week later he withdraws his resignation, staying on in a figurehead role as General Sirik Matak continues to run the government pending his recovery.

10 FEBRUARY 1971
Ground War Four US news reporters – Larry Burrows of *Life* magazine, Kent Potter of UPI, Henri Huett of the AP and Keisaburo Shimamoto of *Newsweek* – die as a Vietnamese helicopter crashes in Laos.

12 & 23 FEBRUARY 1971
Cambodia Two key generals in the Cambo-

dian offensive die – Cambodian Brigadier General Neak Sam fighting Communists on 12 February; and the commander of South Vietnamese forces in Cambodia, Lieutenant General Do Cao Tri in a helicopter crash on 23 February (along with François Sully, a *Newsweek* correspondent). Tri's death stalls the offensive for several weeks, as his replacement, General Nguyen Van Minh reformulates military strategy for the operation.

17 FEBRUARY 1971
USA: Government In his first major news conference since the beginning of the Laotian offensive, President Nixon refuses to set limits on the use of US airpower, barring only the use of tactical nuclear weapons. He also insists that Americans will remain in South Vietnam as long as US POWs are in the hands of the North Vietnamese. On 19-21 February, in a Gallup Poll taken following the Laotian offensive, President Nixon's approval rating falls to the lowest point thus far in his term of office.

20 FEBRUARY 1971
South Vietnam According to the US embassy in Saigon, the United States will give $400,000 to construct 288 isolation cells in the South Vietnamese political prison on Con Son island. These cells will replace the inhumane tiger-cage cells and will henceforth house only common criminals.

20-23 FEBRUARY 1971
Air War In renewed 'protective reaction' strikes, US jets bomb North Vietnamese anti-aircraft artillery and missile sites near the Laotian border. This action is taken after, according to the US command, SAM (Soviet-built surface-to-air missile) firings are directed at US aircraft bombing Ho Chi Minh Trial supply lines.

22 FEBRUARY 1971
USA: Domestic In a different antiwar strategy on campuses, former Senator Eugene McCarthy introduces an antiwar teach-in at Harvard University, in which concerned students are uged to employ political tactics instead of violence. On the same day at Yale University, former US Paris peace talk delegation head W Averell Harriman leads another teach-in.

25 FEBRUARY 1971
USA: Government In both houses of con-

South Vietnamese troops captured quantities of weapons during operation Lam Son 719 in Laos.

gress, legislation is initiated to forbid US military support of any South Vietnamese invasion of North Vietnam without congressional approval. Foreign Relations Committee chairman Senator J William Fulbright (D-AR) declares the Laotian invasion illegal under the terms of the repeal of the Gulf of Tonkin Resolution which allows the president only the mandate to end the war. On the same day, in his State of the World address, Nixon emphasizes the 'grave risk' of US under-involvement if the burden of the war is shifted too swiftly to the South Vietnamese.

1 MARCH 1971

USA: Domestic A bomb explodes in the Capitol building in Washington, DC, causing an estimated $300,000 in damage, but hurting no one. A group calling itself the Weather Underground claims credit for the bombing, which protests the US-supported Laos invasion.

Operation Phoenix According to a newly instituted pacification program endorsed by the US and South Vietnamese comands, the intelligence-gathering mission known as Operation Phoenix is a part, is to be expanded to include the killing or jailing of 14,400 Vietcong agents in an attempt to destroy the Vietcong political organization within South Vietnam. The Saigon government program, of which Operation Phoenix calls for an augmentation of the People's Self Defense Force from 500,000 to four million rural civilians, including women in combat roles and children over seven in support units. In addition, a huge 'people's intelligence network' is to be organized in order to gather covert information about Communist activity. This pacification program attempts to address the continuing problem of persistent Vietcong influence.

2 MARCH 1971

Cambodia Vietcong and North Vietnamese shelling of Kompong Som's oil refinery destroys 80 percent of the nation's main fuel storage facility.

5-8 MARCH 1971

China Premier Chou En-lai visits Hanoi and, in a 10 March joint communiqué with North Vietnamese Premier Pham Van Dong, vows all-out Chinese support for the North Vietnamese struggle against the United States.

6 MARCH 1971

Operation Lam Son 719 Reinforced South Vietnamese troops push into Tchepone, the main North Vietnamese supply depot on the

CHRONOLOGY

Ho Chi Minh Trail. They find the base deserted and almost completely destroyed as a result of American bombing raids. Fighting near the Vietnam border intensifies and in the second week of March, Saigon troops abandon four fire bases in Laos and more than 6000 of some 21,000 ARVN soldiers are withdrawn as casualties soar on both sides. Allied officials declare that the offensive is still going according to plan. Fierce Communist counterattacks are seen as the reason for the allied pull back. On 15 March, the operation's rear support base at Khesanh comes under relentless Communist mortar and rocket fire.

10 MARCH 1971
Negotiations A group of 171 US pacifists meet in Paris with all delegations to the peace talks to determine the 'requisites for peace.'
Australia John Gorton is ousted as the nation's prime minister, following a crisis in which Defense Minister Malcolm Fraser resigns, and after a dispute with the army over Vietnam policy.

17 MARCH 1971
New Zealand Partial withdrawals are set for the nation's Vietnam combat force of 264 men. A 23 April meeting of allied ministers reaches an agreement that New Zealand, Australia, South Korea, and the United States will keep support forces in South Vietnam as their combat troops are withdrawn.

20 MARCH 1971
Ground War In Operation Lam Son 719, near the Laotian border, 53 men of the First Cavalry, Americal Division, disobey orders and refuse to retrieve a disabled helicopter and an armored vehicle from a battle zone. The soldiers are reassigned, with no disciplinary action taken, and their commanding officer is relieved of his position. Another armored unit rescues the equipment the next day.

21-22 MARCH 1971
Air War North of the DMZ, US jets attack North Vietnamese missile emplacements, destroying three. In a related incident, the first North Vietnamese missile in two years brings down a US Air Force F-4 plane 35 miles inside North Vietnam. The two crewmen are rescued on 23 March.

22 MARCH 1971
Ground War In Operation Lam Son 719 after

an intensive two-day shelling of the Laotian capital's airport, some 3000 North Vietnamese and Pathet Lao troops attack government positions near Luang Prabang. On 24 March, three Laotian battalions push back the Communists.

24 MARCH 1971
Ground War Operation Lam Son 719, the South Vietnamese invasion of Laos, ends as the last ARVN units pull out under heavy communist assaults. (The operation officially ends on 6 April.) The 45-day toll is high for both sides. In revised casualty figures, Saigon lists 1160 killed, 4271 wounded and 240 missing. An AP dispatch, citing privileged information, reports casualty figures of nearly 50 percent – 3800 dead, 5200 wounded and 775 missing. According to the South Vietnamese report the US losses include 450 dead, 104 helicopters downed, 608 damaged and five planes destroyed. Saigon claims 13,688 Hanoi troops dead, 167 taken prisoner, along with 6657 weapons captured, 120 tanks and 297 trucks destroyed, and tons of ammunition, weapons and food taken. Unreported masses of South Vietnamese equipment, including tanks, artillery and helicopters were also lost. The North Vietnamese claim a 'complete victory,' as does South Vietnamese Premier Nguyen Van Thieu on 31 March. Traffic on the Ho Chi Minh Trail is soon back to its previous levels, and only the annual monsoons slow it down.

25 MARCH 1971
Air War Citing the violation of the DMZ's neutrality by the massing of North Vietnamese antiaircraft and artillery in the buffer zone, the US State Department warns of retaliatory air strikes. DMZ raids by US planes occur on 30 March.
Negotiations Hanoi and Vietcong chief delegates to the Paris peace talks boycott the March sessions to protest US bombing and what they say are US 'threats of war.'

28-31 MARCH 1971
Ground War The South Vietnamese northern district capital of Ducduc is laid waste by two North Vietnamese regiments. Reportedly, some 100 civilians are left dead, 150 wounded, and 800 houses are burned. On 28 March, in a one-hour battle, communist forces partly overrun a US artillery base in northern Quangtin Province, leaving 33 Americans dead and 76 wounded. They are driven off by

artillery and air strikes, leaving behind 12 dead.

29-30 MARCH 1971
Cambodia The Communists again seize control of a 10-mile stretch of Route 4 near Pnompenh, as North Vietnamese and Vietcong troops push back a Cambodian convoy of several battalions. The fight for the strategic road continues through April.

31 MARCH-1 APRIL 1971
Ground War With US air support, South Vietnamese commandos raid North Vietnamese positions inside Laos as part of Operation Lam Son 719. On 6 April, some 200 South Vietnamese commandos carry out a 10-hour raid in the same area, destroying fuel supplies, weapons, food supplies and storage huts.

31 MARCH-12 APRIL 1971
Ground War A battle rages around Fire Base 6, the Saigon stronghold in the Central Highlands, as Communist troops wage a continuous assault against the garrison of 5000-6000 men, and US bombers pound the heavy Hanoi troop concentrations around the base, dropping explosives and napalm. In an effort to break the siege, on 12 April US C-130 cargo transports begin dropping 7.5 ton bombs.

1 APRIL 1971
USA: Government War critics in congress are denounced as Senate Republican leader Hugh Scott (R-PA) charges some Democrats with 'giving comfort to the enemy.' In a similar vein, Vice President Spiro Agnew calls the war critics 'home-front snipers.' Agnew insists the majority of citizens fell the US soldiers in Vietnam have acted patriotically, but that the antiwar activists have garnered all the publicity, and thus have made veterans feel guilty for having fought for an immoral cause.

14 APRIL 1971
Ground War In a followup to Operation Lam Son 719, some 5000 South Vietnamese begin a push in the Communist-held Ashau Valley along the Laotian border, but make no major contact along the communist infiltration route. Some 400 US troops also participate. On 21 April US helicopters airlift 1500 South Vietnamese marines north of the valley, followed two days later by 525 more troops.

Saigon newspapers term the Ashau operation only a 'training exercise' for the replacements for those troops lost in Lam Son 719. Brigadier General Vu Van Giai, commander of Lam Son 720, announces the operation will extend until October.

16 APRIL 1971
Ground War In effect since 31 March, the siege of Fire Base 6 is announced broken by the South Vietnamese command after 400 Saigon reinforcements are airlifted in, although the 6000 to 10,000 North Vietnamese surrounding the base do not yet allow reinforcements to arrive by foot. On 14 April, four of the five US advisers were airlifted out of Fire Base 6. During the week that follows, a Saigon counteroffensive begins on the surrounding North Vietnamese.

18 APRIL 1971
South Vietnam Vice President Nguyen Cao Ky says that the recently concluded Operation Lam Son 719 was no victory. He also reports that Vietnamization is going very slowly; and he denounces US Democratic presidential aspirant George McGovern for his stated interest in investigating charges that Ky allegedly is implicated in opium smuggling.

18-23 APRIL 1971
Air War US jets carry out the 30th raid since 1 January against missile sites and antiaircraft positions inside North Vietnam in the heaviest six-day period of raids to date since the November 1968 bombing halt. In one of the deepest penetrations of North Vietnam since November 1970, two sites 125 miles south of Hanoi are hit.

19-26 APRIL 1971
USA: Domestic As a prelude to a massive antiwar protest, Vietnam Veterans Against the War begin a five-day demonstration in Washington, DC. The generally peaceful protest, called Dewey Canyon 3 after the February-March Laos drive, ends 23 April with some 1000 veterans throwing their combat ribbons, helmets, uniforms and toy weapons at the Capitol steps. Earlier they had lobbied with their congressmen, laid wreaths in Arlington National Cemetary and staged a mock 'search and destroy' mission. On 24 April a massive rally of some 200,000 takes place on the Mall. A simultaneous protest by 156,000 in San Francisco, described as the

The Ho Chi Minh Trail in Laos was an intricate system of roads, paths and trails.

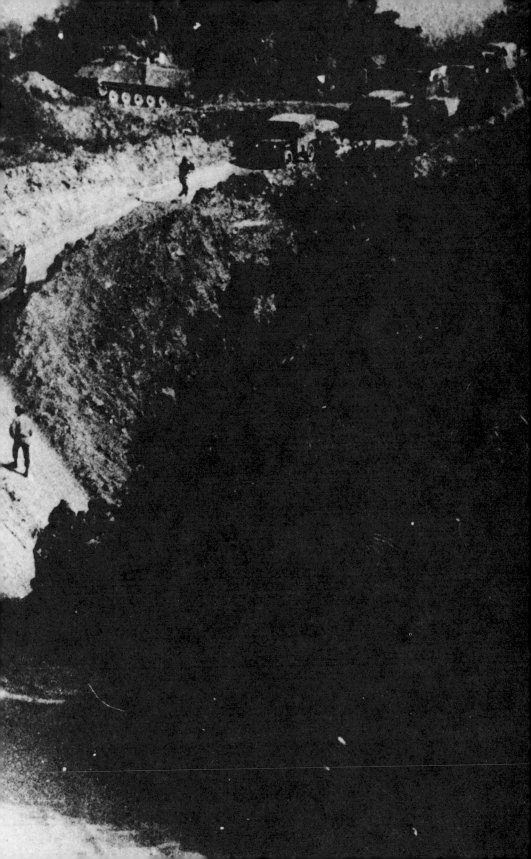

CHRONOLOGY

largest such rally to date on the West Coast, is disrupted by radical groups and militant Mexican-Americans who charge the peace movement is 'a conspiracy to quench the revolution.' Washington's week of orderly demonstrations ends on 26 April as militant leaders take over and the tactics are changed to aggressive 'people's lobbying,' with the avowed purpose of 'shutting down the government.' But some 5000 Washington police, backed by 12,000 troops, out-maneuver them.

20 APRIL 1971
USA: Military The Pentagon releases figures confirming that fragging incidents – named after the fragmentation grenades used by soldiers against their officers – are on the rise. In 1970, 209 such incidents caused the deaths of 34 men, as compared to 1969 when 96 such incidents cost 34 men their lives.

22-28 APRIL 1971
USA: Military Veterans Against the War testimony before various congressional panels reveals that G Company in the 7th Battalion of the 9th Marine Regiment partici-pated in Operation Lam Son 719 inside Laos, contrary to congressional ban, for a two-week period in February; that officially reported US battle death tolls are lower than actual casualties; and that US soldiers have partici-pated in various specific war crimes against the enemy as well as against South Vietnam-ese civilians.

24-27 APRIl 1971
Ground War Hostilities resume as North Vietnamese troops hit allied installations throughout South Vietnam. In the most devastating attack, the ammunition depot at Quinhon is blown up. On the 27th, the avia-tion fuel tanks at Danang air base are ex-ploded by communist fire. In the three-day period, 54 South Vietnamese soldiers and civilians are reported killed, with 185 wounded. The United States lists seven dead and 60 wounded.

26 APRIL 1971
USA: Military The US command in Saigon announces that the US force in Vietnam is the lowest since July 1966, having dropped to 281,400 men.

29 APRIL 1971
USA: Military US casualty figures for 18-24 April are released. The 45 dead bring total US losses for the Vietnam War since 1961 to 45,019, making Indochina losses fourth only to US losses in the Civil War, World War II and World War I. And on 17 May the Defense Department issues figures showing a drop in the combat death rate for black soldiers in 1970 from the previous years. This serves to allay somewhat the controversy over whether disadvantaged social groups have been bear-ing an unfairly heavy combat burden.

3-5 MAY 1971
USA: Domestic The militant antiwar demon-strations in Washington end as police arrest 12,614 protestors – a record high for arrests in a civil disturbance in the nation's history. With inadequate detention facilities, most of those arrested are held 24 hours and the charges against them are subsequently dropped.

8 MAY 1971
USA: Domestic In Washington, DC, the Reverend Carl McIntire leads some 15,000 demonstrators carrying US flags and Bibles in support of a military victory in Vietnam. Members of the Veterans of Foreign Wars and of New York Ironworkers Local 361 (the 'hardhat movement') also participate.

8-10 MAY 1971
Ground War During the truces marking Buddha's birth, allied forces accuse the North Vietnamese of 66 violations of the ceasefire, including a mine explosion of a Quangtri Province ferryboat, killing 36 South Viet-namese civilians.

10-18 MAY 1971
Air War US jets hit North Vietnamese anti-aircraft sites, reportedly destroying 13 em-placements around the Mugia Pass, 75 miles north of the DMZ.

11-15 MAY 1971
Cambodia South Vietnamese troops conduct two drives. On the 11th, some 5000 with US air support sweep from Kandol Chrum south to Kandol Trach in an attempt to clear out communist headquarters and training sites used for attacks inside South Vietnam west of Saigon. On 15 May, over 1000 South Viet-namese troops, with the aid of 320 US heli-copter gunship missions and 32 bombing raids, sweep the Parrot's Beak area of south-eastern Cambodia.

12 MAY 1971
Ground War Operation Lam Son 720's first major battle takes place as North Vietnamese forces hit the same South Vietnamese 500-man marine battalion twice in the same day. Each time the Communists are pushed back after heavy fighting. Earlier, the South Vietnamese reportedly destroy a North Vietnamese base camp and arms production facility in the Ashau Valley. On 19 May, a six-hour battle rages in which thousands of Saigon troops engage the Communists, and three allied helicopters and a reconnaissance plane are downed. Ground fighting, air strikes, and artillery fire continue in the Ashau Valley through 23 May; and the South Vietnamese claim the capture of more communist bunker networks and the destruction of large amounts of supplies and ammunition.
Laos The Pathet Lao Patriotic Front announces its preconditions for peace, which include the end of US intervention and bombing in Laos. Laotian Premier Souvanna Phouma is receptive to immediate peace talks, but does not comment on the Communist demand for a US bombing halt.

13 MAY 1971
Negotiations Still deadlocked, the Vietnam peace talks in Paris enter their fourth year.

16-18 MAY 1971
Laos After bitter fighting, Hanoi forces obtain control of the Boloven Plateau in southern Laos by taking the government strongpoints of Paksong and Ban Houei Sai. North Vietnamese forces destroy 75 percent of Dong Hene, the Laotian military headquarters.

19-22 MAY 1971
Ground War Hanoi forces put pressure on US positions along the DMZ with heavy rocket and mortar attacks. The assault on US base Charlie 2 results in a direct hit on a bunker, killing some 30 soldiers.

23 MAY 1971
Guerrilla War North Vietnamese demolition experts infiltrate the major US air base at Camranh Bay, exploding six tanks of aviation fuel, resulting in a loss of some 1.5 million gallons. US commander General Creighton Abrams is critical of the inadequate security.

24 MAY 1971
USA: Military At Fort Bragg, North Carolina, an antiwar newspaper advertisement signed by 29 US officers supporting the Concerned Officers Movement, results in controversy, but no official action is to be taken against the military dissidents.

26-31 MAY 1971
Cambodia Some 1000 North Vietnamese capture the strategic rubber plantation town of Snoul, driving out some 2000 South Vietnamese as US air strikes support the allied forces. Snoul gives the Communists control of parts of Routes 7 and 13 leading into South Vietnam, as well as of large amounts of abandoned military equipment and supplies. On 31 May Cambodia calls for peace talks if all North Vietnamese and Vietcong forces withdraw. The Communists reject the bid.

27 MAY 1971
Sweden Foreign Minister Torsten Nilsson reveals increased Swedish assistance to the Vietcong, including some $550,000 worth of medical supplies. Similar aid is to go to Cambodian and Laotian civilians affected by the Indochina fighting.

30 MAY 1971
Ground War The North Vietnamese end a series of 48 attacks inside South Vietnam during a 24-hour period. Included in the assaults are five allied DMZ bases, and the US air base at Danang. The following day a Saigon bomb blast levels a government building, leaving three civilians dead and 12 wounded.

31 MAY 1971
Ground War As North Vietnamese attacks along the DMZ continue for the 17th day, some 2500 South Vietnamese begin a drive south of the zone to clear Communist infiltration routes.

1 JUNE 1971
USA: Domestic In support of the Nixon Administration's conduct of the war, a group named the Vietnam Veterans for a Just Peace declares it represents the majority of US Indochina veterans, and calls the protests and congressional testimony of the Vietnam Veterans Against the War 'irresponsible.'

2 JUNE 1971
USA: Military The Army announces that Brigadier General John Donaldson, a former brigade commander in South Vietnam, has

been charged with killing six Vietnamese and assaulting two others. The 42-year-old West Point graduate, a top planner for the Joint Chiefs of Staff, is the highest ranking officer to be accused of killing civilians in the war, and the first general to be charged with a war crime since the Philippine insurrection 70 years before. He is charged in connection with an incident in Quang Ngai Province in March 1969. Lieutenant Colonel William McCloskey, his operations officer in Vietnam, is accused of murdering two Vietnamese in a separate incident.

3 JUNE 1971
North Vietnam After a 24-hour sea voyage to nowhere, prisoners of war spurned by Hanoi are returned to Danang. The last minute refusal to take the captives back in a ship-to-ship transfer comes despite South Vietnam's compliance with details specifically outlined by North Vietnam after Saigon offered to return 570 sick or wounded POWs. The 13 prisoners were the only ones out of 660 screened by the International Red Cross who sought repatriation.

5-6 JUNE 1971
Ground War As part of the increased North Vietnamese DMZ attacks, a fierce battle occurs around South Vietnamese Fire Base Charlie, 12 miles southeast of Khesanh. The North Vietnamese losses are reported as 183 combat dead and 58 slain by US helicopter gunships. On 17 June, 400 North Vietnamese renew attacks on Fire Base Sarge, but are driven back with 25 percent losses. The following day, the 200-man South Vietnamese garrison is reinforced by 1800 additional soldiers.

7 JUNE 1971
Laos In an unusual secret US Senate session to review the American military role in Laos – including some $350 million annually in aid; regular raids by B-52 bombers; and 4800 CIA-financed Thai troops – Stuart Symington (D-MO), J William Fulbright (D-AR) and Edward Kennedy (D-MA) attack Nixon Administration policies. The State Department defends the use of 'volunteer' Thais as predating the 1970 congressional ban on the use of mercenaries.

8 JUNE 1971
Cambodia A four-day battle lull ends as Cambodian government forces are attacked

12 miles northeast of Pnompenh by a 1500-man North Vietnamese force. On 2 June, 2000 South Vietnamese began a drive to block Communist infiltration into the western part of the Mekong Delta region. On 8-12 June, the Communists wage an intensive battle for the control of the Strategic Vihear Suor marshes. On 9 June, the Vietcong capture Srang, 25 miles southeast of Pnompenh, killing many government troops in the 10-hour assault. On 16 June, 20 Communist commandos attack three naval guard posts inside Pnompenh, leaving four Cambodian naval men dead.

9 JUNE 1971
USA: Military A first lieutenant en route to Vietnam goes absent without leave and becomes the first US officer to request asylum in Sweden. According to estimates, some 500 US war resisters and deserters have sought sanctuary in Sweden to date.

12 JUNE 1971
Ground War The Ashau Valley operation, Operation Lam Son 720, continues as 6000 South Vietnamese troops move north to unite with two Saigon marine brigades just south of the DMZ to blockade ever-increasing enemy infiltration through the buffer zone.

13 JUNE-30 DECEMBER 1971
USA: Domestic *The New York Times* begins the three-day publication of leaked portions of the 47-volume Pentagon analysis of how the US commitment in Indochina grew over a period of three decades. The Pentagon Papers disclose closely guarded communiques, recommendations and decisions on the US military role in Vietnam during the Kennedy and Johnson Administrations, along with the diplomatic phase in the Eisenhower years. Their publication creates a nationwide furor, with congressional and diplomatic reverberations as all branches of the government debate over what constitutes 'classified' material and how much should be made public. The publication of the documents precipitates a crucial legal battle between the government and press over 'the people's right to know,' and leads to an extraordinary session of the US Supreme Court to settle the issue.

15 JUNE 1971
Ground War After a 12-hour Central Highlands battle between Saigon paratroopers and

Members of the Special Forces wore camouflage paint on patrol.

the North Vietnamese breaks a three-week siege of Fire Base 5, the South Vietnamese capture a large Communist complex 100 yards from their artillery base.

16 JUNE 1971
USA: Government Congress turns down end-the-war proposals as the Senate refuses twice to set a Vietnam troop withdrawal deadline and the House on 17 June also declines to set a pullout date. However, antiwar forces, defeated twice during the week, make a surprising comeback on 22 June when after a bewildering series of parliamentary maneuvers, the Senate adopts a measure favoring a complete pullout by the spring of 1972, in a 57 to 42 vote. The legislation is conditional on a US-Hanoi accord on the release of American POWs. A White House statement later in the day says the amendment is not binding and warns that if the Communists are to 'assume it to be US policy,' it 'could seriously jeopardize the negotiations in Paris.' The proposal is rejected by the House by a vote of 219 to 176.

17 JUNE 1971
Japan After 21 months of hard bargaining, US Secretary of State William P Rogers and Japanese Foreign Minister Kiichi Aichi sign a treaty returning Okinawa, scene of one of the bloodiest World War II Pacific campaigns, to Japanese rule. Located just 400 miles from communist China for 25 years, it has been the key center through which US supplies flowed in the Korean and Vietnam wars. It is due to remain the most powerful base in the western Pacific, but under terms of the treaty, nuclear weapons are banned from Okinawa and its use as a staging base for wars in Asia is to be limited.

22-28 JUNE 1971
Ground War In a major DMZ area engagement, some 1500 North Vietnamese attack the 500-man South Vietnamese garrison at Fire Base Fuller. Despite US B-52 raids dropping 60 tons of bombs on 21 June and a 1000-man South Vietnamese reinforcement on 24 June, the South Vietnamese have to abandon the base as a North Vietnamese

bombardment has destroyed 80 percent of their bunkers. In an attempt to clear the surrounding area of enemy mortar and rocket sites, the South Vietnamese sweep the region on 25 June. On 28 June, a Saigon spokesman announces that 120 South Vietnamese have reoccupied Fire Base Fuller, but will not rebuild the fortifications. Casualty figures are reported at nearly 500 North Vietnamese dead, with 135 wounded. On 1 July, fighting again flares up around the base, as 300 Communists are pushed back with the help of US and South Vietnamese air power, and with 150 additional South Vietnamese troops.

25 JUNE 1971
Negotiations As announced by the North Vietnamese Paris peace talk delegation, the Pathet Lao renew their peace plan proposal which includes an immediate end to US military involvement and bombing raids in Laos. Laotian Premier Souvanna Phouma rejects the plan by calling for Vientiane as the site of the proposed Laotian peace talks and by calling for the prior withdrawal of North Vietnamese troops from Laos.

30 JUNE 1971
Ground War In an attempt to knock out Communist rocket emplacements that have been shelling US and South Vietnamese bases south of the DMZ during the past two weeks, 14 US F-4 Phantom fighters hit the North Vietnamese region of the DMZ.

1 JULY 1971
USA: Government The 26th Amendment to the Constitution, granting 18-year olds the vote, is ratified and becomes law. The Vietnam war, fought mostly by US soldiers too young to vote, is the major cause for this reform, as antiwar activists have pointed up the injustice of asking those who have no voice in the political decision to sacrifice themselves in battle.

USA: Military In the single largest troop pullout since the phased withdrawal began in 1969, 6100 US soldiers from the Central Highlands depart, beginning the wind-down of the US combat role in that region. The majority of the some 236,000 US troops remaining in Vietnam are in the bitterly contested northernmost provinces of South Vietnam. And by the end of the month, all US Marine combat units are gone. Only Marine advisers and embassy guards remain.

Negotiations The Vietcong present a new seven-point peace plan at the Paris talks, offering release of all US and allied prisoners of war in North and South Vietnam in return for a US troop pullout by the end of 1971. The plan also calls for the end of Vietnamization, the end of all US political and military intervention in South Vietnam, and a phased reunification of both Vietnams. The initial US and South Vietnamese reaction to the plan is noncommital, but at the 8 July session, US Ambassador David Bruce tells the Communists the United States 'cannot possibly accept' the proposal as it stands; but, conceding that the plan has some new elements, he asks for a 'fresh start' in secret negotiations.

8 JULY 1971
Cambodia US helicopters airlift some 1500 South Vietnamese into the Parrot's Beak sector to begin a new drive against some 400 North Vietnamese demolition experts reported there, and to block Communist infiltration into the Saigon region. The drive is halted on 15 July and two-thirds of the South Vietnamese withdraw after no contact is made with the enemy. Later in the month, four separate ARVN drives inside Cambodia occur. On 19 July, 2000 Saigon troops sweep the southeastern Cambodian area to block North Vietnamese infiltration into the Mekong Delta. On 21 July, some 10,000 South Vietnamese already inside Cambodia, aided by an armored brigade and US artillery and helicopter gunships, sweep a more northeasterly region, engaging the communists on 22 July between Krek and Mimot. On 26 July, about 1000 Saigon troops sweep inside Cambodia some 90 miles north of Saigon. And on 28 July, 3500 Saigon forces with 80 armored vehicles begin a drive north of Kompong Trabek near Route 1, the main highway linking Pnompenh to Saigon.

9 JULY 1971
USA: Military The United States complete the DMZ turnover to the South Vietnamese, as some 500 US forces of the First Brigade, Fifth Mechanized Division, at Fire Base Charlie 2, four miles south of the DMZ, hand the stronghold over to Saigon troops, completing the transfer of defense responsibilities for the border area that began in 1969. On the previous day, nearby Fire Base Alpha 4 was turned over to the South Vietnamese. Two separate contingents of 50 US artillerymen each remain at both bases to monitor radar equipment and to operate the artillery.

11 JULY 1971
Air War Inside North Vietnam near the Mugia Pass, two US fighter-bombers destroy an emplacement of antiaircraft guns in the 46th protective reaction strike since the beginning of the year. On the previous day, the North Vietnamese fired three missiles at but missed a US reconnaissance plane 45 miles north of the DMZ.

13 JULY 1971
Laos Laotian tribesmen, reportedly led by CIA advisers in a seven-day drive, take control of the Plain of Jars, meeting little resistance. The Defense Department subsequently denies any participation by US advisers.
USA: Military On 13 July, a US Air Force courtmartial in London finds Captain Thomas Culver guilty of participating in a British antiwar demonstration while in civilian clothes.

14 JULY 1971
China Concluding a 12-day visit to China, Australian Labour party leader Gough Whitlam reveals that Premier Chou En-lai expressed to him China's interest in participating in a new international conference on Indochina, similar to the 1954 Geneva conference. The North Vietnamese, Vietcong, and the Soviet Union react negatively to the Chinese proposal.

15 JULY 1971
USA: Government In a surprise announcement, President Nixon discloses that he will visit Peking, China, before May 1972. The news, issued simultaneously in Peking and the US, stuns the world. Nixon reports that he is going there 'to seek normalization of relations between the two countries and to exchange views on questions of concern to both sides.' This move was preceded by the 6 April invitation to the US Ping Pong Team to visit China, and by Nixon's ending of the 20-year US trade embargo against China. On 22 July, the North Vietnamese announce that they see the forthcoming Nixon visit to China as a divisive attempt by the US.

20 JULY 1971
Laos In a move that indicates Thai troops are permanently occupying a large strip of Sayaboury Province in Laos, they construct several permanent military bases in the 100-mile deep and 20-mile wide area, reportedly with CIA assistance.

22 JULY 1971
USA: Domestic In Washington, DC, four relatives of Vietnam POWs accuse Vietnam Veterans against the War leader John F Kerry of using the POW issue to further his own political goals. The news conference proceeds with a demand for a scheduled withdrawal of US troops from Vietnam in return for the release of North Vietnamese-held American POWs.

26 JULY 1971
Ground War In a mission marking the fourth phase of Operation Lam Son 720, US helicopters drop a battalion of 1600 Saigon troops into the Ashau Valley. They sweep the area over the next two days but meet no enemy.

29 JULY 1971
Negotiations The chief US delegate to the Paris peace talks, David Bruce, announces that he is resigning as of 31 July for reasons of health. William J Porter, US Ambassador to South Korea, is named to succeed Bruce in Paris. In an interview on the following day, head of the Vietcong delegation Nguyen Thi Binh proposes to identify all US POWs as soon as the US designates a deadline for the complete withdrawal of all its troops. She also criticizes Porter for brutal policies in the South Vietnamese pacification program when he was deputy US ambassador in Saigon.

2 AUGUST 1971
Laos In a once top secret classified report, now given clearance by the US Defense and State Departments, the Nixon Administration officially acknowledges that the CIA is maintaining a 30,000-man force of 'irregulars' fighting throughout Laos. The 'irregulars' are recruited and paid directly by the US intelligence agency. Also according to the report, the extent of US financial involvement in Laos in 1970 comes to a total of $284,200,000 to date. In addition, the report notes greatly increased Chinese road-building activity in northern Laos and the concurrent placement of new long-range radar-directed antiaircraft guns along the road from Muong Sai toward Dienbienphu by the Chinese.

3 AUGUST 1971
Cambodia In a Parrot's Beak sector drive, South Vietnamese fighter-bombers and helicopters level two Cambodian villages held by Communists, killing many of the enemy reportedly.

CHRONOLOGY

6 AUGUST 1971
USA: Military The last troops of the first US Army unit to enter Vietnam combat in 1965 – the 4th Battalion, 503rd Infantry of the 173rd Airborne Brigade – are pulled out of the field to return home.

7 AUGUST 1971
Cambodia Ending an 11-day operation to block an essential Communist infiltration and supply route north of Pnompenh, Cambodian government forces overrun the strategic town of Preykry.

15 AUGUST 1971
Ground War As North Vietnamese military activity greatly increases along the DMZ, the US command threatens retaliatory strikes in the interests of self defense. On 12 August, the North Vietnamese conducted three separate assaults against South Vietnamese ground positions. The fighting continues over the next four days, as Communists hit the government bases Alpha 1 and 2 on 13 August, and on the 15th, capture the Saigon marine base of Baho, two miles south of the DMZ. In this action, most of the 180 South Vietnamese defenders are reported as casualties, with Communist losses at 200 dead.

Cambodia According to a report issued on 15 July by the Cambodian Foreign Ministry, South Vietnamese troops have brutally mistreated Cambodian civilians on several occasions earlier in the year. The cited incidents of alleged atrocities arouse such an outcry that the Cambodian high command now officially calls for the withdrawal of all South Vietnamese troops from Cambodia, and for the closing of the Saigon military base at Neak Luong.

18 AUGUST 1971
Australia and New Zealand The prime ministers of both nations tell their respective parliaments that their combat forces will be withdrawn from Vietnam by the end of 1971. According to Prime Minister William McMahon, most of Australia's 6000-man contingent will be home by Christmas; while Prime Minister Sir Keith Holyoake announces that New Zealand's combat force of 264 will leave South Vietnam by year's end. Both nations will leave behind small training forces. Prime Minister McMahon declares that South Vietnamese forces are now able to assume Australia's role in Phuoctuy Province, southeast of Saigon, and that Australia will give South Vietnam $28 million over the next three years in aid for civilian projects. The Australian Defense Minister reports that since 1965, the Vietnam war has cost his nation 473 dead and 2202 wounded and a monetary cost of $182 million for military expenses and $16 million in civilian assistance to South Vietnam.

20-29 AUGUST 1971
South Vietnam General Duong Van Minh, leading opposition candidate in the nation's presidential election race, and Vice President Nguyen Cao Ky – a legal ban on his running lifted by the Supreme Court – throw the campaign into confusion when both withdraw from the contest. Both accuse incumbent President Nguyen Van Thieu of rigging the election, and they resist US pressure to remain in the race. Meanwhile, Thieu holds a firm grip on the National Assembly in the 29 August elections, which Communists try to disrupt. Although opponents make some gains, especially in the cities, candidates backing Thieu swamp the opposition in the Mekong Delta, with a solid majority in the 159-member lower house.

21-22 AUGUST 1971
USA: Domestic In Buffalo, New York, and Camden, New Jersey draft office raids by antiwar protestors associated with the Catholic Left end with the arrest of 25 persons by the FBI and local police. The aim of the dissidents is to confiscate and destroy draft records and military intelligence reports that 'help make the Vietnam war possible.'

22 AUGUST 1971
Air War Two North Vietnamese antiaircraft and missile site targets 38 and 115 miles north of the DMZ are attacked by US jets after the emplacements threaten US planes carrying out bombing missions along the Ho Chi Minh Trail in neighboring Laos.

25 AUGUST 1971
Ground War The Communists begin a widespread campaign of assaults on civilian targets throughout South Vietnam in order to disrupt the 29 August elections. In the period from 28-30 August, they execute 96 reported attacks in the northern part of South Vietnam. US bases also come under artillery fire and air strikes – involved are the Danang base Camp Faulkner, Laikhe base camp and various

The US infantry were armed with the standard M-16 rifle and the M-79 grenade launcher.

other garrisons. The attacks begin with a 13-hour series of explosions of the mammoth US ammunition dump at Camranh Bay.

6-18 SEPTEMBER 1971
Ground War Near the Laotian border, some 12,000 South Vietnamese with major US support begin an offensive Operation Lam Son 810 against some 15,000 North Vietnamese in the region. The goal of the operation is to seek out and destroy communist supply depots and to block enemy infiltration into northwestern South Vietnam expected to culminate in disruptions of the October presidential elections. In support of the operation, US B-52 bombers intensify raids against the southern DMZ.

9 SEPTEMBER 1971
Negotiations At his first Paris peace talk session, new chief US delegate William J Porter renews the US call for secret talks in order to achieve progress at the still stymied conference. The North Vietnamese and Vietcong representatives reject the bid.
South Korea According to a statement by Defense Minister Yoo Jae Heung, his nation will begin the scheduled pullout of its 48,000-man force in South Vietnam in December. All South Korean soldiers are to be out by June 1972.

14-21 SEPTEMBER 1971
Ground War A Mekong Delta offensive begins as South Vietnamese forces, supported by US artillery and air power, sweep into the U Minh Forest to destroy a Communist stronghold there. Intensive fighting characterizes the weeklong operation, leaving a reported 400 Communists dead and 113 South Vietnamese dead and 183 wounded. North Vietnamese gunners bring down 11 US helicopters.

15-16 SEPTEMBER 1971
Laos A bitterly-fought battle ends with the recapture of the strategic Boloven Plateau town of Paksong by seven Laotian government battalions. Communist losses are reported at 279 dead and 600 wounded; and the Laotian casualties include 202 dead, 745 wounded and 195 missing.

16 SEPTEMBER 1971
Terrorism A terrorist bomb explodes in a Saigon nightclub, leaving 14 South Vietnamese and one American dead.

16-20 SEPTEMBER 1971
Ground War Communist attacks in the Saigon area increase as a Vietcong ambush at a Michelin rubber plantation leaves 15 South Vietnamese soldiers and three US advisers

dead. On the 20th, 600 Communist commandos assault a government base near Tayninh, 55 miles northeast of Saigon, leaving 21 South Vietnamese soldiers dead and 64 wounded.

21 SEPTEMBER 1971
Air War In an eight-hour period, 200 US fighter-bombers, protected by 50 escort planes, carry out an intensive series of raids over an area 35 miles north of the DMZ. The goal of the operation is to knock out the greatly increased number of North Vietnamese antiaircraft and missile emplacements in the DMZ area. Communist military fuel storage tanks are also hit. The mission is termed 'protective' by the US Defense Department, and it is also meant to lessen the chance of a large-scale North Vietnamese campaign to disrupt South Vietnam's October presidential elections. On 24 September, Hanoi protests that many civilians were killed or wounded in the air attacks, which mark an intensification of the war. The North Vietnamese delegation boycotts the 23 September session of the Paris peace talks in opposition to the raids.

21 SEPTEMBER 1971
USA: Government The Senate defeats a liberal-led filibuster against the draft bill in a 61 to 30 vote. The House passed the compromise version of the two-year draft extension bill in August. The measure, enabling the president to resume military inductions, halted since the expiration of the previous draft law at the end of June, gives the Nixon Administration the two years it says is needed to work toward an all-volunteer army. The bill also contains a record $2.4 billion military pay raise and authorization for the president to drop undergraduate student deferments.

26 SEPTEMBER-9 OCTOBER 1971
Cambodia Fighting intensifies along the Cambodian-South Vietnamese border, as the South Vietnamese with major US help fight off communist attacks. The allies begin a counteroffensive on 29 September to reopen Route 22 between Tayninh, South Vietnam, and Krek. The 20,000 South Vietnamese in Cambodia are reinforced by 4000 more men, as the US command moves 1500 GIs and armored vehicles to the front just inside South Vietnam. US B-52 bombers batter North Vietnamese positions inside Cambodia. During the offensive, Saigon forces are able to lift two Communist sieges of South Vietnamese bases – at Fire Base Tran Hung Dao on 1 October, and on 9 October of artillery base Alpha inside Cambodia.

28 SEPTEMBER 1971
China In Hanoi, Chinese and North Vietnamese representatives sign a Peking aid package. The treaty is expected to raise Chinese economic assistance over the $200-$250 million it currently grants annually to its Indochina ally.

30 SEPTEMBER 1971
USA: Government A tough Vietnam pullout amendment sponsored by Mike Mansfield (D-MT) is approved by the Senate for the second time. Republicans join Democrats for the 57-to-38 vote backing the rider to the $21 billion military procurement authorization bill calling for withdrawal of US troops from Southeast Asia within six months.

2 OCTOBER 1971
Cambodia Hostilities in the Mekong Delta flare up near Kienthien, leaving 16 North Vietnamese and 18 South Vietnamese dead.

3 OCTOBER 1971
South Vietnam President Nguyen Van Thieu is reelected in a controversial one-man race, garnering 94.3 percent of the votes cast as 87 percent of the nation's eligible voters turn out, according to the official count. The campaign has been marked by protests from students, veterans and Buddhist groups, who charged the election was rigged. Thieu is sworn in for a second four-year term on 31 October amid massive security precautions. To mark the occasion, Thieu frees 2938 Vietcong POWs. In a campaign to disrupt the balloting, Communists gunners fire three rockets into Saigon on 3 October, killing three civilians. Throughout the country, Communist attacks accompany the election.

7 OCTOBER 1971
Air War In the most intensive air strike on North Vietnamese bunkers and artillery sites in over a year, US B-52s drop nearly 1000 tons of bombs on enemy targets near Krek in Cambodia, and around the South Vietnamese city of Tayninh.

8 OCTOBER 1971
North Vietnam Staff Sergeant John V Sexton, Jr, becomes the 22nd American prisoner to be

freed by the Vietcong in 10 years. As a 'reciprocal gesture,' the US releases a North Vietnamese officer in Cambodia, in the hope the move will spur the liberation of other US POWs. On the previous day, a US spokesman announced that two-thirds of the 1618 US servicemen reported missing are assumed to be dead.

Ground War After 399 days, the Thua Thien Province operation Jefferson Glenn involving the US 101st Airborne Division in coordination with the South Vietnamese 1st Infantry Division, ends, with a reported 2026 in enemy casualties. This is the final major operation in which US ground forces are to take part.

11 OCTOBER 1971

USA: Military At allied Fire Base Pace near the Cambodian border, several US soldiers refuse to go out on a night combat patrol. The command is cancelled when it becomes known that a South Vietnamese unit is already performing the mission. On 15 October, Senator Edward Kennedy (D-MA) conveys to the Pentagon for investigation a petition from 65 US soldiers stationed at this same base that says the men are being ordered to participate in offensive combat actions along the Cambodian border, contrary to stated US policy, or face court martials.

16 OCTOBER 1971

Cambodia Premier Lon Nol suspends the National Assembly and announces that he will rule by executive decree, since the 'sterile game of democracy' is hampering the war-torn country in its fight against the Communists. On 22 October, Lon Nol abolishes constitutional rule after declaring a state of emergency. Despite these moves, the US government declares its continuing support for the Pnompenh government.

18 OCTOBER 1971

Air War A US warplane mistakenly drops two 500-pound bombs on a South Vietnamese troop base at Thienghon, near the Cambodian border, leaivng 18 Saigon soldiers dead and seven others wounded.

20 OCTOBER 1971

Cambodia In a new offensive north of Krek, 2500 South Vietnamese begin a drive against an estimated 1600-2000 communists. On 28 October, Saigon reports that the enemy withdrew before the ARVN troops and armored units could engage them.

25 OCTOBER 1971

China In a lopsided vote of 76 to 35, with 17 abstentions, the United Nations General Assembly adopts an Albanian resolution to seat Mao Tse-tung's Chinese Communists and to oust Chiang Kai-shek's Nationalists from the world body after 26 years. The Nationalists' ouster on top of the admission of Communist China comes with a stunning suddenness after a generation of debate, despite US diplomatic efforts to save Taiwan's seat with a 'two-China' policy.

27-29 OCTOBER 971

Cambodia Fighting intensifies as Cambodian government forces battle with Vietcong and North Vietnamese forces northeast of Pnompenh – the major engagements occurring around the provincial capital of Kompong Thom and Rumlong. The Communists begin a siege of these garrisons after their demolition frogmen destroy a crucial Route 6 bridge, thus severing supply lines for the 20,000 Cambodians on the northeast front. Some 400 government soldiers are reported dead as a result of the combat.

29 OCTOBER 1971

USA: Military During this last week of October, US troop strength drops to 196,700, the lowest level since January 1966.

2 NOVEMBER 1971

Cambodia Northeast of Pnompenh, Cambodian government forces lift the Communist siege of Prakham. The Communists, who have surrounded the village for over a week, withdraw, leaving behind 291 dead. On 3 November, 1000 South Vietnamese troops begin a drive against Communist infiltration routes southwest of Kompong Traket that lead toward Saigon. And on 7 November, communists assault Bamnal, 70 miles northwest of Pnompenh, killing 10 government soldiers.

10 NOVEMBER 1971

Cambodia The international airport at Pnompenh is hit by Communist rocket shells that leave 25 persons dead and 30 wounded, and damage nine planes. Concurrently, another North Vietnamese unit attacks a radio transmission facility nine miles to the northwest, leaving 19 Cambodians dead. This assault leaves Pnompenh without access to international communications networks for the next several hours.

An M-113 armored Personnel Carrier with ARVN troops moves along the Ho Chi Minh Trail.

12 NOVEMBER 1971

USA: Government President Nixon discloses another US troop withdrawal of 45,000 more men by 1 February, to bring the troop-level ceiling down to 139,00. Stressing that the US ground combat role in Southeast Asia is at an end and that the troops are 'now in a defensive position,' Nixon says that 80 percent of the forces in Vietnam when he took office have come home, and that the most recent five-week casualties have dropped to less than 10 a week.

13 NOVEMBER 1971

North Vietnam A major North Vietnamese drive down the Ho Chi Minh Trail into Laos and Cambodia is predicted as Saigon military sources report a massive communist build-up of supplies near the Benkarai and Mugia passes in North Vietnam. Intelligence photographs also reveal extensive road-repair activity and new antiaircraft emplacements. In response to this threat, US B-52s step up air raids against communist strongholds in Cambodia, Laos and South Vietnam.

Ground War At a Central Highlands infantry battalion camp near Pleiku, the South Viet-namese defenders ward off an assault by some 600 communists, killing 163 North Vietnamese and Vietcong. ARVN losses total 29 dead and 32 wounded.

Cambodia After almost three weeks of siege, the 400 Cambodian defenders of Rumlong are forced to flee – only 30 reach safety. The others are either captured or killed. In addition, some 400 other Cambodians die as their two reinforcing battalions make an unsuccessful attempt to break the Communist encirclement of Rumlong.

16 NOVEMBER 1971

Cambodia As the battle rages close to Pnompenh, substantially increased US air power lends the Cambodians support. US helicopter gunships also strike at North Vietnamese emplacements at Tuol Leap, 10 miles north of Pnompenh.

17 NOVEMBER 1971

Thailand Citing 'the increasing threat to national security,' Prime Minister Thanom Kittikachorn ends constitutional rule and seizes full power. Backed by military and civilian leaders described as a 'revolutionary council' in the bloodless coup, Kittikachorn also declares martial law and pledges to continue Thailand's pro-US and anti-communist foreign policy.

19 NOVEMBER 1971
USA: Domestic In Washington, DC, the US National Conference of Catholic Bishops endorse their most forceful resolution to date opposing the Vietnam war.

Cambodia The relentless Communist pressure on the capital city of Pnompenh leads to a Cambodian call for South Vietnamese military assistance. Saigon officials reveal that in the previous week an eight-person Cambodian delegation flew to the South Vietnamese capital to request officially South Vietnamese artillery and engineer support for beleaguered government troops.

22 NOVEMBER 1971
Ground War Some 25,000 South Vietnamese begin an offensive against a reported 5000 communists in the Mekong Delta between the U Minh Forest and the Camau Peninsula. They encounter only light resistance.

Cambodia Some 25,000 South Vietnamese, aided by 2500 Cambodians, begin a major offensive against the North Vietnamese around Pnompenh. The drive, aimed at North Vietnamese rear headquarters for three divisions and at supply depots near Chup, initially meets little resistance through 30 November. On 24 November, the South Vietnamese airlift several thousand paratroopers from Krek to Chup. Some 25,000 South Vietnamese are now involved.

23 NOVEMBER 1971
Cambodia US B-52 bombers, helicopter gunships and other planes intensify their strikes on Communist targets in support of the major South Vietnamese offensive. Despite a prohibition on any US ground presence in Cambodia, US military advisers are sighted in Krek and in Pnompenh.

27 NOVEMBER 1971
Ground War Some 15,000 South Vietnamese begin a new drive in the Central Highlands aimed at communist bases there. The United States provides artillery and air support, losing three helicopters to enemy fire.

1 DECEMBER 1971
Cambodia The situation worsens as Communists renew their assaults on Government positions, forcing the retreat of Cambodian forces from Baray, six miles northeast of Pnompenh and from nearby Kompong Thmar. As their resistance deteriorates, the Cambodian government issues a plea for intensified US and South Vietnamese air support. On 2 December, the North Vietnamese overrun Cambodian forces trying to reopen Route 6. Nearly half of the 20,000-man government contingent flees, as hundreds die. The Communists regain control of a 30-mile stretch of Route 6, cutting off thousands of refugees and some 10,000 government troops in the northern Kompong Thmar area. On 6 December, the Cambodian forces abandon the village of Bat Doeung, 16 miles north of Pnompenh, leaving some 50 dead. On the same day, Hanoi radio reports that the Cambodians have lost some 12,000 fighting men in the past week's action. On 7 December, Communists gunners renew their shelling of Pnompenh, firing three rockets into the capital and eight rockets into the international airport. The next day the battle continues nine miles from Pnompenh as 1000 government troops try to hold back the North Vietnamese near the hamlet of Sre Ngei. The capital is inundated by refugees from the surrounding villages. Although on 9 December, the Cambodian forces are successful in recapturing Kleah Sanday, 10 miles south of Pnompenh, two days later they are forced to abandon the Pnombaset garrison overlooking Phompenh's northern defense perimeter, eight miles outside the city.

9 DECEMBER 1971
Negotiations For the first time since the Paris peace talks began, both sides fail to set another meeting date after the 138th session. The standoff is spurred by the Communist refusal to accept a proposal by chief US delegate William Porter that calls for a week's break in the talks. Both sides announce on 28 December that they will not attend the next scheduled meeting. The cancellation makes it the third meeting to be called off in the month. Earlier, Porter had angered the opposite side by postponing the next session of the conference until 30 December, to give Hanoi and the Vietcong an opportunity to develop a 'more constructive approach' at the talks.

14 DECEMBER 1971
Cambodia About 6000 South Vietnamese, aided by 4000 Cambodian troops and by

intensive US air activity, capture Chup, a sanctuary for the North Vietnamese 7th and 9th Divisions. The reported 9000 North Vietnamese stationed there vanish. This achievement follows several days of bloody battle near the hamlet of Dam Be since 8 December, that leave a reported 167 Communists dead. Vietcong radio reports that the South Vietnamese have lost 500 men at Dam Be, while Saigon places the total at 14. On 17 December, the South Vietnamese abandon Chup, other former Communist bases in the area, and the leveled town of Suong in order to consolidate their positions.

17 DECEMBER 1971
Cambodia Cambodian positions in Prakham, 40 miles north of Pnompenh, and their 4000-man Taing Kauk base are the targets of continuing heavy bombardment by the encircling communist forces. The Prakham siege is lifted four days later. On 16 December, enemy fire brings down a US Phantom jet near Pnompenh, bringing to 8053 the total US aircraft lost in the Southeast Asian conflict. As the Communists continue to encircle Pnompenh in the face of weakened Cambodian resistance, antigovernment demonstrations inside the capital break out against the Lon Nol regime. The government reacts by banning all such protests, as well as political meetings, and by authorizing police searches of private houses.

18-19 DECEMBER 1971
Air War Four US F-4 Phantom jets are lost over northern Laos and North Vietnam, three on 18 December – marking the heaviest single-day loss since December 1967 – and one on the 19th.

20 DECEMBER 1971
Laos Overrunning some 6000-7000 Laotian defenders assisted by Thai irregulars, some 15,000 North Vietnamese capture the strategic Plain of Jars. Both sides suffer heavy casualties, according to Laotian reports. Earlier in the month, two North Vietnamese battalions captured the strategic town of Saravane and its air strip at Ban Khot north of the Boloven Plateau on 6 December. On the 21st, the Communists begin a drive against the government base of Long Thieng, defended by CIA-recruited Meo tribesmen. On 28 December, after a 12-hour mortar and ground attack, the North Vietnamese and their Pathet Lao allies seize the town of Paksong, thus gaining control of the complete Boloven Plateau. But they leave the next day, and Laotian government forces move back into Paksong.

22 DECEMBER 1971
China In a blast that emphasizes the rift between the two communist super powers, the Soviet Union accuses China of backing US policies in Vietnam.

23 DECEMBER 1971
North Vietnam In Vientiane, Laos, American entertainer Bob Hope tries to negotiate with North Vietnamese authorities there for the release of US POWs. His proposal suggests the payment of $10 million to a North Vietnamese children's charity in exchange for the release of Communist-held POWs.

23-25 DECEMBER 1971
Ground War Holiday truces go into effect as the communists unilaterally announce a 72-hour Christmas truce for 23-25 December, and the allies proclaim a 24-hour truce for 24-25 December. According to Saigon sources, the Vietcong commit 49 violations, and the Vietcong charge allied forces with 170 violations. US air strikes continue.

26 DECEMBER 1971
USA: Domestic Flying the US flag upside down from the crown of the Statee of Liberty, 15 antiwar Vietnam veterans barricade themselves inside the monument, but end their occupation early 28 December, obeying a federal court order. In Washington on 28 December, over 80 antiwar veterans are arrested after clashing with police on the steps of the Lincoln Memorial.

Air War In the sharpest escalation of the war since the end of saturation bombing in November 1968, US fighter-bombers begin striking at North Vietnamese airfields, missile sites, antiaircraft emplacements and supply facilities for five straight days. On 27 December, US Defense Secretary Melvin Laird says the stepup is in retaliation for the Communist failure to live up to agreements prior to the 1968 bombing halt, citing the shelling of Saigon the week before; DMZ violations, including the building of an infiltration route through the buffer zone; and attacks on unarmed US reconnaissance planes. He adds that in December 'more US planes of all types have been attacked by North Vietnam than in any month' since he assumed his post. Penta-

Draft dodgers and deserters discuss staying in Canada following Nixon's statement of 'no amnesty.'

gon figures show that US planes, with as many as 250 craft participating in some missions, attacked northern targets over 100 times in 1971, a figure comparable to US air activity in the previous 26 months. The intensified bombing spurs new antiwar protests in the streets and in the halls of congress, as critics charge that air war escalation will further jeopardize the release of US POWs.

31 DECEMBER 1971
State of the War The gradual US withdrawal from the Indochina conflict is reflected in reduced casualty figures. The number of Americans killed in action drops to 1386 from the previous year's total of 4204. South Vietnam loses some 21,500 men, while the combined Vietcong and North Vietnamese total is estimated at 97,000. But the cumulative total after ten years of US involvement in the Vietnam war has risen to 45,627 dead American soldiers. The US troop levels, at 280,000 in Vietnam at year's start, are now down to 159,000. The US goal has fully shifted from a military victory to a graceful disengagement, accompanied by Vietnamization as the South Vietnamese eventually assume all combat

responsibility – though with questionable success. But the Communists, with their fierce determination to win coupled with the ability to melt into the landscape when the battle is not of their choosing, strengthen their morale under intensified US air strikes. They make impressive gains in Laos and Cambodia, and still can strike at will almost anywhere within South Vietnam. Meanwhile, allied morale is low, as US soldiers increasingly use drugs, question officers' commands, at times even kill their superiors, and participate in antiwar activity. South Vietnamese disunity is apparent as the presidential election is marked by protests on all sides. The war crimes issue continues. The Pentagon Papers controversy results in a major victory for freedom of the press and for antiwar forces. And the stalled Paris peace talks revive as Communist proposals link faster US withdrawal rates to the freeing of American prisoners of war.

1 JANUARY 1972
Air War US planes make over 200 strikes against North Vietnamese supply lines in Cambodia and Laos. In the first month of 1972 US jets make nearly one-third as many

'protective reaction' strikes on missile sites, antiaircraft batteries and radar installations in North Vietnam as in all of 1971. The intensification of the air war is largely an attempt to disrupt Communist preparations for an anticipated Tet (15 February) offensive.

2 JANUARY 1972

USA: Government President Nixon announces continued troop withdrawals from Vietnam, but says 25,000-35,000 US troops will remain until the North Vietnamese release all US POWs. He says North Vietnamese negotiators in Paris 'totally rejected' considering POW release for a US troop pullout deadline.

Cambodia Some 10,000 ARVN troops pull out of southeastern Cambodia to back up Saigon defenses for the expected Tet offensive. Cambodian troops also withdraw.

3 JANUARY 1972

USA: Domestic Candidate for Democratic party presidential nomination Senator George McGovern says it is not true that Nixon administration negotiators in Paris ever discussed total US withdrawal in return for POW release; he charges that the Nixon administration is using the POW issue to justify bombing of North Vietnam and the continued support of the 'corrupt' Saigon regime of President Thieu.

Laos Meo tribal forces loyal to the Laotian government evacuate Longtieng base, which has been under North Vietnamese artillery fire since 31 December 1971, and deploy to villages and high ground around the base. More than 500 men on each side die in combat throughout the month.

6 JANUARY 1972

Negotiations After a one-month lapse, official peace talks resume in Paris. The Communist delegations restate their position that the release of US POWs is dependent upon (1) the pullout of US forces and (2) the withdrawal of US support for the Thieu regime, adding that (3) the United States must stop Vietnamization, 'a plot to withdraw US troops but still continue the war of American aggression by puppet forces under US direction and with US support and supplies.'

7 JANUARY 1972

North Vietnam India and North Vietnam expand diplomatic relations by upgrading their consulates in Hanoi and New Delhi to embassies. The United States and South Vietnam criticize the Indian action and challenge Indian membership in the International Control Commission (ICC), established at the 1954 Geneva conference.

Ground War In the heaviest shelling of US forces in six months, 18 Americans are wounded by a mortar fire attack on fire support base Fiddler's Green, 20 miles northeast of Saigon.

Cambodia An 1800-man ARVN force begins an operation in northeastern Cambodia to disrupt Communist bases and capture supplies collected for the anticipated offensive.

10 JANUARY 1972

USA: Domestic Former presidential candidate Senator Hubert Humphrey joins the presidential race, saying it is taking longer for President Nixon to withdraw US troops from Vietnam than it did to defeat Hitler. He calls for an end to the war: 'Had I been elected, we would now be out of that war.'

Guerrilla War Seven militiamen are wounded when Vietcong attack the Binhthuan administration office six miles from Saigon. One US soldier is killed and two wounded in the ambush of a patrol 24 miles northeast of Saigon.

12 JANUARY 1972

Ground War With 34 attacks against South Vietnamese military and civilians in the last 24 hours, Communist attacks become more frequent than at any time since last October. The most serious attack occurs 90 miles southwest of Saigon when Vietcong ambush a 30-man platoon of South Vietnamese militiamen in the Mekong Delta.

13 JANUARY 1972

USA: Government President Nixon announces that withdrawals of 70,000 US troops in the next three months will reduce US troop strength in South Vietnam to 69,000 by 1 May. Since taking office Nixon has withdrawn more than 400,000 GIs from Vietnam; US combat deaths are down to less than 10 per week. Nixon's announcement comes in response to presidential challengers' criticism that Nixon is pulling out troops but, particularly by turning to air power, not ending US involvement in Vietnam.

17 JANUARY 1972

Air War Flying more than 200 strikes, US planes hit supply routes and depots in

The US military was responsible for supplying the South Vietnamese with arms and ammunition.

Laos especially along the Ho Chi Minh Trail, in a continuing campaign against the anticipated Tet offensive.

18 JANUARY 1972

War Crimes Seymour Hersh, winner of a Pulitzer Prize for his account of the Mylai massacre, reports that a secret investigation by the US Army Criminal Investigation Division concluded that 347 civilians died at Mylai, a number 'twice as large as has been publicly acknowledged.' Hersh also charges the Army with covering up an incident in which 90 civilians were murdered in the hamlet of Mykhe 4 on the same day.

Air War A US Navy plane downs the first MiG in 22 months, deep inside North Vietnam; US planes from bases in Thailand, South Vietnam, and aircraft carriers fly 250 sorties.

20 JANUARY 1972

Ground War In continued efforts to disrupt the anticipated Communist Tet offensive, a contingent of more than 10,000 South Vietnamese troops begins a sweep 45 miles northwest of Saigon. Speculation that such an offensive will occur, encouraged by high-level US and South Vietnamese officials, is doubted by field officers.

Thailand Government forces totalling 12,000 men heavily armed with US equipment, begin an operation against 150-200 Communist

guerrillas defending a mountain base at Lom Sak in northeast Thailand, about 300 miles from Bangkok.

21 JANUARY 1972

Ground War US soldiers at Fire Base Melanie northeast of Saigon are angry and confused over administration statements that remaining soldiers in South Vietnam are in a 'defensive' posture, not in combat.

Air War US B-52s continue bombing suspected supply dumps in the central highlands.

25 JANUARY 1972

USA: Government President Nixon, in response to criticism that his administration has not made its best efforts to end the war, reveals that his National Security Advisor Henry A Kissinger has held 12 secret negotiating sessions between 4 August 1969 and 16 August 1971 in Paris with Le Duc Tho, a member of Hanoi's politburo, and/or Xuan Thuy, Hanoi's chief delegate to the formal Paris peace talks. Nixon also discloses the eight-point US settlement proposal presented privately to the North Vietnamese delegation in Paris on 11 October 1971, accusing Hanoi of refusing to continue the secret sessions which, unlike the formal talks, 'until recently ... showed signs of yielding some progress.' The main features of his eight-point plan are: withdrawal of all US and allied troops and all Communist troops from South Vietnam,

CHRONOLOGY

Cambodia, and Laos within six months of an agreement; simultaneous release of all military and civilian prisoners of both sides; supervision of the cease-fire, to go into effect with the signing of the agreement, by an international commission; and presidential elections in South Vietnam organized and supervised by a coalition of factions including the Vietcong, with President Thieu and Vice-President Tran Van Huong resigning one month before the voting.

War Crimes Pulitzer Prize-winning journalist Seymour Hersh claims that members of the Army's Americal Division destroyed documents to protect their officers involved in the Mylai murders.

26 JANUARY 1972
USA: Government Revealing more details of the secret Paris peace talks, Henry Kissinger emphasizes two points in Hanoi's nine-point plan (also submitted during the secret talks) which create major difficulties for the United States: the Communist insistence on the end of all US support for the South Vietnamese government; and the Communist understanding that 'withdrawal' means not only withdrawal of US troops but the removal of all US equipment, aid, and arms in the possession of the South Vietnamese army. Kissinger asserts that the abrupt removal of all US aid would guarantee the collapse of the Saigon regime.

Air War US planes strike a radar-missile site near Donghoi, the 19th strike inside North Vietnam since the beginning of the year.

27 JANUARY 1972
Ground War A total of 116 Communist soldiers die during two heavy attacks in the central highlands and the Mekong Delta as the level of fighting rises across South Vietnam.

28 JANUARY 1972
Ground War Ten Americans are wounded when a resupply helicopter is badly shot up in fighting 13 miles southeast of Xuan Loc.
Air War US planes make their 20th strike inside North Vietnam this year.

31 JANUARY 1972
North Vietnam In a communiqué charging President Nixon and Henry Kissinger with 'unilaterally' divulging the substance of the secret talks, creating the impasse at the secret meetings, and distorting the facts, North Vietnam publishes a nine-point plan submitted during the secret talks, its own version of the eight-point US plan, a seven-point Vietcong plan submitted in 1971, and the texts of messages concerning a 20 November 1971 meeting which the United States cancelled. The proposals point up two major differences between the North Vietnamese and US plans: Washington wants the withdrawal of all foreign forces from South Vietnam with the condition of an agreement in principle on a final solution, while Hanoi insists on the withdrawal of US and allied troops from all of Indochina without conditions. Hanoi also wants the immediate resignation of the Thieu regime with elections held by a North Vietnam-South Vietnam-Vietcong replacement government.

FEBRUARY 1972
Cambodia South Vietnamese troops make three separate drives into southeastern Cambodia to counter Communist infiltration into South Vietnam and to disrupt preparations for Communist attacks in South Vietnam's Mekong Delta. On 1 February, 3000 ARVN troops cross into Cambodia in pursuit of the remnants of a 400-man Communist raiding force.

3 FEBRUARY 1972
Negotiations The Vietcong delegation to the Paris peace talks presents a revised version of their seven-point plan of 1971. Although they continue to demand total and unconditional US withdrawal and the immediate resignation of President Thieu, they no longer demand that the United States remove him. The revised plan asks the United States to set a precise date for its withdrawal.

4 FEBRUARY 1972
Thailand A force of 824 soldiers, the last of Thailand's 12,000 troops who served in South Vietnam, depart.
China A statement affirming Chinese support for the Communist struggle in Indochina quotes Premier Chou En-lai saying that China backs the seven-point Vietcong proposal and will back the Communists until they achieve total victory.

5 FEBRUARY 1972
Negotiations The North Vietnamese formally reject President Nixon's eight-point peace plan, which was submitted privately to the North Vietnamese delegation in Paris.

The program of Vietnamization included training in the use of more advanced equipment.

CHRONOLOGY

7 FEBRUARY 1972
Laos About 4000 Laotian troops supported by US air power attempt to relieve pressure on Longtieng by attacking North Vietnamese forces who have been occupying the Plain of Jars in northern Laos since the end of 1971. After a month the North Vietnamese have the Laotians on the run; nevertheless Laotian officials call the operation successful.

9 FEBRUARY 1972
Air War A series of over 100 US air strikes begins against infiltration routes and suspected North Vietnamese buildups in the Central Highlands.
Sea War The aircraft carrier USS *Constellation* joins aircraft carriers *Coral Sea* and *Hancock* off the coast of Vietnam.

10 FEBRUARY 1972
Negotiations Formal weekly peace talks in Paris break down when the US delegation, to protest an anti-war rally set to begin in Versailles the next day, refuses to agree on a date for the next meeting.
Guerrilla War Twenty-five rockets hit the US air base and city of Danang, killing three and wounding 17; and Communist guerrillas attack at three points 15 to 35 miles south of Danang.

11 FEBRUARY 1972
Air War US planes fly 100 missions and South Vietnamese planes fly 101 missions in strikes on northern South Vietnam and the Central Highlands.

12 FEBRUARY 1972
Air War The heaviest US air raids in two years bomb Communist bases for a fifth day along the South Vietnamese/Laotian border.
Cambodia About 6000 Cambodian troops launch a major operation to expel 4000 North Vietnamese troops entrenched around the famous Buddhist temple complex at Angkor Wat, which they seized in June 1970. Fighting continues throughout the month. Even with the addition of 4000 more troops, the Cambodians are unsuccessful, and eventually abandon their efforts to expel the North Vietnamese.

13 FEBRUARY 1972
Air War In one of the heaviest US bombing raids of the war, B-52s fly 19 missions in 24 hours, the largest number for a 24-hour period since records began to be kept in June

1968. Fighter-bombers fly 162 strikes. Targets are Communist infiltration routes and bases west of Kontum, particularly North Vietnam's Army Base Area 609.

16 FEBRUARY 1972
USA: Domestic A Gallup Poll finds that of those interviewed 52 percent approve of President Nixon's handling of the war, and 39 percent disapprove.
Ground War Chief US official in Military Region II J P Vann claims that the Tet offensive has begun with attacks in Binhdinh province; he estimates Communist strength in the Central Highlands at 35,000-60,000 troops, South Vietnamese and allied at 220,000.
Air War The US command announces an operation of 'limited duration' bombing aimed at knocking out North Vietnamese artillery positions in North Vietnam's southernmost Quangbinh province and in the northern sector of the DMZ. One plane has been lost and five artillery pieces have been destroyed in the operation to date.

17 FEBRUARY 1972
Air War Three US planes are shot down by surface-to-air missiles during the 29-hour 'limited duration' bombing of North Vietnam.

19 FEBRUARY 1972
POWs Five captured US flyers tape brief greetings to their families on TV at the International Club in Hanoi, in the presence of journalists and diplomats.

20 FEBRUARY 1972
Guerrilla War Sixty-seven Communist attacks over the weekend, most in the Mekong Delta and Danang regions, result in heavy South Vietnamese casualties. Two Americans die and 10 are wounded in attacks at Bienhoa and Phanrang air bases and in the Mekong.

21 FEBRUARY 1972
International President Nixon arrives in Peking, announcing that his breakthrough visit to China is 'the week that changed the world.' In meetings with Nixon, Prime Minister Chou En-lai urges early peace in Vietnam, but does not endorse North Vietnam's political demands. Nixon's promise to reduce US military presence on Taiwan seems to confirm North Vietnam's fears of a

Chinese-American sellout – Taiwan for peace in Vietnam – and North Vietnamese officials and peace negotiators take a dim view of Nixon's trip, fearing that China and the United States will make a deal behind their backs, as at Geneva in 1954. China continues to supply North Vietnam with levels of aid which increased significantly in late 1971.

24 FEBRUARY 1972

Negotiations Talks resume, but after 17 minutes, the shortest meeting on record, the Communist delegations walk out to protest the US bombing of North Vietnam.

25 FEBRUARY 1972

Guerrilla War Twenty-one Americans are wounded and one is killed in the biggest single US engagement with a guerrilla force in nearly a year. The five-hour action around a Communist bunker line 42 miles east of Saigon accounts in large part for the relatively heavy weekly US casualties – four dead and 47 wounded.

27 FEBRUARY 1972

International In a joint communiqué released by China's Chou En-lai and President Nixon during Nixon's visit to China, the United States reiterates its support of the eight-point proposal advocated by itself and South Vietnam in January for an end to the Vietnam war; and China announces its support of the seven-point proposal presented by the Vietcong in February. The communiqué itself, although apparently presenting conflicting sides, is reportedly the result of intense negotiations.

29 FEBRUARY 1972

South Korea South Korea completes the first phase of the withdrawal of its 48,000 troops from Vietnam; 37,000 South Korean troops remain.

2-3 MARCH 1972

Ground War ARVN troops sweep the western Central Highlands to disrupt suspected Communist plans for an offensive; four Americans are wounded in a booby-trap explosion 20 miles northeast of Saigon.
Air War US planes continue 'protective reaction' strikes against antiaircraft batteries and radar sites as far as 120 miles north of the DMZ, and B-52s continue their fifth straight day of saturation raids against Communist positions in the Central Highlands.

6 MARCH 1972

Air War More than 20 US planes continue raids against antiaircraft installations inside North Vietnam. One MiG is shot down in an air battle over North Vietnam involving about a dozen US planes and MiGs.

7 MARCH 1972

North Vietnam Hanoi and Vietcong radio announce that US bombing in the north is striking 'many populated areas;' US command replies that all targets are antiaircraft defenses.
Air War US jets battle five MiGs and shoot one down 170 miles north of the DMZ in the biggest air battle in Indochina in three years. The total of 86 US air raids over North Vietnam to date this year equals the total for all of 1971.

8-9 MARCH 1972

Diplomatic The US government reports that, on a secret visit to brief Hanoi on his meetings with President Nixon, Chinese Premier Chou En-lai declared that he refused to act as an intermediary for the United States in settling the war.
Guerrilla War Communist rockets and mortar shells hit South Vietnamese bases at 10 points along the DMZ. Eight US soldiers are wounded by a booby-trap nine miles south of Danang.
Air War US planes hit antiaircraft defenses in North Vietnam and in the DMZ for the eighth straight day and continue to bomb below the DMZ around Danang and in the Central Highlands.

11 MARCH 1972

Laos A 4500-6000-man North Vietnamese force threatens Longtieng after taking the village of Sam Thong, defended by a 4000-man Thai force, seven miles to the northwest. Communist artillery closes Longtieng airstrip the next day; the opposing forces continue to battle for strategic ground above the base.

16 MARCH 1972

Ground War Combined with Vietcong shelling of Quangngai and an US base camp the preceding day, Communist forces initiate 41 attacks in 24 hours, most against local militia units, and in Quangngai province.

17-18 MARCH 1972

Ground War ARVN troops supported by air and artillery kill 180 communist troops as they

CHRONOLOGY

The North Vietnamese continued to rely on manpower to transport heavy equipment.

stop and push back an attack by hundreds of North Vietnamese in the area between Hué and the Ashau valley. Over 400 North Vietnamese troops have been killed in the continuing South Vietnamese drive on the eastern edge of the Ashau valley. In the mountains west of Hué ARVN forces succeed in preventing Communist forces from hitting lowland cities from their mountain bases claiming 513 North Vietnamese killed in two weeks of this totally South Vietnamese operation, with 86 South Vietnamese dead and 186 wounded.

Cambodia A total of 8000 South Vietnamese troops continue their drive into eastern Cambodia. Although there is no significant engagement tons of supplies are revealed. South Vietnamese troop strength reaches 10,000 over the next few days.

21 MARCH 1972

Cambodia More than 100 civilians are killed and 280 wounded as Communist artillery and rockets strike Pnompenh and environs in the eaviest attack on that city since the beginning of the war in Cambodia in 1970. Following the shelling, a Communist force of 500 men attacks and enters Takhmau, six miles southeast of Pnompenh, killing at least 25 civilians.

23 MARCH 1972

Negotiations US negotiator W J Porter, announces an indefinite suspension of the Paris peace talks, as directed by President Nixon, pending 'serious discussion' of agenda beforehand. The Communists find these conditions unacceptable. Washington calls for an end to the Communist offensive in Vietnam as a precondition to continuing the talks, the North Vietnamese and Vietcong first call for an end to US bombing of both North Vietnam and South Vietnam, and then agree to talk without the cessation of bombing.

30 MARCH 1972

Ground War A major coordinated Communist offensive opens with the heaviest military action since the sieges of allied bases Conthien and Khesanh in 1968. North Vietnamese troop attacks of South Vietnamese bases and towns along the DMZ herald the eventual participation of 500 tanks and 12 divisions of North Vietnamese regular troops – 150,000 men – as well as thousands of Vietcong, supported by heavy rocket and artillery fire. The 30 March attacks along the DMZ from Dongha to the mountains near Khesanh mark the first communist use of long-range heavy artillery along the DMZ. Thirty-five South Vietnamese soldiers die and hundreds of civilians and soldiers are wounded.

31 MARCH 1972

Ground War The firing of more than 5000 rockets, artillery, and mortar shells on 12 South Vietnamese positions just below the DMZ precedes and accompanies ground assaults against South Vietnamese positions in Tayninh province. The attacks are thrown back, with 87 North Vietnamese killed. South Vietnamese fire support bases Fuller, Mailoc, Holcomb, Pioneer, and two smaller bases near the DMZ are abandoned as the North Vietnamese push the defenders back toward their rear bases. Attacks against three bases west of Saigon force the South Vietnamese to abandon six outposts.

APRIL 1972

Ground War Although landing US Marines in response to the Communist offensive is considered and the 9th Marine Amphibious Brigade takes station in amphibious shipping with four battalion landing teams and two composite helicopter squadrons, no US Marine combat troops go ashore. At this point in the war only 500 Marines – embassy guards, air and naval gunfire spotters, advisors to South Vietnamese Marines – remain in Vietnam.

1 APRIL 1972

Ground War Following three days of the heaviest artillery and rocket bombardment of

US forces supply security to rice farmers harvesting in the middle of the war.

the war, 12,000-15,000 soldiers of Hanoi's 304th Division supported by artillery and antiaircraft units equipped with SAM-2 surface-to-air missiles equalling another division sweep across the DMZ and rout the ARVN 3rd Division, driving them toward their rear bases. The Communist ground objective is apparently Quangtri City, capital of Quangtri province, and then to advance on Hué and Danang further south. The objectives of Hanoi's essentially political offensive are seen as North Vietnam's desire to (1) impress the Communist world and its own people with its determination, (2) capitalize on US anti-war sentiment and possibly hurt President Nixon's chances for re-election, (3) prove 'Vietnamization' a failure, (4) damage South Vietnamese forces and the Thieu regime's stability, (5) gain as much territory as possible before a possible truce, and (6) accelerate negotiations on their own terms.

2-4 APRIL 1972
Ground War Soldiers of Hanoi's 304th Division supported by Soviet tanks and heavy artillery take the northern half of Quangtri province, leaving only Quangtri City, the combat base and Dongha, all under heavy attack, in South Vietnamese hands. South Vietnam's 3rd Division commander Brigadier Geneneral Vu Van Giai moves his staff out of Quangtri combat base to the citadel at Quangtri City, the apparent North Vietnamese objective. The Communist offensive, apparently unexpected at this time, catches both US Ambassador Ellsworth Bunker and MACV chief General Creighton Abrams out of the country on vacation; official US and South Vietnamese response to the invasion is apparent unconcern. Dongha is in flames by 3 April; the next day South Vietnamese troops abandon artillery Fire Base Anne, eight miles southwest of Quangtri City, and their northern line of defense on the Cua Viet River; 20,000-40,000 civilians increase stream flow of refugees south.

3 APRIL 1972
Air War The United States prepares hundreds of B-52s and fighters for possible air strikes. The aircraft carrier *Kitty Hawk* is sent from the Philippines to join the carriers already off Vietnam.

5 APRIL 1972
Ground War Moving out of eastern Cambodia, North Vietnamese troops open the second front of their offensive with a drive into Binhlong province, 75 miles north of Saigon, cutting Highway 13 about 37 miles north of Saigon between Saigon and Anloc. Communist forces continue to advance on Quangtri City and Hué. Observers from Hanoi to Washington see the South Vietnamese response as the deciding factor in the success of North Vietnam's offensive. For the most part, ARVN troops have elected to pull back rather than fight, and US advisors are critical of the South Vietnamese 'defensive mentality' as the action takes on more and more of the quality of a conventional war. In Quangtri the 56th South Vietnamese Regiment has apparently deserted to a man, and Hanoi claims that most of the militia in Quangtri province has defected. Two ARVN bases south of Hué are attacked; Communist operations spread into Thuathien province, which adjoins Quangtri province to the south.

6 APRIL 1972
Operation Linebacker Clear weather for the first time in three days allows US planes and Navy warships to begin the sustained air strikes and naval bombardments ordered by President Nixon after meetings with the Special Action Group on 3-5 April. Hundreds of US planes flying 225 missions by 9 April hit North Vietnamese troop concentrations and missile emplacements above and below the DMZ. Two US planes over North Vietnam are shot down with SAM-2 missiles, a new element in North Vietnamese troop defenses.

7 APRIL 1972
Ground War The North Vietnamese offensive drive in Quangtri province slackens as US and South Vietnamese planes take advantage of good weather to bomb Communist positions. Communist troops take Locninh, a district capital of Binhlong province, and are clearly in control of the northern sector of that province. 15,000 ARVN troops – South Vietnam's 5th Infantry Division – are surrounded by North Vietnamese troops while in retreat from Locninh to Anloc, and heavy fighting ensues.
Air War Saigon reports that US planes on 5 April destroyed Benhai bridge in the DMZ, the only road link between North and South Vietnam.

8 APRIL 1972
Ground War North Vietnamese 2nd Division troops drive out of Laos and Cambodia to

open a third front of their offensive in the Central Highlands, cutting the important highway between Kontum and Pleiku at several points. Anloc is surrounded. The first attacks of the offensive against US installations leave three Americans dead and 15 wounded at Camranh Bay air base, two Americans dead and four wounded at Nuibaden Mountain radio relay station.

9 APRIL 1972
Ground War North Vietnamese troops are thrown back from a major assault against ARVN positions at Fire Base Pedro, ten miles southwest of Quangtri City, losing over 1000 men and 30 tanks in the operation. South Vietnamese losses are also believed to be heavy. Saigon command calls up elements of the 7th, 9th, and 21st Divisions, based in the Mekong Delta, to rescue the 5th Infantry Division still surrounded at Anloc. Fierce Communist resistance prevents the relief forces from getting through. All but one of Hanoi's combat divisions have been committed to battle in the current offensive.

10 APRIL 1972
Air War Although the US command refuses to confirm the location of targets, US B-52s reportedly begin bombing North Vietnam for the first time since November 1967, striking in the vicinity of Vinh, 145 miles north of the DMZ. Target priority is given to SAM-2 missile sites, which have made raids over North Vietnam increasingly hazardous. US officials call Hanoi's SAM-2 defenses 'the most sophisticated air defenses in the history of air warfare.'
Sea War US aircraft carriers *Saratoga* and *Midway* are ordered from Florida and California to join the four other carriers and warships already engaged in the bombardment of North Vietnam.

11 APRIL 1972
Ground War Fire Base Bastogne in Thuathien province, 20 miles west of Hué, is besieged by Communist forces. After five days of heavy fighting the base's 500 troops receive supplies by parachute and some reinforcement from ARVN troops. Holding Bastogne is critical to the defense of Hué's western flank.
Air War B-52 strikes against Communist forces attacking ARVN positions in the central highlands near Kontum remove any immediate threat to that city. US command orders two more squadrons of B-52s to

Indochina. Strikes against North Vietnam are again hampered by poor weather.

12 APRIL 1972
Ground War Fifty of 142 US soldiers of the 196th Infantry Brigade refuse patrol duty around Phubai, 42 miles south of the DMZ, shouting, 'We're not going; this isn't our war . . . why should we fight if nobody back home gives a damn about us; why the hell are we fighting for something we don't believe in?' The 50 soldiers finally agree to go. ARVN 1st Division sets up new artillery positions and brings in a tank battalion and a fresh infantry regiment to secure Route 547, the main artery between Hué and Phuxuan, which has been under attack for several days.

12-13 APRIL 1972
Air War US fighter bombers and B-52s pound Communist troops attacking Anloc west of the city, but fail to halt their advance. B-52s bomb as close as one mile west of the city.

13 APRIL 1972
Ground War Communist forces attack Anloc, capital of Binhlong province, with 40 tanks and 3000 men, taking half the city after a day of close combat. US helicopters, dropping supplies and evacuating wounded, enable the defenders to survive.
Sea War US Navy operations in Vietnam are at their highest since 1968.

14 APRIL 1972
Terrorism Danang and Saigon and many parts of South Vietnam are hit by terrorist attacks; rockets are fired on Saigon and nearby Tansonnhut Airport.
Ground War Communist attacks in South Vietnam – 107 in 24 hours – reach their highest level since the 1968 Tet offensive.
Air War Orders for B-52 strikes against diplomatic, political, and military objectives throughout the 200-mile-long southern panhandle of North Vietnam call for the most extensive use of B-52s thus far in the war.

15 APRIL 1972
Ground War North Vietnamese forces overrun Fire Base Charlie, 20 miles northwest of Kontum, as their offensive in the Central Highlands continues.

16 APRIL 1972
Air War In the first use of B-52s against both Hanoi and Haiphong and the first attacks

against both cities since November 1968, 18 B-52s and about 100 US Navy and USAF fighter bombers hit supply dumps near Haiphong's harbor. Sixty fighter bombers hit petroleum storage facilities near Hanoi, with another wave of planes striking later in the afternoon. Washington makes it clear that the US will bomb military targets almost anywhere in Vietnam; Hanoi reports 13 civilians killed in Hanoi and 47 in Haiphong.

Sea War US missile frigate *Worden* is damaged in the Tonkin Gulf by radiation-seeking missiles fired from US planes; one dead, nine wounded. The destroyer *Buchanan* is hit by one round from a North Vietnamese shore battery; one dead and seven wounded.

17 APRIL 1972

USA: Domestic The first major anti-war protests of the year begin at the University of Maryland with demonstrations against the Reserve Officers Training Corps (ROTC). Hundreds of students are arrested and 800 National Guardsmen are ordered onto the campus. Significant protests continue across the country in reaction to the increased bombing of North Vietnam.

18 APRIL 1972

USA: Military Secretary of Defense Melvin Laird, testifying before the Senate Foreign Relations Committee, says he does not rule out the possibility of blockading and mining Haiphong harbor. He says every area of North Vietnam is subject to bombing as long as the current invasion continues, and that the bombing is for the protection of the 85,000 US personnel still in South Vietnam.

19 APRIL 1972

USA: Domestic The eight Ivy League college presidents and the president of MIT issue a joint statement condemning the renewed bombing of North Vietnam and supporting orderly anti-war demonstrations.

Guerrilla War Vietcong attacks throughout the Mekong Delta rise sharply. All regular South Vietnamese troops from the area have been sent to relieve Anloc.

Ground War All Communist action in the province of Binhlong intensifies, including the siege of Anloc. In the Central Highlands, Communist forces overrun Hoaian, inflicting heavy casualties. Their offensive in the Central Highlands takes on major proportions.

Sea War US 7th Fleet warships bombarding the North Vietnamese coast are attacked by MiGs and patrol boats as Hanoi begins to challenge US naval presence in the Tonkin Gulf for the first time since 1964. The US destroyer *Higbee* is badly damaged in some of the heaviest sea action of the war off

The US Navy provided offshore support for the South Vietnamese troops.

An attack squadron of jets from the aircrft carrier Constellation *prepare to take off.*

Vietnam; 7th Fleet ships dueling with shore batteries engage MIGs for the first time, sinking at least three motor torpedo boats and damaging two. US missile frigate *Sterett* downs one MiG and sinks two torpedo boats.

20 APRIL 1972
USA: Domestic The House of Representatives Democratic party caucus votes to support legislation that will set a termination date for US involvement in Vietnam, at the same time denouncing the current bombing of North Vietnam and North Vietnam's invasion of South Vietnam. Classes are cancelled at Columbia University after police are called to control picketing anti-war students.
Diplomatic Henry Kissinger arrives in Moscow to prepare for President Nixon's coming spring visit. He repeats past US offers for a settlement in Vietnam, adding that North Vietnamese invasion troops now participating in the offensive in South Vietnam must be withdrawn, a demand some see as an indication that the United States is preparing to withdraw its insistence on total mutual troop withdrawal from South Vietnam.
Negotiations The Communist delegations in Paris formally propose resumption of the peace talks for 27 April, whether or not the United States halts its bombing of North Vietnam.
Ground War North Vietnamese troops cut Route 19, which connects Pleiku and Quinhon on the coast, at Ankhe Pass. After a week of fierce fighting, South Korean troops clear the pass, losing 51 men.

22 APRIL 1972
USA: Domestic Anti-war demonstrations prompted by the accelerated US bombing in Indochina draw 30,000-60,000 marchers in New York, 30,000-40,000 in San Francisco, 10,000-12,000 in Los Angeles, and smaller gatherings in Chicago and in cities throughout the United States.
Ground War Fighting in the Mekong Delta is the heaviest in 18 months. During the past two weeks Communist forces of up to one battalion in size have taken a large part of important Chuongthien province.

23 APRIL 1972
Ground War Tanks and soldiers of Hanoi's 320th Division push back South Vietnam's 22nd Division at Tancanh and attack Dakto in the Central Highlands. The North Vietnamese offensive, now in its fourth week, is temporarily slowed at its two other fronts. So far 250,000 civilians have fled from their

CHRONOLOGY

homes, and at least six US advisors and 3000 South Vietnamese have been killed. Communist deaths are estimated at 13,000.

Cambodia The town of Kompong Trach near the South Vietnam border falls to Communist forces after a siege by at least 1500 troops lasting 17 days. During the next three weeks 11 other Cambodian positions fall to the Communists.

25 APRIL 1972

Ground War Hanoi's 320th Division drives 5000 ARVN troops into retreat and traps 2000-3000 others in a border outpost northwest of Kontum, and appears to be on the way to cutting South Vietnam in two across the Central Highlands.

Cambodia Communist troops have by now taken control of all Cambodian territory bordering South Vietnam to the east of the Mekong River with the exception of the provincial seat Svayrieng and a few other government strongholds.

26 APRIL 1972

USA: Government President Nixon, despite the Communist offensive, announces that another 20,000 US troops will be withdrawn from Vietnam in May and June, reducing authorized troop strength to 49,000. Sea and air support will continue; the US Navy has doubled the number of its fighting ships off Vietnam.

27 APRIL 1972

Negotiations Official Vietnam peace talks, suspended by the United States on 23 March, resume in Paris at the proposal of the Communist delegations. The session is described as 'fruitless.'

Ground War North Vietnamese troops shatter defenses north of Quangtri and move to within two and one-half miles of the city. Using Russian-built T-54 heavy model tanks, they take Dongha, seven miles north of Quangtri, the next day, continuing to tighten their ring around Quangtri and shelling it heavily. South Vietnamese troops suffer their highest casualties for any week in the war.

28 APRIL 1972

Ground War Fire Base Bastogne, 20 miles west of Hué, falls to the Communists; Fire Base Birmingham, four miles to the east, is also under heavy attack. Much of Hué's population is now moving south to Danang. 20,000 North Vietnamese troops converge on Kontum, encircling it and cutting it off; US commanders call the defending 22nd Division 'inadequate' and describe its survival as 'problematical.'

29-30 APRIL 1972

Ground War Almost 10,000 civilians and military personnel are evacuated by plane and helicopter from Kontum to Pleiku as North Vietnamese troops tighten their grip on this Central Highlands town. ARVN troops flee southward and North Vietnamese troops move closer to Quangtri City.

Air War US B-52s fly 700 raids over North Vietnam.

1 MAY 1972

USA: Military The number of US troops in Vietnam now stands at 66,300, 2700 fewer than President Nixon's goal of reducing troop strength to 69,000 by this date.

Diplomatic About 60,000 persons demonstrate in Stockholm, Sweden, to protest US bombing in Vietnam.

Ground War North Vietnamese troops capture Quangtri City, the first provincial capital taken during their offensive, consolidating control of the entire province. Hanoi claims 10,000 South Vietnamese and allied casualties and captures in the battle. Eighty percent of Hué's population, already swollen by 300,000 refugees, flees south to Danang. Three districts of Binhdinh province also fall, leaving about one-third of the province under Communist control.

2 MAY 1972

Ground War The panicking 10,000-man South Vietnamese 3rd Division, abandoning Quangtri province, becomes the second South Vietnamese combat division to collapse utterly within a week. The entire defense of the front north of Hué is left to a brigade of several thousand South Vietnamese marines as the fleeing 3rd Division troops rush south.

Negotiations The secret negotiations between Kissinger, Le Duc Tho, and Xuan Thuy resume in Paris. The meeting is unproductive. Kissinger and Tho will meet again in Paris on 19 July, 1 August, 14 August, 15 September, 26-27 September, and 8-11 October.

4 MAY 1972

Negotiations The US and South Vietnamese delegations to the official Paris peace talks agree on an indefinite halt to the talks, citing a

Aircraft on the carrier USS Saratoga *is brought up to the flight deck by elevator.*

'complete lack of progress.' North Vietnam and the Vietcong ask the United States and South Vietnam to return to the conference table 16 May, but their proposal is rejected, as is a 13 June Communist proposal asking the United States to withdraw from Vietnam and return to the conference table.

Air War The aircraft carrier *Saratoga* is ordered to join the other US carriers now operating off Vietnam, bringing the total number of carriers to six for the first time in the war; and 50 fighter bombers are ordered to join the nearly 1000 US combat aircraft currently in Indochina.

5 MAY 1972

Guerrilla War In Mytho province Vietcong guerrillas put the 203rd Civil Guard out of combat, capturing seven prisoners and much matériel.

Ground War The 21st Division ARVN troops trying to reach beleaguered Anloc via Highway 13 are again pushed back by the Communists, who overrun a supporting South Vietnamese fire base. Route 14, briefly reopened the preceding day near Kontum by ARVN troops, is once again closed as Communist troops repulse South Vietnamese paratroopers.

6 MAY 1972

USA: Domestic Sixty presidents of midwestern private colleges, issue a statement calling for immediate and total withdrawal of US forces from Indochina. Letters containing this statement are sent to President Nixon and the Democratic presidential aspirants.

Ground War The remnant of South Vietnam's 5th Division at Anloc continues to receive its daily artillery battering from the Communist forces surrounding it. Saigon announces the evacuation of all civilians from Kontum City south to Pleiku.

7 MAY 1972

North Vietnam In a special broadcast commemorating Vietnam's victory over the French at Dienbienphu in 1954, Defense Minister Vo Nguyen Giap says that the people of Vietnam have defeated three US administrations and are about to complete victory over President Nixon.

8 MAY 1972

USA: Government President Nixon announces that he has ordered the mining of all major North Vietnamese ports as well as other measures to prevent the flow of arms and matériel to the Communists. Foreign

CHRONOLOGY

ships in North Vietnamese ports have three days to leave before the mines are activated; US Navy ships will then search or seize ships, and allied forces will bomb rail lines from China and take whatever other measures are necessary to stem the flow of matériel. These actions will stop only when (1) all US POWs are returned, (2) and an internationally supervised cease-fire begins. If these conditions are met, the United States will 'stop all acts of force throughout Indochina and proceed with the complete withdrawal of all forces within four months.'

8-12 MAY 1972
USA: Domestic A wave of anti-war demonstrations stemming from President Nixon's 8 May announcement of the mining of North Vietnamese harbors leads to violent clashes with police and 1800 arrests on college campuses and in cities from Boston to San Jose, California. Police use wooden bullets and tear gas in Berkeley; 1000 students are arrested in Florida; three police are shot in Madison, Wisconsin; and 715 National Guardsmen are activated to quell violence in Minneapolis.

9 MAY 1972
USA: Domestic US Senate Democrats pass a resolution 'disapproving the escalation of the war in Vietnam,' and a modified version of the Case-Church amendment, for the first time voting for a cutoff of war funds.
North Vietnam Hanoi's delegation to the peace talks in Paris calls Nixon's order for mining and bombing a violation of the 1954 Geneva agreement as well as of the 1968 assurance that US air strikes against the North would end.
Air War US bombing in North Vietnam reaches the levels of 1967-68, when the war was at its height.

10 MAY 1972
International President Nixon's decision to mine North Vietnamese harbors is castigated by the Soviet Union, China, and their eastern European allies, and receives only lukewarm support from western Europe.
Air War The United States loses at least three planes and the North Vietnamese 10 as 150-175 American planes hit targets over Hanoi, Haiphong, and along rail lines leading from China. An F-4J of VF-96 flying from the USS *Constellation* and crewed by Lieutenant Randy Cunningham and Lieutenant (jg)

Willie Driscoll, knocks down three MiGs in one combat mission. Added to two previous victories, this makes them the first American aces of the Vietnam War (and the only US Navy aces).

11 MAY 1972
USA: Military The Department of Defense estimates that the cost of mining North Vietnamese ports and rivers will total $1.5 billion during the next 13 months, and suggests additional appropriations.
South Vietnam President Thieu declares martial law – the first time it has been necessary since the 1968 Tet offensive – in an attempt to cope with problems caused by the current communist offensive. Draft age is lowered to 17 and 45,000 excused draftees are recalled.
USSR The Soviet Union demands that the United States end the mining and bombing of North Vietnam, accusing the United States of 'gross violation of . . . freedom of navigation.'

13 MAY 1972
Ground War Seventeen US helicopters and six US advisors land 1000 South Vietnamese marines behind North Vietnamese lines southeast of Quangtri City in the first South Vietnamese counter-attack since the beginning of the Communist offensive. The marines reportedly kill more than 300 North Vietnamese before returning to South Vietnamese-controlled territory the next day. North Vietnamese tanks and troops begin the long-awaited offensive against Kontum.

14 MAY 1972
Ground War A force of 4000 soldiers of South Vietnam's 1st Division, who have reportedly been engaged in a counterattack for over a week, move to within half a mile of Fire Base Bastogne. About 110 North Vietnamese are killed, and three tons of ammunition and supplies are uncovered.

Mid-MAY 1972
Air War For the first time in the war US Marines make use of Bienhoa airfield. MAG-12 moves in with two A-4 Skyhawk squadrons. The Marine planes offer support to Military Regions I and IV and make some sorties into Cambodia.

15 MAY 1972
Ground War Led by a platoon of 30 soldiers flown in by helicopters, South Vietnamese

troops retake Fire Base Bastogne, a matter of strategic importance, as the recapture of the fire base should prevent the Communists from moving their heavy artillery to within shelling distance of Hué.

Sea War The United States announces it is sending a seventh aircraft carrier, the USS *Ticonderoga*, and at least six other destroyer-type warships to Vietnam. The harbors of Haiphong, Campha, Donghoi, Hongai, Thanhhoa, Vinh, and Quangkhe, and the Red River and other rivers and canals of North Vietnam are being mined. US sources call the mining '100 percent effective;' Hanoi says the mines are being removed as soon as they are dropped and ships are moving without difficulty.

16 MAY 1972
Air War A series of air strikes over the past five days has destroyed all of North Vietnam's pumping stations in the southern panhandle, thereby cutting North Vietnam's main fuel line to the South.

17 MAY 1972
South Vietnam All colleges and universities in South Vietnam are closed to allow for the conscription of students.

Ground War Preceded by five B-52 strikes which reportedly kill 300 North Vietnamese to the south, ARVN forces arrive by helicopter to within two miles of Anloc in continuing efforts to relieve this besieged city.

Sea War Ten Communist supply boats are sunk and 20 others are damaged off the mouth of the Cua Viet River as US warships continue to shell North and South Vietnamese coastlines.

19 MAY 1972
Ground War Units of South Vietnam's 9th and 21st Divisions as well as airborne battalions open new stretches of road near Anloc and reach to within two miles of the besieged city. Preceded by heavy shelling, North Vietnamese troops try to break through the lines of South Vietnam's 23rd Division defending Kontum, and fail.

20 MAY 1972
Diplomatic President Nixon meets with Brezhnev for summit talks in Moscow. Although Vietnam is discussed, there is no change in the Soviet Union's support of North Vietnam, and both parties are apparently unwilling to risk detente over the topic.

Ground War A heavy North Vietnamese attack brings the South Vietnamese column moving up Route 13 to relieve Anloc to a standstill.

23 MAY 1972
Ground War North Vietnam's 1st Division invades the lower Mekong Delta. Their apparent objective is Chuongthien province, known for its weakness in resisting Communist infiltration. Almost all regular ARVN troops have been withdrawn from the Mekong Delta to aid in the battle for Anloc.

Air War The heavy US air attacks which began with Nixon's 8 May interdiction order are widened to include more industrial and non-military sites. In 190 strikes, the US loses one plane, but shoots down four. The strikes concentrate on rail lines around Hanoi and Haiphong, rail lines to China, bridges, pipelines, power plants, troops and troop training facilities.

25 MAY 1972
Ground War North Vietnamese tanks and troops launch a frontal attack on Kontum. Tanks and commandos which previously slipped into the city cut it off from its airport, the besieged city's only means of supply. Some 148 North Vietnamese are reported killed in heavy fighting in Kontum's northeast sector. B-52s begin bombing North Vietnamese troop concentrations in the city.

29 MAY 1972
International In a joint communiqué issued by the United States and the Soviet Union following the conclusion of summit talks during President Nixon's visit to Moscow – the first visit ever by an US president – both countries set forth their standard positions on Vietnam. The United States insists that the future of South Vietnam should be left to the South Vietnamese without interference; and the Soviet Union insists on a withdrawal of US and allied forces from South Vietnam and an end to the bombing of North Vietnam.

2 JUNE 1972
USA: Domestic One hundred protestors gather on the White House sidewalk to begin the second year of an anti-Vietnam war vigil. Originally begun by a Quaker group, the vigil is sustained by various activists.

Air War Thirty to 40 USAF planes and helicopters fly through heavy fire to rescue

South Vietnamese forces follow terrified children after an accidental aerial napalm strike.

CHRONOLOGY

Captain R C Locher, who has been trapped northwest of Hanoi since his Phantom jet went down 10 May.

3 JUNE 1972
War Crimes A 260-page secret Army analysis of the Mylai 4 massacre – known as the Peers report and made public by Pulitzer Prize-winning journalist Seymour Hersh – concludes that the entire command structure of the Americal Division – including Brigadier Generals Koster and Young – wittingly and unwittingly suppressed information on the Mylai incident.

4 JUNE 1972
War Crimes Seymour Hersh further reports that a massacre at Mykhe 4, two miles from Mylai, was perpetrated by Bruno Company, Task Force Barker, Americal Division, on 16 March 1968, the same day as the Mylai massacre. No prosecutions have been made because of lack of evidence. The Peers report acknowledges that 'a large number of non-combatants were killed during the search of the hamlet.'
Ground War North Vietnamese troops repeatedly attack Phoumy, the capital of Binhdinh province, and are beaten back only after US planes kill 60 soldiers.

5 JUNE 1972
USA: Military Secretary of Defense Laird, testifying before a joint Congressional Appropriations Committee, says the increase in US military activity in Vietnam could add $3-5 billion to the 1973 fiscal budget, doubling the annual cost of the war.

6 JUNE 1972
South Vietnam South Vietnamese forces have driven out all but a few of the Communist troops remaining in Kontum, with over 200 North Vietnamese killed in six skirmishes. Several thousand North Vietnamese troops remain in the vicinity.

7 JUNE 1972
USA: Government At the UN Conference on Human Environment in Stockholm, the United States protests Sweden's use of the term 'ecocide' in denouncing US use of herbicides in Vietnam. The United States endorses the concept that countries have new international responsibilities toward each other for actions affecting the environment.
USA: Domestic Senator George McGovern, who has swept the Democratic party spring primaries and was one of the earliest and most vocal opponents of US Vietnam war policy, continues to make the war one of the central issues of the campaign by announcing at a news conference that he would go 'anywhere in the world' to negotiate an end to the war and a return of US troops and POWs.
Air War US planes continue the heaviest bombing of the war. Munitions used in bombing account for most of the increased cost of the war.

9 JUNE 1972
Ground War Part of the relief column composed mainly of 21st Division troops which has been trying to reach besieged Anloc from the Mekong Delta since 9 April finally arrives. These units do not significantly reinforce Anloc, and the two month siege is not lifted; observers feel that the best hope for Anloc is that the North Vietnamese will run out of shells. In Military Region II senior US advisor John Paul Vann is killed in a helicopter crash, probably shot down by a North Vietnamese unit. Military intelligence reports that the entire North Vietnamese 325th C Division has moved into South Vietnam to join the drive against Hué.
Air War Under President Nixon, the number of USAF fighter bombers in Southeast Asia has tripled, the number of aircraft carriers has tripled, and B-52s are being quadrupled. Six carriers are in the Tonkin Gulf, where before there were two, and two more are en route, with a total personnel of 40,000 to 60,000. Because of the USAF commitment to battle-field support in South Vietnam, Navy planes are flying two-thirds of the attack sorties against North Vietnam.

10 JUNE 1972
Air War US Phantom jets destroy Langchi hydroelectric power plant, using 2000-pound bombs guided by laser. Langchi plant supplied electricity to the Hanoi-Haiphong area.

12 JUNE 1972
USA: Military General John D Lavelle, former four-star general and USAF commander in Southeast Asia, testifies before the House Armed Services Committee that he was relieved of his post in March and later demoted after repeatedly ordering unauthorized bombing of military targets in North Vietnam. Court martial charges brought against him by his subordinates,

Guerrillas on patrol in Quang Tri Province.

which also implicated his superiors – particularly General Abrams – are dropped by the Air Force because the 'interests of discipline' have already been served. Lavelle becomes the first four-star general in modern US history to be demoted on retirement, although he continues to receive full general's retirement pay of $27,000 per year.

Covert War The Joint US Public Affairs Office (JUSPAO) in Saigon is closed after four years of directing psychological warfare in Vietnam. Its duties are taken over by the USIA and other agencies; JUSPAO is declared successful in 'winning the hearts and minds' of the Vietnamese people.

China In its strongest statement against the United States since President Nixon's February visit, China for the first time denounces the intensified bombing of North Vietnam, calling the raids, which approach her borders for the first time since 1968, acts of aggression against the Vietnamese people and 'grave provocations against the Chinese people.'

13 JUNE 1972

Ground War Large numbers of fresh South Vietnamese troops are flown into the Anloc area. Although most of the Communist troops within the garrison have been eliminated, North Vietnamese forces still block Route 13 and continue to shell Anloc.

14 JUNE 1972

Air War US planes, flying a record number of strikes over North Vietnam – 340 – sever the main railway line between Hanoi and Haiphong.

17 JUNE 1972

USA: Domestic Five men are arrested for breaking into the Democratic National Committee offices at the Watergate Hotel in Washington DC.

19 JUNE 1972

War Crimes Calling the Mylai massacre 'trifling by comparison,' veteran Vietnam war correspondent Kevin Buckley charges that US soldiers deliberately killed thousands of Vietnamese citizens under the guise of 'pacification.' Buckley cites 1968 operation 'Speedy Express' in which as many as 5000 civilians may have been killed in the Mekong Delta province of Kien Hoa. Records show that Americans list 10,899 fatalities for the operation, but only 748 weapons captured; civilians he interviewed report that most of the enemy fatalities were unarmed farmers working in rice fields.

CHRONOLOGY

20 JUNE 1972
USA: Government President Nixon appoints General Creighton W Abrams, commander of US forces in Vietnam, to be US Army Chief of Staff.
Air War US Marine unit HMA-369 begins flying armed helicopter strikes with the new AH-1J Sea Cobra from the decks of the USS *Constellation*, off the coast of South Vietnam. Flying from the USS *Coral Sea*, A-6 Intruders of Marine unit VMA(AW)-224 make most of their missions into Laos and North Vietnam.

22 JUNE 1972
Ground War South Vietnam's 21st Division, decimated by attempts to relieve Anloc, is replaced by the 25th Division. The siege of Anloc continues. US helicopters fly 18th Division troops to positions south of Anloc to replace badly battered 9th Division troops. In a major Communist drive, 146 North Vietnamese are killed and 18 tanks destroyed against the South Vietnamese defense line west of Hué.

23 JUNE 1972
Ground War US helicopters are required to fly almost all the dangerous missions around Anloc because South Vietnamese crews have panicked under fire. Several US helicopters and their crews have been lost in the last two weeks, causing bitterness among US airmen.

26 JUNE 1972
USA: Domestic Syndicated columnist Jack Anderson makes public four unpublished volumes of the Pentagon Papers which cover Johnson administration efforts to get peace talks started. Anderson defends his disclosure, remarking that President Nixon has made public 'even more sensitive negotiations.' The Democratic National Convention Platform Committee approves a plank making the first order of business for a victorious presidential candidate the immediate withdrawal of US forces from Vietnam.
Air War The United States establishes a 25-mile-wide buffer zone along Vietnam's border with China within which it will not bomb.
Thailand The shift of fighter bomber squadrons involving up to 150 US planes and more than 2000 pilots from Danang to bases in Thailand is completed. The shift was necessitated by the pending withdrawal of the US 19th Infantry Brigade, which provided security for flyers at Danang.

27 JUNE 1972
South Vietnam After over two months of congressional wrangling, President Thieu is granted emergency powers enabling him to rule by decree for six months. The final Senate vote is held after Saigon's curfew, when no opposition members are present, and the Senate later passes a non-binding resolution asserting that Thieu has no authority to rule by decree.

28 JUNE 1972
USA: Government President Nixon announces that no more draftees will be sent to Vietnam unless they volunteer for such duty. A force of 10,000 troops will be withdrawn from Vietnam by 1 September, leaving a total of 39,000.
Ground War Over 10,000 South Vietnamese marines and paratroopers push across the Mychanh River to begin a drive to retake Quangtri province. Supported by at least 17 US cruisers and destroyers and 100 B-52s flying the largest number of missions to date against Communist troop positions, the counteroffensive meets with stiff opposition and makes little headway.

29 JUNE 1972
Negotiations President Nixon agrees to the resumption of peace talks in Paris 'on the assumption that the North Vietnamese are prepared to negotiate in a constructive and serious way.' Talks will begin again 13 July.
Ground War A force of 1000 South Vietnamese marines arrive by US helicopter to join the counteroffensive to retake Quangtri City.

30 JUNE 1972
Ground War More South Vietnamese troops arrive in Quangtri province by helicopter for the third straight day. Supported by continued US air and naval firepower, the counteroffensive troops penetrate to six or seven miles from Quangtri City.

2 JULY 1972
Covert War US military and civilian sources disclose that weather modification techniques such as seeding clouds to suppress antiaircraft fire and hinder troop movements – meteorological warfare – have been used in both Vietnam and Laos since 1963.

7 JULY 1972
Ground War South Vietnamese troops advancing in Quangtri are brought to a

Political cartoons echoed public opinion. Above: Oliphant's War and Peace.

standstill at Lavangha village about two miles from Quangtri City. Heavy Communist shelling of Hué continues; the main highways to Anloc remain blocked.

Laos Premier Souvanna Phouma accepts the offer of Pathet Lao leader Prince Souphanouvong to resume talks to end the fighting. Negotiations will begin 17 October and continue throughout the year, but remain fruitless.

10 JULY 1972
Ground War Although President Thieu claims that his troops have entered or taken the city, fighting remains deadlocked outside Quangtri City, and relatively static on South Vietnam's two other fronts. Military action has increased so much in the last 24 hours in the Mekong area southwest of Saigon that some believe the Communists are opening a new front there.

13 JULY 1972
Negotiations The formal Paris peace talks resume after a 10-week break. Both sides restate their positions; central to the talks is the future of the Saigon government.

14 JULY 1972
USA: Domestic Six national leaders of the 20,000-member Vietnam Veterans Against the War are indicted by a federal grand jury on charges of conspiring to set off an 'armed rebellion' at the Republican National Convention.

15 JULY 1972
Ground War South Vietnamese troops trying to retake Quangtri City finally break through, advancing to within 700 yards of the Citadel, a large walled fortress in the center of town.
Air War B-52s bombing Communist bunkers around Quangtri City kill 300 soldiers in two raids.

17 JULY 1972
Ground War South Vietnamese paratroopers fight their way to within 200 yards of the Citadel in Quangtri City, described as a city of rubble and ash. Citizens emerging from neighborhoods retaken by the paratroopers join the refugees heading south to Hué on Route 1. Many claim they were not badly treated by the occupying North Vietnamese.

19 JULY 1972
Negotiations Washington and Hanoi announce that the secret Paris peace talks have resumed. Henry Kissinger and Le Duc Tho confer for six-and-a-half hours. By mutual agreement neither side reveals details of the meetings.

CHRONOLOGY

Ground War A force of 8000-10,000 ARVN troops preceded by an advance infantry battalion lifted in by South Vietnamese helicopters move north toward district capital Hoaian in Communist-controlled Binhdinh province to open a counteroffensive in this coastal province. Saigon's forces succeed in taking the city two days later, but lose the western half one week after that.

21 JULY 1972
USA: Military The Defense Department acknowledges unsuccessful attempts to destroy rain-forest cover in 1966 and 1967 by starting forest fires, but denies secrecy or desire to create devastating fire storms. During Operation Pink Rose, an area the size of Philadelphia was defoliated and hit with magnesium bombs, but the tropical forest proved too moist for the project, which was undertaken by the Defense Department and US Forest Service experts.

24 JULY 1972
USA: Domestic The US Senate passes the Cooper amendment to a military aid bill, the amendment stipulating complete US troop withdrawal from Vietnam within four months if Hanoi releases all US POWs. The overall bill is killed, in what is seen as a retaliatory victory by the Nixon administration.
United Nations UN Secretary General Kurt Waldheim discloses that he has received information that apparently confirms that US planes and naval vessels have deliberately damaged dikes in North Vietnam that are essential to flood control during the rainy season. The North Vietnamese have repeatedly claimed that their dikes have deliberately been bombed since US air and naval attacks resumed above the 20th Parallel in May. The US Defense Department, President Nixon, and Secretary of State William P Rogers claim that any US strikes against the dikes are accidental, and that damage has been insignificant. Nixon calls Waldheim 'well-intentioned and naive,' asserting that the dike controversy is a deliberate attempt on the part of the North Vietnamese to create an extraneous issue, to divert attention from 'one of the most barbaric invasions of history.'
Air War US fighter bombers attack supply complexes in Hanoi in the first strikes against the capital in a month. Laser guided bombs are used because their pinpoint accuracy allows them to 'hit the target and not the civilians,' despite the cost which is four to five times as much as conventional bombs; laser and TV guided bombs, introduced by the United States in Vietnam, have proven themselves successful and accurate, and have, according to one US official, introduced 'a whole new magnitude' of warfare.

26 JULY 1972
Ground War Although South Vietnamese paratroopers hoist their flag over Quangtri Citadel, they prove unable to hold the Citadel for long or to secure Quangtri City; fighting outside the city remains intense. South Vietnamese troops under heavy shelling are forced to abandon Fire Base Bastogne, which protects the southwest approach to Hué.

28 JULY 1972
USA: Government A CIA report made public by the Nixon administration reveals that accidental minor damage to North Vietnam's dikes has been caused by US bombing at 12 places. The nearly 2000 miles of dikes on the Tonkin plain and more than 2000 along the sea make civilized life possible in the Red River Delta; the destruction of the dikes would destroy centuries of patient work and cause the drowning or starvation of hundreds of thousands of peasants. Bombing the dikes has been advocated by some US strategists since the beginning of US involvement in the war, and has been rejected outright by most US presidents as an act of terrorism unworthy of the United States.
USSR The Soviet Union continues to publicize what it calls the two-month US bombing campaign to destroy the dikes and dams of the Tonkin Delta.

29 JULY 1972
War Crimes Former US Attorney General Ramsey Clark visits North Vietnam as a member of the International Commission of Inquiry into US War Crimes in Indochina to investigate alleged US bombing of nonmilitary targets in North Vietnam. His visit stirs intense controversy at home. Clark reports over Hanoi radio that he has seen damage to hospitals, dikes, schools, and other civilian areas.

31 JULY 1972
North Vietnam Hanoi challenges the Nixon administration on the dike controversy,

Women of the People's Militia in Laos.

claiming that since April there have been 173 raids against the dikes with direct hits in '149 places.'

Cambodia About 2000 South Vietnamese troops begin an operation near Kompong Trabek in the Parrot's Beak region of eastern Cambodia which is designed to cripple a possible Communist operation against Route 4, which links Saigon with the Mekong Delta.

1 AUGUST 1972

Negotiations Henry Kissinger meets privately with Le Duc Tho and Xuan Thuy in Paris. Expecting explicit US agreement that North Vietnamese troops would remain in South Vietnam following a cease-fire (and pending a final settlement), the Communist demand for President Thieu's abdication is somewhat relaxed, although Hanoi is seen as in no hurry to change its terms before the November US presidential election, in which it favors McGovern.

2 AUGUST 1972

Ground War In the heaviest artillery bombardment since the North Vietnamese first attacked Quangtri City, 2000 rounds hit South Vietnamese marines striving to retake the provincial capital. Supported by US B-52s, ARVN troops re-enter Fire Base Bastogne, finding it empty.

5 AUGUST 1972

South Vietnam President Thieu announces a decree requiring every daily newspaper to deposit $47,000 with the government as a guarantee against possible fines and court charges. The government may also shut down any newspaper whose daily issue has been confiscated a second time for 'articles detrimental to the national security and public order.' Sixteen newspapers and 15 periodicals eventually cease publication, leaving only two opposition papers in Saigon.

7-8 AUGUST 1972

Ground War Communists attacking Long-thanh rubber plantations 17 miles east of Saigon, inflict heavy casualties on ARVN troops. On 10 August they succeed in closing Routes 1, 4, and 13, all major supply routes to Saigon. Throughout the next two months highways critical to Saigon's survival are closed by Communist forces, opened, and closed again.

Air War Seasonal bad weather has limited the

Roll call in the People's Liberation Army in Laos, 1972.

usual air strikes throughout North Vietnam, often reducing the usual number by one-third, except for B-52s, which fly above the clouds.

9 AUGUST 1972
Cambodia Over 2000 South Vietnamese rangers clash with North Vietnamese troops. US planes destroyed 14 tanks near Kompong Trabek the day before. A large Communist build-up is under way in Cambodia.

11 AUGUST 1972
Negotiations Calling Vietnamization the main target of the Communist forces, the chief Vietcong delegate to the Paris peace talks maintains that the key issue in the current talks is political settlement in Saigon.
Ground War The last US ground combat unit in Vietnam, the 3rd Battalion, 21st Infantry, is deactivated. Third Battalion's 1043 men guarded the US air base at Danang. Less than 44,600 US servicemen now remain in Vietnam, not including 7th Fleet sailors or airmen, or air force personnel in Thailand and Guam.

13 AUGUST 1972
USA: Domestic Ex-US Army Captain J E Engstrom says that a military report he

helped prepare in 1971 estimating that 25 percent of the lower-ranking military men in Vietnam were addicted to heroin was suppressed and replaced by a 'watered-down' version considered more acceptable to the US command.
Guerrilla War Vietcong guerrillas blow up several thousand tons of ammunition at Longbinh. The relative stability of battle lines in South Vietnam leads some observers to believe that the communists may be reverting to guerrilla tactics.

14 AUGUST 1972
South Vietnam The Interior Ministry denies reports of widespread torture of political prisoners who have been rounded up since the start of the Communist offensive. According to smuggled interviews and documents at least 10,000 persons have been imprisoned in re-education centers, with arrests continuing, and many prisoners are being taken to Con Son jail by the CIA's Air America airline. Critics charge that police make little distinction between those who have Communist connections and those who are merely opposed to the Thieu regime. US advisors on police and prison matters do not deny widespread torture and the use of Air America.
USA: Domestic Former US Attorney General

Ramsey Clark reports after his tour of North Vietnam with the International Commission of Inquiry into US War Crimes in Indochina that if Democratic candidate George McGovern is elected president, all US POWs will be freed by North Vietnam within three months. He reports that the POWs he interviewed in North Vietnam were 'unquestionably ... well treated,' and that he saw damage to North Vietnam's dikes in at least six places, and other extensive destruction in non-military areas.

Negotiations Kissinger again meets privately with Le Duc Tho and Xuan Thuy in Paris.

16 AUGUST 1972

Air War US fighter bombers fly the highest daily total of air strikes against North Vietnam – 370 – of the year as the weather improves, although conditions above Hanoi remain marginal. Fighter bombers fly 294 missions in South Vietnam, most in Quangtri province; and B-52s fly eight strikes in North Vietnam, three in the DMZ, and 24 in South Vietnam.

16-18 AUGUST 1972

Negotiations Kissinger meets with President Thieu in Saigon, 17-18 August, and Le Duc Tho leaves for Hanoi, 16 August, giving rise to rumors that an agreement is close at hand. An official statement says that the meetings in Saigon are a general review of the situation in Vietnam and in Paris.

19 AUGUST 1972

Ground War After a heavy bombardment against northern district capital Queson and neighboring Base Camp Ross, in which the Communists use 130-mm guns with 17-mile range for the first time in the area, Communist forces take the town and the camp. The ARVN troops flee south with hundreds of civilians, leaving behind tanks, artillery, and heavy weapons. This major defeat gives the Communists control of most of Queson district in Quangnam province.

22 AUGUST 1972

USA: Domestic Delegates entering the Republican National Convention are harassed

Captain Steve Richie was the first USAF ace of the Vietnam War.

CHRONOLOGY

by 3000 anti-war demonstrators, many with painted death masks. Thousands of anti-war demonstrators roam Miami Beach during the convention sessions. Hundreds are arrested, and many are injured as police use crowd-controlling gasses.

Ground War Bypassing South Vietnamese strong points around Hué and Danang, the North Vietnamese open a major new front to the south of Quangtri, moving in heavy 130-mm artillery without detection.

26 AUGUST 1972
USA: Military US officials report that the rate of civilian casualties in South Vietnam has risen more than 50 percent since the beginning of North Vietnam's spring offensive. 24,788 civilians have been wounded between 30 March and 31 July, an average of 6197 per month, compared to an average of 2700 for each of the six months preceding.

27 AUGUST 1972
Air War In the heaviest bombing in four years, US planes destroy 96 buildings and damage 78 at Xombai army barracks, 37 miles northwest of Hanoi, and leave Haiduong Barracks West, 23 miles northwest of Haiphong, in flames. Planes also hit bridges on the northeast railroad line to China.

Sea War Four US ships raid the Haiphong port area after dark, shelling to within two miles of the city limits. Cruiser *Newport News* sinks one of two North Vietnamese patrol boats in pursuit, and destroyer *Rowan* sets the other on fire.

28 AUGUST 1972
Air War USAF Captain Richard Ritchie shoots down a MiG over Hanoi, his fifth of the war, to become the first USAF ace of the Vietnam war. Most US missions in South Vietnam and all US missions over North Vietnam are flown from aircraft carriers and bases in Thailand. Bienhoa, a fighter bomber base, is the only US base in South Vietnam.

29 AUGUST 1972
Ground War President Nixon announces the withdrawal of 12,000 more US troops from South Vietnam (from 39,000 to 27,000), to be completed by 1 December.

30 AUGUST 1972
Ground War North Vietnamese artillery hits South Vietnamese marine positions around Quangtri with about 2000 heavy-caliber shells. The shelling is understood to indicate that the North Vietnamese are experiencing no shortages in Quangtri despite allied efforts to cut supply lines.

31 AUGUST 1972
Ground War US command reports five Americans killed, three wounded in the past week, the lowest total since record-keeping began in January 1965.

2 SEPTEMBER 1972
Air War US planes wreck one of North Vietnam's biggest air bases, Phucyen airfield, 10 miles north of Hanoi, shooting down one MiG in a dogfight. Forty-seven MiGs have been shot down since the beginning of the North Vietnamese offensive, and 18 US planes downed by MiGs out of a total of 67 shot down by MiGs for the entire war.

5 SEPTEMBER 1972
Laos US helicopters evacuate Meo tribesmen who have suffered heavy losses following an offensive action around the Plain of Jars that began in mid-August.

6 SEPTEMBER 1972
South Vietnam The Thieu government abolishes popular elections in the country's 10,775 hamlets and supercedes a 1968 law establishing the election of hamlet and village officers. The 44 province chiefs – all appointed by Thieu – are ordered to reorganize local government and appoint hamlet officials. Thieu cites the Communist offensive as justification for the measures – he claims that many hamlet chiefs are Communists and provide support for insurgents – but the decree was in preparation before the offensive.

Ground War Twenty-two soldiers of South Vietnam's 9th Infantry Division are killed and 176 wounded in an attack on its forward command post in the Mekong Delta, 60 miles from Saigon. ARVN troops abandon the district town of Tienphuoc, 37 miles south of Danang, leaving the Communists in control of two-thirds of Quangtin province. Saigon transfers a regiment from Quangtri to Danang, an apparent success of Communist strategy, which is to force South Vietnam to spread its forces thin.

8 SEPTEMBER 1972
Sea War The US Department of Defense reports that the US destroyer *Warrington*,

damaged beyond repair on 17 July, may have been the first victim of the US mining of North Vietnamese waters.

10 SEPTEMBER 1972
South Vietnam The US Embassy in Saigon protests continuing South Vietnamese national radio and TV broadcasts which for four weeks have been calling presidential candidate McGovern a 'mad dog' and 'enemy of the people.'

Guerrilla War Communist saboteurs hit Tansonnhut and Bienhoa, Saigon's two closest major airports. Two South Vietnamese are killed, 20 hurt, and five South Vietnamese planes are damaged at Tansonnhut. Forty Americans are wounded at Bienhoa where one gunship and 50 South Vietnamese helicopters are damaged.

12 SEPTEMBER 1972
USA: Government The CIA and the Defense Intelligence Agency report to the National Security Council that North Vietnam can sustain fighting in the South 'at the present rate' for two years; that while US bombing has caused heavy casualties and prevented North Vietnam from doubling operations, the overall effects are disappointing because troops and supplies have kept moving; that 20,000 fresh North Vietnamese troops have infiltrated into the South in the last six weeks, bringing their total to 100,000 regular troops; that North Vietnamese troops in the Mekong Delta have increased as much as tenfold – up to 30,000 – in the last year; and that a third oil pipeline, like the others nearly impossible to cut by air strikes, has been completed between North Vietnam and China.

15 SEPTEMBER 1972
Ground War In Saigon's most significant victory since the beginning of Hanoi's spring offensive, ARVN troops recapture the Citadel and city of Quangtri after four days of fierce combat. Fleeing North Vietnamese continue to put up resistance from their deployments around the Han River. South Vietnam reports 8135 North Vietnamese and 977 South Vietnamese killed in the four-and-a-half-month battle for Quangtri City.

16 SEPTEMBER 1972
Ground War Communist forces begin an offensive in southern Quangngai province south of the provincial capital Quangngai City

with simultaneous attacks concentrating on district capitals Bato, Moduc, Ducpho, Binhson, and Tunghia. The offensive makes steady progress; Bato falls two days later, indicating that the Communist offensive is far from over.

Air War The USAF reports it has destroyed 90 percent of North Vietnam's biggest railroad yard, 38 miles from Hanoi, on the northeast line running to China.

17 SEPTEMBER 1972
North Vietnam Hanoi ceremoniously releases three US pilots, the first POWs released since 1969, cautioning the United States not to force the freed men to 'slander' Hanoi, and claiming that the 'distortions' about Hanoi's treatment of POWs that resulted from the previous release of prisoners in 1969 caused Hanoi to temporarily suspend the release of POWs. Hanoi's conditions for the pilots' release include that the men (1) do nothing to further the US war effort in Indochina, (2) return home with members of the Committee for Liaison with Families of American Servicemen Detained in Vietnam, the American group headed by Cora Weiss who arranged their release, (3) receive 30-day furloughs if desired, (4) receive medical examinations at either military or private hospitals.

19 SEPTEMBER 1972
Air War USAF ace Captain Charles D DeBellevue shoots down his sixth MiG to become the leading ace of the war.

20 SEPTEMBER 1972
Riverine War The USAF reveals that US planes have been mining the coastal rivers and canals of northern Quangtri province below the DMZ. This may be the first mining of waterways within Vietnam.

22 SEPTEMBER 1972
Ground War The fighting in Quangngai province moves closer to provincial capital Quangngai City, forcing South Vietnamese troops to abandon one fire base to the east and one fire base to the west of the city to attacking North Vietnamese.

26 SEPTEMBER 1972
Air War The USAF announces it is sending two squadrons (48 planes) of F-111 attack bombers to Ta Khli Air Base, Thailand, to strengthen its low-level and all-weather

CHRONOLOGY

capabilities for the approaching monsoon season in North Vietnam.

28 SEPTEMBER 1972
Ground War No US combat deaths occurred in the preceding week for the first time since March 1965. Although North Vietnamese troops make some harassing attacks in Quangngai province, a general lull in ground fighting continues for the sixth straight day.

30 SEPTEMBER 1972
Air War US planes, hitting North Vietnamese air bases Phucyen, Yenbai, Quangland, and Vinh destroy five MiG interceptors on the ground and damage nine others, also on the ground, those hit equal about 10 percent of Hanoi's tactical air force.

1 OCTOBER 1972
Sea War A shell exploding in the barrel of a gun on heavy cruiser *Newport News* results in the deaths of 20 seamen and injury to 37. Towed to Subic Bay in the Philippines for repairs, she is needed so badly on the gun line that she is returned to action with the center port sealed.

3 OCTOBER 1972
USA: Military The Department of Defense reports that more than 800,000 tons of 'air ammunition' has been used over Indochina between 1 January and 30 September, compared with 763,160 for all of 1971. US planes have dropped 7,555,800 tons of bombs on Indochina between February 1965 and 30 August 1972. (Combined allied tonnage during World War II was 2,056,244.)

7 OCTOBER 1972
Ground War Newly-infiltrated Communist troops attack Saigon forces along Route 13 in an area nine to 20 miles north of Saigon in a new phase in the Communist offensive. Mytho is hit by a series of light attacks; there have been over 100 Communist attacks during the last 24 hours. What is left of Quangtri City – 'a wasteland' – is securely under control of South Vietnamese marines. Most of the 300,000 persons who fled Quangtri province during the spring offensive now live in squalid refugee camps at Danang. **Air War** US B-52s continue heavy raids in Bienhduong province aimed at preventing Communist infiltration toward Saigon. US planes fly 300 strikes over North Vietnam.

Cambodia In one of the heaviest raids inside Pnompenh since the beginning of the war, about 200 Vietnamese Communists blow up a bridge over the Tonle Sap, less than two miles from the center of Pnompenh, killing 36 Cambodian soldiers and civilians and losing 28 of their own force.

8-11 OCTOBER 1972
Negotiations Lengthy meetings in Paris between Le Duc Tho, Xuan Thuy, Henry Kissinger, and Major General Alexander Haig, who met recently with President Thieu in Saigon, give rise to rumors that a breakthrough has occurred in the peace talks. Le Duc Tho, presuming the Americans are eager for peace in Vietnam before the elections, proposes that the United States and North Vietnam arrange a cease-fire governing all military matters between themselves, leaving the political questions to be settled by the Vietnamese sides, who will be governed by a 'National Council of Reconciliation' until a final settlement is reached. Hanoi and Saigon will remain separate entities and will continue to occupy the territory each presently controls until then. Kissinger, who considers Hanoi's offer a great breakthrough, explicitly agrees to North Vietnamese troops remaining in the South. He cables President Thieu to 'seize as much territory as possible,' and the Pentagon begins to furnish Thieu with $2 billion of matériel – Operation Enhance Plus – which would be replaceable under the agreement. US military bases that would have to be dismantled are transferred to South Vietnamese ownership. By the end of Operation Enhance Plus, which lasts six weeks, South Vietnam has the fourth largest air force in the world.

9 OCTOBER 1972
Guerrilla War Although Saigon forces drive guerrillas out of one hamlet near the capital and infiltration in the area is relatively minor in comparison to the spring, several hundred Vietcong continue to control at least three hamlets within 20 miles north of Saigon. US and South Vietnamese planes continue heavy bombing in areas of suspected guerrilla activity.

11 OCTOBER 1972
Air War US Navy planes attacking the Gialam railroad yard three miles to the northeast are responsible for the accidental bombing which heavily damages the French

Correspondents for the major news media continued to report from the front.

diplomatic mission in Hanoi and results in the death of Delegate General Pierre Susini. The nearby Algerian and Indian missions are also hit.

12 OCTOBER 1972

South Vietnam President Thieu, in a speech in Saigon, says 'coalition with the Communists means death' and that the Communists will have to be killed 'to the last man' before there is peace.

USA: Military The US Senate approves the nomination of General Creighton Abrams, commander of US forces in Vietnam since mid-1968, as Army chief of staff. Consideration of his approval was sidetracked for months by Senate hearings into unauthorized bombing raids against North Vietnam ordered by General John Lavelle, whose testimony before the House Armed Services Committee sometimes implicated General Abrams.

USA: Domestic Senators Harold Hughes (D-IA) and William Proxmire (D-WI) say Congress will demand more hearings into unauthorized bombing of North Vietnam

unless the Department of Defense immediately improves command and control procedures.

Negotiations The 163rd session of the regular peace talks is held in Paris.

Ground War Communist troops hit the US Special Forces camp at Benhet with 1500 rockets, overrunning it. One US military instructor is killed and one wounded in an ambush of a South Vietnamese Army convoy 25 miles southeast of Saigon. South Vietnamese troops retake Bato, south of Danang. North Vietnamese maintain their control of at least two hamlets within 20 miles of Saigon.

12-13 OCTOBER 1972

Sea War Forty-six black and white crewmen aboard the aircraft carrier *Kitty Hawk* off Vietnam are injured in racial brawls involving more than 100 sailors. Twenty-one black crewmen are eventually charged with assault and rioting and face court-martial in San Diego. Further racial clashes in San Deigo in November result in the reassignment of 123 mostly black seamen aboard the aircraft carrier *Constellation*, who refuse to board the ship after shore leave because they 'fear for their lives.' Late in November black/white clashes occur between 30 seamen at the naval station at Midway Island in the Pacific and among 33 seamen at the Navy Correctional Center in Norfolk, VA.

16 OCTOBER 1972
Ground War Communist attacks concentrate on major roads in the Saigon area and shelling disrupts traffic. Nearly 100 harassing attacks occur in the last 24 hours.
Air War US planes carry out the heaviest raids of the year against North Vietnam, with at least 370 strikes; B-52s hit Communist positions in Cambodia and Laos.

17 OCTOBER 1972
Negotiations After another meeting in Paris, Henry Kissinger flies to Saigon for four days of talks with President Thieu, who has for two days denied the requests of US Ambassador Ellsworth Bunker to see him. There is a growing feeling that the secret peace talks in Paris have reached a critical stage. US Army Chief of Staff General Abrams is en route to Saigon; Pacific Commander in Chief Admiral Noel Gayler is also in Saigon, possibly to work out the military details of a cease-fire.
Ground War Saigon's supply of food is affected and driving outside the city is hazardous due to continued Communist activity against the highways around the capital.

19 OCTOBER 1972
USA: Military Faced with growing congressional concern over the unauthorized bombing of North Vietnam, Defense Secretary Laird announces revised command procedures aimed at 'further strengthening' civilian control of the military. A new group of inspectors general will conduct regular checks to see if orders from Washington are being carried out, and inspectors general from the various service branches will henceforth report to their civilian service secretaries as well as their military chiefs.

20 OCTOBER 1972
USA: Military The United States formally admits that US Navy planes accidentally dropped the bomb which 'inadvertently struck' the French Embassy in Hanoi 11 October. The United States had asserted that the damage was done by a North Vietnamese SAM-2 missile; many Frenchmen consider the incident a result of the United States' using the bombing of North Vietnam to test new weapons.

21 OCTOBER 1972
Negotiations North Vietnam's Premier Pham Van Dong announces that Hanoi will accept a cease-fire as the first step in a peace settlement. As outlined by Pham Van Dong, the cease-fire is to be followed by the withdrawal of US forces, with all POWs to be released when the settlement is agreed upon. Saigon and the Vietcong will join in a coalition followed by general elections within six months. President Thieu is not mentioned.

22 OCTOBER 1972
Negotiations Henry Kissinger meets with President Thieu in Saigon to try to secure Thieu's agreement to the cease-fire draft, particularly to Vietcong participation in postwar South Vietnam. Thieu, who wishes South Vietnam to be recognized as a sovereign state, accuses the United States of conspiring with China and the Soviet Union to undermine his regime, and rejects the proposed accord almost point for point. Kissinger, who is due to initial the draft in Hanoi at the end of the month, cables President Nixon that Thieu's terms 'verge on insanity,' and flies home.
Ground War Bienhoa airport is hit by a barrage of Communist rockets; South Vietnamese commanders report that they do not feel that the peace talks have affected military action.
Air War US B-52s continue bombing Communist positions in an arc north of Saigon; US planes fly 220 missions over North Vietnam.
Laos Increased fighting erupts as both Communist and government forces attempt to gain ground before an anticipated Indochinese cease-fire. Governmment troops begin a drive to retake the southern village of Saravane, and succeed six days later; the village changes hands four more times by the end of the year.

24 OCTOBER 1972
Negotiations The White House orders all bombing north of the 20th Parallel temporarily halted as a signal of US approval of recent North Vietnamese concessions at the secret peace talks in Paris. Bombing within South Vietnam has increased. According to Nixon administration sources, the principal obstacle to a cease-fire is in Saigon, where

President Thieu broadcasts a denunciation of the cease-fire treaty, calling all peace proposals discussed by Kissinger and Hanoi in Paris unacceptable, and urging his troops to wipe out Communist presence in the South 'quickly and mercilessly.'

26 OCTOBER 1972

North Vietnam Hanoi broadcasts a summary of the US-North Vietnamese nine-point cease-fire draft treaty agreement and accuses the United States of trying to sabotage it by claiming difficulties in Saigon.

USA: Government Hoping to reassure the North Vietnamese of US sincerity and President Thieu of US determination to see the treaty through, Henry Kissinger announces at a White House news conference that 'We believe that an agreement is in sight.' In his first public report on the secret peace talks, Kissinger confirms Hanoi's announcement that a breakthrough occurred 8 October, with both sides reaching an over-all agreement on a nine-point peace plan. Although he denies that the United States agreed to sign the document by 31 October, Kissinger says he believes a final agreement could be reached in one more meeting with the North Vietnamese lasting 'not more than three or four days.' The substance of the breakthrough is a settlement in two stages: a military cease-fire, followed by the Vietnamese parties settling their political problems among themselves.

Negotiations Xuan Thuy announces at a Paris news conference – the only one he has conducted personally since the 31 October 1968 announcement of the bombing halt agreement over North Vietnam – that Hanoi and the United States reached an agreement on 17 October on all but two points: the release of POWs and post-cease-fire arms shipments. He claims that since North Vietnam decided to accept the US proposals on these points, the US refusal to sign the treaty on 31 October and its request for more talks creates an 'extremely serious situation.'

29 OCTOBER 1972

South Vietnam All citizens must possess a South Vietnamese flag and produce it on demand, or face arrest; possession or display of a Vietcong flag is punishable by death. President Thieu is working on a decree that would make being a Communist or associating with a Communist punishable by death.

Negotiations The United States announces that the peace accord will definitely not be signed by 31 October, although optimism is expressed concerning early settlement of the remaining details.

Ground War Communist troops intensify infiltration around Saigon, occupying 17 hamlets within 40 miles of the city. Route 1 is cut east and west of Saigon. Communist attacks throughout South Vietnam – 138 – are the highest number for any single day in 1972.

Air War US B-52s and fighter bombers hit North Vietnam below the 20th Parallel. US B-52s fly 23 missions and fighter bombers make 313 strikes against Communist positions in South Vietnam.

31 OCTOBER 1972

Cambodia Hoping to expand their control of South Vietnamese territory before a truce goes into effect, several thousand North Vietnamese and Vietcong troops move out of Cambodia into South Vietnam's Mekong Delta and Saigon areas, leaving the burden of fighting Cambodian government troops to the Khmer Rouge.

1 NOVEMBER 1972

South Vietnam In further clarification of his objections to the draft peace treaty, President Thieu denounces it as a 'surrender of the South Vietnamese people to the Communists' and 'only a cease-fire to sell out Vietnam.'

Negotiations Xuan Thuy, in a TV interview in Paris, asserts that the problem with the peace settlement is not one of major or minor points, as the US claims, but the seriousness of the United States altogether. Hanoi does not object to another Kissinger-Le Duc Tho meeting; what Hanoi desires is that the United States keep its word.

Ground War Twenty-two Americans are killed in a helicopter crash near Mytho in the Mekong Delta.

Air War Heavy US bombing concentrates on North Vietnamese base areas in Laos and Cambodia.

Laos Pathet Lao and North Vietnamese Communist forces kill 200 government troops and force another 300 soldiers and 1000 civilians into Thailand as they overrun Namthorn Buk Kwang garrison, about 90 miles east of Vientiane. The operation is part of an offensive launched 28 October to gain ground before an expected cease-fire.

2 NOVEMBER 1972

Negotiations President Nixon announces that there will be no signing of the truce draft

Mass is said during a search and clear operation

agreement until all remaining issues are resolved. Hanoi radio announces that the US delay in signing forces North Vietnam to increase fighting on all fronts.

Ground War South Vietnam reports 142 Communist attacks in South Vietnam in the last 24 hours.

Air War The White House discloses that the South Vietnamese Air Force will receive hundreds of aircraft more than previously agreed upon. The increase is seen as another attempt to coax President Thieu into early acceptance of a cease-fire.

7 NOVEMBER 1972

USA: Domestic Richard Nixon is re-elected president, carrying all states but Massachusetts for 97 percent of the electoral votes, with only 55 percent of the electorate voting, the lowest turnout since 1948. The Democrats widen their majority in Congress, picking up two Senate seats. Nixon pledges himself to secure 'peace with honor in Vietnam.' US B-52s set a record for concentrated bombing of a single province – Quangtri – in a single day.

8 NOVEMBER 1972

South Korea South Korean troops cease all combat operations in South Vietnam and retire to rear bases at the request of the American and South Vietnamese governments. The 37,000 troops of its 48,000-man presence who remain are scheduled to depart in December.

10-12 NOVEMBER 1972

South Vietnam Hard-line Communist troops in the South led by General Le Vinh Khoa allegedly rebel against the Vietcong in protest over the pending negotiated settlement. The rebellion ends when Hanoi's Pham Van Dong gives clear orders in support of the Vietcong. Hanoi denies reports of the rebellion, calling them examples of CIA psychological warfare.

11 NOVEMBER 1972

Ground War The US Army turns over its Longbinh headquarters base to South Vietnam. The transfer of Longbinh, once the largest US military installation outside the continental United States, symbolizes the end of direct US participation in the war after seven years. About 29,000 US soldiers yet remain in South Vietnam, most of them advisors to ARVN troops, helicopter crewmen, and maintenance, supply, and office

staff. Communist shelling around Quangtri City is the heaviest in the area since the summer. The United States and Hanoi continue to move supplies into South Vietnam in preparation for a cease-fire.

14 NOVEMBER 1972

USA: Government One week after his re-election, President Nixon extends to President Thieu his 'absolute assurance' that the US will 'take swift and severe retaliatory action' if Hanoi violates the pending cease-fire once it is in place. He instructs Kissinger to present Le Duc Tho with 69 amendments to the treaty draft submitted by Thieu, despite Kissinger's protestations that the changes are 'preposterous' and may wreck the treaty.

15 NOVEMBER 1972

South Vietnam Senior official of the US pacification program in South Vietnam Willard E Chambers resigns after six years, 'in sheer disgust.' Chambers says that although he always supported the US policy of preventing a Communist takeover in South Vietnam, those in charge have been unequal to the task: a 'parade of overranked non-entities whose actions reflect their own ignorance of Vietnam, of the peculiarities of a people's war and of the requirements of counterinsurgency.'

Air War US planes make over 800 tactical air strikes in North Vietnam's southern panhandle, one of the heaviest days of raids in the war.

20-21 NOVEMBER 1972

Negotiations The twenty-first session of secret peace talks begins in Paris. The two major differences reportedly concern the nature of the international supervisory force (Canada, Hungary, Indonesia, Poland) which will monitor the agreement, and which the United States envisions as a force of several thousand, North Vietnam as not more than 250; and South Vietnam's sovereignty, which President Thieu insists upon.

22 NOVEMBER 1972

South Vietnam A captured North Vietnamese directive signed by Le Duan orders Communist forces in South Vietnam to observe a cease-fire scrupulously for the first 60 days, and repeats instructions to take as much territory as possible before a cease-fire. The directive predicts that South Vietnam will violate the cease-fire with arrests and attempts to retake territory.

Air War The first B-52 of the war to be shot down is hit by a SAM missile and lost near Vinh, North Vietnam, on the day when B-52s fly their heaviest raids of the war over North Vietnam. The Communists claim 19 B-52s shot down to date.

23-25 NOVEMBER 1972

Negotiations Secret talks resume in Paris. Break-up of the talks with no resumption scheduled before 4 December leads to speculation that the talks have reached an impasse. At issue is the implementation of the international supervisory force, as well as Saigon's insistence on the withdrawal of all North Vietnamese troops from South Vietnam.

27 NOVEMBER 1972

South Vietnam Sources in Saigon reveal that US officials have been secretly building up US civilian personnel under Department of Defense contracts. About 10,000 US advisors and technicians have been instructed to stay in South Vietnam after a cease-fire, essentially taking over the roles of departing military advisors.

Ground War There is heavy fighting in northern South Vietnam, in the foothills of Quangtri. The North Vietnamese have lately favored artillery, mortar, and rocket attacks, possibly reflecting loss of personnel during the lengthy fighting.

30 NOVEMBER 1972

USA: Government White House Press Secretary Ronald Ziegler says that no more public announcements concerning US troops withdrawals from Vietnam will be made now that the level of US presence has fallen to 27,000 men.

USA: Military Defense Department sources say that there will not be a full withdrawal of US forces from Vietnam until a final truce agreement is signed, and that such an agreement will not affect 54,000 US servicemen assigned to Thailand or the 60,000 aboard 7th Fleet ships off the Vietnamese coast.

Ground War Bad weather slows attempts by South Vietnamese troops to regain control of Quangtri province before the expected cease-fire.

Air War US B-52s make heavy bombing runs in Quangtri province and North Vietnam's southern panhandle; US fighter bombers fly 40 strikes despite bad weather.

Negotiations In two separate meetings, President Nixon and Henry Kissinger meet with the Joint Chiefs of Staff to brief them on the Paris talks, and the Joint Chiefs of Staff approve the terms of the projected truce settlement. Kissinger expresses the belief that a final agreement is near.

4 DECEMBER 1972

Negotiations Secret talks resume. Commenting on the problematical negotiations, Henry Kissinger says that the North Vietnamese have changed their position on all of the principal points agreed to by 20 November. Contradictory rumors about concessions, agreements, pressures, and plans continue to rise around the talks.

Ground War The second rocket attack in four days hits Bienhoa air base. The rockets are directed at pre-cease-fire stockpiling of US aircraft.

6 DECEMBER 1972

Negotiations Secret talks resume in Paris after a twenty-four-hour break during which US negotiators received new instructions from the White House.

Ground War Tansonnhut, one of two major airports near Saigon, is hit by the heaviest Communist rocket attack in four years. One US rescue helicopter is destroyed and a fuel dump is set ablaze. US planes bomb suspected Vietcong positions within 10 miles of the airport; the strikes are followed by ARVN troop attacks against the area from which the rockets were fired. Fighting continues around Quangtri; fighting in the Central Highlands has been heavy in the last few days.

7 DECEMBER 1972

USA: Government The US State Department announces that 100 Foreign Service officers are on the alert to go to South Vietnam after a truce, to report their observations to the US government and to relay possible truce violations to the international supervisory commission.

Negotiations Key issue at the secret Paris talks is currently Saigon's and/or Washington's insistence that all North Vietnamese troops be withdrawn from South Vietnam. Communist delegates at the formal talks renew their demand that the United States sign the 17 October draft agreement without any changes.

South Vietnamese marines are instructed in the use of an 81mm mortar.

Air War US B-52s drop in excess of 600 tons of bombs in and around the DMZ; 85 of the 242 strikes flown in the last 24 hours hit South Vietnam's northern military region.

9 DECEMBER 1972
Air War Heavy bombing of Communist troops and supply depots along the DMZ continues for the third straight day. US fighter bombers fly 60 missions in North Vietnam, and 208 in support of South Vietnamese troops in the South.

10 DECEMBER 1972
Negotiations Technical experts of both sides begin to work on the language of the accord, giving rise to expectations that a final agreement is close. General Haig, who has been briefing President Nixon on the Paris talks in Washington, is alerted to fly to Saigon with the document, so that Saigon could sign at the same time as the United States and Hanoi in Paris.
Ground War Fighting occurs near Tamky and Quangtri City, although Communist ground attacks are down; Vietcong attack two militia outposts in the southern Mekong Delta.
Air War US B-52s bomb both sides of the

DMZ for the fourth straight day, fighter bombers making 90 strikes in North Vietnam, 218 in South Vietnam.

12 DECEMBER 1972
Laos The Pathet Lao proposes an immediate truce to be supervised by a commission formed by representatives of both sides and the existing International Control Commission (ICC). The Laotian government will respond with a counter proposal on 19 December which is rejected by the Pathet Lao, whose own cease-fire proposal includes the withdrawal of all US and foreign troops within 90 days, and the formation of a coalition government, which the Laotian government rejects as unconstitutional.

13 DECEMBER 1972
Negotiations After meeting with Le Duc Tho for six hours, Henry Kissinger flies to the United States. The central issue of political power in South Vietnam – President Thieu demands that Hanoi withdraw its troops or at least recognize Saigon's sovereignty over South Vietnam, which would make North Vietnam's presence illegal – remains unsettled. Kissinger suggests to President Nixon

in Washington that he step up bombing of North Vietnam now or defer such action for one more try at negotiations in January, resuming aggressive bombing should new talks fail.

Ground War Fighting is heavy in Pleiku and in Quangtri province.

Air War US B-52s strike at 100 tanks and several thousand North Vietnamese troops heading south over the Ho Chi Minh trail in Laos. Heavy rains limit tactical air strikes in North Vietnam to 20, although 323 are flown in support of troops in South Vietnam in the last 24 hours.

14 DECEMBER 1972

USA: Government President Nixon issues a demand that North Vietnam begin talking 'seriously' or suffer the consequences, at the same time directing Chairman of the Joint Chiefs of Staff Admiral Thomas Moorer to prepare the most intense bombing of the war against sites in and around Hanoi and Haiphong. The Joint Chiefs of Staff have long lobbied for permission to bomb this area.

15 DECEMBER 1972

Thailand The publication of a new interim constitution ends 13 months of absolute rule by Field Marshal Thanom Kittikachom, who led the coup of 17 November 1971. Martial law continues and Thanom becomes premier, minister of defense and minister of foreign affairs in a government dominated by military men.

16 DECEMBER 1972

Negotiations In a presentation seen as repetitive and defensive, Henry Kissinger breaks the silence on the secret talks and announces at a news conference in Washington that the talks have failed to achieve what President Nixon regards as a 'just and fair agreement to end the war.' The deadlock centers on the nature of the international supervisory team and on US insistence on Saigon's sovereignty over South Vietnam. Kissinger charges that Hanoi is to blame for the failure to reach an agreement, and asserts that the United States will not be blackmailed, stampeded, or charmed into an agreement. North Vietnam once again criticizes the United States for breaking the agreement to maintain silence on the secret talks. The Vietcong delegation to the formal Paris peace talks blames the United States for preventing a final agreement by proposing the withdrawal of North

Vietnamese troops from South Vietnam and the re-establishment of the DMZ.

Thailand Thai Premier Thanom Kittikachom gives approval and MACV and the 7th Air Force Headquarters announce that planning has been completed for removal from Saigon to Nakom Phanom air base in Thailand. The move will take place in the event of a cease-fire. MACV will be renamed Military Assistance Command Southeast Asia (MACSEA).

18 DECEMBER 1972

North Vietnam Hanoi claims that the United States has begun bombing above the 20th Parallel again, around Haiphong and dropping more mines off Haiphong harbor.

USA: Government The Nixon administration announces the resumption of bombing and mining of North Vietnam, saying that the full-scale raids will continue until 'such time as a settlement is arrived at.' Strikes are ordered at targets not previously bombed. White House Press Secretary Ronald Ziegler says that the bombing will end only when all US POWs are released and an internationally recognized cease-fire is in force. US aircraft, beginning the most concentrated air offensive of the war – known as Linebacker II – will drop 40,000 tons of bombs, mostly over the densely populated area between Hanoi and Haiphong.

Ground War Heavy fighting continues for the third day around Quangtri City, where South Vietnamese paratroopers supported by US B-52s have been battling for control of Fire Base Anne, eight miles southwest of Quangtri City. Over 150 North Vietnamese reportedly die in the fighting.

Australia Australia's involvement in the Vietnam war ends with the withdrawal of a final group of about 60 military advisors from Saigon. The Australian combat role ended November 1971.

19 DECEMBER 1972

North Vietnam Hanoi's foreign ministry, calling the new B-52 raids against Hanoi, Haiphong, and six provinces 'extremely barbaric,' accuses the United States of premeditated intensification of the war and calls the action insane.

Negotiations North Vietnam's negotiator Xuan Thuy rebuts Henry Kissinger's assertion that additional demands by Hanoi stalled the talks, claiming that the United States wrecked the talks when Kissinger brought in

US B-52s caused massive damage in Hanoi.

126 changes to the October draft to the 20 November meeting, issues of 'fundamental importance.'

Air War US military in Saigon reports three B-52s and two fighter bombers lost since resumption of the bombing and mining above the 20th Parellel. Fifteen flyers are listed as missing. More than 100 B-52s and hundreds of fighter bombers have participated in the raids.

Sea War The USS *Goldsborough*, shelling North Vietnam, is hit by return fire which kills two and wounds three.

19-20 DECEMBER 1972

International Italy, the Netherlands, and Sweden officially condemn the resumption of American bombing above the 20th Parallel, as do China and the Soviet Union. *Le Monde* compares the attacks to the bombing of Guernica; the *Manchester Guardian* calls the bombing 'the action of a man blinded by fury or incapable of seeing the consequences of what he is doing.' Pope Paul VI and UN Secretary General Kurt Waldheim express concern for world peace.

20 DECEMBER 1972

North Vietnam Hanoi radio reports 215 persons killed, 325 wounded in Hanoi by the US raids of 18 and 19 December; 45 killed, 131 wounded in Haiphong on 18 December; and thousands of homes and civilian buildings destroyed or damaged. Nixon administration officials claim that the raids have caused heavy damage to military targets.

21 DECEMBER 1972

Negotiations The Communist delegations walk out of the formal Paris peace talks in protest over the bombing of North Vietnam, calling for another session for 28 December. Citing reports of heavy casualties and million of new refugees, Thich Nhat Hanh, Chief of the Vietnamese Buddhist Peace delegation to Paris, says Buddhists are astonished to read that most Americans think the war is over, because suffering in Vietnam is at its worst in ten years.

Ground War Although ground action elsewhere is relatively light, major fighting continues in the Quangtri City region.

Air War Eight B-52s and several fighter

bombers have been lost since 18 December, with at least 43 flyers captured or killed during the same period. The Cuban and Egyptian embassies have been hit in Hanoi, as have Russian and Chinese freighters in Haiphong.

Cambodia Cambodian and South Vietnamese troops join in an operation to clear insurgents from an area in southeast Cambodia 35 miles south of Pnompenh.

22 DECEMBER 1972

North Vietnam Bach Mai, Hanoi's largest hospital, is hit by US planes; the Indian Embassy in Hanoi is damaged.

USA: Domestic Forty-one US religious leaders issue a pastoral letter condemning the bombing of North Vietnam. The intensified bombing has revived anti-war protests.

Air War Ten B-52s, each costing $8 million, have been lost since 18 December, along with at least 55 flyers listed as missing, a number equal to 13 percent of the POWs held by Hanoi before the raids.

23 DECEMBER 1972

North Vietnam The East German Embassy and the Hungarian commercial mission in Hanoi are hit in the seventh day of US bombing; reports persist that a POW camp has been hit, with US POWs killed and wounded.

Air War USAF officials, announcing that 97 percent of US B-52s make it through Hanoi's Russian SAM-2 bomber defense system, which was designed as a defense against B-52s, say this proves that B-52s can penetrate Russian defenses.

24 DECEMBER 1972

South Vietnam Comedian Bob Hope gives what he says is his last Christmas show to US servicemen in Saigon. The show marks his ninth consecutive Christmas appearance in Vietnam. Hope endorses President Nixon's bombing of North Vietnam to force it to accept US peace terms, and receives South Vietnam's highest civilian medal for his 'anti-Communist zeal.'

Air War US officials report the loss of an eleventh B-52, and announce a temporary Christmas halt to the bombing, to roughly correspond with the 24-hour Christmas truce being observed by South Vietnam and the Communists.

25 DECEMBER 1972

USA: Military US military strength in South Vietnam is reduced by 700 men this week to a total of 24,000, the lowest total in almost eight years.

Ground War Communist forces shell Danang air base and surrounding areas, damaging five US helicopters.

Air War Intense US bombing is resumed above the 20th Parallel after a 36-hour lull because, according to US officials, Hanoi has sent no word that it was ready to resume peace talks. The amount of bombs dropped on North Vietnam between 18 December and 24 December equals half the tonnage dropped on England during World War II, or 20 of the atomic bombs dropped on Hiroshima.

26 DECEMBER 1972

Negotiations Nguyen Thanh Le, spokesman for the North Vietnamese delegation at the formal Paris peace talks, says Hanoi is willing to resume peace negotiations once the United States stops bombing above the 20th Parallel.

Air War US planes stage the most violent attack of the war on Hanoi, raining bombs on downtown Hanoi for more than 40 minutes and losing at least five B-52s.

27 DECEMBER 1972

South Vietnam President Thieu, on the day before the expiration of his special powers, signs a decree which will eliminate virtually all of South Vietnam's political parties except for his own Democracy party, which was formed in November.

Ground War Fighting in the Quangtri area continues, with the South Vietnamese command reporting 56 Communist ground attacks in the last 24 hours.

Australia Australia ends its military aid to South Vietnam and its training program for Cambodian troops. Some observers feel that this surprise aid cut will adversely affect Nixon administration efforts to obtain military aid from Congress.

28 DECEMBER 1972

North Vietnam Hanoi announces heavy damage and destruction of densely populated civilian areas in Hanoi, Haiphong, and their suburbs. Newsmen touring Hanoi's usually animated Kham Thien street – which has been 'carpet bombed' – and a prison for US pilots – confirms this assessment.

Ground War More than 1900 mortar and artillery shells hit South Vietnamese troops in Quangtri province. North Vietnamese troops beat back a South Vietnamese attempt to

Cleaning up after the B-52 air raids in Hanoi.

recapture Artillery Base November in the Central Highlands.

Australia The Seaman's Union of Australia announces a boycott of US ships in Australian ports, to protest US bombing in North Vietnam.

29 DECEMBER 1972

International Italy, the Netherlands, Sweden, Belgium, and Austria have officially protested the US bombing of North Vietnam. England, France, and West Germany maintain official silence despite public demands for official condemnation.

30 DECEMBER 1972

USA: Government In response to a scheduled resumption of the secret peace talks for January 1973, President Nixon orders a halt to bombing and naval shelling above the 20th Parallel. Bombing below the 20th Parallel will continue. It is unclear whether the initiative for a new round of talks came from Hanoi or Washington.

31 DECEMBER 1972

USA: Military The most intense US bombing operation of the Vietnam war ends. The North Vietnamese launched their entire stock of more than 1200 surface-to-air missiles against the US planes. Fifteen B-52s and 11 other US aircraft are lost, along with 93 flyers downed and killed, missing or captured. Many government officials believe the bombing and naval bombardment of North Vietnam was counter-productive because of heavy US losses, international opposition, and growing congressional opposition.

Negotiations In a statement issued in Paris, the Hanoi delegation to the regular peace talks asserts that the US bombing did not succeed in 'subjugating the Vietnamese people,' and calls attention to the losses of US planes and the unfavorable world reaction to the raids.

31 DECEMBER 1972

State of the War As the year draws to a close, the end of the war – or, more realistically, the end of this phase of the war – does finally seem to be in sight. For whatever the critics of Nixon's strategy and tactics may say, the bombing operation that has just ended, Linebacker II, does seem to have caused the

Several B-52s crashed in Hanoi during the bombing raids.

North Vietnamese to agree to return to the conference table. The whole year that has been expended to arrive at this point has been one of the most frustrating – and destructive – years of the war. For although US combat forces were brought down from about 159,000 to some 24,000, the fighting raged throughout the year, killing some 4300 US servicemen.

8-19 JANUARY 1973
Negotiations Kissinger and Tho resume peace negotiations in Paris. An agreement is reached on 9 January, and a joint US–Vietnamese announcement issued 18 January says Kissinger and Tho will meet again on 23 January 'for the purpose of completing the text of an agreement.'

15 JANUARY 1973
Negotiations Citing 'progress' in the Paris peace negotiations, President Nixon suspends the most concentrated bombing of the war, as well as mining, shelling, and all other offensive action against North Vietnam. The cessation of hostilities against North Vietnam does not extend to South Vietnam.

18-26 JANUARY 1973
Ground War South Vietnamese and Communist forces engage in heavy combat in the South in order to gain as much territory as possible before the cease-fire goes into effect.
Air War Between 17 and 25 January US planes make nearly 3000 strikes in the South.

23 JANUARY 1973
Negotiations President Nixon announces that Kissinger and Tho have initialed an agreement in Paris that day 'to end the war and bring peace with honor in Vietnam and Southeast Asia.' The cease-fire is to go into effect at 0800 hours 28 January, Saigon time (1900 hours 27 January Eastern Standard Time).

24 JANUARY 1973
Negotiations Kissinger announces that a truce is also expected in Laos and Cambodia.

27 JANUARY 1973
South Vietnam Saigon controls about 75 percent of South Vietnam's territory and 85 percent of its population. The South Vietnamese Army is well-equipped via last-minute de-

337

liveries of US weapons, and will continue to receive US aid after the cease-fire; the South Vietnamese Air Force is now the fourth largest in the world. The CIA estimates North Vietnamese presence in the south at 145,000 men, about the same as the year before.

USA: Domestic Defense Secretary Melvin Laird announces the end of the military draft in America. The law remains on the books for use in emergencies.

Ground War The last US serviceman to die in combat in Vietnam, Lieutenant Colonel William B Nolde, is killed by an artillery shell at Anloc at 2100 hours (eleven hours before the truce). Four Americans were killed in the last week.

Negotiations 'An Agreement Ending the War and Restoring Peace in Vietnam' is signed in Paris by the United States, North Vietnam, South Vietnam, and the Vietcong. Due to South Vietnam's unwillingness to recognize the Vietcong's Provisional Revolutionary Government, all references to it are confined to a two-party version of the document signed later by North Vietnam and the United States. Displaying little variation from the agreement of the preceding October (or from the 1954 Geneva agreement), the settlement includes: a cease-fire throughout Vietnam; withdrawal of all US troops and advisors (totalling about 23,700) within 60 days; the dismantling of all US bases within 60 days; release of all US and other POWs within 60 days; continuance in place of North Vietnamese troops in South Vietnam; withdrawal of all foreign troops from Laos and Cambodia, and prohibition of bases in and troop movements through these countries; agreement that the DMZ at the 17th Parallel will remain a provisional dividing line with eventual reunification of the country 'through peaceful means'; establishment of an international control commission composed of Canadians, Hungarians, Poles, and Indonesians, with 1160 inspectors to supervise the agreement; continuance of South Vietnamese President Nguyen Van Thieu in office pending elections; respect by North Vietnam for 'the South Vietnamese People's right to self-determination;' no military movement across the DMZ; and no use of force to reunify the country.

28 JANUARY 1973
Cambodia Lon Nol proposes a cease-fire in Cambodia. His proposal will be rejected by Prince Sihanouk on 9 April.

12-27 FEBRUARY 1973
POWs The return of US POWs begins with North Vietnam's release of 142 of 587 US prisoners at Hanoi's Gialam airport. The first 20 POWs arrive at Travis Air Force Base in California on 14 February to a subdued welcome in keeping with the low-key tone of Operation Homecoming, and are quickly dispersed to homes and hospitals across the country. The release program continues after a delay on 27 February, when North Vietnam accuses the United States of 'encouraging' Saigon to make difficulties for the Four-Party Joint Military Commission and claims that Saigon has conducted 20,000 military operations since the beginning of the cease-fire.

15 FEBRUARY 1973
Negotiations Following four days of talks between Henry Kissinger and Pham Van Dong in Hanoi, the United States and North Vietnam agree to establish a Joint Economic Commission to administer US reconstruction aid to North Vietnam.

21 FEBRUARY 1973
Laos Souvanna Phouma's Laotian government and the Communist-led Pathet Lao announce they have reached a cease-fire agreement, ending 20 years of war despite some continued fighting. The agreement provides for cessation of all military activities in Laos, including US and North Vietnamese.

MARCH 1973
North Vietnam General Tran Van Tra, one of the leading Communist commanders in the South, is summoned back to Hanoi to attend a high-level meeting. Spurred by recent gains by Thieu's army and the absence of US B-52s, Hanoi launches a huge logistical program to prepare for a major offensive. An all-weather road is built from Quangtri to the Mekong, and work begun on a 3000-mile oil pipeline from Quangtri to Locninh, the main headquarters 75 miles northwest of Saigon. A modern radio grid enables Locninh to communicate directly with Hanoi. Allied officials meanwhile report that Communist forces are building up supplies and military equipment in the border province of Tayninh, northwest of Saigon.

15 MARCH 1973
USA: Government President Nixon hints that the United States might intervene again in

The Pathet Lao operated anti-aircraft units during the war.

Vietnam to prevent Communist violations of the truce. Nixon has previously assured President Thieu that 'We will respond with full force should the settlement be violated by North Vietnam.'

27 MARCH 1973
USA: Government The White House announces that bombing of Cambodia at the request of Cambodian President Lon Nol will continue until Communist forces end military operations there and agree to a cease-fire.

28 MARCH 1973
South Vietnam The 60-day first phase of Vietnam's cease-fire ends with continued fighting.

29 MARCH 1973
Ground War The last US troops leave South Vietnam, ending nearly 10 years of US military presence in that country. Only a Defense Attaché Office and a few Marine guards at the Saigon American Embassy remain, although some 8500 US civilians stay on.

POWS Hanoi releases the last 67 of its acknowledged POWs, bringing the total number released to 587.

2 APRIL 1973
USA: Government President Nixon and President Thieu end a two-day visit with a joint communiqué expressing 'full consensus' and an US promise of continuing economic aid to South Vietnam. Thieu says he will never ask the United States to send troops back to South Vietnam; Nixon makes it clear that future aid is dependent upon Congressional approval.

5 APRIL 1973
USA: Domestic The US Senate approves 88-3 an amendment forbidding any aid to North Vietnam without prior and specific approval by the Congress.

19 APRIL-8 AUGUST 1973
USA: Domestic Representative Elizabeth Holtzman (D-NY) and four Air Force officers

CHRONOLOGY

file suit in Federal District Court to halt the 'secret American bombing of Cambodia.' On 25 July Federal District Court Judge Orrin G Judd rules in favour of their suit, although the White House requests and receives a stay of Judge Judd's decision from the Court of Appeals two days later. On 1 August Supreme Court Justice William O Douglas orders the bombing halted on an appeal from Holtzman, but is overruled by a full sitting of the Supreme Court a few hours later. On 8 August, the Court of Appeals finally overturns Judge Judd's initial ruling which calls US bombing in Cambodia 'unauthorized and illegal.'

4 JUNE 1973
USA: Domestic The US Senate approves a bill to block funds for any US military activities in Indochina, and the House of Representatives concurs. Nixon and Kissinger lobby to postpone the ban until 15 August, to enable continued bombing of Cambodia.

13 JUNE 1973
Negotiations Representatives of the original signers of the 27 January cease-fire sign a new 14-point agreement calling for an end to all cease-fire violations in South Vietnam. Coming at the end of month-long negotiations between Kissinger and Tho, the settlement includes: an end to all military activities at noon, 15 June; an end to US reconnaissance flights over North Vietnam and the resumption of US minesweeping operations in North Vietnamese waters; the resumption of US talks on aid to North Vietnam; the meeting of commanders of opposing forces in South Vietnam to prevent outbreaks of hostilities. This agreement proves no more efficacious than the original.

24 JUNE 1973
USA: Government Graham Martin is sworn in as ambassador to South Vietnam, replacing Ellsworth Bunker.

29-30 JUNE 1973
USA: Domestic Congress agrees that bombing in Cambodia can continue until 15 August, after which spending for any military activity in Indochina must be approved by Congress.

JULY 1973
Naval War US Task Force 78 completes the clearing of Haiphong and other North Vietnamese harbors of mines laid down by the United States since May 1973, as called for by the cease-fire agreements of 27 January.

16-17 JULY 1973
USA: Domestic The Senate Armed Services Committee begins a probe into allegations that the US Air Force made thousands of secret B-52 raids into Cambodia in 1969 and 1970 at a time when the United States recognized the neutrality of the Sihanouk regime in Cambodia. The Pentagon acknowledges that the raids against Cambodia were authorized by President Nixon and then Secretary of Defense Melvin Laird. Sihanouk denies the State Department claim that he requested or authorized the bombing; Laird and Kissinger deny that they knew of or authorized the by-now-established falsification of records.

14 AUGUST 1973
Cambodia After several days of intense bombing in the area around Pnompenh, the United States ceases bombing Cambodia at midnight, in accord with June Congressional actions. The cessation marks the end of 12 years of combat activity in Indochina. The United States will continue unarmed reconnaissance flights and military aid to Cambodia and Laos. President Nixon denounces Congress for undermining the 'prospects for world peace.'

22 AUGUST 1973
USA: Government President Nixon announces the appointment of Henry Kissinger as Secretary of State, replacing William P Rogers, who resigns the same day.

26 AUGUST 1973
South Vietnam Candidates supported by President Thieu sweep South Vietnamese elections, the first national elections since 1972. Thieu maintains a firm grip on the legislature.

OCTOBER 1973
North Vietnam Pham Van Dong and Le Duan, seeking military aid for North Vietnam, are rebuffed in both Moscow and Peking.

16 OCTOBER 1973
International In a controversial decision, Henry Kissinger and North Vietnam's Le Duc Tho are awarded the Nobel Peace Prize for negotiating the Paris peace accords. Kissinger accepts the award, but Le Duc Tho declines to

accept until peace is truly established in his country.

24 OCTOBER 1973
South Vietnam US intelligence reports that since the cease-fire, North Vietnamese military presence in South Vietnam has been built up by 70,000 men, 400 tanks, at least 200 artillery pieces, 15 anti-aircraft artillery, and 12 airfields. An all-weather road from North Vietnam to Tayninh province has almost been completed.
USA: Government President Nixon vetoes the War Powers Resolution, which would limit presidential power to commit armed forces abroad without Congressional approval. The bill requires the president to report to Congress within 48 hours after commitment of armed forces to foreign combat and limits to 60 days the time they may stay there without Congressional approval. Nixon claims the bill imposes 'unconstitutional and dangerous restrictions' on presidential authority.

NOVEMBER 1973
South Vietnam North Vietnamese tanks and troops seize two South Vietnamese camps near the Cambodian border in a two-day battle, one of the most savage since the 28 January cease-fire.

7 NOVEMBER 1973
USA: Government Congress overrides President Nixon's veto of the War Powers bill.

4 JANUARY 1974
South Vietnam President Thieu claims the war has 'restarted,' asserting that 'we cannot allow the Communists a situation in which ...they can launch harassing attacks against us.'
Ground War ARVN reports 55 soldiers killed in two clashes with Communist forces.

27 JANUARY 1974
Ground War Since the January 1973 truce, 13,788 South Vietnamese soldiers, 2159 South Vietnamese civilians, and 45,057 Communist soldiers have died in the fighting.

22 FEBRUARY 1974
USA: Military The National Academy of Sciences reports, in a study ordered by Congress and commissioned by the Pentagon, that the use of chemical herbicides in the Vietnam war by the United States did damage

to the ecology of South Vietnam that might last as long as a century.

30 MARCH 1974
South Vietnam South Vietnamese Information Minister Hoang Duc Nha warns that North Vietnam is planning a general offensive to reconquer South Vietnam. Fighting in the Central Highlands this month between Kontum and Chuong Nghia is the bloodiest since the cease-fire.

4 APRIL 1974
USA: Government The House of Representatives unexpectedly rejects a White House-sponsored request to increase military aid to South Vietnam.

5 APRIL 1974
Laos A new coalition government is formed with Souvanna Phouma as premier and Prince Souphanouvong, leader of the Pathet Lao, as one of the deputy premiers.

MAY 1974
South Vietnam North Vietnamese General Tran Van Tra estimates that North Vietnamese units have recaptured all of the territory in the Mekong Delta captured by the South Vietnamese following the cease-fire.

9 MAY-30 JULY 1974
USA: Domestic The House of Representatives Judiciary Committee opens impeachment hearings against President Nixon, voting to impeach him on three counts on 30 July.

5 AUGUST 1974
USA: Domestic Congress places a $1-billion ceiling on military aid to South Vietnam for fiscal 1974. This figure will be trimmed to $700 million by 11 August. Military aid to South Vietnam in fiscal 1973 was $2.8 billion; in 1975 it will be $300 million.

8 AUGUST 1974
South Vietnam US officials report continued Communist attacks around Danang. North Vietnamese forces in the South are estimated to be stronger than at any previous time.

9 AUGUST 1974
USA: Domestic Richard Milhous Nixon resigns as president of the United States. Vice-President Gerald Ford succeeds to the presidency.

CHRONOLOGY

A wounded Khmer Rouge *insurgent begs for mercy.*

NOVEMBER 1974
South Vietnam Following rioting and protests by anti-government demonstrators in Saigon which lead to violent clashes with police, several leading South Vietnamese opposition members publicly denounce President Thieu and his 'repressive' policies.
Diplomatic Kissinger concludes from discussions with Russia and China that both nations consider Saigon doomed and are concentrating on expanding their own spheres of influence: the Chinese in Cambodia and the Russians in Vietnam. The promise of aid from the Soviet Union encourages Hanoi to accelerate plans for military operations.

3 DECEMBER 1974
South Vietnam South Vietnamese intelligence reports that it has obtained documents indicating that the Communists are planning a sharp increase in fighting for the coming season.

31 DECEMBER 1974
South Vietnam South Vietnamese Command reports that 80,000 persons have been killed in fighting throughout the country this year, the highest total for any year of the war.

6 JANUARY 1975
Ground War Phuoc Long Province and its capital Phuoc Binh, about 60 miles north of Saigon, fall to the North Vietnamese. Phuoc Binh is the first regional seat taken from Saigon since the fall of Quangtri on 1 May 1972. The South Vietnamese Air Force loses 20 planes defending the province, many to SA-7 missiles. The total lack of reaction from US forces convinces North Vietnam that the Americans will not return to Vietnam; it also encourages Hanoi's Le Duan to urge more aggressive action to create a general uprising by 1976.

28 JANUARY 1975
USA: Military President Ford asks Congress for an additional $522 million in military aid for South Vietnam and Cambodia.
Ground War President Ford reveals that North Vietnam now has 289,000 troops in South Vietnam, and tanks, heavy artillery, and anti-aircraft weapons 'by the hundreds.'

5 FEBRUARY 1975
South Vietnam North Vietnamese General Van Tien Dung goes south to take command of Communist forces.

MARCH 1975
Ground War By early March the North Vietnamese have encircled Ban Me Thuot in the Central Highlands. This strong troop presence, together with information from prisoners, intercepted radio transmissions, and captured documents, indicates that a major North Vietnamese offensive is in preparation.

10-13 MARCH 1975
Ground War The North Vietnamese attack Ban Me Thuot, overrunning most of the town by midday, as heavy fighting erupts in the Central Highlands. ARVN's 23rd Division is devastated, and Ban Me Thuot, capital of Dar Lac province, finally falls on 13 March. Many soldiers of the 23rd Division desert to try to rescue their families; this protective drive on the part of individual soldiers is a phenomenon that contributes heavily to the collapse of South Vietnam over the next few months.

14 MARCH 1975
Ground War Meeting with his commanders, President Thieu orders the withdrawal of ARVN forces from the Central Highlands and the northern provinces of South Vietnam to the coast. Five days later he orders Hué held at all costs.

16 MARCH-1 APRIL 1975
Ground War The withdrawal from Pleiku and Kontum begins, as thousands of civilians join the soldiers streaming down Route 7B. By 17 April, civilians and soldiers are both under heavy Communist attack; the withdrawal, scheduled to be completed in three days, is still underway on 1 April. Only 20,000 of 60,000 soldiers ever reach the coast; of 400,000 refugees, only 100,000 arrive: the fate of the rest is unknown.

24 MARCH 1975
North Vietnam The 'Ho Chi Minh Campaign' begins. Hanoi hands General Dung a new timetable calling for the liberation of the South before the rains begin in May. To achieve this North Vietnamese troops must reach Saigon no later than the last week in April, before South Vietnamese forces can regroup to defend it.

25 MARCH 1975
Ground War The order is given to evacuate Hué by sea and abandon it to the Communists. By now more than one million

refugees, driven by memories of the Communist slaughter of civilians during the 1968 Tet offensive, are streaming toward Danang, which is already under heavy rocket fire.

28 MARCH 1975
USA: Military President Ford announces he has ordered US Navy transports and 'contract vessels' to assist in the evacuation of South Vietnamese coastal cities.

29 MARCH 1975
Ground War Danang falls to the Communists. Many citizens die in the general chaos while attempting to escape from the airport, docks, and beaches.

1 APRIL 1975
Ground War Of the 10,000 men who formed South Vietnam's 22nd Division a week earlier in Binhdinh Province, pushed south by waves of refugees from Quangngai Province and North Vietnamese tanks and artillery, 2000 are evacuated by sea from Quinohn. More than half of South Vietnam's territory is now controlled by the North Vietnamese. During the first week in April Communist forces coming from the south push into Long An Province, just south of Saigon, threatening to cut Highway 4, Saigon's main link with the Mekong Delta.
Cambodia Lon Nol flees Cambodia.

4 APRIL 1975
South Vietnam A major US airlift of South Vietnamese orphans begins with disaster, as an Air Force C-5A cargo jet crashes shortly after take-off, killing more than 100 children. Two thousand others, most of them orphans of US servicemen, are eventually taken to the United States for adoption,

6-15 APRIL 1975
Ground War Two regiments from the ARVN 2nd Division and one brigade of airborne troops are landed at Phanrang airport, on 6 April, in hopes of mounting a counteroffensive. After three days of relative quiet, the airborne brigade is sent to Xuan Loc (10 April) where a major battle is developing; it is replaced by a ranger group. North Vietnamese troops and tanks overrun Phanrang and extinguish ARVN presence in the region.

7 APRIL 1975
Ground War Le Duc Tho arrives at Communist headquarters in Locninh to oversee the final Communist offensive drive. Well over two-thirds of Vietnam is now under Communist control.

8 APRIL 1975
USA: Military After a week-long mission to South Vietnam, General Frederick Weyand, US Army Chief of Staff and former Vietnam commander, reports to Congress that South Vietnam cannot survive without additional military aid. Questioned later by reporters, who ask if South Vietnam could survive with additional aid, he replies there is 'a chance.'

8-21 APRIL 1975
Ground War The ARVN 18th Division in Xuan Loc begins battling two North Vietnamese divisions at the last South Vietnamese defense line before Saigon; it will become the last battle in defense of the Republic of South Vietnam. During the first week a regiment of the ARVN 5th Division and an airborne brigade arrive as reinforcements, while two more North Vietnamese divisions arrive to join the attackers. The ARVN forces are well dug in, and manage to hold out against the attackers until they run out of tactical air support and weapons, finally abandoning Xuan Loc to the Communists on 21 April.

12-16 APRIL 1975
Cambodia The US ambassador to Cambodia and his staff leave Pnompenh on 12 April. On 16 April the Lon Nol government surrenders to the Khmer Rouge, ending five years of war. The People's Assembly headed by Pol Pot, established in December, will cause two to four million deaths over the next three years.

21-25 APRIL 1975
South Vietnam With the fall of Xuan Loc, President Thieu resigns and transfers authority to Vice-President Tran Van Huong before any of the several plots against him can be implemented. On 25 April he flees Saigon.

23 APRIL 1975
USA: Government President Ford says the war is finished, 'as far as America is concerned. Today, Americans can regain the sense of pride that existed before Vietnam. But it cannot be achieved by re-fighting a war.

28 APRIL 1975
South Vietnam Vice-President Tran Van Huong transfers authority as chief of state to

Some Vietnamese were evacuated from Saigon with the aid of US forces.

General Duong Van Minh (who helped overthrow Diem in 1963); Duong is the South Vietnamese official with whom the Communists have indicated they are willing to negotiate.

29-30 APRIL 1975
South Vietnam Option IV, the largest helicopter evacuation on record, begins removing the last Americans from Saigon including US Ambassador Graham Martin. In 19 hours 81 helicopters carry more than 1000 Americans and almost 6000 Vietnamese to aircraft carriers riding offshore. Two US servicemen become the last Americans to die in Vietnam when their helicopter crashes near an aircraft carrier taking part in the evacuation. By dawn on 30 April Communist forces are moving into Saigon, where they meet only sporadic resistance; that morning President Duong Van Minh announces unconditional surrender to the Communists. Colonel Bui Tin, who accepts the surrender from General Minh, explains, 'You have nothing to fear. Between Vietnamese there are no victors and no vanquished. Only the Americans have been beaten. If you are patriots, consider this a moment of joy. The war for our country is over.'

MAY 1975
Laos The coalition government formed a year ago is close to collapse, and there is fighting between the Pathet Lao (supported by North Vietnamese troops) and rightist factions. Demonstrations by students and others are increasingly aimed at US buildings and operations. By the end of the month, many of the top right-wing officials of the government have resigned under pressure from pro-Communist forces.

1 MAY 1975
South Vietnam Prostitution, dance halls, and 'acting like Americans' are banned by the Provisional Revolutionary Government.

7 MAY 1975
South Vietnam A rally in Saigon attended by 30,000 celebrates the capture of the city, and

also commemorates the 21st anniversary of Vietnamese victory over the French at Dienbienphu.

USA: Military President Ford issues a proclamation designating this as the last day of the 'Vietnam era' for military personnel to qualify for wartime benefits during the period which began 5 August 1964.

12 MAY 1975

Cambodia The US merchant ship *Mayaguez*, with 39 seamen aboard, is seized in the Gulf of Siam by the Cambodian Khmer Rouge government, who claim the ship is part of a spy operation. Diplomatic appeals fail.

14 MAY 1975

Cambodia Rescue operations begin as US Marines attack Tang Island and bomb Ream Air Base, in the first use of US troops on foreign soil under the War Powers Act. Thirty-eight Marines die in the operation, with 50 wounded and three missing; the crewmen of the *Mayaguez* are released unharmed the same day.

16 MAY 1975

Refugees Congress appropriates $405 million to fund a refugee aid program and authorizes resettlement of South Vietnamese and Cambodian refugees in the United States. Over 140,000 refugees are flown to the United States under the program in the next few months.

3 JUNE 1975

North Vietnam At a meeting of the National Assembly Premier Pham Van Dong calls for normalization of relations with the United States, conditioned on US economic aid to Hanoi and a pledge to observe the 1973 Paris cease-fire.

14 NOVEMBER 1975

USA: Government Secretary of State Henry Kissinger announces that the United States is prepared to hold talks with North and South Vietnam and Laos and Cambodia on normalizing relations.

3 DECEMBER 1975

Laos The Communist Pathet Lao, now in control of most of the territory and cities of Laos, abolishes the coalition government, ends the 600-year-old monarchy, and establishes the Peoples Democratic Republic of Laos.

20 DECEMBER 1975

Refugees The last of 140,000 refugees who arrived under the resettlement program leave Fort Chaffee, the last of four processing centers established in the United States. Since 2 May, 50,796 refugees have been processed at Fort Chaffee.

FEBRUARY 1976

South Vietnam A decree by the Provisional Revolutionary Government of South Vietnam, concurring with a resolution passed by North Vietnam's National Assembly in December 1975, establishes the organization of all of Vietnam into 38 provinces.

20 MARCH 1976

Thailand The Thai government orders the United States to close all its military installations in Thailand and to withdraw all US personnel except for 270 military advisors.

25 APRIL 1976

Vietnam All-Vietnam elections are held for a new National Assembly and 249 deputies are elected from the North and 243 from the South, 60 seats of the total of 492 being reserved for minorities. The united National Assembly will meet for the first time on 24 June.

2 JULY 1976

Vietnam The National Assembly proclaims the official unification of Vietnam as the Socialist Republic of Vietnam. North Vietnamese Prime Minister Pham Van Dong becomes prime minister in the new government, and all but one high office go to former leaders of North Vietnam. Hanoi is declared the capital, and the North Vietnamese flag, anthem, and emblems are approved as official symbols of the new nation. The North Vietnamese constitution becomes the national constitution, until a commission appointed by the Assembly can draw up a new instrument.

2 NOVEMBER 1976

USA: Domestic James Earl Carter is elected President of the United States.

15 NOVEMBER 1976

USA: Government The United States casts the single Security Council veto on Vietnam's admission to the United Nations, claiming that Hanoi has failed to give an accounting of at least 800 US servicemen still listed as missing in Vietnam. Vietnam asserts that it is

US Marines recapture the merchant ship Mayaguez.

impossible to furnish a complete list of those missing in action.

14-20 DECEMBER 1976
Vietnam In Hanoi the Vietnamese Workers Party convenes its first congress since 1960. A five-year-plan for 1976-1980 projects extensive expansion of industry and agriculture, foreign trade, and reinvestment, as well as large-scale redistribution of the nation's population. The Workers Party is renamed the Communist Party, and Le Duan is reconfirmed as the nation's top leader.

21 JANUARY 1977
USA: Government In his first major presidential act, President Carter pardons almost all the draft evaders – about 10,000 – of the Vietnam war era. Carter says he will immediately address the problem of upgrading the discharges of the nearly 100,000 deserters.

20 MARCH 1977
USA: Diplomatic The first US-government mission to Vietnam since the fall of Saigon in 1975 returns with the remains of 12 US pilots and a firm pledge of assistance from Hanoi to

CHRONOLOGY

President Ford relays news of the release of the Mayaguez *crew.*

co-operate in discovering the fate of other missing Americans.

2-4 MAY 1977

USA: Diplomatic The United States and Vietnam open the first round of negotiations in Paris on normalizing relations. The United States promises not to veto Vietnam's admission to the United Nations, and to lift its trade embargo against Vietnam once diplomatic relations are established.

19 MAY 1977

USA: Government The US State Department releases a classified letter from President Nixon pledging $4.75 billion in US postwar reconstruction aid to North Vietnam. This letter, dated 1 February 1973, is often cited by Hanoi as constituting a US commitment. On this same day, in a televised interview with David Frost, former President Nixon portrays himself as a wartime president who took action to save a nation 'torn apart' by dissent. He regrets not moving 'stronger, sooner' in Cambodia and Laos.

12-19 JUNE 1977

Refugees *The New York Times* reports in several dispatches that the number of refugees from southern Vietnam and the rest of Indochina is increasing, and that refugees are finding it more difficult to find haven in neighboring Asian countries.

8 AUGUST 1977

Vietnam Washington reports that heavy fighting raged along the Cambodian-Vietnamese border in May, forcing Vietnamese to evacuate two southern border towns, on land claimed by the Cambodians.

26 AUGUST 1977

Vietnam The Vietnamese Communist Party Central Committee acknowledges 'big mistakes in leadership,' especially in the field of agriculture, and announces the launching of a 'productive labor movement' to rectify the situation. Continuing economic woes are attributed to the war, reliance on small-scale production, 'poor material,' and technical shortcomings.

20 SEPTEMBER 1977

Vietnam Sponsored by a record number of countries, Vietnam is admitted to the United Nations at the 32nd General Assembly.

28 OCTOBER 1977

Refugees President Carter signs a bill which opens the way for refugees to apply for US citizenship and extends federal aid programs for refugees who have come to the states following the 1975 Communist victories in Vietnam, Laos, and Cambodia.

31 DECEMBER 1977
Cambodia The Cambodian government breaks diplomatic relations with Vietnam, giving 'ferocious and barbarous aggression' by Vietnam as the reason. Earlier in December fierce border fighting occurred when Vietnam occupied the 'Parrot's Beak' area of Cambodia, after a Cambodian raid into Tayninh Province killed or injured 2000 persons.

3 JANUARY 1978
Vietnam US officials assert that Vietnamese-Cambodian fighting is a 'proxy war' between China and the Soviet Union. Vietnamese troops now occupy 400 square miles of Cambodia in the border region of the two countries; China sides with Cambodia in the border dispute.

1 MAY 1978
China Hundreds of ethnic Chinese flee Vietnam following the nationalization of privately-owned businesses in Saigon. Peking accuses Vietnam of abusing and expelling 70,000-90,000 Chinese since 1977, and announces at the end of the month that it is cutting aid to Vietnam and sending ships to evacuate its Chinese.

29 JUNE 1978
Vietnam Vietnam becomes a member of Comecon (the Council of Mutual Economic Assistance), the Soviet-Bloc East European economic community.

3 JULY 1978
China Citing Vietnam's treatment of ethnic Chinese, China announces the termination of all economic assistance to Vietnam. Following two major cutbacks since the beginning of the year, the cut-off is perceived in diplomatic circles as China's reaction to Vietnam's growing friendship with the Soviet Union. China recalls its ambassador from Vietnam on 16 July.

15 AUGUST 1978
China Talks in Hanoi between Vietnam and China collapse when China recalls its delegation. Each side accuses the other of initiating a border clash involving refugees, during which Vietnamese forces occupied Chinese territory.

3 NOVEMBER 1978
Vietnam Vietnam and the Soviet Union sign a 25-year pact of mutual aid and friendship providing for co-operation in the development of Vietnam and 'mutual consultation' in case either nation is attacked. China calls the pact a 'threat to the security' of Southeast Asia.

5 NOVEMBER 1978
Vietnam US intelligence reports indicate that Vietnam plans to launch a major offensive against Cambodia in December.

4 DECEMBER 1978
Refugees Malaysia temporarily reverses policy and announces it will admit Vietnam's 'boat people' – refugees who flee or are expelled from Vietnam in crowded, unseaworthy boats. As in other neighboring Asian countries, there is deep-seated hostility to Vietnamese settlement in any numbers. There are many sinkings, drownings, shellings, murders, and even attacks by pirates as the boat people are frequently turned back and refused asylum.

15 DECEMBER 1978
USA: Government President Carter announces full-scale diplomatic relations between the United States and China, beginning 1 January 1979. Formal US-Taiwan ties are broken the same day.

21 DECEMBER 1978
Cambodia A major invasion by Vietnamese troops into southern Cambodia halts 40 kilometers from the Mekong River port of Kratie. As early as 14 December, Vietnamese troops had been reported as far as 112 kilometers into southern Cambodia.

7 JANUARY 1979
Cambodia The Cambodian government of Pol Pot is overthrown when Pnompenh, the capital of Cambodia, falls to Vietnamese forces and the Hanoi-backed Cambodian National United Front for National Salvation.

17 FEBRUARY 1979
China China launches an invasion of Vietnam, largely as a retaliation for Vietnam's invasion of Cambodia; 200,000-300,000

Chinese troops supported by aircraft and artillery strike along most of the common 480-mile frontier. Vietnamese forces put up stiff resistance. While criticizing Vietnam for invading Cambodia, the United States calls for China to withdraw from Vietnam. The Soviet Union warns China to 'stop before it is too late,' and Vietnam requests the United Nations 'to force the Chinese aggressive troops to withdraw from Vietnam.'

5 MARCH 1979
China China announces that all Chinese frontier troops are withdrawing. During this operation China penetrated up to 40 miles into Vietnam and took the provincial capital of Langson, ostensibly to punish Vietnam for an alleged 700 armed 'provocations' along the border in the last six months. China later claims that 20,000 Chinese and 50,000 Vietnamese troops were killed or wounded in the fighting.

18-28 APRIL 1979
China Vietnamese and Chinese negotiators fail to agree on a peace settlement that would normalize relations between their nations. China continues to insist that Vietnam withdraw all forces from Cambodia and Laos.

21 JULY 1979
Refugees At an international conference in Geneva on the dramatically worsening plight of Indochinese refugees Vietnam promises to stem the flow of these people. The US State Department calculates that the number of people fleeing Vietnam, Cambodia, and Laos has increased almost tenfold during the year, to 300,000. At least 147,000 refugees are in camps in Thailand, 51,000 in Malaysia, and 20,000 in other countries, where most are unwanted for permanent settlement. At least 30,000 Cambodians have been repatriated.

5 AUGUST 1979
Vietnam Hoan Van Hoang, a close colleague of the late Ho Chi Minh and deputy chairman of Vietnam's National Assembly, defects to China. Hoan charges that Vietnam's treatment of its ethnic Chinese is 'even worse than Hitler's treatment of the Jews.'

25 SEPTEMBER 1979
Cambodia Although total victory over Pol Pot forces was claimed on 22 July, Vietnamese troop strength in Cambodia is estimated at 180,000 at the start of a new offensive against the Pol Pot Khmer Rouge troops, estimated at 40,000. Operations continue to wipe out pockets of guerrillas before they can regroup.

14 OCTOBER 1979
Refugees Arrivals of boat people throughout Southeast Asia have dwindled dramatically. Refugee officials report that arrivals from Vietnam during September numbered only 6600, compared to 55,000 arrivals in June.

16 OCTOBER 1979
Cambodia The largest food shipment to date – 1500 tons – arrives to relieve the famine in Cambodia. Months of effort to relieve widespread starvation have been frustrated by lack of agreements between various factions.

24 NOVEMBER 1979
USA: Domestic The US General Accounting Office reports that thousands of US troops deployed in South Vietnam were exposed to Agent Orange herbicide, despite previous Defense Department denials of such assertions. About 4800 former Vietnam servicemen have asked the Veterans' Administration for treatment of disorders they believe were caused by contact with Agent Orange, which contains the toxic chemical, dioxin.

6 DECEMBER 1979-1 JANUARY 1980
Cambodia Early in December the International Red Cross reports that little of the 33,000 tons of food it has delivered to Cambodia has been distributed. Although Oxfam blames technical and logistical problems, the United States accuses the Pnompenh government and Vietnam of deliberately blocking distribution. By 1 January UNICEF director James Grant is able to announce, after a visit to Cambodia, that the thousands of tons of food and medicine piled up in warehouses is finally reaching the people.

9 MARCH 1980
China Chinese Premier Hua Kuo-feng pledges full support for Cambodian guerrillas fighting the Vietnamese-supported Cambodian government. Peace negotiations between China and Vietnam stall out again when Vietnam refuses to discuss its invasion of Cambodia.

21 MARCH 1980
Cambodia Despite optimistic pronouncements in preceding months, UNICEF now

Laotian forces attack a Thai position as the war continues.

states that 'The prospect of famine [in Cambodia] has significantly increased,' due to a second harvest failure and logistical problems.

23 JUNE 1980
Refugees Vietnamese troops in Cambodia cross into Thailand and battle Thai troops for two days near a camp holding some 200,000 Cambodian refugees. The Vietnamese seek to halt the repatriation of Cambodian refugees, many of whom they fear will join the fight against the Vietnamese. Some 100,000 Cambodian refugees are driven into Thailand.

4 JULY 1980
Vietnam Vietnam accuses China of shelling Vietnamese territory earlier in the week, causing many deaths and heavy property damage. The next day China sends a note to Hanoi accusing Vietnam of 'incessant armed provocation' along the frontier.

22 OCTOBER 1980
United Nations The United Nations General Assembly, voting 97 to 23, with 23 abstentions, approves a resolution calling on Vietnam to withdraw its troops from Cambodia.

4 NOVEMBER 1980
USA: Domestic Ronald Reagan is elected president of the United States.

16 DECEMBER 1980
Cambodia Saying the need has eased, the International Red Cross ends its distribution of food across the Thai-Cambodian border, but continues its medical care of Cambodian refugees.

28 JANUARY 1981
Vietnam Vietnam says it is prepared to withdraw an unspecified number of troops from Cambodia if Thailand stops assisting Cambodian guerrillas opposed to the Viet-

CHRONOLOGY

Members of the People's Liberation Army in Laos under attack.

namese-supported Pnompenh government. Thailand denies any aid to guerrillas.

8 NOVEMBER 1981
International A survey of changes in Southeast Asia since the end of the 1975 Indochina wars finds that the standard of living and state of peace in those countries that have rejected Communism continues to rise, while Vietnam, Cambodia, and Laos are mired in war, social upheaval, and economic stagnation or decline.

12 DECEMBER 1981
Vietnam The Vietnamese government invites a group of US war veterans to Vietnam to discuss such issues as Agent Orange and the fate of US servicemen still missing in action. The four veterans who go are criticized for serving Vietnamese propaganda purposes. Foreign Minister Nguyen Co Thach advises them that his country would welcome a study on the impact of Agent Orange use during the war.

25 JANUARY 1982
USA: Domestic A draft of an unpublished US Air Force document written by Major William J Buckingham Jr for the Office of Air Force History reports that the United States secretly sprayed herbicides on Laos during the Vietnam war and openly sprayed them on South Vietnam only after debate at the highest levels of government over whether other nations would criticize it for conducting chemical warfare. The document is disclosed by the National Veteran Task Force on Agent Orange.

22 OCTOBER 1982
USA: Government President Reagan signs legislation to make it easier for thousands of Asian-born children of US servicemen to enter the United States.

The Vietnam War Memorial, dedicated on 13 November 1982.

13 NOVEMBER 1982

USA: Domestic A memorial to America's 2.7 million veterans of the Vietnam war, and to the memory of the 57,939 US soldiers killed or missing in the Vietnam war, is dedicated in Washington, DC. The memorial, designed by Yale architectural student Maya Ying Li, consists of two black granite walls forming a 'V,' listing the names of all the Americans killed in the war. The monument is criticized by some veterans' groups because it carries no inscription identifying the war.

24 DECEMBER 1982

USA: Domestic A group of unemployed Vietnam veterans begins a round-the-clock candlelight vigil at the site of the Vietnam Veterans Memorial in Washington, DC, to call attention to the 1421 US servicemen still missing in action.

28 JANUARY 1983

USA: Domestic President Reagan, at a meeting of the National League of Families of American Prisoners and Missing in Southeast

CHRONOLOGY

Asia, says US intelligence agencies are 'fully focused' on the problem of servicemen still missing and that the goal of full accounting is of 'highest national priority.'

31 MARCH 1983
Refugees Vietnamese troops and artillery assault a refugee camp on the Thai-Cambodian border, forcing thousands of Cambodians into Thailand. Red Cross doctors must abandon the camp hospital and flee with the refugees.

10 JUNE 1983
USA: Military Acting with unusual unanimity, the senior generals of the US Army announce that they oppose any US military intervention in Central America without clear, unequivocal support of Congress and the American people. Their views are interpreted as reflecting scars of the Vietnam experience.

5 JULY 1983
USA: Domestic According to documents made public by Federal Judge George C Pratt Jr, the Dow Chemical Company knew as early as the mid-1960s that exposure to dioxin might cause serious illness or death, but the company withheld this knowledge from the government and continued to sell herbicides contaminated by dioxin to the US Army and the public. Judge Pratt is hearing a multi-billion-dollar lawsuit by 20,000 Vietnam-era veterans against several chemical companies.

29 OCTOBER 1983
USA: Domestic The Reagan administration's sharp curbs on press coverage of the Grenada invasion are traced to deep military resentment of Vietnam war reporting, when journalists had virtually free movement in Vietnam war zones.

30 OCTOBER 1983
Vietnam In an article on life in Vietnam, Craig R Whitney says that Vietnam's leaders seem overwhelmed by the problems of feeding 54 million people without the war's great influx of foreign aid and supplies. Average per capita income is $150 per year.

12 FEBRUARY 1984
China China accuses Vietnam of shelling Chinese border villages during Lunar New Year celebrations, killing a farm worker.

30 APRIL 1984
Vietnam Vietnam charges that Chinese gunners have fired thousands of artillery rounds into Vietnam's northern provinces this month, and that Chinese reconnaissance

A US infantryman on alert.

squads have penetrated as far as one-and-a-half miles into Vietnamese territory, raising tension all along the border. Visits by journalists to the largely undamaged Lang Son Province buttress the contention of some Western diplomats that the fighting is largely a war of communiqués.

7 MAY 1984

USA: Domestic Federal District Judge Jack B Weinstein announces a $180 million out-of-court settlement against seven chemical companies in a class-action suit brought by 15,000 Vietnam veterans against manufacturers of the defoliant Agent Orange. At least 40,000 veterans are involved in various suits against manufacturers of the defoliant, with potential claimants in the hundreds of thousands.

28 MAY 1984

USA: Domestic On Memorial Day the only American Unknown Soldier from the Vietnam war is laid to rest at ceremonies at Arlington National Cemetery in Washington, DC, attended by 250,000, including Congressmen, members of the international diplomatic community, and Vietnam veterans in fatigues. Many see the burial as a national gesture that lays to rest the polarization of the Vietnam era. President Reagan, named honorary next-of-kin, delivers the elegy at the hero's funeral, and urges greater efforts to locate the more than 2400 servicemen still missing.

JULY 1984

International At a meeting of ASEAN (Association of Southeast Asian Nations) in Indonesia, the region's foreign ministers condemn Vietnam's 'illegal occupation' of Kampuchea (Cambodia).

15 JULY 1984

Vietnam Fighting breaks out along the border between China and Vietnam. The Chinese charge that the Vietnamese invaded first and were repulsed after 10 hours; the Vietnamese charge that the Chinese began the fighting by shelling border villages and then moving troops into Vietnam. Many observers feel that the Chinese continue incursions in northern Vietnam to distract the Vietnamese and prevent them from mounting a full-scale offensive against Chinese-backed guerrillas in Kampuchea.

1 SEPTEMBER 1984

USA: Domestic The Reagan administration is reported nearing a decision to offer asylum to 6000-15,000 Vietnamese political prisoners, currently held in 're-education camps,' who worked for US programs during the Vietnam war era. Vietnam has repeatedly offered to allow this group of prisoners to leave for the United States, but until now US officials have questioned the good faith of the offer and declined to test its sincerity.

Refugees Nearly ten years after the Communist takeover of Saigon and five years after the Vietnamese invasion of Cambodia, more than 130,000 Indochinese refugees remain in Thailand awaiting resettlement abroad. The United States has resettled about 300,000 of the 600,000 refugees who have entered Thailand since 1975; hundreds of thousands of refugees also remain in camps in Cambodia and Laos. International refugee officials have worked out a plan to encourage boat captains to rescue 'boat people.' Previously, captains had refused to pick up Vietnamese refugees at sea because of difficulty in finding ports at which they would be allowed to disembark.

11 SEPTEMBER 1984

USA: Government Secretary of State Shultz announces that the United States will ask Vietnam to release an estimated 10,000 political prisoners currently held in 're-education' camps for resettlement in the United States over the next two years. Most of these prisoners are anti-Communists who worked for US programs. Shultz also announces that the United States will admit 8000 Vietnamese children fathered by US servicemen over the next three years. These children, whom the law regards as US citizens, are persecuted in Vietnam because of their non-Asiatic features. Such groups as Human Rights Advocates International protest treating the children as refugees and the slowness of their resettlement. US officials claim such processing is the only way by which the childrens' mothers, who are not citizens, may accompany them to the United States, and the sole means of providing the children with language training and medical care before their arrival.

11 NOVEMBER 1984

USA: Domestic A statue of three Vietnam War infantrymen is dedicated at the War Memorial on Veteran's Day.

THE PRICE OF WAR

THE PRICE OF WAR

Personnel Some 8,744,000 Americans served in the four branches of the US military – Army, Navy, Marines, Air Force – during the main period of hostilities (August 1964-January 1973), which makes the Vietnam War second only to World War II in numbers of personnel involved. But because of the constant rotation of US servicemen in Vietnam – primarily one-year terms – a greater percentage of personnel saw duty in Vietnam. The average age of US combat personnel in Vietnam was only 19 – compared to 26 in World War II. Black Americans constituted about 13 percent of the total troop force in Vietnam, about the same as their proportion of the total US population, but 28 percent had combat assignments, and only 2 percent of the officers were black. Meanwhile, about 15,000,000 eligible American youth avoided the draft by gaining student or occupational deferments; an estimated 250,000 simply didn't register for the draft; an estimated 1,000,000 committed draft offenses; some 25,000 were indicted for draft-related charges, but only some 3250 spent any time in prison.

Casualties The US military lost 47,253 in combat and another 10,449 died in Vietnam; there were 313,616 wounded, of whom 153,300 were classified as seriously wounded. Only a small percentage of the US military personnel actually fought against large Vietcong or North Vietnamese units, although 76 percent were the targets of enemy mortars or rockets, and 56 percent witnessed their comrades being killed or wounded. Due to the use of helicopters for evacuation, and the advanced medical facilities available, 82

Vietcong prepare for an attack.

percent of Americans seriously wounded were saved (compared to 71 percent in World War II and 74 percent in Korea) – the highest survival rate of any modern war. Only 2.6 percent of those who reached hospitals died. However, because of the enemy's use of booby traps, mines, ambushes, and other guerrilla tactics, some 10,000 US servicemen lost at least one limb (more than all those in World War II and Korea combined). Another 81 US servicemen were killed in Laos and Cambodia. Some 1340 Americans were listed as Missing in Action when the war ended. Some of these would be identified and their bodies returned to the United States in the years that followed, but most would remain listed as MIAs.

South Vietnam reported 185,528 of its military personnel killed in the war, with 499,026 wounded. North Vietnam and the Vietcong reportedly lost 924,048 dead in combat. Vietnam is estimated to have lost 415,000 civilians in the war, with at least 935,000 wounded.

South Korea lost 4407 troops fighting in Vietnam; Australia and New Zealand lost 475, with 2348 wounded; and 350 Thais were killed fighting in Vietnam.

Costs It is roughly, but reasonably estimated that the war cost the United States $150 billion in direct expenses. Indirect expenses would probably total at least that, while still other costs – such as payments to veterans, interest on debts incurred, etc – are all but unending. On an average day, US artillery expended 10,000 or so rounds; at about $100 per shell, this item alone cost $1 million per day. One sortie by a B-52 cost $30,000 in bombs alone. Some 4865 US helicopters were lost in the war, each costing about $250,000, and 3720 other aircraft were destroyed. The total tonnage of bombs dropped over North Vietnam, South Vietnam, Cambodia, and Laos came to about 8 million (about four times the tonnage used in all of World War II); 2,236,000 tons of bombs were dropped on the infiltration routes in Laos alone between 1965-71. Although the bombing inflicted an estimated $600 million worth of damage on North Vietnam, it is calculated that the United States spent about 10 times that on these raids, in which thousands of US fliers were killed, wounded, captured, or missing. The Soviet Union and Communist China are estimated to have provided about $3 billion worth of aid to North Vietnam and the Vietcong.

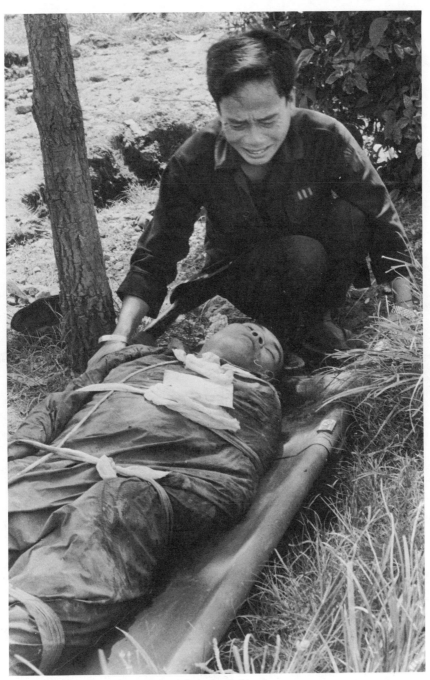

A South Vietnamese trooper weeps over the body of a friend.

LAND FORCES IN VIETNAM AND THEIR WEAPONS

BY IAN V HOGG

LAND FORCES

The course of the continued war in Vietnam, from 1945 onward, saw several different armies and types of armies involved in several different modes of combat, and it is necessary to bear this in mind from the outset. In the days of French rule there was the French regular army pitted against a guerrilla force; later years saw the appearance of the regular armies of North and South Vietnam and the United States, as well as guerrilla and irregular forces from all three combatants. The actual conduct of war varied from small unit actions between regular forces, employing regular tactics and weapons, to set-piece battles, by way of guerrilla actions, internal security actions and confused and chaotic conflicts in which every sort of troop formation found itself involved. At various times, too, air and naval cooperation overlaid the basic land battle and introduced complications in assessment.

The conflict in Vietnam can be said to have begun, in intent if not in actual fact, with Ho Chi Minh's establishment of a 'Democratic Republic of Vietnam' in September 1945. Within three weeks French troops stormed the headquarters of the Ho Chi Minh government, arrested several members and hoisted the French flag.

In the early days there was an uneasy truce as the French came to a form of agreement with the Vietminh, but in December 1946 a Vietminh revolt signalled the start of a phase of low-level guerrilla warfare. At that time the Vietminh commander, General Vo Nguyen Giap, well appreciated the superiority in equipment and firepower enjoyed by the French, though he was less aprehensive about their tactical ability. If, therefore, he could 'keep the pot boiling' by small actions against small French units he felt that at these levels the superiority in firepower would be offset by maladroit handling and that there was a fair chance of inflicting damage. If he could thus inflict visible damage to the occupying forces, this would strengthen the Vietminh's popular support.

By 1949 the French had some 150,000 troops in Vietnam, armed with a motely collection of weapons, largely American and German equipment salvaged from the European Theater or donated after the war in order to provide the French Army with a base of equipment until their own designs went into production. Giap's forces were ill-equipped, relying mainly upon stocks of weapons acquired in the aftermath of the Japanese defeat. Thus while the French could deploy artillery, a small amount of armor, and heavy weapons, the Vietminh were confined to small arms – bolt action rifles and various types of machine guns – and a few mortars capable of being manpacked. Such a technical imbalance virtually decided the tactics, since Giap's men could not sustain a major attack for long. They could move through the jungle in scattered formation, concentrate close to a carefully selected objective, launch a sudden and brief attack, do as much damage as they could in as short a time as possible and then disengage, withdraw, disperse, and vanish into the undergrowth once more to re-assemble several miles away. By keeping up this sort of pin-prick warfare, Giap managed to tie down an inordinate amount of French troops into positions of relative uselessness. Instead of being able to concentrate a major striking force at any one point, the French were forced to disperse their troops in small units in an attempt to impose an appearance of security over as large an area as possible. Most of the French effort in 1948-49 was expended in simply patrolling stretches of road, guarding supply lines and conducting sporadic searches of areas in which guerrillas were reputed to be hiding.

At Christmas 1949 the Chinese Communist forces finally overcame the remnants of the Nationalist Army in China. This had immediate benefits for Giap in that a supply of arms was now freely available across the border, the Chinese having ample weapons to spare. As before, much of this was ex-Japanese equipment, but it also included such items as ex-American recoilless rifles, rockets, mortars and light artillery, anti-aircraft weapons and mines. It was some time before the French appreciated this threat, and even when they finally realized what was happening they severely underestimated both the scale of supply and the speed with which it could be distributed, assimilated and put to use. Moreover they were confident that whatever weapons were acquired by Giap, US aid would more than counterbalance by the supply of more and better weapons from the United States.

In fact Giap received sufficient arms, together with instructional assistance, to be able to organize three full-sized and properly organized infantry divisions by the latter end of 1950, a total of probably 35,000 fully-equipped and trained men. This was an extremely dangerous strength which the French

French troops armed with British equipment arrive in Vietnam.

The French also used captured Japanese tanks in the defense of Phnom Penh, in 1945.

Damaged French artillery at Dienbienphu.

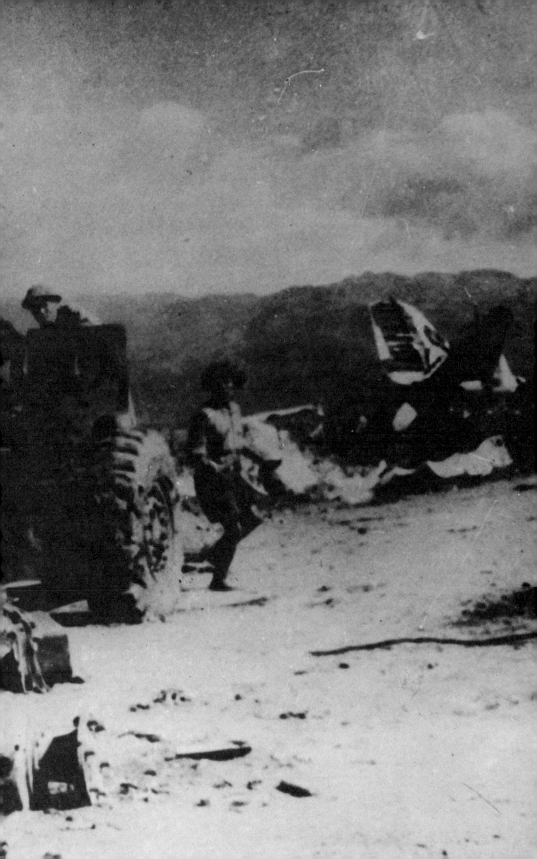

failed to assess properly, and as a result of this accretion of power Giap now moved from minor guerrilla raids to full-scale open warfare. He was, though, careful to make battle in places of his own choosing.

In September 1950, with two divisions formed and waiting, Giap began his campaign by concentrating what approximated an infantry brigade against Dong Khe, a small French outpost close to the Chinese border. Dong Khe, garrisoned by about 250 troops of the French Foreign Legion, suddenly swamped by concentrated mortar fire. When this stopped, infantry attacked in successive waves, then withdrew while another mortar bombardment took place. The infantry attacked once more. By this time the survivors of the outnumbered French, decimated by the attack, managed to escape individually from their perimeter and leave Dong Khe in the hands of Giap's troops.

This defeat was rapidly followed by another attack on a border post and then on a French column moving up to reinforce and retake the fallen posts. The column was caught in open ground and was torn apart, scattered and driven into disorganized retreat. Within a period of a few weeks Giap cleared the French out of the border region of North Vietnam, inflicting a 60 percent casualty rate and capturing vast amounts of booty – almost 1000 machine guns, 125 mortars, 13 artillery pieces, 10,000 rifles, over 400 trucks and quantities of ammunition.

The clearance of North Vietnam led to some far-reaching consequences. The French Government, suddenly aware that they could lose Vietnam if they weren't careful, sent General Jean de Lattre de Tassigny, a well-respected and competent soldier, to take charge of affairs; moreover they gave him a good deal more autonomy than any previous French commander had enjoyed, leaving him to make the decisions and produce the results. US equipment also began to flow into Vietnam to reinforce the French, who had suffered considerably in trying to maintain an army at the end of a tenuous supply line.

On the other side of the battle lines Giap felt confident enough to take on the entire French Army at once, if necessary. He now had his third full division mustered and equipped, arms were still flowing in from China, and recruits were flocking to his banner. The arrival of de Tassigny merely gave him a focus for his efforts.

De Tassigny began by putting his new equipment to good use and involving the French Air Force to a much greater degree than before. Frequent air patrols made the Vietminh reluctant to move by day, since they attracted immediate attack by cannon, bomb and napalm whenever they were seen. In order to bring things to a head, Giap decided on a set-piece attack on a French post, and brought up two divisions against Vinh Yen, some 40 miles from Hanoi. The French got warning of Giap's concentration, mustered 8000 troops and brought in artillery and air support. The land battle was fierce and bloody, and Giap lost a major part of his force before being forced to retreat.

The French, having repulsed the attack, were in good heart but entirely failed to follow up their victory by pursuing Giap and destroying him entirely. The French defense was completely static; their reliance upon mechanical transport tied them to roads, and their dislike of jungle operations led them to throw up defensive lines which encircled the Hanoi-Haiphong district in an endeavor to keep the attackers out. So long as the Vietminh were outside this line the French were satisfied, but it left Giap in virtual command of a large area of the country. He made two further large-scale attacks against the Hanoi area, but both were repulsed, principally by artillery fire.

After these battles there was a lull. The Vietminh were torn by argument and recrimination because of their military defeats and spent the summer of 1951 in reorganizing and re-equipping. The French, whose morale had improved due to their victories, spent the time in building up their forces and acquiring more modern weapons. Unfortunately General de Tassigny died of cancer in January 1952, just as his troops were engaged in operations to extend French influence and carry the battle to the Vietminh. French forces had begun to move out from the Hanoi complex and occupy outposts once more, but this gave Giap the opportunity, once again, of concentrating his forces and defeating these outposts. During this period, too, the French finally began to bring the South Vietnamese into the war, forming Vietnamese regiments and training Vietnamese officers. During their colonial days the French had been reluctant to give any form of advanced military training to 'native troops' and their change of heart left insufficient time to give these forces the basic training needed to be of any use.

By 1954 the French had acquired a large

amount of armor; some 450 tanks and 2000 armored cars, almost all of American origin and all of World War II vintage. This, though, gave them little advantage against Giap, largely due to their inept use of the matériel. The armor was scattered around in small groups of two or three tanks at each outpost, without any appreciable reserve. Moreover the tanks were, like the rest of the French Army, confined to a small strip of land some hundreds of yards to either side of the roads. In their tactical use the tanks were invariably employed as support for marching infantry, their speed being tied to that of the men on the ground, so that there was no independent action and no utilization of the mobility and speed of the tanks. This, as much as anything else, contributed to the long-held belief that 'Vietnam is not tank country.'

The final confrontation of Giap and the French came in the spring of 1954. The French commander, General Henri Navarre, decided to block the Vietminh reinforcement and supply route which led to Laos, and late in 1953 he sent three battalions of paratroops to take and hold a small village called Dienbienphu. There they built two airstrips and established three strongpoints around them, protecting these in turn by four smaller outposts. More troops and artillery, light tanks and ground support aircraft were flown in; the hope was that once this defense had been established, Giap would be tempted to throw his troops against it, whereupon they would be destroyed by superior French firepower.

On 10 March 1954 Giap attacked, preceded by an artillery barrage that astonished the French, since they believed that no-one could manhandle artillery into a firing position through the surrounding jungle. Three of the outposts were overrun, and the Vietminh set up anti-aircraft weapons that effectively prevented the re-supply of the French base by air. A protracted siege then took place, which culminated on 7 May with a total Vietminh victory and the loss of some 13,000 French soldiers. This, so far as the French were concerned, was the last straw, and they washed their hands of Vietnam. In accordance with the agreement hammered out in Geneva, the last French soldier left the country early in 1956.

The equipment used in this first ten-year phase of the Vietnam War was a vastly varied assortment but basically obsolescent. The French Foreign Legion, traditionally responsible for the defense of Vietnam from the days

when it was French Indochina, were principally armed with French weapons: the MAS Mle 49 rifle and the MAS-38 submachine gun, the Mle 24/29 light machine gun, and the 60mm and 81mm Brandt trench mortars. The MAS-36 rifle has the distinction of being the last general-issue military bolt-action rifle to be designed. Designed more with an eye to production than to service, it was robust and reliable. Paratroops had a special version in which the butt was made of aluminium and folded forward, alongside the stock, to make it more compact during a parachute drop.

The MAS-38 submachine gun had a remarkably good design, particularly when it is recalled that in the 1930s designers tried to make weapons which would do everything, giving them bayonets, bipods, optimum sights graduated to 1000 yards and similar useless addenda, all of which added weight. But the French designers of the MAS created a simple and compact weapon for short-range shooting. Their only mistake was to design it around a French 7.65mm cartridge that was low powered and never used by anyone else. Nevertheless, it was a reliable and effective little weapon, and many of them are still to be found in Vietnam, although modified to accept the more common 9mm cartridge.

The same 7.65mm cartridge was also used in the MAS-35 pistol; this had been designed by a private company and was undoubtedly the best-looking and best-performing French weapon of the 1930s. A modified Colt in design, it was too good for mass production and an alternative model, the MAS-35S, of somewhat more severe outline, was eventually developed in an attempt to get sufficient pistols into the hands of troops before 1939. Redesigned in post-war years to take a 9mm cartridge, it is still in use by the French Army.

The Mle 24/29 machine gun was the result of two decisions taken shortly after World War I; one was to replace the existing French 8mm rimmed Lebel cartridge with a rimless design, and the other was to develop a practical light machine gun, a weapon sadly lacking in the French wartime armory. The cartridge appeared in 7.5mm caliber in 1924, and with it came the machine gun, but the combination proved disastrous. The cartridge was re-designed in shorter form, and the gun modified to suit, leading to the '24/29' nomenclature, after which it was used by the French until the 1950s. It resembles most light machine guns of the period, using a top-mounted 30-shot box magazine and being

LAND FORCES

Throughout the war the Vietcong used captured US equipment.

operated by a gas piston.

Once the French Army began to reinforce the Foreign Legion, and as US aid began to flow, more weapons made their appearance. The basic artillery weapon was the elderly French 75mm field gun, first produced in 1897 and subsequently modified by the addition of pneumatic tires. It was still a perfectly sound gun within its limitations. It had restricted elevation, so that the maximum range was no more than 7 miles, and the 16 lb shell had limited destructive powers. On the credit side it had a very high rate of fire, but this was of little use in Vietnam where ammunition supply was a perpetual problem.

With the arrival of US equipment came the standard US Army M1 howitzer. This was a more modern weapon, but its maximum range was identical with that of the '75' though it fired a much more effective shell. Finally there was a small number of US 155mm howitzers, so small a number that, for example, only four were deployed at Dienbienphu. This fired a useful 75 lb shell to 10 miles, and eventually proved to be among the most useful artillery pieces in Vietnam; but, again, ammunition supply was a limiting factor in its use by the French.

The armor sent by the Americans consisted largely of ex-wartime M4 Sherman medium tanks and M8 Greyhound armored cars, later augmented by M24 Chaffee light tanks. There was nothing intrinsically wrong with any of these, but their location at the end of a long supply line meant that they were often out of action for repair, awaiting spare parts.

The Vietminh began the war with arms acquired in the aftermath of World War II and the Japanese surrender, when there were virtually unlimited quantities of arms to be found. As a result their fundamental weapon was the Japanese Arisaka rifle in 6.5mm caliber, a bolt action weapon that was little more than a modification of the well-tried Mauser design. This was supplemented by a variety of Japanese machine guns, notably the Type 11, Type 99 and Type 92. The Type 11 was the Japanese squad light machine gun and, like most Japanese machine gun designs, was based on the French Hotchkiss. However, since it had been designed to accompany the rifle squad, the designer gave it a peculiar feed system unlike any other weapon in the world. On the left side was a hopper into which the gunner dropped clips of ammunition, as used by the riflemen of the squad. The feed mechanism of the gun then stripped the cartridges from the clips and fed them to the gun, spitting out the empty clip as it did so. The theory was that the gun could be supplied by any convenient rifleman at any time, instead of relying upon special magazines. Unfortunately, experience showed that this gun, due to its high rate of fire, battered the feed mechanism to pieces, and a special low-powered cartridge was provided for it. It is doubtful if the Vietminh ever had extensive supplies of this special ammunition, but their use of the weapon in guerrilla attacks probably meant that it saw furious action once a week, so the wear load evened out over a period of time.

The Type 99 was the gun which the Japanese designed to replace the Type 11. This was a considerable technical step forward, being copied from a Czechoslovakian gun which the Japanese had captured from the Chinese Nationalist Army in the 1930s. At the same time the Japanese had decided to re-equip their army with a new cartridge in 7.7mm caliber, and this was one of the first weapons designed for it. It was an extremely good machine gun and was the favorite of the Vietminh.

The Type 92 was a slightly modernized version of a design that appeared in 1914 and was a copy of the French Hotchkisss which the Japanese had used in 1905. The '92' version had been modified to take the 7.7mm cartridge and it had a slow rate of fire – about 450 rounds per minute – which gave it an easily recognizable cadence; Allied troops had called it the 'Woodpecker'. It was heavy, but had been designed so that it could be easily picked up by three men who could then move remarkably quickly across country with it. It was a reliable and robust gun capable of delivering accurate supporting fire to quite long ranges.

When the Chinese Communists began sending weapons into Vietnam in 1950, their first supplies were the same ex-Japanese equipment which the Chinese had removed from Japanese arsenals and dumps in Manchuria in 1945. When this source began to run dry, the next was the stockpile of Soviet weapons which had been built up by the Communists from their liberal supplies received from the Soviet Army. This made up for the lack of a Japanese submachine gun by providing large numbers of Soviet PPSh-41 and PPS-43 weapons, the ideal guerrilla small arm, and, at that time, virtually the trademark of Communist-backed irregular forces. Both had been produced in enormous numbers during the war – some experts have estimated a total production of perhaps 6 million of both types. Both were crudely finished but robust and reliable, firing the 7.63mm Mauser cartridge rather than the more usual 9mm Parabellum, which tied the Vietminh fairly firmly to Communist sources for their ammunition.

The small amount of artillery which Giap was able to muster at vital moments was also Japanese in origin and consisted of a mixture of 75mm and 105mm field guns and 90mm mortars. Heavier guns and mortars might have been available, but these three calibers represented the best compromise between firepower and portability; lighter weapons would not have been sufficiently destructive, while heavier weapons would not have been possible to manhandle into position, as were the guns at Dienbienphu.

When the country was divided into North and South Vietnam by the Geneva Agreements of 1954, the two halves set about organizing their own armies; the North Vietnam Army (NVA) looked to Communist sources for its organization and equipment, and the Army of the Republic of (South)

LAND FORCES

A North Vietnamese unit using US-made 75mm howitzers.

Vietnam (ARVN) looked to the United States for guidance. But while the NVA was a coherent body from the moment of North Vietnam's birth, the ARVN took time to organize, because the South Vietnamese military structure was fragmented and made up of disputatious elements. In the beginning the South Vietnamese Army (SVA) was formed on more or less conventional lines, owing allegiance to the state, since it was the continuance of the local forces which has been put together under French rule.

Eventually the remaining Southern forces were organised into the ARVN, with a nominal strength of about 135,000. This force was totally equipped with US matériel; the standard infantry weapon was the .30 M1 Garand semi-automatic rifle, accompanied by the ubiquitous M1 Carbine and the M3 submachine gun. Infantry support was provided by the 60mm, 80mm and 4.2-inch mortars, and the standard artillery piece was the 105mm howitzer M1. The backbone of the ARVN was its 10,000-man infantry divisions, supported by artillery and a small amount of American-made armor left behind by the French. One armored regiment was deployed in each of the four military districts, each regiment being equipped with M8 'Greyhound' armored cars, M3 half-tracks, M3 scout cars and a number of towed 75mm howitzers. This strength was later augmented by a squadron of M24 light tanks obtained under the US Military Aid program.

For some three years after 1954 there was an uneasy truce between the two states as they grappled with the problems of administering their newly-acquired territory, but once these difficulties were under control it was time to take stock of the political situation. By that time the Communist cadres in South Vietnam had completed their own organization; they had collected weapons, ammunition and recruits, set up bases, organized intelligence, and begun training men in guerrilla warfare. They came to be known as the 'Vietcong', although their formal name was the 'National Front for the Liberation of South Vietnam.' In 1957 Le Duan, the senior Vietcong leader in the South, traveled to Hanoi to confer with the senior Communist leaders and received his orders. He returned to the South and began active guerrilla warfare against the South Vietnamese regime.

The techniques used by these Vietcong bands were primitive but effective. They relied almost entirely on surprise and sudden firepower to achieve their limited objects, and made sure that whether the attack was a success or a failure it lasted no longer than a few minutes. After that the guerrillas would disengage, melt into the jungle to reassemble miles away. Their weapons were small arms and grenades, weapons which could be easily carried and easily concealed, so that the armed guerrilla who vanished into the trees would reappear some distance away as an innocent peasant.

Supplies were soon reaching the Vietcong forces in South Vietnam by the so-called Ho Chi Minh Trail, a supply route which had been hacked through the jungle from Laos and which rapidly became the principal source of weapons and reinforcements. Since this was an unpaved track through jungle, its utility varied with the weather. As a result the operations of the Vietcong began to be regulated by this supply and, consequently, by the weather, though it was to be the late 1960s before this factor was recognized by the US and ARVN commanders.

By 1961 the guerrilla activity throughout South Vietnam had escalated into a running war, with over 600 incidents every month. At the same time the unpopular government of Ngo Dinh Diem was widely criticised for its inability to contain the guerrilla activities. By September 1961 the Vietcong was sufficiently powerful and audacious to attack and capture a major town, Phuoc Vinh, and publicly execute the provincial governor. The ARVN attacked and retook the town on the following day, but in a part of the world where 'face' was important, the Vietcong had gained and the Diem government had lost. In the aftermath of this affair Diem finally agreed to accept military aid; and the first US military forces, two helicopter companies, arrived in December.

It should be stressed that at this time the US and Vietnamese intention was simply to provide technical advisers and instructors, to stiffen and reorganize the ARVN. As the 'Military Assistance Command Vietnam' (MACV), the US military began a program of instruction and rationalization which rapidly

Peasants in North Vietnam aided the Vietcong by transporting supplies.

The French Foreign Legion using crab amphibious vehicles in the marshes south of Saigon.

improved the ARVN's capabilities, particularly by introducing new equipment into the ARVN. In April 1962 two companies of M113 armored personnel carriers (APCs) were shipped in and issued to the 7th and 21st ARVN infantry divisions. The intention was to issue these vehicles to well-trained infantry companies, then give them further training in operations with APCs; the troops allotted proved to half-trained and their unit commanders were taken from an ARVN armored unit and knew nothing of infantry tactics. As a result it took far longer to bring the units up to combat readiness.

Even when their training was completed, the handling of the armored infantry left a lot to be desired, largely because the ARVN command had absolutely no experience of armored warfare, nor were they inclined to listen to their US advisers. Their first real success came in the Plain of Reeds in late 1962. An attack was mounted against a Vietcong force; the APCs ran through flooded paddy fields to the position where the enemy were thought to be and ran into an ambush, as Vietcong appeared on all sides. The ARVN troops sat tight in their APCs and returned fire, and stalemate ensued. The US adviser prevailed on the commander to dismount the troops – the classic mechanized infantry tactic in Western Europe but one which proved disastrous in South Vietnam. Once the ARVN troops leaped from their carriers they were in waist-deep water and pinned down by accurate Vietcong fire. After an hour in which casualties mounted and control was almost lost, the ARVN remounted their APCs and used the mobility of the vehicles to drive through the area and flush out the Vietcong, discovering 150 dead, capturing 38 men and a useful quantity of weapons. This action showed the basic fault of 'European thinking'; what was a good tactic or maneuver in Western Europe was not necessarily good in Southeast Asia. In particular, it became obvious that fighting on foot and leaving the APCs stationary, was not suited to ARVN operations; it was more effective to teach the infantrymen to fight from their vehicles and teach the vehicle commanders to use their mobility to outmaneuver the Vietcong.

The M113 was a useful vehicle in many respects; it was lightly armored with aluminum, carried a .50 caliber Browning heavy machine gun on the roof, had room for 11 infantrymen in addition to the driver and machine gunner, and could swim across rivers and canals if necessary. Its tracks give it excellent cross-country ability and it was practically the only vehicle that could cope with flooded muddy paddy fields. Although it was only a protected personnel carrier, it came to be used almost as a light tank by the ARVN, and at that period of the war the Vietcong had little or no method of stopping the M113.

The success of the two ARVN armored infantry companies warranted expansion, and more M113s were sent, as well as the newly-developed M114 reconnaissance vehicle. By the middle of 1963 each of the four ARVN armored regiments had one squadron of M24 tanks, one of M8 armored cars, one of M14s and two mechanized rifle squadrons with M113s. The rifle squadrons were similar to their predecessors, the mechanized rifle companies, but carried more firepower; they were provided with their own integral support in the shape of three 81mm mortars and a 57mm recoilless rifle.

An armored force composed in this way set out in January 1963 to deal with a force of Vietcong reported at Ap Bac, on the Plain of Reeds. The Vietcong had selected a sound position on a canal bank and they had decided to provoke a fight to size up the ARVN opposition. Intelligence reported the Vietcong as a single infantry company, but in fact there were three companies well reinforced with heavy machine guns and mortars and backed up by local guerrilla units. The ARVN attack was to be by an armored force, and with helicopter-lifted infantry positioned behind the Vietcong in order to cut off their retreat. In the attack the ARVN commander lost his nerve and halted the armored advance, the helicopters ran into severe anti-aircraft machine gun fire, the machine gunners on the APCs, exposed as they stood in their hatches to fire, were cut down, chaos ensued and in the night the Vietcong melted away. The ARVN lost the battle insofar as they did not inflict very serious damage on the Vietcong, and the Vietcong had their morale reinforced by their discovery that they could take on a heavily armed and armored force and get the better of it.

Ap Bac was also notable as being one of the occasions when the ARVN Airborne troops were used. An airborne force had been trained to a fairly high level of competence, and was subsequently used several times successfully, but at Ap Bach it was dropped in the wrong place. Altogether Ap Bach was a milestone in that it forced US commanders to look

A machine gunner keeps watch over the Tuy Hoa Valley.

very critically at the ARVN results and realize that, in fact, the ARVN had very little stomach for fighting.

The M114 reconnaissance vehicle was also discovered to be wanting in several respects. Devised as a cross between a scout vehicle and a light tank, it was smaller and more nimble than an M113 APC and was armed with a pair of machine guns. But while it had performed adequately on test in the United States, operations in Vietnam disclosed that it had poor traction cross-country and had difficulty in entering and leaving the water. By November 1964 all M114s had been withdrawn and replaced by additional M113s, but the lesson of Vietnam appears to have been ignored in the United States and in spite of complaints the M114 continued in service in other parts of the world until 1973.

Late in 1963 Diem was finally displaced. US aid was stepped up and direct assistance in the form of aerial bombing and naval support increased. But the ground battle continued to run in favor of the Vietcong until by 1965 they controlled large rural areas and were gradually moving closer and closer to Saigon and other major towns. What finally led the Americans into direct intervention with ground troops was the realization that there were some 6000 Vietcong within striking distance of the principal US air base at Danang.

In February 1965 the Danang base was provided with a battalion of HAWK air defense missiles to prevent any North Vietnamese air attack in retaliation for the constant US bombing of Hanoi, and on the 26th of the month President Johnson authorized the deployment of US Marines to defend the base.

By the time the first US ground forces began to arrive in Vietnam the opposition had become a great deal more complex and formidable. In the first place the three years of bombing raids against North Vietnam by US covert planes had led to the development of a highly sophisticated air defense system around Hanoi and other major targets. Early in 1965 US air photographs revealed that Soviet surface-to-air (SAM) missiles were being deployed in increasing numbers.

The missile battalions were backed up by generous supplies of anti-aircraft guns, ranging from 37mm to 130mm in caliber, all of Soviet origin. The 37mm was an old weapon, copied from a pre-World Wart II Bofors design, but it could fire 80 1.6-pound shells a minute to a height of 9000 feet, which made it a useful low-level defense. More dangerous was the Soviet 57mm S-60 gun, a design which was largely based on a German development which was uncompleted at the end of World War II. This fires a useful 6-pound shell at 70 rounds a minute to a height of 15,000 feet and is radar-controlled, giving it the capability of day or night firing.

The heavier defenses, to deter the high-flying US bombers, were built up from 85mm, 100mm and 130mm guns. The 85mm M1944 fired a 20-pound shell to 30,000 feet at a rate of about 20 rounds a minute; the 100mm could reach up to 45,000 feet with a 35-pound shell at a rate of 15 rounds a minute, and the 130mm, an ex-naval gun of considerable power, sent its 74-pound shell to 45,000 feet at a rate of 12 rounds per minute.

The Soviets could afford to be generous with anti-aircraft guns largely because by the middle 1960s the anti-aircraft gun, particularly in major calibers, was obsolete; the Soviet Union was defended by that time entirely by missiles. The anti-aircraft gun had also had its day in the United States, but instead of shipping their adolescent weapons to South Vietnam for the ARVN to man, the United States defended its bases there by sending its own anti-aircraft battalions, equipped with the HAWK missile. HAWK stood for 'Homing All-the Way Killer,' and was developed during the latter 1950s as a system capable of dealing with low-altitude targets and of traveling with a field army. As eventually produced it was a cumbersome and expensive system, but it had the supreme virtue of working, at a time when there was nothing comparable in other armies. With subsequent improvement, it is probably the most widely-installed Western missile system and is in use throughout the world.

HAWK first saw employment at Danang Air Base in February 1965. Driven by a two-stage solid fuel rocket, the missile carried a 120-pound warhead of the type known as 'continuous rod'; this has the cylindrical casing of the warhead fabricated from steel rods welded together alternately at top and bottom, so that the detonation of the explosive causes the rods to expand outwards in a continuous circlet of steel that will slice through any aircraft it encounters like wire going through cheese. The launcher is a simple trailer carrying three missiles, but the backup was enormous; a long train of heavy vehicles with three radars, command vehi-

Clearing the vines on an immobilized tank with a machete.

cles, computer vehicles and generators to supply power. Nevertheless, it could unerringly seek out and destroy any aircraft up to an altitude of 35,000 feet and a distance of up to 25 miles. Several HAWK battalions were eventually deployed in sensitive areas of South Vietnam, but due to the north Vietnamese lack of long range air capability they saw very little action.

The next major US introduction was armor. For some years it had been universally held that Vietnam was 'not tank country' and little armor, other than the ubiquitous M113 armored personnel carrier, was used. There were a number of aging M8 armored cars in use by ARVN, and they also received a number of Cadillac Gage V-100 'Commando' armored cars, but the early days of US involvement brought no new equipment. A secondary factor, it might be added was that until 1963 the US Army was not organized to fight in a country like Vietnam; the 1950s had seen the construction of the 'pentomic division' built up of five heavily armed and armored 'battle groups,' the whole set-up being designed for nuclear war in a European theater. But the early 1960s brought some re-thinking and in 1963 the monolithic structure was dismantled and re-organized along more traditional lines, giving a battalion-regiment-brigade structure, far more flexible and capable of being usefully deployed in 'small war' scenarios.

The armor actually arrived as a by-product; in 1965, when the US Marines were sent to protect Danang, their formation was such that a battalion landing team contained a tank platoon. Far from finding no employment in a country 'not for tanks' the Marine M48s were soon hard at work supporting infantry, acting as anchors in strongpoints and assisting search missions and patrols. In mid-August 1965 the tanks were used in Operation Starlite, a spoiling attack against a Vietcong force mustering to attack the Chu Lai airfield close to Danang. They were extremely successful, even though seven were severely damaged in the battle.

In spite of this the Marine use of tanks was castigated as being 'not appropriate to counter-insurgency operations' and there was no attempt to follow up the idea by using Army armored battalions. Indeed, due to the peculiar system of allotting troops to Vietnam, infantry units were considered preferable since a higher proportion of an infantry battalion's manpower was actually in contact with the enemy, and so within a given figure

for manpower it was more effective to employ infantry. However, when the 1st Infantry Division was scheduled for deployment in Vietnam in early 1966 they were permitted to retain one squadron of M48 tanks in order to test whether armor had anything useful to contribute.

In practice, when the tanks did arrive they were mishandled. Since the old Vietnam hands saw no use for tanks, the M48s were withdrawn from service and stored in a base depot. After six months of argument by the divisional commander, the tanks were eventually restored to the unit, but a request for a second squadron to be sent out from the United States met with refusal.

Eventually experience showed that tanks could move through the jungle, if some intelligent assessment of the terrain was made, and tanks could support infantry in Southeast Asia just as well as they could in Europe or any other theater of war. A certain amount of re-education was needed, since the tanks were now being used for their original purpose. In 1916 the first tanks were purely mobile guns to support infantry, but in the intervening years they had become more concerned with fighting other tanks. But in South Vietnam there were no enemy tanks to be seen, and so the US armor reverted to basic infantry support function.

The M48, though, was thought to be somewhat cumbersome for operations in this close country, and commanders began requesting something with good firepower but smaller, more nimble, and amphibious. In 1969 the first issues of the M551 'Sheridan' were made. The M551 was variously called an 'Amphibious Combat Vehicle' or an 'Airborne Assault Vehicle' but in fact it could equally well have been called a light tank. With aluminum armor it weighed 15.5 tons, was air-portable and amphibious, and it was armed with a remarkable weapon, the 152mm gun/missile launcher. This weapon could either fire a conventional type of gun shell, by using a rather unconventional combustible-cased cartridge, or it could function as the launch tube for the 'Shillelagh' wire-guided missile. Such a combination gave the M551 a powerful potential, but it also demanded a powerful collection of electronic gadgetry to control it.

Unfortunately the M551 failed to live up to its promise. The electronics were unreliable in the heat and damp of South Vietnam; the engine, transmission and cooling system gave perpetual trouble; and the revolutionary combustible-cased cartridge system proved to be dangerous. By this time the Vietcong had begun using mines, and an M551 which ran over a mine was likely to have its store of ammunition ignited by the explosion, leading to complete destruction of the tank and its crew. By comparison, an M48 running over a similar mine would suffer a broken track and might have a wheel blown off, but the crew would generally be unharmed and it would be amenable to fairly quick and simple repair.

The missile system was never put to use in Vietnam, since it was primarily an anti-tank device and there was no call for it. But the remainder of the M551s' equipment, and particularly the gun ammunition, gave sufficient trouble to cause the troops to dislike them. Gradually, however, as they became more used to the vehicle and its foibles, and commanders learned to deploy the M551 in situations where its lack of size and amphibian capability were advantageous. Eventually almost every cavalry unit in Vietnam was equipped with them.

The Vietcong employment of mines had been a feature of the war from its earliest days, and it was merely stepped up when more armor appeared. Indeed, one of the objections to the employment of US armor was the ease with which primitive mines could be laid and the difficulty of detecting them. Like every Western army, the US Army had its quota of electronic mine detecting devices which could be carried by troops, but these had been developed with sophisticated mines in mind, mines in metallic cases which would trigger the circuits and signal their presence. The Vietcong, although it had a few of this type of mine, relied far more on makeshift devices using little metal – blasting explosive in a wooden box was a favorite method – which could not be detected by sophisticated methods. It required a man on the ground prodding the earth with a metal spike to physically find the mine before it could be rendered harmless. This is a labor-intensive method not to be recommended in the situation the Americans were in, since it removed men from combat.

Other Vietcong mines were more easily discovered, if detection devices were in use; artillery shells buried in the ground, their fuses replaced by a simple pressure switch were highly favored. But the sheer size of the problem, the difficulty of sweeping mile upon mile of road and thus of slowing down the movement of troops, was such that practical measures for mine detection became impractical, and it became more a matter of preventing mining by constant and erratically-timed road patrols than of trying to detect mines after they had been planted. Many US troops using M113 APCs tried to devise their own methods of countering mines, by layering the floor of the vehicle with sandbags, but this usually ended by overloading the vehicle and burning out its transmission. Another popular move was for the crews of APCs to ride on top, rather than inside; they were likely to be blown off by a mine exploding beneath the vehicle, but any injury so sustained would be less damaging than the injury they would have suffered had they been inside. The most common move was to use a tank as lead vehicle, since it would survive a mine blast better than would an APC. Eventually armoring kits were developed and applied to the undersurfaces of APCs, giving them better protection; the vehicle still sustained considerable damage but at least the major force of the explosion was confined to the outside.

The final device to counter mines was the 'Expendable Mine Roller,' a collection of steel wheels mounted on a framework and pushed ahead of an M48 tank. There were two sets of wheels, or rollers, positioned ahead of the tank's tracks so that any mine threatening the track would be detonated by the pressure of the rollers. The rollers would be damaged, but could be rapidly replaced, while the framework carried them sufficiently far ahead of the tank to ensure that the blast did not damage the vehicle. Initial trials of the mine roller were not very successful, since the tank was pushing 20 tons of dead weight, a load that told on the engine and transmission and demanded extra maintenance. But in the end some 27 of these devices, imperfect as they were, were in use.

In default of any lightweight tanks the M113 APC gradually evolved into an ACAV or 'Armored Cavalry Assault Vehicle.' These came into being when armored cavalry platoons were re-equipped with M113s on arriving in Vietnam. But the functions of an armored cavalry unit included positive fighting. So the platoons began modifying their APCs by building armored shields around the .50 caliber machine gun and by adding two pedestal mounts, complete with armored shields, for two more 7.62mm M60 machine guns at the sides. In fact the US troops had re-invented the shielding and arming first developed by the ARVN some three years before, but scorned at the time.

The use of armor by the North Vietnamese Army was slight. The first occasion was during an attack on a Special Forces Camp at Lang Vei, close to Khe Sanh, in February 1968. A handful of Soviet PT-76 amphibious tanks were used, and succeeded in breaking though the defenses. In the following year US and NVA armor had their sole encounter during the fight for Ben Het. This was another Special Forces camp, overlooking the Ho Chi Minh trail, and in order to draw attention from NVA troop movements down this trail an attack was launched against the camp. The camp held a battery of 175mm guns, some anti-aircraft artillery and infantry, and in order to counter the build-up of enemy,

elements of an armored battalion were sent to strengthen the defense.

For some days the camp was subjected to heavy artillery fire, and eventually, during a night bombardment, a quick-witted tank sergeant heard the noise of engines and tracks through the masking noise of the shelling. Infra-red searchlights were used but without detecting anything; then a defensive anti-tank mine some 1000 yards out suddenly detonated, revealing the enemy's location. Although the mine had stopped the PT-76 tank it had not rendered it incapable of fighting, and it immediately fired its gun at the US positions; this was apparently the signal for the other tanks to join in and seven more were identified by their gun flashes. The US M48s immediately began returning fire and soon destroyed two PT-76s and an APC. After a

'Dusters' were tank bodies converted to deliver 40mm cannon fire.

Helicopters were used to airlift prisoners out of the battle zones.

brief fire fight the surviving NVA tanks withdrew.

The PT-76 was no match fof the M48; it was principally developed as a reconnaissance vehicle and its greatest virtue lay in its amphibious capability. It weighed 14 tons, the thickest armor was 14mm, and the gun was a 76mm of moderate velocity and penetrative power. The M48, on the other hand, was a main battle tank, wighted 47 tons, had armor up to 120mm thick, and had a high velocity 90mm gun which could, and did, rip open the PT-76 like a paper bag. By contrast the only PT-76 shot which hit a US tank at Ben Het did no significant damage to the tank.

The first major armored battle between ARVN and NVA came in 1971, in the aftermath of Operation Lam Son 719 in which ARVN had driven into Laos to cut the NVA supply lines. In their counter-attack the NVA threw in a tank battalion, but this was met by an ARVN M41 tank squadron. In a bitter battle for a landing zone the NVA lost 16 PT-76 and six T54s, the first time that the heavier T54 had been put into combat. The ARVN lost none of their M41s, but in spite of this armor victory the NVA had superiority in infantry and pushed the ARVN off the landing zone.

Stopping T-54s with the M41 was a considerable morale-booster to the ARVN. The T-54 was, at that time, considered to be one of the world's more potent tanks; it was a direct descendant of the all-conquering T-34 of World War II fame, weighed 36 tons, had almost 100mm of armor on the hull front and 200mm on the turret front, and mounted a powerful 100mm gun capable of beating up to 373mm of armor at any range. By contrast the M41 'Walker Bulldog' was a by definition a light tank; it weighed 23 tons, had a maximum of 38mm of armor on the turret front, and

Some of the weapons captured by the South Vietnamese in Laos.

mounted a 76mm gun which could penetrate some 200mm of armor. On paper the T-54 should have gone through the M41s with no trouble, but the superior training of the ARVN told when it came to the battle.

Since their armor was scant and apparently of little effect when it was put into battle, the NVA and Vietcong looked for other methods of defeating US and ARVN armor. While the mine was proving effective, it had the disadvantage that it was a dormant weapon. The first effective anti-tank weapon which the Vietcong adopted was the 57mm recoilless rifle, a weapon developed by the United States in 1945 and used by them in the closing stages of the Pacific Campaign. Eventually numbers flowed from China into North Vietnam and were then shipped down the Ho Chi Minh Trail. The 57mm RCL was a useful weapon for guerrillas; it weighed only 44 pounds and could be fired off a man's shoulder or from a machine-gun tripod. It fired a 2.7 pound shaped charge anti-tank shell which could defeat about 70mm of armor and it also had a useful anti-personnel high explosive shell, so that as well as an anti-tank gun it was an infantry support weapon. Although useless against modern tanks, it was still capable of penetrating the aluminum armor of the M113. Nevertheless a hit on the hull of an APC with a 57mm HEAT shell could cause injuries to the crew, and it rapidly became a popular weapon.

Its defect was that, like all recoilless guns, it blew out a column of flame and smoke from the rear end when it fired, and this 'signature' immediately gave away the firer's location, after which retaliation was inevitable and swift. So a 57mm gunner had to make his first short count. This led to holding fire until the target was within quite short ranges; this, in turn, meant that the gunner was often trapped by accompanying vehicles or infantry and the gun was lost.

If the weapon had to be used at short range, and if there was a danger of losing it, then it made sense to have something less cumbersome and more expendable, and in the late 1960s the Vietcong began to receive supplies of the Soviet RPG-2 grenade launcher. The RPG-2 was developed from the German 'Panzerfaust' and was a light tube with grip and trigger which the man rested on his shoulder; into the muzzle end he inserted a projectile with a warhead twice the diameter of the tail boom and carrying a shaped charge. At the end of the tail boom was a propelling charge. On firing, this charge shot the missile out of the front end and gave the usual recoilless back-blast from the rear end. As the missile left the launcher a set of fins unwound so as to stabilize it, and it could be accurately fired to a range of about 150/175 yards. On impact it could defeat at least three times as thick armor as the 57mm shell.

The RPG-2 was soon replaced by the RPG-7 which rapidly gained a formidable reputation, not only as an anti-tank weapon but also as a bombardment weapon against defended positions. Although it resembled the RPG-2 it was a much more sophisticated weapon, so much so that even now, 20 years later, it is still among the leading weapons of its type. The principal difference was that the projectile contained a rocket motor. On firing, the recoilless charge merely launched the rocket at low velocity; then, after about 15 yards of flight, the rocket motor ignited and accelerated the rocket, sustaining it to a range of 500 meters. The warhead was also improved and could defeat 320mm of armor and greater thicknesses of wood, concrete or other types of protection. The object of this two-stage launch was to protect the firer from the back-blast of the rocket. By making the launch in two stages the operator was in no danger, the rocket could sustain for longer flight, and the signature of the recoilless launch was extremely small.

In 1972 a third and potentially far more dangerous weapon was added to the NVA armory. In April of that year the ARVN 20th Tank Regiment was operating near Dong Ha when their M48s were attacked by NVA troops using the Soviet 'Sagger' guided missile. This was a wire-guided rocket carrying a powerful shaped charge warhead; it was fired from a small launch pad that was simply placed on the ground in a convenient place and connected to a periscopic sight some distance away. The operator found a target and fired the rocket; as it flew, so it unreeled a fine wire connected to the control unit, and the operator, looking through his sight, merely had to push and twist a joystick control to make the rocket fly where he wanted until it struck the target. It had a maximum range of 3000 meters – governed by the length of the wire – and could blow a sizeable hole through 18 inches of armor.

The first use of the Sagger at Dong Ha resulted in an M48 tank and an ACAV being destroyed, but the ARVN troops, once they had got over their initial surprise, soon discovered that the solution was to locate the launch point, then locate the sight unit and its operator, and then spray him with gunfire. This took his mind off the precise business of guiding the missile so that it usually flew off course. Even so, initial surprise could frequently land some effective hits before the tank men could retaliate; in a second battle some three days later the same regiment lost another three M48s.

The use of recoilless guns was not confined to the NVA and Vietcong. The US Army had improved them considerably and two more modern and more powerful weapons, the 90mm and 106mm rifles, were available to both US and ARVN forces. These were principally used as direct-fire support weapons for infantry, particularly where attacks on strongpoints had to be made. Under the hand of the infantry company or battalion commander they were 'instant artillery' and were invaluable for dealing with obstacles that suddenly presented themselves.

When it came to personal weapons, the Vietnam War was a milestone in small arms development because it gave impetus to the small-caliber assault rifle; a trend which gained momentum until in the 1980s, it has become virtually an international standard for infantry.

After 1945 the US Army analyzed wartime infantry actions and developed the M14, virtually a Garand with a 20-round magazine. But at the same time several programs were begun to evolve a smaller, lighter weapon that would be effective at ranges to about 400 yards, which analysis had shown was the maximum rifle range for perhaps 95 percent of infantry shooting. These various programs finally came together in a demand for a lightweight rifle firing a small-caliber bullet at high velocity and the Armalite Company developed a rifle firing a new .223 (5.56mm) cartridge. Tests in 1958 were followed by some small modifications and a recommendation that the AR-15 rifle be considered as a replacement for the M14. The US Air Force was looking for a lightweight short range weapon for airfield guards, and in 1961 bought 8500 rifles. Many of these were sent to Vietnam for USAF use, and there they caught the eye of South Vietnamese Army officers. A light rifle was just what was wanted by the small-stature ARVN soldiers. The US troops saw the ARVN using the AR-15 and demanded it, which led to purchases and issue, as the M16. Its debut was, in fact, somewhat marred.

One of the major public-relations claims made on behalf of the M16 was that it did not require as much cleaning as did the older M14, but unfortunately the troops chose to interpret this as meaning it needed no cleaning at all. Then came a rash of defects, failures to eject, failures to feed, mysterious stoppages in action. This led to a Congressional inquiry that discovered there had been an unannounced change in the composition of the powder used in the 5.56mm cartridges. The new powder, while more powerful and ballistically superior to the old, generated more carbon fouling which, allied with the lack of cleaning, led to the defects. The soldiers were issued cleaning equipment and bombarded with a massive educational program, the rifle was redesigned with a chrome-plated chamber, and the rifle's rate of fire was reduced so that it did not get so hot.

The universal rifle of the Vietcong and NVA, after the division of the country, was the Soviet Automat Kalashnikov 47 (AK47). The Soviets came out of World War II intent upon finding a serviceable lightweight rifle for their infantry, and they had been considerably impressed by the German development of the 'Sturmgewehr' which used a cartridge of standard German 7.92mm caliber but with a shorter case. Other things being equal, a short-cased cartridge means that the weapon can be more compact and the soldier can carry more ammunition. The Germans had begun their study as far back as 1936 and before the war began had decided that a short cartridge capable of accurate fire out to 500 yards or so was all that the average soldier needed. They eventually managed to produce the cartridge and weapon in 1943, and the combination made an indelible impression on the Russians. They, in turn, developed their own short-cased cartridge, the 7.62mm Model 1943, and invited weapon designs to suit.

Kalashnikov was a tank sergeant who had been badly wounded in 1941 and, during convalescence, had become interested in firearms theory and design. No longer fit for front line duty, he was assigned to a weapons factory. After designing a submachine gun and a carbine that were not accepted for service, he designed his Model 1947 rifle and this became the standard Soviet arm in 1951. In 1959 he improved the method of production and the new design became the AKM; he then went on to apply the same mechanical principles to a family of machine guns.

Like the M16, the AK47 is gas operated,

The Vietcong were armed with Chinese and Russian weapons.

but using a conventional piston mechanism to open the bolt, whereas the M16 uses the direct blast of gas. Both fire automatic or single shots, both use a removable box magazine, and in spite of the disparity in caliber have similar performance out to about 400 yards range, after which the bullets tend to lose accuracy. The original AK47 used a machined receiver, expensive to produce, and Kalashnikov's 1959 improvement was to develop a pressed-steel receiver, which made it a cheaper weapon without affecting its mechanical reliability. Without doubt the AK is the most successful assault rifle ever developed, and in the hands of the Vietcong and NVA it soon made an impression on the US troops who faced it.

One of the situations in which it made an impression was in ambushes, a favorite Vietcong tactic, and as a result the US Army began looking at possible ways of countering the ambush. The essential part of an ambush is the surprise element, and, equally, the

essential part of the counter-maneuver is rapid and massive response. US troops were soon adept at taking cover and opening automatic fire with their M16 rifles and M60 machine guns, but something more drastic was necessary. Grenades were effective but their range was short, particularly when the man throwing it had his mind on taking cover. The US Marine Corps began issuing shotguns to their patrols. Shotguns had been used before by the Marines, as far back as World War I, and as quick-response weapon they are extremely effective. The model favored for military use is the slide-action 'riot gun' pattern with a short barrel that gives a good spread of shot, instead of the sporting 'Number Six Shot' cartridge, the military loading was 'OO Buck,' nine lead balls each 0.36 inch diameter. These would kill out to 30 yards and inflict serious wounds for another 30. The drawback was the load of only nine balls which soon spread out so far that it was possible for them to miss a man-sized target.

By the middle 1960s, there was a great deal of experimenting going on in the United States with alternative missiles for small arms, and one of those selected for test was the 'flechette,' best described as a one-inch nail with fins. Although the flechette weighs very little it can be fired at high velocity, and it was demonstrated that this gave it a powerful wounding or killing ability, since it rapidly lost what stability it had on entering flesh and 'dumped' its considerable store of energy in one massive blow. Unfortunately there were a lot of severe technical problems in making a single-flechette rifle cartridge, but it occurred to someone that a bunch of flechettes might make a very potent loading for a shotgun shell. 20 cadmium-plated flechettes, each weighing 7.5 grains, were packed into a shotgun pattern cartridge, known as the 'Beehive' cartridge – from the noise of the darts flying through the air. These darts were so light that they left the barrel at almost 2000 feet per second, and they were capable of penetrating armored vests and steel helmets at 500 yards range. The only defect was that they were poor at penetrating multiple layers of jungle, so that a man behind a yard or two of bush was relatively safe.

The Beehive principle was also applied to artillery. The 105mm howitzer was provided with a shell carrying some 90,000 flechettes and fitted with an adjustable time fuse. This could be set to burst at any point between the muzzle and the maximum range, and bursting the shell released the cloud of flechettes, which continued along the shell's trajectory. Since the shell was up in the air when it burst, and showered the flechettes downward, there was rarely any foliage between the flechettes and their targets. The artillerymen rapidly found another use, which had not been planned; fired to burst at the muzzle, the Beehive shell scythed down the grass in front of the gun position, clearing a field of fire for the local defense machine gunners and denying cover to any marauding Vietcong. It was also found to be useful for flushing snipers from the undergrowth, since the artillery flechettes were heavier and could penetrate further into the bush.

So even the flechette shotgun cartridge was not the complete answer to ambushes, and something even more destructive was sought. In 1965, Springfield Arsenal produced the M79 40mm Grenade launcher. This was a single-shot weapon which resembled a sawed-off shotgun and broke open in similar fashion

to load. It fired a six-ounce high explosive grenade at 250 feet per second and could send it to a range of 450 yrds. In skilled hands it was highly accurate to 200 yards and a gunner could plant the grenade precisely where he wanted it to that range, which was ample for dealing with ambushes. The launcher used an unusual method of firing, called the 'High-Low Pressure System' which had been developed in Germany during World War II. The aluminum cartridge case carried the small propellant charge in a small chamber in front of the cap; this chamber had a number of carefully-sized holes leading into the part of the case where the grenade rested. When the cap was fired, the propellant exploded and created a high pressure inside the chamber; this bled out into the main part of the cartridge case to produce a low-pressure impulse that launched the grenade at an adequate velocity without producing excessive recoil.

The grenade contained a charge of high explosive inside a steel casing that produced fragments and would blast out to a lethal radius of five yards around the point of impact, the lethal radius being defined as that within which 50 percent of exposed troops would become casualties. Shortly after the M79 Launcher arrived in Vietnam a second loading was provided, a plastic casing which was loaded with about 45 flechettes, and then another 'multiple projectile' loading carrying 27 00 Buckshot balls. Both these proved highly effective at short range.

Springfield Arsenal also developed the M203 Grenade Launcher. This was a short tube which clamped beneath the M16 rifle and had a slide-operated breech. The soldier could thus carry a standard rifle, but with a loaded grenade discharger underneath it, and he could fire either. Not only did this give the grenadier some personal protection, it worked the other way and gave more soldiers the ability to fire grenades. Because of the shorter barrel, the maximum range was down to 350 yards and the accurate range to 150 yards, but this was a small loss for a considerable tactical gain.

From suffering ambushes to mounting ambushes was the obvious progressive step for the US and ARVN forces, and where Vietcong bands became too set in the routine this could prove profitable. Once a route became established it could be staked out with a platoon or even more, and with weapons such as the M79 and M203 a terrible blast of firepower could be launched at the decisive

US Paratroops firing mortars during the monsoon rains.

moment. The difficulty with ambushes is to make sure that the entire enemy force is contained within the killing ground, and to help in this the United States developed the 'Claymore' mine, one of the most lethal weapons for its size ever produced.

The Claymore, or Mine, Anti-Personnel, M18A1, was another idea based on German wartime development, a slab of explosive with a slightly hollowed front face, lined with a thick steel plate, as an anti-tank weapon; when the explosive was detonated it threw the plate forward in one piece with sufficient velocity to drive through the front plate of a heavy tank at fifty yards range. Fortunately for Allies the development was never perfected into a service weapon. At the time of the Korean War they adapted the German idea to fire several small pieces of steel as a counter to

the North Korean and Chinese mass-attacks, but before this experimental device was put into action the Korean War was over. Seeing no further use for their idea they passed the results over to the US Army who modified it yet again. This time they used a curved plastic box, filled with explosive, in the face of which were buried 700 steel slugs. The curvature of the casing and the face of the explosive was such that when the explosive was detonated it blasted the slugs out in a fan-shaped arc some 60 degrees wide, with a velocity that was lethal to a range of 80 yards. The slugs flew in a narrow band from one to five feet above the ground, so that none were wasted by going too high or too low. This was the Claymore mine.

The Claymore was detonated electrically, either by command or by some form of trip

LAND FORCES

device. Placed at both ends of an ambush killing ground and fired as soon as the victims were inside the perimeter, the mines devastated both ends of the column and left the rest paralyzed with shock while the ambush party opened fire. They could also be planted on jungle trails, with trip-wires, and left to be triggered by anyone passing that way.

Much basic research that had been begun in the 1950s was by the 1960s beginning to show results, and technology was catching up with some of the wilder ideas. One result of this was a variety of sensing devices that could detect movement by the vibration of the ground or by particular frequencies of noise set up by moving men. These could be strung along a trail, wired to a central listening post, or relayed by radio to a distant listening post; a skilled operator could detect movement on the trail and even tell which direction it was flowing and roughly how many men were there. It was a small step from that to wiring up Claymore mines in the same area, so that when the operator detected movement he

could fire one or more mines to catch those moving.

The other considerable scientific advance that appeared in the hands of US troops in Vietnam was the image-intensifying night sight for weapons. Before this, darkness had meant the cessation of organized warfare, although, in fact, much night action went on, illuminated by flares and pyrotechnic devices which gave a fitful and deceiving light. As a result, night operations were disliked and rarely as successful as they should have been.

During the latter stages of World War II the US Army had developed an infra-red sight for rifles. The device was abandoned fairly rapidly after the war but the idea of night vision was pursued. With the advances in electronics a technique was developed to use an optical lens to detect what small amount of light there was, convert this into electronic signals and amplify it electronically, then reconvert it back into a visual picture which could be seen in an optical eyepiece. It did not work in total darkness; it required some contrast between

Machine guns carried on patrol south of Danang.

Two Marines examine captured enemy 12.7mm anti-aircraft guns.

objects so that there was something to be amplified, but the contrast was magnified by up to 60,000 times, which meant that a scene in starlight, apparently black to the naked eye, could be viewed as if it were daylight through the image intensifier. The other great advantage which this sight possesses is that it does not emit any visible signal, as did the infra-red sight, and thus it cannot be detected by the enemy. The first indication he has is when the bullets begin to strike, at ranges up to 300 yards. Heavier sights were developed for use on machine guns and recoilless rifles which allowed them to fire at even greater ranges. Not every man had this type of sight, but not every man needed it; it was sufficient for sentries, point men or heavy defensive weapon crews to have the ability to see in the dark, so that they could begin the action with well-placed shots. Once the fire fight was under way, the conventional pyrotechnics could be used; it was the initial surprise that counted.

The final technological addition that should be mentioned is, of course, the helicopter; although this properly belongs to the Air Force story, its use by ground troops added a completely new dimension to warfare, in-creasing mobility by an enormous factor. In this respect the Vietnam war is a milestone in military tactical development. During the Korean War the helicopter had first seen extensive use, but principally as a liaison machine and as a means of rapidly evacuating casualites. It served in these roles in Vietnam too, but its greatest breakthrough was its adoption as the means of transportation for 'air cavalry.' By using the helicopter, troops could leapfrog over defences and be positioned in the enemy's rear, a particularly useful maneuver when the opposition was composed of small groups of Vietcong. The helicopter allowed heavy weapons, including artillery, to be lifted and positioned in ideal tactical locations which would have been impossible to reach by any other means. It allowed units to be moved rapidly from one area to another to reinforce or to change the axis of an attack. Small scouting forces could be rapidly thrown forward and positioned, left for a short while to pick up information, and then as quickly brought back or shifted to another area. Without the helicopter to transport the other weapons the US and ARVN forces would have been sadly handicapped in the Vietnam war.

AIR FORCES IN
VIETNAM

BY ANTHONY ROBINSON

The origins of the air war in Vietnam lay in France's struggle to reimpose colonial rule on French Indochina. Air support for the French ground troops struggling to combat the Vietminh had come from a miscellany of World War II fighter aircraft, including Grumman F6F Hellcats, Supermarine Spitfire Mk IXs, DH Mosquito FB Mk V1s and Grumman F8F Bearcats. In 1950 the situation improved when the United States supplied the *Armée de l'Air* with B-26 Invader bombers, thus greatly increasing the French forces' firepower. Yet an even more urgent need remained for transport aircraft. The *Armée de l'Air* had deployed AAC-1 Toucans to the theater in 1946 and they took part in some noteworthy air assault operations in which paratroop batallions were dropped to secure important communications centers. There was even an attempt to capture the Vietminh's 'provisional government' by this means.

Increasing numbers of C-47s also became available and eventually four *groupes de transport* operated this aircraft. With the ending of the Korean War in 1953 further C-47s became available from USAF stocks and the US government agreed to expand the capacity of the *Armée de l'Air*'s transport force still further by making Fairchild C-119s available. However, by the time that the crucial battle of Dienbienphu was fought, only a few French aircrews had been trained on the type. As air supply of the French forces beseiged at Dienbienphu was of vital importance, mercenary aircrew were hired from Major General Claire Chennault's Civil Air Transport company to operate the remainder. Heavy groundfire greatly hampered the resupply operations and the fall of the surrender of the Dienbienphu garrison signaled the end of French rule in Indochina.

The US Air Force's involvement in the Vietnam War began in 1961 with the dispatch of a detachment of the 4400th Combat Crew Training Squadron to Bien Hoa in South Vietnam. As its designation suggests, this specialized counterinsurgency unit was primarily responsible for training Vietnamese aircrew but it was also to be used in ground attack, reconnaissance and air supply operations in support of the ARVN (Army of the Republic of Vietnam). A further objective was the development of tactics and techniques of counterinsurgency warfare under combat conditions. The detachment, codenamed 'Farm Gate,' was equipped with World War II vintage Douglas B-26 Invaders for bombing and reconnaissance duties and Douglas C-47 transports. In addition the more modern North American T-28D Nomad, which had first entered USAF service as a trainer in 1950, was used for close air support, as were A-1E Skyraiders in the early phase of Farm Gate.

Because of its origins as a basic trainer, the T-28D was ideally suited for the operational training of South Vietnamese aircrew, and the Farm Gate aircraft were generally crewed by a USAF pilot with a South Vietnamese Air Force (VNAF) trainee in the back seat. Powered by a 1425hp Wright R-1820 radial engine, the T-28D had a cruising speed of 207mph and a maximum range of 2700 miles. Its armament comprised two 0.5in machine guns, each with 350 rounds of ammunition and up to 1800lb or ordnance. Other modifications to the trainer design to adapt it to a combat role included the fitting of self-sealing fuel tanks and armor protection for the crew. As well as serving with the 4400th CCTS, T-28Ds were supplied to the air forces of South Vietnam, Laos, Cambodia and Thailand. So long as groundfire was light, the aircraft performed its attack mission effectively. However, with the deployment of North Vietnamese Army units into South Vietnam in the mid-1960s, anti-aircraft fire became considerably more intense. Furthermore the T-28s were nearing the end of their airframe lives and a number of aircraft were lost due to structural failure. Consequently it was decided to replace the Nomads with Douglas A-1 Skyraiders in 1964.

The A-1 Skyraider piston-engined attack aircraft was a veteran of the Korean War, where it saw considerable service operating from the US Navy's aircraft carriers. By the early 1960s it was being gradually replaced in Navy service by the A-4 Skyhawk jet attack aircraft, so a large number of surplus Skyraiders were available for transfer to the USAF and VNAF. These included single-seat A-1J and H versions and A-1Es, which provided side-by-side seating for an instructor pilot and pupil. It was the latter variant which first entered service with the Farm Gate detachment, although later in the war the single-seaters were extensively operated by the USAF's Special Operations Wings on close air support and combat rescue escort missions. The US Navy also flew the type off its smaller carriers until it retired them in 1968 and Skyraiders became the mainstay of the

An Army CH-47 helicopter lifts a disabled UH-1 out of the battle zone.

VNAF's close air support effort. In many ways the A-1 was an ideal counterinsurgency aircraft, as it was rugged and dependable. With a maximum speed of 318mph, it was much better able to pick out and attack fleeting targets in the south Vietnamese jungle than were the faster and less maneuverable jets. Yet ironically it was the jets that were to bear the brunt of the close air support effort in Vietnam; in 1969 the USAF's F-100 jet fighter-bombers carried out over 52,000 combat sorties, whereas the A-1s flew only 2055 missions. The Skyraider was armed with four 20mm cannon and it could lift up to 8000lb of ordnance on 15 weapons stations. Thus the A-1 could be armed with a variety of weapons – napalm, cluster bombs, rockets and conventional bombs – so that it would be able to deal with any target encountered. For example, napalm was most effective against enemy troops in the open, but targets sheltering beneath the jungle canopy or protected by fortified bunkers required high-explosive bombs.

The twin-piston-engined Douglas B-26 Invader (originally designated A-26, then redesignated B-26) was used by the Farm Gate detachment both as an attack aircraft and for reconnaissance. It could carry a bomb load of 6000lb and had a nose-mounted armament of six 0.5in machine guns. It had a combat radius of 400 miles and could loiter over the target area for up to 45 minutes. Therefore until the advent of the A-1 Skyraider, the B-26 Invader was the most effective attack aircraft to operate in South Vietnam. However, the stresses of combat flying proved to be too great and following a number of crashes due to structural failure this 20-year old aircraft was withdrawn from use in 1964. Yet this was not the end of the Invader's fighting career, because 40 aircraft were refurbished as B-26Ks (later reverting to the original designation A-26A). These were operated by the 56th Special Operations Wing from Nakon Phanom in Thailand during 1966-69, carrying out night attacks on truck convoys along the Ho Chi Minh Trail.

The Douglas C-47, nicknamed the 'Gooney Bird,' served in the transport role not only with the USAF's Farm Gate detachment, but also with the air forces of South Vietnam, Cambodia and Laos. A specially modified version, the SC-47, was used in Southeast Asia. This was fitted with a strengthened undercarriage and it had provision for jet-assisted take-off in order to operate from short, unsurfaced airstrips. Although it lacked the payload and cargo capacity of postwar tactical transports such as the C-119, C-123 Provider and C-130 Hercules, it nonetheless performed a useful task in supplying isolated army outposts during the early 1960s. Thereafter, although largely superseded in the transport role with USAF units, the C-47 remained in service to undertake a variety of specialized roles. Most notable of these was the night attack mission carried out by AC-47D 'Dragonships' fitted with a sideways-firing, multibarrel machine gun armament. Less spectacular duties included psychological warfare, which involved broadcasting propaganda to Vietcong units through a battery of loudspeakers mounted on the aircraft, or dropping leaflets. RC-47s flew visual and photographic reconnaissance missions over South Vietnam, while specially-equipped EC-47s attempted to intercept Vietcong radio communications and pinpoint the positions of the transmitters.

It soon became apparent that the 4400th CCTS's SC-47s were unable to meet the demands of the air transport mission in South Vietnam and accordingly in January 1962 the USAF deployed 16 Fairchild C-123 Providers to Tansonnhut, near Saigon. This detachment, codenamed Mule Train, was doubled in strength later in the year and the Provider continued to provide airlift support for ground forces for the remainder of the war, latterly with the VNAF. The C-123 was powered by two 2300hp Pratt & Whitney R2800 radial engines (supplemented with two 2850lb thrust J85 auxiliary turbojets in the C-123K version) giving it a maximum speed of 245mph and a range of 1470 miles. The Provider was well-suited to the conditions of the Vietnam War, being a robust aircraft with a good short-field performance and thus able to operate from primitive sirstrips. Until the appearance of the C-130 hercules in the mid-1960s, it was the most important tactical transport in the theater of war. UC-123s fitted with spray equipment also took part in the controversial Ranch Hand mission, dispensing defoliants over jungle areas adjacent to roads in order to deny cover to the Vietcong and also destroying the crops in Vietcong-controlled areas to reduce the insurgents' food supplies.

The air war in Vietnam intensified in 1965, following the Gulf of Tonkin Incident, the USAF jet aircraft went into action against targets in North and South Vietnam. The

North American F-100 Super Sabre, nicknamed the Hun, became the most widely used close air support aircraft. The F-100D version was powered by a 16,950lb thrust Pratt & Whitney J57 turbojet, which gave it a maximum speed of Mach 1.3 and a combat radius of some 500 miles. Armament comprised four 20mm M39 cannon, each with 200 rounds of ammunition, and up to 7000lb of bombs could be carried. F-100s were operated by the 3rd, 31st, 35th and 37th Tactical Fighter Wings from bases in South Vietnam in the late 1960s. So important was this aircraft type to the close air support effort, that only five F-100 squadrons remained in the United States in mid-1967 and re-equipment of the Air National Guard with the type was delayed in order to keep the combat squadrons in Vietnam up to strength. At this time some 800 sorties a day were flown by close air support aircraft in South Vietnam and the Hun bore the brunt of this effort. A variety of ordnance was carried on these missions, including high-explosive bombs; Snakeye bombs fitted with extending fins to slow the weapon's fall during low-level release; cluster bomb units; napalm and 2.75in rockets. In order to avoid fire from the Vietcong's automatic weapons, it was desirable for the F-100s to pull out from their attacking dives at an altitude of 2000ft; but in the heat of action, aircraft often attacked from much lower levels.

In addition to flying close air support sorties over South Vietnam, F-100s took part in the early Flaming Dart attacks on targets in the North. Most F-100s deployed to South Vietnam were fitted with Combat Skyspot equipment, which allowed them to carry out 'blind' bombing at night or through overcast under the direction of ground radar. These aircraft could also act as pathfinders for other fighter-bombers, such as Republic F-105s, which were not fitted with the combat Skyspot receivers. Far more hazardous 'Night Owl' missions were flown against ground targets in the south, with only the light of air-dropped flares to guide pilots onto their targets. Under such conditions depth perception was impaired and there was a real danger of the pilot misjudging his altitude and flying into the ground. Although the F-100 lacked the necessary performance to carry out fighter-bomber attacks against the North once the Communist air defenses had been strengthened, it was found to be useful as a forward air control (FAC) aircraft in the region. The slow piston-engined aircraft used for FAC duties in the

South would not have survived long in such a hostile environment but the faster F-100s were found to be ideal for the target marking mission.

Two-seat F-100Fs were generally used as FAC aircraft, because it was useful to have a second crewmember to act as an observer on these sorties. The F-100F was originally produced as a conversion trainer, but it did retain a measure of combat capability. The cannon armament was reduced to two M39s and bomb load was 5000lb. It was this version of the Hun which pioneered the USAF's 'Wild Weasel' mission, operating against North Vietnamese surface-to-air missile (SAM) sites. Seven F-100s were fitted with special electronic warfare equipment which enabled them to detect and home in on the emissions of SA-2 Guideline SAM's fire control radar. Once detected, the SAM sites could be attacked by bombs, rockets or the specialized AGM-45 Shrike antiradiation missiles. The Wild Weasel F-100F began operations from Korat Air Base in Thailand with the 388th TFW late in 1965. However, operational experience showed that the Hun lacked the performance necessary for this very hazardous mission and in 1966 it was replaced by the F-105F.

In an attempt to produce a close air support aircraft better suited to conditions in South Vietnam than the fast and relatively unmaneuverable F-100, the USAF converted its standard basic jet trainer, the Cessna T-37, as a light attack aircraft. Known as the A-37 Dragonfly, it was powered by two 2850lb thrust, General Electric J85 turbojets, giving it a maximum speed of 507mph and a range with maximum weapons' load of 460 miles. Armament comprised a single 7.62mm GAU2 rapid-fire machine gun, with 1500 rounds of ammunition, and up to 5600lb of bombs carried on eight underwing hardpoints. Dragonflies first went into action with the USAF's 3rd TFW in 1969. However it was with the VNAF that the Dragonfly was to see extensive service. Its side-by-side seating for two pilots made it an ideal operational training aircraft and it was easily maintained by inexperienced ground crewmen. Consequently the Dragonfly became the VNAF's principal attack aircraft and at peak strength after the American withdrawal more than 200 A-37s equipped nine South Vietnamese squadrons.

The USAF's Vought A-7D Corsair II attack aircraft saw relatively little combat over Vietnam, as the 354th TFW only deployed to Korat Air Base, Thailand, with the aircraft as late as October 1972. However, it did participate in the Linebacker campaigns against North Vietnam, carried out interdiction missions and close air support sorties over Laos, and escorted rescue helicopters. The A-7D was a development of the US Navy's A-7A, but was powered by a 14,250lb thrust Allison T41 turbofan (a license-built Rolls-Royce Spey) rather than the naval aircraft's Pratt & Whitney TF30. Another notable difference was the arming of the A-7D with a 20mm M61 Vulcan rapid-fire cannon in place of the earlier A-7s two 20mm conventional cannon. Although the A-7D could not match the F-100's supersonic top speed, it had a considerably better payload and range, being able to carry 4000lb of ordnance over a radius of 700 miles. Navigation and weapons' aiming was also much improved, due to the fitting of a very accurate inertial navigation system and an ASN-91 digital computer.

In Vietnam there were no well-defined battle lines and consequently the precise control of air strikes, particularly in the vicinity of friendly troops, was a matter of considerable importance. All missions within South Vietnam were coordinated from the Tactical Air Control Center at Tansonnhut Air Base, with Direct Air Support Centers attached to each corps-sized army formation. In addition to these ground-based control centers, there were forward air controllers airborne over the target area, who could mark aiming points with smoke rockets and direct the attacks of the fighter bombers by radio. FACs were usually themselves tactical fighter pilots with recent combat experience. FACs also performed a general reconnaissance and intelligence-gathering mission. Individual pilots were assigned to a particular area and soon became familiar with the terrain and the pattern of life in the rural communities. Consequently they were well placed to detect any unusual activity which might give a clue to enemy troop movements. During the early years of the war, the standard FAC aircraft was the Cessna 0-1 Bird Dog, a two-seat, piston-engined observation type which had first seen service in the Korean War. It was powered by a 213hp Continental 0-470, had a maximum speed of 115mph and a range of 530 miles. Target-marking rockets were carried underwing, but the aircraft was otherwise unarmed except for the crew's personal weapons. This together with the lack of armored protection was one of the 0-1's principal defects in the FAC role. It also lacked the long endurance desirable for this mission. Nonetheless, 0-1s were in widespread use with the USAF until the late 1960s and thereafter with the VNAF.

Many of the 0-1's shortcomings were rectified by the introduction into service of the Cessna 0-2A in 1967. This was a military adaptation of the civil Skymaster and was powered by two 210hp Continental IO-360 piston engines mounted in an unusual 'push-pull' arrangement with one in the nose and the second in the rear fuselage driving a pusher propeller. The 0-2's top speed was some 200mph and range was 1060 miles – double that of the 0-1. The 0-2 had no built-in armament, but it was fitted with four underwing hardpoints, and machinegun pods could be carried in addition to marker rockets. the 0-2B was a psychological warfare variant, with a loudspeaker and leaflet dispensers.

Although it was a considerable improvement over the 0-1, the 0-2 was essentially a stopgap. Its successor, the North American Rockwell OV-10A Bronco, was designed from the outset for FAC and counter-insurgency operations, serving with the USAF, US Marine Corps and US Navy in Vietnam. It was powered by two 715shp Garrett T76 turboprops, giving it a top speed of 280mph and a maximum range of 1140 miles. A crew of two was carried, comprising a pilot and observer, seated in tandem with excellent visibility from the cockpit. Armored protection was provided for them and a weapons load of up to 3600lb could be carried in addition to the built-in armament of four 7.62mm machine guns. Therefore the Bronco could itself act as a light attack aircraft, as well as carrying out the FAC mission. The first OV-10As reached the USAF's Tactical Air Support Squadrons in South Vietnam in 1968. Marine Observation Squadrons also began operations with the Bronco in that year, using the aircraft as tactical mission coordinators during helicopter assault operations and as scouts, rather than as FACs. The US Navy's Light Attack Squadron VAL-4 also flew the OV-10A in South Vietnam, escorting river convoys and supporting ground operations in the Mekong Delta in 1971.

One of the major tactical innovations of the war in Southeast Asia was the use of fixed-wing gunship aircraft for night fire-support and interdiction missions. These were essen-

A helicopter crewman waits with Marines during an enemy artillery barrage.

tially converted transport aircraft fitted with a heavy armament of sideways-firing rapid-fire machine guns and cannon. Fire from these weapons could be concentrated into a relatively small area by the pilot flying a carefully banked turn around his target. The idea was the brainchild of Captain Ronald Terry of the USAF's Aeronautical Systems Division and was first applied to the C-47, producing the AC-47D gunship, variously nicknamed 'Puff the Magic Dragon,' 'Dragonships,' or 'Spooky' (after the AC-47's radio callsign). Its armament consisted of three SUU-11A Minigun six-barrelled machine guns with a rate of fire of 3000 or 6000 rounds per minute and ammunition capacity was 24,000 rounds. The weapons were aimed and fired by the pilot, using a gunsight mounted on the portside window. Target illumination was by the simple expedient of dropping parachute flares out of the rear cargo door.

The AC-47Ds were used within South Vietnam to provide fire support for protected hamlets and isolated outposts which frequently came under Vietcong attack at night. However, a further mission for the fixed-wing gunship was envisaged – namely night interdiction against truck convoys along the Ho Chi Minh Trail. This network of jungle tracks, leading from North Vietnam through southern Laos and Cambodia, was the principal route through which supplies and reinforcements were channelled to Vietcong and North Vietnamese Army Forces operating in the south. Because there were few obvious choke points, such as bridges or defiles, along the Trail, it was necessary for the USAF to attack individual trucks, which generally moved under cover of darkness. The AC-47Ds lacked sufficient reserves of power to operate successfully in this region, where mountainous terrain and enemy anti-aircraft fire often necessitated violent evasive maneuvers. Consequently gunship versions of the Lockheed C-130 Hercules and Fairchild C-119 were developed for such missions.

The four-turboprop AC-130 Spectres carried the heaviest armament of any fixed-wing gunships. The early versions were fitted with four 7.62mm Miniguns, Vulcan cannon and 40mm Bofors, while the ultimate armament modification introduced a 105mm howitzer in place of one of the Bofors. The AC-130s also carried a wide range of target acquisition sensors, including radar, infrared, low-light TV, a searchlight and flares. It became the most effective truck-killing

system in the USAF's armory, although its effectiveness was lessened in the early 1970s as the North Vietnamese deployed more powerful AA artillery and surface-to-air missiles along the Trail. The AC-119G gunship was produced as a replacement for the AC-47D and was armed with four 7.62mm Miniguns. However, the AC-119K version, powered by two 2850lb thrust J85 auxiliary turbojets in addition to the twin 3700hp Wright R-3350 radials, was used for night interdiction missions over the Ho Chi Minh Trail. Accordingly, the AC-119K's armament was increased by the addition of two 20mm multi-barrel cannon and radar and infra-red target-acquisition sensors was fitted.

An alternative approach to the problems of truck-killing resulted in the Project Black Spot NC-123K conversion of the Provider transport. This was fitted with a similar range of target detection devices as was carried by the gunships, but its armament consisted of cluster bomb units rather than guns. These were scattered from chutes fitted to the aircraft's rear cargo ramp and, as they were area attack weapons, they did not have to be so precisely aimed as the guns. Although only two NC-123Ks were produced, both saw service in Southeast Asia, operating against truck convoys in Laos and inland waterways in South Vietnam. The pair were credited with the destruction of more than 400 trucks and 50 sampans. A single US Navy squadron, VAH-21 based at Cam Ranh Bay, flew AP-2Hs gunships. These were modified P-2 Neptune patrol bombers, fitted with target acquisition sensors and armed with Miniguns, 20mm cannon and high explosive and incendiary bombs.

By the mid-1960s the USAF had few light bomber aircraft in service and largely depended upon fighter-bombers for its air strike missions. However, two squadrons of Martin B-57 Canberra light bombers, the 8th and 13th Tactical Bomb Squadrons, did see extensive service in Southeast Asia in 1964-69, flying bombing missions inside South Vietnam and interdiction missions along the Ho Chi Minh Trail. The B-57B was a variant of the British Canberra produced in the United States by the Martin Company under license. It was powered by two 7220lb thrust Wright J65 turbojets, had a top speed of 582mph and a range of 2300 miles. Up to eight 750lb bombs could be carried on wing pylons and in the internal weapons bay and the built-in armament comprised four M39 20mm cannon with 200 rounds per gun. The British version of the Canberra also served in Vietnam, as No 2 Squadron Royal Australian Air Force operated English Electric Canberra B Mk 20s from Phan Rang from 1967 until 1971.

A specialized night interdiction version of the B-57 was produced for truck-killing missions over the Ho Chi Minh Trail. This was the B-57G which was fitted with radar, low-light TV and FLIR (forward looking infrared) for target detection in darkness. The FLIR could also penetrate camouflage, a useful capability because the North Vietnamese truck convoys usually rested in concealed truck parks during the hours of daylight. Once a target had been detected, the B-57G would mark it with a laser designator and then attack with laser-guided bombs. The aircraft's highly-efficient computer was capable of making a fully-automatic attack and the B-57G could operate independently of all support aircraft, such as flare-droppers and FACs for target marking. It has been estimated that 80 percent of bombs released by B-57Gs fell within 15ft of the aiming point. However, the aircraft's remarkable capabilites were only achieved at high cost; not only were laser-guided bombs expensive weapons to use against such targets as trucks, but the B-57G's systems had been costly to develop and acquire and furthermore there were only sufficient aircraft to equip one front-line squadron. Eleven B-57Gs deployed to Ubon Air Base, Thailand, in September 1970, serving with the 8th Tactical Fighter Wing. They remained on operations until April 1972, achieving an average truck kill rate per sortie of 2.3.

In terms of individual bomb load, the most powerful strike aircraft of the Vietnam War was undoubtedly the Boeing B-52 Stratofortress. Although it had been intended primarily for the nuclear mission, the B-52 was capable of lifting a large conventional bomb load. An unmodified B-52F could carry a 38,000lb bomb load internally and a B-52D, with the Big Belly modification, could increase this to 60,000lb. In addition the bombers could carry 24, 500lb or 750lb bombs on underwing racks. Strategic Air Command's Stratofortresses began operations over South Vietnam in June 1965, flying from Andersen Air Force Base on Guam. Two years later a second force of B-52s went into action from U-Tapao Air Base in Thailand, from which targets in South Vietnam could be attacked without the need for the bombers to refuel in flight. Powered by eight 13,750lb thrust Pratt & Whitney J57 turbojets, the B-52D had a maximum speed of 556mph at 40,000ft and an operational radius of over 3000 miles. The 'Arc Light' sorties over South Vietnam were usually directed against concentraions of enemy troops. Accurate bombing was achieved by making use of Combat Skyspot ground-based radar, which was more precise than the aircraft's own navigation and bombing aids. Indeed, B-52s were allowed to bomb targets within 300 yards of friendly forces. Because the high-flying B-52 formations could not be heard from the ground, their unheralded attacks on VC/NVA troops were devastating both in psychological and material effects. However, as Arc Light missions needed to be planned many hours in advance, they sometimes went astray and attacked areas evacuated by the enemy. This gave ammunition to those critics of the Arc Light offensive who claimed that the B-52s were doing no more than turn portions of Indochina into a lunar landscape. The opposite view was taken by General William Westmoreland, commander of the US Military Assistance command Vietnam, who pointed out that the B-52s had played a decisive part in defeating the VC/NVA assault on Khe Sanh, by preventing enemy troops from concentrating for a full-scale assault on the base. At the time of the siege in early 1968 the B-52s were flying an average of 60 sorties per day over South Vietnam. The high point of the B-52s' war in Southeast Asia came in December 1972, when the bombers penetrated the heavily defended Hanoi-Haiphong region during the Linebacker II campaign. More than 700 sorties were flown during an 11 day period, at the end of which the North Vietnamese, with their stocks of SA-2 Guideline surface-to-air missiles exhausted and their capital at the mercy of the USAF bombers, were ready to return to the Paris Peace talks. The bomber force had lost 15 B-52s to North Vietnamese SA-2s, but to achieve this result some 900 SAMs had been fired. Two North Vietnamese MiG-21 interceptors fell to the fire of B-52 tail gunners without themselves scoring any successes. During the B-52s' involvement in the Southeast Asia conflict, they had flown 126,615 combat sorties, six percent of these against North Vietnam. A total of 29 Stratofortresses were lost on operations in Southeast Asia, although only 17 of them were brought down by enemy fire.

AIR FORCES

One of the most hazardous missions of the war was reconnaissance over North Vietnam, which, unlike the bombing offensives, was carried out without a break throughout the conflict. The USAF's standard tactical reconnaissance aircraft in the mid-1960s was the single-seat McDonnell RF-101 Voodoo. These aircraft made an early appearance in Vietnam, as a detachment of four RF-101s was deployed to TansonNhut in October 1961. As demands for photographic coverage of the Southeast Asia region increased, RB-26 Invaders and RB-57E Canberras joined in the work. However, it was the Voodoos which operated over the North, until the build-up of Communist air defenses in 1967 made these sorties too hazardous. In June 1966 alone a total of seven RF-101s fell to North Vietnamese antiaircraft fire. From 1967 until they were withdrawn from the combat theater in 1970, the RF-10s were restricted to reconnaissance missions over South Vietnam and Laos.

The RF-101C Voodoo was powered by two 14,500lb Pratt & Whitney J57 turbojets, giving it a maximum speed of 1000 mph and a range of over 2000 miles. It carried four cameras for oblique photography in the nose compartment and a further two for vertical reconnaissance in a fuselage bay, thus being suitable for missions at low and medium altitudes. The Voodoo could easily outpace North Vietnamese MiG-17 interceptors, provided that it had a sufficient warning of their approach, but it was outperformed by the MiG-21. Its successor, the McDonnell Douglas RF-4C Phantom, had a maximum level speed of Mach 2.2 (1450mph) and so was better able to evade interception. The RF-4C's radius for a low-altitude reconnaissance mission was over 500 miles, when carrying a 600-gallon drop tank on the fuselage center-line and two 370-gallon tanks underwing. It was equipped with a range of sensors for day and night reconnaissance, including vertical and oblique cameras, an infra-red sensor and sideways-looking radar. The aircraft first reached Southeast Asia in October 1965 and two years later they equipped four tactical reconnaissance squadrons in the theater. RF-4Cs often accompanied strike aircraft in order to obtain photographs for post-attack assessment, as this meant that they were protected by the main force's fighter and electronic warfare escorts. However, it had the disadvantage that the target might still be partially obscured by smoke from bursting bombs.

Losses of RF-4Cs to the North Vietnamese defenses remained within acceptable limits, but were by no means light. Consequently the USAF developed unmanned reconnaissance drones in order to cover heavily-defended objectives at low level. These high-speed, low-level aircraft, codenamed 'Buffalo Hunter,' were developed from the Ryan-Teledyne Firebee target drones. They were launched from Lockheed DC-130A director aircraft and recovered at the end of their mission by Sikorsky CH-3 helicopters. Although not immune from interception, they provided more elusive targets than the much larger manned tactical reconnaissance aircraft. Another means of evading North Vietnam's air defenses was to operate at high altitude; the USAF's strategic reconnaissance aircraft flying at altitudes above 80,000ft were beyond the reach of the enemy's interceptors and missiles. Lockheed U-2s began to operate over North Vietnam in 1965 and they were joined by Mach 3 Lockheed SR-17As later in the decade. Unlike the tactical reconnaissance aircraft, which were responsible for covering potential targets and assessing the results of bombing missions, the strategic reconnaissance aircraft had the wider responsibility of general intelligence gathering. They provided the overall picture of the build-up of North Vietnam's air defenses and the massive operation to reinforce and supply NVA/VC units operating in the South.

Surveillance of the Ho Chi Minh Trail was a highly-specialized reconnaissance mission, which required the development of a range of sensors able to detect the movement of personnel and vehicles in darkness. Under the codename 'Igloo White,' a field of sensors was sown along the length of the Trail by USAF and US Navy aircraft. They were of various types, but the most common were the Acoubuoy and Spikebuoy, which picked up the sounds of enemy movement, and the Adsid, which detected ground vibrations. This information was transmitted via an airborne relay aircraft to the Infiltration Surveillance Center at Nakhon Phanom in Thailand, where the data was processed and collated. Initially Lockheed EC-121 aircraft were used as relay aircraft, until the specialized Beech QU-22 became available. A modified Beech Bonanza, the QU-22 was operated by the 553rd Reconnaissance Wing from Korat Air Base in Thailand. Although it was generally flown on operations by a pilot, the QU-22 could be operated as a pilotless drone. An equally bizarre reconnaissance aircraft was the Lockheed YO-3 'Q-Star,' a powered glider that could operate silently at low altitude to detect enemy troop movements by night. Although it did not see widespread service, a number of Q-Star prototypes were deployed to Vietnam in 1969-70, fitted with infra-red reconnaissance equipment. Electronic-intelligence (ELINT) was another specialized mission, which was undertaken by USAF Douglas RB-66 Destroyers over North Vietnam. They were responsible for locating and classifying enemy air defense radar, by monitoring their emissions. A related activity was communications intelligence (the detection of radio transmissions), which was carried out by USAF EC-47s and US Army RU-21s over South Vietnam.

Tactical transport operations were one of the USAF's most vital support missions of the war, as ground communications in South Vietnam were poorly developed and road and river supply lines were often cut by Vietcong ambushes. Until the mid-1960s the brunt of this effort was borne by the obsolescent Fairchild C-123K Providers. Thereafter the four-turbo-prop Lockheed C-130 Hercules played an increasingly important role; at the peak of the USAF's involvement in Southeast Asia, 15 C-130 squadrons were committed to the war. Powered by four 3750shp Allison T56s, the Hercules had a payload of some 15 tons and a range of over 2000 miles. In general the C-130 was used for cargo transport, often landing on short and unsurfaced airstrips – sometimes under enemy fire – to resupply isolated outposts. During the four-month siege of Khe Sanh in early 1968, the USAF delivered 12,400 tons of supplies to the Marine garrison and 90 percent of this airlift was provided by Hercules transports. When enemy fire made landing on Khe Sanh's airstrip impossible, supplies were delivered by parachute. Airborne operations were infrequent during the Vietnam War, but C-130s did take part in the only battalion-strength parachute assault of the conflict during Operation Junction City in early 1967. Numerous specially-modified Hercules variants took part in the war. The AC-130 gunships and DC-130 drone launchers/ directors have already been noted; other missions included the Blind Bat flareship and FAC sorties; rescue support with modified HC-130s which could refuel helicopters in flight; airborne command post duties; and

Special Forces support using C-130E-I aircraft (later redesignated MC-130E).

From 1963 until 1967 the US Army operated de Havilland Canada C-7 Caribou twin-engined transports in South Vietnam. However, these were then transferred to USAF control following a ruling by the Joint Chiefs of Staffs that their mission was an Air Force responsibility. The rugged and dependable C-7 was powered by two 1450hp Pratt & Whitney R2000 radials, it had a top speed of 216mph and a maximum range of 1300 miles. Maximum payload was 8740lb, but its more useful characteristic was its excellent short-field performance; a Caribou could take off and clear a 15ft high obstacle within a distance of 1185ft. Six USAF squadrons operated the Caribou in Vietnam, together with a single similarly-equipped squadron of the Royal Australian Air Force. The Caribou's role was to transfer supplies from the major airfields, where they were unloaded from USAF long-range transports, to the Army units in the field. A similar mission was undertaken in Laos and Cambodia by the CIA-funded airline Air America, which flew such antiquated transport aircraft as the C-47 and Curtiss C-46 Commando as well as more modern STOL (short take-off and landing) aircraft and helicopters.

The logistical support of the Vietnam War was a massive and complex undertaking which involved civil as well as military air transport resources. In 1967 the USAF's Military Airlift Command (MAC) flew a total of 210,000,000 miles and carried sufficient personnel to man 85 infantry divisions. The efforts of the active-duty units were supplemented by the airlift units of the Air National Guard and Air Force Reserve, with most of the trooping flights being carried out by civil airlines under charter. The mainstay of MAC's strategic transport fleet in 1965 comprised 21 squadrons of Douglas C-124 Globemaster IIs. Powered by four 3800hp Pratt & Whitney R4360 piston engines, the C-124 could lift a payload of 50,000lb over a range of 4050 miles at a cruising speed of 230mph. Its capacious cargo hold (with 10,000 cu ft of usable space) enabled all but the largest Army vehicles to be lifted, but its slow cruising speed meant that a flight from California to Saigon and back would take two weeks. The turboprop-powered Douglas C-133 Cargomaster was faster, with a cruising speed of 310mph. Its 90ft long cargo hold,

Supplies and equipment were also dropped by parachute.

US Army paratroops prepare to jump during Operation Junction City.

with a capacity of 13,000 cu ft, could accommodate loads as large as a Titan intercontinental ballistic missile. However, only three C-133-equipped aquadrons were in service. The Boeing C-135 transport, with a cruising speed of 530mph and a range of 4000 miles, had the necessary performance for the trans-Pacific reinforcement mission, but it lacked cargo capacity and so was usually employed on troop lift and casualty evacuation duties.

The strategic airlift situation considerably improved in August 1965 when Lockheed C-141 Starlifters began to operate into South Vietnam. The Starlifter was powered by four 21,000lb thrust Pratt & Whitney TF33 turbofans, had a cruising speed of 495mph and

maximum range of 6140 miles. Maximum payload of the C-141A was 70,850lb and 90 percent of all air-portable military equipment could be accommodated in its cargo hold. By mid-1968 14 squadrons of C-141s were in MAC service and the aircraft became the most important strategic transport to operate into South Vietnam. On return flights to the United States the Starlifters were often fitted as aerial ambulances and could accommodate up to 80 patients on litters. Between 1965 and 1972 C-141s carried out some 6000 medical evacuation sorties. MAC's heavy lift capabilities were much increased with the appearance of the Lockheed C-5A Galaxy, which began to operate into South Vietnam in

August 1971. The Galaxy was powered by four General Electric TF39 turbofans, giving it a cruising speed of 537mph. Maximum payload was 265,000lb and range with maximum fuel and an 80,000lb payload was 6500 miles. The C-5As 120ft-long cargo hold could accommodate such outsized items of equipment as a CH-47 Chinook helicopter, self-propelled howitzers or main battle tanks. During the North Vietnamese spring offensive against the South in 1972, Galaxies airlifted 26 tanks into Danang in ten sorties. The C-5s also participated in the final evacuation of Saigon in 1975 and during this operation one aircraft was tragically lost when its cabin pressurization failed shortly after take-off.

The USAF's war against North Vietnam, mounted in conjunction with the carrier air wings of the US Navy, was not a continuous operation, but was interrupted by lengthy bombing halts and hampered by numerous restrictions on target planning. The early 'Flaming Dart' missions were mounted in retaliation for the North Vietnamese torpedo boat attacks on US destroyers in the Gulf of Tonkin. From 1965 until 1968 the 'Rolling Thunder' campaign sought to bolster South Vietnamese morale, punish the North for its aggression and hamper the flow of supplies and men southwards. The air attacks began against targets in the southernmost provinces of North Vietnam and were gradually extended northwards. However, the air offensive was limited in scope, with enemy airfields, for example, being off-limits for much of the time. President Johnson feared to provoke the People's Republic of China into military action and so each new major target had to be personally approved by him before it could be attacked. The Rolling Thunder attacks ended with a bombing halt, which it was hoped would encourage the North Vietnamese to seek a negotiated settlement. However, this expectation was disappointed and bombing north of the DMZ was restarted following North Vietnam's 1972 spring offensive. The Linebacker I attacks were directed against bridges, storage dumps, rail systems and power plants throughout the North. It was followed in December 1972 by the short and intense Linebacker II offensive, which succeeded in its aim of forcing the North Vietnamese to resume peace negotiations in Paris.

The USAF's standard fighter-bomber aircraft during the early campaigns was the Republic F-105 Thunderchief, nicknamed 'the Thud' by aircrews in Southeast Asia. It was flown by the Thailand-based 355th and 388th Tactical Fighter Wings, which operated over the southern panhandle of Laos and from there into the North. The F-105D, powered by a single Pratt & Whitney J57 turbojet, developing 24,500lb of thrust with afterburning, was primarily intended to carry out tactical nuclear strikes during a major war with the Soviet Union. Consequently it was fast at low altitude, with a maximum speed of Mach 1.25 at sea level, it could lift a heavy ordnance load (up to 16 750lb bombs), and its range with maximum fuel was over 2000 miles. It could be refueled in flight using either the USAF's boom-and-receptacle method or the Navy's probe-and-drogue system. A typical weapons' load on operations over the North was six 750lb bombs carried on the fuselage centerline; this arrangement allowed two 450-gallon auxiliary fuel tanks to be carried on the inner wing pylons and ECM jamming pods on the outboard underwing stations. The F-105D was fitted with a 20mm M61 Vulcan multi-barrel cannon, with 1029 rounds of ammunition. This proved to be a highly-effective weapon for self-defense and no fewer than 22 North Vietnamese MiG-17s fell victim to F-105s' cannonfire.

F-105s flew more combat missions over North Vietnam than any other USAF aircraft and consequently suffered the heaviest losses in action. By the end of the 1960s it was necessary to replace Thuds with F-4 Phantoms in the fighter-bomber role. However, the Thunderchief continued to serve as a Wild Weasel aircraft, attacking North Vietnamese surface-to-air missiles. A typical Iron Hand defense-suppression mission was carried out by a flight of four Thuds; two of them were standard F-105D single-seaters armed with bombs and rockets, while the other pair were specially-modified F-105F two-seaters. The latter were equipped with radar-warning equipment, which allowed them to detect the emissions of SAM guidance radars and home onto their source. The SAM sites could then be attacked by anti-radiation missiles, such as the AGM-45 Shrike or the AGM-78 Standard ARM, which were launched against the SAM radars. Alternatively the F-105s backseater – nicknamed 'the bear' by Wild Weasel crews – could guide the flight of F-105s into a direct attack on the missile site, using bombs, rockets and cannonfire.

The latter method was the surer of the two and it resulted in damage to the missiles themselves as well as the radar. However, it was also the most hazardous, as it exposed the Thuds to groundfire from the AA batteries which inevitably ringed the SAM sites.

The multi-role McDonnell (later McDonnell Douglas) F-4 Phantom not only replaced the F-105s on strike missions over North Vietnam, but from the earliest days of the bombing offensive provided fighter escort for the fighter-bombers. USAF Phantoms also provided close air support for the ground forces fighting in the South and in the modified RF-4C version flew tactical reconnaissance missions. F-4s also served in considerable numbers with US Navy and US Marine Corps fighter squadrons and indeed and aircraft originated as a two-seat shipboard fleet air defense fighter for the US Navy. In November 1961 the Phantom was adopted by the USAF to meet its tactical fighter requirement, which emphasized the close air support, interdiction and air superiority missions. Yet few changes were necessary to adapt the versatile Phantom to this new operational environment and the major difference between the Navy's F-4B and USAF's F-4C was the change from the Naval probe-and-drogue in-flight refueling system to the USAF's receptacle-and-boom method. In 1966 the F-4D entered USAF service and it was deployed to Southeast Asia in May 1967 with the 555th 'Triple Nickel' TFS at Ubon Air Base in Thailand. This variant had an improved bombing capability in comparison with the F-4C. In the course of its combat career, the F-4D was further modified to adapt it for the Wild Weasel anti-SAM mission and to enable it to operate with laser-guided and electro-optical 'smart' bombs.

The Phantom was powered by two 17,900lb thrust General Electric J79 turbojets and had a maximum speed of Mach 2. When fitted with auxiliary fuel tanks, the F-4 had a combat radius of over 900 miles. When operating in the air superiority role it was armed with four medium-range AIM-7 Sparrow semi-active radar homing AAMs and four short range AIM-9 Sidewinder infrared homing AAMs. Some F-4Ds carried AIM-4D Falcon AAMs instead of Sidewinders, but the AIM-9 was the more popular weapon. In the air-to-ground roles, up to eight tons of munitions could be carried, including bombs, rockets and air-to-surface missiles. Bombs were usually mounted on triple or multiple ejection racks, which allowed three to six bombs to be carried on a single stores station. In addition to offensive armament, ECM pods were carried for operations into high-threat areas and later in the war a laser-designator pod could be carried to mark targets for laser-guided bombs. One of the major shortcomings of the F-4C and F-4D was the lack of a built-in gun armament, which was considered anachronistic at the time that the aircraft was designed. However, combat experience soon showed that a gun armament was very useful in both air-to-air and air-to-ground engagements. A short-term solution was to fit a pod-mounted 20mm M61 Vulcan cannon to the Phantom. However, this was unsatisfactory for a number of reasons: the gun pod should ideally occupy the fuselage centerline stores station, which was more often needed for a 600-gallon auxiliary fuel tank; the pylon mounting was not as rigid as an internally fitted gun and therefore accuracy suffered; furthermore the drag caused by the gun pod reduced aircraft performance in air-to-air engagements.

Many of the lessons learned in combat over Southeast Asia were incorporated into the design of the F-4E Phantom, which first flew in June 1967. F-4Es first deployed to the combat theater in November 1968, but production was slow and only 72 were in Southeast Asia in mid-1971. The new aircraft featured a built-in M61 cannon, thus correcting the most serious fault of earlier aircraft, but the installation was not entirely satisfactory as room could be found for only 640 rounds of ammunition. As the Vulcan cannon had a rate of fire of 6000 rounds per minute, this ammunition load would be quickly expended – even the SUU-16A pod-mounted weapon was provided with 1200 rounds. The F-4E's maneuverability was improved by fitting extendable slats to the wing leading edge. These automatically opened during high angle-of-attack maneuvers, providing the F-4E with 33 percent more lift. Consequently turn radius was improved and the risk of the aircraft departing from controlled flight in the vicious 'spin/stall,' which was one of the F-4's less desirable characteristics, was reduced. Other refinements introduced on the F-4E included an improved APQ-120 radar and armored protection for vital aircraft systems. One problem experienced with earlier Phantoms was not eradicated with the F-4E, however. This was the distinctive twin

A Phantom II fighter is hooked at the waist catapult aboard USS Nimitz.

plumes of exhaust smoke produced by the J79, which made the aircraft easy to spot at long range.

The early F-4 missions over North Vietnam were carried out by the 8th Tactical Fighter Wing, nicknamed the 'Wolfpack,' which began operations from Ubon Air base in Thailand in December 1965. During 1966-67 the Wing was commanded by Colonel Robin Olds, a World War II fighter ace, who succeeded in shooting down four North Vietnamese MiGs during his combat tour in Southeast Asia. On 2 January 1967 Olds masterminded Operation Bolo – a successful attempt to lure the North Vietnamese MiGs into combat under unfavorable conditions. The outcome was the destruction of seven enemy aircraft in the largest fighter-versus-fighter battle of the war. The 12th Tactical Fighter Wing operated Phantoms from South Vietnam from November 1965 until November 1971, flying F-4Cs and F-4Ds on close air support missions. The 366th TFW was also based in South Vietnam until it moved to

Thailand in mid-1972. In 1969 the 388th TFW exchanged its veteran F-105s for F-4Es at Korat Air Base in Thailand and the 432nd Tactical Reconnaissance Wing – a composite unit incorporating tactical fighter squadrons and tactical reconnaissance squadrons – also operated Phantoms from Thailand. This last unit produced the only USAF aces of the war: pilot Captain Richard S Ritchie and weapons systems operators Captains Charles DeBellvue and Jeff Feinstein. Ritchie and Feinstein were credited with five victories and 'backseater' DeBellvue with six. In all, USAF Phantoms were responsible for the destruction of 107 enemy fighters. The F-4D version was responsible for 44 of these, the F-4C for 42 and the F-4E (with a much shorter period in combat) for 21 'kills.'

In contrast to the F-105 and F-4 fighter-bombers, which operated over North Vietnam in squadron or even wing-sized formations, the General Dynamics F-111As operated singly relying on their low altitude and ability to fly at night and in bad weather to

A CH-47 Chinook comes in for a landing during Operation Thayer II.

evade interception. And whereas the F-4 and F-105 strike forces were accompanied by an armada of support aircraft (including escort fighters, ECM escort, Wild Weasel defense suppression flights, tankers, airborne early warning and communications relay aircraft), the F-111s could operate independently of these. The F-111 was produced to meet the joint-service TFX requirement of 1960, which was intended to provide a successor to the USAF's F-105 strike fighter and also to meet the US Navy's needs for a carrier-based fleet-defense fighter. In the end, the two requirements proved to be incompatible and the US Navy withdrew from the F-111 program amid much recrimination. This was not the end of the F-111 controversy, however. In early 1967 a six-aircraft detachment of F-111As was rushed to Southeast Asia to carry out a evaluation of the design under operational conditions and within two months three aircraft had been lost during combat missions. In view of the fact that the F-111 had yet to complete its full test program and also that the aircraft incorporated much new and untried technology, these losses are not surprising. Yet they inevitably aroused a storm of controversy and it was not until September 1972 that the aircraft was considered truly combat ready.

The F-111A was powered by two 20,000lb thrust Pratt & Whitney TF30 afterburning turbofans, giving it a maximum speed of Mach 2.2 at 35,000ft and Mach 1.2 at low level. Its range when carrying maximum internal fuel was 3300 nautical miles and an ordnance load of 20,000lb could be lifted. A 20mm M61 Vulcan cannon could be fitted in the aircraft's internal weapons bay, as this was seldom used for tactical bombing missions in Southeast Asia. The F-111A's navigation and attack systems, operated by a weapons systems officer seated beside the pilot, comprised a terrain-following and attack radar, together with a very accurate inertial navigation system and weapons delivery computers which enabled blind bombing attacks to be carried out automatically. Its variable-geometry wing, with angle of sweep variable between 16 degrees and 72.5 degrees, gave the F-111 both excellent low-speed characteristics during cruising flight and landing approach, coupled with supersonic dash capability at low level with the wing fully swept.

In September 1972 two squadrons of the 474th TFW deployed from Nellis AFB, Nevada, to Takhli Air Base, Thailand, to recommence the F-111A's combat career after its false start in 1968. A total of more than 3000 missions was flown up until the ceasefire of January 1973, including raids into the heavily-defended Hanoi-Haiphong area during Linebacker II. When the F-111A's sophisticated equipment worked, it performed impressively, as was shown on 8 November 1972 when F-111As carried out 20 bombing missions over North Vietnam in weather that had grounded the other USAF strike aircraft. Yet this complex aircraft continued to suffer maintenance problems with its avionics systems and engines throughout its second deployment period in Southeast Asia. As a result of its protracted development problems, the F-111A saw relatively little combat in the Vietnam War and the greater part of the USAF's bombing campaign against North Vietnam was carried out by the less complex fighter-bombers of an earlier generation.

Aerial refueling was an essential support mission not only for the B-52s making the long overwater flight from Guam to Southeast Asia, but also for the tactical fighter-bombers operating within the combat theater. At the peak of the USAF's involvement in 1968 the tanker force comprised some 90 Boeing KC-135 Stratotankers. Forty of them were based at U Tapao in Thailand primarily to support tactical fighter-bombers; 35 were at Kadena Air Base on Okinawa; the remainder were at Ching Chuan Kang on Taiwan. During 1968 the tankers carried out 129,000 aerial refuelings, the majority of them being in support of tactical aircraft. If fighter-bombers could rely on refueling in flight, they could then carry the maximum bomb load on long-range missions, rather than reduce this in order to lift sufficient fuel for the entire mission. Furthermore, when operating over North Vietnam, the US strike aircraft were often forced to use full afterburner for long periods in combat with the air defenses and this quickly burned up fuel. Consequently tankers were required to rendezvous with the strike force on their homeward flight and refuel those aircraft with insufficient fuel to regain base. Although the tankers never ventured within range of North Vietnamese air defenses and so none were lost in combat, four were destroyed in crashes. In view of the fact that a total of 194,687 sorties were flown during the period, this accident rate is remarkably low.

The KC-135A tanker aircraft is similar in appearance to the Boeing 707 civil airliner, both aircraft having been developed from the Model 367-80 of 1954. The standard crew comprised the aircraft captain, co-pilot, navigator and boom operator. It is powered by four 13,750lb thrust Pratt & Whitney J57 turbojets and has a maximum speed of 600mph. Its total fuel load comprises 31,200 gallons, any proportion of which may be transferred to a receiver aircraft according to the tanker captain's judgment. The normal rate of fuel transfer is at 900 gallons per minute. Refueling is achieved by the tanker aircraft lowering an extendable boom from beneath its rear fuselage to connect with a receptacle mounted on the receiver aircraft. The latter must position itself beneath the tanker and maintain formation while the tanker's boom operator makes the connection. However, it was sometimes necessary to fit the boom with a drogue adapter which could be trailed to provide a refueling connection for the US Navy's probe-equipped aircraft. In fact the Navy usually provided its own tanker support with KA-6D Intruders and KA-3 Skywarriors. Nonetheless, the fact that the two services operated entirely different systems for refueling in flight inevitably meant that there was some lack of flexibility in US tanker operations. The KC-135A was adaptable in other ways, however, and could lift up to 83,000lb of cargo or 80 passengers when used as a transport. Specialized variants of the Stratotanker were used in Southeast Asia for electronic reconnaissance (RC-135) and as airborne command posts (EC-135), while some KC-135As acted as radio relay aircraft.

Electronic countermeasures support for the USAF air strikes over North Vietnam were provided by Douglas EB-66 Destroyers. Converted from the three-seat B-66 tactical bomber of 1954, the EB-66 was fitted with a pressurized compartment in place of the bomb bay to house four ECM operators and their equipment. The EB-66 was powered by two Allison J71 turbojets, had a top speed of 594mph and a range of 1500 miles. During early operations over North Vietnam the EB-66s flew jamming missions against early warning radars and the SA-2's Fan Song radars to within 30 miles of Hanoi. Yet in 1967 as the defense increased in strength, EB-66s were forced to withdraw to operating areas in Laos and over the Gulf of Tonkin. Fighter escort was provided to prevent them being

shot down by North Vietnamese interceptors, but the SA-2s proved to be more troublesome. Once the EB-66s stopped flying over North Vietnam they were at no risk from the missiles, but the effectiveness of their jamming was much reduced at the longer ranges.

Ground-based radar in South Vietnam and Thailand could provide a measure of control over air strikes operating over the southernmost targets in the North. However, those missions directed against the more heavily-defended regions further north had to rely on airborne command and control from the College Eye Lockheed EC-121s. They provided the strike aircraft with warnings of enemy interceptor activity, advised them of any navigational errors that could lead to violation of Communist Chinese airspace, and acted as an information center for meteorological and intelligence information. If a strike aircraft was shot down over the North and its pilot ejected, then the College Eye EC-121 would co-ordinate the rescue attempt. The EC-121s patrolled at stand-off ranges over Laos and the Gulf of Tonkin to evade the North Vietnamese air defenses. Its radar coverage over water was good, but ground returns over the land made detection of low-flying aircraft difficult. However, ECM (electronic support measures) could often provide a clue to enemy activity by monitoring and analyzing North Vietnamese radar and radio emissions. The EC-121D was an adaptation of the Lockheed Super Constellation civil air transport, fitted with massive radomes above and below the fuselage to accommodate radar antennae. It carried a crew of 27, including an airborne controller and his battle management staff. Powered by four 3250hp Wright R3350 turbocompound radials, the EC-121 had a maximum speed of 320mph at 20,000ft. Its service ceiling was 20,600ft and range was 4600 miles. In 1972 the improved EC-121T began operations under the codename Disco. It had a somewhat improved radar performance in comparison with the EC-121D, but the problem of low-level overland surveillance remained.

The exposed seaward flank of North Vietnam was open to attack from the aircraft carriers of the US Navy's Seventh Fleet operating from 'Yankee Station' in the Gulf of Tonkin. A major part of the air offensive against the North was taken by carrier-based aircraft, which also contributed to the close air support missions in South Vietnam and

AIR FORCES

An Assistant Catapult Officer gives the signal to launch.

carried out interdiction sorties along the Ho Chi Minh Trail. Carriers newly arrived in the South China Sea would be given a period of 'working up' on Dixie Station, operating against targets in the South, before they moved northward to launch their air groups against North Vietnam. The composition of a carrier air wing varied according to its area of deployment and the accommodation available aboard the ship. The smaller carriers were unable to operate heavy jets and usually carried some 70 aircraft in contrast to the larger carrier's complement of 90. However, the basic structure of the air wing was constant, comprising a two-squadron fighter element, a three-squadron attack force, smaller detachments of reconnaissance, airborne early warning and electronic warfare aircraft, and a helicopter squadron for rescue

and utility duties. The small *Hancock*-class carriers (modified *Essex* class) typically carried two squadrons of F-8E Crusader fighters, two attack squadrons of A-4 Skyhawk jet fighter-bombers and a third attack squadron flying piston-engined A-1 Skyraiders. Photographic reconnaissance was undertaken by RF-8 Crusaders, AEW by E-1 Tracers, EW by EA-1 Skyraiders and helicopter support by UH-2A Seasprites. The longer carriers, including the nuclear-powered *Enterprise*, embarked F-4 Phantom fighters rather than Crusaders and later in the war A-6 Intruder-equipped attack squadrons and RA-5C Vigilante reconnaissance aircraft, none of which could be accommodated aboard the smaller ships.

The single-seat Vought F-8 Crusader shared the battle for air superiority over

North Vietnam with the F-4 Phantom during 1965-68, escorting naval air strike forces and itself carrying out attack missions. During the early air battles F-8s are credited with the destruction of 19 MiG fighters, but on the debit side 38 Crusaders were lost in combat – many to groundfire rather than enemy interceptors. The F-8J was powered by a single 18,000lb thrust Pratt & Whitney J57 turbojet and had a maximum speed of Mach 1.8 at 36,000ft. Combat radius was 440 miles and a small warload of 2000lb could be carried when operating in the attack role. Ground attack ordnance loads included two 1000lb bombs, or two AGM-12 Bullpup air-to-surface missiles, or eight Zuni unguided rockets. Built-in armament consisted of four 20mm cannon with 84 rounds of ammunition per gun and four AIM-9 Sidewinder missiles were carried for air-to-air combat. The RF-8A tactical reconnaissannce version of the Crusader carried four cameras in a nose compartment, replacing the fighter's cannon armament. During reconnaissance missions over North Vietnam, they usually operated with an escort of fighter Crusaders, flying at an altitude of 4000ft in order to avoid light AA fire, yet remain below the effective reach of the medium-altitude SA-2 SAM. But these tactics could not protect the RF-8As against fire from heavy AA weapons and losses were comparatively heavy – amounting to some 25 per cent of all Crusaders lost in combat.

The F-4B Phantom, a larger, heavier and more powerful fighter than the Crusader, performed less well against the North Vietnam MiGs than its more agile stablemate in 1965-68. This was due to faulty tactics on the part of the Navy fighter pilots (the USAF experienced similar problems) and was rectified by the inauguration of project 'Top Gun.' This provided naval pilots with practical and theoretical instruction in air fighting with small and agile opponents, such as the MiGs. Enemy fighters were simulated by A-4 Skyhawks and F-5E Tiger IIs during the Top Gun training sorties. The improvements obtained in combat were dramatic. In 1968 the US Navy shot down two MiGs in air combat for every one of their own fighters lost to this cause. When fighting over the North resumed in 1972 a kill-to-loss ratio of twelve-to-one was quickly established. Although such factors as better missile reliability played a part in this result, the primary reason was improved tactical skills. In air combat the US Navy's Phantoms accounted for a total of 36

enemy fighters – 26 of them in the period 1969-73. Yet the F-4B's usefulness was not confined to fighter missions, as its bomb load of 16,000lb made it a powerful strike aircraft, which added considerably to the carrier air wings' attack capabilities.

In general the F-4B's performance was similar to that of the USAF's F-4C Phantom, as was its armament. The improved F-4J version had a more capable radar and bombing computer, but both Navy Phantom subtypes lacked a built-in gun armament. Yet despite this shortcoming, it was in air combat that the F-4J made its most notable contribution to the war. The best-known F-4J fighter crew were Lieutenant Randy Cunningham and his 'backseater' Lieutenant (jg) Willie Driscoll, who became the first American aces of the war. Flying with VF-96 aboard USS *Constellation*, this crew scored their first victory on 19 January 1972 over a North Vietnamese MiG-21. A second kill, a MiG-17, followed on 8 May. Then two days later Cunningham and Driscoll were part of the escort for a large strike force attacking the Hai Duong railyards near Saigon. An air battle developed with more than 20 North Vietnamese interceptors over the target area and Cunningham shot down two MiG-17s with AIM-9 Sidewinder AAMs. When withdrawing, Cunningham noticed another MiG-17 flying low and dived down to engage it. A dogfight developed, but Cunningham finally gained the advantage and despatched his fifth victim with an AIM-9. Although the North Vietnamese pilot has never been publicly identified by American intelligence, it is believed that he was the 13-victory ace Colonel Tomb. Cunningham and Driscoll's eventful mission nearly ended in disaster, because as their F-4J crossed the coast it was hit by an SA-2 missile. However, Cunningham nursed his crippled fighter part of the way back to the *Constellation*. He and Driscoll were then forced to eject, but were soon recovered from the sea by helicopter.

The bomb-laden strike aircraft had fewer opportunities to engage enemy fighters, although they were more often cast in the role of victim. However, on one notable occasion in June 1965 a flight of four A-1 Skyraiders operating with VA-25 from USS *Midway* was intercepted by a MiG-17 and, turning the tables on their antagonist, the piston-engined attack aircraft shot down the North Vietnamese jets. This was repeated by another Skyraider from VA-176 in the following year.

AIR FORCES

Yet as the North Vietnamese defenses became stronger, the skyraiders were increasingly relegated to missions over the South and in 1968 the type was withdrawn from Navy service altogether. Thereafter the Naval attack squadrons were exclusively equipped with jet-powered fighters, notably the Douglas A-4 Skyhawk. This compact, single-seat attack aircraft was able to carry an 8200lb warload, in addition to a built-in armament of two 20mm cannon. Early versions were powered by a 7700lb thrust Wright J65 turbojet, but this was replaced on the E-model and subsequent versions by a 8500lb thrust Pratt & Whitney J52. The A-4E had a maximum speed of 675mph and a range of 700 miles. The Skyhawk proved to be well suited to the demands of the Naval air war over Vietnam, as in addition to its excellent payload/range characteristics, it was maneuverable and robust. Skyhawks also operated ashore in South Vietnam with the Marine Air Wings and the type flew more bombing missions during the war than any other Naval aircraft.

The Vought A-7 Corsair II, which first deployed to the combat theater aboard USS *Ranger* in December 1967, was a larger and heavier aircraft than the A-4 which it was intended to supersede. In the end, the two types served on together for the remainder of the war with US Navy attack squadrons, and the Marines continued to operate Skyhawks in preference to the new design. The A-7A was powered by a 11,350lb thrust TF30 turbofan and had a maximum speed of 679mph. Tactical radius was over 700 miles and warload was up to 20,000lb of ordnance. The new A-7E, which entered combat in 1971, was powered by the 15,000lb thrust Allison TF41, had an improved navigation/attack system and was fitted with a single 20mm M61 Vulcan rapid fire cannon in place of the A-model's twin 20mm conventional cannon. The accuracy of the A-7E's weapons' delivery system allowed the aircraft to operate effectively at night against interdiction targets along the Ho Chi Minh Trail. Yet pinpoint attacks at night or in bad weather was really the forte of the A-6A Intruder medium attack aircraft. It was powered by two 9300lb thrust Pratt & Whitney J52 turbojets and had a maximum speed of 640mph. Range with maximum ordnance load of 15,000lb was 1077 miles and if external tanks were fitted this could be extended to 3100 miles. The crew of pilot and bombadier/navigator were seated side-by-side and the latter was responsible for operating the aircraft's advanced navigation and attack systems. Known as DIANE (Digital Integrated Attack Navigation Equipment), the A-6's avionics allowed small precision targets, such as bridges, barracks and fuel depots to be located and attacked in all weather conditions, day or night. One of the A-6's notable exploits of the Vietnam War was the destruction of the Hai Duong bridge between Hanoi and Haiphong.

The Intruder's airframe was modified for two important support missions, namely in-flight refueling and electronic warfare. The KA-6D tanker version of the Intruder, which retained a limited secondary attack capability in clear weather, could offload 15,000lb of fuel at a distance of 288 miles from the parent carrier. Fuel was transferred by means of a drogue refueling system fitted beneath the rear fuselage. The EA-6B Prowler electronic warfare aircraft was a four-seat development of the intruder (the two-seat EA-6A served with the Marines). Fitted with the ALQ-99 jamming system, it operated against North Vietnamease air defenses during 1972. The shipboard EW mission had earlier been undertaken by the EA-1E version of the Skyraider and the EKA-3 Skywarrior – a combined tanker and EW aircraft.

The A-3 Skywarriors were originally employed as a heavy attack aircraft, but when their usefulness in this mission was outlived, a number were converted as EKA-3s and others as RA-3 reconnaissance aircraft. Powered by two 12,400lb thrust Pratt & Whitney J57 turbojets, the A-3 had a maximum speed of 610mph and an operational radius of 1050 miles. Like the Skywarrior, the A-5 Vigilante no longer served in its originally intended heavy attack role in the mid-1960s. However, converted for the reconnaissance role as the RA-5C it proved to be a highly-effective warplane capable of penetrating the most heavily defended areas of North Vietnam. Powered by two 17,000lb thrust General Electric J79 turbojets, the RA-5C had a maximum speed of Mach 2.1 and a range of 2650 miles. Its reconnaissance equipment included cameras, an infra-red sensor, sideways-looking airborne radar and electronic intelligence-gathering sensors. A large and heavy aircraft, it could only be operated by the bigger carriers and its complex reconnaissance equipment made great demands on maintenance personnel.

M-60 machine guns were mounted on the sides of a UH-1B helicopter gunship.

Although the US Navy's carriers never came under air attack when operating off North Vietnam, a constant watch was maintained for hostile air activity by E-1 Tracer and later E-2 Hawkeye AEW aircraft. Apart from these defensive duties, the AEW aircraft were used to direct air strikes and warn the strike force of MiG activity, direct aircraft to rendezvous with tankers, and to coordinate search and rescue operations. The E-1 Tracer, powered by two 1525hp Wright R1820 radials, was equipped with an APS-82 search radar. The later E-2 Hawkeye, with two 4590 Allison T56 turboprops, had the improved APS-120 radar. Rescue operations were undertaken by UH-2 Sea Sprite and SH-3 Sea King helicopters, which were assigned to the carriers for plane guard and utility transport duties. In peacetime they would usually operate near the carriers and rescue any crews forced to ditch in the sea. In Vietnam they had often to penetrate the North Vietnamese defenses to pick up crews who had parachuted into enemy territory.

Consequently they needed to be fitted with armor protection and a machine gun armament. Endurance was often a critical factor in such missions and, in order to extend the helicopters' operating radius to the utmost, destroyers or frigates operating offshore would act as refueling platforms.

Not all of the US Navy's air operations in Vietnam were conducted from aircraft carriers. Shore-based patrol aircraft undertook the important Operation 'Market Time' – the surveillance of coastal waters and inland waterways to detect shipments of arms and supplies for the Vietcong. Most of these missions were carried out by twin-piston engined Lockheed P-2 Neptunes, later replaced by four-turboprop P-3 Orions. However, some of the early patrols were flown by Martin P-4 Marlin flying boats, marking the last use of such aircraft on operations by the US Navy. The convoluted waterways of the Mekong Delta were an area of special concern to the Navy, and the Seawolves of helicopter Light Attack Squad-

A seven tube pod for two rockets mounted on UH-1B helicopter gunship.

ron 3 operated there with UH-1 Huey helicopter in support of the river patrol boat flotillas. In 1971 they were joined by the OV-10 Broncos of Light Attack Squadron 4 – the 'Black Ponies' – and this unit became the last US Navy unit to operate in South Vietnam.

It was the French who first introduced the helicopter into the war, with Hiller O-23 Ravens flying observation missions and Sikorsky H-19s carrying out casualty evacuation. In many ways the helicopter was the ideal vehicle for the guerrilla war in South Vietnam, as it could operate into areas that were inaccessible to tracked or wheeled vehicles and move troops at a speed that was likely to outpace even the elusive Vietcong. As the US involvement in the war grew during the 1960s, so the helicopter came to play an increasingly important role in the Army counterinsurgency operations. Airmobile units, which depended on the helicopter

rather than ground vehicles as their primary means of transportation, proliferated; reconnaissance was carried out by troops of heliborne air cavalry; logistic support, casualty evacuation and the recovery of damaged vehicles and aircraft all depended more and more on helicopters; finally the gunship helicopter was evolved to meet the Army's need for fire support during close-range jungle firefights and to escort vulnerable troop carrying assault helicopters. Vietnam became the helicopter's war, and many thousands of these machines were deployed in combat. Losses were on a similarly massive scale, with over 16,000 helicopters brought down by enemy fire or by accidents.

The first US Army helicopters to see service in Vietnam were the troop-carrying Vertol CH-21 Shawnees of the 8th and 57th Transportation Companies (Light Helicopter). They arrived at Saigon aboard the former escort carrier USNS *Card* in December 1961 and were soon in action ferryng ARVN trops. The CH-21 was a twin rotor helicopter powered by a single 1425hp Wright R-1820 radial engine. Its maximum speed was 130mph and initial rate of climb was 1080ft per minute. In addition to its crew of two, 20 troops could be carried, or an underslung load of 5000lb lifted. The CH-21 not only lacked the performance of the later turbine-powered helicopters, but it also lacked adequate armament. This deficiency was partly rectified by fitting the CH-24 with door-mounted 7.62mm machine guns.

Early in 1962 the first UH-1 turbine-engined transports arrived in South Vietnam. They were assigned to the 57th Medical Detachment (Helicopter Ambulance) for casualty evacuation, but soon troop transport UH-1s appeared and by September 1964 there were 250 helicopters of this type in South Vietnam. Nicknamed the 'Huey' (its original designation had been HU-1), the UH-1 became the standard assault transport and air ambulance helicopter of the war. In its UH-1B version it was powered by a 960shp Lycoming T53-L-5 turboshaft, which was later replaced by the 1100shp T53-L-11. Its performance included a maximum speed of 147mph and an initial rate of climb of 2600ft per minute. The cabin of the UH-1B could accommodate eight troops or three casualties on litters, whereas the later UH-1D had an enlarged cabin with seating for 12 troops. A variety of armaments were fitted to Hueys in Vietnam. Most carried pintle-mounted 7.62mm M60 machine guns mounted in the doorways and outriggers on the fuselage sides carried various combinations of 0.3in and 0.5in machine guns, podded 20mm cannon, 2.75in rocket pods and 40mm grenade launchers. Troop-carrying UH-1s, known as 'Slicks,' would be escorted by armed UH-1 'Hogs,' which would lay down suppressive fire around the landing zones prior to an assault and deal with any groundfire encountered en route.

Casualty evacuation missions by helicopter (given the codename 'Dust Off') were of great importance to the care of the wounded, as they ensured prompt medical attention at well-equipped field hospitals. The UH-1D and UH-1H could carry six patients on litters, as well as a flight crew of two pilots, a crew chief and a medical attendant. Although any transport helicopter could be pressed into service to carry casualties if the need arose, in general this job was performed by specializing helicopter ambulance units. More than 100 Hueys were assigned to this duty in Vietnam by 1968; between 1965 and 1969, 372,947 casualties were evacuated. Often emergency clearings had to be hacked out of the jungle for the helicopter ambulances, using chain saw and high explosives, but if this proved to be impractical the casualty could be winched aboard the hovering helicopter by means of a hoist.

Helicopters proved to be invaluable for a wide variety of heavy lift and 'flying crane' tasks in Vietnam, often carrying out these tasks in areas inaccessible to any other vehicles. Mountain-top fire support bases were established by helicopters lifting in construction materials, howitzers and ammunition stocks and thereafter resupply missions were flown by the helicopters at regular intervals. The first medium-lift helicopter to be used in Vietnam was the slow and cumbersome Sikorsky CH-37 Mojave. Powered by two 1900hp Pratt & Whitney R-2800 piston engines driving a single five-bladed main rotor, the CH-37 had a maximum speed of 130mph, an initial rate of climb of 910ft per minute and a service ceiling of 8700ft. Its cargo cabin, reached through clamshell nose doors, could accommodate two jeeps or a 105mm howitzer and underslung loads of up to 10,000lb could be lifted, The far more capable Boeing-Vertol CH-47 Chinook first reached South Vietnam in 1965 and thereafter rapidly superseded the Mojave. Powered by two 3750shp Lycoming T55 turboshafts, the twin-rotor Chinook had a maximum speed of 180mph, an initial rate of climb of 2880ft per minute and a service ceiling of 15,000ft. The CH-47A variant could carry a cabin load of 10,000lb of cargo or 33 troops, while underslung loads of up to 16,000lb could be lifted. It was usually found that the Chinook ran out of cabin space long before the maximum weight limits were reached and so when transporting cargo it was usually carried as an underslung load. More specialized flying crane tasks were carried out by the Sikorsky CH-54 Tarhe, with its 20,760lb underslung payload.

On occasions the Chinook was pressed into service in a more warlike role than its originally intended mission. Chinook 'bombers' attacked Vietcong bunkers with barrels of riot gas or napalm, which were rolled out of the rear cargo door and fused by a static line once clear of the helicopter. Three specially-

HH-53 Super Jolly helicopters on the flight deck of USS Midway.

modified CH-47s were tested as heavy gunship helicopters by the US Army's 1st Air Cavalry Division in 1966. Nicknamed 'Go-Go-Birds,' they were armed with nose-mounted 40mm grenade launchers, 20mm cannon and 2.75in rocket pods on the fuselage sides and 0.5in machine guns firing from the cabin windows. Although these machines performed reasonably well in service, it was concluded that the Chinook would be used to better effect in its primary transport role and so no further gunship versions were produced.

The specialized attack helicopter which was produced for service in Vietnam was a very different machine from the lumbering Go-Go-Birds. Based on the design of the UH-1, the AH-1G Huey Cobra used the engine, rotor and transmission of the transport helicopter mated to a new streamlined fuselage seating a pilot and gunner in tandem. Its performance included a maximum speed of 219mph, initial rate of climb of 1580ft per minute and range of 387 miles. A 7.62mm Minigun six-barrel machine gun was mounted in a turret beneath the nose and 2.75in rocket pods or pod-mounted machine guns and cannon could be fitted beneath the helicopter's stub wings. This armament was soon augmented by a 40mm grenade launcher, mounted alongside the Minigun in the nose turret. AH-1Gs acted as escorts for troop or cargo-carrying helicopters, reconnoitred landing zones, and laid down suppressive fire, or they carried out armed reconnaissance missions. Working in pairs, with a scout helicopter to find targets for them (a combination known as 'Pink Team'), the AH-1s could operate safely in close proximity to friendly troops, unlike the faster fixed-wing close air support aircraft. They could also make use of such natural cover as trees or vegetation to mark their approaches, but nonetheless the Huey Cobras were vulnerable to enemy fire. The crews were protected by armored seats and often wore armored flak jackets as additional protection.

Early in the war such piston-engined scout helicopters as the Hiller OH-23 Raven and Bell OH-13 Sioux were used in South Vietnam, but their performance was never entirely satisfactory. An improvement came when the turboshaft-powered Hughes OH-6 and later the Bell OH-58 became available. The OH-6, officially named the Cayuse but invariably known in Vietnam as the 'Loach,' was powered by a 317shp Allison T63 turboshaft. Its top speed was 150mph, initial rate of climb 1840ft per minute and service ceiling 15,800ft. It was generally operated by a crew of two, but an additional four passengers could be carried in the rear compartment. In Vietnam the Loaches often carried the helicopter's crew chief, armed with a 7.62mm machine gun, to provide defensive fire. A 7.62mm Minigun or 40mm grenade launcher could also be mounted on the port side of the fuselage. However, the primary task of the Loach was not to fight, but to find the enemy. Operating often at heights below tree-top level, the OH-6 crews could spot such signs of enemy activity as footprints in soft ground or the smoke from campsite fires. The OH-58 Kiowa did not reach Vietnam until 1969 and so saw less service than the Loach. It too was powered by a 317shp Allison T63 turboshaft, and had a maximum speed of 138mph, initial rate of climb of 1780ft per minute, and a service ceiling of 19,000ft.

A number of important observation and reconnaissance tasks were carried out by fixed-wing US Army aircraft in Vietnam. In the early years of the American involvement, O-1 Bird Dogs carried out observation missions. More sophisticated reconnaissance tasks could be undertaken by the twin-engined Grumman OV-1 Mohawk. Powered by 1100shp Lycoming T53 turboprops, the OV-1 had a maximum speed of some 300mph and a range of 1000 miles. It could be equipped with a variety of sensors, including cameras, infrared and SLAR, according to the mission requirement. Some of the Mohawks operated in Vietnam had an armament of underwing machine gun rocket pods, but most were unarmed save for target-

marking rockets. Signals intelligence, the monitoring and location of enemy radio transmissions, was carried out by US Army Beech RU-21s. Other fixed-wing aircraft in Army service included de Havilland Canada U-1 Otter and U-6 Beaver light transports and the Beech U-8 Seminole liaison aircraft.

In contrast to the US Army, which relied on the USAF for close air support, the Marine Corps operated its own ground-attack aircraft as well as transport and attack helicopters. The Marine Aircraft Wings operated much the same aircraft as the US Navy, with F-4 Phantoms, A-6 Intruders and A-4 Skyhawks all deployed to Vietnam in support of Marine ground forces. The Marine's helicopter units, however, differed considerably from those of the Army, because they were primarily intended to support amphibious assault landings. The first Marine helicopters to reach Vietnam were the Sikorsky UH-34s or HMM-362, which occupied the former Japanese airfield at Soc Trang, southwest of Saigon, in April, 1962. The piston-engined UH-34D, powered by a single Wright R-1820 of 1525hp, had a top speed of 130mph, an initial rate of climb of 1570-ft per minute and a service ceiling of 9500ft. It could accommodate 12 fully-equipped troops or lift an underwing load of 5000lb. Its successor, the Boeing-Vertol CH-46 Sea Knight, could carry 17 troops, or 10,000lb of underslung cargo. The first CH-46s arrived in Vietnam in March 1966 and eventually replaced the UH-34, although the latter's retirement was delayed by a series of accidents to the CH-46 which necessitated modifications. Powered by two 1250shp General Electric T58 turboshafts, the Sea Knight had a maximum speed of 166mph, an initial rate of climb of 1290ft per minute and a ceiling of 12,800ft.

The Marines operated UH-1s not as troop transports, but for observation and airborne command post duties. Although similar to the Army machines, the Marine UH-1s carried a more comprehensive array of communications equipment. Marine UH-1s were also fitted with M60 machine guns and 2.75in rocket pods and the gunship role became one of its most important tasks, with two-thirds of all UH-1 sorties in 1966-67 being attack missions. Heavy lift was the mission of the Sikorsky CH-53A Sea Stallion, which began to supersede the Marine's CH-37Cs from early 1967 onwards. It was powered by two 3695shp T64 turboshafts and had a maximum speed of 196mph, an initial rate of climb of

2000ft per minute and a service ceiling of 21,000ft. Its cargo hold could accommodate 38 troops or 24 casualty litters, or such loads as a 1½ ton truck and trailer or a 105mm howitzer. The Sea Stallions were capable of carrying out a wide variety of logistical, engineering and artillery support missions, but their primary task became the recovery of crashed helicopters and during the period from January to May 1967, the first four CH-53As to serve in Vietnam recovered a total of 103 crashed machines.

Undoubtedly the most hazardous support mission of the war was the combat rescue work undertaken by the USAF's Aerospace Rescue and Recovery Service over North Vietnam. Over 3000 airmen were rescued from the jungles or coastal waters during the war and many of these recoveries were made under enemy fire. Consequently losses were comparatively heavy among the rescue crews; 71 airmen were killed and 45 aircraft lost during these operations. During the early years of the air war against the North, the USAF relied on the Kaman HH-43 Huskie helicopter and Grumman HU-16 Albatross amphibian for combat rescue work, yet neither was entirely suitable for the missions. The HH-43 had originally been developed for crash rescue and firefighting in the vicinity of its base. Therefore it lacked the performance – and especially the range – needed for rescue operations in Vietnam. The HH-43A was powered by an 860shp Lycoming T53 which drove twin, intermeshing rotors. Maximum speed was 120mph and range 235 miles. Various methods of improving the Huskie's range were tried, including installing extra fuel tanks and using forward bases in jungle clearings and remote hilltops as refueling points. Combat experience also showed the need for armor protection for the crew and the fitting of a 250ft-long cable so that rescues could be carried out in densely forested areas. Yet in spite of these efforts to improve upon the Huskie's shortcomings, it remained an unsatisfactory rescue helicopter for the Southeast Asia theater.

The HU-16 Albatross had a considerably better range than the HH-43, but was of course a far less versatile machine. Powered by two 1425hp Wright R1820 radials it had a top speed of 236mph and a range with maximum fuel of 2850 miles. Provided that an airman could nurse his damaged aircraft to the coast before abandoning it, he stood a good chance of rescue by the HU-16s.

Between mid-1964 and the end of 1965 these amphibians had saved the lives of 60 aircrew. Yet many American airmen were forced to parachute into enemy territory and the Aerospace Rescue and Recovery Service had a pressing need for a long-range helicopter which would be able to fly into any part of North Vietnam. This requirement was met by the Sikorsky HH-3E – usually known by its nickname the 'Jolly Green Giant.' A development of the US Navy's SH-3 Sea King, the HH-3E was powered by two 1500shp General Electric T58 turboshafts. Its top speed was 164mph and range, carrying two auxiliary fuel tanks, was 760 miles. Its radius of action could be further extended by refueling in flight from a HC-130 Hercules that carried hose and drogue equipment in underwing pods, the HH-3E having a nose-mounted probe. Other equipment required by the demanding conditions of the combat theater included armor protection, self-sealing fuel tanks and defensive machine gun armament. The rescue helicopter was usually escorted by four A-1 Skyraiders, which were intended to deal with hostile fire over the rescue area or en route.

The first HH-3E reached the combat theater in November 1965 and in the course of the following year took an increasing share in rescue missions over the North. Although it was an immense improvement over the earlier HH-43/HU-16 combination and it could reach any region of the North from bases in South Vietnam and Thailand, the USAF nonetheless felt the need for a helicopter with an even greater mission endurance. This would allow it to loiter over the rescue area for long periods, an advantage when hostile gunfire had to be suppressed by fixed-wing aircraft before the helicopter could make its rescue. Therefore a Super Jolly Green Giant appeared in Southeast Asia in 1967. This was the Sikorsky HH-53, a variant of the Marine Corps CH-53A Sea Stallion heavy-lift helicopter. The largest, most powerful and fastest helicopter in the USAF inventory, it could carry up to 38 people in addition to its normal crew of five. It was powered by two 2910shp General Electric T64 turboshafts, had a maximum speed of 195mph and a range on internal fuel of 540 miles (extendable by carrying auxiliary tanks and by in-flight refueling). The helicopter was protected by 1200lb of armor plate and defensive fire was provided by three 7.62mm rapid-fire Miniguns.

Special Forces operations were supported

by CH-3 and CH-53 helicopters which were similar to their rescue counterparts except that they lacked provision for in-flight refueling. Both HH-53 and CH-53s took part in the Son Tay prison camp raid in 1970 and in the operation to secure the release of the American freighter *Mayaguez*, which was illegally seized by Cambodia in May 1975. Little has been published about covert operations by US Special Forces troops in Southeast Asia, but it is known that the C-130E-I version of the Hercules operated from Nha Trang with the 14th Special Operations Wing. This aircraft was specially equipped for low-level infiltration missions at night and could recover equipment and personnel from enemy territory using the Fulton STARS device. This 'skyhook' equipment comprised a pair of caliper-like arms attached to the aircraft's nose, which could snatch a cable raised by a helium-filled balloon. The load or person attached to the other end of the line was pulled into the air and could then be winched into the aircraft. It is not known how extensively this system was used on actual operations, but as it remains in USAF service in the 1980s presumably its record was a successful one.

The North Vietnamese air defenses comprised the interceptors of the Vietnamese People's Army Air Force (VPAAF) together with surface-to-air missiles and anti-aircraft artillery. The VPAAF was never a very large air force, but its interceptors often proved to be effective against bomb-laden US strike aircraft. Operating under the close supervision of their ground controllers in the Soviet fashion, the VPAAF's MiGs could often achieve surprise and knock down US fighter-bombers before their fighter escorts had the opportunity to intervene. The mainstay of the VPAAF's fighter force were Soviet-supplied MiG-21 and older MiG-17 single-seat interceptors, but from 1968 onward these were supplemented by Shenyang F-6s (Chinese-built MiG-19s). The VPAAF had been formed in May 1955, following the French withdrawal from Indochina, but it was slow to develop. The first North Vietnamese fighter regiment was not formed until February 1964 and this unit first went into action in the spring of 1965. Organization and tactics closely followed Soviet practice. The North Vietnamese pilots received their training in the Soviet Union and were then assigned to units of the VPAAF forming in the People's Republic of China. Operational training was

carried out in the sanctuary of Chinese airspace, before the combat-ready fighter regiments flew to their operational bases in North Vietnam.

The VPAAF fighter force steadily increased in strength during the course of the war. In mid-1966 there were 65 interceptors in service, 50 of them MiG-17s, while a single squadron (a regiment was normally made up of three squadrons) flew MiG-21s. A year later there were 100 fighters on strength, nearly half of them MiG-21s, and by the spring of 1972 this force had doubled in strength. By that time the VPAAF was operating from 13 airfields, many of them grouped around the important Hanoi-Haiphong area. The North Vietnamese took advantage of the 1968 bombing halt to improve a number of airfields in the south of the country to allow them to operate jets. Yet the VPAAF played little part in the North Vietnamese spring offensive in 1972; even during the final advance on Saigon in 1975, when airfields at Khe Sanh and Dong Ha south of the former DMZ were available to the VPAAF. The small North Vietnamese bomber force, equipped with only a handful of Il-28 twin-jet bombers, played little or no part in the war. Yet North Vietnamese pilots were sometimes skillful and aggressive. Two of them at least scored a dozen or more aerial victories – Captain Nguyen Van Bay, the VPAAF's first ace, and Randy Cunningham's probable last victim, Colonel Tomb. According to North Vietnamese claims, the VPAAF shot down 320 enemy aircraft during the war; but US records tell a different story, with 92 aircraft lost in combat with enemy fighters in return for 193 VPAAF aircraft destroyed. There can be no doubt that in the battle for air superiority the VPAAF were the losers, yet they nonetheless fought bravely and well.

The oldest fighter in the VPAAF inventory was the MiG-17, a 1950s-vintage aircraft that had been developed from the MiG-15 of the Korean War. Although its 7590lb thrust Klimov VK-1 turbojet was fitted with an afterburner, the MiG-17 was not able to reach Mach 1 in level flight. Yet its lack of acceleration was to some degree compensated for by its high maneuverability. The MiG-17 had a maximum speed of just over 700mph at 10,000ft, is rate of climb was 12,800ft per minute and service ceiling was 55,000ft. Standard armament was three nose-mounted 23mm NR-23 cannon. The VPAAF's MiG-17s usually operated at low level, defending such important targets as airfields or covering likely approach routes to Hanoi and Haiphong. Although no match for the US F-105 or F-4 under normal circumstances, the MiG-17s attempted to intercept aircraft weighted down with bombs and lure them into a turning dogfight in which the Vietnamese fighter could gain the advantage.

The Shenyang F-6, like the MiG-17, was highly maneuverable and it was capable of a maximum speed of Mach 1.3 at 20,000ft. In performance it fell roughly midway between the MiG-17 and MiG-21, but it saw comparatively little combat over Vietnam. The first Shenyang F-6s did not reach the VPAAF until after the start of the 1968 bombing halt, so the only large-scale fighting in which it took part were the Linebacker assaults of 1972. The twin-engined fighter was powered by two 7150lb thrust RD-9 turbojets. Its maximum rate of climb was 22,600ft per minute and service ceiling was 57,000ft. One of its most outstanding features was its heavy armament of three 30mm NR-30 cannon, two of which were mounted in the wing roots with a third in the starboard lower fuselage. It could also carry two AA-2 Atoll infrared guided missiles. Thus, although an outmoded design by the late 1960s, the Shenyang F-6 was a dangerous opponent for a heavily-laden fighter-bomber by virtue of its excellent maneuverability and heavy armament.

The Mach 2 MiG-21 was by far the best fighter aircraft available to the North Vietnamese. An agile and fast point-defense interceptor, it was well suited to the conditions of the air war over North Vietnam where its short range was no handicap as it operated within easy reach of friendly airfields. Several versions of the MiG-21 served with the VPAAF, including the MiG-21F clear weather interceptor armed with two AA-2 Atolls and a single 37mm cannon and the much improved MiG-21PFMA with all-weather capability and an armament of twin 23mm cannon and four AA-2s. The later versions were powered by a 13,700lb thrust Tumansky R-11 afterburning turbojet, had an initial rate of climb of 36,000ft per minute and a service ceiling of 59,000ft. In comparison with its principal antagonist, the F-4 Phantom, the MiG-21 was more maneuverable and could accelerate faster at subsonic speeds. It also outperformed the F-4 at supersonic speeds above 25,000ft. The MiG-21 was far less easy to spot than the massive US fighter with its distinctive engine smoke trail. Yet these advantages were counterbalanced by the Phantom's superior supersonic performance below 25,000ft and its heavy missile armament of four medium and four short-range AAMs. In general the VPAAF MiG-21s tried to avoid combat with the US fighter escorts and used hit-and-run tactics against the bomb-laden strike fighters.

In accordance with Soviet air defense doctrines, the North Vietnamese relied to a great extent on surface-to-air missiles and AA artillery for the protection of high-value targets. Early in 1965 about a thousand AA guns were deployed by the North Vietnamese, defending such potential targets as bridges, storage depots, industrial sites and military installations; by the end of the year their numbers had doubled. The guns ranged in caliber from 37mm up to 100mm and they could be supplemented by heavy machine guns, which were effective against low-flying aircraft. The standard SAM employed by the North Vietnamese was the SA-2 Guideline, a two-stage missile armed with a 285lb warhead, which had a maximum range of 30 miles. SA-2s were usually emplaced in clusters of six, surrounding a control center and surveillance radar. The SAMs first went into action over North Vietnam in mid-1965 and at peak deployment about 200 SA-2 sites were operational. Most of them covered the Hanoi-Haiphong region, but as the missiles were easily transportable their sites were often shifted. Although they undoubtedly posed a serious threat to US strike aircraft, in general the Wild Weasel sorties and ECM jamming proved to be effective antidotes, and by 1972 the North Vietnamese were firing 150 SA-2s for every US aircraft brought down. However, the SAMs by their very presence had an inhibiting effect on US air operations, forcing the strike aircraft to fly at low levels where they were at serious risk from ground-fire.

The South Vietnamese Air Force traces its origins to an army air component established under French tutelage in 1951. Its primary duties were observation, liaison and light transport, for which it was equipped with Morane Saulnier MS500 Criquets (a French-built derivative of the German Fieseler Storch) and various light communications aircraft. After the French withdrawal the Vietnamese Air Force (VNAF) came into existence in mid-1955 as an independent service. Its equipment, for the most part handed on by the *Armée de l'Air*, consisted of

Grumman F8F Bearcat fighters, Cessna L-19 observation aircraft and C-47 and AAC-1 Toucan (license-built Ju 52 trimotor) transport aircraft. The piston-engined Bearcats were armed with four 20mm cannon and could lift up to 2000lb of ordnance. They were the only effective combat aircraft available to the South Vietnamese until T-28Ds and A-1 Skyraiders were supplied by the United States from 1960 onward.

By 1965 the Skyraiders had entirely superseded the T-28Ds and the VNAF was considered by its US instructors to be ready to convert to jets. Its first such aircraft was the Northrop F-5A. VNAF pilots trained on this type in the United States in 1966 and the F-5A equipped 522nd Squadron became operational at Bien Hoa in the following year. Powered by two General Electric J85 turbojets each producing 4080lb of thrust with afterburning, the F-5A could attain a maximum speed of Mach 1.4 at 36,000ft. It could lift up to 4000lb of ordnance and carried two 20mm cannon mounted in the nose. The F-5A had been evaluated in combat over South Vietnam during operation 'Skoshi Tiger' in 1965-66 by the USAF's 4503rd TFW and was found to be suitable for operation by the VNAF. Eventually eight VNAF squadrons operated the type and a number of the improved F-5Es (with more powerful engines and greater fuel capacity) were supplied. Together with the F-5, the A37 Dragonfly became the mainstay of the VNAF fighter squadrons. Three squadrons were converted from A-1s to A-37s between 1967 and 1969 and eventually all Skyraiders were placed in storage and replaced by the jets.

The process of 'Vietnamization,' began by the Nixon administration in 1969, was intended to produce a VNAF which would be capable of supporting the South Vietnamese ground forces without help from US air forces. This policy resulted in a considerable expansion of the VNAF, which grew from a force of 29,000 men and 20 squadrons in mid-1969 to one of 42,000 men and 49 squadrons in December 1972. In addition to its A-37 and F-5 squadrons, the VNAF operated AC-47 and AC-119 gunships, O-1 FAC aircraft, C-7, C-119, C-123 and C-130 transports and UH-1 and CH-47 helicopters. When the cease-fire agreement of January 1973 cut off US aircraft supplies, the VNAF with a total of 2075 aircraft on strength was the fourth largest air force in the world in terms of the numbers of aircraft in service. The hollowness of this position was revealed in 1975 when the VNAF did little to hamper the North Vietnamese Army's *Blitzkrieg* assault on Saigon. It is true that South Vietnam's air force lacked sufficient spares to back its massive aircraft inventory and that there was a serious shortage of trained maintenance personnel, but the fundamental problem was a near total collapse of morale.

A USAF C-47 drops leaflets over the Ashau Valley.

THE NAVAL WAR
IN VIETNAM

BY ANTONY PRESTON

THE NAVAL WAR

Although the French conducted riverine operations against the Vietnamese insurgents between 1946 and 1954, full-scale naval war in Vietnam effectively began on 2 August 1964 in the Gulf of Tonkin, when the destroyer USS *Maddox* was completing a sweep outside the 12-mile limit. Three motor torpedo boats were seen closing at high speed, and despite warning shots from the *Maddox*, the trio maintained an interception course. The destroyer then opened fire in earnest, disabling one with a 5-inch shell and scoring a hit on another. Two torpedoes were seen to pass 200 yards away, but when supporting aircraft from a US carrier appeared, the two hostile MTBs sheered off and made their escape.

The *Maddox* and other US Navy units had been operating in the Gulf of Tonkin to interrupt North Vietnamese coastal traffic carrying arms and food to the Vietcong. Previously the small North Vietnamese Navy, comprising 18 ex-Soviet and ex-Chinese motor torpedo boats and a force of about 60 minor patrol craft and minesweepers had shown no wish to oppose the mighty Seventh Fleet. The motive for this rash attack has never been revealed. Possibly it was retaliation for Seventh Fleet covering operations for South Vietnamese commando raids against the North. Another explanation is that it was meant to embarrass President Lyndon Johnson at the start of his presidential campaign. Whatever the motive, it failed to tempt President Johnson into retaliation, and he contented himself with a warning to Hanoi that no more attacks on US warships would be tolerated.

Only two days later, on the evening of 4 August, the *Maddox* and another destroyer, the *Turner Joy* were patrolling at about 20 knots when a radar operator aboard the *Maddox* identified five small targets approaching at high speed. Both destroyers sounded Battle Stations and opened fire; they later claimed to have sunk two MTBs and damaged another two. The reaction of the US Government was swift, and the carriers *Constellation* and *Ticonderoga* were ordered to launch air strikes against four bases and fuel depots in North Vietnam.

As these strikes escalated the war and sank an estimated 25 torpedo boats and patrol craft, and in addition destroyed 90 percent of North Vietnam's oil stock in exchange for two USN carrier planes shot down and two damaged, it must be asked if the incident justified such heavy reaction. Intelligence sources were later to cast doubt on what the radar operator had seen, and it was suggested that he might have mistaken his own ship's wake for a series of 'blips' on the screen.

The destroyer patrols in the Gulf of Tonkin, code-named 'DeSoto', were suspended for a while, but as soon as they were resumed the harassment began again. On the night of 18 September another pair of destroyers, the *Morton* and *Parsons*, detected what they took to be radar contacts and opened fire. But in spite of two 'engagements' involving the firing of more than 300 shells, at no time was there visual contact and no torpedoes were detected. It is reasonable to suggest that the original attack on the *Maddox* had made people jumpy, and that there may not have been any subsequent attacks by the North Vietnamese. What is certain is that the Johnson administration did not regard two 'engagements' as sufficient provocation, and all that was permitted was continuing but discreet support for the South Vietnamese Navy's clandestine operations off the coast, which were trying to prevent supplies from reaching the Vietcong.

Only in February 1965 did the US Navy launch further air strikes, in retaliation for a Vietcong attack on Camp Holloway, near Pleiku. As US Air Force bases had not yet been established south of the DMZ the Navy's carriers were the only means of striking back quickly. That quick reaction meant that the Navy's aircraft continued to play a major role in the air war, even after the USAF started its 'Rolling Thunder' operation on 2 March. The Seventh Fleet, 125 ships and 64,000 men, was an immensely powerful force, well equipped for the task. Its carrier Task Force, TF77, included the attack carriers *Hancock* (CVA.19), *Coral Sea* (CVA.43) and *Ranger* (CVA.61), operating a mix of strike, interdiction and reconnaissance aircraft.

TF77 was first ordered at the end of 1964 to rendezvous on Yankee Station, a point in the Gulf of Tonkin 75 miles offshore. At the start of February 1965 the scale of Vietcong operations against South Vietnam appeared to be waning, but as soon as the *Hancock* and *Coral Sea* were withdrawn, the attack on Camp Holloway occurred, and they had to be called back to take part in the retaliatory strike, code-named Flaming Dart One. Once Rolling Thunder started, the airspace over North Vietnam was divided into seven 'route packages,' covered jointly by the Air Force

A member of the Vietnam Junk Forces searches a native fishing vessel.

and TF77.

Although the United States would be bitterly criticized by some for escalating the war without thought for the consequences, strict rules of engagement were imposed on the pilots flying these early missions. Targets had to be authorized by the Pentagon, and thereafter each individual mission had to be approved. No follow-up attacks were allowed, and all hostile aircraft had to be identified positively.

The Navy's surface forces had an equally important, if less glamorous task, to enforce a tight blockade of the coast. Surveillance centers were set up at An Toi, Danang, Nha Trang, Qui Nhon and Vung Tau, and a Vietnam Patrol Force, Task Force 71, was established under Seventh Fleet control. A new operation, Market Time, was initiated, as was a riverine counterpart, code-named Game Warden. The main task of the offshore patrol was to monitor the movements of junks, but as there were about a thousand of these moving on the river *daily* there was only a random chance of identifying clandestine craft taking food and ammunition to the Vietcong.

The first specialized ships sent to deal with the problem were a dozen radar picket ships (DERs), former destroyer escorts released from early-warning duties in the North Atlantic and Pacific. The DERs had high endurance, as well as good accommodation, so they could 'loiter' on station, providing relief crews, food, water and fuel for small patrol craft. In time they became virtually HQ ships for the offshore patrols.

Even more useful was Coast Guard Squadron One, with its 50-ft 'Swift' type patrol craft. They had an armament of twin .50 caliber machine guns on the deckhouse, and a combined .50 caliber, and 81mm mortar aft, and were crewed by an officer and five enlisted men. So successful was the first squadron that an eventual total of 104 'Swift' boats were ordered. The Coast Guard also sent 26 of its 83-ft cutters, but other more specialized craft did not prove so successful. The 164-ft *Asheville* (PG.84) class aluminum-hulled gunboats, with their combined diesel/gas turbine drive, proved too complex for the task. Also over-sophisticated for the job was the experimental hydrofoil *Tucumcari* (PGH.2), which served for only a short while in Vietnam.

The surveillance operations were greatly enhanced when patrol aircraft were assigned. By the end of 1965 P-5 Marlin seaplanes were operating from seaplane tenders and P-3A Orion land-based patrol aircraft were also available. The Marlins patrolled from Vung Tau down as far as Phu Quoc Island, off the south coast of Cambodia; the Orions operated between Vung Tau and the 17th Parallel. The seaplanes were, however, later replaced by P-2 Neptune land-based patrol aircraft operating out of Tan Son Nhut, the big airbase at Saigon, and later Camranh Bay and Thailand.

It was only a matter of time before the US Marine Corps was asked to provide amphibious support for operations on the seaward flank of the Vietcong and the North Vietnamese Army. The 9th Marine Expeditionary Brigade (MEB) was on the spot in amphibious ships and transports, and went ashore at Danang to protect the big air base. Two battalions went ashore on 12 March, followed by a third battalion on 10 April, making a total of nearly 9000 Marines ashore by the end of that month. Four more battalions went ashore in May and the MEB was expanded to become 3rd Marine Amphibious Force (MAF). There was also an artillery unit in support and elements of 1st Marine Aircraft Wing (MAW), the first Marine Corps F-4 Phantoms flying from Danang on May 6. The air component was built up to four Marine Air Groups (MAGs), two flying fixed-wing aircraft and two helicopters.

To demonstrate the flexibility of amphibious forces, a Short Airfield for Tactical Support (SATS) was set up at Chu Lai. This was achieved by laying a 4000 ft strip of aluminum matting, complete with arrestor wires capable of stopping a carrier aircraft. This land-based 'flight deck' would eventually have a catapult, but for the first two years Marine pilots took off using rocket-boosters.

The USMC had always demanded maximum gunfire support as well as air cover, and when on 14 May the US Navy was given permission to bombard shore positions, the Seventh Fleet destroyers were assigned to the task. It was soon clear, however, that their 5-in guns lacked range and the right 'punch' to inflict severe damage on well-constructed bunkers. The destroyers also carried too few guns to sustain a heavy bombardment; the older ships were armed with two twin 5in/38 caliber mounts and the newer classes had only one or two single 5in/54 caliber.

The problem of gunfire support was met by bringing forward a number of cruisers, some of them from reserve. One of the biggest cruisers in the US Navy, the 17,000-ton *Newport News* (CA.148) was transferred from the Second Fleet in the Atlantic in September 1967. She opened fire with her nine 8-inch guns on 9 October, in Operation Sea Dragon, intended to harass and curtail the flow of supplies southward across the DMZ. By the time her tour of duty ended in April the following year, she had fired 59,000 shells of various calibers. Her second tour of duty from December 1968 to June 1969 was also successful but her third tour started in late 1971 was marred by an accidental explosion which destroyed a gun and wrecked No. 2 turret.

The 8-inch gunned cruisers could land a 335 pound shell on a target 14-15 miles away, but even this was to be eclipsed when the battleship *New Jersey* (BB.62) was brought forward from the 'mothball fleet' in mid-1967, for her 16-inch guns could hit targets 25 miles away with 3000 pound shells. The *New Jersey* was given an overhaul and recommissioned in April 1968, amid remarkable scenes of nostalgia. Her service on the Gun Line was a spectacular success, for she spent 120 days at sea, 47 of them continuous. In all she fired 5688 16 inch shells and 15,000 rounds of 5-inch. Surprisingly she was then decommissioned in December 1969; the Marine Corps argued against her withdrawal but the US Navy's manpower shortage was now acute, and her large crew was needed to man more important ships.

With so many ships operating off the coast of Vietnam it was important to maintain a Combat Air Patrol, for there was a constant risk of attack from the North Vietnamese Air Force MiG-17s, MiG-19s and MiG-21s. The sinking or even the crippling of an US ship would have had such propaganda value for Hanoi that it had to be guarded against, and in spite of numerous attempts no ship was hit. Much of that immunity stemmed from a very effective air defense system called the Positive Radar Advisory Zone (PIRAZ).

The PIRAZ ships were stationed in the Gulf of Tonkin, and included missile-armed cruisers, frigates and destroyers (CGs, CLGs, DLGs and DDGs). One outstanding example of how PIRAZ worked is the engagement fought by the heavy cruiser *Chicago* (CG.11) in May 1972, while she was supporting the airborne mining of Haiphong. Her main task was to cover the low-level flights of the minelaying aircraft, for the timing of these flights was critical if they were not to sustain heavy losses. As the aircraft approached the entrance to Haiphong Harbor the *Chicago* detected MiGs on radar, heading to intercept the heavily-laden mine-layers. A salvo of Talos long-range missiles knocked down one MiG at a range of 48 miles and forced the remainder to turn away, leaving the minelaying aircraft to complete their mission without opposition.

Not long after, the *Chicago*'s air controllers directed Air Force and Navy pilots so skilfully that they shot down no fewer than 12 MiGs,

and throughout 1972 the MiGs only once attempted to penetrate the 'umbrella' created by PIRAZ. On that occasion the *Biddle* shot down the leading MiG and the rest of the attacking wave broke off and headed for home.

PIRAZ ships had another important mission, to control the helicopters on their Search And Rescue (SAR) missions. Many Air Force and Navy pilots owed their lives to the SAR helicopter crews, many more were spared the horrors of a North Vietnamese prison camp. On occasion the ships also fired anti-radiation missiles (ARMs), missiles fitted with warheads capable of homing on North Vietnamese radars ashore.

Meanwhile the less glamorous campaign offshore to intercept North Vietnamese junks and other small craft went on. At the beginning of August 1965 the Seventh Fleet lost responsibility for the Market Time operation, with the creation of Task Force 115. This force, also known as the Coastal Surveillance Force, was put under the command of Rear

Detachable landing platforms were installed on troop carriers.

THE NAVAL WAR

Admiral Norvell G Ward, the Chief of the Naval Advisory Group. On 18 December the river operation was designated Task Force 116, although still under the overall control of Rear Admiral Ward. Then on 1 April the following year Rear Admiral Ward was appointed Commander, Naval Forces, Vietnam (COMNAVFORV), recognition of the growing complexity of the naval operations in Vietnam.

The river war, which went on parallel with the main naval effort, was on a different scale, but in many ways proved a bloodier and more intensely fought campaign. It was, of course, no more than a continuation of the murderous conflict between French and Vietminh forces from 1946 to 1954.

Nearly 90 percent of the lines of communication in southern Vietnam are rivers and canals, not roads; during the monsoon season roads become impassable and in the dry season the Vietcong found it all too easy to cut the limited road network. The Mekong Delta covers nearly a third of what was then the Republic of South Vietnam. It is covered by rice paddies and swamps, intersected by drainage canals or rivers, making it all but impassable to vehicles in many areas. The annual rainfall of 80 inches falls mostly in the summer, another reason why regular armies are at such a disadvantage against lightly armed, highly mobile guerrillas such as the Vietcong.

The foothills of South Vietnam, known to the French as Piedmont, are less cut up by watercourses and considerably drier, but further north the narrow coastal plain reverts to the flat marshes and rice paddies seen further south. Rainfall is an average 65 inches per year, falling mainly in September-November. Cross-country movement becomes all but impossible, and even flying is dangerous, as the visibility is poor.

The French Navy, during the war against the Vietminh, had created an efficient riverine force, using principally converted LCAs and LCVPs acquired from the British at Singapore. They were divided in River Assault Divisions or *Dinassaults*, and their pattern of operations was followed closely by the South Vietnamese and their American allies in the early days of the Vietcong operations.

The problems of the coastal forces have already been mentioned, but the river problem was much worse; some 50,000 junks operated in the Mekong Delta. Many of these were peaceful craft but some were inevitably used to smuggle arms and food to the Vietcong. Operation Game Warden began in 1965, and to implement it Task Force 116, a River Patrol Force under the command of Captain Burton B Witham Jr was established.

The US forces used a new type of river patrol boat (PBR), a 31-ft 8-ton fiberglass hull armed with two .50 caliber and a single .30 caliber machine gun. Twin waterjets enabled them to operate silently but at high speed in as little as three feet of water. However veterans preferred the slower and well-protected landing craft left over from the French days. As these were converted World War II landing craft they were in varying degrees of decrepitude, and replacements had to be designed and built.

The most unusual were a series of 'river monitors' created by converting two dozen Mk 6 mechanized landing craft (LCM(6)s). A variety of infantry weapons was mounted, including 81mm mortars, flamethrowers and machine guns, and in addition 40mm Bofors and 20mm Oerlikon guns. Twin diesels drove them at 8 knots. An improved type of 'monitor' was given a 10-inch (105-mm) howitzer, and a new form of bar armor was provided to keep out grenade fragments. In all, 42 of these larger monitors were built.

Predating the PBR was the River Patrol Craft (RPC), which had a welded steel hull and twin diesel engines. They were typically armed with twin revolving .30 caliber machine guns forward and a single .30 caliber above the conning position. Other special types developed included Command and Control Boats (CCBs), boats acting as headquarters for commanders of the River Assault Flotillas. Like the monitors they were converted from LCM(6) hulls, and a similar conversion produced the Armored Troop Carrier (ATC). These craft could carry troops, wheeled vehicles such as jeeps, field artillery and stores, and some even had a light steel helicopter pad fitted over the open well deck in the forepart of the boat. This feature made the ATC particularly useful for 'casevac' or casualty evacuation. Others were fitted with fuel tanks to enable them to refuel other river craft.

One of the most unusual craft was the 'mini-ATC', intended to land special forces and swimmers behind the enemy lines. Unlike most riverine craft they were designed for high speed, and to enable them to reach 28 knots some were driven by gas turbines. Their aluminum hulls were protected by ceramic armor (Kevlar) and even at top speed they drew no more than a foot of water, while carrying up to 20 troops.

The river war in Vietnam was too fragmented to be recorded and described in detail. It also took place for the most part away from the inquisitive eye of the media, but it was always an important part of the military effort to contain the Communist insurgency in South Vietnam. It was essential to keep control of the rivers. However, looking back on contemporary records, it is easy to slip into the error of seeing the campaign as a repetitive series of small-scale firefights.

The river forces first came to prominence when they were used in an operation code-named 'Chieu Hoi' (Open Arms), intended to win over defectors from the Vietcong. It was a Psychological Warfare Operation ('psyops' in the jargon of the military), sending boats up the canals to broadcast appeals and to distribute leaflets. During the period of pacification river craft were used to carry Popular Force units from village to village, and from December 1965 Marine Corps units of the

Game Warden force began to reinforce them. In January 1966 the Marines began a Combined Action Program (CAP) in the Phu Bai region, and the area of operations was soon extended to Danang. As the Game Warden personnel began to arrive in strength they were joined by the first USN Sea and Land (SEAL) platoons, forces specially trained in counterinsurgency techniques.

In its early stages the Vietnam campaign was seen as a good testing-ground for new equipment and technology. In May 1966 the first pair of air-cushion vehicles (ACVs) arrived. It was hoped that the Bell SK-5s would provide greater flexibility, as they could cross paddyfields at high speed but they needed such a high level of maintenance that they became a burden to the operators. By the end of 1966 there were 40 Game Warden craft in the Rung Sat waterways, and some 80 in the Mekong Delta. The establishment of Helicopter Support Squadron One with US Navy 'Huey' UH-1 Iroquois helicopters made a great difference as these gunships could bring gunfire support to bear rapidly. The helicopters were divided into two unit fire

Armored assault boats tied up alongside a self-propelled barracks ship.

teams, known as 'Seawolves.' In February 1967 another river assault force, Task Force 117, was formed, to take the offensive against the Vietcong in the Rung Sat and the Delta. The whole Game Warden command had for some time been a separate command, under COMNAVFORV.

By 1967 the river operations had become very sophisticated. Typically the forces would be organized in a Mobile Afloat Force (MAF), using floating barracks and supply craft known as a Mobile River Base (MRB). The MRB was protected by Assault Patrol Boats (ASBs) and monitors, as well as US Army or South Vietnamese Army (ARVN) units and artillery ashore. The ASPBs were also there to prevent the escape of any Vietcong units by water, and in this they could also call on ground attack aircraft and helicopters. Armored troop carriers (ATCs) would land the assault troops, and other units could be airlifted inland by helicopter, to get into position to cut off the enemy's escape route.

While the landing was in progress the ASPBs and monitors would provide supporting fire. Another group of ATCs were grouped into a Ready Reaction Force, ready to support any part of the assault which had run into stiff opposition. A MAF operating at battalion strength was capable of fighting for a period of four to six days over a 15-square-mile area, but at the end of that period the troops would need to be withdrawn by helicopter or by boat. The constant fear of an ambush was understandable, but in addition the heat and humidity was enervating. Accounts from veterans of this type of warfare stress the physical exhaustion more than the strain of combat, and it was necessary to pull crewmen out for a period of rest.

The earliest SEAL teams were set up as Mobile Support Team Two (MST-2), with six converted LCM(6) landing craft. The engines were specially muffled for night operations, with soundproofed enginerooms and underwater exhaust outlets. Armor plating kept out .50 caliber machine gun fire down to 100-yards range, and engine rooms and steering positions were protected against bazooka rockets. Weapons varied according to personal wishes of the crew, but the boats were armed with 106mm recoilless rifles and 81mm mortars. They were designated Heavy SEAL Support Craft (HSSCs), and one was given a 7.62mm Minigun.

The success of the HSSCs led to more conversions, using surplus LCPL Mk 4 hulls. The conversion was less elaborate, and protection was on a less lavish scale. Even so one of these craft escaped from a Vietcong ambush with over 200 hits. All but one of the 13 men aboard were wounded, and the crew undoubtedly owed their escape to the fact that a 57mm rocket projectile had passed right through the fuel tank without exploding. MST-2 was manned from the Naval Amphibious Force at Coronado, California. Tours of duty lasted 180 days, but this does not include additional time spent in the Vietnam Theater, for their knowledge and specialized skills were in great demand.

One of the outstanding achievements of the river war was the construction of a large secure base in the Mekong Delta, to allow Game Warden craft to be based much closer to the battle zone. In two years US Navy Construction Battalions (the legendary Seabees) created an artificial island, using hydraulic suction dredgers to excavate a square mile of basin. Vietcong saboteurs did their best to hinder the work, but despite the sinking of three dredgers, the work was finally completed. This enormous feat was never given any praise by the US media, for it took place well away from the main combat zone.

Meanwhile, the mounting domestic pressure to end the war meant an inevitable falling off of effort of the sea war. In February 1969 the process of 'Vietnamization' began, and within a year the bulk of the Market Time and Game Warden craft had been turned over to the South Vietnam Navy or sent back to the United States. This had the ludicrous effect of transforming the South Vietnam Navy into one of the largest navies in the world, in numbers if not quality. It already possessed some 460 craft, ranging from 640-ton PCEs (coastal escorts) down to minor supply craft, and in 1969 it received an additional 242 patrol craft. This does not include a Junk Force of 500 motorized junks established in 1960 to maintain the coastal blockade. By 1972, when the Americans pulled out, the South Vietnamese Navy had been swollen to 40,275 officers and enlisted men, and 13,800 marines. The ships included former Coast Guard seaplane tenders, 1750-ton cutters and two radar picket destroyer escorts.

The 'Vietnamization' process was almost calculated to wipe out the gains of the preceding four years. Hundreds of craft were dumped on the South Vietnamese Navy, whose personnel suddenly had to learn how to

As part of the program of 'Vietnamization,' ships – like USS Brattleboro – changed hands.

use sophisticated equipment. Although attempts were being made to create rudimentary training facilities, the sudden expansion was quite beyond Vietnamese resources, and standards rapidly fell off. This is no reflection on Vietnamese capabilities, for other navies have suffered in this way, and it was foolish for anyone to hope for any other result.

The Mobile Riverine Force was disbanded formally in 1969, and in its place was set up a force of ARVN marines, aided by US Navy advisers. The value of the craft transferred was officially put at $7.7 million, and the force was given the grandiloquent title of 'Sealords', from the acronym for South East Asian Lake Ocean River Delta Strategy. To commit the Sealords force to a major operation so soon was almost certain to lead to disaster. When in April 1970 the Saigon Command launched a major offensive against the Vietcong sanctuaries in Cambodia, it had to rely heavily on the rivers for access, for the Mekong flows from Phnompenh down through Vietnam. Cambodian forces failed in May to keep the river open, and the task had to be left to the Vietnamese gunboats. They succeeded in this difficult task, which was

fortunate, for when the offensive finally collapsed the Mekong was the only route by which the invaders could escape.

The withdrawal of US forces in 1972 hastened the collapse, despite efforts of the US advisers to keep up morale and efficiency. We know little of the last days before the Communist victory, but we can guess that the riverine forces gradually lost their cohesion. A few craft made their escape after the fall of Saigon on 30 April 1975 but the majority fell into Communist hands. It is doubtful whether the 500 or more craft believed to be still in existence are all operational.

At sea, bombardments continued right up to the end of 1972, to support operations by ARVN units. In May 1972 President Nixon, exasperated by the refusal of Hanoi to negotiate, ordered the mining of Haiphong and other harbors in North Vietnam. This was achieved entirely by aircraft, and sweeping the mines proved virtually impossible for the North Vietnamese. So sophisticated were the mines that after hostilities had ceased the US Navy had to sweep the minefields themselves. The operation achieved its objectives, trapping Soviet and other Eastern Bloc merchant shipping in harbor, but it did little to effect the outcome of the war.

All units of the US Navy played a part in the evacuation that followed the debacle in April 1975. The carriers and amphibious ships were almost swamped by refugees. Nobody who watched the scenes aboard US ships at that time can forget the sight of helicopters being pushed off the flight decks of US ships to make way for more loads of frantic refugees. Some tens of thousands of Vietnamese were picked up by the ships, while boatloads reached Thailand after terrible hardships in open boats. For years afterwards the 'boat people' continued to brave the horrors of a boat voyage from Vietnam, gambling their lives in attempts to reach Thailand, Singapore or Hong Kong.

Hoping to profit by the confusion of the American withdrawal, the Cambodians decided to capture a merchant ship. On 12 May Cambodian patrol boats seized the SS *Mayaguez*, en route to Thailand, taking the captain and 39 crewmen as hostages. Presumably it was hoped to extract a groveling apology from the US Government, and to get as much political advantage as possible from the unwillingness of the US Government to sacrifice the prisoners' lives. It was a well-tried technique, which had worked satisfactorily for North Korea in the similar *Pueblo* incident seven years earlier but it did not work this time.

The US Navy acted resolutely, putting up a combat air patrol over the *Mayaguez*, which was kept at anchor close inshore. This isolated the ship, sinking or driving off any boats which tried to get alongside. The rescue operation started unfortunately, when an Air Force helicopter crashed. Then the assault wave of eight CH-53 helicopters ran into heavy ground fire, and five machines were lost. But three more CH-53s managed to get their Marines on board a destroyer escort, and from there the *Mayaguez* was recaptured. The captain and crew were found on shore nearby, and were also rescued, and the Marine assault group was airlifted out by helicopter that night.

The *Mayaguez* incident was nearly a disaster, due to hasty planning and poor intelligence, but it succeeded at a time when the United States' reputation was at its nadir. Prompt action showed both friends and enemies that the US Government was still capable of acting to protect its interests.

Most of the naval operations in the Vietnam War seem very mundane, being largely confined to air strikes and gunfire support, and at first sight it is hard to see what important lessons were learned. But that is a superficial view, for the intensity of operations tested ships, weapons and men in a way that had not been seen since Korea.

Although ships sustained damage, most of it was self-inflicted. Several carriers suffered damage when ordnance exploded on board, and in one or two cases severe fires followed. What was significant about these potentially fatal accidents was the speed with which the ships' damage control organizations coped with them, and in all cases the area of damage was confined. More bizarre was the accident which befell the missile-armed frigate *Worden* (DLG.18) in 1973. While cruising offshore she was 'attacked' by a US Shrike anti-radiation missile, released accidentally by a Phantom flying high overhead. The Shrike armed itself and performed exactly as designed, homing on the frigate's main surveillance radar and exploding about 80 ft overhead. The blast and fragmentation warhead showered splinters over the *Worden*'s superstructure, severing waveguides and cabling. The wheelhouse was severely damaged and all electrical power was cut off, putting the ship out of action for six hours.

It was well known that modern warships are highly vulnerable to blast and splinter damage to their sensitive radar arrays, but close examination of the *Worden* showed something much more alarming. Blast had shattered the aluminum panels in the ship's upperworks, causing fragments and uprooted panels to wreck the wheelhouse and other spaces. It was later estimated that more than 60 percent of the damage had been caused by the aluminum fragments, and not by the warhead of the missile. This lesson has had very important effects on the design of current USN warships, and it is significant that the latest destroyers are being built with all-steel superstructures.

The long periods spent at sea tested the design of all types of warship. The aircraft carriers in particular are limited in operational efficiency by their ability to sustain operations, and during the Vietnam War carriers broke previous records for continuous operations. Machinery was also subjected to great strain by sustained operations, but above all, personnel were tested under something approaching battle conditions.

The PIRAZ operations already mentioned tested techniques of air control by warships,

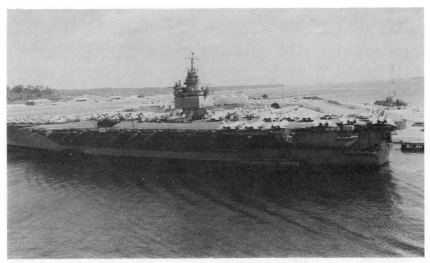

USS Enterprise *served off Vietnam during Operation Frequent Wind.*

of vital importance to naval operations in the 1980s and the future. The US Navy became the first in the world to conduct missile warfare against aircraft, matching the expertise of the Israelis in surface missile warfare.

Vietnam confirmed the US Navy's belief that the big aircraft carrier is vital, for carrier air power remains the only valid form of power-projection in today's world. Not only can carrier aircraft intervene effectively in a land conflict, but they are invariably able to come into action quickly. The strategic direction of the war has been bitterly criticized but nobody can fault the precision and flexibility of the US Navy and Marine Corps pilots, who performed brilliantly.

The principal naval strike aircraft used was the F-4 Phantom in its various marks. This remarkable aircraft could perform a variety of roles, using its unique combination of high performance and heavy payload. The A-4 Skyhawk, being smaller and cheaper, was used in greater numbers than the Phantom for ground-attack, but both types were outshone by the veteran A-1 Skyraider. In spite of being a piston-engined aircraft which had first flown in 1945 and had been operational in the Korean War, it was still ideal for ground-attack. It could loiter over the battle-zone, unlike the fuel-hungry jets, and could carry as much as 15,000 pounds of ordnance, more than twice the payload of the Skyhawk. Out of some 3000 Skyraiders manufactured, over

a thousand were sent to Southeast Asia.

The Skyraider suffered casualties from ground fire when first sent to Vietnam, but it was soon realized that the aircraft was vulnerable only at medium altitude. When flown low it was very hard to hit with machine guns and 20mm gunfire from jungle clearings, as the aircraft was in sight for only a short time. Once the tactics were changed the 'Spad' became highly popular with the aircrews, and the noise of its big radial engine became a constant scourge to the Vietcong.

Backing up the carrier-borne Phantoms, Skyhawks and Skyraiders, there was also the A-6 Intruder. This aircraft was used in three variants, the E-6A all-weather ground attack aircraft, the KA-6D tanker, and the EA-6B Prowler electronic warfare aircraft. The KA-6D was used to refuel aircraft on deep-penetration missions. As the enemy deployed more and more sophisticated missiles the role of electronic warfare became more crucial, and both EA-6B Prowlers and the big RA-5C Vigilantes were used to jam hostile radars. The Vigilante was a multi-sensor reconnaissance aircraft, carrying cameras and infra-red sensors.

Like their USAF counterparts the Navy and Marine Corps pilots had to evolve new tactics to defeat the ground-to-air and air-to-air missiles. It soon proved possible to defeat the missile, but what came as an unpleasant surprise was the discovery that US missiles were also fallible. It had been assumed for many years that missiles had very high kill-rates, but in combat they proved disappointing, and as electronic countermeasures improved, it became clear that the day of the manned aircraft was far from over. Today's aircraft and weapons owe much to the lessons learned in the skies over Vietnam.

For years the Marines had been developing techniques of 'vertical envelopment,' the use of helicopters to carry infantry far inland. When the US Navy's carriers were sent into the Gulf of Tonkin to support Rolling Thunder a number of SH-3A Sea King helicopters were hurriedly converted to a support role. With increased fuel capacity and 7.62mm Miniguns in rear sponsons, their role was to rescue downed pilots, from the jungles ashore and the Gulf. Later the 'Huey' was to achieve even more success as a 'gunship,' giving supporting fire to ground troops.

All classes of warship served in Vietnam, from the 60,000-ton 'super carriers' and the 80,000-ton nuclear carrier *Enterprise*, down to the smallest river craft. The creation of a wide range of specialized small craft was all the more remarkable when it is remembered that the US Navy entered the war with few small strike craft such as motor gunboats or motor torpedo boats. Not all of the new craft developed were successful, but overall the great effort produced a large number of useful inshore and riverine craft for the unusual conditions found in Vietnam. As a 'blue water' force, the US Navy did not deserve censure for failing to foresee the need for light craft, but Vietnam did show how unsuited large warships are in such conditions.

Although the big destroyers and frigates were oversophisticated for such mundane tasks as patrolling the coast and bombarding Vietcong positions, the missile-armed ships were superbly equipped to direct and control air traffic. The long-range surveillance radars needed for air defense provided a 'picture' of the surrounding air space, and the experience provided useful data for the next generation of air defense ships.

The Marine Corps won its fight to get a battleship back in commission, if only for a short while, but the majority of the 8-inch and 6-inch gunned cruisers which did such sterling service on the 'Gun Line' were too old to see much further service. A few survive in the US Reserve Fleet, but for heavy gunpower the Navy now relies on the four *Iowa* class

A vessel of the River Assault Group on patrol.

Two sailors man .50mm 'over-under' weapon aboard a Navy 'Swift.'

battleships. The *New Jersey* was recommissioned in 1982 and in 1984 was joined by her sister *Iowa*, while two others were undergoing modernization. As a direct result of Vietnam the US Navy developed a lightweight 8-inch gun for destroyers, but in spite of successful trials it was never put into production. Arguments continue about how to restore gunpower to the smaller types of warship.

Although vociferous critics had been trying to get rid of the big attack carriers for years, Vietnam showed that they had a considerable role to play. More nuclear-powered carriers are being built, to maintain a total of 15 carrier battle groups in service. The Phantom has given way to a new generation of powerful carrier aircraft, the F-14 Tomcat interceptor and the dual-role F/A-18 Hornet, and new helicopters are in service, but fundamentally the surface strike element of the US Navy has the same sort of capability that it had in Vietnam.

Critics claim that the performance of the US Navy in Vietnam was exaggerated, for the North lacked the ability to launch effective attacks on US warships. Had the North Vietnamese possessed shorebased anti-ship missiles they might have been able to force ships to keep their distance, which would have reduced the amount of gunfire support the ships could provide. Had the North possessed submarines, the threat would have forced the Seventh Fleet to behave more

circumspectly in the Gulf of Tonkin, even if the submarines had never got within range.

The argument is contentious, for if these threats had existed the Navy would have taken them into account, and undoubtedly energetic steps would have been taken to neutralize them. With numerous local ground, sea and air forces available to the United States and South Vietnam, it is unlikely that the North would have been left alone to mount missile attacks on US warships, and even if hostile submarines had not been sunk, their bases would have been put out of action. It is significant that after the initial attacks by motor torpedo boats in August 1964, that particular threat was never deployed again in any way that interfered with Task Force 77.

The effectiveness of the US Navy in the Vietnam War has to be measured against the performance of US forces as a whole. Weaknesses and errors of policy prevented the Navy from reaping the full reward for its efforts, just as they did for the land and air forces. Conversely, the naval effort remained crucial right up to the end, and there can be no doubt that it mitigated the scale of the disaster. The river campaign, although comparatively low-key, did much to delay the final collapse of South Vietnam. What can be said with certainty is that without the US Navy's enormous efforts, the war could not have been prolonged to 1975.

IRREGULAR FORCES IN VIETNAM

BY KEVIN GENEROUS

IRREGULAR FORCES

By all twentieth-century Western military traditions, the hostilities in Vietnam were 'unconventional.' To the French, Vietnam was *la guerre sans fronts*, a 'war without fronts.' The Americans called their Vietnam experience alternately a brushfire war, limited conflict, externally-supported Communist insurgency or simply, guerrilla war. To Ho Chi Minh's Vietnamese Communists, it was always the 'people's war.'

Frustrated Western military leaders faced a guerrilla army from an undeveloped colonial society that appeared primitive in weapons, tactics and military traditions, possessing virtually no modern transport, firepower or air force, and which steadfastly refused – even with its 'main force' units – to fight a European-style conventional war of maneuver. Instead, the Vietnamese Communists fought with traditional guerrilla tactics – stealth, surprise, deception and ambush – adapted to local geography, climate and customs. Ho's army combined Mao Tse-tung's 'revolutionary warfare' (guerrilla 'fish' swimming in a 'sea' of peasants) with fierce Vietnamese nationalism, producing a quasi-religious doctrine of *dau tranh* or 'struggle.' This struggle molded the Vietminh and later, the Vietcong, into a disciplined 'people's army' with a singular purpose that legitimized assassination, kidnapping and terrorism.

A Western commentator has called the Vietnam wars a clash between two distinct military philosophies: one based on mobility of the individual soldier, the other on the mobility of professional armies. But although French and US armies generally clung to conventional military doctrine in Vietnam, a few Western commanders realized that in the inhospitable jungles, mountains and swamps of Indochina, one well-trained irregular equipped with stamina and individual fortitude was worth a platoon of regulars. The need to wage counterguerrilla war required irregular units for pacification (to clear a region of insurgents), intelligence collection and special operations.

Irregular forces sprang up in an *ad hoc* manner. What worked remained in operation; what did not was dropped in favor of something that did. This improvisation led to a crazy-quilt spectrum of irregular units – covert political-psychological ('psywar') teams, private tribal armies and paramilitary groups, counterguerrilla commandos and elite special forces units – whose collective mission was to fight the Communist guerrilla at a grass roots level, employing his own tactics.

Ironically, US military involvement in Southeast Asia began in 1945 with the wartime forerunner of the Central Intelligence Agency, the Office of Strategic Services (OSS). The OSS mission in Asia provided paramilitary support to Ho Chi Minh's embryonic guerrilla movement based in Tonkin.

In late 1944, a well-organized Vietminh underground funneled valuable military intelligence on Japanese troop movements to the OSS and aided downed flyers from Major General Claire Chennault's 14th Air Force. As a token of its appreciation, OSS-China supplied the Vietminh guerrillas with six revolvers and 20,000 rounds of ammunition. The 300 Free French *maquisards* (underground resistance fighters) receiving OSS commando training in China viewed the OSS-Vietminh contacts with growing suspicion; despite a limited military presence, France demonstrated every intention of returning to their pre-war colonial domination of Indochina. But French-OSS commando units never played an important military role before the Japanese surrender.

A notable exception was Project Comore, a June 1945 OSS raid against the Japanese 22nd Division headquarters at Lang Son. Five OSS sabotage experts and 100 French and Vietnamese commandos led by OSS Captain Lucien Conein, a French-speaking ex-Foreign Legionnaire and commando expert, emerged from the jungles and blew up Japanese fuel and ammo dumps. The commandos captured two Japanese prisoners and a cache of documents before melting back into the jungle. Comore reaped an intelligence bonanza on Japanese military operations in Southeast Asia, while suffering only a single casualty.

But the Vietminh remained the dominant underground movement in Tonkin. The OSS extended the Comore concept to the Vietminh after Ho volunteered 1000 'well-trained' guerrillas for anti-Japanese operations. A seven-man OSS advance team, codenamed Deer, parachuted into Ho's jungle camp 75 miles southwest of Hanoi in July 1945. The team adopted guerrilla garb and trained 200 handpicked guerrilla troops in the latest US commando tactics. Deer also supplied US small arms and a communication link to Allied leaders for Ho's request for post-war Vietnamese independence. Deer members later accompanied Vo Nguyen Giap's troops into Hanoi on their 'victory march' in September 1945.

OSS 'Mercy Teams' parachuted into Vietnam in August 1945 to collect intelligence and protect 10,000 Allies in Japanese POW camps. A 12-man Mercy Team landing in Hanoi discovered the city adorned with red and gold Vietminh flags and in *de facto* control of Communist militia. Welcoming OSS Lieutenant Colonel Archimedes Patti's Americans, the Vietminh promptly placed four accompanying Frenchmen in 'protective custody.' Patti's team later reviewed Giap's troops on Vietnamese Independence Day, 2 September 1945.

Two hundred miles south in Saigon another Mercy Team led by OSS Major Peter Dewey landed in the middle of bloody atrocities between French civilians and armed Vietnamese groups. On 22 September, as French military forces began returning to Saigon, the French-speaking Dewey was killed by anti-French guerrillas who apparently took the American for a Frenchman. Dewey became the first US soldier serving in Vietnam to die in action. In October 1945, amid escalating violence, the OSS evacuated its Mercy Teams.

Between 1945 and 1954, the French deployed over 250,000 French Union Forces (FUF) – plus 200,000 troops of the national armies of Vietnam, Laos and Cambodia – against the Vietminh. All FUF troops were hardy volunteers, including the 20,000 crack Foreign Legionnaires, one of the world's foremost regiments. These professional mercenaries, including 7000 displaced German nationals, formed into elite infantry and paratroop units. Anticipating an easy campaign, the FUF deployed conventional light infantry, armored cavalry and artillery.

The guerrillas facing the FUF had humble origins, although they would number over 330,000 by 1954. The Vietminh of 1944 consisted of a few thousand poorly armed militia and a single 34-man Propaganda and Liberation Unit, armed with two revolvers, 17 rifles, 14 flintlocks and one light machine gun. Aided by 4600 OSS-supplied small arms and crude, jungle weapon factories, the Vietminh spent the war's initial phase building a country-wide guerrilla network, with occasional forays against French outposts.

Communist forces were organized into three types of units. Guerrilla-militia units (*dan quan*) in 30-man platoons were the true foundations of 'people's warfare.' Operating at the hamlet level, these part-time militia units (over 100,000 by 1954) guarded villages, harrassed FUF patrols and prepared the local defenses – the mines, *punji* stakes and booby

Members of a US Navy SEAL team wore camouflage on patrol.

traps that claimed so many casualties among Western troops in both wars. Although armed with a handful of bolt-action rifles and homemade hand grenades, the guerrilla-militia served as a manpower pool for better armed units.

The 70,000 regional guerrillas (*dia phuong*), organized into 85-man district companies and 300-man province battalions, backed up the militia and acted as a local strike force. When fully equipped, regional units could engage equal-sized FUF forces in sustained combat for short periods. Regional and guerrilla-militia insurgents emphasized small-unit actions: ambush, sabotage, armed terrorism and harrassing fire. Their primary mission was to wear down French morale, forcing them to protect isolated outposts. Dispersal of French forces allowed the Vietminh to build up their 'main force' units (*chu luc*), consisting of highly mobile 400-man light infantry battalions carrying recoilless rifles and 60mm mortars for artillery support. After the Communist Chinese victory in 1949, Mao made available training bases and captured US arms to beef up Vietminh main forces from a few battalions to full regiments and, by 1950, five 10,000-troop infantry divisions.

Main force battalions closely followed the doctrine 'strike to win, strike only when success is certain.' Main force tactics demanded fast cross-country movement and rapid concentration from many dispersed points of departure prior to attack. Large-scale operations – such as Dienbienphu – required prepositioned stores and months of rehearsal by assault troops using maps and scale-model sand tables. Guerrillas also relied on tactics using stealth and surprise. At Xon-Pheo in early 1952, a Vietminh sapper unit followed a returning Legionnaire patrol through a minefield and then quickly overran carefully prepared defenses.

Some main force units infiltrated the famous 'de Lattre Line,' shielding the ostensibly secure Red River Delta. By 1954 over 80,000 Vietminh had infiltrated the delta. The elite 42nd Independent regiment operated permanently within the de Lattre Line, despite all French attempts to annihilate it.

Vietminh saboteurs engaged in covert activities behind French lines caused an estimated 40 percent of French military equipment to be delivered with wrecked gears, torn wiring or sugar poured into gas tanks. Saboteurs at times had an impact disproportionate to their small numbers. At the height of the Dienbienphu siege, one determined Communist sapper crawled through a mile of sewers under the large French airbase at Cat Bi, evading electrified wire, minefields and guard dogs. Emerging inside the aircraft park, the guerrilla blew up 18 transport planes badly needed to sustain the besieged French garrison.

In an elusive search for set-piece battles and as a counter to the Communists' rapid cross-country thrusts, the French deployed several composite combat units of tremendous firepower and mobility. *Groupe Mobiles* were armored maneuver units (patterned after US regimental combat teams) consisting of scout cars, tanks, mechanized infantry and *commandos* – small shock troop units used for reconnaissance. Historian Bernard Fall called the mobile groups 'an ever moving microcosm of an army.'

Finding mobile operations difficult in the marshy deltas, the French organized six unconventional river flotillas called *dinassauts* – Naval Assault Divisions – to support ground units along Vietnam navigable rivers. A typical 1500 man *dinassaut* consisted of 12 surplus US armored landing craft: LSSLs (Landing Ship Support, Large) flagship and LCMs (Landing Craft Material) serving as armored 'monitors' or 81mm mortar batteries for fire support. Other armored craft carried two companies of Marine commandos, and larger *dinassauts* even used LCTs (Landing Craft, Tank) to carry tanks and reconnaissance aircraft. The French *dinassaut* proved very successful in projecting French power far upriver where mobile ground units dared not venture. The river units demonstrated their strategic value in the 1951 Red River Delta campaigns, participating in one of Giap's few major defeats. And at Hoa-Binh salient in January 1952 French LCMs probed 250 miles into the Tai Highlands on the Black River to duel Vietminh shore batteries in one of the most bloodiest river battles since the US Civil War. To counter the *dinassauts*, the Vietminh employed mines and even frogmen against the shallow-draft monitors. A major tactical innovation, the *dinassaut* concept would later be revived by the US Riverine Force in the 1960s.

To challenge the Communists on the village level, the French enlisted numerous anti-Communist paramilitary groups originally aligned with the Vietminh. Although anti-French in temperament; a combination of

The Vietcong maintained food caches throughout South Vietnam.

Communist strong-arm tactics and political opportunism brought these nationalist groups over to the French. These forces included a Catholic Militia and the ultra-nationalist Dai Viet party in Tonkin. In southern Vietnam, where the Vietminh held far less sway, several private armies jealously controlled whole regions around Saigon. Led by river kingpin Bay Vien, the Binh Xuyen gangsters controlled the Saigon River approaches and the city's lucrative vice parlors with a 6000-man private army.

In the rubber forests northwest of Saigon, the Cao Dai religious sect operated as virtually a state within a state with its 15,000 troops armed by the Japanese during wartime collaboration. Dissident Cao Dai units, like the Lien Minh under general Trinh Minh The, fought against both the Communists and the French. The 20,000-man Hoa Hao army also turned to the French after its leader was assassinated for refusing to submit to Vietminh control.

The flimsy loyalties of the private armies, however, were no match for the efficient Communist organization operating in the densely populated lowlands. To outfox the Vietminh at their own game, the French trained 52 special Vietnamese Army commando battalions – the *Tieu-Doan Kinh Quan* (TDKQ) – light infantry designed to support local militia. Heavily promoted as a 'secret weapon' by the French psychological warfare (psywar) office, the TDKQ commandos were immediately targeted for destruction by Vietminh command, fearing the TDKQ potential against its hamlet guerrillas. With heavier French units bogged down elsewhere, Communist main forces quickly chopped up several TDKQ units in Tonkin. An embarrassed Vietnamese Army quietly dropped the promising TDKQ in 1954.

Far greater success was achieved in organizing ethnic tribesmen as auxiliaries (*suppletifs*) and counterguerrilla units to fight in rugged mountain regions – another concept later adopted by Americans in the 1960s. These tribal groups – Nung, T'ai, Meo, Muong and the *Garde Montagnarde* – were led by a few French officers and NCOs who capitalized on the highlanders' intense hatred of ethnic Vietnamese.

Respected for their fierce jungle fighting abilities, natives were often integrated into

IRREGULAR FORCES

Sandbags create a bunker for protection during Vietcong attacks.

elite units like the *Battalion de Marche Indochinois*, a composite battalion of Europeans, Cambodians and tough tribesmen reportedly among the best FUF combat units. Even *le BEPs*, the tough Foreign Legion Paratroopers, maintained a company of ethnic Indochinese in each battalion to guide Legionnaires in unfamiliar territory.

French ground commanders also experimented with mixed paratroop-native units. At Dienbienphu, intelligence sorties with T'ai irregulars and 8th Parachute Assault Battalion scouts, confirmed the Communist ring closing around the camp months before attack. Also fighting at Dienbienphu were 11 T'ai Irregular Light Companies that reconnoitered the Vietminh approach – although at frightful cost. Twenty-one hundred T'ai

suppletifs fought a hellish 10-day battle around the garrison, dogged by the elite 148th Vietminh Mountaineer Regiment (the Communist recruited highlanders also). Whole companies simply vanished without a trace in fierce but forgotten jungle battles. Only 175 irregulars returned to Dienbienphu. These units however, demonstrated the utility of mobile irregulars in long-range reconnaissance.

The French developed two types of counterguerrilla forces. *Groupements Commandos* were special strie forces working in coordination with conventional combat forces, often led by a native officer with French NCOs. The true counterguerrillas however, were the semi-autonomous Composite Airborne Commando Groups

IRREGULAR FORCES

(*Groupement de Commandos Mixtes Aeroportes*), or GCMAs. The GCMA mission was to organize native *maquis* behind Communist lines, confuse logistics and collect intelligence on Vietminh movements. Major Roger Triniquier commanded 15,000 GCMA counterguerrillas between rubber plantations north of Saigon and the Communist Chinese border, operating in 300-400 man units up to 200 miles inside Vietminh territory. Communist troops took special care to avoid GCMA operating areas deep within their territory, such as the infamous 'Cardamom' zone near the Chinese border.

GCMA cadres who parachuted behind enemy lines were a special breed – handpicked as much for their reputation as troublemakers as for their command of native dialects. French GCMA cadres 'went native,' even marrying into a tribe to gain the respect of local chieftains. Life for the French commandos was exceedingly hazardous. Like Vietminh, the GCMA fought without quarter for the war's duration, dependent upon occasional supply drops and the trust of his irregulars. French GCMAs feared only broken health and the possibility that one of his irregulars might be a member of the 421st Vietminh Intelligence Battalion, a special clandestine unit that gathered intelligence on GCMA guerrillas.

GCMA and GC commandos reported directly to French Central Intelligence – a situation analogous with the CIA's clandestine sponsorship of similar counterguerrilla groups in the 1960s. Other special intelligence units – such as the 610th Recon Commandos operating on the Vietnam-Laos border – worked directly for the French High Command in Hanoi.

Although tactically effective, French counterguerrilla forces appeared too little and too late for any strategic impact. Undisputed masters of irregular warfare, the Vietminh were omnipresent throughout Indochina. The ultimate demonstration of this reality came at Dienbienphu, where 40,000 crack Vietminh troops using eighteenth-century siege warfare tactics overwhelmed an elite French garrison of over 16,000 Foreign Legion paratroopers and elite colonial infantry.

The French investment at Dienbienphu – designed to lure Giap's main forces into an elaborate 'kill zone' – was an irresistible challenge to the Vietminh. Logistical preparations requiring methodical road and depot construction hundreds of miles from Communist base areas took months. Incoming supplies were distributed to assault units on bicycle and foot by thousands of impressed porters. The entire supply system – from the Chinese railhead to concentric circles burrowed around French fortified positions – proved impervious to air interdiction. One hundred tons per day flowed to Giap's siege troops.

Unorthodox artillery and anti-aircraft tactics were ingeniously employed. Rather than Western-style massed interlocking fire, Vietnamese dragged individual pieces into escarpments in hillsides overlooking the garrison. Gunners took care to leave the foliage undisturbed to disguise both the gun's location and muzzle flash from French counterfire. Surprise was total; in the battle's opening phase Vietminh artillery knocked out 40 percent of French artillery guns, destroyed 14 parked aircraft and rendered the dirt runway useless.

Instead of defending individual targets, Communist anti-aircraft platoons fired 20mm cannons, BARs and .50 caliber machine guns into a continuous 200-plane French airlift that flew along murderous flak corridors to drop supplies on a shrinking garrison. Among the 48 aircraft shot down was a C-119 flown by two US contract pilots of Civil Air Transport (CAT), a covert CIA airline. The pilots were the only American combat fatalities of the French war.

Like a giant octopus, the Vietminh siege trenches choked the French garrison. Outflanking French strongpoints, Giap followed the dictum 'isolate and overwhelm.' As waves of Vietminh infantry swelled toward the final outpost on 7 May 1954, 600 surviving Legionnaires of the crack 13th Half-Brigade – knowing that the battle, indeed the war, was lost – fixed bayonets under the light of parachute flares and charged.

For a few French soldiers the war did not end with the July 1954 cease-fire. French military broadcasts instructed all GCMA guerrillas to fall back toward Hanoi. But many commandos remained with their native guerrillas until the bitter end. For the next five years, 10 Vietminh main force battalions hunted down the last GCMA units. One by one, the GCMA radios fell silent. French authorities disclaimed the GCMA remnants.

In 1956 a radio message, in perfect French, was heard in South Vietnam: 'You sons-of-bitches, help us! Parachute us at least some

Secretary of the Navy John Chafee (left center) inspects a SEAL team.

IRREGULAR FORCES

US troops parachute into the war zone.

ammunition so we can die like fighting men, not slaughtered like animals.' Tragically, the last guerrillas of the First Indochina War were French-led irregulars.

Before July 1954, no international rules governed either side's conduct of the war. Both the French and the Vietminh treated Indochina as a single geographic unit, irrespective of national borders and saw little need for covert cross-border activities. But the Geneva Accords changed all this.

The existance of an International Control Commission (ICC) after 1954 to supervise foreign military advisory missions and to police military activities across borders soon forced Communist and Western-backed regimes to expand their covert warfare capabilities. Even the most passive Geneva requirement, a 300-day population 'regroupment' period, became a vehicle of East-West clandestine intrigue. Nearly 900,000 Vietnamese, mostly anti-Communist Catholics, elected to resettle in the south, while some 90,000 Vietminh 'regroupees' left behind families to march north. These troops were eventually absorbed into the 324th and 325th North Vietnamese Army (NVA) divisions.

Mindful of the South's political weakness and confusion, Ho Chi Minh ordered some 10,000 Communist agents in the South underground with enough arms to field 6000 troops. These 'former resistance cadres' set about destabilizing the fledging South Vietnamese nation through political agitation/propaganda, and would provide the seeds of an 'indigenous' southern insurgency should Ho order one. These 'stay-behind' networks were a Communist insurance policy against failure of the Geneva-sponsored 1956 elections that Western intelligence services predicted Ho's party would easily win.

The United States was now rapidly replacing France as the dominant Western power in Southeast Asia. The cutting edge of the US effort to cement a viable anti-Communist government in Saigon was the Saigon Military Mission (SMM) led by Air Force Colonel Edward G Lansdale. Ostensibly the US Embassy's assistant air attache, Lansdale was actually an innovative CIA operative whose growing reputation – based on his role in defeating the Communist Huks in the Philippines – inspired two best-selling Cold War novels, *The Ugly American* and *The Quiet American*. Lansdale's 'Cold War Combat Team' quietly arrived in Saigon after Dienbienphu's surrender to assist the Vietnamese

in paramilitary and political-psychological operations against the Vietminh. After the Geneva Conference, this mission changed to preparing paramilitary teams for action in Communist-held Tonkin (North Vietnam). Before the 300-day regroupment period ended, the 10-man SMM located, selected, exfiltrated, trained, infiltrated and equipped two paramilitary teams, 'Binh' and 'Hao.' Both teams trained at secret Pacific bases, including one provided by the non-profit Freedom Company backed by Lansdale's old Filipino contacts.

Before French withdrawal from Hanoi, 'Binh' – led by now-Major Lucien Conein – prepared for 'delayed sabotage' of Hanoi's buses and railroads by contaminating engine oil and equipment assisted by special CIA technicians flown in from Hawaii. 'Binh' also took extensive note of potential targets for future paramilitary activities as US adherence to the letter of the Geneva Accords precluded 'active' sabotage against Tonkin's power plants, water facilities, harbors and bridges.

The Geneva regroupment period provided a perfect cover for SMM preparations. CIA-owned CAT – which had secured a French contract to airlift Catholic refugees with Lansdale's help – provided covert air transport, while the US Navy Task Force 98 smuggled caches of arms along Tonkin's rivers and coastlines. However, the operational lifetime of SMM agents within the strictly regimented Communist society proved short, as the Vietminh quickly mopped up the 'Binh' and 'Hao' teams.

Lansdale's SMM also performed black 'psywar' operations designed to discourage civil cooperation with the Communists. In one successful operation, SMM spread 'Vietminh' leaflets in Tonkin describing proper civilian behavior and property reform under Communist rule. Within days, the leaflets tripled refugee registration and drastically devalued Vietminh currency. Subsequent efforts by Vietminh radio denouncing the 'psywar' operation were dismissed by rank-and-file Vietminh as a French trick. Under SMM the South Vietnamese Army 1st Armed Propaganda Company was formed to distribute leaflets in southern Vietminh villages instructing prospective regroupees to bring warm clothing when embarking on Communist bloc ships. A whisper campaign then spread rumors that regroupees were being shipped to China as railroad workers.

IRREGULAR FORCES

Special forces cross a rice paddy in the South.

The Communists performed 'delayed sabotage' of their own. HO's Central Committee placed a high priority on subverting the fledging South Vietnamese Army (ARVN), perhaps the only group in the South with the organization and communications to forge a viable nation. One hundred specially-trained Communist cadres were infiltrated into ARVN's ranks to wreck Army-peasant relations, a condition conducive to fomenting a renewed 'struggle' later. Only years later would these moles – in some cases high-ranking South Vietnamese officers involved in key pacification projects – be revealed as Communist agents. Such action encouraged mutual suspicion and paranoia among South Vietnamese leaders.

Lansdale eventually became head of the joint US-French Training Relations and Instruction Mission (TRIM) national security division – charged with coordinating all US civilian and military efforts in Vietnam. To Lansdale, Vietnam's national security started with President Ngo Dinh Diem. Yet the odds were heavily stacked against Diem's uniting the nation: Army Chief of Staff General Hinh was openly plotting Diem's ouster, encouraged by the the French intelligence service openly hostile to the anti-French Vietnamese president. In faction-riddled Saigon, the French armed and supported Binh Xuyen gangsters while Cao Dai and Hoa Hao sects jockeyed for power. Binh Xuyen leader Bay Vien had even bought control of Saigon's police from absent Emperor Bao Dai.

Lansdale developed a close personal relationship with the insecure and monkish Diem. He arranged for Filipino aid to train Diem's Presidential Guard Battalion and supplemented Diem's Catholic Militia loyalists with 3000 dissident Cao Dai (the Lien Minh), who secretly received CIA funding. In October 1954, when SMM learned of Hinh's planned attack on Diem's palace, the Americans lured two pro-Hinh officers to Manila and thwarted the coup. In April 1955, under Lansdale's guidance, Diem's forces moved against the 6000-man Binh Xuyen. After a series of fierce street battles, Diem routed the Binh Xuyen and broke the backs of the sect armies. The disorganized remnants fled to the countryside, some becoming minor Communist auxiliaries. With SMM's aid, Diem appeared to have performed a miracle.

When it became clear that the Geneva-sponsored elections would not be held, the US Army developed a South Vietnamese Army (ARVN) along conventional lines to repel a North Vietnamese multi-divisional attack across the DMZ. A CIA-trained unit was also estabished in February 1956 as a unconventional force based on the old 'Binh' concept. The 1st Observation Group was a 300-man special forces-type unit designed to operate in 15-man teams, preparing its own 'stay behind' units near the DMZ in case of a Communist invasion. It reported not through regular ARVN channels, but directly to Diem. After consolidating his power, Diem turned his attention to the 10,000 Communist underground cadres. Various SMM-sponsored community aid organizations, such as the 500 technicians of the Eastern Construction Company and the medical teams of Operation Brotherhood, also cooperated with Diem's army and police forces to target Vietminh 'stay behind' networks. These US-backed Filipino projects and Diem's 1956 'Communist Denunciation Campaign' cut deeply into Communist underground organizations; by 1959, party membership in the South had dwindled to 5000, with only 2000 mostly old Vietminh troops and sect remnants.

In 1957 Hanoi ordered its nearly extinct cadres to start armed propaganda and recruitment among the peasants. With several hundred party cadres infiltrated from North Vietnam, the Vietcong (a pejorative term for 'Vietnamese Communist') unleashed a terror and assassination campaign against government officials, teachers and village leaders. Over 2500 assassinations took place in 1959, more than double the previous year. Sabotage and terrorism, previously localized, became widespread.

In May 1959, the Central Committee formerly authorized an 'armed struggle' in the South and dispatched the 559th Transportation and Support Group (Doan 559) to prepare for large scale infiltration through Laos and by sea. Between 1959 and 1964, an estimated 44,000 regroupees skirted the heavily defended DMZ, slipping in through Laos. These highly-trained cadres and technicians provided a solid leadership core for a formidable guerrilla force. Doan 559 was charged with securing, expanding and operating what soon became known as the Ho Chi Minh Trail.

During the 1950s a deteriorating political situation in Laos between rightists, neutralists and Communists had allowed some 7000 NVA troops and supporting Pathet Lao guerrillas to seize the strategic Laotian panhandle from the inept Royal Lao Army. Prevented by Geneva Accords from maintaining a large military advisory mission in Laos, the United States established a 'Program Evaluation Office' (PEO) in 1958 as a CIA cover for a wide-range of covert political actions against Communist forces. These included cultivation of highlanders straddling the Laos-North Vietnam border – tribes such as the Meo abandoned by the French. A small pilot Meo guerrilla program, begun in 1958 to bring ethnic representation to CIA-backed Lao political organization, soon became the largest clandestine army in CIA history. In July 1959, 107 US Special Forces White Star teams under the command of Lt Colonel Arthur 'Bull' Simons were assigned as PEO 'civilians' to train 12 Royal Lao Army battalions and Lao paramilitary groups in behind-the-lines guerrilla warfare. Together with a few CIA officers and 99 elite Thai Border Police, White Star teams organized over 9000 Meo the first year to blow Communist supply dumps and harrass NVA/Pathet Lao logistics lines. Under Meo leader Vang Pao (an alumnus of a French *Groupe Commando* near Dienbienphu) the Meo army grew within ten years to over 40,000 guerrillas, becoming the most effective fighting force in Laos.

The CIA covert airline, known now as 'Air

IRREGULAR FORCES

America' (AA), supported the Meo as well as other CIA-backed clandestine armies operating against Communist China. AA transports and helicopters were the CIA's aerial guerrilla force, whose motto was: 'We fly anywhere, anyplace, anytime – professionally.' AA contract pilots flew 'black missions' over China, North Vietnam and, increasingly as the Ho Chin Minh Trail expanded, the Laotian panhandle. When the Trail doubled its infiltration capacity after 1961, the covert Vietnamese war had entered a newer, more deadly phase.

Five years after his SMM tour, Edward Lansdale returned to Saigon as a Brigadier General in the Pentagon's Office of Special Operations. He discovered 'a downhill and dangerous trend' in South Vietnam: over 8000 government officials assassinated in 1960; some 14,000 armed Vietcong were again developing a three-tiered organization (main-force, regional and local guerrilla/ militias) in six former Vietminh bases; President Diem had just narrowly defeated a coup attempt by officers of the elite airborne brigade. Moreover, the US-trained ARVN seemed incapable of managing the growing insurgency.

Lansdale's January 1961 report labeled Vietnam 'a combat area of the Cold War, requiring emergency treatment' and concluded that Vietnam's survival required unconventional strategies and tactics to beat the Vietcong at their own game. The report sparked the interest of a new president who wanted to combat Communist 'wars of national liberation' with US-directed 'counter-insurgency' efforts.

President John F Kennedy quickly followed up Lansdale's suggestion with concrete action, directing a CIA 'Combined Studies Group' to prepare for covert guerrilla operations in North Vietnam and ordering a major expansion of US unconventional warfare assets, then numbering only a few thousand troops. In March, Kennedy asked Congress to provide him the means to defeat 'small, externally supported bands of men.' With Laos in crisis, he ordered the White Star teams to don uniforms and shed their PEO cover.

Kennedy also approved a counterinsurgency plan for Vietnam that increased ARVN by 20,000 men, beefed up the poorly armed paramilitary Civil Guard to 68,000 and Self-Defense Forces to 40,000 and improved ARVN elite forces. In 1960, Ranger companies (*Biet-Dong-Quan*) had been created in each ARVN infantry battalion. Some 9000 BDQ in 65 companies – later expanded to 86 companies by 1963 – received improved training by US Special Forces at the Duc My Ranger School etablished in 1961. But Diem kept other elites – 600 Vietnamese LLDB (*Luc Luong Duc Biet*) Special Forces and the 4800-man airborne brigade – under tight personal control as 'coup insurance' following the aborted 1960 coup.

In May 1961, 400 US Special Forces advisors and other US units arrived to train the Vietnamese in counterinsurgency techniques. Organized in the 1950s to conduct sabotage, disrupt communications and organize guerrillas behind enemy lines, the Special Forces had never numbered more than 2500 men. Kennedy expanded the force fourfold, allowed the troops to wear their distinctive green berets – then in disfavor among Army brass – and gave them a counterguerrilla mission. The basic unit was a 12-man A-Team with each man cross-trained in intelligence, weapons and communications in addition to special language, medical, airborne and survival instruction. The navy organized its own elite counterinsurgency forces – the sea, air and land teams (SEALs) – while the Air Force developed the Air Commandos, who carried Armalite AR-15 rifles and flew specially modified propeller-driven T-28 C-47 and World War II vintage B-26 aircraft. In April 1961 the Air Commandos formed the 4400th Combat Crew Training Squadron. Nicknamed 'Jungle Jim,' the 350-man 4400th was soon shipped to Vietnam to teach Vietnamese counterinsurgency techniques: interdiction, air reconnaissance and ground support. With a Vietnamese pilot-trainee aboard, Air Commandos could fly combat missions, under the code-name Farmgate. The 4400th was redesignated 1st Air Commando Squadron and joined by a second Farmgate squadron in October 1964, both re-equipped with A-1E fighter-bombers.

Jungle Jim followed other air units discreetly inserted into Vietnam in 1961. The 67-man 507th Tactical Control Group, the nucleus of a mobile tactical air support system, arrived in country with all radar equipment identification markings painted out. At the same time, a Combat Development and Test Center was created in Vietnam to destroy Vietcong food sources and strip away jungle ambush cover with chemical agents. A special 69-man USAF unit began

Montagnard *commandos patrol the hills.*

Ranch Hand defoliation operations in early 1962 with six specially equipped C-123 Providers. The US Army 23rd Special Air Warfare Detachment, flying turboprop OV-1 Mohawks armed with cameras and .50 caliber machine guns, performed visual/photo reconnaissance to seek out guerrillas for ARVN ground units.

The first Green Beret training group arrived in Nha Trang in May 1961 to set up four separate ARVN training centers. By late summer over 70 ARVN companies had been trained in rudimentary combat skills and commando tactics. Other Green Berets were called in to support a CIA-sponsored pilot program that would become the largest most innovative and effective unconventional warfare program in Vietnam: The Civilian Irregular Defense Group (CIDG). In late 1961 the CIA had begun organizing the isolated tribal minorities that populated nearly 75 percent of South Vietnam's rugged interior. Based on the French example in mobilizing indigenous tribes and the CIA's

Meo success, the CIDG program was designed to train indigenous units in self-defense, contest Communist control of the strategic central highlands and relieve some of ARVN's defense burden.

Strictly defensive in nature, the initial 'Village Defense Program' began with SF Detachment A-113, a few CIA advisors and the Vietnamese LLDB at Buon Enao, a Rhade village in the southern highlands, where *montagnards* swapped their traditional spears and crossbows for Swedish K-sub-machine guns. By early 1963, 13 months later, the CIDG network included over 200 villages, 12,000 defenders and 26 A-Teams. Communist activity in CIDG areas fell off sharply. Expanding the CIDG program to other tribes, ethnic Cambodians, Nungs, Cao Dai, Hoa Hao, even Diem's Republican and Catholic Youth paramilitary groups, swelled the program to 75,000 in 1964.

Unlike Diem's unpopular and unsuccessful 'Strategic Hamlet' program, the CIDG program did not involve peasant resettlement.

IRREGULAR FORCES

A Green Beret sights a rocket during a counter-insurgency course.

Typically, a Special Forces A-Team recruited a small local 'strike force' for full-time duties that included patrolling, intelligence collection and setting ambushes, and a larger, unpaid force of hamlet defenders – trained in small arms and radios – organized to build and man defenses in case of attack. Special Forces medical and civic action projects greatly impressed the montagnards more accustomed to neglect and abuse by ethnic Vietnamese. When, in 1964, several CIDG camps rebelled against and massacred their Vietnamese advisors, US Green Berets drew upon this reservoir of goodwill to quickly end the rebellion.

As part of a world-wide turnover of CIA paramilitary operations in October 1963 known as 'Operation Switchback,' the CIDG became a Special Forces responsibility along with four other irregular CIA projects: over 650 personnel in Combat Intelligence Teams and about 5000 Border Surveillance and Mountain Scouts – trained to watch and interdict Vietcong movements – were absorbed into the CIDG. In addition, 450 Civilian Airborne Rangers, who performed covert intelligence and sabotage operations in Laos and Cambodia, were militarized and incorporated into the Vietnamese LLDB. These patchwork projects experimented with border control operations and prepared the way for later 'special recon' projects.

Ironically, the CIDG program was not, at its inception, a well-thought-out approach to counterinsurgency. It was almost an accidental success, like many of CIA's *ad hoc*, scattershot 'political actions.' The CIA and later the Special Forces developed and discarded several paramilitary techniques as the need arose, or, like the CIDG and Mountain Scout programs, turned them over to another sponsor with a different *modus operandi*.

After Switchback, the CIDG program evolved away from strictly defensive operations toward more aggressive, hit-and-run commando raids, that included Ranger strike forces along the Vietnam-Cambodian-Laos borders. By mid-1964, 24 CIDG camps had been established in the triborder area and CIDG strike force companies became standardized. This trend reflected a Special Forces style and organization as well as a need to stem swelling Communist infiltration.

The CIA also sponsored several local pacification projects in the early 1960s such as the 'Cinnamon and Shrimp' irregulars. This 500-man paramilitary group was formed by a wealthy Saigon businessman (at Diem's behest) to secure the Saigon-Vung Tao road – a region noted as a guerrilla sanctuary – for commercial traffic. Agency operatives built on the leaders' previous combat experience and a knowledge of Vietminh tactics, opening a small training center near Vung Tao to expand the black-pajama irregulars. Armed with mortars, recoilless rifles and submachine guns, these small mobile units provided valuable intelligence and support to local ARVN units. In the populous Mekong Delta, the CIA borrowed successful ideas from Lansdale's Huk experience. 'Census-Grievance Teams' were formed to comb the Mekong hamlets, conduct a census, hear out peasant complaints while recruiting government agents and identifying local Vietcong. 'Special Intelligence Teams,' disguised as ordinary farmers but armed with 9mm pistols, performed a similar function. More action-oriented 'Counter-Terror Teams' called 'X-Teams' by some operatives, targeted the local Vietcong infrastructure (VCI), employing favorite Vietcong tactics – kidnapping, ambush or assassination – against the local Vietcong infrastructure. Although small and decentralized, these counterinsurgency pro-

The Special Forces trained South Vietnamese guerrillas in the use of modern weapons.

US Infantry fire on North Vietnamese positions during an attack on Saigon.

IRREGULAR FORCES

Hand-to-hand combat was part of Special Forces training.

jects developed techniques applied on a national scale a few years later.

Following Kennedy's 1961 order to organize a clandestine war in North Vietnam, the CIA expanded ARVN's 1st Observation Group from 340 to 805 members. The group was augmented by a special Vietnamese Air Force C-47 Air Transport Squadron that dropped agents by parachute. After October 1961, when the group began operations in Laos, Kennedy approved US participation 'as necessary.' Green Berets and Navy SEALs trained the Vietnamese in special tactics and sea infiltration.

CIA agent drops brought few dividends, however. North Vietnamese captured many teams soon after infiltration and caught others trying to exfiltrate after aborted missions. Captured agents were thoroughly interrogated, and then served as useful propaganda weapons. After Switchback, the Military Assistance Command, Vietnam (MACV) inherited five 'in place' teams in North Vietnam (assumed to be under Communist control) and the CIA's special operations mission. To work with the Vietnamese LLDB 'Special Branch' (later the Special Exploitation Service or SES) MACV organized the 'Studies and Observation Group' (SOG) in January 1964. Ostensibly formed to glean lessons from the US military advisory experience, SOG actually conducted highly classified special operations throughout Southeast Asia. The Special Assistant for Counterinsurgency and Special Activities (SACSA) to the JCS in Washington exercised tight control over SOG operations; knowledge of SOG operations remains on a 'need-to-know' basis even today. Total SOG personnel included about 2000 Americans and over 8000 indigenous troops.

SOG was divided into individual 'study groups' assigned to specific operational plans. A 'Psychological Studies Group' ran black psywar activities (Oplan/ops 33) such as false Communist radio broadcasts from powerful radion transmitters at Hue and Tay Ninh. An 'Air Studies Group' specialized in intelligence and agent insertions into 'denied areas' (ops 32) and maintained its own air force – 90th Special Operations Wing – composed of USAF UH-1F 'Green Hornet' helicopters, a covert C-123 'blackbird' squadron piloted by Nationalist Chinese, a C-130 squadron and the 219th Vietnamese AF H-34 helicopter squadron. A 'Maritime Studies Group' engaged in commando raids against the North Vietnamese coast (Oplan 34A) and in the Mekong Delta (ops 31) with US Navy SEALs, Vietnamese Underwater Demolition Teams (UDTs) and fast patrol boats. Oplan 34A operations in August 1964 are credited with triggering the famous Gulf of Tonkin incidents that resulted in greater American military involvement in Southeast Asia.

SOG's 'Ground Studies Group' (Oplan 35) performed the largest missions: cross border operations, monitoring locations of Allied

The Special Forces assisted in village bridge-building.

IRREGULAR FORCES

POWs and downed airmen for escape and evasion (E&E) raids and a variety of sensitive 'black' missions: kidnapping, assassination, document retrieval, even insertion of rigged ammunition rounds into enemy supply dumps (known as Project Eldest Son). All SOG personnel were volunteers. Colonel 'Bull' Simons, who ran SOG's Ground Studies Group, typified the special breed of unconventional soldier that SOG attracted: World War II Ranger and jungle specialist, Green Beret and twice commander of the Laotian White Star project.

SOG's earliest cross-border operations, code-named Leaping Lena, began in May 1964 when all-Vietnamese teams parachuted into Laos to reconnoiter the Ho Chi Minh Trail. Although not highly successful – Doan 559 troops proved adept at mopping up the 6-man teams – Leaping Lena demonstrated the potential of long-range reconnaissance in denied areas. In September 1965, SOG began Shining Brass missions: American-led 12-man recon teams (RT) targeting NVA installations in Laos for aerial attack. Later Shining Brass operations included insertions of company-size SLAM (Search-Location-Annihilation-Missions) reaction forces to exploit targets located by smaller recon teams.

Until the arrival of regular US combat forces in 1966, SOG operations inside Laos were conditioned by policy considerations stemming from the 'neutralization' of Laos at the 1962 Geneva Conference. Even RT-directed air strikes required permission of the US Ambassador in Vientiane, Laos. Many unconventional soldiers – aware of flagrant Communist violations – chafed under these restrictions. Briefly in 1961, Bull Simons believed the United States might have checked large-scale Communist operations in the Bolovens Plateau, the southern extension of the Ho Chi Minh Trail. In a scant six months, Simon's project 404 (60 Special Forces and over 600 Kha tribesmen) had virtually cleared the Bolovens of Pathet Lao. Given time, Simons hoped to organize 10,000 Kha guerrillas to clear the border areas before Doan 559 tightened its grip on the Laotian panhandle. But after the phony 1962 neutralization, all US military advisors were pulled out under ICC supervision and not allowed to return. The Kha program quickly died.

An estimated 10,000 North Vietnamese in Laos did not leave. After Geneva, Hanoi ordered Doan 559 to develop a mechanized transport capacity and new trails routes on an 'urgent' basis. Older routes were deemed too vulnerable to interdiction by unconventional SOG and White Star units. By 1970, Doan 559 grew from a few hundred to between 20-30,000 personnel, along with an awesome commitment of vehicles and weapons devoted to trail defense and expansion. Doan 559's mission remained simple: keep open an unimpeded route to funnel men and material into South Vietnam. Soon after the Laotian 'neutralization,' battalions and regiments of NVA – no longer regroupees – were swelling the Ho Chi Minh Trail by the thousands.

Americanization of the Vietnam War in 1965 overshadowed what had been largely an unknown unconventional conflict. While US Special Forces technically remained 'advisors' to the South Vietnamese, some Green Berets feared their irregular capabilities might be misused, or worse, ignored altogether by conventional minded MACV brass in Saigon. Eventually, however, the irregulars proved invaluable in support of US regulars and MACV's special intelligence needs.

The 5th Special Forces Group, Airborne (5th SFG) activated its headquarters at Nha Trang in October 1964. The 5th SFG consisted of five 20-man C-Teams each with three B-Teams. In turn, each B-Team controlled four 12-man A-Teams. Although is authorized strength peaked in 1969 at 3740 members of the Green Berets, 5th SFG controlled some 40,000 irregulars during the war, and worked in tandem with US and ARVN regulars and paramilitary Regional and Popular Forces (RF/PF), South Vietnamese militia nicknamed 'Ruff-Puffs.' Although conventionalization of the CIDG – a phased takeover of CIDG that transformed many irregulars into LLDB/Ranger units – began in 1964, the process moved slowly; the CIDG remained an irregular force – only its mission changed. The old hamlet militias were dropped and the smaller strike forces enlarged. CIDG training and orgnization stressed border surveillance and offensive operations. As aggressive 'hunters' of the VC/NVA, the CIDG became the core element of evolving 5th SFG mobile strike forces whose mission included exploitation of small unit contacts, reconnaissance-in-force, and extraction of compromised recon teams.

A small, airmobile strike force dubbed 'Eagle Flight' was formed in October 1964 to serve as a ready-reaction, ambush and raiding

US Infantry take cover behind an earthen dike during the fighting in Cholon.

force, supporting both CIDG and regular operations under direct 5th SFG Command. Five Americans and 36 highly trained *montagnards*, with its own helicopter airlift and UH-1 gunships, made up an Eagle Flight. Strike Forces continued to evolve with the 'Apache Force' and 'Eagle Scouts,' Special Force/CIDG units that also oriented newly arrived US combat battalions in VC/NVA small unit tactics.

In June 1965, MACV authorized formation of Mobile Strike Force Commands (MSFC) in each of the four Corps Tactical Zones (CTZ) and at 5th SDFG's Nha Trang headquarters. These five Mike forces combined all strike force missions with brigade-sized units under 5th SFG command. A Mike force consisted of a permanent A-Team, several 552-man CIDG battalions, a 135-man recon company and an elite airborne-qualified 227-man HQ/service company staffed by either Nungs or ethnic Cambodians who, like the Nungs, were prized soldiers. The Nha Trang 5th MSFC was the largest (2570 personnel by 1968) and saw action in all CTZs; the 4th MSFC in the Mekong Delta also operated in floating bases, complete with helicopters and swift airboats. All Mike forces were rapidly airmobile.

Another 5th SFG priority was development of long-range reconnaissance patrol (LRRP) capabilities to report on enemy troop movements in Communist controlled territory. Project Delta (Detachment B-52) began in May 1964 as SOG's Project Leaping Lena to train CIDG and Vietnamese LLDB in LRRP tactics. When 5th SFG inherited the LRRP mission in May 1965, Project Leaping Lena became Delta, specializing in LRRP intelligence collection, placement of airstrikes or artillery on NVA/VC bases or conducting various classified 'special ops.' Delta consisted of 450 men in 12 recon teams, six (later 12) Roadrunner teams, a Nung security company and the 91st ARVN Ranger Battalion as a fulltime reaction force. Roadrunners were indigenous soldiers dressed as NVA/VC who mingled with Communist troops, either reporting their positions or leading them into Delta ambushes. Delta also worked with regular combat units, as in the October 1965 relief of Plei Me CIDG camp under siege by two regular NVA regiments.

Impressed at Delta's performance, General Westmoreland authorized two more special recon projects (Sigma and Omega) in 1966 and gave Delta the additional mission of training regular US infantry units in LRRP tactics. Omega (Detachment B-50) and

IRREGULAR FORCES

The US military advisors to the Vietnamese Coastal group were armed with M-16s.

A captured 75mm recoilless rifle is examined by Marines.

Sigma (Detachment B-56) were smaller (about 900 CIDG/ARVN and 125 US) than Delta. The special recon projects advanced the strike force concept toward independent long-range guerrilla task forces called Mobile Guerrilla Forces (MGF). MGFs consisted of a Special Forces A Detachment, a 150-man mobile guerrilla company and a 34-man combat recon platoon. Like the old GCMAs, mobile guerrillas operated in remote Communist areas for an extended period, conducting surveillance, reconnaissance, and interdiction. MGF missions, known as Blackjack operations, commenced in October 1966 with Blackjack 21 – a 30-day patrol deep into Kontum Province. The airborne-qualified special recon projects and MGFs possessed the same tenacity, mobility and deceptive tactics that made the Vietcong so effective. They always strove to hit first, hit hard and melt back into the jungle. With normal resupply impossible in enemy territory, supplies were airdropped in dummy 500-lb napalm canisters, during actual airstrikes by USAF Air Commandos, so as not to reveal recon team positions. In mid-1967 MGF and Mike force, with their respective missions, were integrated into Mobile Strike Forces (MSFs).

Concurrent with mobile guerrilla developments, SOG expanded its cross-border operations. In 1965, SOG initiated Prairie Fire in Laos and, in 1966, Daniel Boone operations in Cambodia. SOG also ran intelligence operations called Kit Cat deep in North Vietnam. Until 1966 SOG operations

IRREGULAR FORCES

were launched from four forward operating bases (FOBs) located at Phu Bai, Kontum, Khesanh and Danang. In 1966 Colonel John K Singlaub reorganized SOG into three operations, each responsible for a specific area: Command and Control Central (CCC) covered North Vietnam/Laos; Command and Control North (CCN), the triborder region of South Vietnam/Laos/Cambodia; and Command and Control South (CCS) Cambodia. After 1967 all Special Forces posted to SOG for clandestine missions were given a 5th SFG cover designation 'Special Operations, Augmented, 5th SFG.'

Like the old GCMAs, SOG, mobile guerrillas and special recon projects brought the war directly to the Communists. Although their main task was to collect intelligence for MACV and conventional combat forces, just as important was their psychological impact on the enemy. They kept the Communist soldier off-balance, doubtful of the 'safe' trail just ahead, wary that the next mortar round might be rigged to explode in his face, or that the 'comrade' sharing his rice at a rest station could be a CIDG roadrunner. Thus the objective was to deny the enemy the sense of security in the bush that he had previously enjoyed.

Despite the success of mobile guerrilla force and SOGs unconventional operations, the irregular warfare concept was not applied on a large scale by US conventional units. Even ARVN – composed of Vietnamese who should have felt more comfortable in the field than US irregulars – remained very much a reflection of its conventional US training and equipment.

Some US regular elite troops found that combat in Vietnam demanded special capabilities in the field. An excellent example of an elite force adapting to local conditions were the US Marine Corps recon units that spearheaded the Marines' deep reconnaissance efforts. Recon Marines served as raiders, conducted helicopter insertions in enemy areas and saw combat near the Lao border in I Corps with Vietnamese LLDB and SF/CIDG units. At the MACV Recondo (Reconnaissance and Commando) School in Nha Trang, Delta personnel instructed US and ARVN Rangers, CIDG and Vietnamese Special Forces in LRRP tactics to give regular and irregular units a build-in long-range recon capability. Special LRRP Ranger units became integral to US regular combat battalions. Besides the Ranger 'Lurps' platoons,

Vietnamese 'Kit Carson Scouts' worked closely with US combat forces. Kit Carson Scouts, ex-Communist soldiers who defected through the Chieu Hoi ('Open Arms') campaign, were expert at directing US regulars past unseen Communist ambushes and booby traps.

US Navy SEALs also operated in a variety of unconventional warfare roles. The first SEAL platoons arriving in-country in 1966 staked out the marshy Mekong Delta as their natural habitat. SEALs set up surveillance posts and mounted 3-man hunter-killer raids in Vietcong operating areas. Supported by US Navy Task Force 116 – the US successor to the *dinnasaut* – SEALs proved instrumental in wrestling control over much of the Mekong Delta from the Vietcong. Like the Vietcong, the 'green-faced frogmen' were nocturnal creatures who could also operate from swift airboats and Seawolf helicopters. SEALs performed many missions for a variety of sponsors: TF-116, SOG, Phoenix and in combined operations with SF/CIDG units.

TF-116's riverine operations, codenamed Game Warden, began in 1965 with a motley collection of 24 old French-converted LCM monitors. In time, Game Warden's 'brown water navy' contained over 750 vessels, including 450 8-ton fiberglass river patrol boats (PBRs), armored troop carriers (ATCs) and fast air-cushioned vehicles (PACVs). Four heavily armed River Assault Squadrons patrolled the Mekong with a US 9th Infantry Division brigade, a composite amphibious force of tremendous firepower and mobility when projected deep into the Vietcong's Mekong sanctuaries.

One of the least known special units was the Air Force Aerospace Rescue and Recovery Service (ARRS), pararescue specialists trained as medics, paratroopers, frogmen and Rangers, ready for any contingency involving downed US flyers. The first ARRS team arrived in Vietnam in April 1962 and as the air war picked up after 1965, ARRS flew in specially equipped HH-3E Jolly Green Giant helicopters and HU-16 Amphibious aircraft. The 3rd ARRS Group was activated in 1966 with responsibility for all of Southeast Asia, although all services continued to mount their own local rescue operations. ARRS teams rescued 3883 pilots and crews between 1962-73, while losing 71 members and 45 aircraft.

Besides highly classified 'special projects,' SOG and MGFs also performed dangerous rescue and recovery operations. One of the

A captured Vietcong is brought back by a member of a Navy SEAL team.

IRREGULAR FORCES

Colonel 'Bull' Simons explains the attack on Son Tay POW camp.

most daring recovery operations occurred in December 1966, when 5th SFG Captain James 'Bo' Gritz led his 1st Mobile Guerrilla Force – 12 Americans and 250 Cambodian mercenaries – to recover the 'black box' of a crashed U-2 spyplane in Cambodia. President Johnson personally ordered the recovery of the supersecret U-2 black box to prevent secret codes from falling into Soviet hands. After four days of methodically combing dense jungle, Gritz's team found the wrecked aircraft, but the box was missing. Following sandal tracks away from the crash site, Gritz and his Cambodians located, then shot their way into a nearby NVA base camp. After recovering the black box, the guerrillas retreated safely into the jungle. Gritz's success led SOG to initiate regular Daniel Boone cross-border operations into Cambodia.

Another famous rescue mission was the 21 November 1970 raid on the Son Tay POW camp inside North Vietnam. Colonel Bull Simons and a select Special Forces team executed a near-perfect helicopter assault on Son Tay, only to find the POW camp empty –

a result of faulty intelligence. But the raid demonstrated that Special Forces could operate even deep inside North Vietnam. A former SOG commander, Colonel Donald Blackburn, contends that the US Special Forces should have conducted more such raids on North Vietnamese dams, power plants and bridges – the type of active sabotage denied US commandos after 1954.

The same month as the Son Tay action, a 15-man SEAL team successfully raided a Vietcong camp in the Mekong Delta and freed some POWs. Such rescues were perhaps the most difficult and hazardous special operation in Vietnam. Communist guards had strict orders to shoot their charges in the event of a rescue attempt and the Vietcong constantly moved US POWs, making prisoner location almost impossible. Some 45 recorded Special Forces rescue attempts (1966-70) yielded only a single rescued prisoner, who later died from wounds inflicted by a guard. Despite the danger, attempts were made when possible. In 1983, many years after his successful Cambodian operation, Bo Gritz returned to probe

Southeast Asian jungles as a civilian on an unauthorized private search for yet-unaccounted for US POWs reported to be living and still held in Communist Indochina.

Throughout the Vietnam War, US combat commanders grappled unsuccessfully with pacification, the village-level conflict known as 'the other war.' The village provided the Vietcong guerrilla concealment, food, clothing and intelligence, making the separation of guerrilla from villager extremely hard for US combat units. Vietcong terror also continued to play a part in village life. The assassination of over 8000 government officials and other community leaders between 1964-67 had succeeded in sending a well-defined political message to the people that Saigon could not adequately protect them. For years Saigon's answer was a series of ill-designed, and poorly executed pacification programs, while perhaps the most successful model of village defense, the early CIDG Village Defender program, was ignored outside the Highlands. In August 1965, US Marines brought an imaginative approach to pacification with experimental Combined Action Platoons (CAP). Based partially on CIDG concepts, CPAs consisted of a 14-man US Marine rifle squad, a Navy medical corpsman and a 38-man Popular Force platoon and were responsible for the security of a specific village. While CAP villages averaged much higher security than non-CAP villages, MACV believed the CAP program drained precious manpower from the task of destroying enemy main force units. The CAP program remained small.

The first national pacification effort begun in May 1967, the Civil Operations and Revolutionary Development Support (CORDS), signalled a new emphasis on pacification. CORDS oversaw several paramilitary programs designed to attack the Vietcong infrastructure (VCI). At the CIA's old 'Shrimp & Cinnamon' camp in Vung Tao, a Revolutionary Development (RD) Center produced 59-man RD teams assigned to instill a sense of security and government interest in the population, while Vietnamese Information Service (VIS) and Son Truong cadres (armed propaganda teams) performed a similar RD ideological function.

After the 1968 Tet offensive decimated and exposed the Vietcong infrastructure, Saigon moved quickly with an Accelerated Pacification Program to fill the vacuum. Improved and re-equipped Regional and Popular Forces contributed to increased village security. Combined 'Ruff-Puff' and US operations led to a greater appreciation for the 'Ruff-Puff' by the Americans. By 1970, these paramilitary forces constituted 51 percent of Saigon's military strength.

A 120,000-man National Police Field Force and paramilitary Provincial Reconnaissance Units (PRU) led a much publicized campaign known as the *Phuong Hoang* (Phoenix) Project, a CIA-directed effort to improve intelligence collection started in 1967. The stated Phoenix objective was the 'neutralization' of the VCI, with 'neutralize' defined as those Vietcong cadres captured, rallied (under *Chieu Hoi*) or killed.

In its relatively short bureaucratic existence (1968-71), Phoenix acquired an international reputation as a CIA assassination program, perhaps due to the central role played by CORDS chief William Colby, a career CIA official. However, the numbers actually killed never exceeded 40 percent of the total 'neutralized'; many died in the course of normal military or police actions. Most 'neutralized' cadres were low ranking Vietcong who were captured, interrogated, then released. But some high-ranking Vietcong cadres clearly were targeted for assassination. Average Americans were shocked at press reports on Phoenix, and, unfamiliar with the underlying political nature of systematic Vietcong terrorism, were not used to having their government officially involved in activities of dubious morality.

National Police and PRU units served as the enforcement arm of Phoenix, although the PRUs gained the most notoriety. The CIA-financed PRUs were airborne-qualified irregulars trained and supervised by 50 Green Berets at the PRU center in My Tho. Excelling in unconventional tactics, PRUs often worked closely with US Navy SEALs in Mekong Delta Communist strongholds. Along with their reputation for aggressiveness grew rumors that many PRU troops were recruited out of South Vietnamese jails. Their backgrounds aside, PRUs were considered man-for-man the most effective anti-VCI unit in South Vietnam.

'Vietnamization' and increased emphasis on pacification after the 1968 Tet offensive coincided with the drawdown of US combat forces and shifted the strategic focus of the war. Subsequent major Communist offensives in 1972 and 1975 became essentially conventional affairs, with increased use of

IRREGULAR FORCES

Tanks maneuver across the rice fields.

heavy artillery and tanks by both ARVN and the NVA.

Because of their familiarity with local Communist supply bases, Omega and Sigma did see action during the 1970 Cambodian and 1971 Laotian incursions. A few former special recon and SOG types returned during the 1972 NVA Easter invasion to call in airstrikes in enemy territory. But it was a last hurrah. Five weeks after the Son Tay raid, the Special Forces ended its role in the CIDG program; CIDG units became either ARVN Ranger or LLDB regulars, as originally planned in 1964. On 1 March 1971, the 5th Special Forces Group redeployed back to Fort Bragg, North Carolina.

A large US military presence in Southeast Asia had guaranteed that Air America could operate in relative obscurity. With little fanfare throughout the war, the CIA propriety airline fought in the frontlines of unconventional war. In its glory days Air America supported numerous clandestine guerrilla armies, acting as both an aerial guerrilla force and the CIA's commuter airline of the Far East, and flying Meo troops in lightning advances deep into Pathet Lao territory.

As the war in Vietnam expanded, selected AA pilots with special clearances flew, 'sanitized' aircraft – laundered nonattributable airplanes – on top secret 'black' projects along the Ho Chi Minh Trail from numerous secret bases in Vietnam, Laos and Thailand.

Other AA pilots serviced 'McNamara's Fence,' a $3 billion sophisticated electronic device designed to locate NVA infiltrators. Unfortunatley it proved to be a failure. AA flew in every type of aircraft from 727 jets to small Cessnas and junk aircraft, transporting everything from combat troops (alive, wounded or dead) to baby chicks, dropping rice to refugees and specially trained Nung trailwatchers into denied areas. AA contracted both with the Drug Enforcement Agency (to track international drug smugglers) and with the Meo (to haul its annual and valuable opium crop).

As US forces pulled out, Air America picked up the slack, straining to maintain the status quo. It was not easy. Strong and confident NVA and Pathet Laos forces took the offensive in the early 1970s, driving the Meo out of their traditional mountain homelands. As the once-strong Meo retreated, Air America found itself in the position of hauling (and feeding) tens of thousands of refugees. Domestically, there were difficulties as the CIA fell under intense Congressional scrutiny of its world-wide paramilitary activities and public pressure to divest itself of Air America.

South Vietnam's rapid collapse in 1975 – which saw Air America involved again, as in 1954, in a mass evacuation – also signified the end of the clandestine war that began in Vietnam thirty years earlier.

An Air America helicopter lands on an amphibious command ship.

BIOGRAPHIES

BIOGRAPHIES

CREIGHTON W ABRAMS, 1914-74

General Creighton Abrams was made a four-star general at the beginning of the Vietnam War, bringing to his rank the experience gained as a commander in World War II and the Korean conflict. Named by President Johnson as a deputy commander in Vietnam in 1967, Abrams was responsible for the rural pacification program that relocated over two million people to 'safe military areas.'

With the departure of General William Westmoreland in 1968, Abrams was named commander of the half-million US soldiers in South Vietnam. He faced a formidable task, given that President Johnson had decided to de-escalate the conflict, thereby in effect mandating a no-win military policy and turning US hopes to negotiation.

Abrams continued as commander in the next administration. President Nixon wound down US military commitments under the 'Vietnamization' program, and the President and Henry Kissinger took direct responsibility for running the war. Abrams did his best to function despite ever-tighter restrictions and withdrawals of US troops. He changed his tactics from 'search-and-destroy' missions, depending increasingly on bombing and artillery attacks, supplemented by small night patrols.

In 1970-71 Abrams was a major advocate of the US incursions into Cambodia and Laos, which were intended to buy time for the Vietnamization process. Becoming Army Chief of Staff in 1972, it was Abrams' duty to return to the United States to go before the Senate Armed Services Committee to defend his and the army's actions in those secret invasions. He managed to squelch the investigations as far as the army's responsibility went. In the waning months of the Thieu government, Abrams supervised massive military aid to the doomed government. Abrams died in 1974, remembered as one of the few generals in history given the assignment of not winning a war.

GEORGE BALL, 1909-

A liberal lawyer and European trade-policy specialist who had been in and out of government service since the New Deal, George Ball was a seasoned bureaucrat when he entered the Kennedy administration. Named under-secretary of state in 1961, he became a strong critic of the Diem regime and was one of those favoring a coup during the discussions before Diem's fall. President Johnson's deepening commitment to war in 1964-65 produced a war of memoranda within his administration; but in that hawkish atmosphere, Ball's cautions and protests were hardly tolerated. Nonetheless, Johnson kept Ball around as a devil's advocate, knowing he would not publicly step out of line.

Finally giving up the fight, Ball returned to private law practice in 1966. Two years later he was one of the council of 'wise men' Defense Secretary Clark Clifford convened to advocate de-escalation of the war to the President. At last, Ball's ideas prevailed. As a political commentator during the next administration, he became a prominent critic of Nixon's Vietnam policy and of Kissinger's style of diplomacy. In later years Ball was to state his opinion with stark simplicity: the Vietnam war, he said, was 'probably the greatest single error made by America in its history.'

BUI TIN, 1924-

Although never high in the Communist Hierarchy nor well known to the general public, Bui Tin was typical of the many Vietnamese who had devoted their adult lives to bringing about an independent and unified Vietnam, and he ended up playing one of the most dramatic of all roles in attaining this goal. Born to aristocratic Vietnamese family in Hué, Bui Tin grew up with a veneer of French culture, but as a young man he joined the Vietminh in 1945 and fought in the major campaigns against the French, including that in the Red River Valley and the final battle for Dienbienphu. After partition, Bui Tin remained in the North where he came to be included in the inner circle of the senior Communists in Hanoi. In 1963, he was selected to join a team of about a dozen military and civilian specialists assigned to South Vietnam, where they were to assess the situation and needs of the Vietcong. Even before he returned, Hanoi's leaders had decided to throw their full support to the Vietcong: the Ho Chi Minh Trail was to be enlarged for the increased traffic, ammunition, weapons and food were to be sent in large quantities, and North Vietnamese Army troops were poised to move into the South. (Bui Tin would be among those who admitted after the war that the North Vietnamese had taken these steps well before the United States committed its troops in any number.)

During the next decade, he rose to the rank

of colonel in the North Vietnamese Army and assumed the deputy editorship of its official newspaper, *Quan Doi Nhan Dan*, and it was this joint status that provided Bui Tin with his rendezvous with history. As a leading journalist, he was accompanying the Communist forces in their final campaign against Saigon in 1975 and he found himself attached to one of the leading armored units that burst into Saigon early in the morning of 30 April. As it chanced, Bui Tin as a colonel turned out to be the ranking Communist, so it was his duty to accept the surrender of the South Vietnamese government. As a journalist, Bui Tin was also in the position of being able to report his own eloquent handling of the situation.

McGEORGE BUNDY, 1919-

McGeorge Bundy was one of the very 'best and brightest' of the Eastern intellectuals whom President Kennedy gathered around him in the early days of his administration. As national security adviser to both Kennedy and Johnson, Bundy was also one of those most responsible for the United States' slide into war in Vietnam. He came from an old New England family with a record of public service (his brother William was also an adviser to Kennedy and Johnson) and had been a professor and dean at Harvard University before Kennedy took him into his inner circle.

Bundy brought to Washington an analytical mind and a gift for expediting matters, but also a philosophy of keeping options open as long as possible. The latter aptitude did not stand the government in good stead in regard to the coup that overthrew Diem.

Staying on into the Johnson administration, Bundy became convinced that the United States must make a strong stand against Communism; he therefore was one of the strongest proponents of increased US involvement in Vietnam. As part of the 'bureaucratic layer cake' that Johnson created within his administration to analyze data and recommend policy, Bundy was increasingly involved in the war effort. Publicly, Bundy was an eloquent advocate of the war policy he helped Johnson create and pursue, and frequently represented the President on troubleshooting and factfinding missions around the world.

In 1965 Bundy resigned, ostensibly over disagreements with Johnson's personal style. Whether or not he then had doubts about the war, by 1967 he was privately urging the President to de-escalate the conflict. The next year Bundy publicly called for a winding down of the war, and was one of the council of 'wise men' convened by Clark Clifford to promote that policy. In 1973 Bundy added a curious footnote to his involvement in the war when he appeared as a witness for the defense in the *Pentagon Papers* trial of Daniel Ellsberg.

WILLIAM P BUNDY, 1917-

Along with his brother McGeorge, William Bundy was part of President Kennedy's inner circle of advisers and among those who urged US intervention in Vietnam; and along with his brother he stayed on in the Johnson era to broaden that intervention into war. When Bundy joined President Eisenhower's Commission on National Goals in 1960 he came from 10 years' experience in the CIA. The next year Kennedy named him as an assistant defense secretary in charge of international security affairs.

Always the quiet bureaucrat, Bundy nonetheless was to have a profound impact on the course of the war. Early on he advised 'hard-hitting' support for the Diem government, and in the last months of the Kennedy administration he first suggested the idea that became the Tonkin Gulf Resolution. Later, Bundy wss the chief author of the prototype of that resolution; drafted some months *before* the Tonkin incident, the document seemed to mandate limited presidential power to respond but in fact gave Johnson extraordinary powers to wage war without the approval of Congress.

One of the leading hawks of Johnson's staff, Bundy quickly followed up the Senate approval of the Tonkin Resolution by advising against negotiations and proposing instead a series of escalating military responses, including massive bombing and mining the harbor of Haiphong. Many of his suggestions eventually became policy. During the war the Bundy brothers were part of the team in Washington that chose bombing targets in Vietnam (the President made the final decisions).

Though dubious about committing extensive US ground forces, Bundy supported Johnson's decisions in that direction, meanwhile promoting the use of strategic bombing. By 1967 Bundy was opposing further escalation and advising against mining Haiphong; nonetheless, he advised 'sticking it out.' He resigned from government service in 1969, later becoming editor of *Foreign Affairs*.

BIOGRAPHIES

ELLSWORTH BUNKER, 1894-1984

Named by President Johnson as ambassador to South Vietnam in April 1967, Ellsworth Bunker brought to the post a reputation as 'America's most accomplished diplomat.' In a government career going back to 1951, he had been ambassador to several countries and a successful mediator in the Dominican Republic. But in Vietnam the stately and dignified Bunker was to lose his image as a disinterested negotiator. After his appointment to Vietnam, Bunker vigorously countered Defense Secretary McNamara's criticisms of Johnson's war policy, and also opposed US bombing halts in late 1967. After the disastrous Communist Tet offensive of January 1968, Bunker proclaimed an US victory even though Vietcong commandos had penetrated his own embassy compound. Later that year he supported US incursions into Laos and Cambodia.

With the advent of the Nixon Administration, Bunker stayed in his ambassadorial post, urging active prosecution of the war and applauding the 1970 invasion of Cambodia. In 1971 he played a backstage role in the South Vietnamese elections, including possibly trying to bribe Duong Van Minh to make a show of opposing Thieu. After advising at the Paris peace talks, Bunker resigned as ambassador in 1973. He later headed the US team that secured the Panama treaty of 1978.

WILLIAM LAWS CALLEY, JR, 1943-

There was no doubt that on 16 March 1968 a massacre of civilians – including women and children – took place at the hamlet of My Lai, in the South Vietnamese district of Son My. It was proved in court that Lieutenant William Calley was involved and in large part responsible for the deaths of those 102 apparently unarmed civilians. It is also true that, though several others were tried, Calley was the only military man convicted of murder in the incident.

A graduate of Officers Candidate School, Calley was assigned in Vietnam to the command of Captain Ernest L Medina, who ordered the operation on the suspected Vietcong stronghold of My Lai. In his court-martial Calley testified that Medina had ordered him to kill everyone in the village. In any case, that is what Calley did, herding the civilians into a ditch and mowing them down with a machine gun.

Like everything else in the war, the massacre was photographed and recorded, and in 1969, when an US veteran reported the slaughter, there was plenty of evidence for the ensuing courts-martial. Calley was found guilty in March of that year and sentenced to life imprisonment.

After several appeals Calley was released in 1974 and given a dishonorable discharge. He entered the insurance business. Commenting on the Calley case, General Westmoreland perhaps came close to the truth when he said: 'Had it not been for educational draft deferments . . . Calley probably would never have been an officer. The Army had to lower its standards.'

CLARK CLIFFORD, 1906-

In appointing Clark Clifford as secretary of defense in January 1968, President Johnson was welcoming an old adviser, an outspoken supporter of his policy in Vietnam and a close personal friend. It was a measure of the inescapably rising tide of opposition to the war that even Johnson, the consummate politician, had read his man wrongly: Clifford was then already turning against the war, and in his first weeks of office would engineer a virtual conspiracy from within the government to begin the process of extracting the United States from what had become a hopeless cause.

A distinguished Washington lawyer, Clifford had been a strong anti-Communist from his days as an adviser to President Harry S Truman. In and out of government posts since that era, he became one of the closest advisers to his old friend Lyndon Johnson. However, a fact-finding trip to Southeast Asia in 1967 led Clifford to question US policy. His confirmation as secretary of defense came directly after one of the most critical events of the war – the Communist Tet offensive of early 1968. Despite official US claims of victory, Clifford had seen that the Communists could strike anywhere in Vietnam at will, and no real progress had been or could be made.

Upon entering the cabinet, Clifford first looked for reassurances from military men and government supporters of the war. Finding none, he moved quickly to try to impress on President Johnson the necessity of winding it down. There was a sudden chill in the friendship between the two men, but the President nonetheless listened. Clifford quietly collected a group of supporters for his position and persuaded others – including hawks Dean Rusk and Walt Rostow – to come over to his side. This council of 'wise men' that Clifford convened to make recommendations on war policy had a sudden and dramatic effect: in his speech of 31 March the President proposed peace initiatives and announced he would not run for re-election. Retiring from office in early 1969, Clifford publicly called for unilateral US withdrawal from Vietnam. Years later he observed: 'Countries, like human beings, make mistakes. We made an honest mistake. We felt that we were doing what was necessary. It proved to be unsound.'

LUCIEN CONEIN, 1919-

Part of the tangled web of overt and covert American operatives in Vietnam during the early 1960s was CIA agent and 'dirty tricks' expert Lucien Conein, who became the primary liaison between ambassador Henry Cabot Lodge and the generals plotting to overthrow Diem. The French-born Conein was an experienced 'spook' with a thirst for high adventure when he arrived in the country in 1962, on his third assignment in Indochina. As ordered, he mounted a series of counter-insurgency and sabotage operations.

In June 1962 Conein's old friend Tran Van Don began hinting about a coup against Diem. Conein relayed this information through channels and, after Diem and Nhu's suppression of the Buddhists in August, Ambassador Lodge quickly decided to support the coup and directed Conein to encourage the plotting generals. In a talk with General Minh, Conein was given the information that Lodge was waiting for: all the United States had to do was 'not thwart' the coup. But though Conein was not actually to shoot anybody, his function in the coup was far from passive.

He began meeting regularly with Don in a Saigon dentist's office, giving encouragement and advice. Don responded with more and more details of the coup. All was reported back to Lodge. When anti-coup US General Paul Harkins got word to Don, Conein reassured the plotters of higher-level support. In November, during the coup itself, Conein notified his CIA superiors of its onset and shepherded around a briefcase containing $40,000, in case the conspirators needed cash. Directly after the coup Lodge sent Conein to prod Minh to come up with a better alibi for the murders of Diem and Nhu.

Having played his role in a professional manner, Conein returned to normal intelligence work. A month after the coup he was informed that General Khanh planned a second coup; his report on those plans was ignored. Later Conein was considered for a place on the 'plumbers' team that eventually triggered the Watergate affair. Conein was passed over for that operation, but later commented he would have done a better job.

BAO DAI, 1913-

The pathetic last emperor of Vietnam, Bao Dai, unquestionably desired true independence for his beleaguered country, but he lacked the courage and strength of character to resist the several powers who used him as a pawn throughout his reluctant public career. Born into the old ruling family in 1913, he was educated in France and in 1932 was installed by the French as puppet emperor. The French quickly squelched his efforts at reform (which included naming Ngo Dinh Diem as a minister); lonely and powerless, Bao Dai then retreated to the self-indulgent way of life that would occupy most of his time thereafter.

When the Japanese took over Vietnam during World War II, Bao Dai consented to govern under their aegis; he was fearful of retribution if he did not comply, and the Japanese at least were not the French. After the war, finding Ho Chi Minh's Vietminh seeming to hold the cards, Bao Dai abdicated with manifest relief in favor of Ho's Democratic Republic of Vietnam. For a time he served as 'supreme adviser' to the new government, then returned in 1946 to his playboy life in Hong Kong and the French Riviera.

But the French had no intention of giving up their hold on Vietnam or on Bao Dai. They began courting him in 1947, promising greater independence for the country if he would become head of state. Trapped and outsmarted by the French, Bao Dai was practically dragged into office. Most Western nations, for anti-communist reasons, recognized the corrupt Bao Dai government and the United States began secretly paying him several million dollars a year.

After the French defeat at Dienbienphu in 1954, Bao Dai appointed as his prime minister Ngo Dinh Diem, whom he perceived as the man finally to supplant the French. It was his last major move as head of state. After the Geneva settlement created a separate South Vietnam, Diem ousted Bao Dai in a flagrantly rigged election in 1955. Having served for the last time as a pawn in someone else's game, Bao Dai retired to France.

BIOGRAPHIES

The Emperor Bao Dai

JEREMIAH DENTON, JR, 1924-
One of the first US prisoners to be released by North Vietnam after the 1973 peace agreement, Commander Jeremiah Denton captured the national interest on his return.

A self-described 'average product of Middle America and its values,' the Alabama-born Denton became a crack naval pilot in the 1950s, going to Vietnam as an attack squadron commander in June 1965. One month later his jet was shot down during a raid 75 miles south of Hanoi. Denton bailed out and fell into enemy hands. For the next seven years he was a prisoner of war.

During that time, in a series of North Vietnamese prisons, Denton endured confinement in coffin-sized cells, beatings, starvation and over four years of solitary confinement. Throughout, he remained actively uncooperative with his captors and ordered his fellow prisoners to do likewise. The US POWs maintained a chain of command and developed elaborate communications systems based on Morse code. During a televised interview which was shown in the West, Denton blinked the word 'torture' in Morse code with his eyelids. The message was received, Denton remained similarly clever and recalcitrant for the rest of his confinement.

A national hero after his return, Denton received the Navy Cross in 1974 and was able to parlay his fame and conservative politics into becoming the first Republican Senator from Alabama since Reconstruction.

NGO DINH DIEM, 1901-63

Seldom are a people on the verge of creating a nation-state offered a clear-cut choice between two leaders who are mirror-images of one another; this was arguably the case with the Vietnamese as confronted by Ho Chi Minh and Ngo Dinh Diem. In the end, Diem lost – on all counts, including his own life – but he was no less dedicated than Ho in his search for a Vietnam free of foreign influences.

Ngo Dinh Diem came from a family that had converted to Christianity in the seventeenth century and had long served as mandarins to the imperial court. Although Diem's father had resigned his position to protest French actions, Diem attended a French Catholic school and once considered becoming a Catholic priest (as did his brother Thuc, later Archbishop of Saigon). Diem studied in a French-run school for training government officials, and by the age of 25 was a provincial governor, and soon was competing in the field with Communists. In 1933 he became minister of interior under Bao Dai, but within three months Diem resigned to protest French restrictions. Diem and his family were harassed by the French during the next decade, and when the Japanese took over in 1942 he failed to convince the Japanese to give Vietnam its freedom. When World War II ended, Diem was captured by the Vietminh in September 1945, but Ho Chi Minh personally released Diem. But the Vietminh condemned Diem to death *in absentia* and in 1950 he left Vietnam, ending

up in the United States, where he spent two years in a Maryknoll Seminary in New Jersey. Clearly a dedicated nationalist, opposed to both French and Communist rule of Vietnam, he gained the support of many prominent Americans, but he could not get any commitment from the Eienhower administration. In June 1954 the emperor Bao Dai simply appointed him prime minister and Ngo Dinh Diem flew back to his country.

No matter what he did from this point on, Diem was out of touch with his people, even when he ousted Bao Dai in 1955 and created the Republic of South Vietnam. His regime was troubled from the outset by the incessant struggles with the Communists and other rivals for power, and his overt hostility to the Buddhists – who were a majority – plus his nepotism did little to gain him popular support for even his well-intentioned policies. He refused to participate in the nationwide elections called for by the 1954 Geneva Agreements but got himself elected in the South by blatantly rigged majorities. Although he managed to put down two coup attempts, discontent over his policies and style spread. Finally, in November 1963, Vietnamese military leaders, with the tacit and secret support of the Kennedy administration, staged a successful coup in which Diem and his brother, Ngo Dinh Nhu, were assassinated.

TRAN DO, 1922-

As one of the foremost military men of North Vietnam, General Tran Do was deputy commander of Communist Forces in the South. During the war he shared the deprivations of his North Vietnamese and Vietcong troops – often living underground, moving through the jungle on primitive trails, constantly changing headquarters to avoid detection. It was the informality and flexibility of these operations and the minimum of supplies they required, that baffled US strategists: there were simply no established headquarters to bomb.

In organizing Vietcong guerrilla operations in the mid-1960s, Tran Do ran afoul of many of the factional resentments that troubled all Communist operations: during and after the war, South Vietnamese were suspicious of Northerners and resented the Hanoi-based leadership. Tran Do was a major planner of the early-1968 Tet offensive that in retrospect came to be seen as one of the turning points of the war. But at the time, Tran Do later

BIOGRAPHIES

admitted, the multi-faceted offensive failed to attain many of is objectives, particularly in stimulating sympathetic uprisings in the South. Nonetheless, the Tet offensive dealt a telling blow to US morale, and the Communists were to reap many and unexpected benefits from that fact.

PHAM VAN DONG, 1906-
For over 30 years Pham Van Dong was one of the 'Iron Triangle' that directed the Vietnamese revolution from its inception to its victory (the other two being Ho Chi Minh and Vo Nguyen Giap). Ho referred to Dong as 'my other self.' He was the diplomat and administrator of the triumvirate, though he also did his share of fighting.

Born into a mandarin family, Dong attended the same French lycée in Hué as his classmates Giap and Diem. After finishing school he became a nationalist revolutionary. Sophisticated and articulate as a diplomat, Dong was prime minister of North Vietnam during the war with the United States, managing the complex problems of his country through the years of steadily escalating fighting. Following Ho's death, Dong issued a string of diplomatic initiatives to South Vietnam and the United States, meanwhile giving frequent interviews to the Western press and encouraging the US anti-war movement. Since his peace initiatives were based on US withdrawal, they were steadily rejected. Dong also had his problems with allies China and Russia, whose support was lukewarm.

After the war Dong remained as prime minister of a reunited Vietnam, turning to the difficult problems of peace in a country ravaged by nearly 30 years of war. As he told an US reporter in 1981, 'waging a war is simple, but running a country is very difficult.

LE DUAN, 1908-
Le Duan was one of the small group of leaders who early gathered around Ho Chi Minh, fired by his dream of an independent Vietnam. Like Ho and Pham Van Dong, Le Duan throughout his career had to function in several capacities – soldier, strategist, diplomat and bureaucrat.

A native of the central part of the country, Le Duan was thereby conversant with the often contrasting ideas and styles of North and South. He became secretary-general of Ho's Lao Dong Party in 1959 and was his principal deputy during the 1960s. During the war, Le Duan was much occupied with military and intelligence operations in the South, and it was he who approved the campaign that finally conquered Saigon in 1975. Several times in the 1960s he journeyed to Moscow and Peking to solicit aid from the North's nominal Communist-bloc supporters. Often as not (despite the US obsession with monolithic Communism) China and Russia failed to respond. Taking over the leadership of North Vietnam after Ho's death, Le Duan was to find after the war that the problems of peace were often more difficult than those of war.

JOHN FOSTER DULLES, 1888-1959
Dulles might seem an unlikely individual to appear involved in the Vietnam War, but as Eisenhower's Secretary of State, he laid down policies and took decisions during the 1950s that would in many respects set the course for the US role in Vietnam in the 1960s.

A lawyer by training, Dulles had spent his life working to stabilize the world through international negotiations – from the Versailles Conference in 1919 to the founding of the United Nations in 1945. In particular, Dulles viewed Communism and the Soviet Union as the greatest threats and tests of the West's commitment, and he argued that the United States must be prepared to go to 'the brink' of war to stop their spread. As Eisenhower's Secretary of State in 1953, Dulles was in a position to exercise considerable influence on world affairs. And in the context of the times – China having recently been taken over by the Communists, a war in Korea just ended – it was not unreasonable for Dulles to be concerned about events in Southeast Asia, particularly in Vietnam.

The United States had begun aiding the French in this war in 1950, before Dulles took over, and what began as a relatively modest sum had escalated over the years; by the time the French were defeated at Dienbienphu in May 1954, the United States would have provided at least $1,000,000,000 directly to the French and an equal sum to the Vietnamese Government. But Dulles changed the terms of US aid and commitment to Vietnam. Even before the Geneva Accords were signed, he sent Colonel Lansdale to Vietnam to head a team that would engage in covert operations designed to thwart the Communists in North Vietnam. Dulles called for the buildup of a Vietnamese National Army, with the clear implication that the United States

John Foster Dulles

BIOGRAPHIES

would support it. Dulles ignored the warnings of the experienced French that Diem was not the appropriate individual to support and that the United States would do better to deal with Ho Chi Minh in Hanoi lest he turn to the Communist world. Instead, Dulles all but ignored the Geneva Accords and supported Diem in his refusal to participate in nation-wide elections in 1956.

With these and related actions, Dulles set the United States on the path in Vietnam that would eventually lead into the quagmire of the war. There was no denying Dulles' total sincerity and commitment in his efforts to stem the spread of Communism. Dulles chose the path that seemed the best at that time; 20 years later, many would doubt his course.

VAN TIEN DUNG, 1917-

Most of the leaders of the Communist movement in Vietnam shared with their opponents a rather privileged, French-educated background. One exception to that rule was General Van Tien Dung, a peasant-born protegé of General Giap who became his second in command during the war. It was Dung who commanded the Communist push to Saigon in 1975.

In the 1954 Communist victory over the French at Dienbienphu, Dung had been the primary logistical planner of that complex operation. As Giap's second in command during the 1960s, Dung was a competent if unimaginative leader, but one of considerable wit and charm. In late 1974 he received General Tran Van Tra's plans for invading Saigon without enthusiasm, believing his army not yet strong enough. But Tran found others more sympathetic, and after some exploratory operations succeeded beyond expectations, the campaign gained momen-tum. The South Vietnamese army proved to be weak and US response to the new Com-munist offensive was virtually nonexistent.

Finally Dung took over the operation in spring 1975. With a many-faceted offensive, feinting and suddenly striking, he quickly took Banmethout in early March, and then marched into Pleiku, Kontum, Hué and Danang. Under the name of the Ho Chi Minh Campaign, the push to Saigon began. The city fell into panic, refugees streamed out, the South Vietnamese army was virtually impo-tent. On 30 April Dung's forces roared into Saigon. After the war Dung became Giap's successor as defense minister, and wrote a popular book about the campaign.

DANIEL ELLSBERG, 1931-

Ellsberg achieved a certain notoriety as well as a footnote in the history of the Vietnam War by releasing in 1971 the secret Defense Department study that became known as 'the Pentagon Papers.' Whatever Ellsberg's motives, the Pentagon Papers helped to change many Americans' information, views and attitudes about the war, in general leading to a lessening of support.

Ellsberg was an honors graduate from Harvard who volunteered in 1953 for two years with the US Marine Corps, service that seemed to bring out his feeling that a strong military approach was necessary to sustain the United States' international obligations. After military service, Ellsberg completed his graduate studies at Harvard, then went on to work for the Rand Corporation, one of the major 'think tanks' heavily committed to supporting the US government's activities. Wanting to be closer to the center of power and action, in August 1964 Ellsberg joined the Defense Department. He openly pro-moted his 'hawkish' views on the war then expanding in Vietnam, and in July 1965 he volunteered to assist General Lansdale in setting up counterinsurgency and pacification programs in Vietnam itself; ever the macho intellectual, Ellsberg volunteered to accom-pany military patrols into action.

By now Ellsberg was beginning to have his doubts about the US role in Vietnam, and these were fully confirmed when in late 1967 he was invited by Secretary McNamara to become one of the 36 researchers preparing a history of the US role in Vietnam since 1945. (This was to be a secret internal project that McNamara personally commissioned – for reasons never fully explained.) By the time Ellsberg was through with his section he was convinced that the crisis over Vietnam was very much the result of unjustified presiden-tial intrusions. On his return to the Rand Corporation in 1968, Ellsberg began to send for copies of the Defense Department study – he had top secret clearance and claimed they were needed for his current studies – until he had 18 of the volumes. In the autumn of 1969, he began to photocopy each volume.

At first Ellsberg thought that by making the documents known to such officials as Senators J William Fulbright (D-AR) and George McGovern (D-SD) he would provoke a formal protest; when these men failed to act, Ellsberg decided to 'leak' them to *The New York Times*. On 13 June 1971, the *Times* began to publish installments (and *The Washington Post* and *Boston Globe* began to publish also, using other sources). Ellsberg had accepted from the outset that he might be arrested for his actions, and on 28 June he was. Charged with numerous crimes, he said he was ready to 'go to prison to help end this war.' After his trial, however, all charges were dismissed on 11 May 1973, for by this time Ellsberg had been drawn into what was known as 'Watergate': his phone had been illegally bugged, his former psychiatrist's office broken into, and President Nixon himself had offered the directorship of the FBI to the trial judge in an effort to influence him. Ellsberg had spent close to a million dollars, but he was free – and something of a hero to the anti-war activists he had once opposed. In the years since he has remained in the public eye as an anti-nuclear and arms control activist.

BERNARD B FALL, 1926-67

In one of the many subtle ironies of the Vietnam War that he himself was so fond of pointing out, Bernard Fall was among the few individuals whose professional reputation was advanced during the war – yet he ended up literally losing his life in that war. Fall was born in Vienna but spent his formative years in France where during World War II he fought with the French underground. He first went to Indochina in 1953 to observe the end of the French rule there, then came on to the United States where he took his doctorate in history from Syracuse University. In the years that followed, Fall returned frequently to Vietnam to gain firsthand experience for seven books and some 250 magazine articles about Vietnam and Southeast Asia. He became a professor of international relations at Howard University in Washington, DC, and although he retained his French citizenship he was planning to take US citizenship at the time of his death.

Fall's writings about Vietnam combined scholarship and relevance, detachment and passion, knowledge and experience. In person he was a mixture of intensity and informality, known for his piercing questions and undisguised ambition to become, in his own words, 'the foremost military writer of my generation.' Because he analyzed all sides with the same relentless critical spirit, his writings could be read by all sides looking for support for their views, so that Fall was quoted – and attacked – by both hawks and doves.

Typical of the man who had always sought out experience at firsthand, Fall deliberately chose to go out with a US Marine patrol along the stretch of seacoast northwest of Hué, a road known as 'The Street Without Joy' (which Fall had used for the title of one of his books about Vietnam) where on 21 February 1967 he was killed by a Vietcong mine.

J(AMES) WILLIAM FULBRIGHT, 1905-

Fubright, the Senator from Arkansas from 1945-74, was one of a number of Americans who at first used their position and prestige to support the government's actions in Vietnam but who became dissillusioned and turned against the war. Fulbright stood out from even this minority for several reasons. He had been a Rhodes Scholar and an academic before coming to Washington, so he retained an aura of the great intellect. In the aftermath of World War II he devised what came to be known as the Fulbright Scholarships: by providing money to US students to study abroad and foreign students to study in the United States, these are designed to promote understanding among the peoples of the world – and above all, to use their intellects to settle differences, not their guns. Meanwhile, Fulbright was chairman of the Senate Foreign Relations Committee, generally conceded to be one of the most influential positions in the US government. And finally, Fulbright, as a liberal Southern Democrat, was a special friend of Lyndon Johnson.

Fulbright was among those summoned to the White House on 5 August 1964 and given a special briefing whie being asked to lend his particular power and prestige to get the Tonkin Gulf Resolution pushed through the Senate. Fulbright would later disagree with Johnson's supporters as to just how much he was told about the true nature of events in the Tonkin Gulf, but he did lend his support, win over the hesitant Senators, and beat down attempts to modify the resolution.

Fulbright soon became uneasy with what he had done, for he felt he was simply supporting US retaliations against future 'unprovoked' attacks; when the United States began to put combat troops into Vietnam in March 1965, he warned Johnson of the disaster that would result from a major war in Southeast Asia. By mid-1965, when Johnson asked Fulbright to speak to the Senate with total support for the

BIOGRAPHIES

administration's Vietnam policies, Fulbright instead spoke with obvious misgivings. From this point on, Johnson refused to speak to his old colleague, and in the months that followed he began to think of Fulbright as a traitor. In January-February 1966, Fulbright held hearings before the Senate Foreign Relations Committee that were clearly critical of the administration's policies and allowed them to be televised nationally. Then in April 1966 Fulbright gave a series of lectures at Johns Hopkins University in which he referred to 'the arrogance of power' demonstrated by the United States in Vietnam. From this point on, Fulbright remained a known critic of the US role in Vietnam.

However, it should also be recognized that Fulbright never relinquished his own somewhat detached-restrained approach: thus, although he was one of the first to whom Daniel Ellsberg secretly gave a set of what became known as The Pentagon Papers, Fulbright chose not to hold public hearings on them. Fulbright thus found himself criticized by some who felt his attacks on the war were less than absolute. His was the inevitable fate of a man of intellect and principle who tried to steer a moderate course through a time of tumultous extremes.

VO NGUYEN GIAP, 1912-

Although never as well known to the world at large as Ho Chi Minh, Giap was an equally dedicated revolutionary. As the leader of the Communist Vietnamese military organization, Giap was the mastermind behind over 30 years of struggle that withstood two of the most sophisticated military powers in the world – France and the United States.

Born in central Vietnam, Giap was one of the founding members of the Indochinese Communist Party in 1929; he became a history teacher and studied law at the University of Hanoi, continuing to work for the Communist cause. When the French threatened to crack down on such Communists in 1940, Giap (along with Pham Van Dong) fled to southern China, where for the first time he met the leader-in-exile of the Vietnamese Communists, Ho Chi Minh. Giap and Ho quickly became trusted allies, and by December 1944 Giap was in command of the first Propaganda Unit for National Liberation. Possessing an encyclopedic knowledge of military history and an analytical mind, Giap developed the strategy that culminated in his victory at Dienbienphu.

Giap had several years to develop the army of North Vietnam before he squared off against the United States. Utilizing his knowledge of his country and its people, exploiting every possible weakness of his oponent's strategy, Giap slowly but inexorably wore down the will of the US war machine. At the same time, Giap made his share of mistakes. The Tet offensive, although it proved to be a psychological victory beyond the Communists' calculations, was at the time a tactical defeat for Giap's forces, and his attempt to turn Khe Sanh into another Dienbienphu was another costly defeat. Even the most admiring student of Giap's achievements would have to admit that at least part of his succcess came simply from his willingness to sacrifice any number of lives.

Giap's response to that, of course, would be that the goal was just, necessary and absolute, and in the end he triumphed. His country finally independent and united, Giap effectively retired from public life in 1975. Those who know him describe him as both forceful and imaginative, and if he was less cosmopolitan and multifaceted than Ho, Giap was no less singleminded.

ALEXANDER HAIG, 1924-

Though he served in a variety of military and government posts in his career, perhaps the nation's most enduring memory of Alexander Haig is as the grim-faced White House chief of staff who kept the curious at a distance at the end of the Nixon presidency. A low-ranking West Point graduate, Haig early showed a propensity to float toward the top in a series of military and government posts. In the early 1960s he joined Secretary of the Army Cyrus Vance's staff, soon leaving that post to command an infantry battalion in Vietnam.

Haig reappeared in government service in late 1968, joining the staff of national security adviser Henry Kissinger. There he acquired a reputation as a loyal worker, dutifully supporting controversial actions like the bombing of Hanoi late in the war. In 1970 Haig began a series of trips to Vietnam to report to President Nixon on conditions there. Two years later he was engaged in full-scale shuttle diplomacy between Washington and the Thieu government, and was chiefly responsible for securing Thieu's acquiescence to the 1973 cease-fire. Haig became closer to Nixon when he served as advance man for the President's 1972 China visit.

Vo Nguyen Giap

BIOGRAPHIES

Thereafter Haig served as Army Vice-chief of Staff, but gradually assumed more power as one White House staff member after another toppled during the Watergate debacle. During those months President Nixon increasingly turned to Haig, who encouraged him to hang tough and assembled a legal staff for him. Haig also presided over the transfer of power when the 'smoking gun' tape was revealed and, some say, advised the President to resign. Haig emerged from the Nixon presidency mildly tainted by Watergate but, at least, with no legal charges lodged against him. He went on to become head of NATO and, briefly, Secretary of State under Ronald Reagan.

PAUL D HARKINS, 1904-

A World War II protégé of General George S Patton, General Paul D Harkins brought great experience to his 1962 appointment as head of the US Military Assistance Command in Saigon, which was still called an 'advisory mission.' Escalating US involvement, President Kennedy directed Harkins to initiate large-scale counterinsurgency operations. However, Harkins, who had been trained in conventional warfare and thought in those terms, proved ill-prepared to deal with the realities of guerrilla warfare.

Harkins pressed on the Diem regime the concept of fortified 'strategic hamlets'; the program, promoted with a vengeance, succeeded only in alienating many of the peasants it forcibly relocated. As this and other troubles mounted, Harkins maintained high optimism in his reports, and demanded the same from his officers.

This enforced optimism soon caught up with Harkins, but efforts to secure more accurate military assessments met with adamant resistance. Harkins was a strong supporter of the Diem regime, while Ambassador Henry Cabot Lodge supported the generals who eventually deposed and killed Diem. The coup did nothing to improve relations between Harkins and Lodge. In 1964 Harkins was relieved by Secretary of Defense Robert McNamara, who had become disillusioned with the reliability of Harkin's reports and with his progress. Awarded a distinguished service medal by President Johnson, Harkins retired from service in 1964.

ROGER HILSMAN, JR, 1919-

Though one of the team who advocated and planned early intervention by the United States in Vietnam, Roger Hilsman was one of the first to object to escalating military involvement. A professor of international politics at Princeton in the 1950s, Hilsman was taken into the Kennedy administration as the State Department intelligence director, and in 1962 became Harriman's successor as head of the Far Eastern Bureau.

In early 1962 Hilsman turned his attention to Vietnam, formulating a plan that advised against military intervention while promoting simultaneous political and counterinsurgency efforts. At the end of 1962 Hilsman returned from a tour of Vietnam to report the failure of the strategic hamlets and to give a pessimistic assessment of the corrupt and inept Diem government. As his objections to Diem and Nhu mounted, Hilsman co-drafted the 24 August 1963 cable to Ambassador Lodge; the message obliquely stated US support for the coup. Though Washington quickly backtracked, that cable was just what Lodge wanted to hear, and was what he acted on. Though Hilsman for a time remained in favor of US political and counterinsurgency efforts in Vietnam, he objected to the increasingly militaristic tone of policy in the Johnson administration and resigned from the government early in 1964. Three years later he published a book highly critical of Johnson's war policy.

HUBERT HUMPHREY, 1911-78

Among the casualties of the Vietnam War were the convictions and programs of old-fashioned liberalism, and also the reputation of their most tireless champion, Vice-President Hubert Humphrey. When he came into office with President Lyndon Johnson, Humphrey had been a fighting liberal senator whose name was on some of the most significant progressive legislation of the century; bills on civil rights, health care for the aged, a nuclear-test-ban treaty and a flood of others.

Through the years of Humphrey's Senate career, a close friend and mentor was Lyndon Johnson, and it was only natural that he would become Johnson's running mate in the 1964 elections. When in early 1965 Johnson first began escalating US intervention in Vietnam, Humphrey expressed misgivings; Johnson forthwith banished him from deliberations for over a year. Finally, loyal to his old colleague, Humphrey came around, turning his ebullient style to promoting Johnson's war.

When Johnson declined to run in 1968, Humphrey survived the challenge of Eugene McCarthy to be named the Democratic nominee in the stormy Chicago convention. Despite making efforts in September to distance himself from Johnson and his war policy, he lost to Richard Nixon by less than one percent of the vote.

LYNDON BAINES JOHNSON, 1908-73

Whether Lyndon Baines Johnson is regarded as a tragic figure, betrayed by his own vacillating countrymen, or a 'sick Texan with an ego problem,' as one of his anti-war critics called him, the war in Vietnam was undeniably the scar of LBJ's psyche, career, presidency, country and era.

Nothing in the first 56 years of his life quite seemed to prepare him for such an end. From a rural Texas background, Johnson began as a modest schoolteacher who by his own bootstraps (and perhaps a bit of political hankypanky) raised himself to a career in Congress. By 1955 he was Senate Democratic majority leader and an influential force in liberal domestic policies. But he had little experience of the world at large – his World War II Navy service having been about seven months in the Pacific as a special representative of President Roosevelt – and when he was chosen by John F Kennedy to be Vice-President it was a case of conventional ticket-balancing. Thrust into the presidency after Kennedy's assassination in November 1963, Johnson found he had inherited a widespread and complex commitment to Vietnam.

During the early months of his administration, Johnson – not unreasonably – deferred to the accumulated experience and knowledge of many of the senior Kennedy advisers who stayed on. But it is equally true that Johnson, on his own and wholeheartedly, espoused their basic premise, simplistically summed up as 'the domino theory.' Furthermore, from the outset, Johnson was receiving opposing views from various experts inside and outside the governmment.

Johnson chose to listen to the experts and views he wanted to hear, and so he took the country deeper and deeper into the war in Vietnam. The record shows that he often opposed the 'harder' line of certain more extreme 'hawks' and he sincerely sought what he regarded as a fair negotiated end. But many of his decisions were compromised by political considerations: he refused to call up the reserves, he avoided the taxes needed to pay for the war, he scheduled military operations to influence elections. He definitely withheld much information from the American people, and the record also shows him saying one thing to his inner circle and another to the world at large. And as the casualties mounted and the war bogged down, LBJ adopted a 'bunker mentality' that isolated him even more from alternative views.

Not that Johnson was oblivious to the casualties and conduct of the war in the field. Perhaps no American president since Lincoln became so directly involved in the day-to-day progress of a war. Johson had scale models of some of the major battle sites and insisted on daily briefings, even picking many of the actual targets for bombers.

When he announced in March 1968 that he would not run again for President, Johnson was clearly a man trying to make the best of a bad situation. His health deteriorating, he retired to his ranch, worked on his memoirs, and watched 'Johnson's war' become 'Nixon's war.'

JOHN F KENNEDY, 1917-63

As the years after his death went by, the image of President John F Kennedy's 'Camelot' era was steadily and inevitably tarnished by the accumulation of facts. Among those was the realization of how Kennedy and his advisers had led the nation into Vietnam. Yet Kennedy's tragic death rescued him at least from the final responsibility, and left history a lingering, unanswerable question: would Kennedy finally have gone to war in Vietnam?

As a senator, Kennedy had favored US aid to the French in the Indochina war, and later touted the Diem regime as the 'finger in the dike' against encroaching Communism. Though his image was liberal, Kennedy in fact was rather conservative, and he never questioned the dream of American democracy and culture as the savior of the world. This abiding dream was one of the foundations of the Vietnam War, and arguably the chief fatality of that war.

Kennedy's confident, ebullient and youthful style fitted perfectly into the mood of a country at the zenith of its power and prosperity. When in his inaugural address Kennedy proclaimed that the United States would 'pay the price, bear any burden ... to assure the survival and the success of liberty,' no one questioned the rightness of that credo.

But after the debacle of the Bay of Pigs and later bullying at the hands of the Soviets, Kennedy began to feel the United States needed to make a show of muscle – and Vietnam, he once observed, was the place.

Inexorably, the little country in Southeast Asia moved from a subsidiary to a principal concern of his administration, gaining steadily more attention, more aid, more US military advisers. Nonetheless, Kennedy resisted pressure from Edward Lansdale and others to send combat troops, relying instead on more covert, and cheaper, forms of aid in support of Diem. In October 1961 Kennedy sent General Maxwell Taylor and Walt Rostow to Vietnam; when they recommended sending combat troops, he balked again but agreed to send more and more advisers until by 1963 there were some 16,000 of these and US pilots were covertly flying combat sorties. In public, Kennedy firmly denied that any US troops were fighting in the country.

Clearly, Kennedy was undecided, waiting and seeing, still uncertain of his power as President, loath to commit massive fighting forces but unwilling to get out. The result was a continual seesawing of policy and opinion. This waffling extended into virtually the last major efforts of his presidency – his on-and-off encouragement of the coup that overthrew Diem, which was being promoted by Ambassador Lodge. Learning of the death on Diem on 1 November 1963, Kennedy was visibly horrified. Three weeks later Kennedy himself was dead, and another President with far fewer misgivings took over what he had begun.

NGUYEN KHANH, 1927-

Among the Vietnamese leaders the United States promoted for a time after the fall of Diem, General Nguyen Khanh was perhaps the most spectacularly corrupt and incompetent. A field commander who played a minor role in the 1963 coup, Khanh felt himself slighted by the generals and soon planned a coup of his own. In January 1964 he easily took over the government and installed himself as prime minister.

A swaggering and blustering figure, Khanh quickly demonstrated his lack of ability as a politician, but at the same time he was wily enough to maintain US support: he was not a neutralist and would never seek accommodation with Hanoi. Ambassador Lodge responded by extolling Khanh to Washington (though not without misgivings) and McNamara toured the country touting Khanh to the Vietnamese as the 'best possible leader' for their country (but wrote a pessimistic report to Washington).

In short order Khanh managed to antagonize nearly everyone. Nor was he able to stop Vietcong gains in the countryside. Spending most of his energies scheming to consolidate his power, he had little patience with military or political demands. Both the governmental and military apparatus eroded steadily while Washington made plans to increase aid and to intervene directly against the Communists.

After the Tonkin incident in August 1964, Khanh tried to exploit the new situation by promulgating repressive decrees and assuming the presidency. The result was an even more tumultuous situation: riots and violence in the streets, plots and counterplots flying among various generals as in a bad comic opera, Khanh in and out of power from one day to the next. Khanh was ousted finally in February 1965. Sent into exile, he was last heard of running a shabby restaurant in West Palm Beach, Florida.

HENRY KISSINGER, 1923-

Always quick to see the irony in a situation, Henry Kissinger cannot have failed to appreciate one of the more offbeat paradoxes of the Vietnam War: that he shared a Nobel Prize for Peace for negotiating the end to a war he had openly supported. But Kissinger's career was a succession of twists and turns. The son of a German-Jewish family that fled Nazi Germany in 1938, Henry Kissinger found himself back in Germany seven years later, helping to administer the temporary government at the end of World War II. He then went on to Harvard, where he taught government and gained recognition outside academic circles by writing on foreign affairs and defense issues. And through his directing an international seminar at Harvard, he built up a network of personal contacts that would later provide access to many influential people around the world.

Kissinger's involvement in the Vietnam issue actually began during the Johnson administration in July 1967 when, in a secret episode, he was contacted by French acquaintances to serve as liaison between President Johnson and Ho Chi Minh. After Nixon became President and appointed Kissinger his National Security Adviser, Kissinger in

Henry Kissinger

BIOGRAPHIES

August 1969 began the secret negotiations with the Vietnamese in Paris that, along with the public negotiations, eventually resulted in the cease-fire agreement of January 1973.

Nevertheless, during the first four years of the Nixon administration, Kissinger was instrumental in promoting policies that advanced the war. Kissinger's role, indeed, bears special scrutiny, for he often tried to distance himself from the Nixon style; for example, he tried to maintain his contacts and status within the academic community (by then largely opposed to the war) while simultaneously providing lists of subordinates whose phones were to be 'bugged.' And Kissinger was not above playing politics with the war – on the eve of the 1972 presidential election announcing that 'Peace is at hand' and then within weeks concurring with the brutal bombing of North Vietnam.

Kissinger was rewarded for his loyalty to Nixon by being appointed Secretary of State and remained supportive of Nixon through the latter's final days in office. Kissinger then stayed on as Secretary of State through the Ford administration. After the inauguration of Carter in 1977, Kissinger retired to a life of writing, lecturing and teaching.

ROBERT KOMER, 1922-

Another of those 'best and brightest' who brought their undeniable energies and intelligence to the war in Vietnam, Robert Komer is almost unknown to most Americans except those with inside knowledge of events, but he had immense, if transitory, influence. A graduate of Harvard College and its Business School, Komer became a CIA analyst and then an expert on US overseas aid programs under Presidents Kennedy and Johnson. By 1966 he was giving special advice on Vietnam to President Johnson. Komer had read all the relevant writings, knew the history of the French efforts, and brought the approach of the analyst and business school to the problems, and he was convinced that the war could succeed if the United States gained the support of the Vietnamese people. So in mid-1967, when he got himself assigned to go to Vietnam to serve under General Westmoreland's MACV, he had the chance to put his ideas into practice with an operation that he himself had essentially conceived: the Civil Operations and Rural Development Support (CORDS).

Komer set about to gain the support of those Vietnamese he felt were truly dedicated to the greater good of their country. Always unconventional in his manner, Komer had a free-swinging approach that led to his cables being dubbed 'Komergrams' while his nickname in Vietnam became 'Blowtorch,' And Komer did want to substitute grain for bombs, pacification programs for military operations. After the Tet offensive of 1968, under pressure to get quicker results, Komer devised what he called the Accelerated Pacification Campaign (APC), but before he had much time to test this he was recalled to Washington. His parting gift to Vietnam, however, was another program which became known as the Phoenix Operation. It turned into a CIA-sponsored operation that simply killed known or suspected Communist leaders or sympathizers. Komer himself became a Defense Department analyst in the Carter administration.

VICTOR H KRULAK, 1913-

A US Marine Corps general, Krulak bore the label of 'the leading authority on counterinsurgency and guerrilla warfare,' and it was this reputation that allowed his optimistic views on conditions in Vietnam to influence US early involvement in events there. A graduate of Annapolis, a veteran of World War II and Korea, Krulak rose to become a major general in the USMC and by February 1962 he was named the special adviser to the JCS for counterinsurgency and special activities. The high-level civilian officials of the Kennedy administration tended to be impressed by Krulak's military experience and his forceful manner. At first he advocated backing the regime of President Diem (although he approved the directive to Ambassador Lodge that effectively assured US support to the dissident generals). In early September 1963 Krulak was sent on a special 'fact-finding mission' to Vietnam for President Kennedy, with Joseph Mendenhall, a State Department official who had served in the Saigon embassy. They reported back to Kennedy after their whirlwind four-day trip, and not unexpectedly, each had seen primarily what he expected to see. Mendenhall, the civilian, saw a government close to collapse and lacking popular support; Krulak, the military man, claimed that the military was making progress against the Vietcong. It was after this session that President Kennedy asked, 'You two did visit the same country, didn't you?'

With the deaths of Diem and Kennedy,

Krulak's status was somewhat uncertain. In March 1964 he was promoted to commanding general of the Fleet Marine Force in the Pacific, where his ideas on counterinsurgency were not as applicable. Passed over as a candidate for commandant of the Corps, he retired in May 1968.

NGUYEN CAO KY, 1930-

The flamboyant Nguyen Cao Ky – was a fixture of the whole US era in South Vietnam. As commander of the air force and later prime minister and vice-president, he made his mark on the era but, despite much devious maneuvering, he was never able firmly to seize power. As air force commander, Ky first came to prominence in 1964 when, in a typically extravagant gesture, he threatened to bomb the headquarters of squabbling generals during the Khanh regime. But after Khanh and Ky received an ill-advised tongue-lashing from US Ambassador Maxwell Taylor, Ky helped Khanh survive a coup attempt in February 1965. Soon after, mindful of his own interests, Ky cooperated with Khanh's banishment.

In spring 1965 Ky became prime minister, sharing power with head of state Nguyen Van Thieu. Speaking before President Johnson in a Hawaii conference in 1966, Ky gave a mighty speech promising a 'social revolution' in Vietnam. For his own part, Ky had no intention of challenging the corruption of his government. Ky returned home to suppress the Buddhists more viciously – and successfully – than Diem ever had.

Ky became Thieu's vice-president in the 1967 elections, after a backstage deal that gave him considerable power. But Thieu thereafter managed to outmaneuver Ky despite the latter's notable deviousness, and though Ky remained in office until 1971, his power waned. His challenge to Thieu in the 1971 elections ended when Thieu had him disqualified. Ky fled before the Communist offensive in 1975 and eventually opened a liquor store in California.

EDWARD G LANSDALE, 1908-

A quiet, self-effacing CIA man with a passion for adventure and considerable expertise in intrigue, Edward Lansdale was one of the people most responsible for early US involvement in Vietnam. He came there from successful efforts in the Philippines, where he had developed for the US-backed regime a repertoire of sabotage and counterinsurgency techniques as well as what he called 'psychwar'. A former advertising executive, Lansdale seemed to view war to some extent as an exercise in US-style public relations.

In Vietnam from 1954 to 1956, Lansdale became a close personal adviser to Ngo Dinh Diem, helping that leader to consolidate his power. Some of Lansdale's notions for gaining the loyalty of peasants were the basis of the later rural pacification programs. His efforts in Vietnam during the 1950s were notorious enough to immortalize him in two novels – *The Ugly American* by William Lederer and Eugene Burdick and Graham Greene's *The Quiet American*.

Lansdale returned to Vietnam in 1961 to report to Washington on conditions there. That far-reaching report was critical of Diem's assorted failures, but lambasted the lack of US commitment to the premier and recommended extensive covert support for the Diem government. President Kennedy was impressed with the document and considered making Lansdale ambassador to Vietnam. But George Ball, McNamara and Maxwell Taylor did not agree with it and were decidedly not enthusiastic about Lansdale personally. US involvement in Vietnam thereafter increased largely due to Lansdale's efforts, but not at the levels he wanted. Lansdale was not sent to Vietnam again until 1965, when he came as an assistant to Ambassador Henry Cabot Lodge and helped implement the ill-fated rural pacification programs. He stayed on as head of a counterinsurgency team.

HENRY CABOT LODGE, 1902-84

President Kennedy's appointment of Henry Cabot Lodge as ambassador to South Vietnam in June 1963 was a canny decision for a number of reasons. Lodge was a member of a distinguished family and the appointment thus demonstrated the importance Kennedy gave to the situation in Vietnam. Too, it showed generosity toward Kennedy's longtime political opponent and an indication of bipartisan support for the Democratis' Vietnam policy.

Lodge arrived in Saigon in August 1963, during the first wave of Buddhist protests against Diem. After surveying the situation, Lodge quickly made up his mind that Diem had to go; on 29 August he cabled Washington, 'We are launched on a course from which there is no respectable turning back: the overthrow of the Diem government.'

BIOGRAPHIES

Nguyen Cao Ky

As both Washington and Saigon sank into a morass of plots, counterplots, misinformation and misunderstanding, Lodge never swerved from his convictions about Diem and managed to manipulate the confusion for his own purposes. He kept Washington appraised of the conspiracy, received regular reports from the plotting generals and prodded them despite both Washington's and their own wavering. When in the last hours before the 1 November coup Washington sent word to quash it, Lodge suppressed the cable and notified his government that he was powerless. During the coup he stalled Diem on the telephone; directly afterward he personally welcomed and congratulated the generals who had murdered Diem and Nhu.

The overthrow of Diem set into motion a chain of events that Lodge labored in vain to control. He left his ambassadorial post in May 1964 to seek the Republican presidential nomination. In 1965 he returned for another two-year stint as ambassador in Vietnam, where he vigorously promoted the rural pacification program. The program proved to be a costly failure, as were Lodge's efforts to mediate between then-president Ky and militant Buddhists. Resigning his post in 1967, Lodge was named in the next year to the council of 'wise men' who ultimately persuaded President Johnson to wind down the war. Lodge remained in government service until his retirement.

MIKE MANSFIELD, 1903-

An unusually mild and scholarly man for a politician and even more so for Lyndon Johnson's successor as Senate majority leader, Mike Mansfield for over ten years led a quiet rebellion against US involvement in Vietnam. A former professor of Far Eastern history and a Congressman and Senator from Montana since 1942, Mansfield had long been a friend and protégé of Johnson, whose dictatorial style perhaps led Johnson to choose the accommodating Mansfield for a right-hand man.

But diplomatic as he was, Mansfield was never afraid to speak his piece. Knowing he had been a supporter of Diem, President Kennedy sent Mansfield on a fact-finding tour to Vietnam in 1962. When Mansfield returned with a pessimistic assessment of Diem and a strong recommendation for the United States to stay out of Vietnam, Kennedy was at first openly hostile, but later admitted Mansfield was probably right. Though he voted with most of the Senate in favor of the Gulf of Tonkin Resolution, Mansfield during 1964-65 privately urged President Johnson not to 'enlarge the morass in which we are now already on the verge of indefinite entrapment.' But when Johnson responded with increased escalation, Mansfield made his objections public and relations between the two men cooled.

Loyal party man that he was, however, Mansfield could not bring himself to an all-out attack on a Democratic president; rather, he cajoled, remonstrated, pressed futilely for negotiations. During the Nixon presidency Mansfield's actions became more pointed – he deplored the usurpation of Congressional warmaking power by the presidency (which was really Johnson's doing) and in 1971 introduced an end-the-war bill that passed the Senate but failed in the House. In 1976 Mansfield retired from the Senate; the following year President Carter named him ambassador to Japan.

GRAHAM MARTIN, 1912-

Graham Martin finished his long career in foreign service with the unenviable post of US ambassador to Vietnam. He came to Vietnam after serving in the same capacity in Thailand, where he had negotiated for US military installations to operate against Communists.

Martin arrived in Saigon in March 1973, three months after the signing of the Paris Peace Agreement. Prickly, inflexible, and frail in health, he proved unable to handle the declining situation there – the Communists were advancing (hostilities resumed in June 1973), the Thieu government had lost its credibility and support within Vietnam and in the US Congress. The latter voted to cut off aid to the Thieu government after 15 August 1973. Nonetheless, President Nixon ordered Martin to reiterate US support of Thieu.

Ignoring the signs of a coming Communist victory, Martin failed to make adequate preparations for the evacuation of US and South Vietnamese government personnel. The result was the chaotic pullout which the world saw on television. Among the last to leave, by helicopter from the chancery roof, was Martin, clutching his embassy flag. It was his last diplomatic post.

EUGENE McCARTHY, 1916-

It is a typical irony of politics that Eugene McCarthy, the man who harnessed the tide of anti-war sentiment in the 1960s to unseat

BIOGRAPHIES

Lyndon Johnson, was a strong contender for Johnson's running mate in 1964. A gentle, scholarly man and sometime poet, McCarthy had been a liberal Congressman and Senator from Minnesota for many years and a frequent supporter of Johnson before he grew disenchanted with the Vietnam War in the mid-1960s. But McCarthy had never been a dynamic leader, and his first public statements against the war were timid. In 1967, angered by President Johnson's broadening personal power in pursuing the war, McCarthy extended his attacks, finally in October publishing *The Limits of Power*, a critique of US foreign policy. A month later he announced his candidacy for the presidency, objecting to the war and to the policies of President Johnson.

It seemed a hopeless cause. But no one knew the extent of anti-war feeling in the country, especially among the young. Crowds of young McCarthy campaign workers spread into the primary states; and in March, to the astonishment of everyone, McCarthy came within a few hundred votes of beating Johnson in the New Hampshire primary. Two weeks later, Johnson announced he would not seek re-election.

McCarthy had unseated one of the most powerful leaders in US history, but the rest of his campaign was a strange anticlimax. Robert Kennedy entered the race and won most of the Democratic primaries until his assassination. Then at the chaotic Chicago convention McCarthy showed an inexplicable lassitude; the nomination went to Humphrey, who as vice-president had supported the war.

McCarthy retired from the Senate in 1971. But his effect on national politics was lasting: he had brought a new, youthful spirit into the Democratic party and reform to its election procedures, and he had proved the potency of anti-war feelng in the country.

ROBERT S McNAMARA, 1916-

Robert McNamara was Secretary of Defense from 1961-68, the longest term anyone ever occupied that post. One of the prime architects of the war in Vietnam, he did not mind it being dubbed 'McNamara's War.' But the war that he designed to break the will of North Vietnam ended by nearly breaking him. In his farewell to the government in 1968, an anguished McNamara spoke to reporters of the utter futility of the air war, which was the linchpin of both Johnson's and,

later, Nixon's strategy.

McNamara came to the Kennedy cabinet from being president of the Ford Motor Company, which he had helped revitalize after World War II. He brought to the cabinet post an extraordinary logistical and analytical mind that improved the efficiency of the military while briging it firmly under civilian control. He was Johnson's partner and foremost supporter in the early months of the war, promoting the Gulf of Tonkin resolution and the escalation of US involvement in 1965.

But late in that year the first doubts began to appear. Although his official statements remained dutifully optimistic, in November he wearily observed to reporters, 'It will be a long war.' McNamara convinced Johnson to halt the bombing in December of that year, but the gesture came to nothing. The issue of bombing increasingly divided Johnson and McNamara after that point, as did McNamara's sensitivity to the growing anti-war sentiment in the United States.

Although he publicly stuck to the Administration position in 1966, the following year McNamara was openly skeptical about military prospects. He began, fruitlessly, to look for diplomatic openings. The inevitable break came in November 1967, when McNamara announced his resignation, which had been forced by the President. Johnson, remaining loyal to his supporter despite their bitter break, saw to it that McNamara was named president of the World Bank. He remained at that post into the 1980s.

PIERRE MENDÈS-FRANCE, 1907-82

It was appropriate that to Pierre Mendès-France, the courageous and brilliant maverick of mid-century French politics, fell the unenviable task of implementing France's capitulation in Indochina. Throughout the long war Mendès-France had condemned it as a military, fiscal and moral sinkhole, and the nation naturally turned to him when it had grown sick of the whole disastrous venture.

At 21, Mendès-France had been the youngest lawyer in France; at 25 he was elected as a Radical Socialist to the Chamber of Deputies. Imprisoned as a Jew during World War II, he escaped and became a flyer with the Free French. After the war he resumed his role as 'the pitiless gadfly of French politics.' In 1954, a month after the fall of Dienbienphu and in the midst of the Geneva conference, Parliament named

Mendès-France premier. He vowed to reach a settlement in Geneva within four weeks or to resign. In the final hour, he kept his promise.

He did it with the aid of an unlikely ally – Chinese representative Chou En-lai, who was just beginning his career as one of the great diplomats of the century. Chou suggested the concept of a divided Vietnam, thus selling out the Vietminh but making an agreement possible. The fateful agreement signed, Mendès-France returned home to tell the French Assembly, 'I have no illusions ... as to the contents of the agreements. Their text is sometimes cruel ... but the best we could hope for under the circumstances.' Mendès-France went on to forge a settlement in Tunisia; but a year later he was forced out of office. He remained a voice of caution and sanity in his nation's affairs until his death in 1982.

HO CHIN MINH, 1890-1969

It is a sign of his tenacity of purpose that Ho Chi Minh, leader of a small country in Southeast Asia, is remembered alongside Lenin and Mao Tse-tung as one of the towering Communist leaders of the century. Though like Mao a poet and polemicist, Ho was less concerned with niceties of doctrine than Mao and Lenin; his genius was for political action, and his ideology was capable of considerable stretching as long as it tended toward the purpose that obsessed him: the independence and unification of Vietnam.

Born Nguyen Van Thanh in central Vietnam on 19 May 1890, he attended a French school in Hué before setting off in 1910 to explore the world. During his years of wandering he became a professional revolutionary, laboring constantly for the cause of independence. His travels took him to France, Russia, China, the United States and elsewhere; meanwhile he wrote tracts under a number of aliases and founded the Indochinese Communist Party (1930).

In 1941 he finally returned to his homeland, creating the Vietminh as an army of liberation and taking the name Ho Chi Minh: 'He Who Enlightens.' After leading guerrilla actions against the Japanese during the war, Ho proclaimed Vietnamese independence in 1945. After nine years of fighting the French, the victory at Dienbienphu in 1954 brought the partial achievement of his dream – he became president and premier of North Vietnam, but the country was still divided.

Ho remained in office until his death, directing the war effort against the United States as much as his health would permit, never flagging in pursuit of his goal of unification. A quiet, studious, and frail man with considerable charm and a winning sense of humour, Ho also possessed a will of steel and a concomitant ruthlessness. At his death on 3 September 1969, he had never doubted the eventual success of the cause to which he had devoted his life with utter singlemindedness.

DUONG VAN MINH, 1916-

It seemed to be Duong Van Minh's fate always to be a front man for those more ambitious but less popular than himself. An affable and Gallicized veteran general who participated in overthrowing Diem but claimed his only real interests were tennis and horticulture, he nonetheless managed to act on his own now and then, with sometimes profound results.

Known as 'Big Minh' due to his bulk, he first came to prominence as a Diem loyalist in leading the operation that suppressed the anti-Diem sects in 1956. Disaffected with Diem by 1963, he joined the generals plotting the coup. Because of his considerable popularity, he became the nominal leader though the real instigator was the devious head of the army, Tran Van Dong.

As Lodge manipulated Washington's confusion, the plot went ahead. By the time of the coup it had become the assumption that Diem and Nhu were flown out of the country. But Minh, apparently acting on his own, ordered their murder. It was again Minh who stonewalled the other generals and the Americans about the murders afterward.

Minh briefly chaired the council of generals who attempted to rule after the coup, but he had neither the gifts nor the patience for the business of governing. Soon Khanh seized power, retaining Minh in yet another figurehead position. When Ky took over after Khanh's floundering, he quietly edged Minh out.

Without appearing to desire it particularly, Minh kept resurfacing. In 1971, wishing the appearance of a fair election, US officials pressured Minh to make a show of opposing Thieu, but he refused. In the chaotic days of the Communist victory and the crumbling of the Thieu government, Minh somehow became the nominal head of state, and as such surrendered to the Communists entering

BIOGRAPHIES

Ho Chi Minh

Saigon. Minh stayed on until 1983, when he was allowed to emigrate to France.

HENRI NAVARRE, 1898-

When General Henri Navarre was named commander in chief of French forces in Indochina in May 1953, the French people were already disgusted with the 'dirty war' after seven years of stalemate. But the dour, solitary, and dutiful Navarre vowed nonetheless to take the offensive and win.

Navarre had been a soldier since World War I, had fought the Arabs in Morocco and been a hero of the Resistance during World War II. He came to his post in Vietnam vowing to 'revalorize' the demoralized French troops and pursue an offensive strategy. Instead a series of strange misunderstandings and disastrous miscalculations occured. He failed to understand that his government wanted not an offensive but rather a stable situation as a base for peace negotiations. Underrating his opponent, General Giap, he failed to predict the big Communist offensive on his base at Dienbienphu. During the battle itself, Navarre, comfortably ensconced in Saigon, failed to commit reinforcements and matériel to the besieged French forces, which were outnumbered. After the ensuing defeat, the French government hastened to negotiate and Navarre was consigned to the history books as presiding over the losing side in one of the worst military debacles of modern times.

NGO DINH NHU, 1911-63

Ngo Dinh Nhu, younger brother of Ngo Dinh Diem, was born into a prominent Roman Catholic family near Hué. Educated in France during the 1930s, Nhu came to see himself as an intellectual and philosopher, evolving a political doctrine called 'personalism' that was later to have much influence on his brother's regime.

After Diem came to power in 1954, the chain-smoking Nhu became a shadowy and pervasive force behind the scenes of the government, only emerging into the international spotlight in the last few months before the regime was deposed. Nhu became known as the 'Oriental Richelieu,' controlling the government's secret police, which was organized around a secret society called the Can Lao. This organization attempted to suppress any signs of disloyalty to the Diem regime. Nhu also ran a pro-government newspaper and exercised close control over the trade unions.

Said to be a strong influence on his brother's repression of the Buddhists, which initiated the final erosion of the Diem regime, Nhu was assassinated with his brother in the coup d'etat of November 1963.

MADAME NGO DINH NHU, 1924-

One of the most visible and troubling figures in the regime of Ngo Dinh Diem was his brother's wife, Madame Ngo Dinh Nhu, who, since Diem was unmarried, served as the first lady of South Vietnam. Madame Nhu first attracted the world's notice by her considerable beauty and glamour; but it was soon her words that claimed the attention, most notably in her callous response to the anti-Diem self-immolations of Buddhists in 1963: they were a 'barbeque' she declared; 'Let them burn, and we shall clap our hands.'

Born into an aristocratic and thoroughly Gallicized family (she spoke French and was barely fluent in Vietnamese), she married Nhu in 1944. Installed in Diem's palace, Madame Nhu was the only woman close to the president. Over the years her activities became more public and egregious, her style ever more arrogant. But in becoming an increasingly powerful figure in the Diem government, she could only demonstrate how corrupt and indifferent to the people it was.

In 1963, after the Buddhist revolt, Madame Nhu went on a speaking tour of the United States to defend Diem and her husband. She was received with delight as a glamorous jetsetter and an amusing presence. Following her around the country was her father, who had become an opponent of Diem and rebutted her speeches. But perhaps more than anyone else Madame Nhu embodied the bankruptcy of the cause she represented. After the overthrow and murder of Diem and her husband, Madame Nhu retired to a comfortable widowhood in Rome.

NGUYEN THI BINH, 1927-

Even now the name of Nguyen Thi Binh is not immediately recognized except by the best informed, but for some years she was a familiar figure in the Vietnam drama, particularly after her surprise appearance as head of the negotiating team for the National Liberation Front when it showed up in Paris in November 1968. To the supporters of the NLF, however, this petite, trim woman had been known as 'the flower and fire of the revolution,' and to the world at large she proved to be a most eloquent and persistent advocate of the Communist-Vietnamese search for independence.

Nguyen Thi Binh (her given name means 'peace' in Vietnamese) was born into a middle-class family in Saigon long prominent in their nation's struggles and she became an outspoken opponent of foreign rule as a young student. In 1951 she was arrested in a demonstration that burned French and US flags; sentenced to three years, she was tortured in prison. After the Geneva Accords of 1954, she married a doctor and taught in the countryside but she was now committed to opposing the government of Ngo Dinh Diem. Soon after the National Liberation Front was formed in December 1960, Nguyen Thi Binh joined, and by 1962 she was named to its central committee and became a 'roving ambassador,' traveling around the world to explain the NLF's goals and successes. She also headed the Women's Liberation Association from 1963-66, working to include women in the revolutionary struggle and to assure more rights for women in the new society it hoped to establish.

When the Paris peace talks were opened to the NLF and Nguyen Thi Binh appeared in Paris in 1968, there was understandably much comment; since most people did not know of her prominence within the NLF, there were snide suggestions that she was little more than public relations window dressing. But she soon demonstrated that she was far from a public relations 'front,' and as the negotiations continued in the ensuing years, she proved to be a most articulate, competent, and even tough representative for her cause. She did not personally participate in all the negotiations, public or secret, but she traveled throughout the world, making speeches, writing articles, giving interviews, to promote the NLF's goals. When the peace accords were finally signed in January 1973, they were in part a tribute to over four years of labor by Nguyen Thi Binh. She became the minister of education in the Socialist Republic of Vietnam.

RICHARD MILHOUS NIXON, 1913-

When Richard Nixon assumed the presidency in January 1969 after one of the most tumultuous and divisive years in US history, he bore the aura of a campaign charged with his promise that he had a plan 'to end the war and win the peace.' There was a feeling among even those Americans who did not care for Nixon's general politics that at least he had been given a mandate to rid the country of what had become 'Johnson's war.' Yet when Richard Nixon left the White House five years and seven months later, he left a nation more unsettled and divided than ever.

In retrospect, Nixon's handling of events in Vietnam might have been expected. As a young Congressman from California, Nixon had made political capital out of his dedicated opposition to Communism, and after losing to Kennedy in the presidential election of 1960, Nixon continued to speak out strongly against anything he perceived as the Communist threat, whether in Cuba or China. When he spoke out on the war that began to rage through Vietnam in the 1960s, it was usually to call for even tougher responses than those of the Democrats. Yet for all his tough talk, there was a side of Richard Nixon that could, in the end, relent and negotiate.

Soon after taking office, Nixon did seem to achieve some success in changing the direction of the war. He proclaimed a policy of 'Vietnamization,' slowly reducing US troop commitments while attempting to build up the role of the South Vietnamese military, and he supported the negotiations, both secret and public, that would ultimately lead to a cease-fire. But as the months and then years dragged on, it was Nixon's old and implacable anti-Communism that kept him on the same war path that Johnson had taken. Nixon did not maintain the same day-to-day hands-on involvement in the war as Johnson but he pursued the war knowingly and purposefully.

And as unrest and protest swelled throughout the United States, particularly after the 1970 invasion of Cambodia, it was Nixon's response to this domestic opposition that led to his own downfall. For it was his determination to find those who were 'leaking' secrets about his conduct of the war that led Nixon to go along with the 'plumbers,' the illegal wiretaps, the harassment of dissenters, and finally the break-in at Watergate. Nixon was re-elected in 1972, and then after one final spasm of bombing, he obtained the cease-fire that he had been elected to obtain four years earlier. But by now his own presidency was about to explode. From this point on Nixon was never able to gain the support of Congress or the American people for any further support of the South Vietnamese. So it was that the man who said he would never 'be the first President ... to lose the war' became just that, as well as the first to resign his nation's presidency.

LON NOL, 1913-

When General Lon Nol seized power in Cambodia in March 1970, he supplanted the man who was not only his ruler but also his friend and mentor – Prince Norodom Sihanouk. A product of French colonial schools, Lon had worked his way up through government and military posts for nearly 20 years when Sihanouk rewarded him for his support with a series of appointments beginning in the 1950s. In 1966 Lon was elected premier of a Cambodian government that was trying desperately, if ineffectually, to maintain its neutrality.

Like many Cambodian officials, Lon was not above profiteering in weapons sales to Communists even though his government and his beliefs were strongly anti-Communist. Obviously by no means uncorruptible, Lon was nonetheless effective in his role as premier. But in 1970, as the power of the Communists – both Vietnamese and the Khmer Rouge – increased in Cambodia, Lon took advantage of Sihanouk's absence to stimulate anti-Communist 'demonstrations.'

These demonstrations quickly became a bloodbath, a harbinger of horrors to come. But the immediate, and intended, result was to consolidate Lon's power. In March 1970 the Cambodian National Assembly ousted Sihanouk and gave Lon full power. He immediately announced a policy of 'active neutrality.' But he lacked either the imagination or the power to maintain this neutrality, being in poor health, arrogant, superstitious and not notably intelligent. Inevitably, he did little to halt the advance of the Khmer Rouge and the country's slide toward civil war and chaos.

Lon at first protested, then welcomed intervention; but when the United States invaded Cambodia in May 1970 he was not even informed in advance. He condemned the invasion, but soon said its effect had been 'favorable.' By 1971 the Khmer Rouge controlled most of the country. In response, Lon abrogated most democratic rights and rigged an election that made him president and his power absolute. With massive US aid his army was able to stymie the Khmer Rouge for a time, but in 1975 Pnompenh fell and Lon Nol fled to exile in Hawaii before the victorious forces of Pol Pot, who was to engineer one of the worst genocidal bloodbaths in history.

PRINCE SOUVANNA PHOUMA, 1901-

Like many twentieth-century leaders of Southeast Asia, Prince Souvanna Phouma of Laos was a French-educated man who championed the cause of independence from France. He helped his country achieve that goal with comparative peacefulness in the 1950s and, after a series of ups and downs in his political career, became prime minister of Laos for the third time after the Geneva conference of 1962.

On assuming that position, Souvanna, a neutralist, attempted to reconcile the left and right. But after the Communist Pathet Lao resumed its revolt in 1963 he joined forces with the right in opposition to the insurrection. In 1964 the United States began pressuring Souvanna to allow operations against Vietnamese Communists, whose Ho Chi Minh Trail cut through the panhandle of Laos. Thus began Souvanna's dilemma: in attempting to preserve Laotian neutrality against inroads by Communists, he had to accept military and economic aid from the United States. Nonetheless, he possessed the skill to handle this delicate situation tolerably well; despite much overt and covert US activity in Laos during the late 1960s, the concept of Laotian neutrality was never seriously questioned even by the Communist powers. This was partly because Souvanna strenuously, if ineffectively, protested many of the military incursions into Laos. At the same time, Pathet Lao control of eastern Laos broadened steadily.

In 1971 came the disastrous South Vietnamese operation on Communist positions in Laos, over the protests of Souvanna. This operation devastated much of the country, paving the way for increased Pathet Lao strength. Though he had managed to save his country from the worst of the ravages seen in Vietnam and Cambodia, Souvanna could not stop the gradual encroachment of Pathet Lao power that took over the country and deposed him in 1975.

POL POT, 1928(?)-

Pol Pot was the pseudonym of Saloth (or Salot) Sar, who in the mid-1970s led an almost unprecedented genocidal war on the people of his own country, Cambodia (now called Kampuchea). The son of peasants, Pot fought under Ho Chi Minh in the 1940s and in the

BIOGRAPHIES

anti-French underground in the 1950s. He became secretary of the Cambodian Communist party in 1963, the same year that he retired to the jungle to organize the Khmer Rouge, a Communist guerrilla army. The turmoil following the US invasion of Cambodia swelled the ranks of the Khmer Rouge, who overthrew the Lon Nol government in 1975.

In an effort to destroy cities, to eliminate intellectuals and the educated and to create an agricultural utopia, the entire population of Pnompenh, Cambodia's capital, was forcibly evacuated by the Khmer Rouge. The country effectively became one large concentration camp, the entire population under forced labor in the countryside, death the penalty for any slacking or questioning. Books, temples, all surviving evidence of a glorious past, were smashed or put to the torch. An estimated two million people perished. UN Secretary General Kurt Waldheim called it 'a national tragedy that may have no parallel in history.' Though he functioned within committees, most of the responsibility for this madness seemed to lie with Pol Pot.

In 1978 a Vietnamese invasion ousted Pol Pot and installed a Vietnamese-backed government, the People's Republic of Kampuchea. Pol Pot and the remains of the Khmer Rouge retired to the jungle and resumed active guerrilla warfare.

TRI QUANG, 1922-

In the chaotic factional and sectarian conflicts that raged in South Vietnam between 1963 and 1966, one of the most visible figures was Tri Quang, militant leader of Vietnam's Buddhists. A man of mystical demeanor and iron will, he nonetheless failed to develop a program definable enough to rally around, and in the end his movement, for all its political sophistication, was not able to sustain a voice in government policy.

A monk since his youth, Tri Quang headed Vietnam's Central Buddhist Association when the Diem government massacre of Buddhists propelled him into the spotlight in 1963. A potent political activist, he responded by organizing protests that included the self-immolation of monks. At first Diem's Catholic government stonewalled the growing unrest until Nhu ordered active suppression of the Buddhists. During the ensuing turmoil Tri Quang took refuge in the US embassy.

After the overthrow of Diem, Tri Quang organized resistance to the government of General Khanh, who also seemed pro-Catholic. Once again, Saigon fell into factional and sectarian chaos, though Tri Quang was ultimately able to gain some concessions from Khanh. Finally in 1966 Tri Quang formed an alliance with political opponents of then-prime minister Ky, and extended his efforts to anti-US protests. Once again there was violence in the streets, monks burned themselves and the Buddhist propaganda machine went to work; but Ky, along with the Americans dismissing Tri Quang as a Communist, maintained the upper hand. At length Ky arrested Tri Quang while he was on a hunger strike, and the Buddhist movement soon lost its momentum. In 1975 the Communists banished Tri Quang to a monastery.

WALT ROSTOW, 1916-

It has long been observed that US involvement in Vietnam was heavily promoted by the Ivy League alumni who worked in the CIA and in the Kennedy and Johnson administrations. Walt Rostow was among the most aggressive of those advisers. A Yale-educated Rhodes scholar, he taught at MIT in the 1950s and had CIA connections. He also had some economic theories, which he believed to be a fatal counterblow to Marxist doctrine; these theories were contained in his 1960 book *The Stages of Economic Growth: A Non-Communist Manifesto*.

Having worked as a consultant for Eisenhower, Rostow found his way into Kennedy's inner circle of advisers during the 1960 campaign. Named an assistant to national security adviser McGeorge Bundy after the election, Rostow quickly turned his attention to Vietnam, saying that Communists there were 'scavengers of the modernization process,' interfering with the historical stages of economic growth. He became a tough-talking hawk. Rostow during two administrations would promote fight against the threat of Communism.

Despite Rostow's prophesies that Southeast Asia could be the 'last great confrontation' with Communism, Kennedy balked at Rostow's requests for massive military commitments. But in the Johnson administration Rostow's ideas fell on more receptive ears. He asserted that only escalating military action could effectively counter Communist insurgency. Formally disavowed and even suppressed by the Defense Department, this thesis nonetheless had considerable influence in the Johnson administration; many of its ideas, such as systematic bombing of the North, and military campaigns in Laos eventually became policy.

In 1966 Rostow succeeded McGeorge Bundy as Johnson's national security adviser. As Defence Secretary McNamara's doubts about the conduct of the war grew, Rostow remained a belligerent and optimistic advocate of escalation and, as late as 1967, proposed a major invasion of North Vietnam. Increasingly, Rostow defended the President's policy to the public: in 1968 he chaired a committee that fed favorable reports to the press.

But the tide was running against Rostow even within the administration. When in March 1968 Clark Clifford convened his council of 'wise men' to promote disengagement, Rostow, who was a member of the committee, did not challenge their conclusions. Having been one of the most visible hawks throughout the Johnson years, Rostow left government service to find that the academic community had in effect expelled him: he was 'banished' to a teaching position in Texas. Over the years he continued vigorously to defend the US role in Vietnam.

DEAN RUSK, 1909-

As Secretary of State throughout the Kennedy and Johnson administrations, Dean Rusk was one of the most implacable adherents of US involvement in Vietnam. A Rhodes Scholar who served in World War II before entering government service, Rusk was aware that the Allies' failure to challenge the Nazi threat in the 1930s had led to that war. He was determined not to let such aggression go unchecked again.

Rusk was almost passive during the Kennedy years, as the President directly ran foreign policy. When troubles mounted in Vietnam, Rusk became one of those who tilted the administration away from the Diem regime. In the Johnson era Rusk promoted the escalation of the war as necessary to stop Chinese Communist expansionism, which he regarded as the real meaning of the conflict. As the President's chief adviser, Rusk pressed consistently for more troop commitments and more bombing, meanwhile opposing negotiations with Hanoi. He was also a major public voice in defending Johnson's policy, often citing the appeasement of the Nazis at Munich.

As Defense Secretary McNamara and others sought a cease-fire Rusk stood fast. When, after the 1968 Tet offensive, the President began to shift toward de-escalation, Rusk's primacy and power began to fade; he had little to do with the onset of peace discussions. After leaving office he became a professor of international law at the University of Georgia.

JEAN SAINTENY, 1907-

A Hanoi banker and French colonial official in Vietnam, Jean Sainteny was to play a significant role as a go-between at the beginning of the long war and as a peacemaker at the end of it. Sainteny was sent by de Gaulle to negotiate with Ho Chi Minh in 1945. At first Ho kept his distance from the French, preferring to cultivate the Americans – who gave him some aid at that time. The following year Ho decided his best bet was to seek some kind of accommodation with the French, and he and Sainteny became friends. Through the course of their negotiations pressures mounted, and French military forces gathered in the North.

Finally Ho and Sainteny agreed to a referendum on a separate Cochinchina in exchange for a theoretical independence. The accord was never formalized. Instead, Ho was outmaneuvered in negotiations in France, and French troops took over in Cochinchina. By the end of 1946 the war was on. Throughout Ho and Sainteny maintained contact.

Sainteny reappeared on the scene in 1969, when he acted as go-between from the Nixon administration to Ho Chi Minh. He also arranged the first secret meeting of Henry Kissinger and Xuan Thuy, which took place in his apartment. In 1972 he brought Kissinger and Le Duc Tho together for the beginning of the talks that were finally to end the war, whose beginning Sainteny has been unable to forestall.

JAMES BLAIR SEABORN, 1924-

Unknown to all except a few insiders at the time, James B Seaborn played a crucial role in the progress of the Vietnam War: as the Canadian representative on the International Control Commission (ICC), Seaborn was operating as a secret envoy on behalf of the United States to the governmment of North

BIOGRAPHIES

Vietnam, one of many individuals throughout the world who tried in their way to effect a negotiated end to the war. A career diplomat in Canada's foreign service, with experience abroad and in Toronto, Seaborn was asked in 1964 to serve as the senior Canadian on the ICC that had been set up after the Geneva Accords of 1954 to monitor the agreements. Seaborn did not know at the time that in April 1964 US Secretary of State Dean Rusk had asked Canada's Prime Minister Lester Pearson to allow Canada's ICC representative to serve as a secret emissary to Hanoi. (Since the commissioners routinely traveled back and forth to Hanoi, no journalists or others would ever suspect Seaborn's role.) Seaborn was thus handpicked for this delicate role, and US officials went to Toronto to brief him for his first trip to Hanoi in June.

The initial understanding by Canada was that Seaborn would simply present the US position in general terms – a vague 'carrot' of economic aid, a vague 'stick' of US military involvement. But Seaborn also found that he was being asked to gather, through his observations and contacts, intelligence about the condition of North Vietnam, its economy, war capacity and general state of mind. Although this ran somewhat counter to the role of an international diplomat, Seaborn agreed because he felt he might thereby contribute to improving relations between the two nations.

Seaborn held three meetings with high Vietnamese officials – the first in June 1964, another in August – after the US bombing that followed the Tonkin Gulf incidents – and again in March 1965, after the escalation of 'Rolling Thunder' raids. Inevitably, Seaborn found the North Vietnamese increasingly hostile to any overtures he might offer from the United States. Furthermore, Seaborn's astute assessments of the situation in North Vietnam and of its leaders' views were never given serious consideration by US officials, nor was he ever authorized to offer any tangible changes in the US position. Although the US officials who dealt with Seaborn characterized him as an 'alert, intelligent and steady officer,' and he himself behaved with the highest motives, his mission was effectively meaningless.

ULYSSES S GRANT SHARP, 1906-

Like his namesake, Admiral U S Grant Sharp was a military man who believed in bold and decisive action. But in his incessant efforts to promote bombing as a way of winning the war in Vietnam, he ran afoul both of his superiors and of the facts. A veteran destroyer captain from World War II, Sharp worked his way through the ranks to be named commander of all US Pacific military operations in 1964. Soon after came the Gulf of Tonkin incident.

On 2 August 1964 US ships repulsed an ineffectual Communist attack in the Gulf. Immediately Sharp began planning air attacks on North Vietnamese coastal bases and, in an apparently deliberate provocation, sent two destroyers into the Gulf. On 4 August these ships erupted in a storm of fire against enemy vessels that quite possibly did not exist. After this second 'attack,' Defense Secretary McNamara pressed Sharp to confirm the incident. Under vigorous pressure from Sharp to 'confirm absolutely' the attack, the commander of the ships more or less did so. Meanwhile, President Johnson had already mounted 'retaliatory' air raids on the coast.

On 7 August the Senate passed the Tonkin Gulf Resolution, and the war was underway. Promoted vigorously by Sharp, air raids against the North mounted until, under the title Operation Rolling Thunder, they had become a full scale war. Massive strategic bombing began in mid-1965. Sharp successfully urged sending the Marines to South Vietnam; and, working with General Westmoreland, he achieved expansion of both the ground and air war during 1966-67. But then Sharp began to run afoul of McNamara, who had become disillusioned with the air war. The conflict of the two men was symptomatic of the conflict that by then divided the government and military apparatus. After signals of coming disengagement began in early 1968, Sharp retired. A virulent critic he later proclaimed, 'The war was lost in Washington, not on the battlefield.'

PRINCE NORODOM SIHANOUK, 1922-

Norodom Sihanouk became king of Cambodia in 1941 when the French installed the 18-year-old as their puppet ruler, but by 1954 he had extracted his country from French rule. Thereafter, as head of state rather than king, he tried to maintain Cambodia's delicate neutrality in the face of Chinese and Vietnamese power.

When the United States backed South Vietnam in the war, Sihanouk disavowed the Americans and shifted toward China. In response to North Vietnamese buildups in his country, he leaned back toward America and allowed military excursions against the Communists in Cambodia. Finally in 1969 he acquiesced, under heavy US pressure, to the bombing of Communist sanctuaries. His country slipping toward chaos, Sihanouk in March 1970 went to Russia to request aid in expelling the Communists from Cambodia. While there learned his government had been overthrown by General Lon Nol.

Sihanouk then flew to Peking to seek aid; China received him warmly, but would or could do nothing about the anarchy raging in Cambodia. In April 1970 the United States invaded the country. Sihanouk thereafter lived in China and North Korea, looking for a way to return to power. Blustering and wavering but nonetheless utterly devoted to his country, Sihanouk had failed to do what perhaps no one could do: preserve his ancient people from the violence at their borders.

WILLIAM H SULLIVAN, 1922-

William Sullivan was another unknown who played an important if peripheral role in the conflict in Southeast Asia. For over four years, Sullivan personally directed the 'secret war' that spilled over into Laos from Vietnam. Sullivan had spent his life in national service, first with the US Navy in World War II, then in the Foreign Service. His first post with the latter was in Thailand in 1947, followed by posts in India, Japan, the Netherlands, and Vietnam. He was hand-picked by Averell Harriman to be his deputy at the Geneva conference of 1961-62 that produced the accords intended to establish a neutralist government for Laos. Sullivan came to be highly regarded for his generally moderate views on Southeast Asia, and by January 1964 he was assigned by President Johnson to chair the so-called Vietnam Working Group – an interdepartmental committee with representatives from the Pentagon, State Department, CIA and Johnson staff who were to plan for and manage the obviously growing crisis in Vietnam. Again, Sullivan so impressed his colleagues and superiors that in December 1964 he was named as ambassador to Laos.

Shortly after arriving in Vientiane, Laos's capital, Sullivan found himself directing an increasingly broader and more intensive secret operation. Its narrow goal was to stop the intrusions into Laotian territory by Communist forces, whether those from North Vietnam who used the Ho Chi Minh Trail that passed through Laos or those from South Vietnam who took refuge in Laos when pressed by ARVN or US forces. Essentially it was an air war that involved both Laotian and US pilots, and Sullivan did his best to interpret his mandate in the strictest sense – which brought him into contact with General Westmoreland and other US military leaders. They wanted the air forces from Laos to play a more extensive role and wanted eventually to bring ARVN and US troops into Laos. Sullivan held almost daily briefings, co-ordinated all bombing sorties, and exercised almost total control over the air war in Laos. Although Sullivan had the support of his superiors back in Washington, his was not an enviable job.

When Nixon assumed the presidency in January 1969, Sullivan was recalled and assigned as deputy assistant secretary under William Bundy, but he remained in close touch with affairs in Laos and Vietnam. Sullivan was one of the few Americans in a position to know and exert influence who recognized the fundamental revolution – and dangers – then current in Iran, and when the Carter administration refused to take his advice, he resigned.

MAXWELL TAYLOR, 1901-

As President Kennedy's favorite general (soon to be his chairman of the Joint Chiefs of Staff) World War II and Korean veteran General Maxwell Taylor was a natural choice to head the President's fact-finding mission to Vietnam in 1961. Taylor's recommendations brought about the first significant escalation of US involvement in the area.

As chairman of the JCS, Taylor reported developments in Saigon to Kennedy, including the on-and-off progress of the plot to overthrow Diem. After Diem's and Kennedy's deaths, Taylor replaced Lodge as President Johnson's ambassador to Vietnam in 1964. He set about the difficult task of trying to prop up the Khanh regime and move toward civilian government. He brought to this task little understanding of Vietnam's people or politics and he was apt to be condescending and arrogant in his demands.

At first a supporter of increased bombing, Taylor began to advise against US escalation, especially the commitment of combat troops. But when General Westmoreland asked for such troops Taylor agreed, thus helping pave the way for massive US combat involvement. In 1965 Lodge returned to the ambassador's post and Taylor became a special presidential consultant, but with little policymaking power. His stance remained hawkish for the duration of the war.

NGUYEN VAN THIEU, 1923-

It was never widely known by the Americans who supported Nguyen Van Thieu (whose name means 'one who ascends') as the relentlessly anti-Communist president of South Vietnam that he began his political career as a member of the Vietminh under Ho Chi Minh. Thieu attended a French missionary school as a youth, but on the return of the French in 1945 he joined the Vietminh. Disliking its Communist tendencies, he left after one year, entered a French-supported military academy, and after earning his commission in 1949 fought in several campaigns against the Vietminh. Thieu further removed himself from his indigenous roots by marrying into a prominent Vietnamese Catholic family and converting to Catholicism. Perhaps if more Americans had been aware of these aspects of Thieu's life they would have better understood why he could not gain the full loyalty of his countrymen.

Instead, US military advisers saw him as a promising young officer after the French defeat in 1954 and sent him to the United States for more training. As a colonel in the South Vietnamese army he played a role in the coup against Diem in 1963, and then

Maxwell Taylor

continued his plotting until he became the military chief of state in 1965. With US support, and with considerable backstage string-pulling, Thieu was elected president of South Vietnam in 1967 and 1971. Throughout his tenure, Thieu battled the Communists with undeniable dedication, but he did little to combat the corruption and inefficiency that crippled his regime. Suspicious and indecisive, he was never popular with his people and was often intractable to the very Americans he depended on. But the United States, with no evident alternative, backed him to the end, which came in 1975 when Saigon was overrun by the Communist forces and Thieu fled, eventually settling in Great Britain.

LE DUC THO, 1911-

It is ironic that many of the leaders of the Vietnamese revolution were of middle class or mandarin origin and were French-educated. This was also the background of Le Duc Tho who was one of the early members in Ho Chi Minh's circle, all of whom became revolutionaries early in life and together founded (in 1930) the Indochinese Communist Party. Tho spent over 10 years in French jails for his activities, but it never dampened his commitment to independence.

In the mid-1960s Tho settled in the south to supervise military and political activities during the war. In 1968, he left the front to become the chief negotiator for the North Vienamese in the Paris peace talks.

Tho proved to be a tough bargainer, prepared if necessary to wait years for a favorable settlement. He did wait, and got his concessions. In spite of his frustration, Henry Kissinger came to admire his opponents' tenacity. The agreement they signed in January 1973 was greeted with worldwide acclaim – and the Nobel Prize, which Tho refused. But it was clear that for Le Duc Tho the agreement was only another step toward the goal that was finally realized when he saw his army march into Saigon in 1975.

SIR ROBERT THOMPSON, 1916-

Having been an adviser to the US war effort for years, Sir Robert Thompson in 1969 gave President Nixon his peroration on the whole affair: 'The future of Western Civilization is at stake in the way you handle yourselves in Vietnam.'

A British Army officer and veteran of counterinsurgency operations in Malaya, Thompson came to South Vietnam in 1962 as an adviser to President Diem. Thompson urged the concept of 'strategic hamlets,' a plan that had worked well in Malaya. But the scheme, heavily backed by Washington, was bungled by Nhu, as Thompson was quick to realize.

During the war Thompson advised General William Westmoreland to stick to counterinsurgency tactics rather than relying on big military operations. This advice was largely unheeded. Thompson's final role was as a consultant to the Nixon administration. Giving his approval to the 'Vietnamization' process, with its emphasis on counterinsurgency, Thompson told the President that the South Vietnamese army could finally hold its own against any Communist threat. Nixon was glad to hear it; the advice proved, however, to be wholly unsound.

XUAN THUY, 1912-

When the United States and North Vietnam finally arrived at the bargaining table in Paris in 1968, the Communists were represented by one of their most experienced diplomats, Xuan Thuy. In dealing with his opposite number, Averell Harriman, Xuan maintained the unyielding posture his government expected – the Communists had been outmaneuvered at the bargaining table in the 1940s and 1950s and were determined never to be again, regardless of how long it took. First meeting with Henry Kissinger in 1969, Xuan stonewalled US demands, insisting on the dissolution of the Thieu government.

One of the old generation of nationalists, Xuan had fought the French, been imprisoned by them, and met them again as a diplomat. Before coming to Paris he had been North Vietnam's foreign minister in 1963-65. In Paris he issued a stream of propaganda in public, meanwhile using informal private sessions to do the real work; in these sessions, progress inched forward. Finally in 1970 Hanoi sent Le Duc Tho to head its negotiating team, and Xuan Thuy became his deputy in dealing with Henry Kissinger.

TRAN VAN TRA, 1918-

One of the second generation of Vietnamese Communists who devoted themselves to taking over a unified Vietnam, Tran Van Tra was among the leaders who achieved this –

and then found himself pushed from power because of his own critical accounts of the struggle. Tra was born in Quanghgai, the coastal province in central Vietnam; as a young man he worked on the railroad until he joined the Vietminh in the fight against the French at the end of World War II. Tra rose to become senior officer in the Vietminh, but when Vietnam was partitioned in 1954 he went to the North, and subsequently received training in the Soviet Union and China. In 1963 Tra made his way down the then-developing Ho Chi Minh Trail and took charge of the Vietcong resistance in the Mekong Delta. By 1968 Tra had risen to become deputy commander of the Communist military forces in South Vietnam and was entrusted during the Tet offensive of 1968 to lead the attack on Saigon.

After the cease-fire of January 1973, Tra went to Saigon as a member of the armistice commission, but by March he was called to Hanoi to confer with other top Vietnamese Communists on their plans for the future – that is, how to take over and unify Vietnam. All agreed that the Communist forces in the South were then seriously threatened by the Saigon forces and that the Communists should attack only when they had clearcut superiority. Tra reportedly was among those who argued this most forcefully. At a new Communist command post near Locninh, 75 miles northwest of Saigon, Tra began to make the plans for the assault on Saigon. After much persuasion on the feasibility of his plan, he was finally authorized to start operations with limited forces. To the Communists' surprise, the ARVN resistance crumbled so quickly that by early 1975 Tra was among the Communist leaders who assembled at the Locninh command post to plan the final assault on Saigon. In 1982, Tra published his critical accounts of such matters as the Tet offensive of 1968 and the internal debates among his fellow Communist leaders, subsequently he found himself purged from the Communist Party he had served so faithfully.

WILLIAM C WESTMORELAND, 1914-

When General William Westmoreland took over command of US operations in Vietnam from General Paul Harkins in June 1964, it was clear that Washington had committed 'the pick of the crop.' A graduate of West Point, a decorated combat hero in both World War II and Korea, superintendent of West Point until he was assigned as Harkins' deputy

in 1963, 'Westy' was almost the Hollywood image of a general. What made him valuable to the Johnson administration was that he was *not* a showboat general in the manner of Patton; he was an efficient, disciplined, organization man.

Westmoreland immediately requested combat troops so that his army could get into the fight. In ever-increasing allotments, the US troops arrived – until by mid-1968 there were a half million. Leaving the South Vietnamese army to protect major population centers, Westmoreland planned to secure the coasts, block infiltration of North Vietnamese into the south and then wage a war of attrition with 'search-and-destroy' missions into the countryside, using helicopters for rapid deployment and evacuation. But Westmoreland's strategy never really worked. The body count of the enemy mounted but the number of Communists, whether northern or southern Vietnamese, continued to swell. Massive US bombing could not halt the flow of enemy supplies carried by foot and on bicycles. The 'pacification' program in the countryside was a dismal failure. Westmoreland's response to each development was 'send more troops.' And as the fighting dragged on, Westmoreland's public pronouncements remained optimistic.

In January 1968, Communist forces rose up in cities all over South Vietnam, including downtown Saigon. The attacks gained no significant territory and Communist losses were heavy; Westmoreland pronounced the Tet offensive an allied victory. But the Communists had shown that no part of South Vietnam was safe from their operations, and set against such previously optimistic appraisals as those of Westmoreland himself – and undoubtedly blown out of proportion by the US media – Tet was turned into a psychological victory.

In the wake of Tet came another review of US policy by the Johnson administration. When it was decided to de-escalate the war, halt the bombings, and go to the bargaining table, Westmoreland was reassigned to Washington as chairman of the Joint Chiefs of Staff, a post in which he remained till his retirement in 1972. It was the best that a grateful government could do for a loyal soldier, but after his retirement Westmoreland was free to openly criticize the Johnson administration's handling of the war. A subsequent law suit in 1983 against CBS for misrepresentation was withdrawn.

EARLE GILMORE WHEELER, 1908-75 Commanding from a desk for most of his long military career, General Earle Wheeler was Chairman of the Joint Chiefs of Staff during most of the Vietnam War; in that period he worked tirelessly for the interests of the Pentagon. A protégé of General Maxwell Taylor, Wheeler moved up through the ranks to become Kennedy's appointee for Army Chief of Staff in 1962. There he worked in harmony with Secretary of Defense McNamara in modernizing the army.

Named chairman of the Joint Chiefs of Staff by President Johnson in 1964, Wheeler quickly urged escalation in Vietnam; despite army studies showing it wouldn't work, he advocated bombing of the North. Therafter he promoted the President's war policy with his own considerable political clout. During the Tet offensive of early 1967, Wheeler maneuvered General Westmoreland into

calling for additional troops; Wheeler thereby hoped to convince Johnson to mobilize the reserves and widen the war into Cambodia and Laos. Johnson saw through the move and foresaw the ominous political consequences. Throughout the war, Wheeler was a strong critic of anti-war protesters in the country, saying they showed the Communists weakness of purpose in the United States.

Surprisingly, however, Wheeler seemed to concur with the pessimistic assessment of the war put forth by new Defense Secretary Clark Clifford in early 1968. During the first two years of the Nixon presidency, Wheeler went along with the winding down of US involvement and the 'Vietnamization' process. Wheeler resigned as chairman of the JCS in 1970. He reappeared in the public eye in 1973, testifying before the Senate and Armed Services Committee that Nixon had personally ordered the secret bombing of Cambodia.

General William C Westmoreland

BIBLIOGRAPHY

Austin, Anthony. *The President's War.* Philadelphia: J B Lippincott, 1971.

Baker, Mark. *Nam: The Vietnam War in the Words of the Men and Women Who Fought There.* New York: William Morrow, 1981.

Bator, Victor. *Vietnam: A Diplomatic Tragedy.* Dobbs Ferry, NY: Oceana, 1965.

Beckwith, Colonel Charles and Knox, Donald. *Delta Force.* San Diego: Harcourt, Brace, Jovanovitch, 1983.

Berman, Larry. *Planning a Tragedy: The Americanization of the War in Vietnam.* New York: W W Norton, 1982.

Bloodworth, Denis. *An Eye for a Dragon.* New York: Farrar, Straus & Giroux, 1970.

Blum, Robert. *Drawing the Line: The Origin of the American Containment Policy in East Asia.* New York: W W Norton, 1982.

Bodard, Lucien. *The Quicksand War: Prelude to Vietnam.* Boston: Atlantic-Little Brown, 1967.

Braestrup, Peter. *Big Story.* Boulder, Colorado: Westview Press, 1977.

Buttinger, Joseph. *Vietnam: A Dragon Embattled.* New York: Praeger, 1967.

Carhart, Tom. *Battles and Campaigns in Vietnam.* Greenwich, Connecticut: Bison Books, 1984.

Cincinnatus. *Self-Destruction: The Disintegration and Decay of the United States Army During the Vietnam Era.* New York: W W Norton, 1978.

Dawson, Alan. *55 Days: The Fall of South Vietnam.* Englewood Cliffs, NJ: Prentice-Hall, 1977.

Department of State. *Aggression from the North: The Record of North Vietnam's Campaign to Conquer South Vietnam.* Washington, DC: US Government Printing Office, 1962.

Duiker, William. *The Communist Road to Power.* Boulder, Colorado: Westview Press, 1981.

Ennis, Thomas. *French Policy and Developments in Indochina.* Chicago: University of Chicago Press, 1956.

Fall, Bernard. *Hell in a Very Small Place: The Siege of Dien Bien Phu.* Philadelphia: J B Lippincott, 1966.

—— *Street Without Joy: Insurgency in Indochina 1946-1963.* Harrisburg, PA: Stackpole Books, rev ed. 1963.

—— *The Two Viet-Nams: A Political and Military Analysis.* New York: Praeger, 1963.

—— *The Viet-Minh Regime.* Ithaca, New York: Cornell Univerity Press, 1956.

FitzGerald, Frances. *Fire in the Lake.* Boston: Atlantic-Little Brown, 1972.

Goodman, Allan. *The Lost Peace.* Stanford, California: Hoover Institution, 1978.

Gravel, Senator Mike ed. *The Pentagon Papers.* Boston: Beacon Press, 1971.

Greene, Graham. *The Quiet American.* New York: Viking Press, 1956.

Halberstam, David. *The Best and the Brightest.* New York: Random House, 1972.

—— *The Making of a Quagmire.* New York: Random House, 1964.

Hammer, Ellen. *The Struggle for Indochina.* Stanford, California: Stanford University Press, 1954.

Henderson, William. *Why the Vietcong Fought.* Westport, Connecticut: Greenwood, 1979.

Herr, Michael. *Dispatches.* New York: Knopf, 1978.

Herring, George. *America's Longest War.* New York: Wiley, 1979.

Hoopes, Townsend. *The Limits of Intervention.* New York: McKay, 1970.

Johnson, Lyndon. *The Vantage Point: Perspectives of the Presidency, 1963-1969.* New York: Holt, Rinehart, 1971.

Kalb, Marvin and Abel, Elie. *Roots of Involvement*. New York: W W Norton, 1971.

Karnow, Stanley. *Vietnam: A History*. New York: Viking, 1983.

Kinnard, Douglas. *The War Managers*. Hanover, New Hampshire: University Press of New England, 1977.

Kraslow, David and Lorry, Stuart. *The Secret Search for Peace in Vietnam*. New York: Random House, 1968.

Lacouture, Jean. *Ho Chi Minh: A Political Biography*. Translated by Peter Wiles. New York: Random House, 1968.

Lake, Anthony, ed. *The Legacy of Vietnam*. New York: New York University Press, 1976.

Lansdale, Edward. *In the Midst of Wars*. New York: Harper & Row, 1972.

Lewy, Guenter. *America in Vietnam*. New York: Oxford University Press, 1978.

Mecklin, John. *Mission in Torment*. New York: Doubleday, 1965.

Mueller, John. *War, Presidents and Public Opinion*. New York: Wiley, 1973.

The New York Times Index, 1960-1974. New York: The New York Times Company.

Patti, Archimedes. *Why Viet Nam? Prelude to America's Albatross*. Berkeley: University of California Press, 1980.

Porter, Gareth, ed. *Vietnam: The Definitive Documentation of Human Decisions*. Stanfordville, New York: Coleman Enterprises, 1979.

Robinson, Anthony, ed. *The Weapons of the Vietnam War*. Greenwich, Connecticut: Bison Books, 1983.

Salisbury, Harrison. *Behind the Lines: Hanoi, December 23, 1966-January 7, 1967*. New York: Harper & Row, 1967.

Santoli, Al. *Everything We Had: An Oral History of the Vietnam War by Thirty-Three American Soldiers Who Fought in It*. New York: Random House, 1981.

Schandler, Herbert. *The Unmaking of a President*. Princeton: Princeton University Press, 1977.

Senate Committee on Foreign Relations. *Causes, Origins, and Lessons of the Vietnam War*. US Government Printing Office, 1973.

—— *Background Information Relating to Southeast Asia and Vietnam*. 7th ed. US Government Printing Office, 1975.

—— *The Gulf of Tonkin, 1964 Incidents*. US Government Printing Office, 1968.

Shawcross, William. *Sideshow*. New York: Simon & Schuster, 1979.

Shulimson, Jack and Johnson, Major Charles. *US Marines in Vietnam: The Landing and the Buildup 1965*. HQ USMC, Washington, DC, 1978.

Simpson, Charles. *Inside the Green Berets*. Novato, California: Presido Press, 1983.

Smith, R Harris. *OSS: The Secret History of America's First CIA*. New York: Delta Publishing, 1972.

Snepp, Frank. *Decent Interval: An Insider's Account of Saigon's Indecent End*. New York: Random House, 1977.

South Vietnam: US-Communist Confrontation in Southeast Asia. New York: Facts-on-File, 1966-1973.

Spector, Ronald. *Advice and Support: US Army in Vietnam, The Early Years*. Washington, DC: Center for Military History, 1983.

Stanton, Shelby. *Vietnam Order of Battle*. US News Books.

Stevenson, Charles. *The End of Nowhere: American Policy Toward Laos Since 1954*. Boston: Beacon Press, 1972.

Thompson, James. *Rolling Thunder*. Chapel Hill: University of North Carolina Press, 1980.

Thompson, W Scott and Fuzell, Donaldson, eds. *The Lessons of Vietnam*. New York: Crane, Russak, 1977.

Webb, James. *Fields of Fire*. Engleside Cliffs, NJ: Prentice-Hall, 1978.

INDEX

INDEX

INDEX

INDEX

PICTURE CREDITS

ADN: 364-5.
Bison Books: 14, 34, 36, 40, 42, 74, 79, 130, 156, 165, 170, 198, 202, 221, 224, 234, 247, 295, 297, 302, 312-313, 317, 321, 334, 336, 337, 339, 342, 347, 351, 352, 358, 359, 370, 372, 385, 397, 448, 450, 470-71, 479, 483, 490, 494, 505.
CTK: 368.
Department of Defense: 17-32 (inclusive), 176, 182, 266, 285, 418, 423, 427, 429, 436, 441, 446-7, 502.
Dept of Defense, USAF: 321, 390-91, 393, 404, 444.
Dept of Defense, US Army: 4-5, 6-7, 10-11, 46, 49, 52, 57, 58, 59, 63, 71, 77, 81, 87, 92, 96, 106, 113, 117, 123, 137, 139, 140, 150, 153, 159, 165, 169, 172, 179, 191, 199, 205, 209, 210, 218, 236, 240, 248, 253, 260, 263, 269, 271, 273, 277, 280-81, 289, 292, 299, 303, 325, 354, 356-7, 376, 379, 380-81, 382, 387, 402-3, 408-9, 443, 454, 455, 456-7, 458, 459, 461, 466, 468.
Dept of Defense, USMC: 145, 193, 197, 328-9, 345, 388, 389, 435, 453, 463.
Dept of Defense, US Navy: 2-3, 66, 175, 189, 215, 230, 243, 251, 306, 332, 360-61, 407, 412, 415, 416, 418, 423, 424-5, 431, 433, 437, 462, 465, 469.
ECP Armées: 33, 363 top and bottom, 438-9.
FPG/International: 74, 166, 184-5, 187, 203, 256, 348, 374, 476, 487.
National Archives: 39.
New York Daily News: 97.
Private Collection: 237, 368, 371.
Smithsonian Institution: 353.
Universal Press Syndicate: 317.

ACKNOWLEDGEMENTS

The publisher would like to thank the following people who helped in the preparation of this book: Jan Swafford, who wrote biographies; William Hartford, Thomas Mooney, Raymond Quirnbach, Eva Weber and Joel Zoss, who wrote sections of the chronology; Elizabeth M Montgomery, who edited it; Chris Simon, who designed it; Mary R Raho, who did the picture research; Cynthia Klein, who prepared the index.